STREETWISE®
SMALL BUSINESS
BOOK OF LISTS

Hundreds of lists to help you reduce costs,
increase revenues, and boost your profits

Edited by Gene Marks

BUSINESS

Avon, Massachusetts

Published by
Adams Media, an F+W Publications Company
57 Littlefield Street, Avon, MA 02322. U.S.A.
www.adamsmedia.com

ISBN 10: 1-59337-684-7
ISBN 13: 978-1-59337-684-0

Printed in United States of America

J I H G F E D C B A

Library of Congress Cataloging-in-Publication Data

Streetwise small business book of lists / edited by Gene Marks.
    p. cm.
  ISBN 1-59337-684-7
  1. Small business—United States—Management—Handbooks, manuals, etc. I. Marks, Gene. II. Title:
Small business book of lists.

  HD62.7.S877 2006
  658.02'2--dc22

2006014708

This publication is designed to provide accurate and authoritative information with regard to the subject
matter covered. It is sold with the understanding that the publisher is not engaged in rendering legal,
accounting, or other professional advice. If legal advice or other expert assistance is required, the
services of a competent professional person should be sought.
                    —From a *Declaration of Principles* jointly adopted by a Committee of the
                    American Bar Association and a Committee of Publishers and Associations

Many of the designations used by manufacturers and sellers to distinguish their product are claimed as
trademarks. Where those designations appear in this book and Adams Media was aware of a trademark
claim, the designations have been printed with initial capital letters.

This book is available at quantity discounts for bulk purchases.
For information, please call 1-800-872-5627.

CONTENTS

Acknowledgments

This book would not have been possible without our top-notch research team of marketing and business professionals. My thanks and appreciation go out to: Kimberly Albrecht, Ben Attanasio, Kelly Dougherty, Valerie Fiordaliso, Greg Foley, Peg Foreman, Amy Laing, Andrew Milauskas, Maria Pantoja, Maria Sciamanna, Kalyani Shah, and Eric Stickle.

My mom, Elaine Marks, did a great deal of excellent work in getting our experts' permissions together during a particularly tough year for her.

Thanks also go out to Susan Vestal who kept track of the all of the finances and to the great team at Adams Media, particularly Larry Shea and Jill Alexander, who somehow kept their sanity during this process!

This project rested significantly on the shoulders of Caryn Maenza who created lists, found experts, and handled every issue with grace and professionalism.

Dedication

This book is dedicated to all the experts who contributed their knowledge for our readers' benefit.

Introduction
Top Reasons You'll Keep This Book on Your Desk

Welcome to the Streetwise® Small Business Book of Lists! You've purchased something that you're going to keep on your desk and refer to frequently. Why? We asked our expert, who is also the author and editor of this book, to give you his reasons and here they are:

1. Before you buy something

Whether it's a fax machine, a new computer, or a phone system, you'll turn to this book first, so you can find out from our experts who are the top manufacturers, the most reliable models, and the things you should be considering before you cough up the dough.

2. Before you hire someone

Here our experts list all the things you should consider before you bring on that new employee or even hire an attorney. Forms you need to fill out, questions you should ask, and pitfalls to avoid.

3. When you fire someone

Our experts provide lists that will help guide you through the emotional, legal, and financial maze of terminating an employee. It's never easy.

4. Before you begin (and end) a new business

What's the best organization for your new venture? What should you include in your purchase agreement? What steps should you take to shut down your business? Our experts have all the lists here.

5. When you need help managing your business

Our experts know that managing a business is challenging. How can you save money on insurance? When should you outsource? How do you save money on office expenses? What are the signs of trouble? These lists, and many others, will help you face these challenges.

6. Before you go places

Business owners and managers are up and about. In this book you'll find list after list of advice from experts who travel as you do: ways to save money on car rentals, how to find the lowest airfares, best hotels for the business traveler … and many more.

7. When you need money

Whether you're starting up or looking to expand, you'll want to raise some cash from investors or lenders. Here you'll find dozens of lists, such as Best Banks for Small Businesses, Questions to Ask Your Loan Officer, and Popular Government Loan Programs. All with the most up-to-date information.

8. Before you pay taxes

Our experts know that taxes are your biggest expense. What are the top deductions you can take? What tax credits are most overlooked? How can you reduce your taxable income? What steps do you take in case you're audited? Turn to the lists and you'll find out!

9. When you have questions about technology

Laptops, servers, antivirus software—what's the most popular? Who's the most reliable? What should you know before you invest? We've got lists about them all.

10. To improve your sales and customer service

Finding new customers and keeping them happy is the name of the game. You'll want to look at this book before you hire a new salesperson, improve your customer service group, or attend your next trade show. Our experts will show you the best ways to expand your sales without losing your valuable customers.

11. To make more money

Need we say more? The lists say it all; they are concise, easy-to–read, and packed with information.

Source: Gene Marks CPA, author and editor of *Streetwise® Small Business Book of Lists*. Enjoy!

Chapter
one

Chapter
two

Chapter
three

Chapter
four

Chapter
five

Chapter
six

Chapter
seven

Chapter
eight

Starting Up

Buying and Selling Your Business

Ten Things to Look Out for When Buying a Business

Don't have time to build something from scratch? Want to get things going faster? Maybe you're thinking of buying a business. Before you sign on the dotted line, here are a few things our expert will want you to consider.

1. Make sure you're buying the **assets**, not the business

If the seller is a corporation or LLC, under no circumstances should you buy stock in his business. Instead, offer to buy the assets of the business, and form a separate company to act as the purchaser. Why? Two reasons. First, you get a better tax treatment, since your "tax basis" in the assets will be the amount you paid for them, rather than the amount your seller paid for them long, long ago. Second, if he owes money to people or is being sued, you won't assume any of those liabilities if you buy the assets.

2. Ask about sales taxes and payroll taxes

In many states, even if you buy a business' assets, the state tax authority can come after you if they find out the seller owed sales, use, payroll, and other business taxes. If the seller has employees (other than herself), ask if she was using a payroll service, and make sure she's current in her employment tax payments. Then ask the state tax authority to issue a "clearance letter" saying the seller is current in her sales and use taxes on the closing date. This may take a while, but it'll save you tons of heartache down the road.

3. Determine who will deal with the accounts receivable

Chances are, some of the business's customers will owe the seller money on the closing date. Who will be responsible for collecting these overdue debts? There are only two ways to handle this: Either you purchase the accounts receivable at closing (for a discount, to reflect the fact that some of these folks won't pay up), or you let the seller collect them at his leisure. My vote is for you to buy the accounts receivable at closing; that way, if the delinquent customer wants additional work done after the closing, you're in a stronger bargaining position.

4. Find out if you can assume the seller's lease

Is the seller leasing the premises where she conducts her business? If so, you should find out (a) how much time remains on the lease term and (b) whether the landlord is willing to let you assume the seller's lease "as is," without an increase in rent. If the lease has less than two years to run, you might want to spend the money now to negotiate a new lease with a five- to ten-year term. Also find out if the landlord is holding a security deposit (usually two months' rent, but sometimes more). Your seller will probably want you to purchase her security deposit on top of the agreed-on purchase price for the business assets. If the seller is including the security deposit in the purchase price, make sure that's spelled out in writing somewhere.

5. Are there prepaid expenses?

Take Yellow Pages advertising, for example. When you buy a Yellow Pages ad, you normally pay for a whole year in advance. Chances are your closing will take place sometime during the year, and the seller will want to be reimbursed for the portion of the year when you're running the business and benefiting from the Yellow Pages ad. Prepaid expenses—like the seller's security deposit—usually aren't included in the agreed-on purchase price but are tacked on at the closing. Ask the seller now for a list of "closing adjustments" (amounts the seller has prepaid that will have to be "prorated"), so you can budget for them accordingly, and there'll be no nasty surprises at the closing.

6. Negotiate a "letter of intent"

Also called a "term sheet," a letter of intent (or LOI) is a short, two- or three-page agreement between the buyer and the seller of a business that spells out all the important terms and conditions of the sale. For example, it will include the purchase price, how and when the purchase price will be paid, the assets that will be sold to the buyer (and those the seller will keep for his own use), the terms of the seller's noncompete agreement, and so forth. While LOIs are technically not binding on the parties, it's well worth your time and effort to hammer out as many of the business issues involved in an LOI as possible before the lawyers begin drafting the "definitive" legal contracts that will document the sale. A well-drafted LOI helps the lawyers get the sale documents right on the first (or possibly the second) draft, since most of the important terms and conditions will already have been dealt with in the LOI and aren't subject to further negotiation. Without a LOI, you'll end up negotiating the business deal and the "legalese" of the definitive documents at the same time, requiring multiple drafts of the sale documents and tons of money in legal fees.

7. Watch out for bulk sales laws

Most states have done away with these laws, but many states still require the buyer of a business to notify the seller's creditors that the transaction is going on. Failure to get a list of the seller's creditors and send "notices of sale" to them may give the seller's creditors a shot at undoing (or "rescinding") the transaction in order to prevent the seller's assets from being sold out from under them. Even if the seller has no creditors at all, which is a rare occurrence, the state tax authority generally wants a copy of the "bulk sales notice" so it can determine if the seller owes any sales, use, or other business taxes. If the seller does, she'll have to pay them before the closing takes place.

8. Get an indemnity from the seller

Even if you and your advisers have torn apart the seller's books and records, sometimes things are overlooked and you find yourself being sued because of something the seller did (or failed to do) before you took over the business. Get an indemnity from the seller, promising to defend the lawsuit and pay all judgments and fees if that should happen. Likewise, you should be prepared to give the seller an indemnity if he gets sued because of something you do—(or fail to do) after the closing takes place.

9. Make sure the seller sticks around for a while

In many retail and service businesses, the customers have a personal as well as business relationship with the owner. Be sure the seller continues to make an appearance at the business for a few weeks after the closing to introduce you to customers, help you figure out the books, and "ensure a smooth and orderly transition of the business." Consider paying the seller for her time so she has an incentive to stay off the golf course, at least until you're comfortable that you know what you're doing.

10. Get to know the employees

Before you buy a business, make sure the "key employees" are willing to stick around, since they're often the ones who see the customers day to day, operate all the tricky machinery, and know "where the bodies are buried." Many sellers will be reluctant to let their employees know the business is up for sale, for fear they'll quit en masse. In that case, put a provision in the sales contract that reads as follows: "Seller and Buyer will announce the proposed sale to all employees of the Business within forty-eight hours before the Closing, and Buyer will be given a reasonable opportunity to meet with each employee individually before the closing date to determine, to Buyer's reasonable satisfaction, the employee's willingness to continue working for the Business." Then add a provision allowing you to walk from the deal if you're not totally satisfied that the key employees will stay on board at least long enough for you to learn what they already know.

Source: Cliff Ennico, a nationally recognized small business legal expert, is the author of the nationally syndicated newspaper column "Succeeding in Your Business" and the author of *Small Business Survival Guide* (Adams Media, 2005). You can find out more about him at *www.cliffennico.com*. Contact him at 2490 Black Rock Turnpike, No. 354, Fairfield, CT 06825-2400; (203) 254-1727; fax: (203) 254-8195; e-mail: *cennico@legalcareer.com*.

Most Common Things to Include in an Asset Purchase Agreement

The key document involved in a buy-and-sell arrangement is the Asset Purchase Agreement. That agreement will cover all the business assets owned by the seller and sold to the buyer in the transaction. Whether you are the seller or the buyer in this type of transaction, here are some pointers for you to keep in mind when reviewing an Asset Purchase Agreement.

1. Recitals

The seller and buyer should be clearly designated and the essence of the transaction clearly stated; that is, what the seller specifically desires to sell and what the buyer substantially agrees to purchase.

2. Definition of terms

The typical agreement contains a host of legal terms and legalisms that will keep the lawyers in business but is Greek to the average person. These terms (i.e., hazardous substance or inventory) should be defined up-front in the agreement so that the average person can understand them.

3. Purchase and sale of assets

What assets are being sold should be clearly spelled out in the agreement. For example, assets may include real estate, buildings, equipment and inventory, licenses and authorizations, business agreements, trademarks, patents and copyrights, accounts receivable, work in progress, business records, and any cash funds belonging to the business. Normally, the assets will be transferred on the date the agreement is signed.

4. Purchase price and payment

Both seller and buyer will be keenly interested in the agreed-on purchase price of the business and what conditions are attached to the purchase price. Will it be a completely cash transaction, a long-term loan, a promissory note, a mortgage agreement, or some mixture of cash and credit? In the agreement, the purchase price should be allocated among the assets. This allocation may affect the tax treatment of the parties.

5. Noncompetition agreements

Contemporaneous with the execution of the Asset Purchase Agreement, the parties will often enter into a noncompetition agreement in which one party agrees not to compete for a period and in a certain geographic area in the other party's business. Often the noncompetition agreement will be set out in a separate document. If either party fails to comply with the terms and conditions of the noncompetition agreement, then the aggrieved party can seek a temporary restraining order, a preliminary injunction, or similar injunctive relief and monetary damages from the party who breached the noncompetition agreement.

6. Liabilities

The agreement should spell out what liabilities the buyer is assuming, including any payroll liabilities, tax liabilities, or contractual liabilities. It should also be noted that the seller remains responsible for discharging any remaining liabilities and obligations not specifically assumed by the buyer. Usually, the buyer will not assume responsibility for any personal injury or property damage claims arising before the agreement is signed. However, the prudent buyer should confirm that he or she has adequate insurance coverage if any claims do arise. If some or all of the employees in the business are hired by the buyer, it should be stated in the agreement that the buyer will be responsible for all wages, sick leave, vacation time, and other employee benefits arising after the agreement is signed.

7. Closing

The agreement should specify what additional documents the parties need to bring to the closing. If the Asset Purchase Agreement depends on the execution of other documents, those documents should be reviewed by the seller and buyer in advance so that they can be executed contemporaneously with the agreement.

8. Representations of the seller

Since the seller is getting the money in this transaction, it is usually incumbent on him or her to provide certain representations regarding the truthfulness of the financial statements, whether all licenses and authorizations have been paid, the status of the equipment and inventory being sold, whether the real estate is free of any claims or liens, the absence of any liabilities or litigation against the business, and the absence of any employees' problems affecting the business.

9. Indemnification between the seller and the buyer

Despite the best intentions between the seller and buyer, sometimes a third party will intervene with a lawsuit to prevent the transaction or make a claim against the seller and/or buyer after the agreement is signed. Consequently, indemnification agreements between seller and buyer are sometimes drafted to defend against these third-party suits. Also, disputes arising between the seller and buyer can often be expeditiously resolved by drafting an arbitration clause in the agreement.

10. Miscellaneous provisions

Some provisions that either the seller or the buyer may insist on include the assignment of rights to others, formal notifications regarding any claims, and listing all schedules and exhibits as part of the agreement. No verbal understandings should be recognized by the parties unless they are put in writing.

11. Financing

Often, the transaction will come to an abrupt halt if the buyer cannot obtain suitable financing to close the deal. The financing terms should be set out so that both parties know what type of financing the buyer is seeking. An absolute final date that the buyer has to obtain financing should be specified. If the Buyer fails to obtain suitable financing by the specified date, the seller is free to sell the business to another party.

_____

Source: Robert G. Andre of Ogden, Murphy, Wallace PLLC (*www.omwlaw.com*)—Andre handles a wide range of litigation matters, including insurance coverage, code enforcement actions, real property and land use, commercial litigation, medical malpractice, products liability, toxic torts, environmental and regulation issues, and criminal cases, including arsons. He also advises clients on many types of business transactions, including contracts, leases, incorporations, tax matters, liens and collections, unfair business practices, employment discrimination suits, insurance claims, environmental cleanups, secured transactions, and regulatory compliance actions. Contact him at (206) 447-7000; fax: (206) 447-0215; or e-mail: *randre@omwlaw.com*.

Things to Include in a Letter of Intent to Buy a Business

Before you buy a business, one of the key steps in preparing for the final purchase is the drafting of a letter of intent to buy the business. A letter of intent is a nonbinding agreement between the buyer and seller that essentially lays out terms for the sale and allows further negotiations to occur. While it is not legally binding, the agreement is an important part of the purchasing process, and following is a list of the key things to include in the letter.

1. Price

The price to be paid by the buyer for the business will generally have been already agreed on, but it should be included in the letter along with the other terms of the sale.

2. Deposit to be made by the buyer

Along with the letter of intent, the buyer will generally also make a deposit on the purchase price as a way to solidify further the buyer's intent. The deposit will be refunded to the buyer if negotiations fall through and a sale is not completed. Depending on the size of the deposit, the buyer may want to include the exclusive negotiating rights clause.

3. Exclusive negotiating rights (optional)

If the buyer makes a large deposit toward the purchase of the business, the seller may agree to exclusive negotiating rights with the buyer. This means that the seller waives his right to shop the business to other potential buyers while negotiations are ongoing. This is optional, and the seller may not want it included in order to reserve the right to continue marketing his business to other buyers.

4. What exactly is being acquired by the buyer

The price that has been agreed on by the buyer and seller will be contingent on exactly what the buyer is getting. The letter should spell out the specific business to be acquired, as well as all assets and liabilities that will come along with it.

5. Allowance of due diligence by the buyer

Upon the issuance of a letter of intent, the buyer should be given the right to perform due diligence and assess all aspects of the company to get an idea of its legal, financial, and operational situations. Due diligence allows the buyer to learn on her own exactly what she is buying.

6. Permission to contact legal, financial, and other professionals

In the process of due diligence, the buyer should be allowed to contact the seller's attorneys, accountants, bankers, and any other professionals who would be able to give the buyer an idea of the state of the business.

7. Confidentiality agreement

Since the letter is nonbinding, it does not mean a sale will be completed. Should the sale fall through, both sides should agree to a binding confidentiality agreement that forces them to keep secret the terms of the negotiations. Also, the seller should ensure that the buyer keeps confidential any secret company information to which she had access during negotiations.

Source: CCH Business Owner's Toolkit (*www.cch.com*)—The Business Owner's Toolkit provides advice, guides, legal tools, business models, and other resources to small business owners.

Common Environmental Issues When Acquiring a Business

With the many state and federal environmental statutes and regulations enacted, environmental liabilities play a key role in business transactions. Transactions affected by environmental risk typically involve real estate or capital assets, such as industrial or commercial facilities and equipment, or companies holding those assets. Those deals might include land sales, leases, asset purchases, stock purchases, loans, financing deals, and mergers. Buyers risk taking on direct liability for cleanup costs, damages, and personal injury associated with environmental contamination. A buyer may find he cannot use or operate the property in the way he anticipated as a result of environmental contamination, or that the property acquired is devalued. Consequently, environmental liabilities may affect the pricing and structure of a deal. Here's a list of what to consider before closing a transaction.

1. Identify potential environmental risks in the business or property you are buying by conducting environmental due diligence.

The first step in considering a deal is to investigate the property and company to identify, define, and, if possible, quantify potential environmental issues. An environmental due diligence investigation, sometimes referred to as a "Phase 1", includes a review of (1) current environmental compliance, including the status of all permits, licenses, and registrations (known as the "compliance audit"), (2) possible future capital expenditures in connection with future compliance, and (3) potential liabilities in connection with past activities and existing conditions. Historical environmental information is important to consider because under environmental laws buyers can be held liable for historical environmental liability from sellers and other prior owners, depending upon the facts. Phase I investigations are governed by ASTM standards and certain environmental law provisions designed to allow "innocent purchasers" to obtain protection from liability after the deal is completed.

2. Analyze the information from the investigation to determine whether sampling is necessary.

A Phase 1 due diligence investigation typically includes a review of internal documents of the seller's company, including documents related to the current and former assets of the company, communications with regulatory agencies, permits, financial documents, and litigation files. A site visit and discussions with management personnel typically are also necessary. State and regulatory agencies also can provide crucial information. Regulatory databases available on the internet can add information on permitting, compliance, enforcement actions, underground storage tanks, past spills, and involvement by the company at any state or Federal Superfund sites. Typically, a Phase 1 is done by environmental professionals, usually consultants working with lawyers to assess the information. If a Phase I shows there is contamination present or likely on the property due to past activities, a "Phase II" investigation may be needed to determine the extent of the contamination and to estimate the cost of a cleanup. A Phase II investigation consists of sampling soil and groundwater, and can involve excavating underground storage tanks or other sources of contamination.

3. Consult your lender early to determine whether the financial institution requires specific environmental investigation.

Some lenders have a specific requirements about environmental investigations that must be met in order to qualify for a loan or mortgage. Lenders may also require environmental information to be reported in a certain format, or on their own forms.

4. Determine early whether there are any state laws that restrict transfer of contaminated property.

Several states have laws that require notice, investigation, or even cleanup of property before a sale, to address environmental contamination. Identify any state law governing transfer of property early in the transaction, so you can file the information required under state law without delaying closing. In worst cases, failure to comply with these state statutes can void the transaction.

5. Armed with this information about environmental risks, structure the deal to allocate them.

Sellers seek to pass on liability to buyers, retaining as little environmental liability as possible by, for example, structuring deals as stock purchases or transferring all liabilities associated with assets. Buyers may limit their environmental liability by requiring a seller to clean up the property prior to closing; excluding contaminated parcels or assets from the deal; adjusting the purchase price to reflect the liability; requiring an escrow, holdback, or letter of credit to cover future environmental costs; and structuring the deal to manage liability, for example in a fully-funded subsidiary or as an asset deal rather than a stock purchase.

Source: Kathy Robb is a partner with the law firm of Hunton & Williams (*www.hunton.com*) in its New York office, where she has advised buyers, sellers, and lenders on environmental issues in numerous transac-tions, including identifying, analyzing, and allocating potential risk, advising on deal and corporate structure to minimize risk, and negotiating with state and federal authorities on behalf of clients to address environmental issues. She co-heads the firm's environmental practice. She is a member of the Advisory Board of BNA's Environmental Due Diligence Guide, and speaks and writes frequently on environmental issues. Contact her at *krobb@hunton.com*.

Things to Do Before You Buy a Company

Why build when you can buy? When you do decide to buy a company, and once you've decided on which company you want to buy, there are a number of things to do before making a final purchase. Following is a list of the things you must be sure to do before purchasing a company.

1. Seek professional assistance

It may be valuable to enlist the services of an attorney who can help you review the company's legal and organizational documents before you make your final purchase. Also, an accountant can help to review financial documents and assess the financial state of the company.

2. Provide a letter of intent

A letter of intent is not a binding legal contract; instead, it simply lays out the price and terms of the potential sale, thus allowing the seller to release sensitive or confidential information about the company to the buyer. It also allows either side to back out of the deal without legal repercussions.

3. Sign a confidentiality agreement

The seller will often require such a document to be signed, because it will legally bind the buyer to use any confidential information about the company only in his or her decision-making process with respect to buying the business.

4. Review contracts and leases

Be sure to look over any contracts and leases by which the company is currently bound. Check to see if any such agreements can be transferred from the old owner to the new one, or if new contracts and leases must be drawn up.

5. Review financial statements

Assess the company's financial situation by looking over financial statements from the past three to five years. The statements should not be simple assessments by the owner and should have been reviewed and legitimized by an accountant.

6. Review tax returns

Similar to the financial statements, the tax returns will allow you to assess the financial state of the company in terms of profitability as well as outstanding taxes. Review the returns from the past three to five years, just as you did the financial statements.

7. Check other important documents

A number of other documents should be analyzed before buying the business. Analyzing customer lists, sales records, government certifications, payroll information, supplier and purchaser lists, and bank accounts, among others, will allow you to get a better idea of the company's operations, structure, and stability.

Source: Business.gov (*www.business.gov*)—Business.gov is "the official business link to the U.S. government." It provides information and links for starting, growing, managing, and selling businesses.

Top Tax Considerations When Buying a Business

There are a number of things that must be taken into consideration by an entrepreneur seeking to buy an existing business. Among these are tax issues, and while there tend to be more tax issues for the seller, there are some things that a buyer must notice when buying a business as well. Here's a few of the top tax-related issues to consider during the process of buying a business.

1. Allocations to equipment

The equipment includes the assets that the existing business has for conducting business, such as the equipment for making and selling a product. The more money that is allocated to equipment, the better it is for the buyer. Equipment is written off over a five- to seven-year period.

2. Consulting agreement (with broker)

Similar to equipment allocations, the more that is allocated to a short-term consulting agreement with a broker, the better it is for a buyer. Once paid, this agreement is written off as an expense.

3. Other allocations

Other intangible allocations for other assets are not of as much concern to a buyer. Unlike the relatively short period for equipment allocations, these allocations are written off over fifteen years or longer.

Source: Bernie Siegel, a Certified Business Intermediary and founder of Siegel Business Services, a company just outside Philadelphia that specializes in brokerage services for midsize business in the mid-Atlantic region. Mr. Siegel, a former franchise owner of nine Dunkin' Donuts stores, formed his business brokerage company in 1983. He is a fellow of the International Business Brokers Association, as well as its former vice president. He is also a member of the Pennsylvania Business Brokers Association. He can be contacted at the following address: Siegel Business Services, Inc., One Bala Plaza, Suite 516, Bala Cynwyd, PA 19004; (610) 668-9780; e-mail: *bsiegel@siegelbusinessservices.com*

Top Things to Include in a Mutual Nondisclosure Agreement

A nondisclosure agreement—also called an NDA or confidentiality agreement—is a contract in which the parties promise to protect the confidentiality of secret information that is disclosed during employment or another type of business transaction. Generally, it does not matter who furnishes the nondisclosure agreement so long as it contains the basic elements to limit disclosure. Our expert provides us with the five important elements in a nondisclosure agreement, so here they are!

1. Definition of confidential information

Every nondisclosure agreement provides a list of the types or categories of confidential information or trade secrets at issue in the agreement. the purpose is to establish the boundaries or subject matter of the disclosure, without actually disclosing the secrets. For example, an NDA may define confidential information by listing the various types of information considered confidential, such as programming code,

financial information, related software materials, and innovative processes. When reviewing your agreement, make sure something on the list fits your type of disclosure.

2. Exclusions from confidential information

Every nondisclosure agreement excludes some information for protection. The party that receives the trade secret has no obligation to protect the excluded information. These exceptions are based on established principles of law—the most important one being that information is not protected if it was created or discovered by the receiving party prior to (or independent of) any involvement with you. For example, if another company develops an invention with similar trade-secret information before being exposed to your secrets, then that company is still free to use its independently created invention.

3. Obligations of the receiving party

The receiving party generally must hold and maintain the information in confidence and limit its use. Under most state laws, the receiving party cannot breach the confidential relationship, induce others to breach it, or induce others to acquire the secret by improper means. Most businesses will accept these contract obligations without discussion.

4. Time periods

Some agreements require that the receiving party maintain the secret information for a limited period of years, including language such as "the receiving party shall not use or disclose the secret for a period of five years from the date of execution of the agreement." You can often negotiate the time period. Disclosing parties want an open period with no limits; receiving parties usually want a short period. Five years is a common length in American nondisclosure agreements, although many companies insist on two or three years. In European nondisclosure agreements, it is not unusual for the period to be as long as ten years. Ultimately, the length you decide to use will depend on the relative bargaining power of the parties.

5. Miscellaneous provisions

Miscellaneous terms (sometimes known as "boilerplate") are included at the end of every agreement. They include such matters as which state's law will apply in the event the agreement is breached, whether arbitration will be used in the event of a dispute, or whether attorney fees will be awarded to the prevailing party in a dispute. *Always read an NDA before signing.* Some agreements are titled nondisclosure or confidentiality agreements, yet their terms have the opposite effect. Instead of agreeing to secrecy, the party with the secret effectively waives any claim of trade-secret confidentiality. If you sign one of these waiver agreements, you can lose important rights. Since trade-secret protection is based on confidentiality, your waiver could result in the loss of your trade secrets and leave you with no legal recourse.

Source: Schwegman Lundberg Woessner & Kluth (*www.slwk .com*)—A premier provider of intellectual property services to high-tech companies, universities, and individual inventors nationwide. The firm's services include client counseling, licensing, prelitigation advice, opinions, and patent prosecution. Contact them at 1600 TCF Tower, 121 South Eighth Street, Minneapolis, MN 55402; (612) 373-6900; e-mail: *contact@slwk.com.*

Things Every Business Seller Should Know

You've devoted untold time, money and energy to building and running your business. It may well represent your life's work and net worth. Now you've decided that it is finally the right time to sell. Here are six things you should know.

1. Financially, you would probably be better off keeping your business.

Buyers buy businesses for the income they can receive. They look at past profit performance to predict the future, then pay a price that will allow a fair risk-adjusted return. Mid-size businesses sell for 2.5 to 4.5 times pre-interest, pre-tax earnings. If your business generates annual benefits to you totaling $500,000, a buyer might pay four times or $2 million. Some seller financing will probably be required as well. If you are paid cash at closing and you invest this sum and earn 10 percent annually, your income will be $200,000 per year. You've taken a major pay cut.

2. If your primary sales pitch is "This business could . . .", you're likely wasting your time.

Buyers of private businesses are a very conservative bunch. If they are not, their bankers will require them to be. As such, they must rely on solid historical performance to justify purchase prices. Business sellers that try to peg most of the value on what the business "could" do typically waste their time and lose credibility. Buyers don't have to buy. They only put their money at risk when they find a good deal. If you wouldn't do it . . . it's likely nobody else will either.

3. To maximize value, be open to providing some seller financing.

If you ask for 100 percent cash at closing, studies show you'll typically receive a much lower total price. This is because the amount of cash that the buyer has and the amount the bank will lend are usually fixed amounts. The sum of the buyer's cash and bank financing is the maximum you can receive at closing. Now, would you like more? Then offer some seller financing. Worst case is you don't get paid your entire seller-financing portion, but you still received more than the all cash price!

4. They won't appreciate the work that went into building your business.

Unfortunately, buyers look at your business simply as an investment. They won't appreciate the blood, sweat and tears that you put into building it. You'll always have the pride of knowing what you accomplished and the respect of those who watched you do it. Don't expect any more from a buyer than a fair price.

5. Buyers love when you represent yourself.

Few sellers are experienced in business sales or valuation. All sellers are emotional when it comes to selling their "baby." No seller is objective. As the saying goes, "If you represent yourself you have a fool for a client." Do your heirs a favor and hire an expert to assist you.

6. Your competitors aren't good buyers.

Sure, competitors are logical buyer candidates and quite easy to identify. So you contact the owner of XYZ and ask, "Are you interested?" Now he has a free chance to gather information that will help him compete against you. And even if you don't send him your confidential information, he'll use the fact that you want to sell against you . . . starting today. Oh, he competes in a different territory? These buyers won't pay as much because the skill, expertise, processes and methods of your company are less valuable to those already doing what you do. The better (and lower risk) buyers are individuals, financial buyers or companies in related or adjacent industries.

Source: This article originally appeared in The Business Owner (www.TheBusinessOwner.com), the periodical of choice for owners of small and mid-size private businesses. All rights reserved, D. L. Perkins, LLC. Copyright 2006.

Best Methods for Valuing Your Business for Sale

When the time comes to sell your business—whether you're retiring, moving on to a new project, or because the business is not performing well—you must take a number of things into consideration. Not the least of these issues is the selling price. You want to make sure you get a fair deal when selling your company; therefore, you must make sure you properly evaluate the business and set a good price. There are several methods for determining the selling price, which our expert explains in the following list.

1. Cash flow

Cash flow will typically determine the price of the business, and it will be set based on a multiple of the owner's cash flow. Several factors—such as the size of the deal, the industry, and the growth and potential of the company—go into determining this multiple.

2. EBITDA

The price will often include the multiple of the cash flow, as well as a multiple of the earnings before interest, taxes, depreciation, and amortization (EBITDA). This multiple, too, will be determined by the same factors as the multiple of the cash flow.

3. Current market

Much like real estate, the market at the time of the sale will determine the selling price, or at least the range of prices into which the business will fall. When determining a price, it is often wise to work with a professional who is on top of trends in the current market and will be able to use this experience with business transactions to determine the best price for your company.

Source: Bernie Siegel, a Certified Business Intermediary and founder of Siegel Business Services, a company just outside Philadelphia that specializes in brokerage services for midsize business in the mid-Atlantic region. Mr. Siegel, a former franchise owner of nine Dunkin' Donuts stores, formed his business brokerage company in 1983. He is a fellow of the International Business Brokers Association, as well as its former vice president. He is also a member of the Pennsylvania Business Brokers Association. He can be contacted at the following address: Siegel Business Services, Inc., One Bala Plaza, Suite 516, Bala Cynwyd, PA 19004; (610) 668-9780; e-mail: *bsiegel@siegelbusinessservices.com.*

Top Reasons Owners Sell Their Companies

As an entrepreneur looking to buy a business rather than start your own, there are a number of things for you to consider when shopping for a company. Once you locate a business that interests you, you will likely want to know why the current owner is selling it. There are a number of reasons owners decide to sell, and the reason may or may not impact your decision to buy. Here are the most common reasons business owners put their businesses up for sale, from our resident buying and selling expert.

1. Burnout

The owner may simply be burned out on the entrepreneurial world, and this may or may not indicate anything in particular about the company. His burnout may be a result of a long career and not because of poor business operations; he may simply be seeking a new career path.

2. Retirement

Similar to being burned out and seeking a new direction, a business owner may want out of the company simply because she wants to retire. An owner who is retiring will likely have had a plan for retirement in place, meaning the company should be in good shape in preparation for a transfer of ownership.

3. Family reasons

Issues with a business owner's spouse can be both positive or negative and can impact his or her decision to sell the business. On the one hand, the owner could be going through a divorce that would necessitate the sale; or the owner's spouse may have received a new job in another town, and the business needs to be sold in preparation for a move.

4. Personal/health reasons

A business owner may have health issues that require time away from the business and even money from the sale of the business. Other issues such as substance abuse could lead to an owner's needing to sell his business.

5. Poor business performance

This may not necessarily mean that the business is failing, although that could be a reason the owner wants to sell. Instead, a business may not be performing up to the owner's expectations, but the performance could suit the expectations of a potential buyer.

6. To make a profit

Some entrepreneurs make a career out of buying businesses, improving them, and then selling them for a profit. If this is the case, a buyer may pay more but will likely be getting a company that is in good shape overall as a result of the work of the previous owner.

Source: Bernie Siegel, a Certified Business Intermediary and founder of Siegel Business Services, a company just outside Philadelphia that specializes in brokerage services for midsize business in the mid-Atlantic region. Mr. Siegel, a former franchise owner of nine Dunkin' Donuts stores, formed his business brokerage company in 1983. He is a fellow of the International Business Brokers Association, as well as its former vice president. He is also a member of the Pennsylvania Business Brokers Association. He can be contacted at the following address: Siegel Business Services, Inc., One Bala Plaza, Suite 516, Bala Cynwyd, PA 19004; (610) 668-9780; e-mail: *bsiegel@siegelbusinessservices.com*.

Things to Look for in a Business Broker

Looking to buy or sell a business? You're probably going to need a broker. Unfortunately, many people call themselves brokers but are in fact real-estate salespeople who sell real estate as well as sell businesses in addition to their real-estate activities. Your objective is to find a business broker who has listed and sold businesses in the industry or industries that interest you. Here are a few characteristics of a good business broker, provided by our business-exchange experts:

1. Experience

The broker must be experienced with at least two or three year's full-time work behind him in the industry.

2. Education

A good business broker should have a sound knowledge of finances and preferably have accounting qualifications.

3. Specialization

The broker must specialize in businesses and not be involved in real estate or commercial property.

4. Credentials

The broker must be licensed or approved to sell businesses under the regulations in your state.

5. Facilities

The broker should have office facilities available for meetings and to which you are able to direct inquiries by telephone when necessary.

6. Availability

The broker must be available by phone, even if it is just her mobile, so that you can clear queries that arise immediately.

7. Energy

The broker should have sufficient energy to be able to give the time to help find your business quickly. In this regard, age will be a factor. A young broker will not have the experience or maturity to handle the assignment properly, and a broker who is too old will not have the stamina or the energy to do the job quickly.

8. Easy to get along with

Your broker must be someone that you believe you can put your trust in because you will be working with him or her quite closely in the future. He or she must have credibility and bring across to you a sense that you can rely on him or her to secure a good business at the best price in the shortest amount of time.

Source: GlobalBX (*www.GlobalBX.com*) is a free business-for-sale listing exchange that provides a confidential forum to facilitate the buying and selling of businesses with thousands of businesses and franchises for sale as well as comprehensive business information for business buyers and sellers. Members can submit business, equipment and commercial real estate loans to hundreds of lenders for free. Resources include: Buyer & Seller's Guides, Franchise Information, Business Loans, Message Boards, Newsletter, Business Brokers and Advisors. View them at *www.GlobalBX.com* or contact them at 5255 Stevens Creek Blvd., Suite 130, Santa Clara, CA 95051 or via e-mail at *service@globalbx.com*.

Top Tax Considerations When Selling a Business

There are a number of things that must be taken into consideration by a business owner who is selling his or her business. Among these, tax issues are generally more pressing for the seller, as opposed to the buyer who has fewer tax concerns. One reason for this is that the seller will be making a gain on the sale, and that income will be taxed. To help guide the efforts of a seller, the following is a list of the top tax-related issues to consider during the process of selling a business.

1. Tangible assets

For LLCs, partnerships, sole proprietorships, and Sub S corporations, the seller should make sure that all tangible assets (equipment, buildings, etc.) are allocated at book value. Then, the book value is subtracted from the amount paid for the assets, and the difference is called "goodwill." The goodwill will be taxed at no more than 15 percent for the seller.

2. C corporation—stock sale

For C corporations, the corporation pays taxes on the gain from the sale, and the individual owner pays taxes on the money distributed to him from the corporation. Thus, it benefits an owner to have a stock sale in order to have long-term capital gains for which they would pay a lower tax rate than they would on regular income.

3. C corporation—asset sale

If an asset sale is necessary for a C corporation, the tax burden on the seller will be greater, but there are ways to reduce the burden. One way is to take as much of the sale as possible outside the corporation and directly to the stockholders of the corporation with the use of restrictive noncompete clauses and occasionally through personal goodwill.

Source: Bernie Siegel, a Certified Business Intermediary and founder of Siegel Business Services, a company just outside Philadelphia that specializes in brokerage services for midsize business in the mid-Atlantic region. Mr. Siegel, a former franchise owner of nine Dunkin' Donuts stores, formed his business brokerage company in 1983. He is a fellow of the International Business Brokers Association, as well as its former vice president. He is also a member of the Pennsylvania Business Brokers Association. He can be contacted at the following address: Siegel Business Services, Inc., One Bala Plaza, Suite 516, Bala Cynwyd, PA 19004; (610) 668-9780; e-mail: *bsiegel@siegelbusinessservices.com*.

Top Mistakes Owners Make When Selling Their Business

When the time comes to sell your business, a proper exit strategy is the key to a successful sale. To get the maximum sale price for your business, you must be able to maximize value and be in control of negotiations. There are many pitfalls in the sales process, and you must be able to avoid the big mistakes in order to come out of the process satisfied. The following is a listing of the top mistakes that a seller can make throughout the sales process, so be sure to avoid these for a successful transaction!

1. Being reactive

Stay in control of the sale of your business. Do not wait for someone to offer to buy, and then jump at the chance. If you are going to sell, do the proper preparation and stay in control of the transaction. Do not dabble with your business. You are either for sale or you are not.

2. Stating a price up-front

Naming a price for your business at the outset of negotiations will ultimately hurt the sale of the business. The business could potentially go for higher than you expect, so let negotiations run their course and get the highest price possible. Also, by naming a price that is too high, you may scare off potential buyers who were expecting to negotiate a reasonable price.

3. Settling for a low price

Obtain several potential buyers to conduct price and term negotiations and create competition among them. This competition will lead to a higher sale price and will not leave you stuck with having to sell to one buyer at a price much lower than you otherwise would have gotten.

4. Disclosing information about the sale

Keep the fact that the business is for sale only between important players in the deal. The owner, a business broker, and potential buyers should keep the negotiations between them to ensure that those on the outside of the negotiations—such as employees, customers, and suppliers—do not get worried about the business being sold and decide to leave.

5. Representing yourself

Most potential buyers will be working with professionals when shopping for a business. Working alone will put you at a disadvantage when you find yourself negotiating with professionals for the final sale. Hire qualified third parties to help you prepare the business, develop presentation materials, confidentially contact buyers, conduct the negotiations, and complete the final sale of the business.

6. Dealing with only one buyer

Similar to the mistake of selling too low, remain open to offers from many potential buyers throughout the sale process. Negotiating with only one buyer who has no competition could result in drawn out negotiations being controlled by the buyer and ending in a low sale price.

7. Selling to a competitor

Negotiating the sale of the business with a competitor will result in the disclosure of important information about your company, which in turn will make your business less valuable to another competitor who might otherwise want to buy it. Keep your trade secrets away from competitors and sell to an outside buyer.

8. Failing to recognize/maximize value

Be sure to understand everything about your business that makes it valuable and gives it a competitive edge. Aside from profits, there are intellectual properties and other assets that will add great value to the company. Presenting your intangibles so buyers factor them into the sale price is key to obtaining the best possible price for your business.

9. Bad timing when disclosing information

Do not show or provide prospective buyers confidential information too early. Generate interest among buyers with enticing descriptive information about your financial situation and other aspects of the business. Allow the confidential information to come out only when you have accepted a written letter of intent.

10. Failing to prepare in advance

It is never too early to have a plan for selling the business, even if you've just started it. You may not know when you will sell, but keeping a strategy in mind will allow you to tailor daily decisions in contemplation of an eventual sale and improve the business, eliminate obstacles, and add value continuously until it is time to sell, at which point you will garner a higher sale price than you would have without the foresight.

Source: Phil Currie, Managing Partner of Shoreline Partners, LLC (*www.shoreline.com*), a San Diego–based mergers and acquisitions firm.

Typical Contracts Used in a Business Sale

Whether you are buying a business or selling your own, you must be aware of the various legal aspects of such a transaction. The sale of a business can be complex and does not simply involve one person paying another and taking over the operations. Some of the most important aspects of a business sale are the contractual agreements and other legal documents. To help with your business sale, the following is a listing of the key contracts that are typically involved in the transaction.

1. Confidentiality agreements

These agreements ensure that all confidential information about the company, such as financial records (which are disclosed to the potential buyer and the professionals involved), will remain confidential. This means that all parties agree to use the information only for the purposes of evaluating the business and for completing the sale, and not for any outside purpose.

2. Fee agreements with intermediaries

These agreements are made between the buyer or seller and the professionals with whom they are working. Fee agreements simply state that the party agrees to pay the fees of the intermediary and also specify the terms of payment for the specific service to be performed by the intermediary.

3. General proposal letter

This letter is drafted by the buyer as a proposal for the purchase of the seller's business. This letter is not a contract per se, but it does describe the transaction and includes the proposed price, the terms of the deal, and exactly what is being acquired by the purchaser.

4. Term sheet

This document lays out the basic price and terms of the deal. It includes the price, when and how it is to be paid, and the totals. It is essentially a summary of the deal that is to be made.

5. Letter of intent

As its name indicates, this is a letter stating the intent of the buyer to purchase the business. It states that the seller will take the business off the market during negotiations with the buyer and that all information will remain confidential. The letter is nonbinding and is a basic agreement between the parties to conduct a fair negotiation process.

6. Purchase and sale agreement

This document is legally binding and lays out the conditions of the sale, assures each side that the other is financially capable of completing the sale, and indicates the obligations of each party between the signing of the contract and the closing of the sale. Among other things, this contract protects the buyer from undisclosed liabilities and gives him or her leverage in the case of misrepresentation on behalf of the seller.

Source: *Buying Your Own Business*, by Russell Robb (Adams Media, 1995)—This book lays out the basics for an entrepreneur to purchase a business, including the legal considerations, required professional help, contractual concerns, and post-sale responsibilities, among other topics. Russell Robb is an experienced entrepreneur, having bought and sold three businesses. He is the managing director of Tully & Holland, Inc, a Wellesley, Massachusetts–based firm. They are specialists in corporate finance, serving direct marketers, consumer product manufacturers, and distributors. He is also the editor of *M&A Today*, a national newsletter on mergers and acquisitions. More information on Robb is available on his company's Web site at *www.tullyandholland.com*.

Things to Do Before You Shut Down Your Business

Thinking of just chucking it all and playing a round of golf? Well, before you shut down your business, you're going to want to make sure you've taken these steps first to let the government know of your plans.

1. Make final federal tax deposits

Electronic Federal Tax Paying System (EFTPS), or Form 8109-B

2. File final quarterly or annual employment tax form

Form 940, Employer's Annual Federal Unemployment (FUTA) Tax Return

Form 941, Employer's Quarterly Federal Tax Return

Form 943, Employer's Annual Tax Return for Agricultural Employees

Form 943-A, Agricultural Employer's Record of Federal Tax Liability

3. Issue final wage and withholding information to employees

Form W-2, Wage and Tax Statement

4. Report information from W-2s issued

Form W-3, Transmittal of Income and Tax Statements

5. File final tip income and allocated tips information return

Form 8027, Employer's Annual Information Return of Tip Income and Allocated Tips

6. Report capital gains or losses

Form 1040, U.S. Individual Income Tax Return

Form 1065, U.S. Return of Income Partnership

Form 1120 (Schedule D), Capital Gains and Losses

7. Report partner's/shareholder's shares

Form 1065 (Schedule K-1), Partner's Share of Income, Credits, Deductions

Form 1120S (Schedule K-1), Shareholder's Share of Income, Credits, Deductions

8. File final employee pension/benefit plan

Form 5500, Annual Return/Report of Employee Benefits Plan

9. Issue payment information to subcontractors

Form 1099-MISC, Miscellaneous Income

10. Report information from 1099s issued

Form 1096, Annual Summary and Transmittal of U.S. Information Returns

11. Report corporate dissolution or liquidation

Form 966, Corporate Dissolution or Liquidation

12. Consider allowing S corporation election to terminate

Form 1120S, Instructions

13. Report business asset sales

Form 8594, Asset Acquisition Statement

14. Report the sale or exchange of property used in your trade or business

Form 4797, Sales of Business Property

Source: Small Business Notes (*www.smallbusinessnotes.com*)— Provides information and resources for other businesses struggling to provide that same quality in a challenging economic environment. Their purpose is to provide the resources for all the information that a small business needs to operate. Contact the editor of Small Business Notes, Judith Kautz by sending e-mail to *info@smallbusinessnotes.com*.

Starting Your Business

Questions to Ask to Tell If You Have What It Takes to Start a Business

Understanding who you are and what you really want in life are the key areas to address in making a decision to go into business. It is very important to do an assessment of yourself and your relationship to your business idea before you begin your business. Here are some questions posed by our expert, a business coach and writer.

1. Do I have the persistence and patience necessary to be a business owner?

It would be nice if once you wrote your business plan all you needed to do would be to execute flawlessly and everything would fall into place. Maybe it happens to a few businesses but usually in some part of the plan you get different results than you expected. It takes patience to wait for the result in the first place. It takes persistence to keep updating your plan and then trying something else until you find how to make it work.

2. Does this business idea really energize me?

Am I really excited about it? If your vision of this business is really compelling, it will give you the energy to move forward on your idea. The energy allows you to persist even when things are not going as planned and it helps you to generate enthusiasm in others.

3. Can I generate enthusiasm about my idea from others?

New business owners have to spend most of their time marketing initially. If the business owner him/herself can get others excited about his/her business idea, then that is the first step in generating interest from a customer or a strategic partner. The owner must be able to articulate the idea in a way that is convincing to the customer or client.

4. Am I convinced that I am exactly the right person to own this business? Can I articulate why?

Self-confidence is important in the success of the business. You must believe in yourself before others will believe in you.

5. Do I have the commitment necessary to put aside other interests to focus my energy on this business?

There will be lots of distractions while you start your business. Are you willing to commit to whatever it takes to get the business up and running successfully?

6. Am I able to quickly recover from setbacks and not take things personally?

Can you still keep working and feeling confident even on a day that a big client or big prospect decides against using your service or buying your product?

7. Who will support me in this endeavor?

It helps to have people in your life that appreciate you and really want you to succeed. Family support is critical because you'll need to spend large amounts of time working and your family needs to understand this. Mentors, colleagues and coaches also are important for advice and encouragement.

8. Do I have enough financial reserves to carry me until I am profitable?

Your business needs enough capital to get going until it is profitable. You also need money in reserve for your personal expenses if things get tight. Worrying about money will sap your energy.

9. What weaknesses do I have that may get in my way as I start this business? What will I do about them?

Identifying your weaknesses and strengths is an important task. Use your strengths in running your business and find ways to off-load the tasks you are not good at. Shore up those weaknesses as best you can in the beginning when finances are tight. Being aware of them is the first step.

10. What is my intuition telling me about this venture?

Be in tune with your intuition. Business people get caught up in the analytical part of the business. The numbers do help you run your business but don't ignore what your gut tells you. Leave some time in your day to spend time thinking about your vision. (Daydreaming!)

Source: Alvah Parker is a Business and Career Coach as well as publisher of *Parker's Points*, an e-mail tip list and *Road to Success*, an ezine. Parker's Value Program© enables her clients to find their own way to work that is more fulfilling and profitable. Her clients are managers, business owners, sole practitioners, attorneys and people in transition. Alvah is found on the web at *www.asparker .com*. She may also be reached at 781-598-0388. Copyright © 2004 all rights reserved.

Popular Business Organization Types

One of the first decisions you will have to make as a business owner is how the company should be structured. This decision will have long-term implications, so consult with an accountant and attorney to select the form of ownership that is right for you. Here are the most common types of business organizations.

1. Sole proprietorships

The vast majority of small business starts out as sole proprietorships. These firms are owned by one person, usually the individual who has day-to-day responsibility for running the business. Sole proprietors own all the assets of the business and the profits generated by it. They also assume complete responsibility for any of its liabilities or debts. In the eyes of the law and the public, you are one in the same as the business.

2. Partnerships

In a partnership, two or more people share ownership of a single business. Like proprietorships, the law does not distinguish between the business and its owners. The partners should have a legal agreement that sets forth how decisions will be made, profits will be shared, disputes will be resolved, how future partners will be admitted to the partnership, how partners can be bought out, or what steps will be taken to dissolve the partnership when needed. It is hard to think about a "breakup" when the business is just getting started, but many partnerships split up during crises, and unless there is a defined process, there will be even greater problems. They also must decide up-front how much time and capital each will contribute. There are three types of partnerships: general partnership, limited partnership, and partnership with limited liability and joint venture.

3. Corporations

A corporation, chartered by the state in which it is headquartered, is considered by law to be a unique entity, separate and apart from those who own it. A corporation can be taxed; it can be sued; it can enter into contractual agreements. The owners are the shareholders. The shareholders elect a board of directors to oversee the major policies and decisions. The corporation has a life of its own and does not dissolve when ownership changes.

4. S corporations

A tax election only, it enables the shareholder to treat the earnings and profits as distributions and have them pass through directly to their personal tax return. The catch here is that the shareholder, if working for the company and if there is a profit, must pay herself wages, and it must meet standards of "reasonable compensation." This can vary by geographical region as well as occupation, but the basic rule is to pay yourself what you would have to pay someone

to do your job, as long as there is enough profit. If you do not do this, the IRS can reclassify all of the earnings and profit as wages, and you will be liable for all of the payroll taxes on the total amount.

5. Limited liability company (LLC)

The LLC is a relatively new type of hybrid business structure that is now permissible in most states. It is designed to provide the limited liability features of a corporation and the tax efficiencies and operational flexibility of a partnership. Formation is more complex and formal than that of a general partnership. The owners are members, and the duration of the LLC is usually determined when the organization papers are filed. The time limit can be continued if desired by a vote of the members at the time of expiration. LLCs must not have more than two of the four characteristics that define corporations: limited liability to the extent of assets, continuity of life, centralization of management, and free transferability of ownership interests.

Source: Small Business Administration (*www.sba.gov*).

Top Reasons Small Businesses Fail

It's no secret that a large majority of small businesses fail in the first five years. The question is why do they fail and what can I do to prevent problems in my own business? Here are the fourteen top reasons, which may help you to determine why your business isn't growing and thriving.

1. Mistaking a business for a hobby

Just because you love something doesn't mean you should convert it into a business. Too often, businesses fail because the owner feels her passion is shared by others. Research your business idea and make sure it's something that other people are willing to pay for.

2. Poor planning

Yes, you must have a business plan. It can be a simple three-page plan or a huge forty-page plan. The point is that you look at all the aspects of your business in advance and are prepared to handle problems when they arise. Your business plan helps you focus on your goals and your vision, as well as setting out concrete plans to accomplish them. And don't get mellow—revisit and revise your business plan annually.

3. Entrepreneurial excitement

Entrepreneurs often get excited about new ideas but are unable to determine if they're "true opportunities" and/or put them into practice. Test every new idea against your business plan and mission statement before deciding whether to undertake it. Ask yourself two questions: Will this move me toward my business goals, and Do I have the time and skill to implement this?

4. No diversity

Too often, small business owners will have just one product, one service, or one big client. They cling tight to this one thing because it brings in good revenue. But what if that one thing disappears? Variety and diversification will cushion you against the ebb and flow of business tides.

5. Poor recordkeeping and financial controls

Yes, you have to keep financial and business records, you have to review your revenue and expense report each month, and you have to file taxes and other business-related filings. If you don't know how to do these, or don't want to, get help from someone who does.

6. Lack of experience in running a business in general, or in the industry you're entering

There are so many hats you have to wear to run a business effectively: marketing, selling, strategic planning, finance, employee relations. On top of that, you have to understand your industry, the skills required to offer your products and services, and the trends in the industry. If you don't know about these basic skills, educate yourself. Talk to others who are successfully running their own businesses, talk to industry leaders, get a book, find a Web site, get a coach, take a class, do your homework. And keep increasing your business and industry skills by attending classes or reading new books every year.

7. Poor money management

You need to be able to live for one to two years without income when getting started; often businesses are very slow to get off the ground. Also, you have to create and use a realistic business budget and not constantly drain business income on personal spending.

8. Wrong location

If your business runs out of commercial space, you need to make sure that you are convenient to your customers, and near your suppliers and your employees.

9. Competition

Customers will go where they can find the best products and services. It's important to know who your competition is, what they have to offer, and what makes your own products or services better.

10. Procrastination and poor time management

Putting off tasks that you don't enjoy will sink your business faster than anything else. You can't afford to waste time on unimportant tasks while critical tasks pile up. All tasks need to be done; if you don't like to do them (or don't want to spend your time doing them), hire someone to do them for you. If your time management and prioritizing skills are rusty, hire a small business coach or take a class. Don't wait until you're "inspired" to do a task or you'll postpone doing critical business tasks for a long time.

11. Ineffective marketing

Learn the basics of marketing and make sure that you track the success or failure of each marketing technique you use. Understand the concept of a marketing funnel and use appropriate techniques for each level of the funnel. Dump those marketing techniques that aren't working. Learn about newer techniques, especially when it comes to Internet marketing.

12. Ineffective sales techniques

Once you have a potential client, you have to know how to lead them down the sales path.

If you don't understand the basics of selling, get some education on it immediately. If a selling technique doesn't work, try another one.

13. Poor customer service

Once you have a customer, you have to keep them. There are two key points here: make sure you pay attention to what the customer wants (and how these wants can change over time), and make sure you provide quick return of phone calls and e-mails, proper billing, win-win problem solving, and an overall pleasant, professional demeanor.

14. Entrepreneurial burnout

Owning your own business requires a huge investment of time, money, energy, and emotion. It's easy to work long days and forget to take time off. But in the end, this only causes burnout; your motivation and creativity will suffer, and a pessimistic attitude will prevail. You'll find yourself unable to balance your business and personal life, and both will suffer. Schedule self-care time into your work week and be religious about taking time off from your business.

Source: Karyn Greenstreet (*www.passionforbusiness.com*) of Passion For Business LLC helps self-employed people create the business and personal success they want and deserve. They offer consulting and coaching services, as well as educational workshops and teleclasses. Contact them at Passion For Business LLC, PO Box 331, Revere, PA 18953; (610) 346-6601.

Steps to Take When Choosing a Franchise

Franchising is a wonderful way to go into business for yourself. So many things have already been established for your benefit: branding, marketing, processes, products, systems, etc. Building a business through franchising has been so successful that franchised businesses generate jobs for more than 18 million Americans and account for 9.5 percent of the private-sector economic output, according to a study released by the International Franchise Association Educational Foundation. If you are convinced that you want to investigate franchising for your next career move, how do you go about finding just the right one? Here is our expert's recommended list of ideas for determining what to look for in a franchise that will meet your needs, expectations and goals.

1. Determine what you have to offer and what you need from a business

Before you start looking at franchises, take stock of that most important component of the equation—YOU. What skills, experience and interests do you have? Consider your past jobs and determine what you liked best and least about them; then make a list of your strengths and weaknesses. How much money can you invest and how much would you like to make? Are you comfortable managing others or would you prefer to work alone? Where do you want to work? Are you willing to relocate? What hours are you willing to work while the business ramps up and what lifestyle expectations do you have after the business is established? How do you feel about selling and the sales process? By starting with a list of what you have to offer and what you need from a business, you can create a strategy and model for your research.

2. Keep all your options open

Keep an open mind. Whether (at Step 1) you use an outside resource or do your own franchise research via the Internet, it is best to keep all options open when considering a franchise. An inexperienced person may approach the process by thinking, "Well, I love donuts. How about a donut franchise?" And after spending days or weeks of research on Krispy Kreme, Dunkin' Donuts and others, the individual may find he doesn't have the required capital, the territory he wants is not available, and he'd have to give up weekends if owning a food franchise. Another ineffective way to begin your franchise research is to lock yourself in to one or two concepts. If you think, "I'll only look at ice cream and exercise franchises," you may miss finding that that gem of a concept that would mesh perfectly with your needs. With thousands of franchise companies available, keeping an open mind is the best strategy you can employ to get on the ground floor of that new, hot concept or to find something that will really take off in your market.

3. Contact the franchisors and request information about their concepts

Let's say you've found an assortment of franchises that look promising. What do you do next? Contact the franchisors and request information about their concepts. You will probably get call from someone in the franchise development department who will gauge your interest and advise you if the territory you seek is available. You will want to thoroughly view the web site information and any brochures and videos they send you. Keep notes on your impressions. Are their materials professional and up-to-date? Are you treated courteously by a friendly and knowledgeable member of the corporate office? Are your questions and concerns answered to your satisfaction? What you see from the company at this time may be an indication of the type of support you would receive as a franchisee in their system.

4. Read the company's UFOC (Uniform Franchise Offering Circular)

Your next step is to read the company's UFOC (Uniform Franchise Offering Circular), a document every franchise in the United States is required to provide. From this you will learn the history of the company, the training and marketing programs, and what costs, royalties and fees you will be required to pay. Some franchisors also provide earnings claims in the UFOC that will help you estimate the potential of the business. The UFOC is full of information about the franchise and it clearly explains the responsibilities of the franchisee (you) and the franchisor. Your UFOC review and understanding is a very significant part of the research process. By paying attention to what you discover in a company's UFOC, you can weed out franchises that just don't measure up. Some warning signs of a franchise that is facing challenges are extensive litigation with franchisees or a closing rate of units greater than what's being opened.

5. Call existing franchisees

This step is considered to be of monumental importance when judging the likelihood of finding happiness in a particular franchise: CALL EXISTING FRANCHISEES! Existing franchisees are your best source of information for finding out what really happens in a business on a day-to-day basis. You can ask what they like and dislike about the business, if they are happy with corporate support, and even get a feel for the type of earnings a franchise makes. Gather a variety of opinions and you'll get a clear picture of not only the franchise itself but of how you'd fit into the organization. That is why this step is so significant to your being able to make a definitive decision.

6. Narrow down your choices

Your next step is to narrow down your choices. Okay, maybe it's not all that easy. Let's review what you've done so far: Made a list of your strengths, experiences and needs. While keeping an open mind, found some companies that look promising. Requested information. Reviewed the UFOC. Talked with existing franchisees. Hopefully you've now found one or more companies that will meet your needs. When you've made it this far, it's time to go to Discovery Day (an onsite meeting with a franchisor). At this meeting you will be introduced to the top people in the home office and you may make a visit to a local franchisee, allowing you to ask even more questions and maybe to get some hands-on experience with the business. Discovery Days are very interesting and exciting. When you leave, you will have a good understanding of the franchise. Don't forget that this is a two-way street. They'll be evaluating you as thoroughly as you evaluate their business.

7. Make your decision

The last step, of course, is making the final decision. Like any major decision, you will be filled with anticipation and anxiety, excitement and fear. Those are very normal feelings, experienced by almost everyone. But if you've done your homework and followed the steps as outlined, you should be very comfortable with your decision. Congratulations—you're ready to be a franchisee!

Source: FranChoice, Inc.: (www.franchoice.com). FranChoice helps future entrepreneurs realize the dream of owning their own business. Their franchise experts help customers identify franchises that best meet their criteria, and then guide them through the franchise opportunity investigation process. Contact them at: FranChoice, Inc., 7500 Flying Cloud Drive, Suite 600, Eden Prairie, MN 55344, or call them at 952-942-5561.

Fastest-Growing Franchise Organizations

The following are the ten fastest-growing franchises according to *Entrepreneur* magazine.

1. Subway

In 1965, seventeen-year-old Fred DeLuca and family friend Peter Buck opened Pete's Super Submarines in Bridgeport, Connecticut. With a loan from Buck for only $1,000, DeLuca hoped the tiny sandwich shop would earn enough to put him through college. After struggling through the first few years, the founders changed the company's name to Subway and began franchising in 1974. Offering a fresh, healthy alternative to fast-food restaurants, Subway has franchises throughout the United States and in several countries, with locations in traditional and nontraditional sites alike.

325 Bic Dr.
Milford, CT 06460
(800) 888-4848; (203) 877-4281
Fax: (203)783-7329
www.subway.com

2. Pizza Hut Inc.

While college students in Wichita, Kansas, Frank and Dan Carney were approached by a family friend with the idea of opening a pizza parlor. Inspired, the brothers borrowed $600 from their mother, purchased secondhand equipment, and rented a small building on a busy intersection in their hometown. With that, the first Pizza Hut opened its doors in 1958. More than forty years later, Pizza Hut has locations throughout the world serving its specialty pizzas. Pizza Hut is owned by Yum! Brands, parent company of Taco Bell, KFC, A&W Restaurants, and Long John Silver's.

14841 Dallas Pkwy.
Dallas, TX 75254
(866) 298-6986
Fax: (502) 874-8848
www.yumfranchises.com

3. Quiznos Sub

In the kitchen of Footer's Italian restaurant in Denver, the first Quiznos recipes were born. The owners of Footer's used the baguette-style bread, red-wine vinaigrette dressing, and tuna salad created in their kitchen to establish their new venture, opening the first Quiznos in Denver in 1981.

Over twenty years later, Quiznos has locations throughout the United States, Puerto Rico, Canada, the United Kingdom, Japan, and Australia, using the original recipes from Footer's kitchen. Restaurants also serve soups and salads.

1475 Lawrence St., No. 400
Denver, CO 80202
(720) 359-3300
Fax: (720) 359-3399
www.quiznos.com

4. Jan-Pro Franchising Int'l. Inc.

Jacques Lapointe founded Jan-Pro in Providence, Rhode Island, in 1991. It started franchising the following year. Jan-Pro is a commercial cleaning franchise that operates throughout the United States and Canada.

11605 Haynes Bridge Rd., No. 425
Alpharetta, GA 30004
(866) 355-1064
Fax: (678) 336-1781
www.jan-pro.com
E-mail: *melanie.nance@jan-pro.com*

5. Curves

At the age of twenty, premed student Gary Heavin had taken over a failing fitness center in Houston, turning the business around and, within five years, opened six more centers. After ten years and seventeen centers, Heavin's business went under. Not wanting to give up, Heavin took lessons from the strengths and weaknesses of his first chain and decided to open a second. In 1992 Heavin opened Curves for Women, a women-only fitness center, in

Harlingen, Texas. The company began franchising in 1995.

100 Ritchie Rd.
Waco, TX 76712
(800) 848-1096; (254) 399-9285
Fax: (254) 776-2762
www.buycurves.com

6. Jani-King

As a student at the University of Oklahoma in 1968, Jim Cavanaugh worked as a night auditor at a hotel chain. While there, he realized that there would always be a strong need for janitorial services as long as there were office buildings. He began marketing janitorial services by day and cleaning buildings with his friends by night. Within a year, Cavanaugh established Jani-King, and in 1974 he started franchising. A commercial-cleaning service, Jani-King sets up franchisees with a customer base and charges fees depending on the size of that initial base.

16885 Dallas Pkwy.
Addison, TX 75001
(800) 552-5264
Fax: (972) 991-5723; (972) 239-7706
www.janiking.com
E-mail: *info@janiking.com*

7. Jackson Hewitt Tax Service

Started in 1960, Jackson Hewitt is a full-service, year-round national tax service specializing in computerized federal and state preparation of individual returns. It began franchising in 1986, the same year that the IRS introduced electronic filing.

3 Sylvan Way
Parsippany, NJ 07054
(800) 475-2904
Fax: (973) 630-0909
www.jacksonhewitt.com
E-mail: *franchisedev@jtax.com*

8. The UPS Store

Founded in 1980, Mail Boxes Etc. became a subsidiary of UPS in 2001. The company now franchises The UPS Store concept, whose locations provide packaging, shipping, copy and print services, mailbox services, computer time rentals, and more. The UPS Store and Mail Boxes Etc. franchises are located throughout the United States and in more than forty countries.

6060 Cornerstone Ct. W.
San Diego, CA 92121
(877) 623-7253
Fax: (858) 546-7492
www.theupsstore.com
E-mail: *usafranchise@mbe.com*

9. Coverall Cleaning Concepts

Founded in 1985, Coverall Cleaning Concepts franchisees provide a variety of commercial cleaning services to customers throughout North and South America, Australia, and Asia. These services include hard floor care, carpet cleaning, and restroom sanitation.

5201 Congress Ave., No. 275
Boca Raton, FL 33487
(800) 537-3371; (561) 922-2500
Fax: (561) 922-2424
www.coverall.com

10. CleanNet USA Inc.

Mark Salek founded CleanNet USA in 1987 and opened the company's first office the following year in Columbia, Maryland, providing cleaning services to commercial clients in the Baltimore/Washington, D.C. area. Today, CleanNet's uniformed force offers a variety of cleaning services for commercial, retail, and industrial facilities in financial, hospitality, medical, and other industries.

9861 Broken Land Pkwy., No. 208
Columbia, MD 21046
(800) 735-8838; (410) 720-6444
Fax: (410) 720-5307
www.cleannetusa.com

Source: *Entrepreneur Magazine's 2006 Franchise 500, www .entrepreneur.com/franchise500.*

Lowest-Cost Franchises to Start Up

The following lists the Top 10 Low-Cost Franchises for 2006 from our friends at Entrepreneur Magazine.

1. Curves

At the age of twenty, premed student Gary Heavin had taken over a failing fitness center in Houston, turning the business around and, within five years, opened six more centers. After ten years and seventeen centers, Heavin's business went under. Not wanting to give up, Heavin took lessons from the strengths and weaknesses of his first chain and decided to open a second. In 1992 Heavin opened Curves for Women, a women-only fitness center, in

Harlingen, Texas. The company began franchising in 1995.

100 Ritchie Rd.
Waco, TX 76712
(800) 848-1096; (254) 399-9285
Fax: (254) 776-2762
www.buycurves.com

2. Jackson Hewitt Tax Service

Started in 1960, Jackson Hewitt is a full-service, year-round national tax service specializing in computerized federal and state preparation of individual returns. It began franchising in 1986, the same year that the IRS introduced electronic filing.

3 Sylvan Way
Parsippany, NJ 07054
(800) 475-2904
Fax: (973) 630-0909
www.jacksonhewitt.com
E-mail: *franchisedev@jtax.com*

3. Jani-King

As a student at the University of Oklahoma in 1968, Jim Cavanaugh worked as a night auditor at a hotel chain. While there, he realized that there would always be a strong need for janitorial services as long as there were office buildings. He began marketing janitorial services by day and cleaning buildings with his friends by night. Within a year, Cavanaugh established Jani-King, and in 1974 he started franchising. A commercial cleaning service, Jani-King sets up franchisees with a customer base and charges fees depending on the size of that initial base.

16885 Dallas Pkwy.
Addison, TX 75001
(800) 552-5264
Fax: (972) 991-5723; (972) 239-7706
www.janiking.com
E-mail: *info@janiking.com*

4. RE/MAX Int'l. Inc

Founded by Dave and Gail Liniger in Denver in 1973, RE/MAX is now a global network of more than 62,000 real-estate agents. The Linigers created the company to give agents higher commissions. In the RE/MAX system, agents are in charge of their own business, split office expenses equally with other agents, and operate under a maximum commission concept.

PO Box 3907
Englewood, CO 80155-3907
(800) 525-7452; (303) 770-5531
Fax: (303) 796-3599
www.remax.com

5. Liberty Tax Service

John Hewitt, founder of Jackson Hewitt Tax Service, acquired a tax company that had been franchising in Canada since 1973. The company changed its name to Liberty Tax Service and now offers franchises throughout the United States and Canada.

1716 Corporate Landing
Virginia Beach, VA 23454
(800) 790-3863; (757) 493-8855
Fax: (757) 493-0169
www.libertytaxfranchise.com
E-mail: *sales@libtax.com*

6. Jan-Pro Franchising Int'l. Inc.

Jacques Lapointe founded Jan-Pro in Providence, Rhode Island, in 1991. It started franchising the following year. Jan-Pro is a commercial cleaning franchise that operates throughout the United States and Canada.

11605 Haynes Bridge Rd., No. 425
Alpharetta, GA 30004
(866) 355-1064
Fax: (678) 336-1781
www.jan-pro.com
E-mail: *melanie.nance@jan-pro.com*

7. ServiceMaster Clean

ServiceMaster was incorporated in 1947 as Wade, Wenger and Associates. Marion Wade got the idea for his company after an accident with chemicals left him temporarily blind in 1945. Today, it is part of the ServiceMaster Co. franchise family, which includes franchise companies Merry Maids, Furniture Medic, and Terminix. ServiceMaster Residential/Commercial Services is headquartered in Memphis, Tennessee, and has enjoyed more than twenty-five years of consecutive growth.

3839 Forest Hill Irene Rd.
Memphis, TN 38125
(800) 255-9687; (901) 597-7500
Fax: (901) 597-7580
www.ownafranchise.com
E-mail: *brwilliams@smclean.com*

8. Kumon Math & Reading Centers

High school math teacher Toru Kumon developed the Kumon method of learning forty years ago in Japan, when his son was struggling with second-grade arithmetic. Realizing that a strong foundation in the basics—addition, subtraction, multiplication, and division—was essential for higher-level math, Kumon created a series of math worksheets for his son to work on after school. With daily practice, Kumon's son gradually expanded his mastery of mathematical skills, and by sixth grade was able to solve differential equations and integral calculus problems. Today, Kumon franchisees apply this method of daily practice and self-paced advancement to children's math and reading skills. Kumon Centers are now located throughout North America.

300 Frank W. Burr Blvd., 5th Floor
Teaneck, NJ 07666
(866) 633-0740; (201) 928-0444
Fax: (201) 928-0044
www.kumon.com
E-mail: *franchise@kumon.com*

9. Jazzercise Inc.

While teaching traditional jazz dance classes in Evanston, Illinois, in 1969, Judi Sheppard Missett turned her students away from the mirrors and started a "just for fun" class that incorporated dance moves to provide aerobic exercise. After moving to Southern California, she started training other instructors in the Jazzercise program in 1977. Six years later, the company began franchising. Now Jazzercise's CEO, she continues to teach weekly Jazzercise classes and choreograph new dance routines. Based in Carlsbad, California, Jazzercise has more than 5,000 instructors teaching its total-body conditioning program to almost half a million participants each year in the United States and more than thirty other countries. Jazzercise instructors are trained and certified before becoming franchised.

2460 Impala Dr.
Carlsbad, CA 92008
(760) 476-1750
Fax: (760) 602-7180
www.jazzercise.com

10. Chem-Dry Carpet Drapery & Upholstery Cleaning

Robert Harris worked as a carpet cleaner to pay for his law school tuition. He found the cleaning methods being used were not getting the job done and set about developing new solutions to get carpets cleaner. Harris started using his new solution to clean carpets for family and friends, and demand for his services quickly grew. In 1977, Harris founded Chem-Dry to bring his new cleaning methods to more customers. Chem-Dry began franchising in 1978 and now has locations in the United States, Canada, Japan, Australia, and the United Kingdom.

1530 N. 1000 West
Logan, UT 84321
(877) 307-8233
Fax: (435) 755-0021
www.chemdry.com
E-mail: *charlie@chemdry.com*

Source: *Entrepreneur* magazine's 2006 Franchise 500. Visit *www.entrepreneur.com/franchise500*.

Typical Business Start-up Legal Problems

Many businesses start around the kitchen table or on the computer in the basement. As underground businesses, they operate informally and bypass many of the legal requirements. As they grow and enter the mainstream, it's important to "get legal." There is no question, it costs more to operate legally. The transition is costly but necessary to growth. Being smart about how you make the transition can save you money in the long run and enable your business to grow without major problems. Here are some examples of common problems experienced by businesses going mainstream.

1. Scrambling to get a big order

A software business being run from the basement using neighborhood kids to fill orders after school had to really scramble to get that "big order." In order to get a contract from a large company, they had to quickly arrange outsourced manufacturing and quality control procedures. They had to demonstrate that they owned the intellectual property in the software and that their business and employment practices would satisfy their major customer's "audit" procedures.

2. Cash crisis because of higher overhead

A popular baking business found itself in a cash crisis when it expanded to a (legal) commercial kitchen and discovered that its prices were too low to cover its increased overhead. Doubling prices caused a dramatic decline in orders.

3. Employee issues

To pursue commercial opportunities, a cleaning business found itself with a slew of legal problems related to its workers. They had to set up procedures for each worker, including filling out the I-9, an immigration form that requires viewing documents that establish both the identity and the employment eligibility of the employee. They had to set up a payroll service to handle payroll tax withholdings and get worker's compensation insurance and liability insurance. The increased costs required that they increase their rates significantly.

4. Payroll and sales tax penalties

Failure to pay payroll and sales taxes in a timely manner resulted in the tax authorities "levying" on the personal and business bank accounts of a business owner. This caused major problems, disrupting business and personal activities and costing many thousands of dollars in penalties, interest, and legal fees.

5. Not taking advantage of legal protections

You need to consider incorporation (S-Corp, C-Corp, LLC) (protect your personal assets from business liabilities), homestead declaration (protect your home from creditors), and registering your name (and your domain name).

6. Not establishing consistent workplace practices

You need to set up policies and procedures for employees or contractors, training, problem management, profession/industry practices, and noncompete and nonsolicitation agreements.

7. Not using good bookkeeping and accounting practices

Make sure to keep good records and pay your estimated taxes.

8. Wrong business partnerships

Be cautious in forming business partnerships. Business partnerships are like marriages. They are much easier to get into than to exit. So, be sure to put your agreement in writing.

Source: Jean D. Sifleet, Esq., CPA, business attorney, consultant, and author of *Beyond 401(k)s for Small Business Owners—a Practical Guide to Incentive, Deferred Compensation and Retirement Plans* (John Wiley & Sons, 2004). She is also the author of *Advantage IP—Profit from Your Great Ideas* (Infinity 2005) and numerous other books and business publications. Her Web site *www.smartfast.com* is a recognized resource for practical information on business issues. Jean can be contacted at 120 South Meadow Road, Clinton, MA 01510; (978) 368-6104; e-mail: *jean@smartfast.com*.

Top Reasons for Changing Your Corporate Structure

Are you a proprietorship, a corporation, or a partnership? Should you be something else? Is there a better corporate structure for your business? Here's a list of top reasons why people go through the painful processes of changing their corporate structure.

1. Legal restrictions

There are legal restrictions among each of the three structures.

2. Liabilities assumed

Liabilities assumed by a sole proprietorship are sole, while a partnership is the owners, and a corporation is the general owner and the other owners as far as their contribution is concerned.

3. Type of business operation

The business may be looking to expand and need a different corporate structure.

4. Earnings distribution

Sole proprietorships gain all earnings by themselves. In a partnership, earnings are is spread throughout the partners; in a corporation, earnings go to the business and can be dispersed from there.

5. Capital needs

If a company starts off from a sole proprietorship, the money comes from the person or from a loan. A partnership can have multiple owners who contribute to the capital of the company. In a corporation, there are multiple ways to gain capital: debt and equity financing and common and preferred stock.

6. Number of employees

In a sole proprietorship, it may be hard to control all the employees. Changing your structure to a partnership can allow for others to handle employees.

7. Tax advantages or disadvantages

In a sole proprietorship, the individual pays the taxes; however, in a partnership and in a corporation, either the profits or the losses are split among the owners.

8. Length of business operation

A sole proprietorship can be transferred from the owner only if he does so himself. In a partnership, the partner is unable to transfer her portion of her partnership to another without the authority of the other partners. In a corporation, the shareholders vote to dissolve the business unless it is decided by a court.

Source: Small Business Administration (*www.sba.gov*).

Most Common Things to Include in a Shareholder Agreement

Here are some of the main points (i.e., a checklist) to include in a shareholders agreement.

1. Structure

What is the "structure" of the company (and how is equity divided among shareholders)?

2. The kind of agreement

Should the agreement be unanimous and involve all (or just some) of the shareholders?

3. Who will own shares

Who owns (or will own) shares (i.e., the parties to the agreement)?

4. Vesting provisions

Are there vesting provisions (i.e., shares which may be subject to cancellation if a shareholder/manager quits)?

5. Pledge or hypothecate their shares

Are shareholders allowed to pledge or hypothecate their shares?

6. Board members

Who is on the board? What about outside board members?

7. Officers/managers

Who are the officers and managers?

8. Meetings

What constitutes a quorum for meetings?

9. New equity issues

What are the restrictions on new equity issues (e.g., antidilution aspects, pre-emptive rights and tag-along provisions)?

10. Ownership buyouts

How are ownership buyouts handled (e.g., a shotgun-clause approach versus a voluntary-sale approach)?

11. Resolution of disputes

How are disputes to be resolved among shareholders (e.g., an arbitration clause)?

12. Sale of shares

How are share sales handled (e.g., first right of refusal)?

13. Obligations and commitments

What are a shareholder's obligations and commitment (e.g., conflict of interest or commitment, full-time or …)?

14. Shareholders' rights

What are shareholders' rights (what information, financial statements, or reports can shareholders access)?

15. Death/incapacity

What happens in the event of death/incapacity?

16. Valuation

How is a share valuation determined (e.g., to buy out an estate in the event of death)?

17. Insurance requirements

Is life insurance required (e.g., funding for purchase of shares from estate or for key person insurance)?

18. Operating guidelines

What are the operating guidelines or restrictions (budget approvals, spending limits banking, etc.)?

19. Decisions and approval

What types of decisions require unanimous board and/or unanimous shareholder approval?

20. Compensation issues

What are the compensation policies (e.g., remuneration of officers and directors, dividend policies)?

21. Required agreements

Are other agreements required as well (e.g., management contracts, confidentiality agreements, patent rights)?

22. Shareholder restrictions

Should there be any restrictions on shareholders with respect to competing interests?

23. Business dissolutions

What could trigger the dissolution of the business?

24. Liability exposure

What is the liability exposure, and is there any corporate indemnification (and insurance)?

25. Advisers

Who are the company's professional advisers (legal, audit, etc.)?

26. Financial obligations

Are there any financial obligations by shareholders (e.g., bank guarantees, shareholder loans)?

Source: Michael C. Volker (*www.mikevolker.com*)—Michael writes articles that are meant to be introductory in nature to help the budding high-technology entrepreneur and student. Contact him at his Web site or by e-mail at *mike@volker.org*.

Advantages of C Corporations

When you are considering which legal entity to choose for your business, carefully consider the pros and cons of the corporation. A corporation is unlike any other form of doing business because it is considered by federal and state law to be an artificial legal entity that exists separately from the people who own, manage, control, and operate it. It can make contracts and pay taxes, and it is liable for debts. Corporations exist only because state statutory laws allow them to be created. Here are some of the pros of starting a corporation.

1. Limited personal liability

The main reason most businesses incorporate is to limit owner liability to the amount invested in the business. Generally, stockholders in a corporation are not personally liable for claims against the corporation and are, therefore, at risk only to the extent of their investment in the corporation. Likewise, the officers and directors of a corporation are not normally liable for the corporation's debts, although in some cases, an officer whose duty it is to withhold federal income tax from employees' wages may be liable to the IRS if the taxes are not withheld and paid to the IRS as required. States have similar laws imposing personal liability on corporate officers for withheld state income taxes or for unpaid sales and use taxes.

2. Income splitting

By using a corporation, you may be able to split your overall profit between two or more taxpayers so that none of the income gets taxed in the highest tax brackets. The total tax paid by the two taxpayers—you and your corporation—may be less than if all of the income were taxed to you, as in a sole proprietorship.

3. Fringe benefit plan deductions

Federal and state tax laws permit you, as a corporate employer, to provide a number of different fringe benefits to shareholders/employees on a tax-favored basis. These tax-favored fringe benefits include medical insurance plans, self-insured medical reimbursement plans, disability insurance, death benefit plans, and (to a limited degree) group-term life insurance. In addition, a corporation—other than an S corporation—can generally deduct medical insurance premiums it makes on behalf of an employee who is an owner of the business, and the employee is not taxed on the value of the benefit provided. This is far more favorable than payments of salary to an employee, which are fully taxable.

4. Tax break for dividends received by a corporation

C corporations can deduct at least 70 percent of the dividends they receive from stock investments from their federal taxable income.

5. Tax break for investing in small business stock

The tax law provides major tax incentives for investing in the stock of certain small corporations. This incentive is not available for investments in unincorporated businesses or in stock of S corporations. A noncorporate investor who purchases "qualified small business stock" after August 10, 1993, and holds it for five years or more is allowed to exclude from his or her taxable income up to 50 percent of any capital gain reported on the sale of stock. The period in which the first company's stock was held can be counted toward the five-year holding period requirement if the second company's stock is later sold for a gain.

6. Continuous existence

Unlike a sole proprietorship or partnership, a corporation has continuous existence and does not terminate on the death of a stockholder or a change of ownership of some or all of its stock. Creditors, suppliers, and customers, therefore, often prefer to deal with an incorporated business because of this greater continuity. Naturally, a corporation can be terminated by mutual consent of the owners or even by one stockholder in some instances.

Source: Michael D. Jenkins, an attorney and CPA (*www.roninsoft .com*)— He is the author and principal editor of the million-selling state-specific book series, *Starting and Operating a Business in the US.* He is also the owner of Ronin Software and currently authors and publishes the *Starting and Operating a Business* book series as user-customizable electronic books, for each state. Contact him by e-mail at *mdjenk@aol.com.*

Disadvantages Of C Corporations

And, of course, the flip side. Our expert was meticulous enough to tell us of the advantages of forming a corporation. So let's hear the negatives.

1. More red tape

In addition to having more paperwork and recordkeeping requirements—in order to maintain the corporate veil of limited liability—corporations must ensure they meet all annual report filings and, in some circumstances, SEC requirements as well. Incorporation takes a lot of organization and maintenance, and you will want to know all you can about its operations and costs. Of the major types of legal entities, C corporations and S corporations have the most burdensome requirements with regard to the formalities of formation and existence. In addition to filing articles of incorporation with the state where it is organized, it must also adopt bylaws, elect a board of directors, hold organizational meetings as well as regular board and shareholders' meetings, and keep minutes of such meetings. In addition, each state in which it operates has its own corporate requirements, such as qualifying to do business, that must be observed.

2. Cost of incorporating

Besides the usual filing fees required by state agencies for articles of incorporation, name reservation, and issuing stock, and often for appointing an in-state registered agent to receive legal process, legal fees will often run between $500 and $1,000, even for a simple incorporation. If you need to obtain a permit from the state to issue stock or securities, legal fees can be much more.

3. Double taxation

While this section has outlined a number of important tax advantages of incorporating a business, the picture is not all that one-sided. Regular corporations (C corporations) have one major potential disadvantage that usually does not exist for other legal forms of doing business: potential double taxation of its earnings. This problem arises because a C corporation must first pay corporate income taxes on its taxable income. Then, the after-tax earnings may be subject to a second tax on either the individual stockholders if the earnings are distributed as dividends, or as a corporate penalty tax if the earnings are not distributed as dividends.

4. Higher tax rate for personal service corporations

Certain kinds of corporations, called qualified personal service corporations (QPSCs), are taxed at a flat rate of 35 percent, instead of the graduated tax rates found in the currently applicable corporate tax rate table. While it may not always be clear whether an incorporated service business is a QPSC, the IRS defines a QPSC by these characteristics: At least 95 percent of the value of its stock is held by employees or their estates or beneficiaries; and the employees perform services at least 95 percent of the time in the fields of health, law, engineering, architecture, accounting, actuarial science, performing arts, or consulting.

Source: Michael D. Jenkins, an attorney and CPA (*www.roninsoft .com*)—He is the author and principal editor of the million-selling state-specific book series, *Starting and Operating a Business in the US*. He is also the owner of Ronin Software and currently authors and publishes the *Starting and Operating a Business* book series as user-customizable electronic books, for each state. Contact him by e-mail at *mdjenk@aol.com*.

Top Tax Reasons Not to Incorporate

Most tax problems from an incorporated business arise from attempting to avoid a second tax: Shareholders pay taxes when they receive profits as dividends even though the corporation already has paid on those profits. Many times, these dividends are not as obvious as they may seem. Here our expert, a tax attorney, identifies taxable transactions that are incurred by an incorporated business and therefore reasons not to incorporate a closely held business.

1. Bargain sale

If a corporation sells an asset to the shareholder at less than market value, the difference between the sales price and market value is a dividend.

2. Paying personal expenses

If a corporation pays expenses of a shareholder or purchases an asset for the shareholder, it's a dividend. Done often enough, this could result in a fraud penalty or jail time.

3. Loans to shareholders

If a corporation loans money to a shareholder, it can result in a constructive dividend. The key here is whether the corporation treated the loan as a bank would. So you should represent the loan with an interest-bearing note and a payment schedule the shareholder complies with. The shareholder should give the corporation security if a bank would require it.

4. Unreasonable compensation

If a corporation pays a shareholder-employee excessive compensation, the overpayment is a dividend. Therefore, it doesn't get a deduction. The problem especially exists when only shareholders receive bonuses, it has paid little or no dividends compared to profit, the payment's allocation coincided with stock ownership, or the corporation paid compensation as a year-end bonus when it knew the profit amount rather than monthly salary checks. The question courts often ask is would an independent, non-employee shareholder approve such compensation considering the nature and quality of the shareholder-employee's services?

5. Accumulated earnings tax

If a corporation doesn't pay sufficient dividends relative to profits, it has the potential of being subject to the accumulated earnings tax. This is a tax on top of the regular corporate tax. If the corporation accumulated earnings instead of paying dividends, it could be taxed on its excess assets. This includes cash not needed for operations, receivables from officers, and investments unrelated to the business.

6. Liquidation

If a corporation liquidates and distributes assets to shareholders, it's taxed as if it sold its assets for market value. The shareholders are taxed on the market value of what they receive in excess of their stock basis.

7. Moving from a regular corporation

If a corporation moves to LLC status, this will be taxed as if the corporation liquidated.

Source: A. J. Cook (*www.taxfables.com*) now practices as a tax lawyer with the Memphis law firm Pietrangelo Cook PLC. Formerly, he was with the CPA firm Ernst & Young as a partner in charge of tax services in the Memphis office. Contact him by telephone: mornings (901) 754-8925; afternoons: (901) 685-2662; fax: (901) 685-6122. Or write him at 6785 Slash Pine, Memphis, TN 38119. His e-mail is *aj@taxfables.com*.

Reasons So Many Companies Incorporate in Delaware

According to the Delaware Division of Corporations, over a half a million businesses have a legal home in Delaware, a number that includes over 50 percent of U.S. publicly traded companies and 58 percent of Fortune 500 companies. There must be a reason so many companies choose to incorporate in the same state. The following are a number of reasons Delaware is so attractive to corporations.

1. Taxes

Delaware boasts no sales tax or property tax for corporations. In addition, there is no corporate income tax if the company does not conduct business in Delaware, which it is not required to do. There is also no tax on shares of stock for non-Delaware residents.

2. Legal system

The Delaware legal system has a great deal of experience with corporate laws, meaning those laws have been tested in the courts. Also, the state courts have a history of making decisions in favor of corporations. The legal system for courts is under the Court of Chancery, which is a separate court system devoted entirely to business.

3. Out-of-state operations

A corporation formed in Delaware does not have to conduct business in the state, as mentioned. The company also can have a non-Delaware business address, as long as it has a registered agent in Delaware to deal with the state. Furthermore, no corporate records are required to be kept in the state.

4. One-person incorporating

One person is all it takes to form a corporation in Delaware. In contrast to other states that may require at least three people to serve as officers for a corporation, in Delaware, one person can be president, treasurer, secretary, and the director.

5. Low costs

In addition to the previously mentioned tax benefits, there is a low annual franchise tax for corporations in Delaware, as low as $60 per year. There is also no minimum capital required to start a corporation in Delaware, as opposed to a $500 or $1,000 minimum in other states.

6. One corporation, multiple types of business

If incorporation papers are filed with the broadest allowances, one corporation in Delaware can conduct any legal form of business. There is no need to file any additional paperwork for a corporation to conduct a different kind of business, which gives the corporations a lot of leeway.

Sources: Delaware Division of Corporations (*www.state.de.us/ corp/*), which provides information on incorporating in Delaware as well as providing resources to businesses in the state.

Things to Consider Before Incorporating in Another State

If you decide on a corporation as the structure for your small business, there are several things to consider in the process of incorporating your company. Among these considerations is the state in which you will incorporate your business. When selecting a state for incorporation, there are a number of things to consider, and the following list provides a guide to these considerations.

1. Number of incorporators

Be sure to look into how many people are required to start a corporation in a particular state. Some states allow just one person to serve all roles in the formation of a corporation, while others require different people to serve the role.

2. Capital requirements

Check on the requirement of a state for the minimum level of capital needed to start a corporation. There may not be any such level in certain states, but others will have a minimum.

3. Filing fees

Different states charge different amounts for filing the article of incorporation. Fees can range from $50 to $250, so it might be wiser to choose a state with lower fees, if possible.

4. Corporate franchise tax

Much like the differences in filing fees, different states will have different rates for corporate franchise taxes, so it is worth considering what the annual rates would be for your corporation.

5. Corporate income tax

In addition to checking on corporate franchise taxes, you should be sure to consider the corporate income tax rates. Also, since you may be incorporating in one state and operating in another, consider whether the earnings of your corporation in another state can be taxed in the state of incorporation.

6. Location of recordkeeping

Check on whether the state of incorporation requires that you keep records and books in the state, or whether the corporation is allowed to keep records outside the state. This would be a consideration if your company is choosing to incorporate in one state and operate in another.

7. State courts

Look at the record of the state court system with respect to business cases to see if the courts are business friendly or if they have a record of deciding unfairly against businesses.

8. Location of principal place of business

Another consideration if your company wants to incorporate in one state and operate in another is if the state of incorporation allows you to have your principal place of business outside the state.

9. Shareholder issues

Consider whether the state of incorporation requires that the names of shareholders be publicly disclosed, as well as whether there is a state inheritance tax on nonresident shareholders.

10. Corporate bank account requirement

Some states require that corporations have a corporate bank account, while others, such as Delaware, do not. This may be a consideration for financial and accounting aspects of the company.

Source: QuickMBA (*www.quickmba.com*)—An online resource for business administration that provides information on business law, entrepreneurship, and other areas of business and is operated by the Internet Center for Management and Business Administration.

Disadvantages of Limited Liability Companies

There's another side to the story. Here are some reasons why an LLC may NOT be the right choice for your business.

1. Members pay self-employment tax on profits

Professional firms will often find it preferable to operate in the form of professional corporations and S corporation status, rather than as LLCs, since all the earnings of a professional LLC will generally be subject to self-employment tax. If operating as an S corporation, only the salaries paid will be subject to FICA taxes (at the same rate as self-employment tax), and any remaining profit that is earned by the S corporation will be subject only to income tax, not to self-employment or FICA taxes, provided that the amount of salaries paid is not unreasonably low and subject to treatment as tax avoidance by the IRS.

2. Admission of new members

Admission of new members, after the LLC has been in existence for a while, can cause an imbalance in the capital accounts for the members, particularly upon dissolution.

3. Difficult to sell partial LLC business

It may be more difficult to sell a portion of the business to someone else, as compared to selling someone else shares of stock, due to the legal structure of the corporation. New members may be invited and accepted, but there are many complexities in selling the LLC business.

4. May jeopardize continuance if a member assigns economic rights

If a member assigns his or her economic rights, the assignee also receives the right to ask for dissolution of the LLC, if the LLC is at will. Thus the existence of the entity could be affected if the assignment goes in the wrong hands.

5. Unnecessary restrictions

LLCs must usually provide in their articles of organization that the entity will terminate in not more than thirty years, and an LLC must (generally) have more than one owner, unlike corporations. (But many of these provisions, and in particular the one-owner prohibition, have already been repealed by most of the states, now that the IRS final regulations have made such restrictions unnecessary for federal income tax purposes.)

6. Unfavorable federal tax treatment

Even the federal tax treatment of LLCs is no longer uniformly favorable. Perhaps unintentionally, a new partnership tax law provision that was added in the Revenue Reconciliation Act of 1993 may adversely impact professional service firms that are organized as LLCs, rather than as true partnerships. Under the 1993 tax law amendments, certain payments made by partnerships to outgoing partners (for "goodwill" or "unrealized receivables") are no longer deductible to the partnership, except when made to a general partner in a service partnership, such as a law or medical partnership.

Source: FindLaw's Legal Professionals Channel (www.findlaw .com) is designed to help you with your practice-specific legal information needs. There are different area topics for the latest legal news, case law, and analytical articles relevant to your practice. Contact author William J. Cutchin, Cutchin Law Firm, P.C., Suite B, 755 Johnnie Dodds Blvd., Mount Pleasant, SC 29464; (843) 216-0809; fax: (843) 216-0828;

Top Reasons to Form a Limited Liability Company

A limited liability company, or LLC, is a type of business structure that allows a company to combine some of the benefits of a corporation and a partnership. Much like an S corporation, the LLC combines the limited liability of a corporation with the tax benefits of a partnership, but it also provides other benefits not found in an S corporation. Following are the top reasons to form a limited liability company.

1. Limited liability

As the name indicates, an LLC allows its members to have limited liability, meaning the members do not assume the risk for any debts or obligations incurred by the company.

2. Taxation benefits

LLCs pay no federal income taxes because they are viewed as partnerships for tax purposes. The individuals in the LLC write off losses on their personal income taxes.

3. Few formalities

Aside from having to form an operating agreement, there are not the required formalities that accompany a corporation. Holding annual meetings or issuing stock certificates are not requirements for an LLC as they are for a corporation.

4. No minimum or maximum number of members

Like a corporation, an LLC has no limit to the number of members. While there can be as many members in the LLC as desired, there can also, in most states, be as few as one member, allowing for an individual to create his or her own LLC.

5. Members do not have to be individuals

In addition, there is also no requirement that members be individuals. This means that corporations or partnerships, which are legal entities, can also be members of an LLC.

6. Management group can run the LLC

In other forms of business, decisions can only be made by owners, in one form or another. In an LLC, a management group can be hired to run the company, and the members of the management group do not have to be members of the LLC. This allows more options with respect to ensuring effective operations and decision-making in the company.

Source: Andrew J. Sherman is a partner in the Washington, D.C., office of Dickstein Shapiro Morin & Oshinsky LLP, with over 350 attorneys nationwide (*www.dsmo.com*)—Mr. Sherman is a recognized international authority on the legal and strategic issues affecting small and growing companies. He is an adjunct professor in the Masters of Business Administration (MBA) program at the University of Maryland and Georgetown University, where he teaches courses on business growth, capital formation, and entrepreneurship. He is the founder of Grow Fast Grow Right, an education and training company for executives of middle market companies (*www.growfastgrowright.com*) and the author of fourteen books on the legal and strategic aspects of business growth and capital formation. He can be reached at (202) 833-5000 or e-mail *ShermanA@dsmo.com*.

Advantages of Partnerships

In a partnership, two or more people share ownership of a single business. Like proprietorships, the law does not distinguish between the business and its owners. The partners should have a legal agreement that sets forth how decisions will be made, profits will be shared, disputes will be resolved, how future partners will be admitted to the partnership, how partners can be bought out, or what steps will be taken to dissolve the partnership when needed. It is hard to think about a "breakup" when the business is just getting started, but many partnerships split up at crisis times and unless there is a defined process, there will be even greater problems. They also must decide up front how much time and capital each will contribute, etc. Here are a few advantages of partnerships.

1. Easy to form

Partnerships are relatively easy to establish; however, time should be invested in developing the partnership agreement.

2. Flexible

With more than one owner, the ability to raise funds may be increased. As a partner, you are an agent for the partnership and can do anything necessary to operate the business, such as hire employees, borrow money, or enter into contracts on behalf of the partnership.

3. Partnership not taxed separately from its partners

The profits from the business flow directly through to the partners' personal tax returns. Partners in a partnership may deduct their share of the tax losses of the business, if any, subject to various limitations that generally do not apply if the partnership carries on an active business in which the partner is actively engaged.

4. Prospective employees

Prospective employees may be attracted to the business if given the incentive to become a partner. This also is a technique often adopted to attract and retain unique and bright talent.

5. Complementary skills

The business usually will benefit from partners who have complementary skills. A potential partner could bring an expertise into the business that otherwise would have to be brought in by hiring an employee or outside consultant. Having a diverse partnership, with each partner using his or her strengths to improve operations, is often worthwhile in the long run.

Source: Small Business Administration (*www.sba.gov*).

Disadvantages of Partnerships

We've looked at the upside of forming a partnership, but now our expert, the Small Business Administration, gives us the downside. Here are a few disadvantages of partnerships.

1. Jointly and severally liable

Partners are jointly and individually liable for the actions of the other partners. Each partner (except for a limited partner in a limited partnership) is personally liable for all the debts, taxes, and other claims against the partnership firm. If the assets of the firm are not sufficient to pay off the creditors, they can satisfy their claims out of the partners' personal assets. In addition, when any partner fails to pay personal debts, the partnership's business may be disrupted if his or her creditors proceed to satisfy their claims by seeking what is called a charging order against partnership assets.

2. Sharing of profits

Profits must be shared with others. Unlike a sole proprietorship, where the owner makes his own decisions and solely shares the entire profits of the business, a partner by virtue of law is obliged to share his profits with the other partners. This applies only to profits as the partners may decide not to share the losses and not every partner may bear the losses.

3. Possible disagreements among partners

Since decisions are shared, disagreements can occur. A good relationship between partners can make a strong business team, but the downside risk is that the partners may not get along. It is not infrequent to see the partners have totally different views about how the business is to be run, which can lead to dissension, acrimony, deadlock, and in some cases, dissolution of the partnership or even lawsuits.

4. Tax disadvantage

Some employee benefits are not deductible from business income on tax returns. A partnership business may deduct the cost of various fringe benefits from income, but unlike a C corporation, the partners must include the value of such benefits in taxable income, so that such benefits on behalf of one partner are simply a shifting of income from the other partners to that partner.

5. Terminating the partnership

The partnership may have a limited life; it may end upon the withdrawal or death of a partner. The partners may agree differently in the partnership agreement and choose to continue the business. This is in contrast to a corporation, which, theoretically, has perpetual existence. Under the laws of most states, bankruptcy of a partner or the partnership itself will cause the dissolution of the partnership, regardless of any agreement to the contrary.

Source: Small Business Administration (*www.sba.gov*).

Most Common Things to Include in a Partnership Agreement

One of the first decisions that potential business owners must confront is how their for-profit business should be structured and operated. If there is more than one owner or partner in the business, it is even more important to have a clear understanding of the business organization. A written and clearly defined partnership agreement is essential for structured relationships between two or more partners or business entities. Here is a list of some of the most common elements to consider when drafting a partnership agreement.

1. Name of the partnership

One of the first agreements between partners is the name of the partnership. Although it may sound simple, this crucial decision is often overlooked. There are numerous possibilities in choosing a name. One of the most common techniques is to use the last names of the individual partners, such as Smith and Jones. If a fictitious or assumed name such as Eastside Widgets is chosen, must make sure the name is not already in use and also register it with the state. The terms of the partnership agreement may dictate how and why the name can be changed or modified in the future.

2. Life span

Unlike corporations whose lives are generally perpetual, the existence of the partnership is controlled by the contractual agreement. The life span can be set to dissolve after a specific duration (i.e., five years); at the occurrence of a specific event (i.e., the sale of the major asset owned by the partnership); a specific date (i.e., October 2, 2020); upon the death, bankruptcy, or withdrawal of a partner; or at will, meaning until the partners vote for termination. Once a partnership is dissolved, it still continues to exist but only for the purpose of "winding-up." such as liquidation of the assets, payment of bills to outstanding creditors, and settlement of accounts.

3. Contributions

Contributions of each partner should be defined in terms of capital (cash and/or other property) and services. This is the value being given in exchange for an ownership interest in the partnership. Without a written agreement, there is no guideline on what value a partner needs to invest in a business. Contributions can include cash, property, services, or any combination thereof. In addition, the partners must decide what percentage of ownership is gained by such corresponding investments. If contributions vary, a written partnership agreement is even more important; the distribution of ownership needs to be clearly outlined.

4. Duties and obligations

In the formation of a partnership, it is common for partners to bring initial value in exchange for ownership. However, it is important to outline the duties and future obligations of each partner to avoid confusion or miscommunication down the road. In the partnership agreement, specific management and administrative responsibilities can be assigned to each partner. While management needs may fluctuate with time, it is important to address basics such as who is going to be responsible for corporate books, bank accounts, accounts payable and receivable, employee supervision, contract negotiations, marketing, and customer service. Contributions of each partner should be outlined in terms of hours per week or month, performance deadlines, services rendered, or future capital investments that will be expected. Vague, unwritten promises and duties are very difficult to enforce or track if broken. A partnership agreement assigns accountability for the business and also helps to ensure that all partners know exactly what is expected of them.

5. Decision-making

Many partnership disputes start with problems over decision-making. Generally, unless the partnership agreement directs otherwise, each partner is an agent of the partnership and therefore has decision-making authority. This decision-making power can expose the business and each partner to additional personal liability. There is no clear guideline on what works best for all businesses. Some businesses may require the unanimous or majority vote of all the partners for every business decision, while others may allow individual partners to make decisions on their own. The partnership agreement may spell out when it is appropriate for partners to make individual decisions versus when additional partner approval is required. For example, some partnership agreements may prohibit individual partners from entering into new business contracts, borrowing or lending money, executing a mortgage, or buying and selling major property without the consent and approval of the other partners. Some partnerships may dictate that certain partners make agreed capital contributions but have no decision-making authority. Others may give weight to each partner's vote depending on seniority, capital investment, or contribution. In sum, clearly outlining the decision-making process will help to alleviate partner conflicts.

6. Allocation of profits/losses

Another important area that should be discussed in any partnership agreement is the allocation of profits and losses and the manner in which they will be shared. By default, many partnerships assume partners will share profits and losses equally regardless of contribution, time, or effort exerted in the business. The amount assigned can be a fixed number or percentage, based on a formula, based on partner vote, distributed evenly, or in proportion to individual partner contributions. Decisions need to be made not only on how profits are allocated but when. Some businesses entitle partners to regular weekly, monthly, or quarterly draws; others wait until the end of each

year to distribute any profits, while others may require any profits be reinvested in the business. Because the partners have a strong fiduciary duty to the partnership and to each other, this is an area for which planning is necessary in order to avoid conflict.

7. Resolving disputes and differences

Typically, every business will eventually experience some form of dispute or difference. If procedures are not in place to help resolve conflicts, internal turmoil will destroy the business. One or more of the partners may go to court to seek dissolution or recourse on various grounds such as controversy, reckless actions, or inability to perform pursuant to the partnership agreement. To help avoid costly court battles, the partnership agreement may contain an arbitration provision to help the partners work through problems by using alternate dispute resolution methods. Such methods may include a partner voting procedure, or use of an outside arbitration or mediation service. Many partnership disputes can be easily avoided with a properly planned, executed, and monitored partnership agreement and clear communication channels.

8. Admitting new partners

Eventually, there may be growth for the business, and therefore opportunities to add new partners. Agreeing on the procedures, requirements, and timelines for admitting new partners will help reduce conflict when this issue comes up. All the considerations for the initial partnership agreement again come into play when adding new partners, including their contributions, duties, and obligations, decision–making, and allocation of profits or losses.

9. Alienation of rights or dissolution

The number of failed partnerships due to the death or dissolution of one or more of the partners is alarming. To avoid such pitfalls, the partnership agreement should be structured to accommodate the departure of an owner. Some provisions allow the existing partners to buy out partnership units from the former partner; some automatically transfer rights to the spouse or family of the deceased partner, while others will seek to replace the former partner with a new partner altogether. Planning and preparation with appropriate procedures is better than a court- or state-ordered termination of a business.

10. Authority

Before the partnership agreement is put into effect, it is important to consider who has authority to bind the partnership and to modify the partnership agreement. The partnership agreement can have provisions that require one or all of the partners' consent before binding the partnership. In other cases, one or several partners, such as a founding partner, can retain sole rights to bind or change the partnership agreement.

Source: Mathew B. Tully, Esq., is the founding partner of the Albany, New York, law firm of Tully, Rinckey & Associates, PLLC (*www.tullylegal.com*)—Tully, Rinckey & Associates is a full-service law firm catering to individuals, families, and businesses throughout the state of New York and the federal courts. The firm was recently named one of the Top 50 law firms and one of the Great Places to Work by the *Business Review*. Tully can be contacted at 3 Wembley Court, Albany, NY 12205; (518) 218-7100; e-mail: *mtully@tullylegal.com*.

Advantages of Proprietorships

A sole proprietorship is one of the most common ways to organize a new start-up. Many self-employed individuals, home-based businesses, and small cottage industries operate as sole proprietorships. There are lots of advantages to doing business this way, and our expert provides us with a few right here.

1. Easy to organize

The great advantage of operating a new business as a sole proprietorship is that it is simple and does not require any formal action to set it up. You can start your business today as a sole proprietorship. There is no need to wait for an attorney to draft and file documents or for the government to approve them. Of course, you may need a local business license, and a growing number of states require you to register to do business in their state, in addition to the usual local licenses that are required in almost every locality. Most states do not impose any income taxes directly on a sole proprietorship.

2. Profit (or loss) is yours

All of the profit or loss from your business belongs to you and must be reported on your federal income tax return, Schedule C, Income (or Loss) from a Business or Profession, on Form 1040. This can either be an advantage or a disadvantage for income tax purposes, depending on the circumstances. If operating the business results in losses or significant tax credits, you may be able to use the tax losses or tax credits to reduce taxes on income from other sources. Or, if your sole proprietorship generates modest profits—but not more than about $75,000 to $100,000 a year—overall taxes may be less than if incorporated, assuming you need most of the income to live on.

3. Unemployment tax savings

As a sole proprietor, you are not considered an employee of your business. As a result, you avoid paying unemployment taxes on your earnings from the business. Both the state and federal governments impose unemployment taxes on wages or salaries, but not on your self-employment income. Note that a corporation would normally get an income tax deduction for the unemployment tax it paid on your salary, so that the actual after-tax savings from operating as a sole proprietorship would be somewhat less than the gross amount of the unemployment taxes you would avoid paying.

4. Ability to withdraw assets tax-free

Another advantage of a sole proprietorship is that you can shift funds in and out of your business account or withdraw assets from the business with few tax, legal, or other limitations. In a partnership or a limited liability company, you can generally withdraw funds only by agreement. In the case of a corporation, a withdrawal of funds or property may be taxable as a dividend or capital or violate some states' corporation laws, potentially causing a loss of your limited liability protection from creditors.

Source: Michael D. Jenkins, attorney and CPA(*www.roninsoft* *.com*)—He is the author and principal editor of the million-selling state-specific book series, *Starting and Operating a Business in the US*. He is also the owner of Ronin Software and currently authors and publishes the *Starting and Operating a Business* book series as user-customizable electronic books, for each state. Contact him by e-mail at *mdjenk@aol.com*.

Disadvantages of Proprietorships

As we've seen in another list, a sole proprietorship has several advantages. But things are never as good as they seem, right? This type of organization has its downsides too, and here are a few.

1. Personal liability

As the owner of the sole proprietorship, you will be personally liable for any debts or taxes of the business or other claims, such as legal damages resulting from a lawsuit. This is one reason many entrepreneurs prefer to use a corporation or LLC rather than a sole proprietorship. Unlimited personal liability is perhaps the major disadvantage of operating a business as a sole proprietorship.

2. Limited tax savings for fringe benefits

A major disadvantage of sole proprietorships is they cannot obtain a number of significant tax benefits regarding group-term life insurance benefits, long-term disability insurance coverage, and medical insurance or medical expense reimbursements. To qualify for favorable tax treatment regarding these fringe benefit plans, you need to incorporate. A self-employed individual is now allowed to deduct 100 percent of his or her health insurance when computing adjusted gross income, effective since January 1, 2003. However, the health insurance deduction only reduces your income tax, not the federal self-employment tax.

3. Largely eliminates special advantages of corporate retirement plans

While this was formerly an important disadvantage of operating as a sole proprietorship, there are now virtually no differences in the tax treatment of self-employed plans of sole proprietorships and partnerships, as compared with corporate retirement plans.

4. Harder to borrow money

Compared to a corporation or LLC, a sole proprietorship lacks any continuity of existence if the proprietor dies. A corporation continues after the deaths of its stockholders. For that reason, banks or other lenders are often more hesitant about lending to sole proprietors than to corporations or other legal entities.

Source: Michael D. Jenkins, an attorney and CPA (*www.roninsoft* *.com*)—He is the author and principal editor of the million-selling state-specific book series, *Starting and Operating a Business in the US*. He is also the owner of Ronin Software and currently authors and publishes the *Starting and Operating a Business* book series as user-customizable electronic books, for each state. Contact him by e-mail at *mdjenk@aol.com*.

Top Reasons to Form an S Corporation

Under certain circumstances, a corporation can elect to be treated similarly to a partnership for federal tax purposes. The business must first be incorporated as a regular for-profit business corporation with the state and then, once formed and certain conditions are met, can file an election with the Internal Revenue Service (IRS) to be treated as a Subchapter S Corporation. This form of corporation is sometimes called a "Close corporation," but most often is referred simply as an "S corporation." Here are some of the advantages to electing for S corporation status.

1. No "double-taxation"

In a regular corporation, referred to as a C corporation, taxes are imposed on earnings at two different levels. First, a corporate tax is imposed on the corporation itself for earnings. Then, that income is taxed again to shareholders when distributed as dividends. By electing for S corporation status, taxation is avoided at the corporate level. The S corporation acts as a conduit for earnings so they pass through to the shareholders. The income is then taxed only at the shareholder level, at each shareholder's tax rate. Therefore, an S corporation avoids "double-taxation."

2. Avoid disputes with the IRS

If a corporation is going to make payments to shareholders who have, for example, rendered services, rented property, or lent funds to the corporation, the corporation may deduct the salaries, rent, and interest it paid, pursuant to the Internal Revenue Code (IRC). This can result in no corporate tax being owed by the C corporation. However, these deductions can be examined for reasonableness, and there are other requirements that must be met. Thus, an S corporation may be desirable because there is no corporate tax imposed, so it avoids having to take deductions in the first place.

3. Alternative tax rate

A corporation's financial plan may be to accumulate all of its earnings and profits, rather than distribute such income to shareholders. An S corporation may still be desirable in this situation, though, if the tax rates of the individual shareholders are lower than the rate that would be imposed on the corporation.

4. Deduction of losses

The operating losses of the S corporation are passed through to shareholders in accordance with each shareholder's percentage of shares. The shareholders can then deduct those losses to offset their own taxable income, subject to limitations imposed by the IRC.

5. Voting rights

An S corporation is allowed to have only one class of stock. However, a difference in voting rights among the common stock does not, by itself, equate to more than one class of stock. This can be advantageous in, for example, a family-business situation. Parents involved in the corporation with their children can retain the voting stock, while issuing to the children the nonvoting stock. In such a situation, the parents can retain control of the business without violating the children's right of participation. It is permissible for either one, or both, of the parents to hold the voting stock.

Source: Kelly Michael Monroe, Esq., is the head of the Business Planning and Advisement division of the Albany, New York, law firm of Tully, Rinckey & Associates, PLLC (*www.tullylegal.com*)— Tully, Rinckey & Associates is a full-service law firm catering to individuals, families, and businesses throughout the state of New York

and the federal courts. The firm was recently named one of the Top 50 law firms and one of the Great Places to Work by the *Business Review*. Monroe can be contacted at 3 Wembley Court, Albany, NY 12205; (518) 218-7100; e-mail: *kmonroe@tullylegal.com*.

Typical Start-up Costs

This list can help you figure out how much it will cost you to open your doors for business on day one. Your start-up costs can be broken down into the following categories:

1. Hiring professionals

The cost of a lawyer, accountant, and perhaps other professional help.

2. Getting insurance

The cost of protecting your business and personal assets.

3. Planning advertising and marketing

The cost of getting your product or service known in the marketplace.

4. Hiring employees

The cost of hiring people to perform necessary tasks for businesses that require it.

5. Planning the physical space

The cost of setting up your office, store, or other location.

6. Special considerations for retail businesses

Some of the special cost considerations of opening a storefront business, if that's your avenue.

7. Miscellaneous costs

A look at those costs that any business will incur but that are often ignored or forgotten.

8. Raising money

The cost of obtaining start-up money, as well as some suggestions for potential sources of financing.

Source: CCH Business Owner's Toolkit: (*www.toolkit.cch.com*)— The Business Owners Toolkit provides advice, guides, legal tools, business models, and other resources to small business owners.

Ways to Find Your Start-up's Niche in the Market

A market in its entirety is too broad in scope for any but the largest companies to tackle successfully. The best strategy for a smaller business is to divide demand into manageable market niches. Small operations can then offer specialized goods and services attractive to a specific group of prospective buyers. Here's a few good niches supplied by our friends at the Small Business Administration.

1. Study the market

There are undoubtedly some particular products or services you are especially suited to provide. Study the market carefully, and you will find opportunities. As an example, surgical instruments used to be sold in bulk to both small medical practices and large hospitals. One firm realized that the smaller practices could not afford to sterilize instruments after each use as hospitals did, but instead simply disposed of them. The firm's sales representatives talked to surgeons and hospital workers to learn what

would be more suitable for them. Based on this information, the company developed disposable instruments that could be sold in larger quantities at a lower cost. Another firm capitalized on the fact that hospital operating rooms must carefully count the instruments used before and after surgery. This firm met that particular need by packaging their instruments in pre-counted, customized sets for different forms of surgery.

2. Do a market survey

While researching your own company's niche, consider the results of your market survey and the areas in which your competitors are already firmly situated. Put this information into a table or a graph to illustrate where an opening might exist for your product or service.

3. Find the niche

Try to find the right configuration of products, services, quality, and price that will ensure the least direct competition. Unfortunately, there is no universally effective way to make these comparisons. Not only will the desired attributes vary from industry to industry, but there is also an imaginative element that cannot be formalized. For example, only someone who had already thought of developing prepackaged surgical instruments could use a survey to determine whether a market actually existed for them.

4. Create a good database

A well-designed database can help you sort through your market information and reveal particular segments you might not see otherwise. For example, do customers in a certain geographic area tend to purchase products that combine high quality and high price more frequently? Do your small business clients take advantage of your customer service more often than larger ones? If so, consider focusing on being a local provider of high-quality goods and services, or a service-oriented company that pays extra attention to small businesses.

5. Make sure you're consistent

If you do target a new niche market, make sure that this niche does not conflict with your overall business plan. For example, a small bakery that makes cookies by hand cannot go after a market for inexpensive, mass-produced cookies, regardless of the demand.

Source: Small Business Administration (*www.sba.gov*).

Typical Start-up Expenses That Can't Be Immediately Deducted

You're going to incur a lot of costs, known and unforeseen, when starting up your new business. Unfortunately, not all of these costs can be deducted right away. Some of them will need to be amortized and deducted over time. Here's a few typical costs that you won't be able to deduct right away.

1. Costs of investigation

These are the expenses incurred to analyze potential markets, products, or labor supply. Feasibility studies or significant travel expenses may be incurred during this stage. Due diligence efforts can be expensive. For acquiring a business, these costs could also include inspection and analysis of all legal and financial information, in addition to operations, sales, or other business

aspects. In some situations, it may be advisable to form a corporation prior to initiating a search to ensure a tax deduction in the event of an abandoned or unproductive investigation.

2. Pre-opening expenses

These are incurred after the decision is made to create a business, and which one, but before operations begin. These costs can include salaries, training, travel, and professional fees. Costs incurred during this phase that would be an allowable deduction if paid or incurred by an existing and similar trade or business are expenditures treated as start-up expenses. Specifically excluded from the definition of start-up expenses are interest, certain taxes, and research and development expenses. These costs can be deducted during the start-up phase, consequently creating a net operating loss.

3. Litigation to determine the commencement date

Determining the commencement date for when a trade or business begins often has been the subject of litigation. Each case must be considered individually on the facts and circumstances, which often results in an ambiguous answer. The consequence of misjudging this date may result in an invalid election to amortize the start-up costs and result in permanent capitalization. The type of business is a significant factor in determining a start date, as a business is considered to begin when it starts the operations for which it was organized. A manufacturing enterprise usually would begin when the production process commences. Retail operations are generally considered to begin when the doors are opened to the public. Service businesses have less precedent to follow, but what does exist indicates a service business begins when actual services are provided, or you hold yourself out as ready to provide services.

4. Acquiring an existing business

Start-up expenses are applicable to the investigation phase only when acquiring an existing business. After the decisions are made as to whether to enter a business and which specific business to acquire, the investigation phase concludes and the acquisition process begins. Costs incurred related to this process are capitalized. Certain acquisition costs may be depreciated or amortized, depending on how the deal is structured. At the time the business is acquired, the amortization of start-up expenses can begin.

Source: Tamara Campfield is a CPA with Gordon, Hughes and Banks LLP (*www.ghbcpa.com*)—She specializes in the taxation of start-up and closely held businesses. Reach her at (303) 986-2454 or *tcampfield@ghbcpa.com*.

Popular Free Places to get Start-up Help

So you're ready to start your own business and be your own boss ... or are you? There are many time-saving and free resources to help you start formalizing your new business. Our expert consults, trains, and coaches individuals on many various topics of small businesses, so she knows where to look. Here are some great places for you, too.

1. Federal agencies

Receive free help from the Small Business Administration (*www.sbaonline.sba.gov*), U.S. Census—Department of Commerce (*www.census.gov*), Internal Revenue Services (*www.irs.gov*), and Federal Consumer Information Center (*www.pueblo.gsa.gov*).

2. State agencies

Help can be received from the U.S. Attorney General's Office (*www.usdoj.gov/ag/*) and Service Core of Retired Executes (*www.score.org*).

3. County

National Business Incubation Association (*www.nbia.org*) is a great place for help along with colleges for small business centers.

4. City and town

In your area, search for your local chamber of commerce and try to develop a relationship with a banker and a lawyer.

5. The Internet

You can search online at sites such as *www.google.com* and *www.yahoo.com* for free information. Also, use the Web to find and locate former colleagues who may provide help and support. You also can join an e-mail list online for business newsletters.

6. Libraries

Your local library has many books containing valuable information regarding small businesses, so make sure you put it to use.

7. Friends and family

Talking with family and friends, you can receive referrals from them. If they are in the business world, they can also help you out.

8. Other business owners

Ask to take other business owners to lunch and talk about your start-up. You can ask for their advice, referrals, and business card. You also can contact owners who work in the same industry at different locations, who are not competitors.

Source: Maria Marsala *(www.ElevatingYourBusiness.com)*—A former Wall Street trader, Maria is a nationally known trainer, author, and consultant. Since 1998, she has helped more than 1,000 business owners to make more money in less time by creating SIMPLE systems that work.

Top Start-up Considerations for a Non-U.S. Citizen

If you're not a United States citizen, and you're interested in starting up your own business—watch out. It can be done, but you'll have to navigate through a few challenges. This is a list of things that you may want to consider when speaking with an attorney.

1. A taxpayer identification number (ITIN) isn't enough.

An ITIN merely helps you comply with federal income tax laws. an ITIN is issued to people (mostly foreign nationals) who have to pay taxes or file returns with the IRS but who don't have a social security number. Here are a few examples: An ITIN can't be used as legal identification nor can it be used to set up your own business in the United States.

2. You need a green card.

A green card entitles you to remain permanently in the United States and to obtain a social security number. If you don't have a green card, you can get a temporary E-1 or E-2 visa.

3. You can also have a temporary E-1 or E-2 visa.

The E-1 or E-2 visas will allow you to engage in entrepreneurial activities. These types of visas will allow you to set up a company and employ people in the United States. Remember that the green card and the E-1/E-2 visas are not mutually exclusive (in other words, you don't need both).

4. You will need to invest heavily in your business.

The E-1 or E-2 visa may be issued provided you're willing to invest heavily in the business—generally around $1 million—although if you're planning to locate in a rural or inner-city area with higher-than-average unemployment rates, you may only have to invest $500,000 or so.

5. You'll have to renew your visa.

The E-1 and E-2 visas generally allow you to stay in the United States legally for three to five years, and they may be renewed if you can convince the U.S. Bureau of Citizenship and Immigration Services that the business is doing well and that you intend eventually to return to your country of origin.

6. You'll have to retain ties with your country of origin.

To qualify for an E-1 or E-2 visa, you have to retain ties with your country of origin. If you're from France, for example, the bureau will look to see that you continue to have bank accounts, own real estate, or correspond regularly with family members there. If you have no family, bank accounts, or real estate in France, it's a lot less likely that you intend to return there, and they'll be less likely to grant you the visa.

7. You must be from a designated country.

E-1 and E-2 visas are only issued to aliens from certain countries—those with whom the United States has signed treaties allowing for cross-border movement of entrepreneurs.

Source: Gabe Selig of Selig, Duff & Associates, a Connecticut-based immigration legal firm. Contact him at *gselig@seligduff.com*; (203) 866-9400 x704.

Top Ways to Fund Your Start-up Business

It has been said that "it takes money to make money." The aspiring entrepreneur is often pressed to find more funds. Where can you find them? Here are some creative ways to finance start-up businesses.

1. Founder's capital

Prepare for your start-up by saving. It will take much more money than you planned. Consider inviting a wealthy and trustworthy friend or relative to be a cofounder, and perhaps silent partner. Other people and firms who might consider investing want to see that the founders are truly committed to the venture with their own funds.

2. Friends and family

These people believe in you and your ideas. They want you to succeed. They are mostly interested in the founders and if the concept sounds interesting. Many of them say, "If you, the founders, are committed to this, I know it will go far.

Count me in." Usually they do not conduct a complete evaluation, but invest based on faith. Their knowledge of the founders is the key factor that helps them get the risk to a manageable level. Most of these supporters come in prepared to lose their investment in order to support the founders in fulfilling their dream. Sell unregistered securities through a private placement offering (PPO) to friends and family who qualify as accredited and sophisticated investors. Engage security attorneys to ensure compliance with the Security and Exchange Commission (SEC) and state 'Blue Sky' requirements.

3. Government grants

Government funding—at the national, state, and local levels—can support development of new technology at research institutions and support entrepreneurial activity. The technology from research organizations can ultimately be transferred to start-up businesses. Explore what government sources are available for your venture. For example, apply for SBIR (Small Business Innovation Research) grants administered through the various U.S. government agencies.

4. Barter

What services or products do you have or will you have that one of your service providers wants? Rather than pay cash, barter. Explore how you can exchange a product or service instead.

5. Stock options

Talented people can often be enticed to work for equity as a form of compensation. Rather than fork out the firm's limited cash, explore setting up a stock option program for employees as well as consultants and service providers.

6. Corporate fees and grants

Engineering charges for consulting and customized development may be available from commercial accounts interested in applying your technology to their pressing concerns. These corporations get an early look at the product offering and have the ability to greatly influence its direction. Additionally, these firms may evolve into long-term strategic partners.

7. Revenue from product licensing and sales

Once you have a product available, revenues from its licensing and sales activity can help bootstrap the firm. Choose projects that will generate cash to fund your ongoing operations.

8. Angel investors

Angel-investor networks have formed through the country. These high-net-worth individuals are sophisticated investors interested in early-stage private equity investment in emerging firms with great potential. They may also want a management or board position in your firm as part of the deal.

9. Venture capitalists (VCs)

After considerable due diligence, these firms make private equity investments in promising early-stage companies. Venture capitalists' primary goal is to maximize financial return while getting the risk to a manageable level. In exchanging their money for an ownership stake in the company, venture capitalists also bring business acumen, contacts, and seasoned board experience to the firms in which they invest.

10. Debt financing

Some firms find debt financing through banks and other financial institutions and investors. The funds must be repaid plus interest. For example, the Small Business Administration has a business loan program that works in conjunction with banks.

Source: Theresa M. Szczurek, PhD, president and CEO of Technology and Management Solutions LLC, is a leadership development consultant who helps organizations and individuals succeed by aligning their passions with purpose. She works with emerging and established organizations worldwide in marketing, strategic planning, and organization development to re-energize work forces and produce extraordinary results. She works actively for the advancement of women. An award-winning business leader, author, and speaker featured in *Fortune, ABC World News,* and other media, her newest book, *Pursuit of Passionate Purpose: Success Strategies for a Rewarding Personal and Business Life* (Wiley 2005), quickly became an Amazon Bestseller (number 4 Business and number 16 Overall). Visit *www.PursuitofPassionatePurpose .com* and *www.TMSworld.com* for more information. She can be reached at (303) 443-8674 or *tms@TMSworld.com*.

Typical Steps to Create a New Business

Starting your own new business could be a challenging task. You have to be very sure before you jump into the venture of indulging into creating your own business. As it is true in all ventures, if the venture is successful, you would make huge profits, but all businesses come with their associated risks. We asked an expert in small business to provide us with his steps to create a new business and here they are.

1. Evaluate yourself

Begin by taking stock of yourself and your situation. Why do you want to start a business? Is it money, freedom, creativity, or some other reason? What skills do you have? What industries do you know about? Would you want to provide a service or a product? What do you like to do? How much capital do you have to risk? Will it be a full-time or a part-time venture? Your answers to these types of questions will help you narrow your focus and pick a business. Maybe you don't know what kind of business fits your goals. If that's the case, there are many places to get business ideas. Look through the Yellow Pages. Go to trade shows. Buy industry magazines. Check in with the Small Business Association. Read the business section of the newspaper.

2. Analyze the industry

Once you decide on a business that fits your goals and lifestyle, you need to evaluate your idea. Who will buy your product or service? Who would be your competitors? You also need to figure out at this stage how much money you will need to get started.

3. Make it legal

There are several ways to form your business—it could be a sole proprietorship, a partnership, or a corporation. Although incorporating can be expensive, it is well worth the money. A corporation becomes a separate entity that is legally responsible for the business. If something goes wrong, you cannot be held personally liable. You also need to get the proper business licenses and permits. Depending on the business, there may be city, county, or state regulations as well as permits and licenses to deal with. This is also the time to check into any insurance you may need for the business and to find a good accountant.

4. Draft a business plan

If you will be seeking outside financing, a business plan is a necessity. But even if you are going to finance the venture yourself, a business plan will help you figure out how much money you will need to get started, what needs to get done when, and where you are headed.

5. Get financed

Depending on the size of your venture, you may need to seek financing from an "angel" or from a venture capital firm. Most small businesses begin with private financing from credit cards, personal loans, or help from the family. As a rule of thumb, besides your start-up costs, you should also have at least three months' worth of your family's budget in the bank.

6. Set up shop

Find a location. Negotiate leases. Buy inventory. Get the phones installed. Have stationery printed. Hire staff. Set your prices. Throw a "Grand Opening" party.

7. Indulge in trial and error

It will take a while to figure out what works and what does not. Follow your business plan, but be open and creative. Advertise! Don't be afraid to make a mistake. And above all, have a ball—running your own business is one of the great joys in life!

Source: Steven D. Strauss is one of the country's leading small business experts. A columnist for USA Today.com and Microsoft Small Business, he is also the author of fourteen books, including the recently published *Small Business Bible*.

Things to Consider When Writing Your Business Plan

While including the necessary items in a business plan is important, you also want to make sure you consider the right things. The success of business lies not only in a great entrepreneur or a great business model but also in the avoidance of mistakes in the planning stage. Our expert offers some things to consider when writing your business plan.

1. Procrastination

Too many businesses make business plans only when they have no choice in the matter. Unless the bank or the investors want a plan, there is no plan. Don't wait to write your plan until you think you'll have enough time. "I can't plan. I'm too busy getting things done," businesspeople say. The busier you are, the more you need to plan. If you are always putting out fires, you should build firebreaks or a sprinkler system. You can lose the whole forest by paying too much attention to the individual burning trees.

2. Cash flow casualness

Most people think in terms of profits instead of cash. When you imagine a new business, you think of what it would cost to make the product, what you could sell it for, and what the profits per unit might be. We are trained to think of business as sales minus costs and expenses, which equal profits. Unfortunately, we don't spend the profits in a business. We spend cash. So understanding cash flow is critical. If you have only one table in your business plan, make it the cash flow table.

3. Idea inflation

Don't overestimate the importance of the idea. You don't need a great idea to start a business; you need time, money, perseverance, and common sense. Few successful businesses are based entirely on new ideas. A new idea is harder to sell than an existing one, because people don't understand a new idea and they are often unsure if it will work. Plans don't sell new business ideas to investors. People do. Investors invest in people not ideas. The plan, though necessary, is only a way to present information.

4. Fear and dread

Doing a business plan isn't as hard as you might think. You don't have to write a doctoral thesis or a novel. There are good books to help, many advisers among the Small Business Development Centers (SBDCs), business schools, and there is software available to help you (such as Business Plan Pro, and others).

5. Spongy, vague goals

Leave out the vague and the meaningless babble of business phrases (such as "being the best") because they are simply hype. Remember that the objective of a plan is its results, and for results, you need tracking and follow-up. You need specific dates, management responsibilities, budgets, and milestones. Then you can follow up. No matter how well thought out or brilliantly presented, the plan means nothing unless it produces results. One size fits all. Tailor your plan to its real business purpose.

6. Diluted priorities

Remember, strategy is focus. A priority list with three or four items is focus. A priority list with twenty items is certainly not strategic, and rarely if ever effective. The more items on the list, the less important each is.

7. Hockey stick–shaped growth projections

Sales grow slowly at first, but then shoot up boldly with huge growth rates, as soon as "something" happens. Have projections that are conservative so you can defend them. When in doubt, be less optimistic.

Source: Tim Berry is a business planning expert and the author of several books and planning software packages such as Business Plan Pro. Berry is also a successful entrepreneur, a cofounder of Borland International in 1983 and has many books to his credit. E-mail: *tim@planningpeople.com*. Tim is also the founder and CEO of Palo Alto Software (*www.bplans.com*).

Typical Business Plan Mistakes

Okay, you've finally written your business plan. But will it help you secure the funding you need? Will it help you build a successful business? A business plan is a double-edged sword—it allows you to introduce and sell your business, but it also gives the reader an opening to say no. Don't blow your big chance. Now more than ever, you only get one chance to make a good first impression. Here are some key mistakes to avoid from an expert who specializes in helping her clients create successful business plans.

1. Too much jargon

If readers can't understand what you're saying, they won't buy in. Another caution: Go easy on the latest jargon. If your business plan is laden with the latest "sexy" buzzwords, readers' antennae go up. Are you using fancy words to hide a lack of substance? Better to write a user-friendly, straightforward business plan.

2. Great idea, but customers will not pay for it

You may have a great idea, but that's no guarantee that customers are willing to pay for it. An important question to ask is, "What problem am I solving for *paying* customers?"

3. Too many generalizations

Discuss your specific solution to solve the problem. Support your statements. Too often, business plans are filled with superlatives, generalizations and over-the-top optimism—guaranteed red flags.

4. Selling it

Too many entrepreneurs fall into the trap of thinking, "If I build it, they will come." You need to explain how you are going to sell your product or service.

5. Unrealistic assumptions

A good business plan has realistic assumptions. A seasoned investor can spot unrealistic assumptions a mile away. Even if you're self-funding, what good will it do you to be unrealistic? Another caution: The numbers need to support the story.

6. Competitive position that can't be defended

You may have a great idea, but if it's successful and competitors can copycat it, what good is that? Being first is no guarantee of maintaining market share.

7. Don't write your executive summary first

How can you summarize what you haven't yet written? Writing a business plan is a process, and there are no shortcuts. Your business will evolve and take shape as you think through all the issues, big and small. This evolution is a critical part of the plan writing process, and the results will inevitably show in your executive summary. You need to write it last and write it well—once you get in the door, it's the hook that will entice an investor to look deeper.

Source: Diane Tarshis is principal of Springboard Business Plans, LLC, and has been writing business plans for more than ten years. She brings her 20-plus years of business experience to each and every plan, whether for an upscale restaurant, a portfolio of hedge funds (fund of funds), or a floral shop franchise. Diane holds a degree in finance from the Wharton School and spent several years working as an investment banker on Wall Street. She can be reached at (773) 871-0110 or by visiting her Web site at www.springboardplans.com.

Things to Include in a Business Plan

Ready to write that business plan? There are two primary components: (i) the narrative or text portion (i.e., the words) and (ii) the quantitative or financial portion (i.e., the numbers). The words need to clearly explain your business concept, the strategies you plan to implement, the competitive environment, etc. The numbers need to support the words. This will result in a business plan that tells a coherent story and has realistic numbers to support that story. Specifically, our expert says you will need to include the following:

1. Business description

Describe it simply and clearly. What is the opportunity? In other words, what pain are you solving for paying customers? What do customers currently pay to solve that problem? Your business model, i.e., the source(s) of your revenues.

2. Products and/or services offered

What are you selling? At what price? At what cost to you? What are the features and benefits of what you are selling? What makes it different and desirable? Why will customers buy it from you? How will products be manufactured? What are the mechanics of your website if selling via the Internet?

3. Market analysis

Industry overview—describe the size of your industry and its unique characteristics. Define your target markets. What is the size of your target market? What is its growth potential? Is the market competitive? If not, why not? Who are your customers? Give demographic information. Why will they buy from you? How will you reach your customers? What is your marketing/sales plan?

4. Location

Where will your business be located? Are there zoning issues? Do you need to rent or buy space? How much square footage do you need? What characteristics are required? Preferred? At what price? If renting, who pays for utilities? Who pays the real estate taxes? Are renovations or build-out required? Who pays, if renting?

5. Competition

Give an overview of the competitive landscape. What is your competitive advantage? Is it defensible (i.e., if it works, will your competitors be able to copy you)? List your five closest competitors and describe: who they are, their products/services, their strengths and weaknesses and what you've learned from watching them—how will you be better than them?

6. Management

Why are you (and your team) qualified to build/run this business? What is your (and your team's) professional background and experience? Do you have relevant personal experience in this industry? Who reports to whom? Who makes final decisions? Describe any advisors or other professionals who are assisting you (and their backgrounds).

7. Personnel

Who will you be hiring? For what positions? Describe their responsibilities. At what pay rate? Who reports to whom? What is the staffing/hiring plan (i.e., when will you fill each position)?

8. Application and expected effect of investment/loan

How much money are you trying to raise? What, specifically, will it be used for? Why do you need it at this stage?

9. Sources and uses of funding

This is a numerical restatement of the Application and Expected Effect of Investment/Loan section in the narrative portion of your business plan. Here you are listing the specific expenditures you will make with the loan/investment.

10. Capital equipment list

This is the equipment you use to provide your service, manufacture your product or to sell, store or deliver your merchandise, not equipment that you use in the normal course of business. Equipment that you expect to replace frequently (annually or more often) is not included. Capital equipment can include office furniture, computers, store fixtures, machinery used to make products or deliver services, delivery vehicles, etc.

11. Balance sheet

A balance sheet shows the assets, liabilities and net worth of a business at a specific point in time.

12. Breakeven analysis

A breakeven analysis shows the point at which your business will be breaking even, i.e., neither making a profit nor losing money—shown either in dollar sales or unit sales. The basic breakeven formula is: Sales = Fixed Costs + Variable Costs

13. Projected income statement

An income statement (or profit & loss statement) shows a business's financial state over a period of time. It is also important to include an explanation of your assumptions.

14. Cash flow projections

This is your most important spreadsheet because it shows when cash will flow in and out of your business over time. Cash is king, so make sure you have enough to cover slow periods and/or slow paying customers. A good cash flow projection can be the difference between success and failure.

Source: Diane Tarshis is Principal of Springboard Business Plans, LLC, and has been writing business plans for more than 10 years. She brings her 20+ years of business experience to each and every plan, whether for an upscale restaurant, a portfolio of hedge funds (fund of funds) or a floral shop franchise. Diane holds a degree in finance from the Wharton School and spent several years working as an investment banker on Wall Street. She can be reached at (773) 871-0110 or by visiting her Web site at *www.springboardplans.com.*

The Small Business Market

Number of Minority-Owned Businesses, by Region

Although the majority of small business owners are Caucasian, that does not mean that various minorities cannot have success in the entrepreneurial world as well. For any number of reasons, different regions of the country may be more conducive to success for minority business owners. If you are a minority entrepreneur, or simply want an idea of which regions have the most minority-owned businesses, the following is a listing of the number of combined businesses owned by African-Americans, Hispanics, Asians and Pacific Islanders, and Native Americans and Native Alaskans by region, ranked from most to fewest, based on U.S. Census Bureau data as provided by the Small Business Administration.

1. West
Total minority-owned businesses: 960,500
Region includes Arizona, California, Colorado, Hawaii, Nevada, New Mexico, Utah

2. Mid-Atlantic
Total minority-owned businesses: 585,700
Region includes Delaware, District of Columbia, Maryland, New Jersey, New York, Pennsylvania, West Virginia

3. Southeast
Total minority-owned businesses: 567,100
Region includes Florida, Georgia, Kentucky, North Carolina, South Carolina, Virginia

4. South
Total minority-owned businesses: 515,700
Region includes Alabama, Arkansas, Louisiana, Mississippi, Tennessee, Texas

5. Great Lakes
Total minority-owned businesses: 267,900
Region includes Illinois, Indiana, Michigan, Minnesota, Ohio, Wisconsin

6. Northwest
Total minority-owned businesses: 83,900
Region includes Alaska, Idaho, Montana, Oregon, Washington, Wyoming

7. Great Plains
Total minority-owned businesses: 80,800
Region includes Iowa, Kansas, Missouri, Nebraska, North Dakota, Oklahoma, South Dakota

8. New England

Total minority-owned businesses: 75,100

Region includes Connecticut, Maine, Massachusetts, New Hampshire, Rhode Island, Vermont

Source: Small Business Administration (*www.sba.gov*).

Typical Characteristics of Business Owners

With any profession, there are certain characteristics that allow certain people to excel over others who do not possess such traits. The world of entrepreneurship is no different. There are key characteristics that allow business owners to make their companies profitable, earn the respect of their employees, and maintain success over a long period. The following are some of the typical characteristics of a successful business owner.

1. Advance planning

Especially when starting your business, it is important to understand exactly what your product is, who your customer is and their traits, who your competitors are and their traits, and to set goals for your business based on this understanding. Each stage of your business activities should be well planned out to ensure success once you begin taking action on those activities.

2. Advance organization

Once your planning is complete, you must be sure to organize the people and resources you will need to achieve the goals you have set. This will allow the plans laid out originally to be executed smoothly and efficiently. Similarly,

such organization will be key to all undertakings for your business, not just the start-up.

3. Successful employee scouting

Your abilities as an entrepreneur will mean nothing if you do not have the best possible people working toward your goals. A successful business owner must be able to locate and surround himself or herself with the highest quality people who can take the plans made by the owner and put them into action.

4. Ability to delegate

Once the right people are located for the business, the owner must understand what tasks need to be accomplished and who is best suited to work on those tasks. Being able to match the right people to the right tasks and being able to separate yourself from that task, relinquishing control to the employee, is key to success as a business owner.

5. Ability to oversee work

Once the tasks are properly delegated, an owner must be able to monitor the progress of a project to ensure that it is being done properly and on time. While the employee will have control over the project, the business owner is still responsible for its outcome, so he or she must be able to oversee the work being done, without taking over, to ensure its success.

6. Setting standards

In order to ensure that projects are properly done, the owner must set standards for time, quality, and ultimate goals. When the employees working on particular tasks understand exactly what is expected of them, the tasks will be completed more efficiently and more effectively than if they are working with an ambiguous set of expectations.

7. Determination

A business owner's determination may be the most important element to his or her ultimate success. The competitive edge to achieve their goals, outperform competitors, and conquer any obstacles will provide owners and their employees with the motivation needed to ensure success.

Source: Brian Tracy, *Develop the Habits to Win in Business*, from *www.entrepreneur.com*. Brian Tracy is a business coach and a leading authority on entrepreneurial development.

Most Active Small Business Political Action Committees

As a small business owner, you may be concerned about your interests being represented in government and whether Congress will create legislation that will be in favor of business. To ensure that candidates who are business friendly are elected, political action committees exist to make contributions to the campaigns of those candidates. The following is a listing of the most active nationally based small business political action committees, based on contributions from the 2004 election cycle.

1. National Federation of Independent Business

2004 contributions: $754,916
Based in Washington, D.C., FEC Committee ID: C00101105
www.nfib.com

2. U.S. Chamber of Commerce

2004 contributions: $173,150
Based in Washington D.C., FEC Committee ID: C00082040
www.uschamber.com

3. International Franchise Association

2004 contributions: $152,999
Based in Washington, D.C., FEC Committee ID: C00084491
www.franchise.org

4. National Franchisee Association

2004 contributions: $143,000
Based in Washington, D.C., FEC Committee ID: C00329425

5. Business Industry PAC

2004 contributions: $102,352
Based in Washington, D.C., FEC Committee ID: C00001727
www.bipac.org

6. National Association of Small Business Investment Companies

2004 contributions: $92,250
Based in Washington, D.C., FEC Committee ID: C00109991
www.nasbic.org

Source: OpenSecrets.org listing of 2004 PAC contributions by Business Associations. OpenSecrets.org provides data on all areas of finance in U.S. elections, including who gives and gets the money and information on campaign finance laws. The site is run by the Center for Responsive Politics.

Number of Businesses Owned by Women, by Region

Although the majority of small business owners are male, that does not mean that women cannot have success in the entrepreneurial world as well. For any number of reasons, different regions of the country may be more conducive to success for female business owners. If you are a female entrepreneur, or simply want an idea of which regions have the most businesses owned by women, the following is a listing of the number of these businesses by region, ranked from most to fewest, based on U.S. Census Bureau data.

1. West

Total Number of Businesses Owned by Women: 1,043,900

Region includes Arizona, California, Colorado, Hawaii, Nevada, New Mexico, Utah

2. Great Lakes

Total Number of Businesses Owned by Women: 934,100

Region includes Illinois, Indiana, Michigan, Minnesota, Ohio, Wisconsin

3. Mid-Atlantic

Total Number of Businesses Owned by Women: 926,100

Region includes Delaware, District of Columbia, Maryland, New Jersey, New York, Pennsylvania, West Virginia

4. Southeast

Total Number of Businesses Owned by Women: 885,700

Region includes Florida, Georgia, Kentucky, North Carolina, South Carolina, Virginia

5. South

Total Number of Businesses Owned by Women: 702,300

Region includes Alabama, Arkansas, Louisiana, Mississippi, Tennessee, Texas

6. Great Plains

Total Number of Businesses Owned by Women: 343,200

Region includes Iowa, Kansas, Missouri, Nebraska, North Dakota, Oklahoma, South Dakota

7. New England

Total Number of Businesses Owned by Women: 309,900

Region includes Connecticut, Maine, Massachusetts, New Hampshire, Rhode Island, Vermont

8. Northwest

Total Number of Businesses Owned by Women: 279,400

Region includes Alaska, Idaho, Montana, Oregon, Washington, Wyoming

Source: Small Business Administration (*www.sba.gov*).

Best Organizations for Working Women

There are many reasons for a working woman to join an organization including support, contacts, education and training, political advocacy, leadership development opportunities, and working together toward a common cause. Look at your own situation and evaluate various groups based on your needs. Also, consider the philosophy, membership, and activities of the association's local chapter, as appropriate. Often you get more out of membership as you put in more time and effort. Here is a list of some popular organizations that serve the needs of working women. the information is taken from their Web sites.

1. BPW

Business and Professional Women / USA helps women achieve economic self-sufficiency by advancing careers, building businesses, and advocating for workplace equity. With 1,500 local organizations across the country and members in every congressional district, BPW/USA is the leading advocate for millions of working women on work-life balance and workplace equity issues. Formed in 1919, its mission is to promote equity for all women in the workplace through advocacy, education, and information. BPW International exists in more than 100 countries and serves the needs of working women across the globe.

www.bpwintl.com

2. NAWBO

The National Association of Women Business Owners represents the interests of all women entrepreneurs across all industries. Working to propel women entrepreneurs into economic, social, and political spheres of power worldwide, membership is open to sole proprietors, partners, and corporate owners with day-to-day management responsibility. The organization, which has chapters in almost every metropolitan area in the United States, promotes economic development, strengthens the wealth-creating capacity of its members, creates business culture changes, builds strategic alliances, and transforms public policy and opinions.

www.nawbo.org

3. WorldWIT

WorldWIT is a leading global online and offline network for women in business, and WorldWIT is free. All women (and supportive men) in business and technology (including related areas such as law, the media, the arts, government, not-for-profits, consulting, and academia) are welcome to join the conversation in a free, moderated, SPAMless e-mail discussion group. There are more than seventy groups throughout the world.

www.worldWIT.org

4. Your local community

Your local Chamber of Commerce may have an active women's group with participants from companies throughout the community. Likewise medium to large firms, non-profit associations, and government agencies may have an internal group focused on its own women's issues, status, and support. Tailored to meet the needs of the women in the community of interest, these local groups may have agendas focused on specific issues. Also check out if there is a Women's Chamber of Commerce in your area.

5. The Committee of 200

This is the professional organization of preeminent women entrepreneurs and corporate leaders. The organization capitalizes on the power, success, and influence of businesswomen in the global economy. With more than 470 women, members now represent more than eighty industries, including manufacturing, technology, and finance. Entrepreneurs who qualify own and run companies that earn at least $15 million in annual revenues. Corporate executives who qualify are either CEOs or senior executives leading substantial operating divisions, with direct impact on annual revenues of $250 million or more.

www.c200.org

6. International Women's Forum

The International Women's Forum is an organization of top women that furthers dynamic leadership, leverages global access, and maximizes opportunities for women to exert their influence. Membership is by invitation only and is influenced by definitive international standards. Members of the IWF are the world's women leaders who serve and lead their countries, governments, corporations, businesses, academic institutions, arts communities, philanthropic enterprises, and organizations for trade, diplomacy, science, and research. They are heads of state, chief executive officers, entrepreneurs, opinion-leaders, decision-makers, and pathfinders to success. IWF advances women's leadership across careers, cultures, and continents.

www.iwforum.org

Source: Theresa M. Szczurek, PhD, president and CEO of Technology and Management Solutions LLC, is a leadership development consultant who helps organizations and individuals succeed by aligning their passions with purpose. She works with emerging and established organizations worldwide in marketing, strategic planning, and organization development to re-energize work forces and produce extraordinary results. She works actively for the advancement of women. An award-winning business leader, author, and speaker featured in *Fortune*, ABC World News, and other media, her newest book, *Pursuit of Passionate Purpose: Success Strategies for a Rewarding Personal and Business Life* (Wiley 2005), quickly became an Amazon Bestseller (number 4 Business and number 16 Overall). Visit *www.PursuitofPassionatePurpose.com* and *www.TMSworld.com* for more information. She can be reached at (303) 443-8674 or *tms@TMSworld.com*

Top States for New Business Formation

Where do you want to start your new business? Depending on the state in which you start your business, you may be one of many new businesses in a given year, or you may be among only a few thousand others. Certain states have much higher numbers of new business formations each year than others. One of the main reasons is simply that some states have larger populations, but there are other factors that lead to increased business formation. These are the states that have had the most new business start-ups in the past year. Maybe they're on to something?

1. California
New employer businesses: 113,500

2. Florida
New employer businesses: 69,711

3. New York
New employer businesses: 60,569

4. Texas
New employer businesses: 52,677

5. Washington
New employer businesses: 36,136

6. Pennsylvania
New employer businesses: 31,214

7. New Jersey
New employer businesses: 29,236

8. Illinois
New employer businesses: 28,933

9. Georgia
New employer businesses: 24,217

10. North Carolina
New employer businesses: 22,465

Source: Small Business Administration (*www.sba.gov*).

Slowest Industries for Small Business

What are the safest small businesses to start, and what are the riskiest? One measure of risk is to compare relative percentages of profitable and unprofitable businesses in a given industry. Our expert used sole proprietorship data since net income or loss is not affected by owners' compensation. Compiling data on 120 different types of businesses, our expert came up with some interesting results, which are listed here.

1. Clothing and accessories stores
Industry—Retail
59.5% with profits
40.5% with losses

2. Securities and commodity exchanges
Industry—Finance/insurance
59.1% with profits
40.9% with losses

3. Performing arts, recreation, and related
Industry—Entertainment
57.6% with profits
42.4% with losses

4. Utilities
Industry—Utility services
57.3% with profits
42.7% with losses

5. Chemical manufacturing
Industry—Manufacturing
56.8% with profits
43.2% with losses

6. Sporting goods, hobby, book, and music stores
Industry—Retail
55.0% with profits
45.0% with losses

7. Support activities for agriculture and forestry
Industry—Agricultural services
54.9% with profits
45.1% with losses

8. Oil and gas extraction
Industry—Extraction
54.3% with profits
45.7% with losses

9. Miscellaneous store retailers
Industry—Retail
50.7% with profits
49.3% with losses

10. Textile and textile product mills

Industry—Manufacturing

50.5% with profits

49.5% with losses

11. Health and personal care stores

Industry—Retail

49.5% with profits

50.5% with losses

12. Other miscellaneous manufacturing

Industry—Manufacturing

48.8% with profits

51.2% with losses

13. Nonstore retailers

Industry—Retail

48.8% with profits

51.2% with losses

14. Videotape and disc rental

Industry—Rentals

48.4% with profits

51.6% with losses

15. Primary metal industries

Industry—Manufacturing

41.0% with profits

59.0% with losses

16. Nonmetallic mineral mining and quarrying

Industry—Mining

38.3% with profits

61.7% with losses

17. Commodity contracts brokers and dealers

Industry—Finance/insurance

36.6% with profits

63.4% with losses

18. Computer and electronic products

Industry—Manufacturing

35.4% with profits

64.6% with losses

19. Animal production (including pet breeding)

Industry—Breeding

34.5% with profits

65.5% with losses

20. Scenic and sightseeing transportation

Industry—Transportation

33.8% with profits

66.2% with losses

21. Hunting and trapping

Industry—Hunting/trapping

23.6% with profits

76.4% with losses

Source: Bizstats (*www.bizstats.com*)—A leading online source for small business statistics that provides instant access to business statistical information that is useful and meaningful. Contact the editor, Patrick O'Rourke, CPA at *patricko@bizstats.com*.

Your Place of Business

Regions More Friendly to Small Businesses

There may be geographic or demographic reasons for choosing where to start your small business, or you may choose an area for family or other reasons. Whatever the reason, your chances of surviving as an entrepreneur may be greatly impacted by the area in which you choose to set up shop. Different areas of the country have proven to be more conducive to small business survival, and the following list ranks the eight major regions of the country based on the Small Business and Entrepreneurship Council's 2005 Small Business Survival Index, with the lower the number indicating a better environment for business survival.

1. South

Average Small Business Survival Index: 42.857

Including: Alabama, Louisiana, Mississippi, Tennessee, and Texas

2. Northwest

Average Small Business Survival Index: 44.563

Including: Alaska, Idaho, Montana, Oregon, Washington, and Wyoming

3. Southeast

Average Small Business Survival Index: 44.8685

Including: Florida, Georgia, Kentucky, North Carolina, South Carolina, and Virginia

4. Great Plains

Average Small Business Survival Index: 45.5522

Including: Iowa, Kansas, Missouri, Nebraska, North Dakota, Oklahoma, and South Dakota

5. Great Lakes

Average Small Business Survival Index: 47.5782

Including: Illinois, Indiana, Michigan, Minnesota, Ohio, and Wisconsin

6. West

Average Small Business Survival Index: 47.7804

Including: Arizona, California, Colorado, Hawaii, Nevada, New Mexico, and Utah

7. Mid Atlantic

Average Small Business Survival Index: 53.681

Including: Delaware, District of Columbia, Maryland, New Jersey, New York, Pennsylvania, and West Virginia

8. New England

Average Small Business Survival Index: 54.9673

Including: Connecticut, Maine, Massachusetts, New Hampshire, Rhode Island, and Vermont

---

Source: Small Business and Entrepreneurship Council's (www
.sbecouncil.org) Small Business Survival Index 2005, by Raymond J.
Keating, Chief Economist for the Small Business and Entrepreneurship

Council. This report, published in 2005, provides a look at "the policy environment for entrepreneurship across the nation." The index numbers for each state were based on the governmental tax burdens for small businesses and included each state's top personal income tax rate, top capital gains tax rate for individuals, top corporate income tax rate, additional taxes on S-Corporations beyond top personal income tax rate, individual alternative minimum tax, corporate alternative minimum tax, and state and local property taxes. The Small Business and Entrepreneurship Council can be contacted at the following address: 1920 L Street, Suite200 Washington, DC 20036 Phone: (202) 785-0238

Typical Provision of an Office Lease

Although reading a commercial lease can be difficult and time-consuming, the consequences of not reading it can be infinitely more unpleasant. Unfortunately, many contracts have provisions buried in the lease that may have unintended impact on you. The best thing you can do to prepare is to not be surprised. Here's a list of typical provisions of an office lease—understanding them beforehand is very important.

1. Common area maintenance ("CAM") expenses (also known as "operating expenses")

Landlords may try to use this provision as a "profit center." An operating expense or CAM provision requires the tenant to pay its pro-rata share of the operating expenses incurred by the landlord in the operation and maintenance of the building. Unfortunately, landlords have expanded the list of expenses to include every imaginable expenditure. By doing so, some landlords have turned this provision into a profit center. Instead, the provision should only pass through to the tenant legitimate expenses relating to the operation

and maintenance of the common areas. Carefully review the history of the building's CAM charges for at least the three prior years. This will enable you to compare the amount of operating expenses and their annual increases to other comparable buildings to determine whether they are reasonable, and to estimate what the charges might be in future years.

2. Repair and maintenance provision

Landlords may try to use this provision to require you to repair and maintain areas located outside the leased premises. Pay particular attention to any repair and maintenance provision that requires the tenant to repair and maintain items or areas that are traditionally the landlord's responsibility. A typical lease will define repair and maintenance obligations with reference to the interior of the premises. However, depending on the definition of the premises, this may result in the tenant's having to repair and maintain such things as plumbing, sprinklers, HVAC ducts, and the building's structural elements. Try to make certain that the costs of the repair and maintenance for which the landlord is responsible cannot be passed on to you, through, for example, the operating expense provision.

3. Real property taxes

An unsuspecting tenant may have to pay real estate taxes and special assessments for a period beyond the expiration of the lease. The real property taxes provision defines the respective obligations of the landlord and tenant for real property taxes. Landlords have expanded the definition of real property taxes to include any type of tax assessed against the property, the landlord, or for doing business and are increasingly defining taxes to include future taxes of any sort, including rent taxes or income taxes. Be aware that your tax liability may increase dramatically if the landlord sells the property; particularly if the landlord has held the property for a long time and property values have greatly increased. You may wish to limit increases in real property taxes resulting from a change in ownership by, for example, having increases occur incrementally over time or being completely eliminated.

4. Compliance with laws

If you don't appreciate the potential effects of this provision, you may find yourself footing the bill for earthquake retrofitting, asbestos abatement, sprinkler installation, or compliance with the Americans with Disabilities Act. This provision typically requires the tenant to perform potentially expensive replacements, alterations, or improvements of the leased premises to comply with existing or future laws and government orders relating to the leased premises. If the landlord is to bear the responsibility, you must curtail the landlord's ability to "pass on" the cost of compliance through other provisions, such as the operating expense provision. If the tenant is to be responsible for compliance with laws, the landlord should represent and warrant to the tenant in the lease that the building is in compliance with all presently existing laws and limit the tenant's responsibility for compliance with future laws to those items necessitated solely due to his or her particular use of the premises.

5. Assignment and subletting

Asking for permission to assign or sublet the premises may give the landlord the ability to terminate the lease. In the typical commercial lease, the landlord requires the tenant to get his or her consent prior to any assignment or sublet. Negotiate several exclusions from the consent requirements, including assignment or sublet for reorganization purposes and space-sharing arrangements up to a defined square footage (the latter has particular application to office leases or retail leases where the business is seasonal). Where the lease requires consent and the landlord consents to an assignment or sublet, the landlord may get to keep all rents paid by the assignee or subtenant in excess of the tenant's fixed rent obligation to the landlord. Ask for at least a portion of this "excess" rent.

6. Subordination, nondisturbance and attornment (SNDA) provision

If the landlord asks you for what amounts to a favor for the benefit of its lender, be sure to get something in return. This provision defines the important relationship between the landlord's current and future lenders and ground lessors, and the tenant in the event the landlord defaults on loan obligations or obligations to the ground lessor. A subordination clause typically readjusts the priorities that normally would result from general legal rules, by providing, for example, that any existing or subsequent lender of the landlord can elect to deem its deed of trust superior or junior to the lease, regardless of the date on which the lender's deed of trust was recorded. An attornment provision generally obligates the tenant to recognize the foreclosing lender or ground lessor as the new landlord under the existing lease.

7. Tenant remedies (termination and abatement rights)

A lease containing waivers of tenant remedies may leave you with no place to turn if the landlord defaults in its obligations. This clause defines what, if any, remedies are available to the tenant in the event of a default on the part of the landlord. Many commercial leases cause the tenant, by accepting the terms of the lease, to waive a host of remedies provided by the law. Other leases fail to mention tenant remedies entirely. When negotiating a lease, ideally you would like to preserve your "repair and deduct" rights, so if there is a problem, you can remedy the problem and deduct the cost from your rent. In most cases, the landlord will require a waiver of this right. You should, therefore, negotiate a lease that contains abatement and termination rights.

8. Termination, relocation, or expansion rights

If you haven't read the lease carefully, you may be surprised to learn that the landlord has reserved the right unilaterally to terminate the lease or relocate you. A termination provision in favor of the landlord allows the landlord unilaterally to terminate the lease, usually on the occurrence of some condition. A relocation provision allows the landlord to relocate the tenant to other premises within the building. Ideally, do not agree to such clauses. If conditions require acceptance, make certain that you can

only be relocated to a comparable location and position and that the landlord has to pay for all expenses related to the relocation, including the cost of moving the business and installing tenant improvements.

9. Damage and destruction

A trap for the unwary, this provision provides what will happen if the leased premises or the building housing the leased premises is damaged or destroyed. It typically provides that the landlord may elect, in its sole discretion, to continue the lease or to terminate it. In the case of continuation, the provision usually provides for an abatement of rent in the same proportion that tenant's use of the leased premises is impaired. Make sure that the abatement of rent language is fair. Some leases base it on the amount of square footage of the leased premises that is damaged or destroyed. This is unfair since sometimes the entire leased premises may not be usable even where the damage is to a small area. The ability to terminate should reside in both landlord and tenant. Otherwise, you may find yourself bound to a lease under which you are unable to use the leased premises for a significant time. This can throw a real wrench into your business plans.

10. Tenant improvements

Now you see them; now you don't. If improvements are to be made to the leased premises prior to your occupancy, you must understand the economic impact of such improvements and know what you will get. Make certain that the obligation to pay rent and other charges do not begin until the tenant improvements are complete. Before entering into the lease, in an allowance arrangement, you should have final space plans and estimates for the work so that you are not exposed for the cost of improvements in excess of the landlord's allowance or, at the very least, will know how much you will have to pay. An agreement should be made as to the disposition of the landlord allowance if the actual tenant improvements cost less than the allowance. The landlord would like to keep the unused portion of the allowance, but you should attempt to get the landlord to apply the allowance to the costs of other work that is your responsibility under the lease or work letter, pay it to you, offset it against future rent, or allow you to use some portion of it.

Source: Team Skyline (*www.skylineleasing.com*) is an elite group of top-producing agents at Starboard TCN Worldwide who focus on providing clients with a full-service solution to San Francisco office space rentals. Team Skyline's professionals focus on office space leasing and investment sales. They work with many major multiple-market clients and excel at providing them with a single point of contact. Contact them at 26 O'Farrell, San Francisco, CA 94108; (415) 765-6890.

Popular Forms of Leasing

Like anything else, there's not just one of anything. Our great financial minds have come up with lots of new ways to define a leasing agreement. So before you venture into the leasing world, you should check out these most common forms of leasing arrangements.

1. Financial lease

This is the kind of lease most often used by a business to enable it to acquire equipment that would otherwise be purchased. The typical financial lease calls for periodic payments, usually monthly. The term of the lease approximates the useful or economic life of the equipment, and the equipment is returned to the lessor at the end of the lease term. The lease may not be canceled by the lessee, and the lessee usually must maintain the equipment and repair it throughout the term. In short, the lessee enjoys most of the benefits of ownership and also most of the obligations but does not really own the equipment.

2. Gross lease

In this form of lease, the lessor is responsible for all expenses associated with ownership of the equipment such as maintenance, taxes, and insurance.

3. Net lease

A net lease is the opposite of a gross lease. Here, the lessee is responsible for expenses related to the operation of the equipment such as maintenance, taxes, and insurance.

4. Leveraged lease

In this kind of lease, the lessor puts up part of the purchase price of the equipment and borrows the rest from one or more banks or other lenders. The fact that a lease is a leveraged lease should not affect the lessee.

5. Sale and lease-back

The sale and lease-back arrangement is similar to a financial lease. Here, the business that desires use of the equipment purchases it, sells the equipment to a leasing company, and simultaneously leases it back from the leasing company for a specified term. In this type of lease arrangement, the lessor often provides the lessee an option to purchase the equipment at the end of the term.

6. Closed-end lease

This kind of lease is common with automobiles. Here, the lessor and lessee forecast the fair market value of the leased equipment at the end of the term. The periodic lease payments made by the lessee are based on the amount of the equipment value that the lessee will "consume" over the term; that is, the original purchase price minus the forecasted fair market value at the end of the term. If it turns out that the leased equipment is worth less at the end of the term than the parties predicted, the lessee must pay to the lessor the difference in value.

7. Open-end lease

This lease is the opposite of a closed-end lease. Here, the lessee has no obligation to the lessor if the fair market value of the equipment is less at the end of the term than predicted.

8. Residual value

This is the value of the equipment at the end of the term.

9. Capital lease

This is a lease of a piece of equipment or an item that, if purchased, would take a substantial capital investment. According to accounting rules, capital leases must be recorded on the balance sheet of the business directly. The economic value of the capital in the equipment is shown as an asset, and the obligations under the lease are reflected as a liability.

10. Option to purchase

In some leases, the lessee is given the option to buy the equipment at the end of the lease term, either for "fair market value" or for a set price. When negotiating a lease, inquire whether the lessor will grant you an option to purchase. In some cases, a lessor may even grant an option to purchase at the end of the term for some nominal amount, such as $1. While these provisions are enforceable between the lessor and lessee, they are usually dangerous for the lessor. The risk arises if the lessee runs into problems and cannot make the lease payments and meet other obligations. If another creditor attaches the leased equipment, the court may rule that the lease arrangement is really a disguised sales agreement. In that case, the lessor's interest in the equipment is recast as that of a seller who financed the sale of the equipment for the benefit of the lessee/buyer. In that position, the lessor/seller would have only a security interest in the equipment and stands to lose it to other creditors.

Source: SmartText Corporation (*www.smartagreements.com*) develops and sells forms with explanations. The explanations are written by experienced businesspeople with the help of attorneys to provide the most useful guidance and assistance possible without providing legal advice. The company's products are used by law firms, professional accounting firms, Fortune 500 corporations, and thousands of small businesses in more than thirty countries around the world. Contact them at P.O. Box 7489 Shawnee Mission, KS 66207-0489; (913) 269-6589.

Most Common Lease Negotiation Mistakes

The single biggest issue on most tenants' minds when negotiating their office lease is how to achieve the lowest rental rates. Yet, most tenants feel disadvantaged and ill-equipped to achieve this goal. According to our expert, you must position your tenancy as something that is not only desirable but also elusive in order to get the landlord nervous enough to give you the best rates. However, negotiating effectively and positioning your tenancy doesn't have to be as difficult or intimidating as you might expect. Like anything else, if you have a proven system to follow—and know the signals and the language—you can successfully turn the tables in your favor.

1. Starting too late

Many tenants start lease-renewal negotiations too late. Tenants need enough time to implement lease-negotiation strategy and techniques without pressure and to negotiate a new lease elsewhere and relocate if negotiations fail. Allow nine to twelve months before the lease expires. Get time leverage on your side and take it away from your landlord.

2. Bidding blind

What price should you offer when you bid on a location? Is the landlord's asking price too high, or does it represent a great deal? If you fail to research the market in order to understand what comparable spaces are selling for, making your offer would be like bidding blind. Without this knowledge of market value, you could easily bid too much or fail to make a competitive offer at all on an excellent value.

3. Failure to create competition for your tenancy

It is important to create the perception that relocation of your business is an option even if this is the last thing you want to do. If a landlord thinks you have no other real alternatives, you will pay a higher rent than new tenants pay. Engaging a professional to negotiate your lease renewal automatically activates competition especially when the professional lets your current landlord know that you are actively evaluating alternative premises. Get your landlord worried that he will lose a good tenant and possibly face vacant space and the uncertainties of leasing to someone else.

4. Failure to negotiate terms of the lease

Industry estimates show that about 90 percent of small tenants make no changes at all to a lease! Don't make this mistake. A "standard" real-estate lease contains hidden cost clauses that can cost you a lot of money and problems in the future. It can even affect the viability of your business to survive in some cases. Clauses inserted in leases by the landlord's lawyers can end up costing tenants tens of thousands of dollars over the term of the lease. They can also cost many thousands in penalties upon the expiration of the lease. Simple changes to your lease during lease-renewal negotiations can provide the protection you need. Look not only for clauses to delete and change in your lease but also for clauses that are missing and should be added. Down the road, this can even be more important than getting the best rental rates.

5. Leaving money on the table

Many tenants fail to negotiate enough. They leave too much on the table because they simply do not position themselves to get more. Besides getting better rental rates and business protection, it may be possible to get free rent; this is one of the easiest concessions a landlord can give. About 75 percent of renewal tenants can get free rental periods. Be aware of general market conditions, and always ask for more than you think you will get. By being aware of these and other issues and by seeking the advice of an experienced real-estate consultant, your negotiating skills can be more effective in your lease-renewal process. Most renewal tenants can save at least $10,000 in rental costs, free rental periods, and hidden costs of leasing without lifting a finger by hiring a competent real-estate lease consultant. Some lease consultants will *guarantee* their results.

Source: Anthony Dyson (*www.the-real-estate-lease-advisor.com*)—A real-estate lease negotiator for more than twenty years, Dyson has an uncanny knack for negotiating clearly, persuasively, and effectively with landlords without upsetting the apple cart. Contact him at Dyson Realty Corporation, 35 Empress Avenue, Suite 908, Toronto, Ontario (Canada), M2N 6T3; (416) 410-1080; fax: (416) 849-0236.

Key Terms Included in a Commercial Lease

There are many key words you need to know when working with a commercial lease. Don't be surprised—do your homework in advance. Here is some of the basic language that you'll need to know.

1. Escalation clause

This clause spells out how much the rent will escalate with inflation. Ask for documentation on what the percentage has been over the last five years.

2. Renewal option and maintenance

You have the option of renewal under the original base rent under this clause. The lease should spell out what repairs or maintenance items you will be responsible for under the terms of the lease.

3. Insurance

Normally, the lessor will request proof of insurance coverage before the move-in, as well as have adequate liability coverage for injuries. The minimum coverage of the lessor should be included in the lease.

4. Move-in and delivery regulations

If you move into a multiple-occupancy building, it is possible that the management company will have rules regarding hours during which you may actually move in and specific doors and elevators that you must use to do so. Also, there may be restrictions on times and types of deliveries to your office once you have moved in.

5. Storage space

If you require storage space, you should determine if the landlord has such space available and the costs associated with its use. Or will you be allowed to build such an area in the space you lease?

6. Subleasing and restrictions of use

The lease should clarify if a sublease is permissible and the specific terms. The lease should also spell out any restrictions for use within the lease space.

7. Improvements

You may agree to improvements as part of the negotiations; these should be reflected in the lease. The ownership of these improvements must also be addressed in the lease. It should specify what happens to them when the lease terminates.

8. Heating and air conditioning

It is important that the hours of operation for the heating and air conditioning be addressed, and whether they are your responsibility.

9. Renovations and repairs

If there are items that you and the lessor agree should be done to prior to, or even after you move in, these items should be included in the lease.

10. Termination

The terms of your right to end the lease are crucial, as well as in which circumstances the landlord can do the same.

Source: Small Business Administration (*www.sba.gov*).

Advantages of Leasing

The low cost of leasing compared to conventional financing is its most attractive benefit. Companies choose to lease rather than purchase equipment for many reasons. Any of the following advantages could be significant enough for leasing to be the more attractive financing.

1. Off-balance sheet (operating lease) financial reporting

Leasing may result in Off-balance sheet (operating lease) financial reporting, based on underlying assumptions. Leasing may enhance earnings per share and return on assets results, which are important benefits to public corporations.

2. Cost advantage

Leasing may provide a cost advantage over conventional financing by transferring tax incentives (accelerated depreciation) associated with the equipment ownership from the lessor (the owner) to the lessee (the user) in the form of lower lease payments.

3. Minimizes alternative minimum tax (AMT)

Leasing may minimize alternative minimum tax and mid-quarter convention implications. Lease payments are not "preference items" for purposes of determining the AMT.

4. Finances working capital needs

Leasing provides 100 percent financing, conserving cash and preserving lines of credit for working capital purposes.

5. Matches lease payments to revenue

Leasing provides a close matching of the lease term and payments to the revenue produced from employing the equipment.

Source: Ed Perkowski, Northeast regional manager of Chase Equipment Leasing Inc., a subsidiary of JPMorgan Chase Bank, N.A. (*www.chase.com*)—Chase provides a broad array of equipment finance and leasing products and solutions for companies located throughout the United States. Ed Perkowski can be contacted by telephone at (585) 258-6475 or by e-mail at *edward* *.perkowski@chase.com.*

Top Ways to Increase Workplace Security

Opportunistic thieves consider office buildings easy targets. Even a workmate could be a potential thief. Workplace violence is the most important security threat to America's largest corporations, followed closely by crisis management. Workplace security concerns are common in every part of the world, even in Australia where our expert is. Here are ten ways you can increase workplace security, according to the Australian Federal Police.

1. Lock it up or lose it

Thieves usually look for items of value such as laptop computers, mobile phones, and electronic equipment they can easily sell. Staff property, such as wallets and valuables, will also be stolen if not locked up.

2. Make sure you have up-to-date security

Office security needs constant attention. Thieves will always be looking for opportunities. If your building has up-to-date security measures in place and alert staff, it may deter or prevent a theft.

3. Check security procedures for all building entry and exit points

Check for any faults and weaknesses in the security procedures you use. Thieves will take advantage of any opportunities to gain undetected access, such as through faulty fire doors and elevators, unattended loading docks, and unattended reception areas.

4. Encourage staff to approach unknown visitors

Thieves often gain entry to buildings by "tailgating" a legitimate staff member. Security and other relevant staff should question people who are not wearing identification and establish if they have authority for being on the premises. A security process should be in place to deal with this sort of situation.

5. Establish an assets register

Make sure your assets register contains the make, model, and serial numbers of all your office equipment and is kept in a secure area.

6. Nominate a security coordinator

One person in each office should be responsible for security issues. Their role should include conducting a regular security audit of the office, raising security concerns at staff meetings, acting as a liaison with other tenants or offices in the building, making recommendations to improve security, and working with building security.

7. Install security system warning signs

Warning signs at entry points to the building can inform a potential thief of your security systems and deter them from entering the building. (For example, if you use twenty-four-hour video surveillance, put up a sign advertising the fact.)

8. Network with other tenants about security issues

To have a broader understanding of the security issues that affect your office, network with building management and other tenants. This can be mutually advantageous.

9. Report all suspicious or criminal activity to police

If you hear something or see something, say something. All thefts must be reported to police, even if there is no apparent evidence left at the scene and further investigation may not required. Suspicious activity outside or within the building should also be reported to police.

Source: The Australian Federal Police (AFP), Australia's international law enforcement and policing representative, and the chief source of advice to the Australian government on policing issues. More information is at *www.afp.gov.au*.

Things to Consider When Determining the Best City for Your Company

Where to relocate? Will one city encourage your company's growth, and will another stifle it? This question is one of the most important decisions a company will face. There are many factors to consider. These tips should help you make the best strategic decision on where to locate your company.

1. Convenience

Is your company located near a major airport? Does your business require international travel? If your business requires travel, it's important to be located near a major airport to minimize time spent traveling. Additionally, it's important to think about the location of your suppliers and vendors. Not everything can be planned for and emergency deliveries are sometimes necessary.

2. Customers

Where are your customers located? Sales are often driven by face-to-face meetings and traveling to see a customer within your city is much easier than traveling to meet a customer out-of-state. Additionally, it's important to consider in which time zone your customers are primarily located. If you are on the East Cost and your customers are primarily on the West Coast, it's going to be difficult to find a good time to communicate with them throughout the day.

3. Taxes

Some states and cities are much friendlier to new businesses than others. Research the tax laws of each city and state. Some cities even offer incentives for new businesses to move there to encourage growth within their city.

4. Work force

The labor pool in cities is greater than in rural areas and you will have an easier time finding qualified employees to work for you. But it's also important to consider the cost of living in a particular city. If you are located in an expensive city, you will have to pay your employees more to compensate for the higher cost of living. A lot of large companies are currently moving operations to cities like Boise, Idaho, or Salt Lake City, Utah, where they can take advantage of a much lower cost of living. This is a popular new trend termed *farmsourcing* or *onshoring*.

5. Expenses

Once you've narrowed your list to three to five potential locations, ask a realtor for the average cost per square foot. This will help you to determine the bottom-line expense of renting a space in a particular city.

6. Competition

Contrary to common sense, competition is a good thing. Locating your company in an area that is known for a particular kind of business can dramatically improve visibility and growth. For example, moving your technology company to Silicon Valley and getting to know your competitors can lead to innovation at your company, keeping you one step ahead of the game.

7. Growth

Where do you see your company in five to ten years? It's important to evaluate all of these criteria, not only for today, but for the future as well. A move can be expensive, and it is best to plan to minimize that kind of disruption on your operations.

Sources: Rachel Walls, president of The Golden Gate Company, LLC (*www.goldengatecompany.com*)—She plans and organizes relocations for companies, along with helping them to sell any surplus equipment and furniture. She can be contacted at (415) 902-8517.

Common Tenant Responsibilities

Landlord-tenant laws are generally dictated by individual states. For example, under Washington State's Landlord-Tenant Act, the tenant has specific responsibilities which are listed here. Of course, you should check with your own state's laws just to make sure.

1. Rent

Pay rent, and any utilities agreed on.

2. Local requirements

Comply with any requirements of city, county, or state regulations.

3. Cleanliness

Keep the rental unit clean and sanitary.

4. Trash

Dispose of garbage properly.

5. Infestations

Pay for fumigation of infestations caused by the tenant.

6. Systems

Properly operate plumbing, electrical, and heating systems.

7. Damages

Do not intentionally or carelessly damage the dwelling.

8. Waste and nuisance

Do not permit "waste" (substantial damage to the property) or "nuisance" (substantial interference with other tenants' use of their property).

9. Moving out

When moving out, restore the dwelling to the same condition as it was when the tenant moved in, except for normal wear and tear.

Source: Office of the Attorney General, state of Washington, 1996 Landlord-Tenant Law (*http://access.wa.gov*)

Considerations for Choosing a Real Estate Broker

Buying and selling real estate is often the biggest expenditure of a person's life. Consequently, selecting the person who is going to help you with that transaction should be considered carefully. Not all real estate brokers are alike. Buyers and sellers who don't do their homework can wind up with incorrect advice that could cost them a lot of money. Look for brokers by asking friends, relatives and financial advisors for referrals. Then interview them looking for these characteristics.

1. Knowledge of real estate, particularly in the location of interest and in the transaction type

There are a wide variety of real estate transactions and a wide breadth of knowledge needed for each type of transaction. Real estate brokers need to know the law, financial possibilities and institutions, the local and national markets, and good marketing techniques.

2. Experience

Brokers with a track record of successful transactions and loyal clientele are good candidates for managing your transaction successfully.

3. Organization

Real estate transactions are complex. Unforeseen circumstances are almost standard in the industry. Many transactions fail because a deadline was missed or critical information was not communicated.

4. Communication skills

A good broker will keep you informed about what is happening with your transaction on a regular basis. They should also be communicating with other parties to the transaction.

5. Time for you

Don't pick the busiest broker because they are well known. Make certain they have time to meet your needs. A less high profile broker, who services fewer clients, may give you a much higher quality of service because of the time they can devote to your transaction.

6. Honesty, Integrity, Ethics

You need to feel comfortable that private information that you share about financial matters will not be shared with other parties inappropriately. Likewise, the broker should be straightforward and honest with you about what is happening in the transaction. You should be able to trust them to represent your interests appropriately. Brokers that belong to the National Association of Realtors take a pledge to a Code of Ethics.

7. Specialization

Many brokers choose areas of specialization, either in the type of real estate they do or in the area serviced. Some work only with buyers, some only with sellers. Some prefer commercial ventures. A broker who specialized in the type of transaction you wish to pursue may bring an additional expertise that will add value to the quality of the transaction.

Source: Judith A. Kautz, Ph.D., MBA, owner of Small Business Notes (www.smallbusinessnotes.com). Judith Kautz has worked in both the public and private sectors of business for over 30 years. In private industry she has been employed as a systems analyst and manager in computer consulting businesses, in addition to providing private consulting services in computer applications, statistics, and management. Judith also practices real estate in the State of Hawaii. She can be contacted at *editor@smallbusinessnotes.com*.

Typical Responsibilities of an Office Manager

Our expert is an office manager for a local church, and when we asked her what her responsibilities were, she named everything but the kitchen sink! That's because, as office manager, she's responsible for … just about everything. If you're looking for an office manager as good as Rhonda, you should understand the duties that are typically performed by one. Here they are.

1. Does accounting for the books and records and payroll; pay bills

Makes sure that all the bills are paid, as well as the payroll.

2. Manages the database, office budgets, and yearly calendars

Makes sure that the calendar for the year is planned, and each department has its allocated budget.

3. Oversee the support staff

Keeps track of staffs' days off, vacation time, and work.

4. Maintains files on everything related to the office

Keeps and maintains files on everything in the office, such as employees, bills, payroll.

5. Schedules use of conference rooms and handles phone calls

Makes sure there is no conflict in schedules for a conference room and handles phone calls regarding the business.

6. Makes sure equipment is up-to-date

Make sure the computers, Internet, and telephones are running and up-to-date.

7. Handles all contracts

Works with all contracts, which include personnel, equipment, and leases.

8. Meets/speaks to all sales representatives

Meets with all sales representatives from other companies.

9. Maintains office supplies and keeps everything labeled and organized

Makes sure there are plenty of supplies in the office (stationery, pens, pads of paper, stamps, etc.) and also keeps everything labeled and organized so there is no confusion.

10. Makes recommendations to the manager and keeps the Web page current

Gives input to the manager and also keeps the Web page up-to-date.

Source: Rhonda Milauskas, office manager, St. Francis of Assisi (*www.instrumentofpeace.com*), 8300 Old Columbia Road, Fulton, MD 20759; (410) 792-0470.

Best Ways to Lower Your Energy Costs

Because the energy costs and needs of any small business are going to be vastly different, there are no hard-and-fast rules for keeping these expenses down. But here are a few areas you can explore.

1. Make sure equipment is running efficiently

Whether you have a bakery with gas stoves or a manufacturing plant with massive, energy-hungry machines, make sure that all equipment is running correctly. Even a small malfunction could cost you in wasted energy bills. Stick to the recommended maintenance schedule for all machinery.

2. Choose wisely

When it comes to servicing your energy needs, you probably have more choices than you realize. Compare the prices of natural gas versus electric heating and cooling. If you use a generator as your main power source or backup, compare the costs of propane, diesel, and other alternatives. Do your homework or assign an employee the task—you could be pleasantly surprised with the results. Also, find out if your local utility company has any "green power" incentives for making the switch to more eco-friendly energy sources.

3. Investigate alternative energy sources

Although it might not be feasible to convert your whole office to solar energy, you might be able to keep heating costs down in the winter by simply installing more windows and leaving the blinds up. Carpeting also does wonders to keep heat inside.

4. Buy fuel-efficient vehicles and keep them properly maintained

If your business uses a fleet of company vehicles, make sure to buy fuel-efficient models. Read up on consumer reports. Test-drive a hybrid and see what you think. Keeping cars well maintained—checking and changing air filters, keeping tires properly inflated and so on—will also help you get the most mileage for your gas costs. Nationwide companies, such as Flexcar, also offer options to lease cars for as many hours a week as you need them. The price of gas and insurance is included.

5. Be vigilant

If your employees have access to company vehicles, make sure that you keep an eye on mileage. If they're using the vehicles for out-of-the-way personal errands, ask them to make up the difference in gas costs. If you reimburse employees for gas costs in their own vehicles, look over their logs and make sure the mileage estimates are reasonable.

Even though the high cost of energy won't be going away any time soon, you don't have to feel helpless in the face of this problem. A little watchfulness can go a long way in finding the most cost-effective solutions for your energy needs.

Source: Maggie Flynn. This article originally appeared on NFIB .com. The National Federation of Independent Business (NFIB) (*www .nifb.com*) is the largest advocacy organization representing small and independent businesses in Washington, D.C. NFIB's purpose is to impact public policy at the state and federal level and be a key business resource for small and independent businesses in America. Telephone: (800) NFIB-NOW or (615) 872-5800.

Typical Illegal Actions by a Landlord

Landlord-tenant laws are generally dictated by individual states. For example, under Washington State's Landlord-Tenant Act, there are specific actions that, if taken by a landlord, are illegal. These are listed here. Of course, you should check with your own state's laws just to make sure.

1. Lockouts

The law prohibits landlords from changing locks, adding new locks, or otherwise making it impossible for the tenant to use the normal locks and keys. Even if a tenant is behind in rent, such lockouts are illegal. A tenant who is locked out can file a lawsuit to regain entry. Some local governments also have laws against lockouts and can help a tenant who has been locked out of a rental. For more information, contact your city or county government.

2. Utility shutoffs

The landlord may not shut off utilities because the tenant is behind in rent or to force a tenant to move out. Utilities may only be shut off by the landlord to effect repairs and only for a reasonable amount of time. If a landlord intentionally does not pay utility bills so the service will be turned off, that could be considered an illegal shutoff.

If the utilities have been shut off by the landlord, first check with the utility company to see if it will restore service. If it appears the shutoff is illegal, you can file a lawsuit. If you win in court, the judge can award you up to $100 per day for the time without service, as well as attorney's fees.

3. Taking the tenant's property

The law allows a landlord to take a tenant's property only in the case of abandonment. A clause in a rental agreement that allows the landlord to take a tenant's property in other situations is not valid. If the landlord does take your property illegally, contact the landlord first. If that is unsuccessful, notify the police . If the property is not returned after the landlord is given a written request, a court could order the landlord to pay you up to $100 for each day the property is kept (to a total of $1,000).

4. Renting condemned property

The landlord may not rent units that are condemned or unlawful to occupy due to existing uncorrected code violations. The landlord can be liable for three months' rent or treble damages, whichever is greater, as well as costs and attorney's fees for knowingly renting the property.

5. Retaliatory actions

If a tenant exercises rights under the law, such as complaining to a government authority or deducting for repairs, the law prohibits the landlord from taking retaliatory action. Examples of retaliatory actions are raising the rent, reducing services provided to the tenant, or evicting the tenant. The law initially assumes that these steps are retaliatory if they occur within ninety days of the tenant's action, unless the tenant was in some way violating the statute when notice of the change was received. If the matter is taken to court and the judge finds in favor of the tenant, the landlord can be ordered to reverse the retaliatory action, as well as pay for any harm done to the tenant and pay the tenant's attorney's fees.

Source: Office of the Attorney General, state of Washington, 1996 Landlord-Tenant Law (*http://access.wa.gov*).

Signs that a Landlord May Make Concessions

When it's time to negotiate your office lease, it's always a help to get reduced rent or contributions from the landlord. Sometimes, circumstances are right for you to take the upper hand. Here are a few of the indicators you should consider.

1. Signs appear
This is a clear indication of oversupply.

2. Signs stay there
When you can't unload the property, the renter has a negotiating advantage.

3. Waving the flag
Pennants and flags are pulled out of storage and are used to advertise space.

4. Inducements offered
Small inducements begin to be offered for leasing space.

5. Weakness in the market
Physical vacancy rates increase.

6. The value of the property isn't enough
Guarantees are used to justify income, expenses, and capitalization rates for properties being sold.

7. Costs to replace
Replacement costs become a reason to buy.

8. Cash flow isn't everything
Gross rent multipliers are used when cash flow doesn't work.

9. Buzz words pop up
Words such as *discount, below, turnaround, opportunity, unusual,* and *once in-a-lifetime* punctuate investment brochures.

10. Certain ads decline; others increase
Ads for personnel for real-estate companies begin to decline in the classified sections of newspapers. Ads for rental space increase in the classified sections of newspapers. Ads for property sales decline in the classified sections of newspapers.

Source: Cymrot Realty Advisors Inc. (*www.cymrot.com*)—Offers strategic advice (strategy) in regard to real-estate companies, real estate–related companies, real-estate properties, and real-estate litigation. Contact them at 800 El Camino Real West, Suite 180, Mountain View, CA 94040; (650) 964-7100; e-mail: *cymrealadv@batnet.com.*

Common Landlord Responsibilities

Landlord-tenant laws are generally dictated by individual states. For example, under Washington State's Landlord-Tenant Act, the landlord has specific responsibilities, which are listed here. Although these responsibilities are generally consistent throughout the country, you should still check with your own state's laws just to make sure.

1. Health and safety
Maintain the dwelling so it does not violate state and local codes in ways that endanger tenants' health and safety.

2. Structural components
Maintain structural components—such as roofs, floors, and chimneys—in reasonably good repair.

3. Weather

Maintain the dwelling in reasonably weather-tight condition.

4. Security

Provide reasonably adequate locks and keys.

5. Utilities

Provide the necessary facilities to supply heat, electricity, and hot and cold water.

6. Trash

Provide garbage cans and arrange for removal of garbage, except in single-family dwellings.

7. Common areas

Keep common areas—such as lobbies, stairways and halls—reasonably clean and free from hazards.

8. Pests

Control pests before the tenant moves in. The landlord must continue to control infestations except in single-family dwellings, or when the infestation was caused by the tenant.

9. Repairs

Make repairs to keep the unit in the same condition as when the tenant moved in, except for normal wear and tear.

10. Systems

Keep electrical, plumbing, and heating systems in good repair, and maintain any appliances provided with the rental.

11. Contact information

Inform the tenant of the name and address of the landlord or landlord's agent.

12. Water heaters

Set water heaters at 120 degrees when a new tenant moves in.

13. Smoke detectors

Provide smoke detectors, and ensure they work properly when a new tenant moves in. (Tenants are responsible for maintaining detectors.)

Source: Office of the Attorney General, state of Washington, 1996 Landlord-Tenant Law (*http://access.wa.gov*).

Key OSHA Requirements for Your Business

Through its rulings, OSHA has developed a set of requirements that define its expectations of a comprehensive, confined space protection program, including the proper use of confined space entry and retrieval equipment. OSHA standards may require that employers adopt certain practices, means, methods, or processes reasonably necessary to protect workers on the job. It is the responsibility of employers to become familiar with standards applicable to their establishments, to eliminate hazardous conditions to the extent possible, and to comply with the standards designed to provide workers with in-depth protection. Here are the requirements.

1. Access to medical and exposure records

This standard requires that employers grant employees access to any of their medical records maintained by the employer and to any records the employer maintains on the employees' exposure to toxic substances.

2. Personal protective equipment

This standard, included separately in the standards for each industry segment (except agriculture), requires that employers provide employees, at no cost to employees, with personal protective equipment designed to protect them against certain hazards. This can range from protective helmets to prevent head injuries in construction and cargo-handling work, to eye protection, hearing protection, hard-toed shoes, special goggles (for welders, for example), and gauntlets for iron workers.

3. Hazard communication

This standard requires that manufacturers and importers of hazardous materials conduct a hazard evaluation of the products they manufacture or import. If the product is found to be hazardous under the terms of the standard, containers of the material must be appropriately labeled and the first shipment of the material to a new customer must be accompanied by a material safety data sheet (MSDS). Employers, using the MSDSs they receive, must train their employees to recognize and avoid the hazards the materials present.

4. Hazard-free workplace

In general, all employers (except those in the construction industry) should be aware that any hazard not covered by an industry-specific standard may be covered by a general industry standard; in addition, all employers must keep their workplaces free of recognized hazards that may cause death or serious physical harm to employees, even if OSHA does not have a specific standard or requirement addressing the hazard. This coverage becomes important in the enforcement aspects of OSHA's work.

5. Recordkeeping

Every employer covered by OSHA who has more than ten employees (except for certain low-hazard industries such as retail, finance, insurance, real estate, and some service industries) must maintain OSHA-specified records of job-related injuries and illnesses. There are two such records: the OSHA Form 200 and the OSHA Form 101.

6. Reporting

In addition to the reporting requirements described here, each employer, regardless of the number of employees or industry category, must report to the nearest OSHA office within eight hours of any accident that results in one or more fatalities or hospitalization of three or more employees. Such accidents are often investigated by OSHA to determine what caused the accident and whether violations of standards contributed to the event.

7. Employees

Employees must be provided with jobs and a place of employment free from recognized hazards that are causing, or are likely to cause, death or serious physical harm. Employers cannot discriminate against employees who exercise their rights under the OSHA Act. Also employers must provide well-maintained tools and equipment, including appropriate personal protective equipment to all employees. Employers must also provide medical examinations and training required by OSHA standards, and post prominently the

OSHA poster (OSHA 3165) informing employees of their rights and responsibilities.

8. Accidents and injuries

Employers must report to OSHA within eight hours accidents that result in fatalities. They must report to OSHA within eight hours accidents that result in the hospitalization of three or more employees. Records of work-related accidents, injuries, illnesses and their causes must be kept and annual summaries for the required period must be posted. A number of specific industries in the retail, service, finance, insurance, and real-estate sectors that are classified as low-hazard are exempt from most requirements of the regulation, as are small businesses with ten or fewer employees.

9. Notices

OSHA citations and abatement verification notices must be posted at or near the worksite. Cited violations must be abated within the prescribed period. Employers must respond to survey requests for data from the Bureau of Labor Statistics, OSHA, or a designee of either agency.

Source: Environmental Health & Safety Online (*www.ehso.com*)— This group is for EHS professionals and the general public. They find credible public domain sources of research, such as public research institutions and government scientific Web sites; gather the key information from them; organize it, often rewrite it, and publish it. EHSO is one place to easily find the best source of environmental, health, and safety guidance. Contact them at EHSO, Inc., 8400-O Roswell Rd., Atlanta, GA 30350; (770) 263-8700.

Common Building Violations

When purchasing a new property (whether it is an investment property or a new home or even a business) some people take certain things for granted and assume that the building is properly built and shouldn't have any problems or issues associated with it. Here our expert provides us with some of the most common violations. But always remember to contact your Local Township or Borough Office if you have any questions or concerns.

1. Emergency egress windows are too small

The most common Code Violation that home inspectors miss is that at least one window in each bedroom must be of sufficient size to permit the occupants to escape a fire and also allow a fully outfitted firefighter to enter.

2. Construction defects

Some defects are design related—the architect/engineer designed the building that does not work as it was intended. Other are material deficient—use of inferior building materials causing problems such as leaky windows, asphalt roofing, drywall or other problems. There are sometimes construction deficiencies caused by substandard workmanship and building code violations resulting from the failure of the builder to comply with proper codes.

3. Operation of a business in a residential zone

Usually certain types of home businesses are permitted and may require a special license with specific guidelines and restrictions. You should always check with your township or borough and see what your area will allow.

4. Building without a permit

If you are doing any remodeling or construction work whether it is interior or exterior work, you should check with your Township or Borough as to whether or not a Building permit is required. Failure to do so may result in a fine or worse.

Source: Body-Borneman *(www.bodyborneman.com)*. With a loyal client base of over 15,000 customers, many of whom have been with them for almost 40 years, Body-Borneman has grown to become one of the largest insurance agencies in Southeastern Pennsylvania. The agency markets a complete line of property, casualty, life and group products. This is accomplished through a staff of 45 loyal employees, of which 33 are licensed agents. Contact Sean Deviney at 610-367-1100.

Things You Should Do Before Constructing an Office

Ready to start working from home? Well, you've got to have just the right work environment. Here are a few tips for constructing a safe and professional environment for working out of your house.

1. Itemize tasks

Itemize all the tasks you need to do to run your business.

2. Draw up a workflow

Draw up a workflow for the most efficient way to accomplish those tasks.

3. Identify space

Identify space within your home that would accommodate your business.

4. Analyze equipment needs

Look at the equipment and furniture needs of your business.

5. Check electrical and telephone outlets

Check to make certain you have adequate electrical and telephone outlets for your equipment.

6. Lay out equipment and furniture

Lay out how your equipment and furniture will fit in the space, considering efficient workflow.

7. Think about the lighting

Make certain the lighting is sufficient for your work needs.

8. Plan for keeping records

Plan storage of records and supplies into the office arrangement.

9. Choose comfortable furniture and equipment

The ergonomics of your work environment is critical. Choose furniture and equipment that are comfortable to avoid work fatigue and injury.

10. Add comfort features

Take the time to add some comfort features. This should be a pleasant environment.

11. Plan flexibility into the space

If at all possible, plan flexibility into the space with movable equipment and desks and adjustable shelving.

12. Move noisy equipment away

Place noisy equipment away from work areas that need quiet, if at all possible.

Source: Small Business Notes (*www.smallbusinessnotes.com*) provides information and resources for other businesses struggling to provide that same quality in a challenging economic environment. Their purpose is to provide the resources for all the information that a small business person needs to operate their business. Contact the editor of Small Business Notes, Judith Kautz by sending e-mail to *info@smallbusinessnotes.com*.

Questions to Ask Your Architect

Each architect has an individual style, approach to design, and a method of work. So, it's important to find an architect who is compatible with your style and needs. Here are some questions to determine if your architect is right for you.

1. What does the architect see as important issues or considerations in your project? What are the challenges of the project?

2. How will the architect approach your project?

3. How will the architect gather information about your needs, goals, and so on?

4. How will the architect establish priorities and make decisions?

5. Who from the architecture firm will you be dealing with directly? Is that the same person who will be designing the project? Who will be designing your project?

6. How interested is the architect in this project?

7. How busy is the architect?

8. What sets this architect apart from the rest?

9. How does the architect establish fees?

10. What would the architect expect the fee to be for this project?

11. What are the steps in the design process?

12. How does the architect organize the process?

13. What does the architect expect you to provide?

14. What is the architect's design philosophy?

15. What is the architect's experience/track record with cost estimating?

16. What will the architect show you along the way to explain the project? Will you see models, drawings, or computer animations?

17. If the scope of the project changes later in the project, will there be additional fees? How will these fees be justified?

18. What services does the architect provide during construction?

19. How disruptive will construction be? How long does the architect expect it to take to complete your project?

20. Does the architect have a list of past clients that you can contact?

Source: The American Institute of Architects (*www.aia.org*)— Since 1857, the AIA has represented the professional interests of America's architects. As AIA members, more than 70,000 licensed architects and allied professionals express their commitment to excellence in design and livability in our nation's buildings and cities. Members adhere to a code of ethics and professional conduct that assures the client, the public, and colleagues of an AIA-member architect's dedication to the highest standards of professional practice.

Questions to Ask a Sign Company

Like them or not, signs are a vital part of an enterprise. Business identification is a sales and marketing necessity. Plenty of thought goes into the creation and design of signs that not only sell products but are also pleasing to the eye. Our expert, a very popular sign-manufacturing company, suggests you ask these questions.

1. What type and thickness of material will be used on my sign, and may I see a sample piece?

2. If the panel is to be painted, what brand of paint do you use?

3. For painted wooden sign panels, do you gently round all the edges to ensure proper paint adhesion?

4. In addition to the primer coat, how many coats of paint will my panel have?

5. Regarding the graphics, will you use 2 mil high-performance vinyl?

6. Do you recommend my sign be overlaminated with UV or antivandal guard film?

7. If the sign will be installed on a wall, posts, or suspended, will you predrill mounting holes in the panel, so the insides of the holes will receive paint as well?

8. Do you offer sign installation? If not, do you furnish the correct mounting brackets, hardware, and fasteners, and if applicable, a mounting pattern?

9. If you install the sign, will you obtain the proper sign permits if required?

10. If you install signs, are you a C-45 licensed, bonded, and insured sign contractor?

11. If I order my sign today, when will it be ready for pickup or delivery?

12. What is the expected lifespan of this particular sign?

13. Do you offer a guarantee or warranty?

Source: A Graphic Edge Inc.(*www.graphicedge.com*)— A California-based popular sign company specializing in "Gerber Edge Graphics" and "Dimensional" Signs. Contact them at 323 West Grand Ave., Escondido, CA 92025; (760) 735-8494; e-mail: *signs@graphicedge.com*.

High Finance

Borrowing to Grow

The Five Cs of Credit

A bank is not a charitable institution. It is in business to make (not lose) money. Consequently, when a bank lends money. it wants to ensure that it will be paid back. To maximize the possibility of being paid back, the bank wants to make sure that there is sufficient assurance that a person can pay back a loan and that he or she has met such obligations before. According to the Small Business Administration, here are the five Cs that banks use to evaluate potential loans.

1. Capacity

Capacity to repay is the most critical of the five factors. The prospective lender will want to know exactly how you intend to repay the loan. The lender will consider the cash flow from the business, the timing of the repayment, and the probability of successful repayment of the loan. Payment history on existing credit relationships—personal and commercial—is considered an indicator of future payment performance. Prospective lenders also will want to know about your contingent sources of repayment.

2. Capital

Capital is the money you personally have invested in the business and is an indication of how much you have at risk should the business fail. Prospective lenders and investors will expect you to have contributed from your own assets and to have undertaken personal financial risk to establish the business before asking them to commit any funding. If you have a significant personal investment in the business, you are more likely to do everything in your power to make the business successful.

3. Collateral

Collateral or "guarantees" are additional forms of security you can provide the lender. If for some reason, the business cannot repay its bank loan, the bank wants to know there is a second source of repayment. Assets such as equipment, buildings, accounts-receivable, and in some cases, inventory are considered possible sources of repayment if they are sold by the bank for cash, Both business and personal assets can be sources of collateral for a loan. A guarantee, on the other hand, is just that: Someone else signs a guarantee document promising to repay the loan if you can't. Some lenders may require such a guarantee in addition to collateral as security for a loan.

4. Conditions

Conditions focus on the intended purpose of the loan. Will the money be used for working capital, additional equipment, or inventory? The lender will also consider the local economic climate and conditions both within your industry and in other industries that could affect your business.

5. Character

Character is the general impression you make on the potential lender or investor. The lender will form a subjective opinion about whether you are sufficiently trustworthy to repay the loan or generate a return on funds invested in your company. The lender will review your educational background and experience in business and in your industry. The quality of your references and the background and experience of your employees will also be taken into consideration.

Source: Small Business Administration (*www.sba.gov*).

Questions to Ask Before Searching for Financing

In this book, we look at lots of different types of financing. But don't just rush into the market. You first need to ask yourself some important questions, so you don't waste time and effort. Since one of the keys to raising capital is managing your cash effectively, our expert provides us with a few key questions you should ask before you search for financing.

1. What exactly is a cash-flow budget?

One of the three components of your business financial statements (along with the balance sheet and income statement), your cash-flow budget is an estimate or projection of your business' cash inflows—that is, money expected to come in, such as cash from sales or the collection of accounts receivable—and the time period when you expect to receive it. It's also a projection of your cash outflows—all the money you'll need to pay to suppliers, accountants, utility companies, and so on (i.e., your accounts payable). Your cash-flow budget is critical to the success of your business because you could have great profits on paper but still experience a cash-flow shortfall. If you just concentrate on profits, such a cash-flow shortfall could crop up and cripple your business. Keep in mind that if you plan to apply for a loan in the next year or so, your cash-flow and other financial records should reflect a positive picture on how well you manage your cash and the financial aspects of your business.

2. How much money will I need?

If you are a retailer, for example, you may get a loan for 50 to 75 percent of the value of your inventory (your collateral). Keep in mind that most lenders will discount the value of collateral so they don't risk 100 percent of its top market value.

3. When will I need the money to cover my needs based on my projections?

For example, perhaps you plan to buy new equipment in about eight months.

4. Will I need additional money—and, if so, when?

Maybe you anticipate you'll need more money for new business growth in about ten months. But understand that the more you grow your business—that is, the more sales you generate—the less cash flow you will actually have to work with.

5. How long will I need the money?

Some businesses need a short-term bank loan to carry them through slow periods, such as over the summer months when sales slow down.

6. How will I be able to repay the loan?

This, of course, is of primary interest to your lender. According to the Small Business Administration, if you need working capital, the lender may want to know how the loan can be reduced during your business period of greatest liquidity covering the business cycle, or over a one-year period. Conversely, if you are looking for growth capital, the lender may want to know how the loan will be used to make your business more profitable and generate extra cash, which can be used to repay the loan in several years.

7. What if you spot a potential cash crunch?

If your cash-flow projections flag a potential cash crunch, you can start correcting the situation before you meet with the lender.

Source: Richard Siedlecki is a self-employed management consultant who focuses on business and marketing plans, new business start-ups, and direct marketing via direct mail, catalogs, and the Web. Reach him at (404) 303-9900 or sied@mindspring.com.

Popular Forms of Financing

Show me the money! Most businesses need financing to get them off the ground and help fund expansion. Our expert advises and supports small and medium-size businesses in the Richmond, Virginia area, so we thought they could give us a few avenues to raise some cash.

1. Debt financing

Debt financing does not give the lender ownership control, but the principal must be repaid with interest. Length of the loan, interest rates, security and other terms depend on what the loan is being used for.

2. Commercial bank loans

This includes short-term loans that are for short periods (30–180 days), usually made to cover temporary or seasonal needs for inventory or personnel. These are common for established businesses, but may be hard for a new business to obtain. This also includes medium to long term loans which may be repaid over anywhere from one to five to even 20 years depending on how the funds are used. The source of repayment is the cash flow of the business. Typical uses are for equipment, fixed assets, etc. Most loans to start a small business will be of this type. Another type of loan includes real estate financing: Real estate is typically financed over a fairly long term, 10 to 30 years. Expect a down payment of about 20%. And finally, accounts receivable financing are monies loaned against accounts receivable pledged as collateral.

3. Equity financing

Equity is money put into a business by the owner, private investors, and/or venture capitalists. Equity gives an investor ownership and possibly some control of the business. Money invested could be from your own savings: It is nearly impossible to start a business without using some of your personal funds. It is hard to convince someone to take a risk in your idea if you do not. Friends, relatives, business associates, etc. are a good source of equity financing. Most small businesses get started with this kind of help. They may provide some of the cash or may back a loan from a financial institution. Another group of financing are the venture capitalists who invest in a new firm (usually high-tech or innovative concepts) looking for a very high return on investment. Minimum investments are from several hundred thousand dollars to millions of dollars.

4. Internal financing

Customers can be a source of temporary financing if they provide the raw materials or if they pay a cash deposit. This is not feasible in most businesses.

Trade credit in the form of ordering, receiving and selling the goods before the bill is due. Once you have obtained a good reputation with your suppliers you may be able to have credit for anywhere from 30 to 90 days. Profit earned by the entity that is reinvested and used to expand your business is a very healthy source of financing.

5. Leasing

Leasing is simply another form of financing. Leasing reduces the cash needed up front, but like a loan you are obligated to the payment for a certain period of time. Some lease contracts give you ownership of the leased item at the end of the term for a specified amount.

6. Basic 7 (a) loan guaranty

This is the commonest mode of Federal government financing for loans up to $2 million. This is the SBA's most flexible business loan program. The 7 (a) serves as the SBA's primary business loan program to help qualified small businesses obtain financing. Loan proceeds can be used for most business purposes including working capital, machinery, equipment, furniture and fixtures. The typical borrower for this kind of loan is an existing business.

7. Microloan 7(m) loan program

This program provides short term loans for up to $35,000.00 to small businesses and not-for-profit child care centers for working capital or the purchase of inventory, supplies, furniture, fixtures, equipment or machinery. Small businesses must apply directly with the SBA's local intermediary lenders.

8. Community Express

Available to persons who meet the normal requirements, but must also: Be located in a "low or moderate income" urban or rural area, or have a current or proposed business owned (51% or Greater) by a minority, women, or veteran. This loan program makes it easier and faster for selected lenders to provide small business loans for $250,000.00 or less.

9. 504 Loan program

Provides long term fixed rate financing to small business to acquire real estate, machinery or equipment for expansion or modernization. The typical client is a business that requires brick and mortar financing to grow their business or for economic growth of a region and/or community project. This program provides long term loans for up to $1.5 million for a single project and $4 million for manufacturers with a minimum loan amount of $50,000.

Source: The Greater Richmond SBDC, a partnership program between the U.S. Small Business Administration and the Greater Richmond Chamber of Commerce, provides assistance and training to help small business owners and potential owners make sound decisions for the successful operation of their businesses. As part of the statewide Virginia SBDC network the GRSBDC serves a population of approximately one million people in Central Virginia, primarily in the City of Richmond and the counties of Chesterfield, Goochland Hanover, and Henrico,. The GRSBDC offers confidential, individual counseling as well as workshops, conferences and courses at various locations in its service area. Contact Address: 600 East Main Street, P.O. Box 1598, Richmond, VA 23218-1598 Tel: 804.783.9314 Fax: 804.783.9366

Best Banks for Small Businesses

Small business credit markets remain competitive for most small firms and profitable for small business lenders. Our expert, who represents the community of small businesses in this country, devotes a significant amount of time to reviewing banks, large and small, and how well they work with small companies. Here is a list of their top banks.

1. American Express Centurion
4315 S. 2700 West
Salt Lake City, UT 84184
(801) 945-3000

2. BB&T Corporation
200 West 2nd St.
16th Floor
Winston–Salem, NC 27101
(336) 733-2724

3. Regions Financial Corporation
417 North 20th St.
Birmingham, AL 35203

(205) 944-1300
Fax: (334) 832-8419

4. Synovus Financial Corp.
1111 Bay Ave.
Suite 500, P.O. Box 120
Columbus, GA 31902
(706) 649-2401
Fax: (706) 641-6555

5. First Citizens Bancshares
116 E. Main St.
Mount Olive, NC 28365
(919) 658-7000

6. Citigroup Inc.
399 Park Ave.
New York, NY 10043
(800) 285-3000

7. Sky Financial Group Inc.
614 E. Lincoln Way
Minerva, OH 44657
(330) 868-7701
Fax: (330) 868-3460

8. Union Planters Corporation
4928 William Arnold Rd.
Memphis, TN 38117-4238
(901) 485-3387
Fax: (901) 682-9491

9. Wells Fargo & Company
420 Montgomery St.
San Francisco, CA 94104
(800) 869-3557

10. Fifth Third Bancorp
Fifth Third Center
38 Fountain Square Plaza
Cincinnati, OH 45263
(513) 579-5300

Source: Small Business Administration (*www.sba.gov*).

Largest Credit Unions

Credit unions serve their members in a variety of ways. Some credit unions excel at providing their members with their dream home; some put more of their members behind the wheel of their favorite car at affordable rates. Other credit unions focus on performance ratios such as loans-to-shares or ROA. Our expert, a nationally recognized credit union consulting firm, has put together this list for us, ranked by total assets.

1. Navy Credit Union
PO Box 3000
Merrifield, VA 22119-3000
(800) 914-9494

2. State Employees Credit Union
PO Box 27665
Raleigh, NC 27611
(888) 732-8562 or (919) 857-2150

3. Pentagon Federal Credit Union
PO Box 1432
Alexandria, VA 22313-2034
(800) 247-5626

4. The Golden 1 Credit Union
PO Box 15966
Sacramento, CA 95852-1966
(916) 732-2900; (877) GOLDEN 1

5. Orange County Teachers Federal Credit Union
PO Box 11547
Santa Ana, CA 92711
(714) 258-4000; (800) 4OCTFCU;
(800) 462-8328

6. BECU Credit Union
PO Box 97050
Seattle, WA 98124
(800) 233-2328

7. Suncoast Schools Federal Credit Union
PO Box 11904
Tampa, FL 33680
(800) 999-5887

8. Alliant Credit Union
11545 W. Touhy Ave.
Chicago, IL 60666
(773) 462-2000; (800) 328-1935

9. American Airlines Federal Credit Union
PO Box 619001
MD 2100, HDQ
DFW Airport, TX 75261
(800) 533-0035

10. Security Service Federal Credit Union
PO Box 691510
San Antonio, TX 78269
(866) 361-1902

Source: Callahan & Associates, Inc. (*www.creditunions.com*)—This a national credit union research and consulting firm. They believe in the credit union movement and have been at the leading edge of credit union issues for more than twenty years. Their goal is to provide credit union professionals and interested parties with the tools and insights to continually highlight the impact of credit unions on members and the financial services marketplace.

Typical Reasons Loans Are Denied

Rejections don't stop at the high school prom! As a business owner or manager, you may be unfortunate enough to experience the denial of a loan application. Why? Here are typical reasons given by the industry trade group for mortgage bankers.

1. Appraised value too low

One of the factors considered by the lender is the ratio of the loan amount to the sale price or the appraised value of the property, whichever is lower. If the appraisal on the property is substantially lower than the purchase price, the loan-to-value ratio (or LTV) may be higher than the lender will, or can legally, approve. If the purchase price is simply higher than the prevailing prices being paid in the general area, you can try to renegotiate the price with the seller down to a level more in line with the market and one that the lender would accept in order to approve your loan. If this is not possible, your only other solution is probably accepting a lower loan amount, assuming you have sufficient funds to cover the additional down payment.

2. Inadequate funds

Based on the financial information and the verification of deposit, the lender may have determined that you do not have enough cash to make a down payment and cover closing costs. Usually, these funds may not come from borrowing, but a gift from a relative can be used as long as no repayment of the money is expected. Other solutions include getting the seller to take back a second mortgage, which would reduce the down payment requirement (assuming you can still qualify with the additional loan payments), or getting the seller to pay some of the closing costs, such as the origination fees. Finally, you could correct this problem by simply waiting, providing you institute a savings program in the meanwhile.

3. Insufficient income

In assessing your ability to repay the requested loan, lenders look at the amount of your monthly income in relation to your proposed mortgage payments and to all of your monthly debt and installment loan payments. Generally speaking, your mortgage payment should not be more than 28 percent of your monthly gross income, and your total debt, including mortgage payments and other installment payments, should not be more than 36 percent. Sometimes, particularly if your credit card record is very good, if you can show that you are already carrying that much housing expense through rent or mortgage payments, you may be able to convince the lender to reconsider. This is an example of why full and accurate disclosure on the loan application works in your favor, even though it may not be obvious at the time.

4. Too many debts

In some cases, it is not only the amount of debt owed by an applicant that prevents qualifying for the loan. Extensive use of numerous credit cards and revolving accounts with evidence of increasing account balances that close to the card issuers' debt limits may be enough to kill the application. The primary solution to this problem is to pay off some of the accounts to bring down outstanding obligations, as well as the number of creditors.

5. Unsatisfactory credit history

Nothing can be more damaging to your loan request than a history of poor debt repayment practices. If the credit report shows frequent late charges, past-due accounts, judgments, or bankruptcy, chances for approval of the loan are slim. Lenders may stretch their guidelines on debt ratios or income requirements, but they have little tolerance for a bad credit record. Even low loan-to-value ratios and debt ratios cannot offset an unsatisfactory credit history. If your loan is turned down because of a poor credit report, you may request a free copy of the report from the credit report company, which will be identified in a notice from the lender. Examine the credit report carefully to see if it is up-to-date and accurate. The credit bureau must correct any errors in the report. If there are unsettled disputes over certain accounts, it must also include your side of the argument in the report. Many lenders look for one year's clean payment record to offset past credit problems. If the credit report is accurate and you have a questionable credit history, you need to start repaying outstanding balances on time in order to re-establish an acceptable record.

Source: Mortgage Bankers Association (*www.mortgagebankers.org*)—For more information, contact the Mortgage Bankers Association, 1919 Pennsylvania Avenue NW, Washington, D.C. 20006; (202) 557-2700.

Typical Sections of a Loan Agreement

Loans can be very complicated contracts. Make sure you are not missing a section if you are the writer; if you are receiving the contract, make sure that a key section is not missing. Just to make sure, our expert provides a listing of the most common sections you'll find in a loan agreement.

1. Credit facilities

This section talks about the credit extended and how and when to repay the loan.

2. Interest and fees

An interest rate, minimum monthly interest, and loan fees are specified here.

3. Security interest

This section talks about the nonpayment of a loan and the abilities of a lender to secure his or her interest.

4. Conditions precedent

This is that section that deals with status of accounts, minimum liability, landlord waiver, executed agreement, opinion of borrower's counsel, priority of company's liens, insurance, borrower's existence, organization documents, and taxes.

5. Representations, warranties, and covenants of the borrower

This talks about the existence and authority of the borrower, trade names, place of the business, location of collateral, title and maintenance of collateral, books, records, financial condition, tax returns and payments, pension contributions, compliance with the law, litigation, and use of proceeds.

6. Receivables

This includes the representation, schedules, documents, collection, remittance of proceeds, disputes, returns, and verification.

7. Additional duties of the borrower

This has to do with additional duties that are given by the lender to the borrower. This can be financial, insurance, reports, and access to collateral.

8. Term

This section includes the maturity date, early termination, and payment obligations.

9. Events of defaults and remedies

This deals with the events of default, remedies, standards for determining commercial reasonableness, power of attorney, application of proceeds, and cumulative remedies.

10. General provisions

This includes interest computation, application of payments, charges to accounts, monthly accountings, notices, severability, integration, waivers, no liability for ordinary negligence, amendment, time of essence, attorney fees, costs, and charges, benefit of agreement, publicity, paragraph headings, governing law, and mutual waiver of jury trial.

Source: Dean Morrison, Business Development Officer, Baytree Leasing, a wholly owned subsidiary of Baytree National Bank and Trust, an FDIC Insured, Nationally Chartered Bank based in Illinois. Web site is *www.baytreebank.com*

Questions to Ask Your Loan Officer

Financing a business such as a store, office or apartment building can be a confusing and frustrating experience. Borrowers are often subject to unwieldy demands and requirements imposed by traditional lenders (such as banks, lending institutions, etc.) since these lenders are regulated and generally averse to risk-taking. Becoming well informed can save you time and money during the loan origination process and in the future. Here is a list of questions that you should generally ask your loan officer.

1. What will my monthly payment be? Can the amount change? What would cause the payment to change? How much and how often could the payment go up? When will the loan be paid off?

Just because a lender says you qualify for a certain loan amount doesn't mean you are getting a loan that is affordable for you. Make sure you can meet the loan payments now and in the future.

2. Is there a "balloon" payment? If so, when is it due, and how much will I owe?

A balloon payment is a large, lump-sum payment due at the end of the loan term. A balloon loan may keep monthly payments low in the early years, but it must be refinanced or paid off in full at the end of the loan term, and the low payments mean that relatively little of the loan balance has been reduced. For some borrowers, a balloon loan can be very appropriate. For others, the consequences can be costly, perhaps even resulting in the loss of their home if they can't repay or refinance the amount due.

3. What is the APR—annual percentage rate—for this loan? Is this the lowest rate you can offer?

The APR is the total cost of the loan, including interest charges and other fees, expressed as a yearly rate. Comparison-shop among several lenders so you have a good sense of the costs you should be incurring, and then negotiate the best possible terms. Don't be afraid to make lenders compete for your business by letting them know that you are shopping for the best deal.

4. What "points" and fees would I be charged? Are any of these charges being added to the loan balance and increasing my payments? If so, how much extra would I pay each month and over the life of the loan?

Each point equals one percent of the loan amount. Make sure you have a good understanding of all the costs, terms, and conditions of the loan. Compare verbal answers with what is written in your loan documents.

5. Does the loan amount include fees for credit insurance, such as life, disability, or unemployment insurance? If so, why, and how much will it cost me in up-front, monthly, and total fees?

You may not need the extra insurance, or you may get a better deal from your insurance agent or other sources, so shop around. Also, the lender is prohibited from conditioning approval of a loan on whether you buy insurance through the same company. Be very suspicious if the lender pushes single-premium insurance. The one-time payment usually is so big that consumers add the fee to their loan amount and pay interest each month, adding significantly to the monthly payments and to the total cost.

6. Is there a prepayment penalty if I pay off the loan early by refinancing or selling my house? What is the penalty?

On some loans, a prepayment penalty will be charged if you pay more than is required on your monthly payment or pay off the loan before its term ends. Many lenders offer loans with prepayment penalties at lower interest rates than the same loans without prepayment penalties. Depending on your circumstances, a loan with a prepayment penalty can be a good alternative. However, prepayment penalties also can trap you into a loan. For example, if market interest rates drop, you may miss out on a chance to refinance if the prepayment penalty on your loan is too high. Under the Truth in Lending Act, lenders must disclose any prepayment penalty and how it is determined. If the lender says there is no prepayment penalty, there should be a statement to that effect in the documents. You should ask the lender to show you where that is stated in the documents.

7. Do any of the loan terms differ from what was previously discussed or provided? If yes, which terms and why?

Review documents prior to signing them and make sure you understand why any changes in terms and conditions have been made.

Source: The Federal Deposit Insurance Corporation (FDIC) preserves and promotes public confidence in the U.S. financial system by insuring deposits in banks and thrift institutions for up to $100,000; by identifying, monitoring, and addressing risks to the deposit insurance funds; and by limiting the effect on the economy and the financial system when a bank or thrift institution fails. Contact Federal Deposit Insurance Corporation at 550 17th Street NW Washington, D.C. 20429-9990; (877) ASKFDIC [(877) 275-3342].

Common Loan Covenants

What is a loan covenant? It's a condition that the borrower must comply with in order to adhere to the terms in the loan agreement. If the borrower does not act in accordance with the covenants, the loan can be considered in default and the lender has the right to demand payment (usually in full). Why do banks add covenants to the loan agreements?

They do this to maintain loan quality, keep adequate cash flow, improve financial weakness, and keep an updated picture of the borrower's financial performance and condition. If you're getting a bank loan, you should get to know these common loan covenants.

1. Maintain hazard insurance or content insurance

You may be required to keep insurance coverage on your plant or equipment or inventory in order to safeguard against the catastrophic loss of collateral.

2. Have key-man life insurance

This insures the life of the indispensable owner or manager without whom the company could not continue. The lender usually gets an assignment of the policy.

3. Stay up to date with payment of taxes, fees, licenses

You'll agree to keep those expenses up-to-date; failure to pay would result on the assets of your company being encumbered by a lien from the government, which would take precedence to the one from the bank.

4. Provide current financial information

You'll agree to submit financial statements for the continuing assessment by the bank. Financial statements are usually submitted yearly, while accounts receivable can be required every month.

5. Maintain minimum financial ratios

You'll likely be required to maintain a certain level in key financial ratios, such as minimum quick and current ratios (liquidity), minimum return on assets and return on equity (profitability), minimum equity, minimum working capital, and maximum debt-to-worth (leverage).

6. No change of management or merger without prior approval

This guarantees the continuing existence of your business and will impede the deterioration of financial conditions due to a merger with an unknown entity.

7. No more loans without prior approval

This helps assure the bank that you will not take on excessive debt affecting the quality of the original loan.

8. No dividends or withdrawals or limited dividend withdrawl

This occurs in situations where the net worth is being eroded by the extraction of capital in the form of dividends or stockholder's withdrawals. The lender might find it necessary to restrict the amount of money that can be taken out of your company. In subchapter-S corporations, it is not uncommon to limit withdrawals to the owner's tax liability.

Source: Dean Morrison, Business Development Officer, Baytree Leasing, a wholly owned subsidiary of Baytree National Bank and Trust, an FDIC Insured, Nationally Chartered Bank based in Illinois. Web site is *www.baytreebank.com*

Most and Least Expensive Types of Business Loans

There are lots of different ways to finance your business; one is debt financing. Business loans can come in a lot of different forms, and of course, there are some loans that are more expensive than others. This list shows various types of business loans, ranked by their expense to the borrower. We go from most expensive to least expensive.

1. Finance companies

The most expensive loans are available from finance companies. Finance companies often lend to those who cannot obtain credit from banks or credit unions. Typically, the interest rate ranges from 15 to 30 percent. If you are denied credit by a bank or credit union, you should question your ability to afford the higher rate of a loan company. There is, however, one type of loan from finance companies that is currently less expensive than most other credit. These are loans, often at a rate under 10 percent, available from the finance companies of major auto manufacturers: General Motors Acceptance Corporation, Ford Motor Credit, and others. Yet, keep in mind that a car dealer offering you such a rate may be less willing to discount the price of the car or throw in free options.

2. Retailers

Borrowing from car dealers, appliance stores, department stores, and other retailers is also relatively expensive. Interest rates are usually similar to those charged by finance companies, frequently 20 percent or more.

3. Bank-issued credit cards

Banks lend funds not only through installment loans but also through cash advances on MasterCard or VISA cards. Interest is charged on these advances at rates ranging from 14 to 24 percent. Most banks charge 18 to 20 percent.

4. Commercial bank debt

Medium-priced loans can be obtained from banks. New car loans, for example, may cost 11 to 15 percent, used-car loans and home improvement loans slightly more.

5. Credit unions

There are several advantages in borrowing from credit unions. These institutions effectively provide free credit life insurance. Generally, they are sympathetic to borrowers with legitimate payment problems, and they sometimes pay dividends to all their depositors at the end of the year. Unfortunately, membership in most credit unions is restricted to members of a group-trade union, employees of a firm, church, or community.

6. Money borrowed on financial assets

Also relatively inexpensive is money borrowed on financial assets that are held by the lending institution; for example, a certificate of deposit purchased from a bank or the cash value of a whole-life insurance policy. The interest rate on these types of loans typically ranges from 8 to 12 percent. But remember that your assets are tied up until the loan is repaid.

7. Family

Inexpensive loans can be found from parents or family members, They may charge you only the interest they would have earned on the money, as little as the 5 percent earned on a passbook account. Such loans, however, can complicate family relationships.

Source: Better Business Bureau of Greater Maryland (*www.balti more.bbb.org*).

Typical Parts of a Promissory Note

A promissory note is debt you owe (or is owed to you) to a lender such as individuals, family, or outsiders. Our expert, a real-estate attorney, specializes in drawing up these kinds of agreements for clients who buy and sell property. In this list, he gives us some of the more important parts of a promissory note, with an emphasis on real-estate transactions.

1. Verification

Be sure you verify that your name and address are correct.

2. Confirmation that the interest rate is what you were promised by your lender

While you should also analyze the Truth in Lending statement, which must be given to you at settlement, the annual percentage rate (APR) contained in that statement is not the same as your mortgage interest rate, which must be spelled out in the note. The APR represents the true yield to the lender, computed on all of the fees and costs you will have to pay at settlement.

3. First payment due date

Typically, interest is paid in arrears, so when you make your March payment, for example, it is paying the interest that accrued during the month of February.

4. Correct amount of your monthly payment

Make sure that it is correct. However, some lenders will escrow monies for real-estate taxes and insurance, and thus your actual monthly payment will be higher than spelled out in the note. Make sure you know exactly what your real payment will be, before you leave the settlement table.

5. Prepayment penalty

This is a very important issue, and you should know your rights before you complete the settlement. In fact, this is an issue that you should discuss with your lender well in advance of settlement. If there is a prepayment penalty associated with your loan, you may want to shop around for another lender.

6. Grace period

Most commercial lenders will allow you to make your payment up to the fifteenth of each month before calling you in default. However, interest will accrue on your loan until the payment is received—and recorded—on your lender's books, and thus you should try to make your payments as early in the month as possible.

7. Assumable loan

Can someone buy your property and take over your loan? Most loans contain what is known as a "due on sale" clause. In the promissory note, the section will be called "transfer of property or a beneficial interest in Borrower."

Source: Benny Kass is the senior partner with the Washington, D.C., law firm of Kass, Mitek & Kass, PLLC (*www.kmklawyers.com*). He is a specialist in real-estate legal areas such as commercial and residential financing, closings, foreclosures, and workouts. He is also a charter member of the College of Community Association Attorneys and has written extensively about community association issues. Contact him at *blkass@kmklawyers.com*.

Getting Money from the Government

Reasons to Get a Section 504 Loan

The CDC/504 loan program is a long-term financing tool that provides growing businesses with long-term, fixed-rate financing for major fixed assets, such as land and buildings. A certified development company (CDC) is a nonprofit corporation set up to contribute to the economic development of its community. CDCs work with the Small Business Administration and private-sector lenders to provide financing to small businesses. Proceeds from 504 loans must be used for fixed-asset projects, such as purchasing land and improvements, including existing buildings, grading, street improvements, utilities, parking lots and landscaping; construction of new facilities, or modernizing, renovating, or converting existing facilities; or purchasing long-term machinery and equipment. This list summarizes the types of things a Section 504 Loan will fund.

1. Installation or repair of sanitary disposal systems, together with related plumbing and fixtures, that will meet local health department requirements

2. Payment of reasonable connection fees, which may include assessments for utilities (i.e., water, sewer, electricity, or gas), which are required to be paid by the applicant, and which cannot be paid from other funds

3. Energy-conservation measures such as insulation and combination screen-storm for windows and doors

4. Repair or replacement of heating system

5. Electrical wiring

6. Purchasing existing buildings

7. Purchasing land and land improvements, such as grading, street improvements, utilities, parking lots, and landscaping

8. Repair or replacement of roof

9. Replacement of deteriorated siding

10. Payment of incidental expenses such as surveys, title clearance, loan closing, and architectural or other technical services

11. Paying professional fees directly attributable to the project, such as surveying, engineering, architectural, appraisal, legal, and accounting fees

12. Necessary repairs to mobile/manufactured homes provided the loan applicant owns the home and site and has occupied the home prior to filing an application with USDA Rural Development and the mobile/manufacture home is on a permanent foundation or will be put on a permanent foundation with Section 504 funds

13. Additions to dwellings with grant funds (conventional, manufactured, or mobile) only when it is clearly necessary to remove health or safety hazards to the occupants

14. Repair or remodel houses to make accessible and usable for handicapped or disabled persons

15. Payment of application packaging fees under certain conditions

Source: USDA Rural Development (*http://rurdev.usda.gov*)—An arm of the U.S. Department of Agriculture, this agency helps ensure that rural citizens can participate fully in the global economy. By providing technical assistance and programs to rural Americans, USDA believes a stronger economy will emerge as we work to improve the quality of life for our citizens. Contact them at 200 4th Street SW, Federal Building, Room 210, Huron, SD 57350.

The Benefits of Starting a Business in an Enterprise Zone

An enterprise zone is a designated geographical district in which resident businesses are legally entitled to receive special benefits from a government; it is established in economically depressed areas to encourage companies to locate there. We looked to our experts at the Los Angeles Community Development Department to give us reasons a business would want to open its doors there. Some of the actual amounts may change by the time of publication, so please double check with a tax professional.

1. State tax credits up to $31,570 for hiring an eligible employee

Up to $31,570 can be claimed over a five-year period by an enterprise zone business as a tax credit for each eligible hired employee. The employer can take a tax credit of 50 percent of wages paid to a qualified enterprise zone

employee in the first year of employment. Subsequent years decline by 10 percent. Wages, which qualify for the hiring tax credit, range from minimum wage ($6.75 per hour, effective January 1, 2002) up to 150 percent of minimum wage, or $10.12.

2. Sales and use tax credit of up to 8.25 percent

The sales or use tax paid on the purchase of qualifying machinery, machinery parts, and equipment can be claimed as a tax credit when purchased for exclusive use in an enterprise zone. On January 1, 1998, qualified equipment was added to the tax credit. This equipment includes computers, telephone and fax machines, and copy machines.

3. Business expense deduction of up to $20,000

The cost of qualified property purchased for exclusive use in an enterprise zone may be deducted as a business expense in the first year it is placed in service. The maximum business expense deduction for qualified property is the lesser of 40 percent or $20,000.

4. Net interest deduction on loans made to enterprise zone businesses

Income can be deducted on the amount of the net interest earned on loans made to an enterprise zone business. Net interest is the full amount of interest less any direct expenses incurred in making the loan (such as commissions paid to a loan representative).

5. Net operating loss carryover of 100 percent for fifteen years

One hundred percent of net operating losses (NOL) of individuals or corporations conducting business in an enterprise zone may be carried over for fifteen years in order to reduce the amount of taxable income for those years. (This amount is greater than standard NOL carryovers in California for non–enterprise zone businesses.)

6. Electrical rate reduction for five years, starting with 35 percent the first year

The Department of Water and Power (DWP) offers a five-year electrical rate reduction for new and expanding businesses located in the city's state enterprise zones or federal empowerment zone. If a business is eligible, the five-year rate reduction for empowerment zone or enterprise zone businesses is as follows:

Year 1: 35%, Year 2: 30%, Year 3: 25%, Year 4: 20%, Year 5: 10%.

7. Reduced fees for architectural plans in an enterprise zone

Ordinance 168439 provides a fee waiver for the review of commercial or industrial architectural plans for projects 40,000 square feet or larger located in an enterprise zone.

8. Enterprise zones allow site plan reviews in lieu of conditional use permits

Ordinances 165951 and 166127 allow site plan reviews (which are less complex and less costly than variance process) for major developments in an enterprise zone.

9. Enterprise zone businesses may pay sewer hookups in installments over five years

Ordinance 16902 allows enterprise zone businesses to be exempt from the one-time sewer hookup fee so that payment is in installments over a five-year period. The five-year plan, however, requires interest payable on any unpaid balance.

10. Enterprise zone businesses may waive parking space requirements for selected uses

Ordinance 165773 waived certain enterprise zone parking space requirements for office, retail, restaurant, bars, and similar high-trip generating uses in order to allow for continued business growth.

_____

Source: The City of Los Angeles Community Development Department (*www.lacity.org*)—The department provides programs designed to develop and maintain healthy, self-sufficient families; safe, viable neighborhoods; to promote economic development through employment, training, and job-placement; and to assist with the growth and sustenance of small and medium-size businesses using city resources.

Popular Government Loan Programs

The SBA offers numerous loan programs to assist small businesses. It is important to note, however, that the SBA is primarily a guarantor of loans made by private and other institutions.

1. Basic 7(a) loan guaranty

These loans are the most basic and most used type loan of the SBA's business loan programs. The name comes from section 7(a) of the Small Business Act, which authorizes the agency to provide business loans to American small businesses. All 7(a) loans are provided by lenders, called participants because they participate with the SBA in the 7(a) program. The SBA does not fully guaranty 7(a) loans. The lender and SBA share the risk that a borrower will not be able to repay the loan in full. The guaranty is a guaranty against payment default. It does not cover imprudent decisions by the lender or misrepresentation by the borrower. Under the guaranty concept, commercial lenders make and administer the loans. The business applies to a lender for financing. The lender decides if it will make the loan internally or if the application has some weaknesses, which will require an SBA guaranty if the loan is to be made. The guaranty that the SBA provides is only available to the lender. It assures the lender that in the event the borrower does not repay the obligation and a payment default occurs, the government will reimburse the lender for its loss, up to the percentage of SBA's guaranty.

2. Prequalification program

The prequalification loan program uses intermediary organizations to assist prospective borrowers in developing viable loan application packages and securing loans. This program targets low-income borrowers, disabled business owners, new and emerging businesses, veterans, exporters, and rural and specialized industries. The intermediary's job is to work with the applicant to make sure the business plan is complete and that the application is eligible and has credit merit. If the intermediary is satisfied that the application has a chance for approval, it will send it to the SBA for processing. If the SBA decides the application is eligible and has sufficient credit merit to warrant approval, it will issue a commitment letter on behalf of the applicant. The commitment letter, or prequalification letter, indicates the SBA's willingness to guaranty a loan made by a lender under certain terms and conditions. The intermediary then helps the borrower locate a lender offering the most competitive rates. The applicant takes the letter and application documents to a lender for a decision.

3. Certified Development Company (504) loan program

The CDC/504 loan program is a long-term financing tool for economic development within a community. The 504 program provides growing businesses with long-term, fixed-rate financing for major fixed assets, such as land and buildings. A Certified Development Company is a nonprofit corporation set up to contribute to the economic development of its community. CDCs work with the SBA and private-sector lenders to provide financing to small businesses. Typically, a 504 project includes a loan secured with a senior lien from a private-sector lender covering up to 50 percent of the project cost, a loan secured with a junior lien from the CDC (backed by a 100 percent SBA-guaranteed debenture) covering up to 40 percent of the cost, and a contribution of at least 10 percent equity from the small business being helped.

4. Microloans

The Microloan program provides very small loans to start-up, newly established, or growing small business concerns. Under this program, the SBA makes funds available to nonprofit community-based lenders (intermediaries), which, in turn, make loans to eligible borrowers in amounts up to a maximum of $35,000. The average loan size is about $10,500. Applications are submitted to the local intermediary and all credit decisions are made on the local level.

5. Home and personal property disaster loans

If you are in a declared disaster area and are the victim of a disaster, you may be eligible for financial assistance from the U.S. Small Business Administration—even if you don't own a business. As a homeowner, renter, or personal-property owner, you may apply to the SBA for a loan to help you recover from a disaster.

Sources: Small Business Association (*www.sba.gov*).

Popular Government Grant Programs

Good preparation, thoughtful planning, and concise packaging is essential to apply successfully for a government grant. Many departments and agencies offer money to private businesses that further their own aims. Our expert, who specializes in bringing this information together, has determined these programs are some of the more popular government grant offerings.

1. Department of Education grants

The Department of Education was created in 1980 by combining offices from several federal agencies. Its original directive remains its mission today; to ensure equal access to education and to promote educational excellence

throughout the nation. The department's 4,500 employees and $71.5 billion budget are dedicated to establishing policies on federal financial aid for education, and distributing as well as monitoring those funds, collecting data on America's schools and disseminating research, focusing national attention on key educational issues, and prohibiting discrimination and ensuring equal access to education.

www.ed.gov/about/offices/list/ocfo/grants/grants.html

2. Environmental Protection Agency grants

The mission of the Environmental Protection Agency is to protect human health and the environment. Since 1970, the EPA has been working for a cleaner, healthier environment for the American people. The EPA is led by the administrator, who is appointed by the president of the United States. The EPA leads the nation's environmental science, research, education, and assessment efforts. Grants administered by the EPA address air pollution, hazardous waste, water pollution, wetlands protection, and more.

www.epa.gov/ebtpages/envigrants.html

3. Federal Emergency Management Agency

FEMA is part of the Department of Homeland Security's Emergency Preparedness and Response Directorate. FEMA has more than 2,600 full-time employees. FEMA also has nearly 4,000 standby disaster-assistance employees who are available for deployment after disasters. FEMA's continuing mission within the new department is to lead the effort to prepare the nation for all hazards and effectively manage federal response and recovery efforts following any national incident. FEMA also initiates proactive mitigation activities, trains first responders, and manages the National Flood Insurance Program and the U.S. Fire Administration. The agency also offers individual and public assistance programs designed to help rebuild towns after a disaster.

www.fema.gov

4. HUD Community Development Block Grants

Community development activities include many different programs that provide assistance to a wide variety of grantees. Begun in 1974, the Community Development Block Grant (CDBG) is one of the oldest programs in HUD. The CDBG program provides annual grants on a formula basis to many different types of grantees through several programs. It provides eligible metropolitan cities and urban counties with annual grants to revitalize neighborhoods, expand affordable housing and economic opportunities, and improve community facilities and services, principally to benefit low- and moderate-income persons.

www.hud.gov/offices/cpd/communitydevelopment/programs/index.cfm

5. National Institutes of Health

The National Institutes of Health (NIH) is the nation's largest medical research agency, making important medical discoveries that improve health and save lives. Part of the U.S. Department of Health and Human Services, NIH is the primary federal agency for conducting and supporting medical research. Helping to lead the way toward important medical discoveries that improve people's health and save lives, NIH scientists investigate ways to prevent disease as well as the causes, treatments, and even cures for common and rare diseases. It supports the research of nonfederal scientists in universities, medical schools, hospitals, and research institutions throughout the country and abroad.

http://grants1.nih.gov/grants/oer.htm

Source: LibrarySpot.com (*www.libraryspot.com*)—This Web site was created to break through the information overload of the Web and to bring the best library and reference sites together with insightful editorials in one user-friendly spot. Sites featured on LibrarySpot.com are hand-selected and reviewed by our editorial team for their exceptional quality, content, and utility. Most recently, Forbes.com selected LibrarySpot.com as a "Forbes Favorite" site, the best in the reference category, and *PC Magazine* named it one of the Top 100 Web Sites. Contact LibrarySpot.com at 1840 Oak Avenue, Evanston, IL 60201; (847) 866-1830.

Top Rural Loan Programs

Why are you reading this? Shouldn't you be out milking a cow somewhere? Oh, you need some cash to help grow your rural-based business. Well, you've come to the right place. Here's a list of some of the more popular rural financing programs around.

1. Community Facilities direct and guaranteed loan programs

Rural Housing Service (RHS)

The Rural Housing Service administers the Community Facilities direct and guaranteed loan programs to help develop "essential community facilities" for health care, public safety, and public services. Health care facilities such as hospitals, clinics, ambulatory care centers, rehabilitation centers, and nursing homes can apply to RHS for direct loans or loan guarantees. They must be located in rural areas and towns with populations of 20,000 or fewer. RHS may guarantee up to 90 percent of any loss of interest or principal on the loan. It will also make direct loans to applicants who are unable to obtain commercial credit. Funds may be used for facility construction, expansion, or improvement, and for land acquisition.

RHS Community Programs: (202) 720-4323 *www.rurdev.usda.gov/rhs/common/non_profit_intro.htm*

2. Business and industry guaranteed loans

Rural Business-Cooperative Service (RBS)

Loan guarantees of up to $10 million are available through RBS to develop businesses or industry, increase employment, or control pollution in rural areas. The business or industry must be located outside any city with a population of 50,000 or more and its immediately adjacent area. RBS places a priority on projects in areas with a population of 25,000 or fewer. Any legal entity, including individuals, public and private organizations, and federally recognized Indian tribal groups, may be eligible to borrow money. Under the loan guarantee, the Rural Business and Cooperative Development Service contracts to reimburse the lender for losses of principal and interest: up to 90 percent for loans of $2 million or less, 80 percent for loans over $2 million but less than $5 million, and 70 percent for loans over $5 million.

Rural Business-Cooperative Service: (202) 690-4100 *www.rurdev.usda.gov/rbs/busp/bprogs.htm*

3. Distance Learning and Telemedicine Grant and Loan Program

Rural Utilities Service (RUS)

This program was authorized in the 1996 farm bill to support projects that provide distance learning and telemedicine services to rural areas. It replaces the RUS (formerly known as REA) Distance Learning and Medical Link Grants program. Starting in fiscal year 1997, eligible applicants can apply for both grants and direct loans through this program. The program allows for capital equipment purchases (i.e., purchase of end-user telemedicine equipment) but not for building construction or renovation.

RUS Telecommunications Program: (202) 720-9554, E-mail: *DLML@rus.usda.gov. www.usda.gov/rus/telecom/staff/index_staff.htm*

4. Rural Health Outreach Program

Office of Rural Health Policy (ORHP)

The Office of Rural Health Policy (ORHP) allows projects receiving funds under the Rural Health Services Outreach Grant Program to purchase equipment or vehicles, provided that (a) the equipment or vehicle is an essential component of the outreach program, and (b) the purchase does not exceed 40 percent of the federal grant amount. The funds may not be used for the purchase, construction, renovation, or improvement of a building or property.

ORHP: (301) 443-0835

5. Rural Hospital Flexibility Program

Office of Rural Health Policy (ORHP)

This program was authorized by the Balanced Budget Act of 1997 to increase the ability of states and rural communities to identify and address rural health deficits. Funds may be used by states to (a) develop and implement rural health plans with broad collaboration; (b) stabilize rural hospitals by helping them consider, plan for, and obtain designation as "Critical Access Hospitals" (CAHs); (c) support CAHs, providers, and communities as they develop networks of care; (d) help improve and integrate emergency medical services. States may use up to 15 percent of their total grant amount to lease or purchase equipment. Funds cannot be used for construction/renovation/modernization, routine hospital operating costs, routine emergency medical services costs, or individual clinical services.

ORHP: (301) 443-0835

6. Rural telemedicine/telehealth programs

Rural health providers seeking capital support to set up and equip a telemedicine or telecommunications program can turn to a number of agencies for grant information like the *Office for the Advancement of Telehealth (OAT),* which administers the Rural Telemedicine Grant Program. Up to 40 percent of grant funds may be used for equipment. The *National Library of Medicine (NLM)* has several types of grant programs to fund equipment and related costs enabling health care institutions to connect to the Internet. The *National Telecommunications and Information Administration (NTIA)* is part of the U.S. Department of Commerce. The NTIA's Technology Opportunities Program (TOP) (formerly Telecommunications and Information Infrastructure Assistance Program) provides matching demonstration grants to state and local governments, health care providers, school districts, libraries, social service organizations, public safety services, and other nonprofit entities to help them develop information infrastructures and services.

Source: The Rural Information Center (RIC) (*www.nal.usda.gov/ric/ruralres/business.htm*) provides information and referral services to local, tribal, state, and federal government officials; community organizations; rural electric and telephone cooperatives; libraries; businesses; and citizens working to maintain the vitality of America's rural areas. The RIC Web site contains more than 3,000 links to current and reliable information on a wide variety of rural resources and funding sources. Contact them at USDA, Rural Information Center National Agricultural Library, 10301 Baltimore Ave., Room 304, Beltsville, MD 20705-2351.

The Advantages of an SBA Loan

The Small Business Administration (SBA) guaranteed loan programs are set up to handle a full range of small business needs for any industry. An SBA loan can be used to construct new or purchase existing commercial owner-occupied real estate, to expand or modernize facilities, to purchase machinery, equipment, fixtures, leasehold improvements, finance business acquisitions and business start ups or to finance inventory and accounts receivables. Our expert, who finances SBA deals and is an SBA Preferred Lender, offers reasons why small businesses may want to consider this choice for raising needed cash.

1. Keeps cash in your business

Longer terms equal lower monthly payments. SBA loans are usually long-term and could be as long as seven years for working capital, 10 to 15 years for equipment, and up to 25 years for real estate. Higher loans for the value of collateral equal lower down payments. SBA loans allow for up to up to 90% financing for new purchases and offer solutions for financing soft assets such as goodwill. In addition to his, SBA loans give you the ability to finance closing costs versus paying them out of pocket.

2. Preserves management flexibility

SBA loans have option for interest only periods. They have lines of credit with 7-year commitments (non-SBA lines typically are one year). Balloon payments are not necessary. There are limited pre-payment penalties. Pre-payment penalties exist only on loans longer than 15 years and the prepayment penalty only applies to the first three years. There are also limited call features and financial covenants.

3. Minimal costs

Their loan packaging fees are minimal, typically from $250 to $1,000. The SBA guarantee fee is based on the amount of the guaranteed portion of the SBA loan. There are no points or origination fees and interest rate caps are based on deal size.

Source: Cleveland-based KeyCorp (www.key.com) is one of the nation's largest bank-based financial services companies, with assets of approximately $93 billion. Key companies provide investment management, retail and commercial banking, consumer finance, and investment banking products and services to individuals and companies throughout the United States and, for certain businesses, internationally. Contact them at 800-539-2222.

Typical Steps for Getting an SBA Loan

Getting a loan guaranteed by the Small Business Administration (SBA) can be time-consuming. Our expert provides lots of SBA-backed financing and has laid out the specific steps you'll be taking right here.

1. The initial interview

Once you decide that your business needs a loan, you need to decide which SBA lender would be convenient and suitable to your borrowing requirements. Once you have narrowed down your SBA loan lender, an officer assigned to your loan is chosen for his or her experience in your type of business. Not many banks have staff with the experience and knowledge needed to make an evaluation. This is a key step, saving time and effort that could be lost with someone less experienced in SBA procedures and regulations.

2. Information collection

Once the lending officer has made an initial evaluation of your business circumstances, the information collection process begins. There are two parts to this process. First, collect financial and business data routine to running your business and personal affairs. Most business owners are able to put this information together by simply pulling and copying records from files. Second, ascertain how the funds will work to achieve your business objectives. This is where the SBA loan officer can help get the funds you are seeking. An experienced officer would listen to your business objectives, understand how those objectives can be achieved through your loan, and make it work by selling your loan to the bank and the SBA.

3. Bank approval

Since the bank is being asked to lend you the money, the first approval for your loan must come from the lending institution. The SBA guarantees only that you will pay it back, limited to a maximum 80 percent of any default value.

4. SBA loan packaging and submission

This is the one step unique to the SBA approval process. Once the lending institution collects the information needed for internal bank approval, your loan is "packaged" and submitted for SBA approval. In many cases, the lending institution is empowered to preapprove your loan on behalf of the SBA. You get immediate assurance that your loan will close quickly and efficiently.

5. Closing the loan

Depending on the type of loan you choose, the closing may be as simple as a visit to the bank for routine paper signing, or it may involve a little more work, such as a title-company closing for a real-estate loan.

Source: Comerica Incorporated (*www.comerica.com*) is a financial services company headquartered in Detroit, strategically aligned by the Business Bank, Retail Bank and by Wealth & Institutional Management. Contact information: Comerica Tower at Detroit Center, 500 Woodward Avenue, M/C 3391, Detroit, MI 48226; (800) 292-1300; hearing-impaired (TDD): (800) 822-6546

Ways the SBA Can Help a Start-up

The U.S. Small Business Administration (SBA) is an independent agency of the executive branch of the federal government. It is charged with the responsibility of providing four primary areas of assistance to American small business. These areas are advocacy, management, procurement, and financial assistance. Financial assistance is delivered primarily through SBA's Investment Programs, Business Loan Programs. The SBA offers numerous loan programs to assist with starting of small businesses. Here are some ways they can assist the fledging business.

1. Basic 7(a) loan guarantee

This serves as the SBA's primary business loan program to help qualified small businesses obtain financing when they might not be eligible for business loans through normal lending channels. Loan proceeds can be used for most sound business purposes, including working capital, machinery and equipment, furniture and fixtures, land and building and leasehold improvements, and debt refinancing (under special conditions). Loan maturity is up to ten years for working capital and generally up to twenty-five years for fixed assets.

2. Certified Development Company (CDC), a 504 loan program

This program provides long-term, fixed-rate financing to small businesses to acquire real estate, machinery, or equipment for expansion or modernization. Typically, a 504 project includes a loan secured from a private sector lender with a senior lien, a loan secured from a CDC (funded by a 100 percent SBA-guaranteed debenture) with a junior lien covering up to 40 percent of the total cost, and a contribution of at least 10 percent equity from the borrower. The maximum SBA debenture generally is $1 million (up to $1.3 million in some cases).

3. Microloan, a 7(m) loan program

This program provides short-term loans of up to $35,000 to small businesses and not-for-profit child-care centers for working capital or the purchase of inventory, supplies, furniture, fixtures, machinery, and/or equipment. The SBA makes or guarantees a loan to an intermediary, who in turn makes the microloan to the applicant. The microloan program is available in selected locations in most states.

4. Loan prequalification

This program allows business applicants to have their loan applications for $250,000 or less analyzed and potentially sanctioned by the SBA before they are taken to lenders for consideration. The program focuses on the applicant's character, credit, experience, and reliability rather than assets. An SBA-designated intermediary works with the business owner to review and strengthen the loan application. The review is based on key financial ratios, credit and business history, and the loan request terms. The program is administered by the SBA's Office of Field Operations and SBA district offices.

5. SBA's investment programs

In 1958 Congress created the Small Business Investment Company (SBIC) program. SBICs, licensed by the Small Business Administration, are privately owned and managed investment firms. They are vital participants in a partnership between the government and the private sector economy. With their own capital and funds borrowed at favorable rates through the federal government, SBICs provide venture capital to both new and established small independent businesses. All SBICs are profit-motivated businesses. A major incentive for SBICs to invest in small businesses is the chance to share in the success of the small business if it grows and prospers.

6. SBA's bonding programs

The Surety Bond Guarantee (SBG) Program was developed to provide small and minority contractors with contracting opportunities they would not normally have. The U.S. Small Business Administration can guarantee bonds for contracts up to $2 million, covering bid, performance, and payment bonds for small and emerging contractors who cannot obtain surety bonds through regular commercial channels. SBA's guarantee gives sureties an incentive to provide bonding for eligible contractors and thereby strengthens a contractor's ability to obtain bonding and greater access to contracting opportunities.

Source: Business.gov (*www.business.gov.com*)—A U.S. government site that guides its visitors through the maze of government rules and regulations and provides access to services and resources to help them start, grow, and succeed in business.

Businesses That Are Ineligible for an SBA Loan

A vast majority of businesses are eligible for financial assistance from the Small Business Administration (SBA). However, the applicant businesses must operate for profit, must be engaged in, or propose to do business in the United States or its possessions, must have reasonable owner equity to invest, and must first use alternative financial resources including personal assets. So not everyone can get funded. Can you? Here are some of the businesses that are ineligible for financial assistance from the SBA.

1. Real-estate investment firms

Firms exist when the real property will be held for investment purposes, as opposed to loans to otherwise eligible small business concerns for the purpose of occupying the real estate being acquired.

2. Businesses engaged in speculative activities

Those firms developing profits from fluctuations in price rather than through the normal course of trade, such as wildcatting for oil and dealing in commodities futures, when not part of the regular activities of the business are excluded from being eligible for an SBA loan. Dealers of rare coins and stamps are also not eligible. SBA considers speculative activities too risky; it is not the objective of SBA to lend to risky opportunities.

3. Firms involved in lending activities

The SBA lends money to the borrowers to carry out businesses in the normal course of trade of goods and services. Since in the case of banks, finance companies, factors, leasing companies, insurance companies (not agents), and any other firm whose stock-in-trade is money, SBA has specifically excluded them from being eligible for an SBA loan. SBA has excluded since the firms whose business is involved in lending are not actually borrowing the money from SBA for any business operations but are lending the same money borrowed from the SBA.

4. Businesses that use pyramid sales plans

Pyramid sales plans are characterized by endless chains of distributors and subdistributors where a participant's primary incentive is based on the sales made by an ever-increasing number of participants. Since the products in such cases are usually cosmetics, household goods, and other soft goods that lend themselves to this type of business, they are not eligible for an SBA loan. SBA excludes this since this business only prospers if the chain grows but there is no real growth due to business endeavor.

5. Firms engaged in any illegal activities

Illegal activities are by definition those activities that are against the law in the jurisdiction where the business is located. Included in these activities are the productions, servicing, or distribution of otherwise legal products that are to be used in connection with an illegal activity, such as selling drug paraphernalia or operating a motel that permits illegal prostitution. The very nature of the business activities being illegal, they are excluded from getting an SBA loan.

6. Firms in the gambling industry

Gambling activities include any business whose principal activity is gambling. While this precludes loans to race tracks, casinos, and similar enterprises, the rule does not restrict loans to otherwise eligible businesses, which obtain less than one-third of their annual gross income from either (a) the sale of official state lottery tickets under a state license, or (b) legal gambling activities licensed and supervised by a state authority. The outcome in gambling activities is a matter of chance and/or luck. Thus SBA would not lend to any business whose profitability or income is a matter of chance or luck.

7. Charitable, religious, or other nonprofit institutions

Charitable, religious, or other nonprofit or eleemosynary institutions, government-owned corporations, consumer and marketing cooperatives, and churches and organizations promoting religious objectives are not eligible. Again SBA has excluded these institutions since they do not delve into any business endeavor and making profit is not even the objective of these institutions.

Source: Small Business Administration (*www.sba.gov*).

Common SBA Loan Guarantees Required

The Small Business Administration (SBA) was officially established in 1953, but its philosophy and mission began to take shape years earlier in a number of predecessor agencies, due to the pressures of the Great Depression and World War II. Nearly 20 million small businesses have received direct or indirect help from one or another of those SBA programs since 1953, as the agency has become the government's most cost-effective instrument for economic development. Like other lending institutions, SBA would also want to protect the security of its loan advances and thus requires some lenient collateral to be furnished before granting any loans. Here's what you'll need to provide if you want an SBA loan.

1. Collateral: business as well as personal assets

Collateral can consist of assets that are usable in the business and personal assets that remain outside the business. Borrowers can assume that all assets financed with borrowed funds will collateralize the loan. Depending on how much equity was contributed toward the acquisition of these assets, the lender also is likely to require other business assets as collateral.

2. Personal guarantees

For all SBA loans, personal guarantees are required of every 20 percent or greater owner, plus other individuals who hold key management positions. Whether a guarantee will be secured by personal assets is based on the value of the assets already pledged and the value of the assets personally owned compared to the amount borrowed. In the event real estate is to be used as collateral, be aware that banks and other regulated lenders are now required by law to obtain third-party valuation on real estate–related transactions of $50,000 or more.

3. Certified appraisals for loans of $100,000 or more

Certified appraisals are required for loans of $100,000 or more. The SBA may require professional appraisals of both, business and personal assets, plus any necessary survey, and/or feasibility study.

4. Owner-occupied residences

Owner-occupied residences generally become collateral when the lender requires the residence as collateral, the equity in the residence is substantial, and other credit factors are weak. Such collateral is necessary to assure that the principal(s) remain committed to the success of the venture for which the loan is being made. The applicant operates the business out of the residence or other buildings located on the same parcel of land.

5. Resource management

The ability of individuals to manage the resources of their business, sometimes referred to as "character," is a prime consideration when determining whether a loan will be made. Managerial capacity is an important factor involving education, experience, and motivation. A proven positive ability to manage resources is also a large consideration.

Source: Small Business Administration (*www.sba.gov*).

Popular SBA Bonding Programs

The U.S. Small Business Administration (SBA) can guarantee bonds for contracts up to $2 million, covering bid, performance, and payment bonds for small and emerging contractors who cannot obtain surety bonds through regular commercial channels. SBA's guarantee gives sureties an incentive to provide bonding for eligible contractors, and thereby strengthens a contractor's ability to obtain bonding and greater access to contracting opportunities. A surety bond is a three-party instrument between a surety, the contractor, and the project owner. The agreement binds the contractor to comply with the terms and conditions of a contract. If the contractor is unable to successfully perform the contract, the surety assumes the contractor's responsibilities and ensures that the project is completed. Here are the four types of contract bonds that may be covered by an SBA guarantee.

1. Bid

A bid is a bond that guarantees that the bidder on a contract will enter into the contract and furnish the required payment and performance bonds.

2. Payment

A payment is a type of contract bond that guarantees payment from the contractor of money to persons who furnish labor, materials, equipment, and/or supplies for use in the performance of the contract.

3. Performance

Performance is a contract bond that guarantees that the contractor will perform the contract in accordance with its terms.

4. Ancillary

Finally, ancillary contract bonds are bonds that are incidental and essential to the performance of the contract.

Source: Small Business Administration (www.sba.gov).

Popular SBA Investment Programs

In 1958 Congress created the Small Business Investment Company (SBIC) program. SBICs, licensed by the Small Business Administration, are privately owned and managed investment firms. They are vital participants in a partnership between the government and the private sector economy. With their own capital and funds borrowed at favorable rates through the federal government, SBICs provide venture capital to both new and established small independent businesses. All SBICs are profit-motivated businesses. A major incentive for SBICs to invest in small businesses is the chance to share in the success of the small business if it grows and prospers. Here is a list of the various types of investment programs.

1. Seed financing

This is a small amount of capital provided to an inventor entrepreneur to prove a concept and to qualify for start-up capital. This may involve product development and market research as well as building a management team and developing a business plan.

2. Start-up

This is capital provided to companies completing product development and initial marketing. Companies may be in the process of organizing or they may be in business for a year or less, but they have not sold their product commercially. Usually such firms have made market studies, assembled key management, developed a business plan, and are ready to do business.

3. Early stage

This is capital provided to companies that have expended their initial capital (often in developing and market-testing a prototype) and require funds to initiate full-scale manufacturing and sales.

4. Expansion financing

This working capital is for the initial expansion of a company that is producing and shipping, and has growing accounts receivable and inventories. Although the company has made progress, it may not yet be showing a profit.

5. Later-stage financing

This is capital for the major expansion of a company whose sales volume is increasing and that is breaking even or profitable. Funds are used for further plant expansion, marketing, working capital or development of an improved product.

6. MBO/LBO/acquisition

Acquisition financing provides funds to finance an acquisition of another company. Management/leverage buyout funds enable an operating management group to acquire a product line or business.

Source: Small Business Administration (www.sba.gov).

Considerations for Requesting an SBA International (IT) Loan

If your business is preparing to engage in or is already engaged in international trade or is adversely affected by competition from imports, the International Trade Loan Program is designed for you. Here's what you need to be eligible.

1. Show that you're affected by international trade

You must establish that the loan will significantly expand or develop an export market, that you are currently adversely affected by import competition, that you will upgrade equipment or facilities to improve competitive position, or you must provide a business plan that reasonably projects export sales sufficient to cover the loan. A small business concern is engaged in international trade if, as determined by the SBA, "the small business concern is in a position to expand existing export markets or develop new export markets." A small business concern is adversely affected by international trade if, as determined by the SBA, "the small business concern (i) is confronting increased competition with foreign firms in the relevant market; and (ii) is injured by such competition."

2. Must meet the type of business and size requirements

The SBA has many rules about business types and size of business that must be met to apply for any of their loans. Check their Web site for more information.

3. Make sure the proceeds meet specific purposes as defined by the SBA

The proceeds of an SBA international trade loan may be used to acquire, construct, renovate, modernize, improve, or expand facilities and equipment to be used in the United States to produce goods or services involved in international trade or to refinance existing indebtedness that is not structured with reasonable terms and conditions. There can be no working capital as part of an IT loan or as part of any refinancing.

4. Make sure your needs are within the maximum amounts allowed

The maximum gross amount ($2 million) and SBA-guaranteed amount ($1.5 million) for an IT loan is the same as a regular 7(a) loan. However, there is an exception to the maximum SBA 7(a) guaranty amount to one borrower (including affiliates).

5. Maximum guaranteed limits can be increased

The maximum guaranteed amount can go up to $1,750,000 under the following circumstances: (a) the small business has been approved for an IT loan, and (b) the business has applied for a separate working capital loan (or loans) under the Export Working Capital Program and/or other 7(a) loan programs. When there is an IT loan and a separate working capital loan, the maximum SBA guaranty on the combined loans can be up to $1,750,000 as long as the SBA guaranty on the working capital loan does not exceed $1,250,000. In all cases, to receive the maximum SBA guaranty amount of $1,750,000, the financing package for the small business must include an IT loan that was approved after December 7, 2004.

6. Be aware of the maximum guaranty percent that's allowed

For the international trade loan, the SBA can guaranty up to 85 percent of loans of $150,000 and less, and up to 75 percent of loans above $150,000. The maximum guaranteed amount is $1,250,000.

7. Make sure you have the right collateral

Only collateral located in the United States, its territories, and possessions is acceptable as collateral under this program. The lender must take a first lien position (or first mortgage) on items financed under an international trade loan. Additional collateral may be required, including personal guarantees, subordinate liens, or items that are not financed by the loan proceeds.

Source: Small Business Administration (*www.sba.gov*).

Steps for Getting Business from the Federal Government

Interested in doing business with the federal government? There are a lot of opportunities as long as you've got patience and you're willing to follow the rules. Here are some steps to start you on your way.

1. Start with the Small Business Administration

Begin with a visit to your nearest SBA and SBA-sponsored Small Business Development Center or go online to *www.sba.gov*. Here you will find resources, reports, and educational programs to provide you with the necessary information to bid successfully on government contracts.

2. Read the essential tool of federal contracting: the FedBizOpps site

FedBizOpps.gov is the single government point-of-entry (GPE) for federal government procurement opportunities over $25,000. Government buyers are able to publicize their business opportunities by posting information directly to FedBizOpps via the Internet. Through one portal—FedBizOpps (FBO)—commercial vendors seeking federal markets for their products and services can search, monitor, and retrieve opportunities solicited by the entire federal contracting community.

3. Locate your nearest Procurement Technical Assistance Center

The PTACs assist small businesses in marketing and selling products and services to federal, state, and local governments. For locations, call (409) 886-0125 and ask for the Association of Government Marketing Assistance Specialists.

4. Search opportunities to be a subcontractor

This is especially beneficial when you are just getting started; you gain valuable experience and begin to build credibility for your business. Review the site for the "Top 100 Contractors and Their Purchasing History" for suggestions.

5. Be a team player

Team up with a similar business. There is strength in numbers, especially for newcomers. Network with other business owners. Build a list of your own contacts and find out about opportunities through your network.

6. Get your foot in the door

Get to know and visit the contracting agencies that you are interested in doing business with. Visit the Office of Small & Disadvantaged Business Utilization Directory (*www.sba.gov/GC/osdbu.html*). Having contacts who are familiar with you and your company's capabilities are critical when bidding on micropurchases from the government. (Micropurchases are purchases under $2,500).

Source: Business.gov (*www.business.gov*)—A Web site run by the federal government that guides visitors through the maze of government rules and regulations and provides access to services and resources to help them start, grow, and succeed in business

Reasons to Register with the Government's Central Contractor Registration

The Central Contractor Registration (CCR) is the federal government's repository of data common to all contractors. CCR is the single place for contractors to register when conducting business with the federal government. It benefits your business in the many ways listed here.

1. Leads

Increased visibility of worldwide sources for goods and services and their geographical preferences for conducting business.

2. It's simple

One-time registration with the federal government with annual renewals.

3. Contracts and payments

Expedited contract awards and payments by electronically exchanging contractor-specific data with procurement, finance, and other automated information systems (AIS), such as logistics, transportation, and medical.

4. Up-to-date information

Reduced duplicative data entry that can create errors and inconsistent information.

5. Low cost

Decreased data maintenance and storage costs.

6. Data services

The CCR collects, validates, stores, and disseminates data in support of agency acquisition missions.

7. No hassle payments

CCR validates the vendor's information and electronically shares the secure and encrypted data with the federal agencies' finance offices to facilitate paperless payments through electronic funds transfer (EFT). Additionally, CCR shares the data with government procurement and electronic business systems.

Source: The Central Contractor Registration Web site (*www.ccr.gov*)—They can also be contacted at (888) 227-2423.

Top Myths about Government Contracts

Federal, state and local governments spend billions of dollars annually on a wide variety of goods and services. Even so, most small businesses don't go after these potentially lucrative contracts. Why? Because the government has a bad reputation as a customer, and small businesses don't want to deal with the hassle. However, much of this reputation is based on misperceptions and outdated information. We've collected some of the most prevalent myths about doing business with the government to help you separate fact from fiction.

1. Myth: The government isn't a reliable client

Fact: Regardless of how the economy is doing, the government is always in business. During times when the private sector is scaling back, the government still needs to maintain its infrastructure and go about its business. As a result, government contracts can be a steady source of revenue regardless of the highs and lows of the economy.

2. Myth: The government doesn't have any money to spend

Fact: That couldn't be further from the truth. Although government spending is under close scrutiny, there is a great deal of money out there. In many cases, state and local governments are the single largest buyers in their area. Look at your local government's fiscal-year budget to learn when, where, and how much money is being spent.

3. Myth: It will take too long to get paid

Fact: The Prompt Payment Act of 1982 stipulates that federal contractors receive payment within 30 days of submitting a properly prepared invoice. Most cities, states, and other local jurisdictions have followed suit with similar regulations. If payment is late, you are usually entitled to interest for every day it is overdue. In addition, more and more agencies are using

purchase cards and electronic funds transfers, which make payments fast and efficient.

4. Myth: Government paperwork is too long and too confusing to manage

Fact: In the past several years, the government has decreased and simplified paperwork on every level. Also, many agencies now put their contracting forms, regulations, and instructions online, making them easily accessible. That said, the government still takes its paperwork seriously. Contractors must pay careful attention to every detail when working with any government agency.

5. Myth: Small companies don't get government contracts

Fact: Federal, state, and local agencies have programs in place to ensure that small and disadvantaged businesses get a share of government work. For example, the federal government enacted the Very Small Business Program to increase the number of contracts going to businesses with fewer than 15 employees and annual receipts of less than $1 million.

6. Myth: Contracts only go to companies that already work with the government

Fact: These days, many government agencies go out of their way to recruit new contractors, especially among small businesses. There are also systems of checks and balances in place to prevent contracting officials from playing favorites with a particular company.

7. Myth: Government agencies don't communicate, so I'll never know why I didn't get a contract

Fact: Many jurisdictions now mandate that contracting officials list the reasons why one company was chosen over the competition. You can also request a debriefing with officials to sort out your shortcomings and the winning bidder's strengths.

Source: Onvia *(www.onvia.com)*—a firm that helps business-to-government (B2G) companies achieve a competitive advantage by delivering timely and actionable government procurement opportunities and information. More than 17,700 clients across the United States rely on Onvia as a comprehensive resource for tailored, industry-specific information needed to make intelligent sales decisions. Contact them at 1260 Mercer Street, Seattle, WA 98109. Tel: 206/282-5170.

Things to Do Before Writing Your Government Proposal

It is important for you and your business to understand the precautions to take before writing a government proposal. Here are some important things to consider.

1. Research the project before the bid is released

Establish contact with the client in advance, if possible. Use the Freedom of Information Act and Open Records laws with government agencies to learn as much as possible about the project and the precise needs and expectations of the client. Create a dialog with the buyer, if possible.

2. Provide a clear solution to the client's problem

Clients want to feel that you understand the problem that they are trying to solve and that you actually have a solution. On the other hand, they are suspicious of bidders who just tell them what they already know and provide only vague answers to their questions.

3. Make sound bid/no-bid decisions

Your proposal win rate will dramatically increase once you make rational, logical bid/no-bid decisions. You must make a thorough analysis of each bid to scrutinize your organization's fit with the project, your competition on the bid, and the client.

4. Create the impression that your firm is superior to your competitors

The truth is that in most situations, several bidders are equally capable of meeting the client's needs. Your challenge is to create an impression with your proposal that your firm's approach is unique.

5. Know your competitors

Know the advantages and shortcomings of your competitors. It is also important to know their bidding tendencies. By doing so, you can subtly address their shortcomings in your proposal and know how to position yourself against their tendencies.

6. Highlight the major points of your proposal

Use everything from graphic design to repetition to make sure your major proposal points are understood and remembered. All major points should stress the specific direct benefits to the client.

7. Organize your proposal writing effort

Proposal writing is a time-consuming task. Don't waste time and labor with a poorly organized writing plan. Allow enough time to review and edit it before you submit your proposal.

8. Update your business information regularly to prepare for the next proposal

This will allow you to edit your material with an open mind and a fresh pair of eyes and make important improvements on future bids.

9. Perform the "little things" correctly

Don't let small mistakes kill you. Omitting requested information, exceeding page limits, or word counts, ignoring proposal guidelines, placing information in the incorrect place, or failing to repeat or reiterate information in different sections—these are the small things that will cause you to lose points with an evaluation team.

10. Make a strong, positive last impression

Whether it's in final negotiations or on a site visit, give the client a new reason to accept your proposal. Sometimes this means making a price concession or adding more value to your offer. Sometimes it simply means presenting the client with yet more research on their project to show that you're still thinking about it and working on it, even after the bid deadline.

Source: Randall P. Whatley, president, Cypress Media Group (www.cypressmedia.com)—An advertising, public relations, political consulting, and training firm, Cypress Media Group has been a government contractor for twenty years and advises both

businesses and government agencies on the proposal analysis, writing, and production process. Contact them at PO Box 53198 Atlanta, GA 30355-1198; (770) 640-9918.

Tips to Blunder-Proof Your Government Bid

Make sure your proposals are practical—and your paperwork is perfect. You may have the greatest proposal in the world, but if you fail to present it in a sophisticated, professional manner, you won't get the contract. Here are the common pitfalls to avoid when submitting a bid or proposal.

1. Using complex language

Keep your proposal simple and easy to follow. Use easy-to-understand language and avoid long-winded sentences and paragraphs.

2. Applying for a contract that will place your current projects at risk

All too often, businesses submit proposals or bids they can't fully complete. Before applying for a contract, make sure you possess the skills and resources required to finish the project. Otherwise, you'll find yourself scrambling to meet the contract requirements while your other projects suffer.

3. Not accepting credit cards for payment

Many government agencies now prefer to use merchant credit cards and government purchase cards to buy certain goods and services. If you don't accept plastic, you may miss out on these contracting opportunities. Many contractors also are waking up to the benefits of credit-card transactions. Instead of having to fill out detailed paperwork and wait for a check, they receive immediate payment.

4. Pricing an item unit incorrectly

Many experts say this is the most common mistake made in submitting a bid. A typical example is submitting a bid on gallons when the request was for quarts. A simple error such as this could cost you a contract.

5. Submitting a messy bid

Just as you wouldn't send a coffee-stained business card to a potential client, you should not submit a proposal that is unprofessional in style or appearance. Before you seal the envelope, double-check your document for typos, blank pages, unnumbered or mis-numbered pages, smudges, rips, and poor grammar.

6. Having preconceived notions about what specific agencies need

Don't knock yourself out of consideration by assuming an agency doesn't need your products. You never know, the city of Seattle may, in fact, be looking for scuba equipment. Contact the agency before you decide. Businesses are often pleasantly surprised by what agencies will buy.

7. Focusing on frills rather than on fundamentals

Rather than putting all your effort into dazzling government buyers with your marketing flair, you should concentrate on making your proposal or bid rejection-proof. Begin by responding to each and every requirement in the solicitation. This makes it impossible for the agency to reject you as being nonresponsive to the solicitation. Then, make sure your proposal offers a clear, well-thought-out solution that will solve the problem at hand while calling attention to the direct benefits of your proposal. This makes it impossible for the agency to reject you for not being as qualified as other bidders, and the client cannot reject your bid on the grounds that you will not add value to the contract. Finally, make sure you firmly follow the bid/proposal rules.

8. Not allowing enough time

When it comes to bids and proposals, the clock starts working against you from day one. Not only will you need time to check and recheck your documents, but you'll also need time to read any agency-specific rules and regulations and other information that will help you write your submission. Most important, you'll want to begin calculating the time and materials you will need to fulfill the contract. You'll need this information to determine your bid price—a vital part of the proposal. Finally, make sure you allow enough time for your proposal to reach the agency office before the deadline.

9. Ignoring or underestimating your competitors

A crucial goal of your proposal is to differentiate yourself from your competitors. How much more efficiently will you do the job? Why is your price better than theirs? What benefits will the agency receive if it works with your company instead of your competitor? If you haven't taken time to study and understand your competitors, it's unlikely that you'll beat them to the contract.

10. Inconsistency

Last but not least, it's important to review your bid for consistency before you send it off. Is your work plan in agreement with your budget and schedule? Do your figures add up? Are you consistent with measurements and any other elements that are vital to your proposal?

Source: © July 2004 Onvia, Inc. Used with permission. Onvia (www.onvia.com)—a firm that helps business-to-government (B2G) companies achieve a competitive advantage by delivering timely and actionable government procurement opportunities and information. More than 17,700 clients across the United States rely on Onvia as a comprehensive resource for tailored, industry-specific information needed to make intelligent sales decisions. Onvia also manages the distribution and reporting of requests for proposals and quotes from more than 485 government agencies nationwide. Onvia offers unparalleled coverage of 65,500 federal, state and local purchasing entities and across such markets as architecture, engineering, IT/telecom, consulting services, operations and maintenance, office equipment, transportation and medical equipment. Contact Onvia at 1260 Mercer Street, Seattle, WA 98109. Tel: 206-282-5170.

Working with Investors

Popular Forms of Equity Compensation

Paying your people with equity is a great way to keep them motivated and give them part of the action. But be careful. Equity compensation is a large and somewhat technical subject. Here our expert gives us a list of the different forms of equity compensation

1. Stock options: Qualified (ISOs)

Incentive stock plans are qualified to receive special tax treatment under section 421(a) of the IRS tax code.

2. Stock options: Nonqualified

These options are granted outside of a qualified plan that do not meet requirements for favorable tax treatment.

3. Restricted stock

The recipient is granted shares or a right to purchase shares, often at a discount, whose acquisition or sale is subject to restrictions. Restrictions may include employment tenure, personal performance requirements, or corporate performance requirements.

4. Performance-based stock shares

Stock grants in which the ultimate number of shares and/or the value of the stock is based upon other performance criteria (e.g., earnings per share growth over a three-year period).

5. Stock shares

Stock grants in which there are no set performance criteria or limitations.

6. Stock appreciation rights

The recipient is granted rights to receive only the appreciated value of stock at some future date.

7. Phantom stock

The recipient receives "paper" units for which the value is typically based on the book value of the share of stock at the time of the grant.

8. Employee stock ownership plan (ESOP)

This is a qualified, defined contribution to an employee benefit plan that invests primarily in the stock of the employer company. A company creates a trust fund for employees and funds it through contributions of stock, cash to buy stock, or cash to pay back the ESOP's load to buy stock. The stock thus acquired by the ESOP is then allocated to employee accounts.

9. Employee stock purchase plan (nonqualified)

A nonqualified plan allows employees to set aside money for a specified period into a company account, which is then used to purchase company stock at a specific price. The price is typically set below current market value or less than market value at the beginning of the plan period.

10. Employee stock purchase plan (qualified)

A plan qualified to receive special tax treatment allowing employees to set aside money for a specified period into a company account, which is then used to purchase company stock at a specific price. The price is typically set below current market value or less than market value at the beginning of the plan period.

Source: Culpepper and Associates (*www.culpepper.com*)—Founded in 1979, they conduct worldwide salary surveys and provides benchmark data for compensation and employee benefits programs. Their data spans a full-range of jobs, from board members down through every area, function, and level of tech companies. Contact them at 3600 Mansell Road, Suite 310, Alpharetta, GA 30022; U.S. (770) 641-5400.

Top Ways to Find an Angel Investor

Angels are not average investors: They are people who can afford to indulge their love of risk. According to the Center for Venture Research, about 225,000 angels invested about $22.5 billion in 48,000 businesses in the year 2004. Typically, an angel invests less than $1 million in an early-stage company. Angels provide additional value beyond the funds they provide. Many were successful business owners and entrepreneurs who can also bring you valuable industry experience, executive knowledge, creative ideas, and contacts. Our expert, a well-known business strategist, provides these guidelines for targeting angel investors.

1. Build a convincing case

Angel investors may be willing to take on more risk than most, but they still need to see a well-thought-out plan with a product that has a documented "must have" need and a competent team behind it. It is rare that an entrepreneur can raise money from angels without clearly defining the competitive landscape of the business and how the product has a clear competitive advantage over others. Investors will want to know the barriers to entry. Namely, how you will keep competitors from being in the same exact business. Some barriers to entry might include patents, trade secrets, and proprietary processes.

2. Create a prototype and line up beta testers

Angels do get involved in the early stages of a company, but not usually before there is a working model of the product and potential customers have committed to test the product. Having a prototype will greatly increase your chances of attracting angel investors. Demonstrating that you can get paying customers in the real world puts you far ahead of entrepreneurs who simply have a business plan and an idea. Later-stage companies need to show they have accomplished revenue growth and have paying customers who validate their pricing strategy.

3. Ante up

If you want to start a business, be prepared to invest your own money. Entrepreneurs who expect angels to risk money in their venture, better throw something into the pot. Those entrepreneurs who are not willing to assume such risk are not considered serious by investors, and will most likely not receive funding.

4. Focus your search

Identifying angels who are suitable for you up-front will increase your chances of success. To help you identify appropriate angels when pitching, ask them what they look for in a company, how much they typically invest, what kind of return they expect on their money. In addition, concentrate on your industry, target investors interested in your stage company and deal size, and look close to home look for risk–takers.

5. Make connections

While some investors do read plans that come over the transom, plans referred to them by a trusted source, such as a business associate, lawyer, or accountant, get far more attention. Other options to meet people with deep pockets are to present or at the very least attend a venture capital conference or angel club meeting. Network to find out about these opportunities.

6. Connect personally

Angels spend a lot of time with entrepreneurs especially in the early stages of building a company, so getting along is crucial. Chemistry covers whether you like, trust, and are in sync with each other. To have good chemistry, you have to connect personally and have similar expectations, visions, and objectives for the company. Being able to answer angels' questions without feeling threatened is also crucial.

7. Be persistent and patient

Entrepreneurs must be committed, passionate, and thick-skinned. Raising capital is a time-consuming, ego-challenging process. It is not unusual for a start-up entrepreneur to spend 50 to 70 percent of his time raising capital from angel investors, a process that can average three to six months and in an uncertain market, it takes even longer.

8. Do due diligence on angels

Entrepreneurs should be choosy about who finances them. Make certain that you really know your angel. Understand her motivation and expectations for exit strategy and ROI (return on investment). Know what added value she can bring to the table. Knowledgeable angels with good connections can jump-start a company and keep it thriving. Well-connected angels can even make it easier to get additional rounds of financing including venture capital.

9. Don't haggle over terms

Efforts to horde stock and inflate valuations will make the company less attractive to suitors. Let experienced professionals—lawyers and accountants—handle terms and valuations. Heed their advice.

10. Keep angels informed

Angels want to know how the company is doing whether it is good or bad. Staying in touch by phone, e-mail and even a monthly letter will keep investors happy.

Source: Geri Stengel, a business strategist, president of Stengel Solutions (*www.stengelsolutions.com*)—Stengel Solutions is a strategic planning and marketing firm specializing in solutions for industry leaders, growth businesses, and nonprofits. She can be reached at (212) 362-3088.

Top Questions to Ask an Outside Investor

Getting money from an outside investor can be great for your business; but over time, if you have a fearful, intrusive, or controlling investor, you may soon regret being involved. And there usually isn't an easy way out. You want to spend as much time as you can getting to know your potential investors. To help clarify whether a particular investor is a good fit for you, use these questions.

1. Why are you investing in this business?

2. What aspect of this business is most appealing to you?

3. What other businesses have you invested in before?

4. May I call some entrepreneurs you've invested with before?

5. How soon do you expect to see a return on this investment?

6. How would it affect you if you were to lose the money you're investing?

7. If you felt I wasn't capable of building this company to the stage you'd like, what would you do?

8. How do you see decisions being made? By whom?

9. What role do you want, if any, in the company (e.g., board membership)?

10. Do you understand all the risks in making this investment?

Source: Rhonda Abrams is a nationally syndicated columnist, popular speaker, and bestselling author of books for entrepreneurs. Her books include *The Owner's Manual for Small Business, Winning Presentation In A Day,* and *The Successful Business Plan: Secrets & Strategies.* Her syndicated column appears in USAToday.com

and more than 100 newspapers throughout the United States. Her knowledge of the small business market and her passion for entrepreneurship have made her one of the nation's most recognized advocates for small business. She is president of The Planning Shop. You can register for Rhonda's free business tips newsletter at *www.PlanningShop.com.* 555 Bryant Street, No. 180, Palo Alto CA 94301; (650) 289-9120.

Questions to Ask Your Investment Banker

Hiring the most prestigious investment banker doesn't necessarily translate into greater value or better service for your company. Value and service will generally depend on whether there is a good match between the strengths of the investment bank you use and the needs of your company. This underscores the need to interview and do your due diligence before you select an investment banker. Selecting the right investment banker for your company will include the following factors.

1. Is the bank interested in companies of your size or in your size transaction?

This is the foremost question you should bear in mind before you select your investment banker. It could be possible that your company size is targeting domestic as well as international investors, but the investment banker has neither knowledge nor experience in foreign investment.

2. Does the bank have an investment analyst who is recognized as being strong in your industry and will that analyst issue reports about your company?

Make sure the investment banker also has experienced analysts who have specialized experience relating to the industry in which your company belongs. This is also very important because the analyst should not be spending time and effort in learning the specifics of your business.

3. Does the investment bank's customer base match the types of investors you are seeking (e.g., retail vs. institutional investors or U.S. vs. international)?

Again it is important that the bank's customer base matches your customer base. Otherwise, you would be marrying two different poles and attempting to target investors who have no interest in the line of business in which you are involved.

4. Does the investment bank have a good record of supporting the market price after the transaction is over?

The investment banker should have a good brand image and reputation of supporting the market price. If this is not the case, the market price of your business would fall and that would not be a healthy sign for the growth of your business.

5. Is the investment bank strong in other financial services your company needs?

Evaluate whether the investment banker is providing you with any other ancillary services. Other financial services could include helping you with your proposed IPO or helping you manage your debt-equity ratios.

6. Who will sell your deal?

The investment bankers you meet at the "pitch" are not necessarily the ones who will do the work. These senior bankers are very experienced and have impressive resumes. However, in many cases, you will spend your time dealing with bankers who are a year or two out of business school. Ask to meet and interview the team. Also, ask the senior people to describe exactly what roles they will play. Get the home and cell phone numbers of the senior people and use them as needed throughout the deal.

7. What is your industry experience?

Ask what other companies the bankers have represented in your industry. Have them create a list with the type of deal for each industry client. Success in selling is increasingly dependent on knowledge about special industry markets and which investors are interested in each market. Don't make a decision based on a generic deals list that's not industry specific.

8. Are there any conflicts of interest?

Ask the bankers whether they represent any of your competitors. Ask them to check their database. You may not want to educate them with your confidential information, if they're advising a competitor. Ask what happens to you if a larger competitor is doing a bigger deal and wants the banker to drop you. Get confirmation they will continue working for you.

9. Are you registered?

Investment bankers are subject to extensive government regulation. Most states require them to register with the state securities regulators. Many small placement agents and finders fail to register. Ask whether the banker is registered in all the states in which securities are to be sold. Check with the securities regulators about whether there have been any securities violations by the placement agent or finder.

10. Tell me about your clients.

Ask for references to clients of the investment banker. Ask for references to both clients whose deals closed and clients whose deals did not close.

Source: Jim Verdonik is a principal in Daniels Daniels & Verdonik, PA (*www.d2vlaw.com*)—During his twenty-five years of legal practice in New York and North Carolina, Mr. Verdonik has participated in numerous public offerings, venture capital and seed capital investments, mergers and acquisitions, private placements of securities and license, and other corporate partnership transactions on behalf of both public and private companies. He can be contacted at Daniels Daniels & Verdonik, P.A. Post Office Drawer 12218, Research Triangle Park, NC 27709-2218; (919) 544-5444; e-mail: *jverdonik@d2vlaw.com*.

Popular Investment Bankers

Since 1997 or so, the list of middle-market investment banks that have been subsumed into larger rivals or simply evaporated has been unimaginably long. Surviving that winnowing process has been a major accomplishment. Thriving has been another matter altogether, though a handful of boutiques have managed to do exactly that. The following lists the investment banks that continue to thrive.

1. Jefferies

Jefferies Group, Inc.
520 Madison Avenue
New York, NY 10022
212-284-2300
www.jefferies.com

2. Lehman Brothers

745 Seventh Avenue, 30th Floor
New York, NY 10019
212-526-7000
www.lehman.com

3. Raymond James

Raymond James Financial, Inc.
880 Carillon Parkway
St. Petersburg, FL 33716
727-567-1000
800-248-8863
www.raymondjames.com

4. Bear Stearns

383 Madison Avenue
New York, NY 10179
(212) 272-2000
www.bearstearns.com

5. AMEX Broker Dealer

American Stock Exchange
86 Trinity Place
New York, NY 10006
212-306-1000
www.amex.com

6. Merrill Lynch

Merrill Lynch & Co., Inc.
4 World Financial Center
New York, NY 10080
(212) 449-1000
www.ml.com

7. AG Edwards

A.G. Edwards & Sons, Inc.
Attn: Contact Center

One North Jefferson
St. Louis, MO 63103
www.agedwards.com

8. Goldman Sachs & Co
85 Broad St.
New York, NY 10004
(212) 902-1000
www.gs.com

9. Morgan Stanley
1585 Broadway
New York, NY 10036
(212) 703-4000
www.morganstanley.com

10. Charles Schwab
The Charles Schwab Corporation
101 Montgomery Street
San Francisco, CA 94104
www.schwab.com

11. Knight Capital Group
545 Washington Boulevard
Jersey City, NJ 07310
(201) 222-9400
Fax: (201) 557-6853
Toll Free: (800) 544-7508
www.knight.com

Source: Investment Dealers' Digest *(www.iddmagazine.com)* "Middle Market Bank of the Year," The Survivor. Investment Dealers' Digest is the early warning system for trends, new products, and people moves on Wall Street. Its late-breaking news and authoritative data helps you stay on top of what's happening on Wall Street and in the capital markets each week. You'll find essential news and feature stories, plus listings of newly registered securities, new issues and more. Quarterly rankings and Who's Who listings keep you up-to-date on people and events in the U.S. underwriting, M&A, private placement and other specialized markets. Their brand new Investment Banking Database contains information, by sector, that is unavailable anywhere else in the world, including weekly and year-to-date deals, league table and fee information on a half-dozen investment banking sectors including technology, healthcare and media-telecom, among others.

Typical Fees You'll Pay When Going Public

Offering expenses for an initial public offering are generally substantial. The fees of the underwriter generally constitute the greatest offering expense. In many cases, the indirect expenses associated with a public offering are likely to cost about as much as the direct expenses. Here is a list of the typical fees that companies should anticipate incurring when going public.

1. SEC registration fees

The Securities and Exchange Commission (SEC) is authorized to collect for registrations, mergers, and transactions of securities under section 6(b) of the Securities Act of 1933 (for registrations of securities). These fees are based on the size of the offering or the number of shares outstanding after the offering. Typical SEC fees range from a low of $12,500 to as high as $30,000.

2. NASD filing fees

As the world's leading private-sector provider of financial regulatory services, NASD has helped bring integrity to the markets—and confidence to investors—for more than sixty years. NASD licenses individuals and admits firms to the industry, writes rules to govern their behavior, examines them for regulatory compliance, and disciplines those who fail to comply. These fees are based on the size of the offering or the number of shares outstanding after the offering. Typical NASD fees range from a low of $4,000 to as high as $7,500.

3. Stock exchange and NASDAQ listing fees

There are registration fees involved with the Securities and Exchange Commission (SEC), the National Association of Securities Dealers (NASD), and the various states. For example, you have to register securities under the Blue Sky Laws in each state in which the company plans to do business or sell its securities. The fees associated with the Blue Sky Laws can run as low as $20,000 or less up to $60,000 or more depending on the number of states involved. These fees are based on the size of the offering or the number of shares outstanding after the offering.

4. Printing and engraving fees

Printing can be costly, especially if there is an error with the prospectus. Printing can encompass not only the prospectus but also underwriting documents and other legal documents. Typical fees are in the range of $100,000 to $250,000.

5. Legal fees and expenses for company counsel

Attorneys will review and prepare various documents for regulatory compliance as well as perform due diligence. This usually ranges from $125,000 to $200,000.

6. Accounting fees and expenses

Most IPOs require a set of audited financial statements (not just the current year, but prior years as well). Audit fees are in the range of $75,000 to $200,000.

7. Filing fees and underwriters' attorneys fees for state securities law filings (Blue Sky).

Underwriting is the highest cost associated with going public. Underwriters (investment bankers) collect a percentage of the total amount raised in the public offering (usually around 7%). The more complex the offering is, the higher the underwriting costs will be. Also, the more shares that are sold, the lower the commission paid to the underwriter.

8. Underwriters' discount and expenses

Technically, underwriters do not charge the company a commission. The underwriter purchases the stock from the company at a discount from the public offering price and then resells the stock to the public at the higher public offering price. The underwriters' discount for initial public offerings generally ranges from 6 to 10 percent of the public offering price. In addition, underwriters are often compensated in ways other than the underwriters' discount. These methods of compensation include the issuance of warrants to purchase shares of the company's stock in the future for a price equal to a percentage of the public offering price, generally ranging from 110 to 120 percent.

9. Underwriters' fees for the investment banking consulting agreement

Another form of underwriters' compensation is the requirement that the company enter into an investment banking consulting agreement, which requires fixed monthly payments for a period of two to three years. The agreement may also include a right of first refusal for the underwriter to do future public or private financings for the company. This right of first refusal positions the underwriter to demand a payment from the company or to be included in the deal in a lesser capacity in return for waiving its right of first refusal. Finally, underwriters sometimes require the company to pay the underwriters' expenses. The largest expense is generally the fees of counsel to the underwriters. The fee reimbursement is often expressed as a nonrefundable unaccountable expense allowance. This permits the underwriter to charge a reimbursement that exceeds the underwriters' actual expenses.

10. Directors' and officers' insurance

The largest indirect expense is directors' and officers' insurance. The insurance premium may cost $200,000, and premiums in excess of $500,000 are not unknown.

11. Travel expenses

Travel can also constitute a major indirect expense. The underwriters generally pay the travel expenses associated with the road show, but the officers of the company may have a dozen trips to New York and the West Coast to sell the underwriters on doing the offering.

12. Other administrative costs

Other indirect expenses include hiring additional staff or overtime for salaried employees to handle the administrative tasks associated with the offering and legal, accounting, and other expenses incurred during the six months before the offering that are associated with preparing for the offering.

13. Opportunity cost

Finally, during the time management is preoccupied with the offering, the company will often lose out on opportunities to increase sales. This cost of management time can be the most expensive indirect expense of the offering.

Source: Jim Verdonik is a principal in Daniels Daniels & Verdonik, PA (*www.dv2law.com*). He practices corporate and securities law. During his twenty-five years of legal practice in New York and North Carolina, Mr. Verdonik has participated in numerous public offerings, venture capital and seed capital investments, mergers and acquisitions, private placements of securities, and license and other corporate partnership transactions on behalf of both public and private companies. He can be reached at Daniels Daniels & Verdonik, PA, Generation Plaza, Suite 200, 1822 NC Highway 54 East, Durham, NC 27713; (919) 544-5444; e-mail: *jverdonik@d2vlaw.com*

Typical Benefits of Being a Public Company

When your company needs additional capital, "going public" may be the right choice, but you should weigh your options carefully. If your company is in the very early stages of development, it may be better to seek loans from financial institutions or the Small Business Administration. Other alternatives include raising money by selling securities in transactions that are exempt from the registration process. All public offerings must be registered with the Securities and Exchange Commission (SEC). There are benefits and new obligations that come from raising capital through a public offering.

1. Access to capital

Your access to capital will increase, since you can contact more potential investors.

2. Increases awareness of your company

Your company may become more widely known.

3. Financing may come easier

You may obtain financing more easily in the future if investor interest in your company grows enough to sustain a secondary trading market in your securities.

4. Shareholders can more easily sell interests at retirement

Controlling shareholders, such as the company's officers or directors, may have a ready market for their shares, which means that they can more easily sell their interests at retirement, for diversification, or for some other reason.

5. Helps attract and retain quality employees

Your company may be able to attract and retain more highly qualified personnel if can offer stock options, bonuses, or other incentives with a known market value.

6. Better company image

The image of your company may be improved.

Source: Small Business Notes *(www.smallbusinessnotes.com)*—Provides information and resources for other businesses struggling to provide that same quality in a challenging economic environment. Their purpose is to provide the resources for all the information that a small business needs to operate. Contact the editor of Small Business Notes, Judith Kautz by sending e-mail to *info@smallbusinessnotes.com*.

What to Do as an Alternative to the Initial Public Offering (IPO)

It is important to remember that the IPO, a company's first public sale of equity, is the most expensive method of raising capital. The fees required by the investment banker in order to prepare the company for the IPO—a thorough audit of a minimum of five years of financial records, filing of the necessary paperwork with a variety of regulatory agencies, establishing the optimal stock price, dealing with any number of open issues like outstanding lawsuits, product liability, a severe number of customer complaints—can run to millions of dollars. If management's primary requirement is growth capital, there are several avenues that our expert suggests are worth exploring prior to committing to an IPO.

1. Bank loans

Providing the business has a reasonable credit rating and good banking relationships, this is the least expensive method of raising expansion capital, a far less expensive alternative than the sale of equity.

2. Accounts receivable financing of factoring

This is a common asset-based loan, in which a financial institution buys the company's accounts receivables and collects the debt.

3. Equipment loans

Another asset-based loan, these are made by financial institutions for the purpose of buying specific machinery or equipment for the company. The financial institution holds title to the equipment until the loan is paid, in the event of default.

4. Contract loans

Financial institutions will advance funds against a specific contract, based on the credit worthiness of both parties of the bi-lateral agreement. As the contract is fulfilled, the funds are collected and distributed, by prior agreement, by the financier.

5. Loans from current shareholders

Members of the company's management team and its board of directors that are in a position to do so may wish to lend funds to the company in exchange for future considerations such as a favorable interest rate, equity claims, or some other consideration that furthers the lender's self-interest vis-à-vis the business.

6. Friends and relatives of the company

Private equity can be provided from a number of sources, but ideally it should come from a party with an interest in the company's business and not just a money source (e.g., venture capital), which can be as expensive as an IPO. A sibling, cousin, child of an owner with investable funds that is interested in learning and, eventually, managing the business, is an excellent option for owners' plan to sell equity.

7. Strategic Partners

These are companies or individuals with an interest in the business. Typically, these include suppliers, distributors, key customers, or competitors. By investing in your business, these players provide capital for expansion, liquidity for the current owners, and, most importantly, a dedicated interest in expanding the business successfully.

Source: Don Grede has 25 years of experience in business-to-business marketing of leading-edge technologies and services for early and mid-stage ventures. His firm, The Aspen Alliance (www.theaspenalliance.com) provides consulting and management services to companies seeking to increase their market value. He is an effective corporate spokesman, introducing new technologies and services to the investment analyst community, and at trade shows and conferences. As an entrepreneur, Don co-founded, operated and sold the premiere sales application software company in the television industry. He holds an MS/MBA from M.I.T.'s Sloan School of Management. He can be reached at don@theaspenalliance.com

Typical SEC Exemptions for an Initial Public Offering

Most companies will file Form S-1 for full registration with the SEC. However, there are some exemptions to Form S-1 for those that qualify. How can you get around this dreaded process? This list gives you a few ways.

1. Regulation A offerings

Small public offerings (Regulation A) are exempt from formal registration provided that the company is a U.S. or Canadian company, the total offering cannot exceed $5 million over a twelve-month period, the offering cannot represent a resale of stock by an affiliated company if the issuing company has not had income for at least one of the last two prior fiscal years, and the issuing company cannot be an investment or public company. These securities can be freely traded in the secondary market. The advantages of a Regulation A offering as opposed to a full registration are simpler financial statements and generally no Exchange Act reporting obligations after the offering is made. However, you still must file with the SEC on Form 1-A, which includes a set of financial statements in accordance with GAAP (generally accepted accounting principles); but it is not audited.

2. Regulation D Rule 504

This rule is considered by many to be the perfect answer for the small company that needs to raise up to $1 million but can't afford the time or expense to go through the entire SEC registration process. Under the Rule 504 exemption, a company can offer up to $1 million of securities in a twelve-month period. The important characteristics are securities (both debt and equity) can be sold to an unlimited number of persons, general solicitation or advertising can be used to market these securities, and the securities are freely traded and not "restricted." This means investors may sell their securities on the open market without registration or other sales limitations that are on privately placed securities and audited financials are not required.

3. Regulation D Rule 505

Rule 505 provides an exemption for offers and sales of securities totaling up to $5 million in any twelve-month period, selling to an unlimited number of "accredited investors" and up to thirty-five other persons. The issued securities are "restricted" and may not be sold for at least a year without registering the transaction.

4. Regulation D Rule 506

Under this exemption, you can raise an unlimited amount of capital, cannot use general solicitation or advertising to market the securities, can sell securities to an unlimited number of accredited investors and up to thirty-five other "sophisticated" purchasers, financial statements must be certified, and purchasers receive "restricted" securities. Consequently, purchasers may not freely trade the securities in the secondary market immediately after the offering.

Source: The Wall Street Organization (*www.wallstreetorganization. com*)—This state-of-the-art online investment banking and financial public relations firm uses proprietary technology to assist companies interested in learning about various types of securities offerings and corporate issuers seeking alternative capital-formation avenues. Contact them at 67 Wall Street, 22nd Floor, New York, NY 10005-3198; (212) 731-0761; e-mail: *contact@wallstreetorga nization.com*.

Typical SEC Filings for an Initial Public Offering

Although there are more than 360 different SEC form types, the twenty-five most common account for 75 percent of all SEC documents filed each year, and the ten most frequent account for over half. Here are the top ten from one of the top providers of online business and financial filing information.

1. 10-Q (quarterly report): 11.6%

2. 8-K (unscheduled material event): 10.4%

3. SC 13G/A (amended filing of beneficial owner): 5.0%

4. 497 (investment company prospectus): 4.6%

5. SC 13G (filing of beneficial owner): 4.2%

6. DEF 14A (proxy): 3.7%

7. N-30D (fund manager's semiannual report): 3.3%

8. Form 4 (insider sales and purchases): 3.2%

9. 24F-2NT (investment company registration of securities): 3.2%

10. 10-QSB (quarterly report, small business issuer): 3.0%

Source: EDGAR Online, Inc. (*www.edgar-online.com*)—A leading provider of value-added business and financial information on global companies to financial, corporate, and advisory professionals, the company makes its information and a variety of analysis tools available via online subscriptions and licensing agreements to a large user base. Contact them at 50 Washington Street, 9th Floor, Norwalk, CT 06854; (800) 416-6651.

Reasons Not to Go after Venture Capital

A venture capitalist is a highly specialized investor who provides capital to early-stage technology companies for expansion. These companies already have sales to bona fide customers but require additional funding to fuel rapid growth. There are many problems associated with venture capital. It is very important to understand that although venture capitalists provide financing for companies, they are not the entrepreneur's friend. It is common for a venture capital firm to fire the founding team within months of financing and replace them with executives the firm knows and trusts. So the entrepreneur seeking to create a job for himself or herself should forget about this financing source. Here are a few more problems associated with venture capitalists and the pursuit of their money.

1. Provide a tempting distraction from the real work

Chasing venture capital at the beginning is often a tempting distraction from the much more complex and important entrepreneurial tasks of creating something to sell and persuading someone to buy it. Some rookie entrepreneurs chase venture capital as a means of postponing the day of reckoning when the marketplace finally decides if their idea will fly.

2. Invest only in "hot" high-growth sectors

Most venture capitalists behave like sheep investing only in whichever industry happens to be the "flavor of the month." Everyone else need not apply. Many entrepreneurs waste time by not doing their homework to find out what industries a venture capitalist invests in before making contact.

3. Are never in a hurry to do a deal

Typically, companies seeking funding are under financial pressure to close a deal—any deal, in many cases. Meanwhile the venture capitalist, who is looking at a dozen new deals each and every day, feels no pressure to do anything. This imbalance in power gives him a tremendous advantage in negotiations.

4. Often try to extract last-minute concessions

Once financing negotiations begin, some venture capitalists will stall in order to push cash-short companies to the brink of bankruptcy as a means of extracting additional equity and concessions at the last moment.

5. Deal terms

Terms demanded by greedy venture capitalists can often erode and ultimately destroy the founding team's motivation and commitment to building a successful company.

6. May lead to loss of entrepreneur's control

With the first dollar of venture capital accepted, the entrepreneur becomes a de facto employee of the company. He or she may be fired at will and forced to walk away with little or no reward for work performed to date.

7. May result in more bureaucracy

As soon as venture capitalists become involved, the founder's role shifts from critical company building functions to preparing reports, attending endless meetings, writing memos, and hand-holding impatient and/or meddlesome investors. Ironically, many entrepreneurs leave the corporate world to escape these functions.

8. Creates pressure for a liquidity event

Venture capital brings with it tremendous pressure to create a liquidity event, such as an IPO, but this frequently results in bad decisions being made to launch products too early or enter into the wrong markets.

9. Avoids responsibility for bad decisions

The venture capitalist's knee-jerk response to almost every problem faced by a portfolio company is to fire the founders and evade any personal responsibility for driving bad decisions.

10. Costly

Perhaps the most significant reason venture capital is not a preferred option is that it is very expensive. Venture capitalists demand a very high rate of return on their money, which can result in little being left over for those who build the company.

Source: Peter Ireland of the Smart Startup (*www.antiventurecapital. com*)—Providing solutions for startup funding problems for almost two decades, Ireland has raised capital for his own ventures as well as helped other entrepreneurs. In terms of experience, he has held executive positions with a number of corporations both private and publicly held.

How to Approach a Venture Capitalist

Far too many entrepreneurs do not understand the role of venture capital. Many myths and misconceptions abound, and as a result, most entrepreneurs fail to secure capital after approaching a venture capitalist. The following list provides some insights into to the world of venture capital: what works, what doesn't, what they are looking for, and what they are not.

1. Have a going concern (e.g., a real company)

Venture capitalists do not invest in ideas. Friends, family, and fools invest in ideas. If you want to have a chance with raising venture capital, have a real company, one with a developed product, customers, revenues, and ideally, profits.

2. Know what they invest in

Know if a venture capitalist actually invests in your *kind* of company. If you have a software company, you are wasting your time if you contact an investor who only invests in medical device and drug discovery deals.

3. Have a company with a scalable revenue model

They are especially interested in going concerns that feature highly scalable revenue models. Scale means the average sale price is very large (usually six figures or above) and/or sales repeat themselves on a regular basis with little or no added effort by the company. For example, an Internet Service Provider selling monthly subscriptions has a scalable business model.

4. Have a defensible position

This means intellectual property or a well-known (and well liked) brand name.

5. Be objective about your company

Stick to the deal facts; be objective. If you decide to take a subjective approach and tout how great your company is, or if you hard-sell, you'll sound like a snake oil salesman, and you'll lose the deal. If your company has "warts" (and all companies do), it is better to disclose those issues early in the process instead of burying the problems and hoping the investor doesn't discover the problem(s).

6. Give direct answers

You will be asked very direct questions. Learn to provide direct answers.

7. Stick to the facts

Omit a recap of business history in your plan and/or presentations. They know these things. Stick to the facts; namely, how much money the company has already earned, and how much more you'll earn once you get an investment.

8. Know the specifics

Know how, why, and where the investment will be spent, and how, why, and when this will result in revenues and profits.

9. Remember this will not be easy

Prepare to sell your soul. Raising venture capital is the most difficult, most costly, and most frustrating experience you'll ever have.

10. Remember who controls the deal

The person with the money. Entrepreneurs need investors more than venture capitalists need entrepreneurs. Most review hundreds, if not thousands, of plans every year. Most invest in a handful of those deals, maybe five to twenty per year. While an entrepreneur thinks she has a "great idea," remember that VCs see hundreds of "great ideas" every month. The competition is intense.

Source: This list was culled from the writings of Bill Snow, including his e-book *Venture Capital 101*. Bill is the cofounder of VC Fodder, the Internet's top source for down-to-earth, accurate, and humorous assistance and advice for entrepreneurs of all shapes and success levels. Bill is also an investment banker for Chicago-based boutique

Kinsella Group Inc. You can learn more about Bill at *www.vcfodder. com*, or at his personal Web site, *www.billsnow.com*. You can contact Bill by e-mail at *bill@vcfodder.com*.

Ways to Attract Investors

How do I attract investors? That's a question asked by many entrepreneurs. Finding investors is tough, but it's not impossible. If you need outside investment money to start and successfully run your business, this list is a must-read. Investment is a key element of growth for small businesses. But acquiring investors can sometimes seem like an insurmountable task, leaving business owners with the idea that they will have to rely solely on their friends and family members to invest in their company. The fact is that there are plenty of people who are willing to invest in your business, but only if they have a reasonable expectation that they will receive a return on their investment. Your job is to convince them that they will receive a return by laying a solid foundation for investment.

1. Have a business plan

First and foremost, investors want to know that you have a plan for your business. A make-it-up-as-you-go approach simply will not cut it. A good business plan is a well-researched road map that spells out the goals and strategies that will be required to achieve real growth. It should also include information about your competition and market research that indicates how effective your strategies will be in the marketplace.

2. Have written investor agreements

Be prepared to present potential investors with a written agreement dictating the terms of their investment and an exit strategy detailing the process for divestment. A written investor agreement accomplishes several things. It communicates to investors that you are serious about investment and indicates that you have taken steps to prepare for it. It boosts investor confidence because it clearly spells out what will be expected of them should they decide to invest in your business as well as legal security for their investment. At the same time, it safeguards your rights and responsibilities by providing you with a documented agreement regarding the scope of the investment relationship.

3. Track record of growth

One of the most important things you can do to attract potential investors to your business is to demonstrate a track record of growth. Investors like to invest in companies that have a proven ability to achieve bottom line growth. You don't necessarily have to set the world on fire, but you do need to be able to show investors that you are able to consistently set and meet your goals.

4. Produce healthy financial statements

Along with a track record of growth, investors will also want to see financial statements that correspond with the goals and strategies laid out in the business plan. If the numbers indicate that your company is in the midst of a financial crisis or if they don't back up the expectations you have communicated to them, investors will be leery to commit. It's not a bad idea to go over your financial statements with your accountant before you approach potential investors. In some cases, you might be able to take steps to make your financials more attractive for investment.

Source: Gaebler Ventures is a Chicago-based business incubator and holding company that develops and nurtures companies that are shaping the future. For additional information, visit www.gaebler.com.

Common Downsides of Venture Capital Financing

So you've got your company up and running and want to take the next step and accelerate your growth. Time to go get some venture money, right? Maybe not. Few entrepreneurs focus on the laundry list of pitfalls of taking money from venture capitalists. Although there are many benefits to becoming a venture-funded company, there are some downsides that you should consider. Here are a few from our expert VC.

1. One ultimate goal for your company

Plenty of VCs are great people, and many can add value to your business in the form of market insight, connections with customers. Ultimately, however, they invest in your company for one reason: to make money. This means that your business needs to be sold or to go public in order for their investment to be a success. These may be your goals for the company as well, but the pressures of finding an exit will naturally change the decisions you make as you build your business. While venture capitalists may be supportive of some of the other reasons you wanted to found your company (create a great culture, have a fun place to work, build a real company, etc.), this support is about furthering the goal of finding an exit for their investment.

2. A different risk profile than yours

For the most part, they have a very different view of risk than you do. They didn't mortgage their house to start your business; they didn't work for a reduced (or no) salary for several years to get your company up and running; if your business fails, they still have a job the next morning. While good venture capitalists are generally pretty sensitive to the wishes of entrepreneurs, there is a fundamental difference in the risk tolerance they will have for your business; a difference that can lead to different decisions when faced with the same set of facts (for instance, if an early offer comes in to buy the company).

3. A short- to medium-term time horizon

Most venture funds have a ten-year life; that is, after ten years, they need to distribute whatever remains in their portfolio directly to their investors. There are some ways they can extend this, but ultimately every venture fund has a finite life. As the end of that life approaches, there is more pressure to create liquidity events (i.e., sell portfolio companies). Ten years may seem like a long way off in the start-up world, but it can pass more quickly than you think. Also don't forget that this is ten years from the start of the fund, not ten years from the time they invest in your company—depending on where a fund is in its life, they can have as little as five years left in their fund horizon.

4. Venture capitalists' opinions

This should be obvious, but rare is the early-stage venture capitalist that gives a company money, asks for quarterly updates, and then pretty much leaves them alone. For starters, they have a fiduciary obligation to their investors to be good stewards of their money, and part of this obligation is to keep regular tabs on the companies in which they've invested. Mostly though, they believe that they have something to add to the mix. Venture capitalists see lots of different business situations, experience similar challenges across businesses, and believe they can offer the benefit of both their own operating experience (since most have some type of operating background) as well as the experiences of the rest of their portfolio. If you take their money, you are going to hear plenty of suggestions on how to better run your company—"your" business becomes "our" business as well.

5. Lose control

Essentially all investments come with strings attached, in the form of shareholder agreements and protective provisions. At a minimum, these will likely give your investors a seat (if not several seats) on the board as well as the ability to veto certain decisions (such as merging or selling the company, taking on debt, declaring a dividend, etc.). Because of their ownership of your company, they'll have a vote in any shareholder matter, and because they will likely hold preferred shares (and you will hold common shares), they

will be able to exert significant influence on the financing and operating strategy of your company. This includes firing you, if things do not go as planned. While most have a positive relationship with the companies in their portfolio (and their founders), things happen in the course of the life of a business that sometimes create rifts between founders and their venture backers. Remember that when you take venture money, you have a new level of responsibility to your investors—both by virtue of the stewardship you now have of their investment capital and because of the power you gave up to them in the process of taking that capital.

Source: Seth Levine is a principal with Mobius Venture Capital, a $2 billion venture firm with offices in Palo Alto, California, and Superior, Colorado. Seth focuses on new technology investments in the enterprise services, enterprise software, and infrastructure spaces. He's on the board of several early-stage technology companies and an adviser to numerous other businesses. Seth also writes a popular blog about the business of venture capital at *http://sethlevine .typepad.com*. He can be reached by e-mail at *seth@mobiusvc.com*.

Typical Terms of Venture Capital–Financing Agreements

Our expert, a venture capitalist, knows lots and lots of complicated terms that could make any small business owner's head spin! But here he provides us a list of some of the more typical terms you should familiarize yourself with if you're looking into a venture capital deal.

1. Price

All deals have a "price." Unfortunately, the actual price per share of stock in a venture capital deal is rarely the only factor in the actual "price of the deal," although it is often the term that entrepreneurs focus the most on. Venture capitalists will often talk about "premoney" (the valuation before the money is invested in the company) and "postmoney" (the valuation after the money is invested in the company). Price per share in both situations will be equal; the postmoney valuation is equal to the premoney valuation plus the amount invested.

2. Liquidation preference

The liquidation preference determines how the pie is shared on a liquidity event (sale, merger, wind down). Most investors will get their money out first, followed by the common shareholders (founders, employees, and option holders). Liquidation preferences can be simple (e.g., the venture capitalist either gets his liquidation preference or he converts into common stock and gets his percentage of the company) or complex (e.g., with a "participating preferred," he will get his money out first and then convert into common stock and get his percentage of the company).

3. Protective provisions

They typically want to have meaningful control of any company they invest in. One of the ways they do this is through the protective provisions, which are effectively vetoes on certain actions by the company. These provisions require that the venture capitalist agrees for the company to be able to do a number of things, such as issue new classes of stock, sell the company, repurchase stock, change the certificate of incorporation or bylaws, change the board of directors, or borrow money in excess of a certain amount.

4. Antidilution

When they invest, they buy shares at a certain price. They typically include an "antidilution" provision to protect themselves from share sales via investment at a lower price (including shares sold to them in the future). While almost all these deals have something called "weighted-average antidilution" (this gives them some downside protection), some deals will have "full-ratchet anti-dilution" (if shares are issued in the future at a lower price, the previous shares issued will be adjusted down to that same lower price).

5. Redemption rights

Venture capitalists invest with a three- to seven-year time horizon on investments. After holding an investment for five years, they start to consider ways to get liquidity (e.g., sell their investment). The redemption rights clause in a financing agreement gives them some leverage to start to agitate for liquidity, especially if the company is "sort of successful" (e.g., generating some profits, but not growing very fast).

6. Vesting

They want to make sure there is an incentive for the founder and employees to stay at a company after their investment. The primary tool for this is through a vesting agreement where stock and options will "vest" over four years. This means that you have to be around for four years to own all of your stock or options. If you leave the company earlier, the vesting formula applies and you only get a percentage of your stock.

7. Information rights

When they invest, they typically end up with a minority (less than 50%) interest, but they want to make sure that they have a contractual right to be informed of the activities at the company. "Information rights" provides this capability and is a standard feature in venture capital deals.

8. Registration rights

One of the possible successful outcomes of a venture-backed company is an IPO. They fantasize about this when they make their initial investment and correspondingly load up the terms associated with registering their stock in and around an IPO. These terms rarely come into play, both because the IPO is a rare event for a start-up and because most of them get renegotiated in the IPO anyway. Our advice to entrepreneurs: don't worry about these too much.

9. Right of first refusal

When venture capitalists make an initial investment in a company, they almost always expect to make investments again in the company. They want to reserve the "right of first refusal" to be able to participate at least up to the level that maintains their ownership in later financings.

10. No-shop agreement

Once a venture capitalist wants to invest in your company, you negotiate a term sheet that lays out the terms listed here, among others.

This term sheet is simply an outline of the deal; you still have work to do to draft the definitive agreements, have the venture capitalist complete due diligence, and close the financing. During the period between the signing of the term sheet and closing the financing, they will almost always want the company to sign a no-shop provision. This reinforces the handshake that says "okay, let's get a deal done—no more fooling around looking for a better/different one." In all cases, bind the no-shop by a time period; usually forty-five to sixty days is plenty.

Source: Brad Feld is a managing director at Mobius Venture Capital and lives in Boulder, Colorado, and Homer, Alaska. Prior to Mobius, Brad founded Feld Technologies, which was sold to Ameri-Data Technologies in 1993. Brad currently serves on the boards of a number of private companies and several non-profit organizations. He writes extensively on venture capital and entrepreneurship on his blog, which can be found at *www.feld.com*. The best way to contact Brad is by e-mail at *brad@feld.com*.

Where You Work

The Road Warrior

Best Places to Find Cheap Airfare

Our resident travel expert says that to get the best fare you need to use the Internet as your research tool. Most of the major travel search engines will provide you with a baseline of prevailing fares. Check at least two of the sites listed and then go directly to the airline's Web site to see if the airline will give a better price directly. Booking directly also helps you to earn more points and upgrades.

1. TripStalker

This free software program searches or stalk on the Internet for the best airfares. You enter your exact travel criteria for up to three trips (or stalks), which triggers ongoing queries to travel providers. You are alerted via desktop, e-mail, or SMS text messaging on your phone when the price drops below the requested price. Once alerted, you can modify and book directly through your airline. TripStalker is different from other low-fare search engines because it constantly stalks the Internet for your specific travel criteria, giving you the best deal without all the hassle and hard work.

www.tripstalker.com

2. SideStep

This site offers a free plug-in that finds airfares, rental cars, and hotels.

www.sidestep.com

3. BookingBuddy.com

This site compares airfare at the major travel sites. It searches more than airline and travel agency sites to find great low airfares on the Web.

www.bookingbuddy.com

4. Travelocity

Find cheap airfare for your trip with Travelocity's Flexible Dates shopping.

www.travelocity.com

5. Travelzoo

Compare airline tickets on multiple travel sites and then book direct for maximum savings and rewards.

www.travelzoo.com

6. Expedia

A one-stop source for checking airfares.

www.expedia.com

7. CheapTickets

Compare airfare, and sort by schedule or price.

www.cheaptickets.com

8. Orbitz

Sort flights by price, departure time, duration, and airline.

www.orbitz.com

Source: Joel Widzer, PsyD, is an expert on consumer loyalty and frequent-flier programs. He is the author of *The Penny Pincher's Passport to Luxury Travel* and a contributor to MSNBC. His consulting firm, *www.jetready.com*, advises travelers and businesses on a range of issues from maximizing their travel programs to managing travel fatigue. He can be reached at (714) 544-2855.

Largest Frequent-Flier Programs

Frequent-flier programs are popular. Recent figures report that there are more than 163 million members, 112 million within the United States with an astounding 10 trillion miles available for award use. Deciding which program is best for you should center on what airline (and codeshare partners) serves your hometown airport with the routes you're most likely to fly. An additional consideration is your likelihood for achieving elite status. If you're a low-frequency flier you might consider a program that has fewer members so you're not competing with ultra fliers for upgrades and preferred perks. While actual membership's numbers are not released by airlines, the following list is generally consider the ranking order of top frequent-flier programs.

1. American Airlines—AAdvantage
Alliance Partner Oneworld
www.oneworld.com
MD 5400, PO Box 619688
Dallas–Fort Worth Airport, TX 75261-9688
(800) 882-8880
www.aa.com

American AAdvantage is considered the largest frequent flyer program with roughly 46 million members.

2. United Airlines—United Mileage Plus
Alliance Partner Star Alliance
www.star-alliance.com
Mail: Mileage Plus Service Center
PO Box 28870
Tucson, AZ 85726-8870
(800) 421-4655
www.ual.com

3. Delta Air Lines—Delta Sky Miles
Alliance Partner SkyTeam
www.skyteam.com
Delta Air Lines, Dept. 745
SkyMiles Service Center
PO Box 20532
Atlanta, GA 30320-2532
(800) 323-2323
www.delta.com

4. Continental Airlines—One Pass
Alliance Partner SkyTeam
www.skyteam.com
OnePass Service Center
PO Box 4658
Houston, TX 77210-4658
(713) 952-1630
onepass@coair.com

5. Northwest Airlines—WorldPerks
Alliance Partner SkyTeam
www.skyteam.com
WorldPerks Customer Service Center
601 Oak Street
Chisholm, MN 55719-1995
(800) 327-2881
www.nwa.com

6. US Airways/American West—Dividend Miles
Alliance Partner Star Alliance
www.star-alliance.com
US Airways
Dividend Miles Service Center
PO Box 5
Winston-Salem, NC 27102-0005
DividendMiles@usairways.com

7. Alaska Airlines/Horizon Air—Mileage Plan
Customer Care
PO Box 24948
Seattle, WA 98124-0948
(800) 654-5669
www.alaskaair.com

Earn and redeem Mileage Plan Miles on Alaska Airlines or any of their thirteen airline partners.

Source: Joel Widzer, PsyD, is an expert on consumer loyalty and frequent-flier programs. He is the author of *The Penny Pincher's Passport to Luxury Travel* and a contributor to MSNBC. His consulting firm, *www.jetready.com,* advises travelers and businesses on a range of issues from maximizing their travel programs to managing travel fatigue. He can be reached at (714) 544-2855.

Most Popular Hotel-Reward Programs

Hotel-reward programs are an excellent tool for achieving greater productivity and cost savings. As with any loyalty program, consolidation is important. Getting the best benefits come with loyalty. Use at least two programs to provide geographical coverage but not more than three to maximize frequency of visits. If you anticipate only a moderate level of hotel visits (5 to 10 per year), look for a program with fewer members, so that upgrades and more comfortable rooms remain available to you.

Here is a list of the most popular hotel-reward programs, according to our resident travel expert.

1. Marriott Hotel and Resorts
Marriott Rewards
310 Bearcat Drive
Salt Lake City, UT 84115-2544
(800) 450-4442
Fax: (801) 468-4033
www.marriottrewards.com

In sixty countries, there are 2,700 hotels, including Marriott Hotels & Resorts, JW Marriott Hotels & Resorts, Renaissance Hotels & Resorts, Courtyard by Marriott, Residence Inn by Marriott, Fairfield Inn by Marriott, Marriott Conference Centers, TownePlace Suites by Marriott, SpringHill Suites by Marriott, Marriott Vacation Club International, Horizons by Marriott, and The Ritz-Carlton Hotel. Marriott's reward program offers flexibility and hotels ranging from the upscale to less expensive limited-services hotels.

2. Hilton Hotels
Hilton Honors (HHonors)
PO Box 9003
Addison, TX 75001-9003
(800) 548-8690
Fax: (972) 788-1818
www.hiltonhhonors.com
E-mail: *hhonors@hilton.com*

In eighty countries, there are 2,800 hotels: Hilton, Conrad Hotels, Doubletree, Embassy Suites Hotels, Hampton Inn, Hampton Inn & Suites, Hilton Garden Inn, Homewood Suites by Hilton, and Scandic Hotels. Hilton HHonors allows "double dipping," where you can earn both hotel points and airline miles for the same stay. Their reward program has consistently received top rankings from business travelers.

3. Hyatt Hotels and Resorts

Hyatt Gold Passport
Customer Service Center
PO Box 27089
Omaha, NE 68127-0089
(800) 544-9288
Fax: (402) 593-9449
www.goldpassport.com

In forty countries, there are 213 hotels, including Hyatt, Hyatt Regency, Grand Hyatt, Park Hyatt, Hyatt Place, and Hawthorn Suites. Hyatt Hotels consistently offers high–quality, comfortable rooms from their Hyatt Regency to Park Hyatt Brand.

4. Starwood Hotel and Resorts

Starwood Preferred Guest (SPG)
800 Talbot St.
St. Thomas, ON Canada N5P1E2
(888) 625-4988
Fax: (519) 633-8557
www.spg.com
E-mail: *customercare@starwoodhotels.com*

In sixty countries, there are 725 hotels, Sheraton, Four Points, St. Regis, The Luxury Collection, Le Meridien, W Hotels, and Westin Hotels. Starwood Hotels are considered one of the best hotel chains for business travelers, offering a variety of business-oriented hotels. Members earn two Starpoints for every eligible U.S. dollar spent.

5. InterContinental Hotels Group

Priority Club Rewards
PO 30320
Salt Lake City UT 85130
(800) 272-9273

Fax: (800) 725-8232
www.priorityclub.com
E-mail: *PriorityClub@ichotelsgroup.com*

In 150 countries, there are 3,500 hotels, including Inter Continental, Crowne Plaza, Holiday Inn, Holiday Inn Select, Holiday Inn Express, Staybridge Suites, and Candlewood Suites. Priority reward members can earn elite status quickly among a large number of world-wide hotels.

6. Four Seasons Hotels

1165 Leslie Street
Toronto, ON M3C 2K8 Canada
(800) 819-5053
www.fourseasons.com

There are sixty-eight hotels in thirty-one countries. The Four Seasons does not officially offer a reward program. However, past stays are recorded, and upgrades and special amenities are offered based on historical performance with the brand.

7. Leading Hotels of the World

Leaders Club
c/o The Leading Hotels of the World
99 Park Avenue, 10th floor
New York, NY 10016
(800) 650-2582
www.lhw.com
E-mail: *theleadersclub@lhw.com*

With 420 hotels worldwide, the Leaders Club is an invitation-only program. Members are selected by program hotels or directly from the Leading Hotels of the World. A collection of first-class hotels offers unparalleled luxury for business travelers worldwide.

Source: Joel Widzer, PsyD, is an expert on consumer loyalty and frequent-flier programs. He is the author of *The Penny Pincher's Passport to Luxury Travel* and a contributor to MSNBC. His consulting firm, *www.jetready.com*, advises travelers and businesses on a range of issues from maximizing their travel programs to managing travel fatigue. He can be reached at (714) 544-2855.

Top Ways to Get a Hotel Room Upgrade

Our resident travel expert says that one of the biggest hotel aggravations is knowing that while you're crammed into a closet, luxury suites sit empty. Here are a few of his tips for getting luxurious upgrades.

1. Book direct

When you book your hotel rooms directly, you do the hotel a favor by saving them distribution or commission cost. They often return the favor in terms of upgrades. Hotel companies like Hilton, Starwood, Marriott, Radisson, and others offer "best rate" guarantees. So, by booking direct, you can get a great deal.

2. Build your loyalty

By dealing directly with the hotel, you build loyalty. That's important because loyalty can pay off in upgrades. Loyalty can be easily leveraged. If you're in a lobby full of convention attendees who are only in the area for a long weekend, and not likely to return, stress your loyalty to the person helping you. Tell them that you love the hotel and you'd like to come back. You'll be the perfect choice for an upgrade.

3. Time your arrival

Most hotel guests check out between 12 and 2 P.M. Business travelers tend to check in around 5 P.M. and after. Time your check-in between 3 and 5 P.M. so the good rooms are still available. If you can't make it between these times, call the hotel and inquire about your room type. Usually you can get the hotel to block a nice room before your arrival.

4. Think competitively

Call reservations managers at two competing hotels; explain that you're trying to decide which hotel will offer better value and let a bidding war ensue. This can reap inexpensive rooms and a nice upgrade.

5. Get on the list

Call ahead and ask the hotel's manager to place a note in the computer regarding a request for an upgrade. Requests with the boss's name get results.

6. Write for results

Tell the desk agent you would be happy to write a note to management about how helpful they are. Hotel staff members love letters because it becomes a part of their permanent personnel record helping them get raises and promotions.

7. Tip wisely

Getting escorted to your room by a bellperson? Offer them a $20 tip to help you score a nicer room.

Source: Joel Widzer, PsyD, is an expert on consumer loyalty and frequent-flier programs. He is the author of *The Penny Pincher's Passport to Luxury Travel* and a contributor to MSNBC. His consulting firm, *www.jetready.com*, advises travelers and businesses on a range of issues from maximizing their travel programs to managing travel fatigue. He can be reached at (714) 544-2855.

Best Ways to Save Money on Hotel Rooms

As a business traveler, your hotel room becomes your office on the road. Getting the most value for your hotels is easy with these few simple tips.

1. Book direct

The best rates are often found directly on a hotel's Web site. An added benefit of booking direct is upgrades. By booking directly on a hotelier's Web site, you lower their distribution costs, and the favor is often retuned in the form of a nice room upgrade or suite.

2. Remember supply and demand

The first economic principle I learned in college was the law of supply and demand. With hotels, this means offering special incentives when rooms would otherwise go empty. I have often traveled to Manhattan (a city famous for their high hotel rates) and gotten a good deal at the Grand Hyatt when this large hotel has empty rooms. Since most business travelers do not have the luxury of flexibility, the best method for determining where to bring your bags is research. A search on the Internet or quick chat with a travel agent will tell you which hotels are experiencing peak demands and which ones are not.

3. Ask about concierge floors

Concierge or executive floors can offer the busy business traveler great value. Not only can you catch a tasty breakfast and coffee in the morning, they can serve as a nice area to meet with clients or interview prospective employees. Staffed with dedicated agents who can arrange transportation, pick up and deliver dry cleaning, and send faxes, you can really save a bundle of time and money.

4. Make memberships pay

If you can show evidence of membership in organizations such as the American Automobile Association (AAA) or the American Association of Retired Persons (AARP), you'll save an additional 20 to 25 percent. Paying with an American Express Business Card at the Hyatt Hotels will yield a 3 percent savings

5. Leverage loyalty

Now that you've got the best basic price and a well-planned journey, it's time to get a little more luxury than you paid for. Remember that loyalty pays; hoteliers like repeat customers. Even if you travel only once or twice a year, travel providers want to keep you as a customer. So they will reward your loyalty with preferential services, prime upgrades, and special discounts.

6. Make friends

My favorite strategy for getting a great travel experience requires nothing more than being pleasant! When you show appreciation for the hard work of hotel workers, you become a pleasure to do business with. Relax, smile, commiserate, spread some human kindness, and more often than not, rewards will follow.

Source: Joel Widzer, PsyD, is an expert on consumer loyalty and frequent-flier programs. He is the author of *The Penny Pincher's*

Passport to Luxury Travel and a contributor to MSNBC. His consulting firm, *www.jetready.com*, advises travelers and businesses on a range of issues from maximizing their travel programs to managing travel fatigue. He can be reached at (714) 544-2855.

Most Business Friendly Hotel Chains

When you travel on a business trip, you want a competitive edge. Having all the tools readily available at your hotel can help you leapfrog the competition.

1. Hyatt Hotels and Resorts

They offer the best-rate guarantee, and many properties offer business centers with Internet access for no additional charge.

(800) 492-8891
www.hyatt.com.

2. Hilton Hotels

Hilton Hotels offers easy-to-use online reservations. Most properties provide in-room Internet access and dedicated executive floors.

(800) HILTONS
www.hilton.com

3. Marriott

The Marriot brand can meet the needs of the luxury traveler, the thrifty traveler, and those in-between.

(800) 932-2198
www.marriott.com

4. Starwood Hotels and Resorts

Starwood is a global operator of hotels and resorts primarily in the luxury and upscale segment of the lodging industry.

(888) 625-4990
www.starwood.com

5. Four Seasons Hotels

They offer the finest quality service including highly personalized twenty-four-hour service. The Four Seasons embodies a true home away from home for those who know and appreciate the best.

(800) 819-5053
www.fourseasons.com

Source: Joel Widzer, PsyD, is an expert on consumer loyalty and frequent-flier programs. He is the author of *The Penny Pincher's Passport to Luxury Travel* and a contributor to MSNBC. His consulting firm, *www.jetready.com*, advises travelers and businesses on a range of issues from maximizing their travel programs to managing travel fatigue. He can be reached at (714) 544-2855.

Popular Forms of Travel Insurance

Travel insurance is important for you and your business so you can save money if things go wrong before or during a business trip. This can save you and your business thousands of dollars per year. Here are the most popular forms of travel insurance put together by an industry expert.

1. Trip cancellation insurance

This reimburses you if the cruise line or tour operator goes out of business. It also provides coverage if you have to cancel the trip due to sickness, a death in the family, or other calamity listed in the policy. In addition, if you or an immediate family member becomes seriously ill or is injured during the trip, most policies reimburse you for the unused portion of the vacation. The cost is generally 5 to 7 percent of the price of the vacation, so a $5,000 trip would cost roughly

$250 to $350 to insure. Trip cancellation is very different from the cancellation waiver that many cruise and tour operators offer. Waivers are relatively inexpensive, costing approximately $40 to $60. They provide coverage if you have to cancel the trip, but they have many restrictions. They must be purchased when you book the trip and will usually not cover you immediately before departure (the time period most people cancel) or after the trip has begun.

2. Baggage insurance or personal effects coverage

This provides coverage if your personal belongings are lost, stolen, or damaged during the trip. To insure $1,000 worth of personal belongings for a week, it costs roughly $50 per year. Before purchasing this type of coverage, find out how much insurance the airline or trip operator provides for your belongings. Also, check your homeowner's or renter's policy. It will usually provide coverage for off-premises theft. Therefore, if your luggage is stolen, your insurer will pay to replace it, less the deductible. If you are traveling with expensive electronic equipment, jewelry or sporting gear, it might be more cost-effective to purchase a floater or endorsement to your homeowners or renters policy. The cost to insure a $1,000 ring is between $10 and $40 annually. This provides full coverage for the item, anywhere in the world, usually for one year.

3. Emergency medical assistance

This provides insurance and medical assistance for travelers. It covers you if you had to be airlifted off a mountain due to a skiing or hiking accident or had to stay for a prolonged period in a foreign hospital. It also provides coverage if you get seriously sick or injured and needed to be flown home. Some commercial airlines require very sick passengers to travel on a stretcher with a doctor. This means that you might have to purchase ten or more seats on a plane at a possible cost of over $10,000.

Before purchasing this type of coverage, check with your own health insurance carrier. Find out what type of coverage you have when traveling abroad and if there are any limits. Also, ask if it will pay to fly you home or to a country with first-rate medical care.

4. Accidental death

This provides a variety of coverage if you or a family member dies on the trip. If you have a good life insurance plan or have made other financial provisions for your loved ones, this may be duplicate insurance.

Source: The Insurance Information Institute (*www.iii.org*)—Their mission is to improve public understanding of insurance—what it does and how it works. The III is located at 110 William Street, 24th Floor, New York, NY 10038; (212) 346-5500.

Top Ways to Get a Rental Car Upgrade

When you're on the road making sales calls or taking clients out to eat, a nice rental car makes a great impression and also adds joy to your driving experience. Here are a few tips to get the most car for your dollar, from our resident travel expert.

1. Build your loyalty

Join a car rental membership program. Members can bypass the check-in lines, heading directly to their cars with the engine running and air conditioner cooling or heater heating, depending on weather conditions. You also can check your car back in electronically and proceed directly to your airport gate. This will save you valuable time.

2. Book directly

This gives you the best rates and provides the opportunity to ask for an upgrade. If one is not available at the time of booking, ask the agent to notate your record for an upgrade. When checking in, tell the desk agent that you requested an upgrade. Often when they see the notation in your record, they'll comply.

3. Check the rates

A little known secret in the car rental industry is that the price difference between a subcompact to a full-size is a few dollars per day. First, inquire about the price of the subcompact and then ask what the price of the full size is—you'll often be surprised.

4. Reserve a popular car

When making your reservation, inquire what cars are the most popular at the specific rental location. It is more likely that these cars will be sold out and you'll be upgraded to a larger car.

5. Know the game

Often when a rental location is sold out of your car type, they'll try to have you upgrade for a nominal fee ($5 per day). If this happens to you, ask them if cars are still available in your class type. If not, tell them you want the upgrade for no charge.

6. Accept the best

If you reserve a non-smoking car and your car reeks of cigarette smoke, ask for an upgrade. Likewise, if your car is old and dingy, request a newer upgraded car.

7. Ask and you shall receive

The simplest technique for a rental upgrade is simply to ask in a nice polite manner. Often if you're a nice person, the rental agent will upgrade you at no charge.

Source: Joel Widzer, PsyD., is an expert on consumer loyalty and frequent-flier programs. He is the author of *The Penny Pincher's Passport to Luxury Travel* and a contributor to MSNBC. His consulting firm, *www.jetready.com*, advises travelers and businesses on a range of issues from maximizing their travel programs to managing travel fatigue. He can be reached at (714) 544-2855.

Important Questions to Ask at the Rental Car Counter

Renting a car on your next business trip? Our expert advises that, at the very least, make sure that you know the answers to these questions.

1. When do I need to return the car?

Car rental companies charge you in twenty-four-hour increments based on the time you picked up the vehicle. Most companies allow a forty-five-minute grace period beyond your return time, but exceed that and you can find yourself paying for another day's worth of rental fees.

2. How much will the rental actually cost?

Most rental companies and Web sites quote their rate before taxes, airport fees, and surcharges. Avoid surprises and ask what the total charge of your rental will be.

3. What is my liability if I'm involved in fender-bender (or worse)?

A simple accident can be a big hassle, and in some countries could land you in jail, require a large deposit on your credit card, or delay departure until the matter is settled.

4. Do I need extra insurance?

Most business-oriented credit cards such as American Express and Visa Business Card offer added insurance. So does your personal automobile insurance policy. Each year it's a good idea to call your credit card company and personal insurance and determine what coverage you have for both domestic and international car rentals.

5. Where can I drive?

Rental car companies impose restriction of where their cars can be used. If you're renting in Southern California, you'll most likely be prohibited from driving into Mexico. When driving in Europe where you can transverse multiple international boarders in hours, unknowingly, you might be breaking the rules of your rental agreement.

6. What are the terms of my rental agreement?

It's a good idea to call your car rental company or review their Web site to determine the terms and policy of the rental agreement. Be sure to ask about who can drive the car, where the car needs to be parked, what happens if you need to extended your rental, and if the rental company is responsible in case of a mechanical failure.

7. Where do I keep my rental contract?

In most cases, keep it in the car. The rental agreement is usually used as the car's registration, providing ownership and liability information for police officers.

8. What do I do if I have a problem with the car or need to keep it longer than planned?

When you pick up the car, be sure to find out the phone numbers to call in case of an accident, breakdown, or rental extension. You can also call the company's toll-free customer service number.

9. What are my fuel options?

Rental cars usually come with a full tank of gas with drivers responsible for returning their vehicle in the same condition. When you have a lot of driving ahead, one option that can save time and money is the "Fuel Purchase Option" or "Fuel Service Option." This option allows you to prepurchase fuel at slightly under the average market price when you pick up the car. This plan is helpful when you have a tight schedule and know that you will use at least one tank of gas.

Source: Joel Widzer, PsyD, is an expert on consumer loyalty and frequent-flier programs. He is the author of *The Penny Pincher's Passport to Luxury Travel* and a contributor to MSNBC. His consulting firm, *www.jetready.com*, advises travelers and businesses on a range of issues from maximizing their travel programs to managing travel fatigue. He can be reached at (714) 544-2855.

Ways to Save Money on Your Rental Car

Renting the right car can not only save you money, it can add comfort, convenience, and safety to your trips. Here are some good ideas from our resident travel expert.

1. Book wisely

Arriving at a car rental counter and plunking down your credit card in front of the attendant is not the best way to get good value. It's actually the worst. You'll save time and money if you call your travel providers directly or book your reservations on the Internet.

2. Use frequent renter programs

Like airlines and hotels, major car rental companies track their customers' rental histories and offer preferential service to loyal customers. Most of the major companies offer frequent renter programs that earn you upgrades and free rental days.

3. Become a preferred renter

Most major car rental companies also offer preferred renter programs or clubs (one example is the Hertz #1 Club). When you belong to one of these clubs, you get preferential treatment, which allows you to bypass the rental counter. While many of these programs come with a price tag, most programs will waive the fee if you write or call the car rental company and ask them to waive it. They will do it because the car rental industry is very competitive, and they want your business.

4. Maximize your clout

Select at least two different companies for your car rental business. The first is your primary provider; this is where you will put most of your business so you can earn the highest level of preferential service. The second company is your hedge against regional market variations. As in the hotel industry, rates and availability in the car rental industry can vary from place to place; on occasion, one company's rates will be grossly out of whack. By working two loyalty programs, you won't get caught paying inflated prices when your objective is to minimize your business expenses.

5. Getting the best rate

You have to be persistent, and you have to call the car rental companies directly—sometimes several times. It is not uncommon to speak with one rental agent and be offered one rate and then call back a few minutes later and get another rate. If you're renting for three or more days, ask if a weekly rate is available. Often car rental companies offer cheaper weekly rates for as few as three days.

6. Getting upgraded

When making your reservation, ask the agent to document your record for an upgrade based on availability. This will greatly increase your odds of being upgraded when you pick up your car. Another strategy is to call the on-site manager in advance of your arrival, introduce yourself as a loyal, preferred customer, and ask if she can help you nail down that upgrade. It has been my experience that most on-site managers are very accommodating.

7. Work the discounts

Car rental companies offer myriad discounts, ranging from corporate discounts to those affiliated with airlines and hotels. I have found that AAA and American Express often have special rates with car rental agencies; check your monthly airline mileage statement for special offers available from your airline's car rental partners. Also be sure to check the car rental company's Web site for special deals or promotions; there are often discounts for booking online. Finally, individual rental locations will occasionally offer their own specials and promotions, so you should ask at the counter if they have anything for you. Just remember to mention your status as a preferred business customer.

8. Check the mileage

Most rental companies offer unlimited mileage for typical business rentals. However, be certain to verify their policy before renting as exceeding mileage requirements can rack up the cost of your rental.

9. Think small; then think big

Start with the rental companies' smallest car and than find out the rate for the next level car. Very often, you can move from a subcompact to a full-size car for only $2 to $3 dollars a day adding comfort and safety to your travels.

10. Go smokeless

You will increase your odds for getting a newer, cleaner car if you insist on having a nonsmoking car. You will also increase your chances for an upgrade because if a nonsmoking car is unavailable in the class of service you booked (and it might be, since nonsmoking cars are in high demand), you will be upgraded to accommodate your nonsmoking needs.

Source: Joel Widzer, PsyD, is an expert on consumer loyalty and frequent-flier programs. He is the author of *The Penny Pincher's Passport to Luxury Travel* and a contributor to MSNBC. His consulting firm, *www.jetready.com*, advises travelers and businesses on a range of issues from maximizing their travel programs to managing travel fatigue. He can be reached at (714) 544-2855.

Your Home Business

Top Microlenders for Home-Based Businesses

The Small Business Administration's Microloan Program provides very small loans to start-up, newly established, or growing small business concerns. Under this program, the SBA makes funds available to nonprofit community-based lenders (intermediaries), which, in turn, make loans to eligible borrowers in amounts up to a maximum of $35,000. Here are some of the top participating banks in this program.

1. American Express Centurion Bank
4315 S. 2700 West
Salt Lake City, UT 84184
(801) 945-3000

2. Citigroup Inc.
399 Park Avenue
New York, NY 10043
(800) 285-3000

3. MBNA Corporation
1100 North King Street
Wilmington, DE 19884-0131
(800) 362-6255
Fax: (302) 456-8541

4. Wells Fargo & Company
420 Montgomery Street
San Francisco, CA 94104
(800) 869-3557

5. BB&T Corporation
200 West 2nd St.
16th Floor
Winston Salem, NC 27101
(336) 733-2724

6. Lauritzen Corporation
1 First National Center
Omaha, NE 68102
(402) 341-0500
Fax: (402) 342-4332

7. First Citizens Bancshares
116 E. Main St.
Mount Olive, NC 28365
(919) 658-7000

8. Colonial Bancgroup Inc.
1 Commerce St.
Montgomery, AL 36104
(334) 240-5000
Fax: (334) 240-5069

9. Fleetboston Financial Corp
100 Federal St.,
Boston, MA 02110
(617) 434-4645

10. Bank One Corporation
270 Park Ave.
New York, NY 10017
(212) 270-0589

Source: Small Business Administration (*www.sba.gov*).

Best Home-Based Businesses to Start Today

What kind of a home-based business will you start? Here, our expert provides some great home-based businesses to start today. The criteria to make this list were based on high ease of entry, relatively low cost, high future demand, and potentially high return. Individuals and couples must exercise great caution in pursuing home-based business opportunities simply because they show up here. You should first choose a business because you love it and you're skilled in doing it.

1. Internet sales and marketing

Yes, indeed, there are dot-com failures around. But the Internet train keeps gathering steam. If you have a product to sell, this is very likely the way to sell it (or auction it). If you don't have a product, you can sell someone else's from the confines of your home. Opportunities such as e-stores, e-auctions, and site selling have moved this category into the number-one position—that and more than a billion dollars in sales last year. Get a Web site built and you're off and running.

2. Children's products and programs

From toys and furniture to educational programs, this category sizzles with possibilities. The U.S. birthrate is stagnating, but median family incomes are rising and so are parents' efforts to do more while having less time for their children. With so many working parents, after-school and summer programs with substance are desperately needed. Children's furniture, painted murals, and training and exercise programs are other items that will be in demand, he says. Profit potential is moderate, but you will be doing something important.

3. Information detective or researcher

Have a bit of Sherlock Holmes in you? You can make good money by sleuthing for information that corporate executives and others need but don't have time to search for themselves. Government regulations and intelligence regarding competitors are but two areas to pursue. Technology has made information-gathering easier but also has stockpiled the amount of information to plow through. Solve someone's time problem by offering to locate and retrieve the information they need and you'll have people knocking on your door!

4. Home inspector

Home sales depend increasingly on the results of a professional inspection. The inspectors generally are independent contractors who are trained and certified; many also have past experience as homebuilders or in the construction trades. While that experience is helpful, it is not mandatory. But certification is necessary if you want to move beyond having your mother-in-law and best friend as clients. Not only do buyers need home inspectors, but real-estate companies, insurance firms and banks do, too.

5. Internet Web master

Get started by developing Web sites for your church, your child's school PTSA, or your politician friend. But building sites for businesses is where the money is. Training is available through the Web (naturally) at low cost, but you will need a scanner, additional disk storage, a faster Internet connection, and other equipment. But if this is a labor of love for you, and you know how to market yourself, you will never be out of work. You can earn $50 and $100 an hour and hire out as a contractor to businesses for large [Web site] developments.

6. Personal assistant

For many business people today, time is more precious than money. You help them, not by unplugging their clocks, but by doing their shopping, running errands, chauffeuring children, and doing other tasks that effectively give them more personal time. The most ambitious here will also see ways to become virtual business assistants by providing services such as word processing, newsletter writing, even digital photography or Web site design. Serve your clients in as many ways as you know how.

7. Event planner and organizer

Life won't become one big party, but it could become many little ones. Talented organizers for weddings, bar mitzvahs, morale events, and the like are in high demand if they are strong marketers as well. But it takes a creative bone, an entrepreneurial spirit, and an indifference to the traditional workweek. Start-up costs? Antonia Calzetti and Brenda Yagmin spent less than $500 to begin their home-based business in New York in October 1999. The two, who met at a small catering company, have helped build their clientele through direct mailings, press releases, and other marketing efforts. Their new company's sales should reach $100,000 this year, they tell *Entrepreneur*. "We party every day," says Calzetti.

8. Home repairs and landscaping

Home equity enhancement. Cute name, but the real words here are *painting*, *repairing*, and *landscaping*. The more you can do to increase the value of a home in the real-estate market, the more you can make. Selling yourself to real-estate agents is a good first step. How can a PC help? New technology allows you to provide potential clients with a look at their home—with your improvements added.

9. Personal coach

Corporate chieftains, entrepreneurs, and most everyone else could use an objective listener to identify and correct weaknesses. The key here is that you must possess the ability to help someone from skills and experience you have developed in your own life. You also must be a good listener and a good self-marketer. Talane Miedaner used a personal coach in her job at a Manhattan bank—then followed his lead, enrolled in a training program, and became one, too. She now has a business that works with forty clients a month and is generating $150,000 a year in sales. "I love the commute," she tells *Entrepreneur*, referring to her home in New York's Catskill Mountains. "I roll out of bed and I'm coaching away."

10. Technical support

Those who troubleshoot computer system problems at businesses big and small will never be out of work. But you can build a similar business out of your home, offering training and support (even security consulting) to small offices, home offices, and residential customers with PCs. Prerequisites (besides a demonstrated knowledge) include a passion for technology, a customer service bent, hourly rates, and a flexible—but not too flexible—schedule.

Source: Monte Enbysk, formerly the managing editor for the Micro-soft.com Small Business Center, is now a lead editor for the Micro-soft.com network and writes occasionally about technology for small businesses. He has been a writer and editor at MSN Money, *Washington CEO* magazine, and several newspapers in the Pacific Northwest. For more business tips and advice online, please see *www.microsoft.com/business/default.mspx.*

Most Common Home-Based Business Insurance Coverages

Are you running your business out of your home? Maybe you're under the impression that your Homeowner's Insurance will cover you for business liabilities. Wrong! Most Homeowners Insurance policies EXCLUDE incidental business operations. Our expert, an insurance broker and consultant, has provided these most common business insurance coverages for you to consider.

1. Property & Liability Insurance

Home-based business owners need both Property and Liability Insurance. Property Insurance will provide coverage to those special items you use to conduct your business, whether it is musical equipment that is used to teach students or computer equipment that is used for a graphic designer. If your home is burglarized or destroyed by a fire you will want to cover these items from peril. The Liability Insurance provides third party coverage to your customer that comes to your home to conduct business. If they are injured at your home and file a lawsuit against you, your standard homeowners insurance policy may not provide Liability Protection because it specifically excludes business pursuits.

2. Auto Insurance

If you use your personal auto policy to conduct business (i.e., Cosmetic Sales, Food Delivery, Newspaper Delivery etc.) and someone becomes injured, your standard auto insurance policy may provide minimal coverage or none at all. You should contact your insurance agent and see what options are available on their policy or if you need to be re-written on a Commercial Auto policy.

3. Health / Disability / Life Insurance

Don't forget that you will also need to purchase health, disability or life insurance to cover medical expenses you or your employee may incur if you become sick or are injured away from work. Disability Insurance can be purchased if you or your employee is injured or sick for a long period of time and unable to work. And life insurance can be purchased to pay final expenses to a Mortgagee/Loss Payee or grieving loved one.

4. Workers Compensation Insurance

Once you hire an employee you must purchase Workers Compensation Insurance regardless of what their job function is. Most home-based businesses assume that since the Hazard exposure is very low they don't need to purchase Workers Compensation Insurance, when in fact if they don't purchase this type of insurance for their employee and the employee becomes injured you could be faced with fines that could potentially close your business and put you in financial debt for a long period of time. Workers Compensation can be purchased by almost any insurance carriers and in some cases by the State directly. You should contact your insurance agent and discuss the options that are available to you since Workers Compensation laws vary from state to state.

5. Umbrella Policies

Because we all live in a litigious society, many people have purchased Umbrella Policies to protect their assets from excessive lawsuits. If you have a home-based business, your exposure to a third party lawsuit has increased and you may wish to purchase an Umbrella policy to protect yourself. Most Homeowners and Auto policies will only provide coverage up to $500,000 or $1,000,000. If you don't feel as though that is enough you can purchase a Umbrella policy that will increase the Liability Limits on your Homeowners and Automobile policy an extra $1,000,000 or even up to $5,000,000.

Source: Body-Borneman *(www.bodyborneman.com)*—With a loyal client base of over 15,000 customers, many of whom have been with them for almost 40 years, Body-Borneman has grown to become one of the largest insurance agencies in Southeastern Pennsylvania. The agency markets a complete line of property, casualty, life and group products. This is accomplished through a staff of 45 loyal employees, of which 33 are licensed agents. Contact Sean Deviney at (610) 367-1100.

Considerations Before Hiring an Employee to Work from Your Home

Depending on how your home-based business grows, you may need to hire an employee or two to help you out. Before you do, however, you may want to keep these considerations in mind.

1. Provide full disclosure

Prior to an interview, you should let each candidate know about your home office base. Don't give them the impression that you're trying to hide something from them.

2. Ask potential candidates how they feel about working in a home office

This should be one of the first questions you ask—and you'll want to listen carefully to the answers. If you're not satisfied with their answers, follow up with some behavioral questions to find out what they're really thinking. You should give the candidate time to voice any misgivings they may have.

3. Before the employee starts work, set up an appropriate workspace

You need to find a way to balance the limited space in your home with your employee's need for privacy. Let's face it, nobody wants to be in a situation where the boss can hear every single word he or she says. It just breeds discontent and puts more pressure on your employee. Over time, that pressure will build up and create a situation that isn't likely to end well.

4. Establish a separate space for meetings

At the very least, invest in a table you can sit around to hold meetings. In theory, using your desk as a place to sit around during a meeting is a decent idea. In practice, however, it will be difficult to set a professional tone for the meeting if you and your employee are crowded around your desk, trying to work in the midst of all your paperwork.

5. Take bathroom facilities into account

If you don't have a bathroom dedicated primarily to the office space and your employees, you might want to reconsider your plans to hire someone else. Enough said.

6. Have an appropriate exit/entrance to your home office

The path to your home office should ideally not interfere with what goes on in the rest of the house. This rule isn't as critical as the restroom issue, but it helps lend a feeling of professionalism to the entire endeavor if you have an entrance that's as direct as possible.

7. Make the office off-limits to your family

You need to make sure your family understands that your office space—and in particular, the desk and computer of your employee—is a no-go zone. Sure, the office is in your house, but if you want your employee to feel comfortable, this is a line that must not be crossed.

8. Provide generous vacation time

It's my belief, after working in a home office, that the rule should be more vacation rather than less. A home office is an intense work environment, and your employees are much more apt to burn out here than in a standard work environment. An extra week of vacation—and three should be the minimum—is a great way to minimize burnout.

9. Be flexible

Be open to your employee's ideas and needs. Suggest flex-time or working remotely—your employees will thank you for it.

10. Try to laugh a little

The close quarters of a home office can be stifling, and there are no other employees around for your worker to vent to. So figure out how to keep the mood light and learn to laugh about life's daily little annoyances.

Source: Tom Candee, marketing head for an online software store. Tom has been working from his home for more than two years. Tom can be contacted at *tcandee@gmail.com*

Top Ways to Successfully Work from Home

Working at home can be an attractive option for business owners and corporate employees. It does however come with its own set of issues. It can be isolating without colleagues to talk to. There are all sorts of distractions that can interfere with the workers productivity. The more businesslike you make your home office environment and schedule the easier it will be to work from home. Our expert, a business coach and consultant to many home based workers, offers these tips.

1. Maintain a schedule

Maintain regular working hours and stick to them.

2. Get a phone, computer, and printer just for your business

Get a separate phone line, computer and printer that are only used for your business.

3. Keep workspace separate from living space

Keep your workspace separate from your living space. Ideally it should be visually and acoustically separate from the living quarters.

4. Have goals and to do lists

To gauge your progress maintain goals and to do lists. On Sunday night or Monday morning create a plan for the week. At the end of the week take time to reflect on your progress.

5. Talk with other independent workers

Find other independent workers or a personal coach to give you feedback on your ideas and progress.

6. When working with a team, have frequent telephone and e-mail conversations

If you are working with a team, have frequent telephone and e-mail conversations with the members of the team. This helps to keep the project on track and allows team members to anticipate and prepare for problems.

7. Document work

Document your work and learn to do this in laser-like language.

8. Request feedback from clients and managers

Request frequent feedback from clients and managers so that you are sure you are satisfying their expectations continually. Without daily contact it is hard to read people. Most people find it difficult to give negative feedback. At the end of a project they may accept it as is even though they are disappointed with the result. Ongoing feedback helps avoid this problem.

9. Take regular breaks during your day

Be creative in your way of relaxing. Meditation, a cup of coffee, a snack, a walk, are examples of ways to stop what you are doing to re-energize.

10. Set clear boundaries

Neighbors, friends, and family must know that your office is off limits. Even though you are home every day you are working. Have a no-interruption policy during working hours.

Source: Alvah Parker is a Business and Career Coach as well as publisher of *Parker's Points*, an e-mail tip list and *Road to Success*, an ezine. Parker's Value Program© enables her clients to find their own way to work that is more fulfilling and profitable. Her clients are managers, business owners, sole practioners, attorneys and people in transition. Alvah is found on the web at *www.asparker.com*. She may also be reached at (781) 598-0388.

Most Visited Websites for the Home-Based Business

The following lists the most visited sites in all 'home-based' categories

1. WAHM

WAHM is a source for home business information, work at home/work from home jobs. It offers advice for work-at-home moms and dads.
www.wahm.com

2. OzeMedia

Offers a free weekly online marketing newsletter to help individuals succeed with their home business.
www.ozemedia.com

3. Moms Network Exchange

One of the original sites for work at home moms and for those looking to work at home. It offers the best resources, ideas, business opportunities, networking with other work at home moms, free advertising and promotion along with work at home ideas and home business profiles.

www.momsnetwork.com

4. Biz Whiz

Biz Whiz is a community Web site for work-at-home-related information and resources.

http://biz-whiz.com/

5. 4HB.com

4hb.com is an online destination for new and existing small- and medium-sized businesses with a particular slant towards those that maintain an office at home, and/or home-based businesses.

www.4hb.com

6. Work On the Internet

Work On the Internet is a small business and home business online resource center. They are continuously looking for information on running a business online, internet marketing, e-mail marketing, search engine marketing, lead generation ideas, selling online, building your own Web site and just about anything related to how to succeed in the tough world!

www.workoninternet.com

7. FreelanceMom.com

FreelanceMom.com offers business opportunities, freelance jobs, home business ideas, steps to creating your own website, marketing your business and much more.

www.freelancemom.com

8. HBWM

HBWM is a professional association and online community of parents who work at home and those who would like to.

www.hbwm.com

9. Home Biz Tools

Home Biz Tools helps people find the work they love and turn that into income. If you are an existing business, this site can help you acquire a competitive edge and move you towards greater profitability. It is a place to gather tools for success. A place where the average person can get the latest and greatest resources to create income at home.

www.homebiztools.com

10. Bizy Moms

Bizy Moms offers a section on business ideas written by a person with that type of business. Real stories from real people. They offer career kits. Bizy Moms informs you of the latest scams that you may encounter. In addition to this, Bizy Moms offers articles and advice.

www.bizymoms.com

Source: Alexa.com. Founded in April 1996, Alexa Internet grew out of a vision of Web navigation that is intelligent and constantly improving with the participation of its users. Alexa Related Links and Traffic Rankings are the embodiment of this vision, growing and getting better as more people join the Alexa community of smart Web surfers.

Considerations When Starting Up a Home Business

The Small Business Administration estimates that 53 percent of small businesses are home-based. That number continues to rise as workers seek a better quality of work and home life. However, operating a home business is not stress-free. Successful home businesses must be planned as carefully as any other endeavor you undertake if you are going to find the balance that is needed to make it work. Here are some considerations to keep in mind from our small business expert.

1. Family support

To effectively operate a home business you need time uninterrupted by family obligations. Make certain your family is aware of, and willing to respect, the time you need to meet your business obligations.

2. Isolation

Working at home can be very lonely if you don't structure your time to include social interaction. In a traditional job, you have co-workers to exchange ideas with and share your triumphs. Find some way to work that into your home business life by adding time for activities, such as finding other people operating home businesses to network with.

3. A financial plan

Like any business, you need to keep your financial books in order, making certain not to intermingle business funds with your home finances. If you put money from your savings into your business, account for it and pay yourself back. If you are paid in cash for a job, don't spend it on groceries before entering it on the books as income that you have paid out to yourself. Set up a good bookkeeping system from the get-go and follow it to the letter. Make certain you have enough money to operate for a year without having to raid the family cookie jar to keep the business afloat. The fastest way to lose family support is causing them financial hardship to achieve your dream.

4. Organization

Every successful business has a strong organizational structure. For a home business this is even more important because you need to be clear when it is business time and what is business space. That doesn't mean you go into an office and close the door for eight hours every day. It means that you need a schedule that everyone knows about and space that is yours for working. Set up procedures for operating the business that are comfortable for you, but get the work done.

5. Legal regulations

Make certain you are meeting all the legal obligations required by the city, state and federal governments. A home business is a "real" business and needs to follow the laws for operating a business where you live.

6. Office space

Set aside space for an office. Whether it is a closet, a garage, or a spare bedroom, you need someplace that is for the home business. Everything for the business should go there when you stop work. The dining room table may be nice to work at, but precious documents can be lost if they are left around the house. Have a place for everything and keep it there when you are not working.

7. Equipment

Deciding what equipment is needed is a big decision because of the cost and maintenance. Do you need a separate telephone line? A computer dedicated to the business? A fax? A cell phone? A xerox? Most home businesses start small and add equipment as it is needed. Assess what your business should have at a bare minimum and budget for it.

Source: Judith A. Kautz, Ph.D., MBA, owner of Small Business Notes (www.smallbusinessnotes.com). Judith Kautz has worked in both the public and private sectors of business for over 30 years. In private industry she has been employed as a systems analyst and manager in computer consulting businesses, in addition to providing private consulting services in computer applications, statistics, and management. She can be contacted at editor@smallbusiness notes.com.

Items to Include in Your Home Business Budget

While paying rent on external space is usually not a factor in most home businesses, your budget should include many of the same items that any small business must plan for. Our expert says that many items that are normally used in a home can be used in a home business—your computer is a prime example. However, for these items to be deductible as a valid business expense on your income tax return, they need to be purchased separately and not intermingled with other home office supply items.

1. Office supplies

Make certain you have enough money for the basics, including organizational products like filing systems and calendars.

2. Insurance

Insurance is one of the most commonly forgotten items in setting up a home business. Your business computer is not covered by your home fire insurance. You need a separate policy to cover your business equipment. If you are having clients come to your home, you also need to consider getting liability insurance to cover accidents that might occur while they are there. Talk with your home insurance agent to find out what is covered and what extra coverage you might need.

3. Advertising

Advertising may be the second most commonly forgotten budget item in setting up a home business. A Web site is considered advertising. Business cards and your stationery are advertising. In order to get clients you need to advertise. Decide the best way to do that, figure out how much that will cost, and put it in your budget.

4. Telephone

A cell phone may suffice for a home business. Certainly you will want a separate number from your home number with an answering service to take messages when you are not available. With the variety of telephone plans available these days, there are many choices. Cost out the one that will best fit your needs.

5. Travel and entertainment

There are few businesses that require no travel. Keep track of your mileage. This is a deductible expense. When you get together with clients or other businesspeople you are networking with for a meal, that is an entertainment expense. This isn't something that just big businesses do. Allocate funds in your budget for it. It is good for you to get out and about regularly, both to scout what is happening in the world that might be important to your business, but also to get your business known.

6. Dues and subscriptions

Every professional belongs to business organizations and subscribes to business-related journals. That is part of being professional. One of the biggest mistakes home businesses make is operating far too casually. Keep up-to-date on your field and participate in your business community. Your business will thrive from it.

7. Repairs and maintenance

How many businesses have missed deadlines because their equipment breaks down? Do that too many times and you are out of business. Spend the time and money keeping all your equipment in top shape. And, that includes keeping adequate supplies of toner and other supplies.

8. Equipment

For most businesses it is relatively obvious what some of the equipment is that you need. If you are running a sewing business, a sewing machine is an essential. However, there are also items that can be categorized as "nice to have." A fax might fit there. Then there are the pure "luxury" items, like a top-of-the-line desk chair. Budget for the essentials and reward yourself with some "nice-to-haves" and "luxuries" for your successes along the way. If you make a list in each category, not only will you have a carrot to be working towards, but you will have a clear picture of what expenditures to plan for in the future.

9. Software

If you have a computer, you will need software. Plan for not only specialized software for your business, but also word processing, financial and presentation software. As part of operating a professional business you need to have basic software to organize and develop professional materials and accounting. It is an investment you will not regret.

Source: Judith A. Kautz, Ph.D., MBA, owner of Small Business Notes (www.smallbusinessnotes.com). Judith Kautz has worked in both the public and private sectors of business for over 30 years. In private industry she has been employed as a systems analyst and manager in computer consulting businesses, in addition to providing private consulting services in computer applications, statistics, and management. She can be contacted at editor@smallbusiness notes.com.

Typical First Steps for Starting a Home-Based Business

Starting your own business is a big, and sometimes scary step. The best way to be confident is to be prepared.

1. Have you identified a need?

Identify a need in your area that isn't being met, and match your skills to that need. Maybe you and your friends have discussed the need in your area for an affordable scanning service. Why not take a class to learn about scanning and digital image manipulation? Then your skills will meet a need, and you can offer affordable scanning services to your community. Most of all, make certain your idea is practical, and don't get totally hooked on an idea that has no future.

2. Have you analyzed your income needs?

Remember to take into account all the benefits you may be giving up when you quit your current job. Put yourself into a better financial place by eliminating as much of your personal debt as possible. Pay off the credit cards, your car, and any other outstanding debts that eat your income each month.

3. Do you know the law?

Ignorance is not a defense for ignoring zoning and other laws. All it takes is a few phone calls to make sure you are going to operate within the legal guidelines, but foregoing operating within the legal boundaries can cost you a lot of time *and* money. Some communities don't allow any form of business to operate from a residential area. If applicable, check into laws governing product labeling, product safety, interstate commerce, and postal regulations.

4. Do you have a business plan?

Believe me, it will do wonders to focus on exactly what kind of business yours will be, who you are selling to, how you will sell, how much to charge, how much it will take to start up, and where all the money will come from. This is your road map.

5. Do you want your own business?

Do you want your own home business badly enough to work long hours without knowing how much profit you'll end up with? Know how hard you are willing to work without being certain of the outcome.

6. How much of your own money will you have to put in?

Or how much credit you can expect from suppliers? Have you talked to a banker or lender to see what is expected of you?

7. Are you organized?

Organize yourself and your business! Get organized from the beginning, because it won't take long for things to start piling up. Organization equals professionalism, and clients will quickly be able to tell if you are professional or not.

8. Can you run a business?

Do you need to have the ability to organize, prioritize, and manage money, time, projects, and people? Check with your local SBA because they have lots of free resources to help people trying to start a new business. They also have free business templates that you can download at *www.sba.gov.*

9. Have you access to equipment you'll need?

Locate and price all your equipment and supplies. In fact, it is a good idea to talk to others in your business, if possible, and see what equipment and supplies they started with, what things they could have done without, and what things are vital to start-up. Take stock of the supplies you may already have on hand, and see where you stand. Some common supplies of any office-based service will be a computer, decent printer, fax machine or modem fax, business phone line, and a photocopier or scanner. Your business may need even more supplies. Write down every little thing you may need. On the subject of supplies: Don't be wasteful, or buy things you don't need right now. If you can make do with your old equipment until you start making money, don't buy that new computer just yet.

10. How are you going to do your bookkeeping?

Find the proper bookkeeping system for your business. You must keep accurate records of all financial transactions related to your business.

11. Have you thought about advertising or creating a Web site for your business?

Research all the possible avenues of advertising available to you, and choose the methods that will benefit your business. Get a Web site for your business. Even if you aren't selling anything online, get a nice, clean, professional Web site for your business. Remember that the Internet is quickly becoming a preferred medium for business. You can incorporate your Web site address into all your advertising media, such as your business cards and letterheads. This makes your business seem more professional and credible!

Source: At-HomeWorks.com (www.at-homeworks.com/)—At-HomeWorks.com is an online guide and resource community for mothers working from home, and anyone else who wants to find a home-based job or start a home business. The information was found at the following link: www.at-homeworks.com/start_up.htm.

Tests to Claim a Home Office Deduction

More workers with home offices can now deduct some home expenses. A new law could reduce taxes on the return you are now preparing. The change could affect artists, musicians, hospital-based doctors, outside sales people and others who use their home office to keep records or schedule appointments. Until the Internal Revenue Service gets used to the idea, home office deductions may still trigger audits, so back up deductions with records. Here are some tests to claim a home office deduction from our expert.

1. New law

Before, to get the deduction, unless you met customers or patients at your home office, you had to earn income there. This was like soliciting insurance on the phone from home. Now you may qualify even if you do only bookkeeping or schedule appointments at home. One big if limits the opportunity: Your office qualifies if there is no other fixed location where you do administrative work. Typically, if this requirement is satisfied, a house painter who spends much of his time at job sites and a salesperson who visits customers may be allowed the deduction. In one court case an entrepreneur owned a Laundromat a few miles from home. She went there daily to collect money and meet with employees. She then worked two hours a day in her home office keeping books and performing managerial tasks. Before, she couldn't deduct home expenses: now she can.

2. Use space exclusively

The home office need not be a whole room or even marked off by a permanent partition. It only needs to be an identifiable dedicated space. As under the old law the space must be used for business exclusively. If you work on the dining room table you can't serve meals on it. An Ashland, Kentucky, consultant wanted to know if he could deduct some costs for the home office in his spare bedroom. He did computer work at a desk and used the twin beds for work tables when he had no guests. In this example, the area around the beds is not used exclusively for business because guests slept there. But the area around the desk might qualify.

3. Deduction amount

Home office workers can deduct part of the expenses of the entire house or apartment such as the following: rent or depreciation, utilities, housekeeping costs, home insurance and general repairs. No lawn care, however, says the IRS. Compute the deduction by comparing the business area to the area of the whole house or apartment. Consider either the number of rooms or square footage. For example, if a taxpayer has a seven-room home and uses one room exclusively for business, then the deduction is one-seventh of the allowable household expenses. Or, if an apartment is 1,000 square feet and 200 square feet are dedicated as a home office, then one-fifth of the allowable expenses may be deducted.

4. Regular use

You must use the space for business regularly.

5. Must be used for your employer's convenience

If you are an employee, the space must be used for your employer's convenience. Qualifying for the deduction is especially difficult if you already have an office at your employer's place of business.

6. Managing personal stocks and bonds does not qualify

Using your office only to manage your personal portfolio of stocks and bonds does not qualify.

Source: A. J. Cook (www.taxfables.com) now practices as a tax lawyer with the Memphis law firm Pietrangelo Cook PLC. Formerly, he was with the CPA firm Ernst & Young as a partner in charge of tax services in the Memphis office. Contact him by telephone: mornings (901) 754-8925; afternoons: (901) 685-2662; fax: (901) 685-6122. Or write him at 6785 Slash Pine, Memphis, TN 38119. His e-mail is aj@taxfables.com.

Top Home Office Tax Deductions

The home office has a unique set of deductions available to qualifying employees and business owners. However, our expert warns that in order to qualify as a home office deduction, an individual must first prove that the home office is a qualifying home office. Once you've accomplished that great task, then you may be able to take advantage of some of these typical deductions that home office enjoys.

1. Accounting fees

Accounting fees incurred to properly account for your qualifying home office expenses and income are deductible expenses. Personal accounting fees are not deductible as a home office deduction.

2. Attorney's fees and legal fees

Attorney's fees and legal fees incurred in the organization or maintenance of a qualifying home office are deductible home office expenses. Qualifying expenses should be strictly for the home office and not for the formation or maintenance of a separate business entity (business expenses should be deducted on the business return and not as a home office deduction).

3. Capital improvements

A capital improvement in a home with a qualifying home office is an expense subject to the Internal Revenue Code depreciation regulations. A capital improvement adds value to the asset and/or extends its useful life. An example of a capital improvement in a qualifying home office would be the installation of energy-efficient windows or the expansion of the qualifying home office space. When depreciating such an asset, the owner must be cautious not to include expenses considered personal in nature. If the improvement improves personal living space, that portion of the expense does not qualify.

4. Cell phones

Cell phone expenses used exclusively for the qualifying home office or for the convenience of the employer may be included in a reimbursement plan. If the cell phone expenses are reimbursed, then the company will treat the costs appropriately. If the expense is not reimbursed and the cell phone is used for business purposes, the employee may deduct the business expenses on their individual income tax return. The cell phone unit is a listed depreciable item and must be depreciated according to the Internal Revenue Code depreciation regulations.

5. Computers

The costs incurred for acquiring a qualifying home office computer are to be depreciated according to the Internal Revenue Code depreciation regulations. The costs incurred for the qualifying computer maintenance may be expensed as a qualifying home office deduction. The business use of the computer should be logged and the records maintained.

6. Depreciation and equipment

Qualifying home office furniture and equipment must be depreciated under current Internal Revenue Code regulations. Generally, an asset must be depreciated if the home office owner owns the asset, it lasts more than one year, it is used for business, and it has a determinable useful life. Such property may include desks, computers, fax machines, chairs, and tables. If an asset does not qualify, it cannot be deducted. Rental assets used exclusively for business can be deducted as a rental expense under current law guidance.

7. Insurance, homeowner's or an additional rider

The business-use percentage of homeowner's insurance may be expensed as a home office expense. This may include the business percentage of the homeowner's insurance policy and any additional costs incurred in obtaining a business rider for the qualifying home office.

8. Interest

Interest incurred in a home mortgage or other similar loan used to maintain or build a qualifying home office is a deductible expense subject to the business-use percentage limitations.

9. Internet fees

Fees used to gain access to the Internet for the convenience of the employer or home business and not otherwise reimbursed are a qualifying expense, provided they are used exclusively for business in a qualifying home office. Personal Internet access is not deductible.

10. Journals and subscriptions

Business and trade journals sent to a qualifying home office are a deductible business expense. Depending on the nature of the home office, the expense may be an unreimbursed employee expense or a direct business expense for the home business person.

11. Maintenance and repair costs

Maintenance costs incurred to preserve a qualifying home office may be a qualifying expense. Repair and maintenance work is expensed in the year it was incurred. A repair does not add significant value to the property. For example, painting and staining a qualifying home office would be considered maintenance and repair expenses, unless they are included with a capital-improvement project. If they are part of a capital-improvement project, they must be depreciated along with the other capital-improvement expenses.

12. Mortgages

The business-use percentage of the home mortgage is deductible for a qualifying home office.

13. Postage

Home office postage that is strictly business related is deductible.

14. Real-estate taxes

The business-use percentage of the real-estate taxes is deductible for a qualifying home office.

15. Rent

The business-use percentage of the rent is deductible for a qualifying home office.

16. Software

Software expenses used exclusively for your home office for the convenience of your employer may be included in a reimbursement plan. As such the business or individual incurring the expense should own the deduction. If a business purchased the software, it would become a business expense. If the software expense was not covered by an employer, the costs may be deducted as an employee expense, provided they are strictly business related, paid for by the employee, and not reimbursed.

17. Start-up costs

The costs incurred to begin conducting business from a qualifying home office may be a deductible expense. If the costs are incurred to organize or start a new business, then they are to be amortized according to the Internal Revenue Code amortization regulations. An employee cannot take the amortization deduction as a non-reimbursed employee expense. It is a business expense.

18. Supplies

Home office supplies that are strictly business related are deductible expenses.

19. Tools

Tools used in the course of business may be a qualifying home office deduction.

20. Utilities

The business-use percentage of the household utilities is a deductible expense for a qualifying home office.

Source: Michelle Neumeier, EA, owner of Home Business Tax Solutions (*www.hbtsinc.com*)—She assists small and home-based business with their income, sales, and payroll tax responsibilities. She can be reached at W181 N9022 Melanie La., Menomonee Falls, WI 53051; (262) 844-1067, e-mail: *www.michelle@hbtsinc.com*.

Most Risky Home-Based Tax Deductions

As a whole, home-based businesses are a risky venture. The Internal Revenue Service is cautious with home business deductions because they have historically been abused. Remember that an expense must be "ordinary and necessary" in the course of business to deduct the expense. These two points are often at the center of the allowance or disallowance of a particular deduction. Always be prepared to justify the expense as ordinary and necessary in the course of your qualifying home-based business. So here's what our expert thinks are risky home-based tax deductions.

1. Home office expenses

A qualifying home office is a space that is "exclusively and regularly" used for business purposes according to the Internal Revenue Code. Your home office must be the principal place of business for you and/or where you meet and deal with business clientele. If you are an employee, your home office must be for the convenience of your employer and cannot be rented from your employer. If you have a qualifying home office, then the business-use percentage of your home's insurance, mortgage/rent, qualifying interest, and related utilities may be business deductions. Keep in mind that this deduction will have implications when the you sell the residence, whether it was taken when it was applicable.

2. Personal digital assistants

Many business professionals find hand-held technology useful and productive in their businesses, especially the home business professional who utilizes this technology to communicate with a central office or with clients. However, the allowance of this expense is to be determined by its proven necessity to a particular business as well as its status as ordinary. Therefore, it may not be an allowable deduction for the home business professional.

3. Home repairs and improvements

Home offices that qualify as such for IRS purposes may be able to deduct or capitalize the business portion of home repairs and improvements. Often the differentiation between business and personal percentage is called into question. Proper recordkeeping is necessary.

4. Telephone services

The first telephone line into any home is *not* a permissible business deduction. A second line, dedicated to business use or specific charges that are identifiable business charges, may be permitted with proper records.

5. Cable utilities

Cable utilities may be permissible if the expense can be shown to be necessary and ordinary in the course of business for a specific industry. For example, family home day cares typically have access to cable children's networks for the viewing needs of the children in their care. However, only the business portions of these charges are deductible.

6. Internet access

Internet access charges are treated in the same way as cable utilities. If a business can prove they are necessary and ordinary in the course of business then they can deduct the business-use percentage of these charges. Proper recordkeeping is necessary to substantiate the business-use percentage.

7. Computer hardware and software

A qualifying home office or home-based business may be able to depreciate a computer and its software under Internal Revenue Code depreciation regulations, provided it is accomplished using the business-use percentage of these expenses only. It is essential that computers used for business and nonbusiness purposes have a time log to document appropriate business use. The log should record the number of hours the computer is used in business and the number of hours the computer is used for personal purposes. This often becomes a trap for the business owner. If a business computer, kept in a qualifying home office, is *ever* used for nonbusiness purposes, then the space is not *exclusively* used for business and the entire home office deduction will be called into question.

8. Lawn and garden care

If a business professional uses the home to meet with clientele, it is logical that the exterior appearance of the office should have a professional appearance; however, this expense is often too personal in nature to warrant its inclusion as an expense on a business return.

9. Vehicle expenses

Vehicle expenses are one of the most common business expenses and also one of the poorest substantiated expenses. Because many business professionals do not keep adequate vehicle expense records, this deduction can be reduced or eliminated entirely upon review. Keep a vehicle log showing beginning annual mileage, individual trip mileage and ending annual mileage; trip purpose; trip date; and trip destination along with receipts for all vehicle expenses. Keep this information for business and personal use for each car used in the business and keep it with the income tax return.

10. Meals and entertainment

The meals and entertainment deduction is also one of the most abused deductions; therefore, it is one of the most scrutinized. Appropriate substantiation is also required. Substantiate a meal and/or entertainment expense with a receipt showing on behalf of whom the expense was paid, what the item purchased was, when the purchase was made, where the expense was incurred, why the expense was incurred, and how much the item cost. Even with the appropriate records, the expense must be a qualifying meals and entertainment expense subject to the current year's restrictions and limitations before appropriate deductions can be made.

Source: Michelle Neumeier, EA, owner of Home Business Tax Solutions (*www.hbtsinc.com*)—She assists small and home-based business with their income, sales, and payroll tax responsibilities. She can be reached at W181 N9022 Melanie La., Menomonee Falls, WI 53051; (262) 844-1067, e-mail: *www.michelle@hbtsinc.com*.

Most Common Home-Based Business Zoning Issues

Zoning regulations enhance the quality of life by controlling and separating different land uses. Not everyone is thrilled when a commercial enterprise, like a home-based business, does work out of a residential neighborhood, so be careful. Restrictions on home-based businesses used in zoning codes can be classified into the following groups:

1. Physical changes and visibility

Zoning codes often prohibit exterior physical changes. These include requiring that the business use be secondary or incidental to the residential use. A business owner may not purchase a residence and convert it into a business without living there. Most zoning codes restrict the space that a home-based business may occupy. Zoning codes also restrict outdoor activities. Outdoor displays are designed to attract attention. They are inherently and intentionally obtrusive. Zoning codes restrict the use of signage except for residential signs. A few zoning codes also prohibit publishing the business address in a telephone listing or any print advertising. Finally, zoning codes have restrictions on commercial vehicles.

2. Traffic

Traffic generation and parking is a real hot-button issue for home-based businesses. There are three primary aspects of this larger issue. Most zoning codes include restricting the numbers of visitors to a business, including limits on the number of visitors per day, the number of visitors who may be on the premises at any one time, and/or the hours that visitors may come. Zoning codes also restrict the number of employees or prohibit employees altogether. Final zoning codes could include restricting business parking or require that additional parking be provided.

3. External effects

Most zoning codes restrict or prohibit nuisance impacts (e.g., noise, odors, glare). It could, for example, plausibly prevent a professional musician from giving lessons or practicing at home. Another approach is to prohibit such effects when they are caused by equipment used in the business. Some zoning codes restrict the type of equipment used to residential or "hobby" equipment. Others prohibit use or storage of hazardous materials. Zoning codes usually do not allow hazardous substances to be stored, much less used, on the premises.

4. Business activities

Many zoning codes prohibit certain types of businesses in residential areas. Most zoning restrictions apply to all residential zones on a jurisdiction-wide basis. There are limited means for varying the restrictiveness of zoning regulations from zone to zone: Variant definitions of a home-based business can be defined and allowed in different densities of residential zone, or different types of review and permission can be used for different residential zones. The most common practice, however, is to have one definition of home occupation, and one definition of the day care home, which imposes the same restrictions and requires the same level of review and type of permission throughout the jurisdiction.

5. Zoning restrictions

Zoning restrictions on home-based businesses seem to be designed for the most vulnerable residential neighborhoods and then applied on a jurisdiction-wide basis. Flexible performance standards that adapt to different characteristics of individual neighborhoods would be more efficient and are preferable. For example, instead of prohibiting exterior physical changes, any remodeling for a home-based business can be required to conform with the neighborhood's residential character and/or architecture. Traffic concerns can be addressed by requiring that activities of the home-based business may not significantly reduce availability of parking for residents. Although some types of business (e.g., automotive repair shops) may be hopelessly incompatible with residential neighborhoods, most types of businesses can be restricted through performance standards rather than by absolute prohibition.

Source: Small Business Administration (www.sba.gov).

Best Home-Based Franchises

The following are the top ten home-based franchises for 2006 according to our friends at Entrepreneur magazine.

1. Jani-King

As a student at the University of Oklahoma in 1968, Jim Cavanaugh worked as a night auditor at a hotel chain. While there, he realized that there would always be a strong need for janitorial services as long as there were office buildings. He began marketing janitorial services by day and cleaning buildings with his friends by night. Within a year, Cavanaugh established Jani-King, and in 1974 he started franchising. A commercial cleaning service, Jani-King sets up franchisees with a customer base and charges fees depending on the size of that initial base.

16885 Dallas Pkwy.
Addison, TX 75001
(800)552-5264
Fax: (972)991-5723; (972)239-7706
www.janiking.com
E-mail: *info@janiking.com*

2. Jan-Pro Franchising Int'l. Inc.

Jacques Lapointe founded Jan-Pro in Providence, Rhode Island, in 1991. It started franchising the following year. Jan-Pro is a commercial cleaning franchise that operates throughout the United States and Canada.

11605 Haynes Bridge Rd., #425
Alpharetta, GA 30004
(866) 355-1064
Fax: (678) 336-1781
www.jan-pro.com
E-mail: *melanie.nance@jan-pro.com*

3. ServiceMaster Clean

ServiceMaster was incorporated in 1947 as Wade, Wenger and Associates. Marion Wade got the idea for his company after an accident with chemicals left him temporarily blind in 1945. Today, it is part of the ServiceMaster Co. franchise family, which includes franchise companies Merry Maids, Furniture Medic, and Terminix. ServiceMaster Residential/Commercial Services is headquartered in Memphis, Tennessee, and has enjoyed more than twenty-five years of consecutive growth.

3839 Forest Hill Irene Rd.
Memphis, TN 38125
(800) 255-9687; (901) 597-7500
Fax: (901)597-7580
www.ownafranchise.com
E-mail: *brwilliams@smclean.com*

4. Jazzercise Inc.

While teaching traditional jazz dance classes in Evanston, Illinois, in 1969, Judi Sheppard Missett turned her students away from the mirrors and started a "just for fun" class that incorporated dance moves to provide aerobic exercise. After moving to Southern California, she started training other instructors in the Jazzercise program in 1977. Six years later, the company began franchising. Now Jazzercise's CEO, she continues to teach weekly Jazzercise classes and choreograph new dance routines. Based in Carlsbad, California, Jazzercise has more than 5,000 instructors teaching its total-body conditioning program to almost half a million participants each year in the United States and more than thirty other countries.

Jazzercise instructors are trained and certified before becoming franchised.

2460 Impala Dr.
Carlsbad, CA 92008
(760) 476-1750
Fax: (760) 602-7180
www.jazzercise.com

5. Chem-Dry Carpet Drapery & Upholstery Cleaning

Robert Harris worked as a carpet cleaner to pay for his law school tuition. He found the cleaning methods being used were not getting the job done and set about developing new solutions to get carpets cleaner. Harris started using his new solution to clean carpets for family and friends, and demand for his services quickly grew. In 1977, Harris founded Chem-Dry to bring his new cleaning methods to more customers. Chem-Dry began franchising in 1978 and now has locations in the United States, Canada, Japan, Australia, and the United Kingdom.

1530 N. 1000 West
Logan, UT 84321
(877) 307-8233
Fax: (435) 755-0021
www.chemdry.com
E-mail: *charlie@chemdry.com*

6. CleanNet USA Inc.

Mark Salek founded CleanNet USA in 1987 and opened the company's first office the following year in Columbia, Maryland, providing cleaning services to commercial clients in the Baltimore/Washington, D.C., area. Today, CleanNet's uniformed force offers a variety of cleaning services for commercial, retail, and industrial facilities in financial, hospitality, medical, and other industries.

9861 Broken Land Pkwy., #208
Columbia, MD 21046
(800) 735-8838; (410) 720-6444
Fax: (410) 720-5307
www.cleannetusa.com

7. Snap-on Tools

Since 1920, Snap-on Tools dealers have sold a variety of hand, power, and diagnostic tools to professional service technicians. From their mobile showrooms, dealers visit customers once a week—making sales, handling repairs, and introducing new products. Snap-on provides dealerships, body shops, marinas, airports, and other shops where cars, trucks, boats, planes, and various vehicles are repaired with tools and equipment.

2801 80th St., PO Box 1410
Kenosha, WI 53141-1410
(800) 756-3344
Fax: (262) 656-5088
www.snapon.com
E-mail: *franchise@snapon.com*

8. Servpro Industries Inc.

Founded in 1967 by Ted Isaacson, Servpro provides home and business owners with a variety of cleaning and restoration services. In the home, Servpro cleans upholstery, walls, and furnishings and provides disaster protection. For businesses, the company cleans carpets, floors, HVAC systems, and air ducts. In case of fire and other disasters, Servpro cleans, restores, and reconstructs carpets, hard surfaces, and masonry.

801 Industrial Dr.
Gallatin, TN 37066
(800) 826-9586; (615) 451-0600
Fax: (615) 451-1602
www.servpro.com

9. WSI Internet

WSI Internet, founded in 1995, has a network of consultants that spreads across more than eighty-seven countries and six continents, providing Internet services to small- and medium-size businesses. WSI Internet is based in Toronto, Ontario, and has been franchising since 1996.

5580 Explorer Dr., #600
Mississauga, ON L4W 4Y1 Canada
(888) 678-7588; (905) 678-7588
Fax: (905) 678-7242
www.wsicorporate.com

10. Matco Tools

Since 1979, Matco Tools, a subsidiary of Danaher Corp., has been manufacturing and distributing mechanics' tools and service equipment, including everything from hand tools and toolboxes to shop equipment. With more than 1,200 distributors across the United States and Puerto Rico, Matco and its franchisees service more than 825,000 automotive technicians and mechanics worldwide.

4403 Allen Rd.
Stow, OH 44224
(800) 368-6651
Fax: (330) 926-5325
www.matcotools.com

Source: *Entrepreneur* magazine's 2006 Franchise 500. For more information, please visit www.entrepreneur.com/franchise500.

Questions You Should Ask Before Buying a Franchise

Before you buy any franchise, it's important to do "due diligence" and make sure there are no surprises before you sign on the dotted line. After thoroughly reading the franchise's Uniform Franchise Offering Circular (UFOC), meeting with a number of current franchisees, and viewing their operations at close hand, here are some important questions to ask the franchise before you sign up.

1. What will your territory be?

Can the franchise put another franchisee in a location that's uncomfortably close to yours? Are you allowed to advertise your location outside of your "assigned" territory (and, vice versa, can other franchisees advertise in your territory)?

2. Does the franchise plan to offer its products and services directly to consumers?

Does the franchise plan to sell directly to consumers via the Internet or a toll-free telephone number? If they do, how will the franchisees benefit from the direct sales operation?

3. Are you limited to just one location?

If the franchise concept works, is it possible for you to "build an empire" and open several locations in adjacent territories? Will the franchise grant you a "right of first refusal" before they open locations in territories next to yours?

4. Are the deadlines for opening your first location reasonable?

Is the franchise giving you enough time to find a site, negotiate a lease, and complete your "build-out"?

5. If you can't find a suitable location within a reasonable time, what happens?

Sometimes you just can't find a suitable location even though you've been knocking yourself out looking for one. Will the franchise be reasonable in that situation, and let you out? Will the franchise refund a portion of your upfront franchise fee?

6. What are the projected costs of opening your first location?

If it isn't already in the UFOC, ask the franchise to provide you with an itemized estimate of all costs you can be expected to incur before you have your "grand opening." Be sure to factor in "hidden" costs, such as insurance premiums, lease security deposits, and real-estate brokers' fees, and be sure to get quotes from several sources before you commit to the franchise.

7. What is the franchise's commitment to advertising within your territory?

If you are one of the only franchisees in your area, how much of the franchise's advertising fund will be dedicated to your territory?

8. What happens if the franchise merges with another franchise?

Will they allow you to keep operating under the old format? Will they give you a reasonable amount of time to convert over to a new format?

What if the other franchise has a location right across the street from yours?

9. What happens if you are sued because the franchise violates local law?

Generally, you are responsible for making sure your franchised business complies with local laws. But if you're following the franchise manual to the letter, and somebody sues you because of something outside your control (for example, the franchise's name violates a local trademark, or the franchise's exclusive arrangement with a supplier violates state "unfair trade practices" laws), will the franchise stand behind you and pay your legal bills?

10. What happens if the franchise is not renewed at the end of the term?

No franchise is forever; the average term is ten to fifteen years. Do you have the absolute right to renew as long as you've done a good job? If either you or the franchise decides not to renew, do you get paid something for all your time and trouble in building the business? Can you continue in business under another name?

Source: Cliff Ennico, a nationally recognized small business legal expert, is the author of the nationally syndicated newspaper column "Succeeding in Your Business" and the author of *Small Business Survival Guide* (Adams, $12.95). You can find out more about him at *www.cliffennico.com*. Contact him at 2490 Black Rock Turnpike, # 354, Fairfield, CT 06825-2400; (203) 254-1727; fax: (203) 254-8195; e-Mail: *cennico@legalcareer.com*.

Your Store

Things to Ask Yourself Before Purchasing a Bar Code Scanner

If you have inventory to manage, then bar code devices are extremely valuable tools. There are a large variety of bar code technologies with a wide range of prices tags. To get started, you'll probably need to purchase a bar code scanner and a printer. Here are some questions to ask yourself when choosing a scanner.

1. Will you scan "uneven" surfaces like pop cans or bottles?

If so, you don't want a Wand or CCD scanner. You should choose a laser scanner or linear imager that can handle uneven surfaces.

2. Do you need a scanner that operates under bright sunlight?

If so, make sure you choose a CCD scanner, linear imager, or a laser with high visibility. High-visibility laser scanners use a brighter beam of light that will overcome this problem.

3. Do you need to scan items at long ranges?

If you scan items in a large environment (like a warehouse), choose a laser scanner with long-range capabilities. Long-range scanners typically have an aiming beam, which is a bright dot to assist the user in locating the bar code. You can read bar codes up to forty feet away, but the bar code needs to be large and printed on "retroreflective" material that can reflect a lot of light.

4. Will you read small, dense bar codes, such as those found on jewelry tags?

If so, you may need a high-density scanner that will read down to 2-mil bar codes. (The mil is the size of the bar.)

5. Do you want to scan items very fast?

If so, you should consider an omnidirectional scanner. These scanners allow you to check items quickly because it doesn't matter how the bar code is positioned. The rest of the scanners require the bar code to be turned in a specific direction because they only emit a single line. Just think about your last visit to the grocery store. Can you imagine how slow it would be if the cashier has to make sure every bar code was turned a specific direction? Omnidirectional scanners save them a lot of time because it doesn't matter which way the bar code is positioned.

6. Do you want a wireless scanner so you're not restricted by the cable?

If you scan large bulky items or you need to scan items in an area where the cable denies access, then you should consider a wireless scanner. Wireless scanners are just like other scanners except they don't require a cord. They're also nice because you don't have to worry about the cord getting damaged. If you want to carry your scanner around to count your inventory, then you should consider a PDT (Portable Data Terminal), instead of a wireless scanner.

7. Do you want to hold your scanner or do you want it mounted in a fixed position?

If you're like most grocery stores and you need to scan small items very fast, then a fixed-mount omnidirectional scanner could be your best option. They're great because you can quickly move the item in front of the fixed scanner. But if you also scan large items you'll need a hand-held scanner too. So, you'll have to invest in two scanners and spend more money.

Source: Jeff Haefner is a nationally known author and retail technology consultant. He has experience as a programmer, retail consultant, network administrator, POS software salesman, and marketing manager. Jeff's Web site offers *free* tips and an popular newsletter teaching retailers how to get the most out of POS software and technology. The Web site also includes "The POS Software Buyer's Guide—How to Choose POS Software and Avoid Problems." If you'd like to learn more, visit his Web site at *www.possoftware-guide.com*

Things to Ask Yourself Before Purchasing Bar Code Printers

If you plan to use bar code scanners, then you might need to print your own labels and apply them to bins, shelves, booklets, and merchandise that don't include UPC tags. Here are a few questions to ask yourself before purchasing a bar code printer.

1. Should I use a standard printer?

Bar code labels can be printed with standard ink-jet or laser printers, but results can vary. These printers aren't the ideal choice, because scanners require crisp bar codes with at least 300 dpi in order to work reliably. Laser printers also require

sheets of paper, which makes it difficult to print one or two labels at a time. In addition, they cannot produce chemical- or water-resistant labels that will last a long time. That's why most people use thermal label printers. They're designed to produce high-quality labels that last a long time. They also allow you to print one label at a time (instead of an entire sheet).

2. Should I use a direct thermal printer?

Thermal printers are ideal choices when it comes to printing bar code labels. Direct thermal printers have the print head in direct contact with heat-activated thermal paper and no ribbon is required. As a result, costs are lower, but there are several drawbacks. The print color is limited to black, and the printing is not as crisp as that of thermal-transfer ribbon printing. Over time, the labels will turn brown, particularly when subjected to heat and sunlight. Direct thermal printing is popular in the foods industry, since most items are stored away from heat and sunlight, and the label shelf life is less than one year.

3. Should I use a thermal-transfer printer?

In this method, the print head transfers ink (via heat) from a carbon ribbon onto paper—hence, the name *thermal transfer*. The ribbons can be different colors, so the user is not limited to black print. Printing is very crisp and durable, so this method is excellent for high-density bar codes and labels that require longevity. The other benefit is that thermal-transfer printers can print on paper, film, and even foil substrates.

4. Do I need to print in color?

Will you ever need to print labels in colors other than black? If so, you should consider a thermal-transfer printer.

5. How long should the labels last?

Do the labels need to have a shelf life of more than one year? If so, you should consider a thermal-transfer printer.

6. What conditions will it be exposed to?

Will the labels be subjected to heat or sunlight? If so, you should consider a thermal-transfer printer.

7. What kind of surface will you print on?

Will you be printing on a variety of different substrates (i.e., papers, films, and foils)? If so, you should consider a thermal-transfer printer.

Source: Jeff Haefner is a nationally known author and retail technology consultant. He has experience as a programmer, retail consultant, network administrator, POS software salesman, and marketing manager. Jeff's Web site offers *free* tips and an popular newsletter teaching retailers how to get the most out of POS software and technology. The Web site also includes "The POS Software Buyer's Guide—How to Choose POS Software and Avoid Problems." If you'd like to learn more, visit his Web site at *www.possoftwareguide.com*.

Top Reasons to Use Bar Codes

Bar code scanning devices are extremely helpful tools used by retailers, warehouses, distributors, or anyone who needs to track inventory. Scanners will help increase your efficiency by reading bar code information much faster and more accurately than you could type the same information manually. Simply put, bar code scanners translate bar codes into numbers and letters and send the data to your computer. The actual bar code consists of a series of narrow and wide lines printed on a label or tag. Each "bar" represents a character for a bar code scanner to interpret. The scanner measures the widths of the bars and spaces, translates the different patterns back into regular characters, and sends them to a computer or portable terminal. Most scanners auto-detect different types of symbologies. However, you should double-check and find out which symbology you'll use before spending your hard-earned money. Scanners are great tools that allow you to accomplish the following tasks.

1. Serve customers faster and improve service

By quickly scanning bar codes at the point of sale instead of typing a SKU.

2. Reduce pricing and inventory errors

The typical error rate for human data entry is one error per 300 characters. Bar code scanners can be as good as one error in 36 trillion characters.

3. Save time and improve efficiency

If all your merchandise is bar-coded, you can save time by checking out customers faster, instantly implementing markdowns, and eliminating the problem of price tag switching.

4. Reduce costs

If you have UPCs on your merchandise, then you don't have to put the price tag on the product itself, which saves time and reduces handling costs.

5. Improve the accuracy of your inventory

Bar coding reduces errors at receiving and at the point of sale so your inventory stays accurate.

Source: Jeff Haefner is a nationally known author and retail technology consultant. He has experience as a programmer, retail consultant, network administrator, POS software salesman, and marketing manager. Jeff's Web site offers *free* tips and an popular newsletter teaching retailers how to get the most out of POS software and technology. The Web site also includes "The POS Software Buyer's Guide—How to Choose POS Software and Avoid Problems." If you'd you like to learn more, visit his Web site at *www.possoftwareguide.com.*

Popular Features for Cash Registers

The number of items, clerks, and rate of inflows/outflows will determine which cash register is most suitable for a particular operation. The higher-end models have more reporting features, programmable functions, and more sophisticated printing and display capabilities. To choose the right cash register, you will want to consider the following features.

1. Displays

Most cash registers have a front display for the operator and a rear display for the customer. Some rear displays can be adjusted and rotated for convenient customer viewing. Higher-end models may have an alphanumeric front display, where the top line is alphanumeric and the bottom line is numeric only. The alphanumeric display shows item descriptions during sales

registration and alphanumeric prompts during the program mode to assist the user with installation or in the selection of menu options.

2. Printers

Printers come in single, two, or alphanumeric stations and are connected to the register. Single-station printers print out only one paper tape that can be used either as a journal record or a customer receipt. However, some single-station printers print on two-ply paper providing both a receipt for the customer and a merchant copy (journal tape) for recordkeeping.

3. Keyboards

Cash registers come with two keyboard variations: raised and flat. A raised keyboard is similar to that of a PC. It is the optimal solution, if you plan to touch-type or want to enter large texts. A flat keyboard protects against spills and crumbs. It is therefore ideal for the application in bakeries, restaurants, and other hospitality trades. Also, you can then combine your built-in flat keyboard with an extra raised keyboard to input large amounts of text or make PLU modifications.

4. Departments

Departments are numbered keys on the keyboard that represent a grouping or category of items (such as diary products). They can be used for quick and accurate entries of items sold, but are usually used for tracking and reporting. The number of departments ranges from 8 to 99.

5. Price lookups (PLUs)

Commonly referred to as PLUs, these are numbers that can be programmed to represent merchandise or inventory. They are used for quick and accurate entry and tracking of frequently sold items. Once programmed, the user punches in the PLU code (e.g., 99) on the keypad and then presses the PLU button. The product's name and price and any other programmable information will immediately appear on the display. The number of PLUs can range from 1 to 30,000 depending on the model. Certain models also allow the user to assign a name to each PLU number so that each selected item has a name, price, and description all at the touch of a button. This is a valuable feature for items with high turnover.

6. Clerk identification system

Most models have a clerk ID security system that gives clerks an individual ID number, allowing them to sign in and use the ECR. This system serves as a tracking and reporting feature for individual clerk sales.

7. Cash drawers and trays

All models come with at least four slots for coins and four slots for bills in the cash drawer. Higher-end models come with a few extra slot trays or an accessory drawer for additional storage of currency and/or checks.

Source: Quorion Data Systems (*www.quorion.de*)—This young German company develops, manufactures, and sells innovative electronic cash registers. Contact: an der Klinge 6, 99195 Erfurt-Stotternheim, Germany; telephone: +49 362 04 542 0; fax: +49 362 04 542 11; e-mail: *sales@quorion.de*.

Things to Consider Before Purchasing a Cash Register

Looking to buy a new cash register for your business? Here are some considerations before you ring up the sale.

1. How big is your business?

Cash registers are available with a wide array of functions and abilities. If you have a larger department store, you may need department and product codes to be built in to the register. Smaller stores have no need for department codes. Larger businesses will also want to use a product code scanner. Always be sure, before buying a cash register, that it will also support your future needs as well.

2. What functions do you need?

Different registers are available with different functions. Many of these functions include department codes, price lookups, and item codes. Many cash registers are also available with tax computations and security features. Registers vary from 200 price lookups all the way to 1,700 maximum. Department codes vary from 16 to 99, and clerk IDs vary from 8 to 40 maximum. Be sure your cash register has all the functions and features you need.

3. Where is your business located?

Initially you would not think location would be important when purchasing a cash register. Because almost everybody needs to use a cash register, they are available in several different formats. Maybe you should consider lightweight portable cash registers that run on C batteries. These registers are great for use in kiosks and other small locations. Other cash registers are hardwired but are still lightweight for use at fairs, dances, charity events, and other temporary locations. Heavier-duty cash registers are designed for use at fixed locations such as department stores.

Source: ABCO (*www.abcosolutions.com*)—A source for quality office supplies, office machines and equipment, ABCO sells everything from rotary paper cutters, book-binding machines, paper folders, paper drills, collators, pouch laminators, sand roll laminators, shrink wrap systems, money counters, and more. Contact them at ABCO Office Solutions, 1142 West Flint Meadow Drive, Kaysville, UT 84037; PO Box 829, Kaysville UT 84037-0829; toll-free: (800) 658-8788; local: (801) 927-3020.

Top Things Needed to Set Up a Point-of-Sale Station

In order to efficiently run a retail business, a point-of-sale system has become a necessity to help speed up transactions, control inventory, improve customer service, and easily analyze key indicators like sales, inventory turns, and more. Our expert, who knows POS systems, offers you this advice.

1. Standard computer

The *very* first thing you need is a good business computer. Most point-of-sale (POS) systems run on a standard IBM compatible PC with Windows 98, 2000, or XP, but PC minimum requirements vary with the software provider. If you have more than one computer, you'll need a network. Windows peer-to-peer networks are commonly used in small businesses. But some POS systems require UNIX or Linux. So check with the software vendor to get the specs. When

choosing a computer, you should consider buying everything from the POS software vendor. They usually preconfigure and test the computer. This isn't always the cheapest way to go, but it's usually the most reliable method. If the vendor doesn't offer computers, then you should look for a good business computer. Don't buy a cheap "home" computer with Windows XP Home, a bundled printer, scanner, preloaded games, multimedia software, and who knows what else. Find a good-name brand computer that was built for business use, and when it comes to computers, don't buy the cheapest that you can find. You could be asking for trouble.

2. POS workstations

If you're looking for maximum reliability and a space-saving design, you may want to consider a POS workstation (instead of a standard computer). POS workstations are specially designed computers that include a variety of POS peripherals tightly built around the computer. All the components are designed to fit together, resulting in a very compact, space-saving design. Beneath the surface, POS stations include durable components that are built and tested for the demanding needs of the retail environment. As a result, they usually last longer than a standard PC. In addition, POS stations allow you to open the case quickly and upgrade or repair components without the use of tools—making it easy for almost any retailer to upgrade components or fix the computer. When choosing a POS workstation, it's very important to consider the service, support, and longevity of the company that manufactures the workstation. You will rely on them to send upgrades, replacement parts, and help you fix the hardware when you have problems. To protect your investment, choose a reputable company that will be around for a long time. You'll also have a variety of options when choosing a POS workstation.

3. POS software

The next thing you must have is the actual software. There are thousands of different POS software packages, and entire books having been written about choosing POS software. POS software is commonly used in millions of retail businesses throughout the world. They range from simple programs to extremely advanced programs with thousands of different features designed to streamline operations and improve efficiency. In addition, there are about thirty different vertical markets that software companies have customized their POS software to handle.

4. Receipt printer

The next most important device is the receipt printer. As you probably guessed, this device is used to print receipts for your customers. Most receipt printers use paper rolls about three inches wide. This is perfect for retailers that need to quickly print a small amount of information. However, if you repair equipment or sell large-ticket items like motorcycles or tractors, it's more practical to print a full invoice (8.5 x 11inches) on a standard dot-matrix or laser printer.

5. Bar code scanner

Bar code scanners are extremely popular tools at the point of sale. They allow you to check items *much* faster and more accurately at the point of sale than if you type the SKU number on a keyboard. In addition, bar code scanners can reduce pricing and inventory errors. The typical error rate for human data entry is one error per 300 characters. Bar code scanners can be as good as one error in 36 trillion characters.

6. Cash drawer

A cash drawer is an essential item that opens when you ring up a sale—just like a cash register. You can get locking cash drawers, plastic inserts to separate your bills and coins, slots for your credit card slips, and much more.

7. Magnetic strip (credit card) reader

The magnetic strip reader (MSR) provides a way of reading credit cards and sending the information to your POS software—so you don't have to type the information by hand. MSRs are devices that plug into your keyboard and send information to your POS software when swiped. To make your POS software and the MSR work together, you need to configure the software—which is the most difficult part.

8. Keyboard

You might want to consider replacing your standard keyboard with a good POS keyboard. Why? First of all, POS keyboards are built to take everyday retail abuse. They include spill-resistant materials and heavy-duty material that will last longer. POS keyboards also include programmable keys much like the traditional cash register. The keys can be set up to do one-key functions such as total, produce, soft goods, discount, and so on. In addition, you can integrate credit card swipes and scanner ports to save space and add convenience.

9. Customer display

Big retailers like Wal-Mart and Target use customer displays for a good reason—because displays improve customer satisfaction. They will show the customer exactly what you are ringing up. So if there's an error, they can catch it. If your POS software supports displays, then maybe it's time for you to get one.

10. Monitor

Have you considered the type of monitor you should buy? This may not seem important, but most retailers end up wishing they'd bought different monitors (usually smaller monitors or maybe touch screens).

11. Change dispenser

If speeding up customer checkouts and reducing change errors is important to you, then you might want to add a change dispenser to your arsenal. They automatically distribute the correct change, so your cashiers don't have to worry. Most change dispensers work through a serial interface. You'll also need to find one that works with your type of currency (U.S., Canadian, etc.).

12. Pin pad

Pin pads provide an extra layer of security against credit card fraud. Your customers simply swipe their own card and enter a pin, if needed. Most pin pads also allow the use of smart cards, which can help you increase customer loyalty.

Source: Jeff Haefner is a nationally known author and retail technology consultant. He has experience as a programmer, retail consultant, network administrator, POS software salesman, and marketing manager. Jeff's Web site offers *free* tips and an popular newsletter teaching retailers how to get the most out of POS software and technology. The Web site also includes "The POS Software Buyer's Guide—How to Choose POS Software and Avoid Problems." If you'd you like to learn more, visit his Web site at *www.possoftwareguide.com*.

Things to Ask Before Purchasing Point-of-Sale (POS) Software

With thousands of different POS systems to choose from, it's very common for retailers to make mistakes when buying a system. In fact, almost 75 percent of the retail businesses make the wrong choice the first time around. They say that if they could do it all over again, they would choose something different. To help you avoid mistakes and get on the right track, here are ten things to ask before purchasing a POS system.

1. Is the software designed for your industry?

It is important to look for software that's tailored for your industry. Every retailer has very different needs. Another problem is that some POS software companies claim to work for almost any business. They're probably right. The software will work. But you'll probably miss out on a lot of "time-saving" and "profit-generating" features. The trick is to find POS systems that are actually designed for your vertical market.

2. Who uses this software?

It's also very important to find a POS system that is used by other retailers like you. So if there's a special new feature that you need for your industry, the POS developer is more likely to make the change (because hundreds of other users will benefit from the same feature). If you're part of a small group, they probably won't listen to your requests!

3. What size of business do you target?

Each software product is well-suited for a certain size customer. Some POS systems are designed for Tier 1 retailers (doing over $250 million in annual sales). Some POS systems are designed for Tier 5 retailers (doing $50,000 to $500,000 in annual sales). To help you narrow the choices, you need to find a POS system that is marketed to your size of business.

4. Can I get a software demonstration?

One of the best ways to quickly learn about a software system is to get a demonstration from a sales person. If you have high-speed Internet access, most companies can give demonstrations right over the Internet. Make sure that you "fully utilize" the salesperson. Their job is to take the time and show you what they have to offer. Use them for demos and answering questions. Don't try to figure things out yourself. It takes too long! Use the salesperson and you'll save time.

5. Do you have a list of customers in my area?

This is an important step that shouldn't be overlooked. Calling references will help you select the right system and avoid many problems. In fact, calling references can tell you a lot. If you ask the right questions, you can find out if the vendor offers sufficient training, if the software is reliable, if the company offers good service, if the software is easy to use, if the software has any problems, if it's an overall "good" system.

6. What type of training do you provide?

You might think you can train yourself and save money. But I can assure you that "good" software training is extremely important. All too often, I talk to retailers who use POS software, and they think they're using the software effectively. But most of those retailers are making some major mistakes. Unfortunately, POS software does not run itself. It's not very helpful unless you use it properly. In fact, a mid-range to high-end POS system can be very extensive and complicated. In order for you and other employees in your business to use it effectively, you need good training, preferably one-on-one. You can get onsite, classroom, telephone or internet training. I think the best method is to get onsite or classroom training. and then get telephone training three to nine months after the initial installation. It will cost more, but the additional training is worth it. It's also helpful to get training from someone that has experience in your industry. Another training method is computer-based training (through a CD-ROM or the Internet). It's usually a self-paced video tutorial. Those can be effective to get started quickly but not for the initial training. The retailers I've seen take this route experience poor results. Sometimes they are happy with the software, but they aren't using it right, and they're missing out on some major time-saving processes. Plus, it's time-consuming. You have to figure out how to use the software, and then you still have to train your employees. On the other hand, computer-based training is an easy way to teach new employees a few things about the software. The bottom line is that "one-on-one" training is very effective and the best way to go in most situations.

7. What is the average support callback time?

When you invest in point-of-sale software, you're buying a relationship, not just a product. In fact, the "quality" of the software company is usually just as important as the product. Just imagine: You can't print and it takes two days to get help from a support technician. That would be a frustrating and expensive problem. If you want to get a high return on your POS software investment, choose a company that can give you fast and reliable service and support.

8. How long has your company been in business and how many active customers do you have?

There are thousands of POS software companies, and dozens come and go every year. What would you do if you bought a new POS system and the company went out of business a few months later? Find a company that has been established for several years and has a solid customer base.

9. How many businesses are using this software?

This will give you an idea how well the software has been tested. If there are only a few people using the software, it will probably have bugs. There's probably a reason that the software is not popular.

10. What will be my return on investment (ROI)?

Whether you're replacing your old POS software or starting fresh, why do you want a POS system? Whether you have one employee or 1,000 employees—you need to keep this concept in your conscious mind as you're considering every software feature, every aspect of the software company, and every part of the computer system. Create a "return on investment" document for a couple of the POS systems that you are considering. This can help you make the right decision.

11. Do you have the following features?

This is the last, but the most important and difficult issue. It is absolutely critical to create a features checklist (or wish list) to figure out which POS system will give you the highest return on investment (even if you're a small retailer). Unless you're a retail POS expert, it's difficult to sort through countless POS systems and figure out what features you really need. What's more, it's difficult to understand the "true" potential of your POS system. As a result, many retailers overlook important features that would save them a lot of time and money! If you want to avoid this common mistake, it's important to create a thorough features wish list.

Source: Jeff Haefner is a nationally known author and retail technology consultant. He has experience as a programmer, retail consultant, network administrator, POS software salesman, and marketing manager. Jeff's Web site offers *free* tips and a popular newsletter teaching retailers how to get the most out of POS software and technology. The Web site also includes "The POS

Software Buyer's Guide—How to Choose POS Software and Avoid Problems." If you'd you like to learn more, visit his Web site at *www.possoftwareguide.com*.

Popular Point-of-Sale Software

Every retail store, and quite a few nonretail outlets, will need a POS system. Besides ringing up the cash, good POS systems also give a business a new level of control over operations, increase efficiency, and boost profits. A wrong system can be a waste of money and a source of ongoing frustration. We asked a national seller of these systems to list the most popular applications on the market now.

1. Microsoft RMS: Store Operations

Designed to help small retailers, Microsoft Business Solutions Retail Management System Store Operations helps you compete more efficiently and for greater profitability. Starting at: $820.

Microsoft Corporation
One Microsoft Way
Redmond, WA 98052-6399
(800) –MICROSOFT; (800) 642-7676
www.microsoft.com

2. NextPOS Restaurant

NextPOS for Restaurants software solution is the affordable, easy-to-use, feature-rich, and 100 percent multilingual restaurant point-of-sale and store management solution. Starting at: $750.

NextPOS Corporation
14685 Mono Way
Sonora, CA 95370
www.nextpos.com

3. Microsoft Point of Sale

Microsoft Point of Sale is designed for single-store retail businesses that need an application that is affordable and easy to learn and use, with functionality that can eliminate manual processes and increase efficiency. Starting at: $630.

Microsoft Corporation
One Microsoft Way
Redmond, WA 98052-6399
(800) –MICROSOFT; (800) 642-7676
www.microsoft.com

4. PC America CRE Retail

Cash Register Express (or CRE 2004) is a cost-effective computerized cash register that keeps your inventory costs down, reduces theft, and makes more money! CRE 2004 is the first Windows-based POS system exclusively for retail and video stores. Its easy-to-use interface makes it a breeze to manage your store. Starting at: $545.

PC America
One Blue Hill Plaza, second floor
PO Box 1546
Pearl River, NY 10965
(845) 920-0200
Voice: (845) 920-0880
www.pcamerica.com

5. Microsoft RMS: Headquarters

Designed to help small retailers, Microsoft Business Solutions Retail Management System Store Operations helps you compete more efficiently and for greater profitability. Starting at: $2,800.

Microsoft Corporation
One Microsoft Way
Redmond, WA 98052-6399
(800) –MICROSOFT; (800) 642-7676
www.microsoft.com

6. IC Verify Credit Card Processing

One of the most comprehensive payments processing products available for retail and mail/telephone. IC VERIFY software processes all payments types including credit, debit, check, purchase cards, and private label cards. Starting at: $295.

IC Verify, Inc.
(800) 666-5777
www.icverify.com

7. PCCharge Credit Card

Enable businesses with Windows-based system to process credit card, ATM/debit card, EBT cards, checks, and gift/loyalty card on their PCs. Starting at: $220.

VeriFone, Incorporated
Parkway Business Center
5000 Business Center Dr.
Suite 1000
Savannah, GA 31405
www.gosoftware.com

Source: POS Global (*www.posglobal.com*)—One of the leading global sources for affordable point-of-sale and auto ID products. Contact them at 4004 W. Plano Parkway, Plano, TX 75093; (972) 769-7300; fax: (972) 599-9387.

Popular Point-of-Sale Software Features

Most POS systems on the market offer hundreds of different features. But here are just a few of the key features that are important to retailers.

1. Automatic purchase order suggestion and replenishment

This is a huge time-saver for retailers who stock a lot of products. The software will automatically suggest what you need to order based on what has been sold.

2. Sales tax calculations

If you're calculating taxes the old-fashioned way, this is another huge time-saver. Since your POS software is tracking all sales, you can simply run your sales tax report each month and everything will be totaled for you.

3. Special order tracking

This feature allows you to easily track your customers special orders. So you almost never forget to place the order for them. You can also easily check the status of the order to see if it came in.

4. Customer marketing

Many POS systems include marketing features that allow you to identify certain market segments. Then you can easily create a targeted list and send them a promotion. For example, you could easily create a list of all customer that bought XYZ widgets and send them a letter about a sale you're having on a complementary product.

5. Customer history lookup

This is a critical feature that allows you to quickly view all past purchases and transactions for your customers. So you can easily pull up past receipts or check your customers' payment history.

6. End-of-day closeout reports

Another time-saving feature is the end-of-day closeout reports available in most POS systems. In just a few seconds, you can print reports that show your sales totals for the day broken down by department, category, tender (cash, credit card, etc), and more. In addition, you can view information such as your totals for each cash drawer and canceled invoices.

7. User security

Most retailers find it very important to keep employees out of certain areas of their POS system to avoid theft, protect sensitive information, and keep information accurate. User security can be an extremely important feature that allows you to lock certain employees out of desired screens and fields.

8. Accounting software interfaces or integration

By linking with your accounting software, you can save a huge amount of time by avoiding double entry. Not to mention you'll cut down on mistakes. Many POS systems will let you export sales totals into your accounting software to make life easier.

9. Price control

A variety of price control features are available that allow you to change pricing easily based on supplier, customer, price range, and more. So for example, you could easily run a 10 percent discount on all merchandise purchased from XYZ supplier for seven days. Not only does this save time, but it makes it easy for management to control pricing for the entire business.

10. Electronic purchase order transmission

This is another huge time-saver that allows you to send your purchase order to your supplier electronically instead of calling, faxing, or keying the order on to their Web site.

Source: Jeff Haefner is a nationally known author and retail technology consultant. He has experience as a programmer, retail consultant, network administrator, POS software salesman, and marketing manager. Jeff's Web site offers *free* tips and a popular newsletter teaching retailers how to get the most out of POS software and technology. The Web site also includes "The POS Software Buyer's Guide—How to Choose POS Software and Avoid Problems." If you'd you like to learn more, visit his Web site at *www.possoftwareguide.com.*

Day to Day

Liabilities and Insurance Matters

States with the Lowest Auto Insurance Rates

As a small business owner, there are many insurance needs that you must address. If you have company cars, delivery vehicles, or the like, auto insurance will be a major concern. But how much will you be paying for auto insurance? That depends on what state your business is in, as different states have different average insurance rates. To get an idea of what you might have to pay, the following list is of the states with the lowest average annual auto insurance premiums.

1. Iowa
Average annual premium: $638.56
State insurance department: *www.iid.state. ia.us*

2. Idaho
Average annual premium: $669.13
State insurance department: *www.doi.state. id.us*

3. Maine
Average annual premium: $671.25
State insurance department: *www.maineinsurancereg.org*

4. Wisconsin
Average annual premium: $671.39
State insurance department: *oci.wi.gov/oci_home.htm*

5. South Dakota
Average annual premium: $694.46
State insurance department: *www.state. sd.us/drr/reg/insurance*

6. North Carolina
Average annual premium: $697.57
State insurance department: *www.ncdoi. com*

7. Virginia
Average annual premium: $712.69
State insurance department: *www.scc.virginia.gov/division/boi/index.htm*

8. Nebraska
Average annual premium: $712.79
State insurance department: *www.doi.ne.gov*

9. Ohio
Average annual premium: $713.67
State insurance department: *www.ohioinsurance.gov*

10. Vermont
Average annual premium: $734.31
State insurance department: *www.bishca. state.vt.us*

Source: Reprinted with permission by the National Association of Insurance Commissioners (*www.naic.org*). The NAIC does not rank State Average Expenditures and does not endorse any conclusions drawn from this data.

States with the Highest Auto Insurance Requirements

If your business has company cars, delivery vehicles, or uses any other kind of vehicles as a part of doing business, your company will need auto insurance. Depending where your business is, there are different requirements for the types and amount of coverage. The following list provides the eleven states with the highest requirements for auto insurance, ranked by coverages required.

1. Minnesota

Types of insurance required: bodily injury and property damage liability, personal injury protection, uninsured motorist coverage, underinsured motorist coverage

State insurance department: *www.commerce.state.mn.us*

2. Connecticut

Types of insurance required: bodily injury and property damage liability, uninsured motorist coverage, underinsured motorist coverage

State insurance department: *www.state.ct.us/cid*

3. Kansas

Types of insurance required: bodily injury and property damage liability, personal injury protection, uninsured motorist coverage

State insurance department: *www.ksinsurance.org*

4. Maine

Types of insurance required: bodily injury and property damage liability, uninsured motorist coverage, underinsured motorist coverage

State insurance department: *www.maineinsurancereg.org*

5. Maryland

Types of insurance required: bodily injury and property damage liability, personal injury protection, uninsured motorist coverage

State insurance department: *www.mdinsurance.state.md.us*

6. Massachusetts

Types of insurance required: bodily injury and property damage liability, personal injury protection, uninsured motorist coverage

State insurance department: *www.mass.gov/doi*

7. New Jersey

Types of insurance required: bodily injury and property damage liability, personal injury protection, uninsured motorist coverage

State insurance department: *www.state.nj.us/dobi/index.html*

8. New York

Types of insurance required: bodily injury and property damage liability, personal injury protection, uninsured motorist coverage

State insurance department: *www.ins.state.ny.us*

9. North Dakota

Types of insurance required: bodily injury and property damage liability, personal injury protection, uninsured motorist coverage

State insurance department: *www.state.nd.us/ndins*

10. Oregon

Types of insurance required: bodily injury and property damage liability, personal injury protection, uninsured motorist coverage

State insurance department: *www.cbs.state.or.us/external/ins/index.html*

11. Vermont

Types of insurance required: bodily injury and property damage liability, uninsured motorist coverage, underinsured motorist coverage

State insurance department: *www.bishca.state.vt.us*

Source: Insurance Information Institute (*www.iii.org*)—The Insurance Information Institute provides resources to enhance public understanding of what insurance is and what it does. The organization has become a definitive source for insurance information for the media, regulatory agencies, and the government.

Reasons to Have a Computer Disaster Plan

A disaster can strike a business at any time, and it can come in a variety of forms. The loss of data can have a huge impact on a company, and if severe enough, it can wipe out a company entirely. To help prepare to deal with such a disaster, a business owner should have a plan in place to protect computer systems and important information. The following list details some of the main reasons for having such a plan.

1. Disasters will occur.

In all likelihood, a disaster of some degree will strike a business, and having a plan in place to deal with a disaster of any kind will allow the business to recover and maintain operations. From events such as losing computer files or entire computer systems to large-scale natural disasters that hit the business hard, a plan for any disaster will prove valuable.

2. Data loss impacts several key areas.

Because computer systems hold almost all data for a company these days, the failure of those systems can impact many areas of the business. First and foremost, productivity will be hurt because of downtime and the time it takes to recover or re-enter the data. Morale will be hurt because so much important information was lost and the work to get back to normal could be daunting. Finally, profits will be hurt because of the slowdown in productivity.

3. Computer loss could threaten business survival.

With a large-scale loss of data and computer systems, businesses often fail. Studies have shown that there is only a one-in-four chance of a business surviving, immediately after a loss like that. When the business does survive, within eighteen to sixty months following the loss, there has been shown to be a 40 to 93 percent chance of the business closing down.

4. Data is too valuable.

Because the only asset for a company more valuable than data is generally the employees, it is very important to have a plan to back up and maintain data. The information is more important than the computers that hold it, and it is incredibly expensive and time-consuming to try to recover and restore data.

5. Preparedness is a must.

Having a plan in place can eliminate guesswork if and when a disaster does strike, it can reduce the time to identify and address a disaster, it can keep personal opinions out of the picture when dealing with a disaster, and it can reduce legal and financial impacts of disasters.

_____

Source: Jerry Adcock, data backup and disaster recovery expert. Mr. Adcock runs a branch of Subterranean Data Services (*www .sdsvaults.com*), a data storage and protection company, in Vancouver, Washington, and has written articles on the subject of disaster recovery and data loss, and information.

Things to Include in a Disaster Plan

You must plan for a variety of unfortunate events in order to ensure that your business can survive in less-than-ideal situations. One of these events is a natural disaster; with enough severity, such disasters can easily destroy a business. The following list includes the basic components of a disaster plan to ensure that your business will not be entirely wiped out.

1. Duplicate records

Be sure to keep complete up-to-date duplicates of your computerized and written records. Federal law states that your company may be held liable for these records even if they are lost, so be sure to keep duplicates on hand.

2. A list of activities and resources needed to sustain business

You should be able to identify the tasks needed to keep your business afloat and the resources need to perform those activities. While the majority of your business is shut down and recovering from a disaster, you should at least be able to maintain customer service to facilitate a complete recovery.

3. Worst-case scenario recovery plan

Your disaster plans should be geared toward the worst-case scenario to be sure that you are able to address any problems presented by a disaster. Locate alternate facilities, equipment, and supplies to keep your business going, and be sure to know qualified contractors who can literally help you rebuild your business.

4. Emergency response plan

Formulate a plan to respond to an emergency, including who will be contacted and when and what will happen to the company's facilities, equipment, customers, and employees. Be sure that everyone involved in the business is trained in the response plan so that should it ever need to be implemented, it will run smoothly.

5. A stockpile of disaster supplies

Should a disaster ever strike, you may need backup sources of power, such as generators, and backup communications systems, such as walkie-talkies, as well as basic emergency supplies, such as flashlights and first-aid kits. Be sure to have these things on hand in addition to the supplies needed to keep the business going.

6. Emergency contact list

Have a list of phone numbers and addresses of local, state, and federal emergency management agencies (such as FEMA), financial institutions (such as banks), major clients, suppliers, insurance agents, and company employees and management. The list should be copied and kept in several places, so that it is available no matter when or where the disaster strikes.

7. Emergency communications strategy

In addition to the emergency contact list, be sure to have an effective strategy in place so clients, suppliers, and others can contact your company by phone and at a new location to which the company may be forced to move. This strategy can include contacting people by phone, by e-mail, or through advertisements, among other methods.

8. Review your plan regularly

Once you have your entire disaster plan in place, be sure to review it regularly so that you and your employees all know how to deal effectively with a disaster. Be sure to assess the level of disaster risk in your area and keep your plan up-to-date so that your company can bounce back as quickly and efficiently as possible.

Source: The Insurance Information Institute (*www.iii.org*)—A resource that provides information on auto, life, home, and business insurance, among others, to individuals and businesses.

Top Insurance Issues for the Self-Employed

Our expert believes that many self-employed business owners are either over-insured or under-insured. She suggests that business owners address the first three questions below about business insurance needs to themselves. Self-employed people should then consider these specific questions when dealing with insurance agents and other professionals.

1. What are your circumstances?

Is your business conducted in your home, somewhere else, or both? Do you have employees, subcontractors, or do you work alone? Do you provide a product, a service, or both?

2. What can go wrong in your business?

Think of every possibility. What kind of a financial hit can you take without insurance coverage? How quickly could you resume operations in the event of fire or theft or an unhappy and litigious client? Distinguish between what you would like to insure if premium costs didn't matter and the coverage you absolutely must have. And there's always the question of coverage limits. You don't want to buy more coverage than you need. For liability coverage, is $300,000 enough, or do you need protection up to $1 million? Your call.

3. Are your priorities right?

Are you concentrating on damage to your home business equipment, such as your computer, printer, copier—perhaps a $5,000 expense—and dismissing the importance of coverage for injury to a client or employee—a potential multimillion-dollar lawsuit?

4. What are an insurance agent's skills and qualifications?

The agent who handles your personal insurance, such as life and medical, may not have the expertise to understand your business or the work situation of a self-employed individual. For instance, many agents do not know the difference between an employee and an independent contractor.

5. Does your auto insurance cover your business driving situations?

It may cover errands to pick up office supplies and an occasional dropoff to a customer; it may not cover regular or frequent deliveries of your product to customers.

6. Does your home insurance cover your home business?

The short answer is no—although a lot of home-based business owners think otherwise. Your home policy does insure you for liability that involves an invited guest or, depending on the policy, household or maintenance workers. It does not cover employees or freelancers who work for your business. Nor does it cover the delivery driver who falls down your icy steps while delivering the new printer for your business. A modest-sized home-based nonhazardous business might be adequately insured for business property loss and liability for $200 a year. Whether you can get coverage for that amount depends on the nature of your workers—a clerical assistant sitting at your computer one day a week is one thing, five people working every day at industrial sewing machines in your basement is another.

7. If someone works for you, what kind of coverage do you need?

Your first chore is to determine whether the worker is a freelancer or is your employee. This may not be a simple task. A freelancer would be covered by your business liability policy. Your employee would be covered by workers' compensation insurance. State laws and regulations determine whether you need workers' comp.

It's often based on factors like the number of hours worked, or the amount of wages paid per quarter. In some states family members who are your employees do not have to be covered. Start your questions with your state's department of labor. Be warned: Clear, understandable information may not be easy to come by.

8. What about a neighbor who is also a client who trips over your son's tricycle and breaks his leg?

That's why there are civil courts. Whether the home policy or the business policy covers that liability depends on circumstances. If you're covered by both policies the answer will probably be more to your liking. In most cases the policy also covers your legal fees. If you conduct a home business, some companies won't insure your home unless you also buy business coverage. That coverage may be an endorsement to the home policy or a separate in-home business policy.

9. Would a business policy cover liability for your products?

That depends on the policy and the product. You should have product liability insurance if the product you make could cause harm to someone. Make sure you understand all particulars of the coverage—exceptions to coverage (such as gross negligence) would have to be stated in the contract. And remember that some liability cases have a long tail—you can be sued twenty years from now for a software program you made this week. The cost for insuring some products might make you stagger, but the more expensive the coverage the more likely that the risk is large.

10. What about malpractice insurance?

In the industry this is called professional liability insurance, or errors and omissions. It protects the policyholder against malpractice, mistakes, negligence and not exercising due diligence. For some (like physicians) it's legally necessary; for some (like technology consultants) the purchaser of the product often requires it. For many self-employed entrepreneurs the risk of not being covered may not be that great. But don't assume you're one of them; a massage therapist may use an oil that gives the bride-to-be client a skin rash that ruins the wedding and cleans out the therapist's assets to pay for the delayed honeymoon. If you belong to a professional guild or organization, start there with your questions.

11. A business property and liability policy will cover the losses if lightning blows out your computers and the electrical wiring in your home office, but will it replace lost income during the repair time?

Not unless it includes business interruption coverage, which insures against potential lost income. Amounts for income you would earn in the future are based on your recordkeeping for previous earning periods. Policies can also cover inventory losses, relocation costs, and expenses incurred in using a temporary location.

12. And what if you fall down and break your arm and can't work for a couple of months, or have an illness that puts you out of commission for a year?

For that you need disability coverage, an expensive insurance with a lot of curves and hidden valleys. This kind of insurance calls for intensive research on your part to determine its value to your situation.

———————————

Source: June Walker (*www.junewalkeronline.com*) has been a financial and tax consultant to the self-employed for 25 years. Her clients are worldwide and include psychologists, carpenters, IT consultants, and attorneys. June is the author of *Self-Employed Tax Solutions: Quick, Simple, Money-Saving, Audit-Proof Tax and Recordkeeping Basics for the Independent Professional* (Globe Pequot Press, 2005). For more information, e-mail her at *june@junewalkeronline*, or call (888) 219-7771.

Things Every Business Owner Should Insure

Success in business hinges on a number of factors, but solid insurance coverage can be a crucial element, even for small businesses. Uppermost in priority for small business owners is to review their operations and identify the risks that could pose a threat to the business. Here are some factors to consider, provided by the Washington State Office of the Insurance Commissioner.

1. Property coverage

Business owners, like homeowners, need to protect the physical property in which their enterprise operates, as well as the inventory and equipment involved in the business. The threats are the same, too: You need protection against flood, fire, break-ins, vandalism, windstorms, and other natural and human-caused damage or loss. The first tip for many small businesses is to recognize that their homeowner's policy probably will *not* cover their operation even if it is based in the home unless the policy includes extra features that extend to commercial activity.

Normally, home policies also do not cover business equipment, inventory, or other items, even when they are simply being stored on the property. Home policies that extend some coverage may have a low dollar limit on the amount of stored property that will be covered. There also are geographic limits for business property coverage. If you have business property that goes off premises, you will need to consider separate coverage for that property while it is away from your listed, insured business address.

2. Liability and premises medical coverage

Liability and premises medical coverage are important concerns for nearly all business operations because businesses usually depend on customers who physically visit the premises. In addition, liability coverage can also be purchased to apply to losses caused by a business' product(s). Product liability is not always automatic, so ask your agent or broker about the coverage and how it might apply to your unique situation. If you work at customer locations ("completed operations"), consider buying completed operations coverage, too. You should expect your agent or broker to conduct a full review of your business exposures to loss.

3. Professional liability

Certain kinds of professionals face a particular kind of liability. Lawyers, doctors, dentists, and even insurance brokers and agents must have a certain level of qualification to practice their trade, and because they do, their customers have the right to expect that they will act within certain parameters of competence. When actual performance falls below these levels, custom-

ers and clients may seek damages against the person or the business. Coverage that protects the business or the professional is sometimes called "malpractice insurance." (Another popular name is "errors or omissions" coverage.) In a nutshell, this coverage protects these professionals against those circumstances where they face professional liability claims.

4. Special coverages

Businesses may have special needs that insurance can address. Some businesses purchase lost-business protection to guard against the possibility that certain unforeseen circumstances could close the business' doors or keep customers from buying the product. In addition, businesses may have special losses that they would want to cover. For example, the loss of a computerized accounts-receivable file or other business records may force the business to close.

5. Auto insurance

If your business activities involve the use of a vehicle, your regular auto policy probably will not cover them. However, you should talk to your insurer or your agent, since an endorsement or rider may extend coverage to these additional risks. Too often, employers do not take into account their vehicle needs and liabilities even though vehicles may be a key element of the business plan. This can range from pizza deliveries to newspaper reporters racing across town to cover traffic accidents. Who covers the use of these vehicles? Many small employers try to hedge their bets in this area and decline to consider their exposure. But there is a risk and a liability to be considered. For very small businesses and where the business use of vehicles is minimal, you can probably include it in your personal auto coverage. If the commercial use exceeds those limits, you are much better advised to seek the coverage that fits.

6. Health insurance

You may want or need to add health insurance to your coverage for you and your employees. If so, look into the prospect of small group health insurance. Health insurance is often purchased with the help of an insurance broker who will research the market for you and collect different kinds of coverages you can choose between.

7. Umbrella policies

An umbrella policy extends liability coverage you may already have so that you can handle an unusually large loss. The umbrella coverage kicks in when the limits of your underlying policy are reached. Umbrella policies provide additional liability coverage, even though the limits of an underlying policy may not be set that high. This type of coverage is called an "umbrella" because it opens up over these other coverages to protect you. For example, suppose your business insurance provides up to $100,000 worth of coverage against liability, but someone injured on your property establishes a $125,000 claim against you for personal injury. In such a case, your umbrella policy would step in and provide the additional $25,000 worth of coverage.

8. Life insurance

Even small companies may want to invest in life insurance when the owners or operators of the business are crucial to the success or failure of the enterprise. When companies invest in life insurance, it is usually through "key-man" policies, so called because the business itself is the beneficiary in the event that the key person or people die. The coverage will help the business replace those people as well as deal financially with the loss of their expertise.

9. Business interruption

If you are unable to operate your business as a result of a covered peril (e.g., fire, storm damage, vandalism), business interruption insurance steps in to help you cover the losses. Many small businesses often trim this coverage from commercial packages in the hope of pinching pennies. However, this kind of coverage may prove invaluable in those events in which the business suffers because customers are denied access to your business. One caution: Business interruption losses are not always easy to claim. For example, it is hard to establish the precise amount of business lost. Many insurers will require businesses to document these claims very carefully. Be prepared to research your records for several years before an insurer will accept a claim that otherwise merely shows a temporary dip in business.

Source: Washington State Office of the Insurance Commissioner (*www.insurance.wa.gov*)—The Office of the Insurance Commissioner (OIC) is one of the smaller agencies in the state government. It operates under the direction of the State Insurance Commissioner, a statewide-elected official. The OIC employs approximately 200 workers who perform the agency's mission of consumer protection and regulation of the state's insurance industry from a central office located in Tumwater.

Top Reasons to Get Errors and Omissions Insurance

Do you provide a service based on professional expertise? Then you're a prime candidate for professional liability coverage, also known as errors and omissions (E&O) insurance. For consultants, a continually renewed professional liability policy provides the best protection against the effects of current or past errors. Our expert, an insurance broker, lists these reasons for getting E&O insurance.

1. Liable for advice given

Those who hold themselves out to clients as experts can be found liable for advice that results in damage to the client. They can be ordered to pay the cost of both direct and indirect damages. In the case of roofing consultants, costs could escalate beyond structural repairs to replacement of valuable materials or equipment that may be damaged or destroyed.

2. Protect against significant financial loss

Professional liability insurance is intended to protect against the significant financial loss that can result from a lawsuit. Regardless of fault, litigation is costly, time-consuming, and potentially disastrous to a firm's reputation.

3. Defense against liabilities due to errors and omissions

Some firms have relied on their general liability insurance to protect against claims of errors or omissions, but these policies typically cover physical damages to persons or property caused by faulty equipment, facilities, or products. For defense against liability due to errors or omissions, a professional liability policy works best.

4. Low cost

As the use of professional liability has proliferated and as underwriters have developed plans for specific businesses and industries, premium costs have generally dropped into an affordable range. For the same kinds of malpractice insurance that cost medical professionals tens of thousands of dollars, consultants' premiums are measured in the hundreds.

5. Often required in requests for proposals

Professional liability insurance is often required by requests for proposals or in contracts for services. For this reason, some consultants have treated the policies as a form of protection that can be discarded after the period when the possibility of errors would be highest. This is a dangerous practice.

6. "Claims made" provision

Most professional liability policies have a "claims made" provision that states that the policy must be in effect at the time the claim of liability is made—not just when the negligent event occurred.

7. Payment for damages

Any structural deficiencies of roofs, for example, could remain unnoticed for a considerable period. If the consultant discarded the professional liability policy after the work was done, that firm could end up writing checks for considerable damages.

8. Guard against claims after job completed

To guard against claims that occur after a job is completed, most policies offer an extension period beyond the original term, for a prorated premium. This is called the "tail" of the policy. Some job contracts include requirements for the term of professional liability coverage, often for a period of years after a job is concluded.

Source: Dick Goff, president of MIMS International, Ltd. (*www.mimsintl.com*), is an insurance broker and program administrator. Contact him at Dulaney Valley Road Suite 610, Towson, MD 21204; (410) 296-1500; e-mail: *mims@mimsintl.com*.

Popular Types of Life Insurance

There are many different types of life insurance policies for you to consider. Our expert, an insurance agent, lists out the most popular used by small business owners.

1. Term Insurance

Term Insurance does just what the name implies . . . provide protection for a specific term of one or more years. Since protection is only provided for a specific time period it is considered temporary protection. Death benefits are paid only if you die within the term of years for which the policy is written. Term insurance can usually be renewed, often without a medical examination. But premiums will be higher each time you renew because you are older. Term insurance provides you with the greatest amount of coverage per premium dollar. Most policies are "convertible," which means the policy can be traded for permanent life insurance

protection. Premiums for the new policy will be higher than those paid for the term policy.

2. Cash value life insurance AKA mortgage insurance

This is a type of insurance where premiums charged are higher at the beginning than they would be for the same amount of term insurance. The part of the premium that is not used for the cost of insurance is invested by the company and builds up a cash value that may be used in a variety of ways. You may borrow against a policy's cash value by taking out a policy loan. If you don't pay back the loan and interest on it, the amount you owe will be subtracted from the benefits when you die, or from the cash value if you stop paying premiums and take out the remaining cash value. You can also use your cash value to keep insurance protection for a limited time or buy a reduced amount without having to pay more premiums. You also can use the cash value to increase your income in retirement or to help pay for needs such as a child's tuition without canceling the policy. However, to build this cash value, you must pay higher premiums in the earlier years of the policy. Cash value life insurance may be one of several types; whole life, universal life and variable life are all types of cash value insurance.

3. Whole life

The most basic type of permanent insurance is "whole life." Whole life policies develop cash values on a tax-deferred basis. This cash value can be used for a variety of purposes, including: Using the policy as collateral and borrowing up to the current cash value. This is useful for funding short-term obligations. If you die before the loan is repaid, the amount owed and interest is deducted from the life insurance proceeds. Payment of premium is required to keep your policy in force. You may authorize the insurance company to borrow from your cash value to pay the premium due. Use the cash value to fund a paid up policy at a reduced level of protection if you wish to stop making premium payments completely. The cash value of the policy is always available if you elect to cancel the policy. You pay taxes on the cash value only if it exceeds the amount of premiums you paid into the policy.

4. Universal life

Universal life insurance combines features of both term and permanent insurance. Universal life not only offers life insurance protection, but it also accumulates cash that is credited with interest earnings. The amount you earn depends on current interest rates. The premiums you pay are added to the cash accumulation portion of your universal life policy. Each month a deduction from the account value is made to provide for life insurance protection and other benefits and riders. An administrative fee is also deducted from the cash accumulation. Universal life is a type of flexible premium policy, allowing you to vary the timing and amount of your premium payments every year, or even skip a premium payment. Insurance continues as long as there is enough money in the cash accumulation to pay for the insurance charges. You can obtain cash from your universal life policy by borrowing or withdrawing from the account value.

5. Variable life

This is a kind of insurance where the death benefits and cash values depend on the investment performance of one or more separate accounts, which may be invested in mutual funds or other investments allowed under the policy. Be sure to get the prospectus from the company when buying this kind of policy and study it carefully. You will have higher death benefits and cash value if the underlying investments do well. Your benefits and cash value will be lower or may disappear if the investments you chose didn't do as well as you expected. You may pay an extra premium for a guaranteed death benefit.

Source: Body-Borneman (*www.bodyborneman.com*)—With a loyal client base of over 15,000 customers, many of whom have been with them for almost 40 years, Body-Borneman has grown to become one of the largest insurance agencies in Southeastern Pennsylvania. The agency markets a complete line of property, casualty, life and group products. This is accomplished through a staff of 45 loyal employees, of which 33 are licensed agents. For more information, contact Sean Deviney at (610) 367-1100.

Largest Property Casualty Insurers

Among the many insurance considerations you will have as a small business owner is property casualty insurance. This insurance protects your physical property such as offices and warehouses from losses. When searching for a property casualty insurer, the larger the company is, usually the better able they will be to provide you complete, reliable coverage. The following is a list ranking the largest property casualty insurers, by total assets.

1. Berkshire Hathaway Inc.

Total assets: $203,426,000,000

www.brkdirect.com

2. Allstate Corporation

Total assets: $139,808,000,000

www.allstate.com

3. St. Paul Travelers Companies

Total assets: $106,608,000,000

www.stpaultravelers.com

4. ACE Ltd.

Total assets: $53,651,156,000

www.acelimited.com

5. XL Capital Ltd.

Total assets: $45,460,035,000

www.xlcapital.com

6. Chubb Corporation

Total assets: $41,678,000,000

www.chubb.com

7. Safeco Corporation

Total assets: $36,303,300,000

www.safeco.com

8. Allmerica Financial Corporation

Total assets: $23,664,200,000

www.allmerica.com

9. American Financial Group, Inc.

Total assets: $21,275,863,000

www.amfnl.com

10. White Mountains Insurance Group

Total assets: $17,923,900,000

www.whitemountains.com

Source: SNL Financial: Insurance Industry Vital Statistics, Ten Largest Publicly Traded Property & Casualty Companies (*www.snl.com*)—SNL Financial is a research and information company for specific financial sectors, insurance included.

Ways to Speed Your Claim Reimbursement

Insurance adjusters will usually assist business owners in evaluating their claim and fully explain the steps to be taken. Until meeting with the adjuster, continue to conduct your operations as normally as possible, making business decisions as if you have no insurance. Insurance assists businesses recover from the loss. Focus on keeping the doors open and the impaired business functioning, not on what the insurance policy will provide. Our expert here lists a number of things you can do to help the adjuster expedite the claim.

1. Immediately inspect the loss

Immediately inspect the loss to determine the extent of the damage, taking steps to salvage damaged property (professional salvage firms may be able to assist with this task), and prepare a list of the steps required to promptly resume operations on a full-time, or even a part-time, basis.

2. Contact insurance agent or broker

Contact the insurance agent or broker to report the loss to the insurance company so an adjuster may be assigned.

3. Review your insurance policy

Review the insurance policy to verify coverages. The adjuster will help you review the policy, if necessary.

4. Have a copy of your operating statement or income tax return and sales records

Have a copy of the most recent operating statement or income tax return and sales records available for the adjuster to calculate the loss. Subject to policy terms and exclusions, business interruption insurance is specifically written to replace the income the business would have provided had operations not been interrupted. This is usually based on the business' financial history, as well as other local and economic factors.

5. Close out the books as of the date of the loss and maintain records

Close out the books as of the date of the loss and maintain an accurate separate record of the operating expenses that continue during this period. Remember, the adjuster will need to verify these expenses as part of the claim process.

6. Maintain accurate expense records

Maintain accurate expense records for extra expenses incurred to expedite the resumption of operations.

7. Record any communications received

Record any communications received regarding an order to evacuate. How did the business get the word? A written order? A verbal order? Someone heard it on the radio? Save any written orders or fliers received to document the claim.

8. Document activities

If the business interruption involves the loss of electrical power, document, to the best of your knowledge, when it went off and when it was restored. If any written information was received regarding the power interruption, be sure to save it as documentation for the claim.

_____

Source: The International Warehouse Logistics Association (*www .iwla.com*)—IWLA defines the standards of excellence and advances these standards among members and their customers while providing the resources, education, and professional programs designed to advance members' businesses and provide greater value for their customers. The association serves third-party logistics providers throughout North America and has been the voice of the industry since 1891. Contact them at IWLA, 2800 S. River Road, Suite 260, Des Plaines, IL 60018; (847) 813-4699; *e-mail@iwla.com*.

Reasons to Have Workers' Compensation Insurance

Workers' compensation insurance is one of the key insurance concerns for small business owners. It protects the company against claims from employees who are injured on the job and is now required for employers in virtually all states. Aside from this requirement, however, there are compelling reasons for a business owner to have the insurance, and the following list details these reasons.

1. It is required

The most compelling reason to have workers' compensation insurance is that it is required in virtually all states for companies with employees; some states do not require it for companies with fewer than three employees. Independent contractors are not considered employees for the purposes of determining whether a company must have the insurance.

2. Covers liability for injuries

The purpose of the insurance is to cover the costs of medical expenses for an employee who is injured on the job, meaning the company will not have to pick up the tab for medical bills. Typically, the insurance also provides some wage loss replacement.

3. Difficult to self-insure

The main reason to have insurance from an independent carrier, rather than self-insuring, is the regulation on self-insurance. Large cash reserves are required if a company decides to self-insure, and so it is often difficult to have enough cash to insure without a carrier.

4. Easy claims for employees

It is increasingly easier for employees to make workers' compensation claims and collect on them. With the system benefiting the employees, it is wise for the employers to have insurance to avoid paying large bills out of their own pocket.

5. Coverage B

Generally, an employee cannot sue the employer for negligence but can simply collect for their medical bills and partial wage replacement. However, if an employee sues for gross negligence or intentional conduct leading to injury, Coverage B insurance exists to insure the company against pain and suffering claims and other tort damages.

Source: Fred S. Steingold, is a business lawyer in Ann Arbor, Michigan, and is the author of three other books on small business, including *The Legal Guide for Starting and Running a Small Business* (Nolo Press, 2005).

States with Highest Workers' Compensation Rates

As a small business owner, one of the main insurance issues you must address, with relation to your employees, is workers' compensation. Depending on what state your business is located in, you could be paying anywhere from just above $1.00 to more than $6.00 per $100 of payroll for workers' compensation insurance. To see if you fall into the higher end of that range, the following is a listing of the states with the highest rates for workers' compensation insurance, based on the rate per every $100 of payroll, as well as the Web sites of each state's department of workers' compensation.

1. California
Rate per $100 payroll: $6.08
www.dir.ca.gov/dwc/dwc_home_page.htm

2. Alaska
Rate per $100 payroll: $4.39
http://labor.state.ak.us/wc/home.htm

3. Florida
Rate per $100 payroll: $4.20
www.fldfs.com/wc

4. Hawaii
Rate per $100 payroll: $3.73
http://hawaii.gov/labor/dcd/index.shtml

5. Ohio
Rate per $100 payroll: $3.59
www.ohiobwc.com

6. Kentucky
Rate per $100 payroll: $3.48
http://labor.ky.gov/dwc

7. Delaware

Rate per $100 payroll: $3.44

www.delawareworks.com/industrialaffairs/
services/workerscomp.shtml

8. Montana

Rate per $100 payroll: $3.41

http://wcc.dli.state.mt.us

9. Louisiana

Rate per $100 payroll: $3.37

www.ldol.state.la.us/wrk_owca.asp

10. District of Columbia

Rate per $100 payroll: $3.26

http://does.dc.gov/does/cwp/view.a.1232
.q.537428.asp

Source: 2004 Oregon Workers' Compensation Premium Rate Ranking (*www.cbs.state.or.us*)—Oregon's Department of Consumer and Business Services publishes this report on the workers' compensation rates of the fifty states and the District of Columbia. The Department of Consumer and Business Services Information Management Division can be contacted at PO Box 14480, Salem 97309.

States with Lowest Workers' Compensation Rates

As a small business owner, one of the main insurance issues you must address, with relation to your employees, is workers' compensation. Depending on what state your business is located in, you could be paying anywhere from just above $1.00 to more than $6.00 per $100 of payroll for workers' compensation insurance. To see if you fall into the lower end of that range, the following is a listing of the states with the lowest rates for workers' compensation insurance, based on the rate per every $100 of payroll, as well as the Web sites of each state's department of workers' compensation.

1. North Dakota

Rate per $100 payroll: $1.06

www.state.nd.us/risk/workers-comp

2. Indiana

Rate per $100 payroll: $1.24

www.in.gov/workcomp

3. Arizona

Rate per $100 payroll: $1.49

www.ica.state.az.us/workers'.htm

4. Arkansas

Rate per $100 payroll: $1.57

www.awcc.state.ar.us

5. Virginia

Rate per $100 payroll: $1.57

www.vwc.state.va.us

6. Utah

Rate per $100 payroll: $1.63

www.labor.state.ut.us/indacc/indacc.htm

7. Massachusetts

Rate per $100 payroll: $1.70

www.mass.gov/wcac

8. Kansas

Rate per $100 payroll: $1.81

www.dol.ks.gov/wc/html/wc_all.html

9. Iowa

Rate per $100 payroll: $1.91

www.iowaworkforce.org/wc/

10. Oregon

Rate per $100 payroll: $2.05

www.cbs.state.or.us/external/wcd/

11. South Dakota

Rate per $100 payroll: $2.05

www.state.sd.us/dol/dlm/dlm-home.htm

Source: 2004 Oregon Workers' Compensation Premium Rate Ranking (*www.cbs.state.or.us*)—Oregon's Department of Consumer and Business Services publishes this report on the workers' compensation rates of the fifty states and the District of Columbia. The Department of Consumer and Business Services Information Management Division can be contacted PO Box 14480, Salem 97309.

Managing Your Business

Best Books on Business Management

Are you interested in reading some great business books, but don't know which ones are the best? We asked one of our experts, an excellent business consultant, author and speaker, to recommend some of his favorite books on business management. Here's his list.

1. *The Entrepreneur's Guide* by Deaver Brown

Ballantine Books 1981; ISBN 0-345-29634-6. Deaver Brown was president and cofounder of Cross River Co., which developed and manufactured the Umbroller, the first umbrella-style folding child stroller. His book gives specific advice backed up by personal anecdotes. The chapter on finance should be memorized by all business owners; the chapter on operations is especially useful to anyone in manufacturing.

2. *Marketing Warfare* by Al Ries and Jack Trout

McGraw Hill/Plume 1986; ISBN 0-452-25861-8. The best book on marketing strategy, period. Ries and Trout also wrote *Positioning— The Battle For Your Mind* (ISBN 0-446-30041-1) and *The 22 Immutable Laws of Marketing* (ISBN 0-88730-592-X).

3. *Guerrilla Marketing* by Jay Conrad Levinson

Houghton Mifflin 1984; ISBN 0-395-38314-5. It's not really a marketing book; nevertheless, this is a very good book about advertising and promotion for companies with small budgets.

That means every small business in America. The ideas are low-cost and can be implemented immediately. Jay has written other good books, too, including *Guerrilla Marketing Attack* and *Guerrilla Selling*.

4. *Dress for Success* by John T. Molloy

Warner Books 1975 with later revisions; ISBN 0-446-82568-9. Excellent book on correct attire for business. We live in a fast-paced world of short attention spans and sound/vision bites—a world where your first impression may be the only impression. Everyone who has face-to-face contact with customers or clients should read this book. It tells and shows how to dress for various types of clients. It has good pictures, too, so you'll know the difference between a club tie and a regimental stripe tie. Molloy also wrote *The Woman's Dress for Success Book* (ISBN 0-695-80810-9) and *Live for Success* (ISBN 0-553-01359-9). The men's and women's "dress" books have been updated periodically to reflect current fashions. Get the most current edition.

5. *The Secrets of Consulting* by Gerald M. Weinberg

Dorset House 1985; ISBN 0-932633-01-3. A wonderful book that is, in my opinion, badly titled. Because only consultants and consultant wannabes will pick it up. That's a shame because the book is about giving advice and troubleshooting problems, understanding people, and more. It's about the very things you'll be doing in your small to midsize business every day. This book is full of fantastic and entertaining stories.

6. *The Makeover Book—101 Design Solutions for Desktop Publishing* by Joe Grossman

Ventana Press 1996; ISBN 1-56604-132-5. If you have a desktop-publishing program (and many of you do) and you're going to produce a newsletter (and you probably should because it's a great way to help your business grow), or set up a Web site (and you should probably do that, too), then this book is for you! It shows how to design a clean-looking professional document or site that your customers and prospects will read. The book offers before-and-after examples. *The Makeover Book* will show you how to create good-looking documents or Web pages—even if you hire somebody else to do it!

7. *The Business Tune-Up & Repair Guide* by Joseph M. Sherlock

39 Plymouth Press 2002, revised 2005. Joseph Sherlock's business book, the *Business Tune-Up & Repair Guide* offers step-by-step instructions to solve almost any business problem. It distills Joe's forty-plus years of business experience as well as his personal experience in building his own successful company into one fact- and idea-filled business book. This book offers help to every business owner and manager: If you're not yet in business, this book will help you avoid potholes. If you're a start-up business, this book will steer you on the right course. If you have an established business, this book will supercharge your profits. Solutions

and ideas in the book are specific, timely, relevant, and easy-to-implement. The book also includes a fully-annotated sample business plan and a workbook section that helps you create your own business plan. Order directly from *www.joesherlock.com*.

Source: Joe Sherlock (*www.joesherlock.com*)—Joe provides small business consulting services and business advice to small and midsize firms. He is the author of several business books and a professional speaker and seminar leader. Joe is also a business consultant and founder of Sherlock Strategies, a management consulting firm. Contact him at 18617 NE Cedar Drive; Battle Ground, WA 98604; (360) 666-1099.

Ways to Improve Forecast Accuracy

Thinking of creating a forecast so that you can try and figure out, in advance, what your sales or profits are going to be in the future? As you probably know already, predicting the future is a pretty tough task. But there are steps you can take to help you make your forecasts as accurate as possible. We asked an expert in business forecasting to provide us with this list of ways (in his own words) to help improve forecast accuracy.

1. Match the forecasting method to the situation

Experts are no better than non-experts when using their unaided judgment, an evidence-based finding that I refer to as the "Seer-sucker Theory"—no matter how much evidence exists that seers do not exist, people will pay for the existence of seers. Empirical evidence on which method works best in which situations can guide you.

2. Use domain knowledge

Managers and analysts typically have useful knowledge about situations. For example, they might know a lot about the automobile business. While this domain knowledge can be important for forecasting, it is often ignored by forecasters. One useful and inexpensive way to use managers' knowledge is based on "causal forces. Causal forces can summarize managers' expectations about the direction of the trend in a time series. When causal forces conflict with historical trends, accuracy is improved if the trend is assumed to be zero.

3. Structure the problem

One of the basic strategies in management research is to break a problem into manageable pieces, solve each piece, then put them back together. This strategy is effective for forecasting, especially when you know more about the pieces than about the whole. For example, to forecast sales, decompose by level, trend, and seasonality; or by industry sales and the brand's market share; or by inflation, real price and unit sales.

4. Model experts' forecasts

Judgmental bootstrapping offers an inexpensive way to model experts' forecasts. In this method, you make a statistical inference of a judge's model by running a regression of the judgmental forecasts against the information that the forecaster used. This procedure is more accurate and less expensive than asking experts to make forecasts when many forecasts are needed.

5. Represent the problem realistically

Start with the problem and develop a realistic representation. Realistic representations are especially important for problems where unaided judgment fail, as when forecasting decisions made in conflict situations. Simulated interaction, a type of role-playing in which two or more parties act out interactions, is a realistic way to portray situations. For example, to predict how a union will react to a company's intended offer in a negotiation, people play the two sides and they go through negotiations. The outcome is used as a forecast.

6. Use causal models when you have good information

When knowledge about the problem is good and when one has good data, develop a causal model. The forecaster can obtain relevant obtain knowledge from experts and from prior research.

7. Use simple quantitative methods

Complex models are often misled by noise in the data, especially in uncertain situations. Relatively simple models are less prone to mistakes, and more accurate than complex models. Here is a good test for simplicity: if you cannot understand how the forecasts are made, find a simpler method.

8. Be conservative when uncertain

When you encounter high uncertainty (which is common in forecasting) make conservative forecasts. In time series, this means staying close to historical averages, or in the case of a steady trend, staying close to the trend line. However, if the historical trend is subject to variations, discontinuities, and reversals, you should be less willing to extrapolate the historical trend.

9. Combine forecasts

Combining is especially effective when different forecasting methods are available. Ideally, use as many as five different methods, and combine their forecasts using a predetermined mechanical rule. In the absence of strong evidence that some methods are more accurate than others, an equally weighted average of the forecasts should work well. A review of 30 studies found that combining forecasts reduced forecast errors by about 12 percent. In some cases, the combined forecast was more accurate than any of the individual methods that made up the combined forecast. In surveys of forecasting methods, many organizations claim to use combined forecasts. I suspect, however, that most organizations use them in an informal manner and thus miss most of the benefit.

Source: J. Scott Armstrong, Ph.D. (MIT 1968), Professor of Marketing at the Wharton School, University of Pennsylvania was a founder of the *Journal of Forecasting*, the *International Journal of Forecasting*, and the *International Symposium on Forecasting*. He is the creator of the Forecasting Principles Web site (forecasting-principles.com) and editor of *Principles of Forecasting* (Kluwer Academic Publishers, 2001). In 1996, he was selected as one of the first six "Honorary Fellows" by the International Institute of Forecasters. He was named Society for Marketing Advances "Distinguished Marketing Scholar of 2000."

Questions to Ask When Interviewing an Individual Accountant

Choosing the right accountant for your business can mean the difference between success and failure. After all, it's your financial numbers that make or break your business. Unfortunately, once you've selected an accountant, it's a pain to switch. Your accountant gains detailed knowledge of you, your business, and your data—and that makes it very tough to transition to a new accountant. The end result is that many businesses that work with mediocre accountants don't make the change to a better accountant simply because the switching costs are too high. Our expert, a venture capital firm, offers these questions to ask a prospective individual accountant.

1. Do you have your CPA?

Business owners are often confused as to the certified public accountant (CPA) designation. A CPA has surpassed accepted financial education levels and passed state-administered tests to prove competency and periodic re-certification exams. Certain situations, such as audits and many loan applications, require CPA involvement. Not surprisingly, CPAs can charge higher fees than a non-CPA. But there are a great many non-CPAs who excel at small business accounting and financial and technology consulting. Again, getting to know them and your needs is the necessary first step.

2. What kind of creative business advice will you offer me?

A good accountant can deftly handle data and numbers but should also be able to demonstrate quick and creative business acumen. Ask the candidate to offer three quick ideas on how your firm might be able to save money right now. Ask for three examples in which he offered useful business advice to other clients that went beyond just tracking the numbers. While "creative accounting" is usually a negative, having a creative business mind can be a huge asset toward helping your company to grow.

3. Do you consider yourself to be tech-savvy?

Small business accounting software has made powerful accounting tools available to everyone. But these accounting packages, most notably MYOB and QuickBooks, are only as useful as the person who installs them and runs the applications. Even if you are not a techie, do your homework to be able to determine whether the candidate understands the role computer technology plays in turning business information into business intelligence. For example, ask her how she will integrate your computer files with the technology in her office. What role will the Internet play in keeping in touch and interchanging financial information?

4. Who are your other clients?

Imagine this scenario. You hire an accountant based on the assumption that he understands the basics of your business. Then, you find out that he's never had a client like you before. Instead, he's only prepared tax forms for wealthy individuals who don't own businesses. Avoid that possible disaster by asking who the accountant works with. If they are businesses that are similar to yours, that's a good sign. In asking about his clients, you will also want to understand how busy he is and whether he has the time and resources to support you adequately.

5. How do you calculate your fees?

Ask the accountant what you can expect fees to be and will she guarantee that you will not exceed certain amounts that you agree on up-front. In a time-based fee structure, make sure to find out the hourly rate, as well as all fees for expense reimbursement. Find out now whether a simple two-minute phone call or a one-page fax means an hour of billable time. If that's the case, run for the door.

6. Are you active in the local business community?

Who do you know that can help me? Find out whether your prospective accountant can introduce you to people who might be useful to you, including prospective customers, suppliers, bankers, and investors. Since talk is cheap, take it one step further. Ask the accountant for examples of introductions he's made in the past for other clients and how those introductions played out.

7. Why should I use you?

As a final question, it's always good to let the accountant make the case for why you should engage her.

Source: Gaebler Ventures is a Chicago-based business incubator and holding company that develops and nurtures companies that are shaping the future. For additional information, visit *www .gaebler.com*.

Ways to Keep Your Business Expenses under Control

Every business owner knows that it's critical to keep track of expenses. Keeping costs under wraps could mean the difference between staying in business or filing for bankruptcy. Our expert, a small business consultant and author, provides this list of ways to keep these costs from spiraling out of control.

1. Read your general ledger

It ain't a good beach read, but your general ledger will sure tell you a lot about your business. Every month you should print out a full detailed general ledger of all of your company's transactions and read through it. You'll be surprised what tidbits you'll find.

2. Get a flash report

Each day have your accounting manager give you a flash report of open receivables, payables, sales, purchases, and other critical metrics. Compare them to the prior day and week. Anything unusual will be sure to crop up and you can address before it becomes a bigger problem.

3. Start walking around

Get off your butt and walk around the office. Listen to what your employees are talking about. By walking around, you'll see the action from a front-row seat. You'll get back to you seat with a few more cost-control ideas.

4. Start paying early and on specific days

Take advantage of vendor discounts. Set a specific payment schedule and stick to it. This way you can manage your cash flow on your timeline, not someone else's.

5. Outsource

There are so many ways a small business can keep costs under control just by outsourcing. Hire a payroll service. Farm out some manufacturing process. Subcontract a specific job.

6. Monitor revenue by employee

Productivity is the key to cost control. Each employee should be contributing to the overall revenue engine of your company. Don't add employees unless their contribution fuels your growth. Keep track of this number monthly and you'll keep up with your costs, too.

7. Join a group

No matter what business you're in, there's a group to join. Look for chambers of commerce, associations, fraternal organizations—whatever. Many of these groups offer volume discounts on health insurance and other typical business costs to their members. Joining a group is a great way to keep things under control.

8. Avoid and remove the corporate trappings

Do you really need that fancy office space? That state-of-the-art computer system? Some companies, such as corporate law or accounting firms, may need to impress. But won't your customers be happier with just good service and quality products? Don't overspend on corporate extras that don't add to your bottom line.

9. Decide between nice-to-have and must-have

Do you really need gourmet coffee in the office? Expensive copy paper? Multiple digital cameras? A super-powerful computer? Don't buy into the hype of your supplier. Figure out what you really need to have and avoid the nice-to-have stuff, unless you can really justify that it's worth spending the money.

Source: Gene Marks (*www.marksgroup.net*) is a small business consultant and author of *The Small Business Desk Reference*, *The Complete Idiot's Guide to Successful Outsourcing*, and *Outfoxing the Small Business Owner*.

Ways to Reduce Overhead

The lifeblood of any business is its cash flow—that steady stream of dollars and cents that comes from sales and then flows out in the form of wages, inventory, rent, insurance, and other expenses. Unfortunately, there are times when there's more out than in, and only sheer perseverance keeps entrepreneurs trying to close the gap instead of closing the doors. Here's some of the time-tested ways to keep overhead low.

1. Target overstocks

By comparing (a) how many of each item were sold in an inventory year with (b) the item's end-of-year inventory, you can come up with what items are potentially overstocked. Next, list the overstocked items that are selling well enough to warrant holding the excess. Finally, list the overstocked items that would be worth selling at a discount to recover the cash.

2. Add up the little things

Just-in-time inventory management may be your most important way to reduce overhead, but don't ignore the smaller items that can add up to significant amounts. One approach is to list your overhead costs in descending order of expense. The result is a prioritized list of which costs to examine first to see if they can be reduced. Don't dismiss any item as impossible to reduce, until you've scrutinized it carefully and involved your staff in looking for new options.

3. Review employee costs

Analyze results, not efforts, to gauge which employees should stay where they are, which should be retrained, and which should be let go. Determine your ideal number of employees by comparing your needs during your slackest times with your average days. Staff for your minimum needs as long as that level will not compromise service most of the time. It's less costly to pay overtime or bring in temporary help during peak periods than to keep unnecessary employees on the payroll.

4. Look at your facilities

Compare your rent with what you might pay if you moved, and then ask your current landlord if your lease can be renegotiated. If you are willing to sign a longer lease, you may get a price break now or have the rent forgiven or deferred in your slowest months. Also consider shrinking the area you occupy and subleasing some of the remaining space. If you own your building, ask your banker about refinancing at a lower interest rate or over a longer term.

5. Adjust the heating and cooling

How you heat and cool your office and workspace can also make a difference in your overhead costs. Questioning abnormally high bills, adding insulation, replacing old air conditioners with high-efficiency models, and wrapping water heaters are steps that work for businesses as well as homes. Converting to fluorescent lighting will garner considerable savings.

6. Shop for cheaper insurance

Rates vary widely, but so do the products and services when it comes time to make a claim. Know precisely what you are getting in a particular policy, and deal with an A- (or better) rated company.

7. Track responses to your advertising and promotional efforts

To spend your advertising dollars effectively, you need to know what produces leads and what generates profitable sales. For example, several special-category Yellow Page ads may pull better than a single large ad under your major listing.

8. Own your phones

Owning your phones is usually more advantageous than renting, especially when you put the savings into phone services that provide more effective operation. Investigate the different services available for both local and long-distance calls. Ask about volume discounts for certain time periods, to particular geographical areas, and to specific phone numbers.

9. Take a hard look at other costs

Keep only the dues and subscriptions that serve you with valuable information or raise your profile in your industry or community. An expensive golf membership has to be evaluated in terms of whether your income would drop without it. While you're on the golf course, ask your friends about what they're doing to reduce overhead. Networking can find you a better bookkeeper, a less expensive janitorial service, or a tip for trimming your inventory still further so that your business is buoyantly afloat and doing well when the economic tide turns.

Source: Small Business Administration (*www.sba.gov*).

Best Calculations to Measure Financial Health

Our expert strongly believes that if you want to succeed in business, there's no question that you've got to know how to read basic financial information, but merely being able to read the data is not enough. You've also got to know how to interpret the data and draw conclusions from the patterns it suggests. In addition, many people—such as bankers, accountants, business partners, investors, and the government—measure business success primarily in terms of financial outcomes. As a result, it's important to be able to communicate and negotiate in a language that everybody understands. No matter what type of business you're in, or what your educational background is, if you want to succeed, you've got to have a working knowledge of these basic financial concepts.

1. The basic set of financial statements

The basic set of financial statements are the balance sheet, income statement (also known as the profit & loss statement), and the statement of cash flows. Since business results are measured in dollars, it's imperative that you know how to read the basic set of financial statements. Sadly, many smaller business owners wait to learn about financial statements until they need to borrow money. Instead, they tend to focus on components or specific accounts such as cash, accounts receivable, inventory, office expense, and payroll. While this may be fine when starting out, it isn't nearly enough if you want to grow your business. In order to grow, it's essential to see the whole picture. Being able to understand your company's basic financial statements is the first step in mastering your company's finances.

2. Cash-flow projections

Cash-flow projections have the same purpose as the statement of cash flows: *to keep track of cash.* The only difference is that cash-flow projections help you deal with the future while the statement of cash flow shows how you've managed cash in the past. The ability to mange your company's cash is vital to its success. A cash-flow projection is an important financial tool that will help you accomplish that goal. It surprises me how many smaller business owners don't adequately measure and project cash flow. For many, a casual glance at their checkbook balance is the extent of their cash-flow management. Unfortunately, looking at and balancing your checkbook is not the same thing as measuring or projecting cash flow. If you run your business solely by looking at your checking account balance, you're making a critical mistake. A checking account balance represents the past and present. To successfully manage cash flow, you need to deal with the future. You need to know how much money you're going to collect and how much you're going to spend. That's the essence of projecting cash flow. In addition, a cash-flow projection shows you where the money is "tied up" in your business.

3. Ratio analysis

If you're not financial ratio savvy, you're not alone! Many smaller business owners aren't. But then again many smaller business owners aren't as successful as they should be! The fact is, knowledge of even just a few key ratios goes a long way in increasing your ability to analyze and understand your company's financial position. As I explain in *Gold Mine Tactics: The Business Owner's Success Manual,* ratios allow you to see things that would otherwise be hidden from the naked eye. The information suggested by financial ratios can help you to improve results, especially profitability. By analyzing changes and trends over time, ratios allow you to pinpoint and improve specific problem areas. They do a much better job of isolating these areas than do the basic set of financial statements alone. In addition, a ratio becomes an even more powerful tool if you compare it to the ratios of other companies in the same industry (see the next item, trend analysis).

4. Trend analysis

Now let's take ratio analysis one step further. Even though ratios are excellent financial management tools, they're limited because they ignore the time dimension. Success (or failure) tends to be something that happens over time, not in one or two moments. Since ratios are snapshots at one point in time, they may not, by themselves, be able to detect trends or patterns. Ratios are even more powerful when compared and analyzed over time in order to derive meaningful results. That's where trend analysis comes into play. Trend analysis happens to be one of my all-time favorite management tools. It's cost-effective and easy to learn. It can help you to spot either emerging opportunities or impending difficulties. There's no doubt that you need to stay on top of trends in order to build a gold mine business. Trend analysis is simply taking a look at financial and other data, including ratios, and trying to recognize or interpret patterns. In addition, trends can be compared to industry averages, or used in the development of company budgets and forecasts.

5. Forecasts, projections, and budgets

Forecasts, projections, and budgets are reports designed to help you compare anticipated future events with actual results. They are indispensable financial management tools. A budget, for example, can tell you a whole host of things, such as how many employees you can afford or how much money can be spent on advertising and promotions. Unfortunately, few smaller businesses actually use a budget on a regular basis. Forecasts and projections show how your business will turn out under various assumptions. This analysis is critical if you want to grow. For example, a projection can be used to measure a company's expected financial position once it gets required financing. A budget is very similar to a forecast or projection in that it also involves predicting the future. A budget will help you to understand why some of your plans didn't turn out as expected. This is because once a budget is prepared, it can be compared to actual results to determine variances. These variances can be investigated and scrutinized. A budget can also be used to help you control costs and manage resources.

6. Break-even analysis

Break-even analysis is where you determine the point of activity (sales volume) at which total revenues and total expenses are equal. In other words, the break-even point shows you the minimum amount of sales you need to cover your expenses. Do you know your break-even levels? This tool is a *must* when launching a new product or service or when adjusting prices.

Source: Alex Goumakos, CPA (*www.goldminetactics.com*), business consultant, and author of *Business Owner's Success Manual*. His services help clients increase profits in their existing business or start a successful business from scratch. Contact him at MindStudio, Inc., 2402 Lisa Lane, Suite 200, Allentown, PA 18104; (888) 839-2727; e-mail: *alex@goldminetactics.com*.

Things to Include in a Break-Even Analysis

A significant advantage of some business ideas is that the venture can break even at what seems to be an easily achievable volume.

A technique for quantifying that volume, called break-even analysis, examines the interaction among fixed costs, variable costs, prices, and unit volume to determine that combination of elements in which revenues and total costs are equal. Here are some items you should include in your break-even analysis.

1. Fixed costs

Fixed costs are those expenses necessary to keep the business open and are not impacted by sales volume. They will include such things as rent, basic telephone expenses and utilities, wages for core employees, loan or lease payments, and other necessary expenditures. Be sure to include a living wage for yourself as a fixed cost.

2. Salaries

Did you figure in the company's obligation on payroll taxes? Did you allow for additional wages to cover vacations and sick days? Are you providing any benefits? Are you using a payroll service?

3. Occupancy expense

In addition to rent, have you included likely utilities costs? Which are you liable for? Electricity, gas, garbage disposal, and telephone are usually the major ones. Don't forget long-distance calls. Is there Internet service?

4. Sales expense

Have you determined your advertising costs? Are their printing costs? Cell phones probably should be charged here.

5. Other

Some of the more frequently overlooked costs include insurance, fees to professionals (legal, accounting, other), and interest payments.

6. Variable costs

Variable costs include those expenses that change as a result of sales volume. This can be a relatively simple relationship, as in cost of goods sold. For example, the variable cost of baked goods sold at our coffee shop is what we pay the supplier for them, 30 cents each. Variable costs can also be complex; for example, higher sales in one area of our business may increase long-distance charges. Labor costs may be fixed for full-time employees; then, as sales increase, some overtime is incurred until additional personnel can be justified.

7. Contribution margin

A general term often used for the difference between selling price and variable cost is *contribution margin*, or the amount that the unit sale contributes to the margin available to pay fixed costs, and, you hope, generate profit.

Source: Dr. John B. Vinturella of Vinturella and Associates (*www.jbv.com*), a management consulting firm specializing in entrepreneurs and small business. Dr. Vinturella, company principal, has almost forty years' experience as a management and strategic consultant and entrepreneur, and fifteen of those years as an academic entrepreneur-in-residence and adjunct professor. He can be reached at (504) 246-3999, and at *jbv@jbv.com*. His address is 11111 Winchester Park Drive, New Orleans, LA 70128.

Ways to Get the Most out of Your Financial Statements

If you ask small business owners what's their least favorite part of running their businesses, most will probably say to you that it's managing the finances. But without sound financial management, any business, regardless of its size, won't be around for long. This starts with an understanding of basic financial statements and what they can tell you about the financial performance of your company. Here's a list of ideas for getting the most out of your firm's financial statements.

1. Determine whether you need to create financial statements

Any business that files a corporate tax return (partnerships and C and S corporations) must create a balance sheet and income statement. Along with a cash-flow statement, these are the three types of business financial statements. If you apply for a bank loan or any other type of financing, you will need to present credible financial statements. If you're a sole proprietor and only file a Schedule C with your federal tax return, financial statements aren't required, but they can be an invaluable financial management tool.

2. Understand the differences among the three types of financial statements

The balance sheet is simply a snapshot of your financial position at any given time. Usually presented in two columns, it reflects what your company owns (assets) versus what your company owes (liabilities). The income statement (or P&L) tells you how much money you made (or lost) for a given period—usually a month, a quarter, or a year. The cash-flow statement ties the balance sheet and income statement together, reconciling the change in your business' cash position from the beginning to the end of the period being measured (usually a year). In short, it tells you where the cash came from and what the business did with it.

3. Know what your balance sheet is telling you

The three most valuable pieces of information you can glean from the balance sheet are how liquid the company is, how much debt the company is using, and how quickly receivables are being collected. These are critical factors for any business owner to know in order to manage the business finances properly.

4. Look beyond profit or loss on the income statement

Of course, making a profit is your ultimate goal, but a close analysis of your income statement can reveal more than just a profit or loss. Don't just look at the numbers in isolation; compare them from quarter to quarter or year to year to look for trends that can help you improve financial management. For example, if the operating margin (which shows how much money is being made from the basic operations of the business) is improving from year to year, this reflects an improvement in the overall operating performance of the company.

5. Use the cash-flow statement to identify and understand your cash-flow cycle

The cash-flow statement will reveal your business' critical cash-flow or operating cycle: the cycle of cash conversion from inventory to sales to receivables and back to cash again. By monitoring this cycle, you can benchmark everything from a slowdown in collection of receivables to an increase in inventory turnover.

6. Identify key financial ratios

One of the most helpful management tools you can derive from your financial statements is key financial ratios that will help you gauge the financial health of your business. The most important small business financial ratios are as follows:

a. Current ratio: Derived from the balance sheet, this ratio shows how many times current debt could be paid off with current assets. It's used frequently by investors and lenders to measure liquidity.

The formula: Current Assets / Current Liabilities

b. Debt-to-equity ratio: Another balance-sheet ratio, this ratio measures your debt capacity. Not surprisingly, lenders are also very interested in this ratio.

The formula: Total Debt / Shareholder's Equity

c. Accounts receivable (AR) days: This measures how long it takes you to collect the money that's owed to you. Compare your AR collection time to your terms of sale and industry averages to see how well you're doing against your peers and your own internal standards.

The formula: AR × 365 : Annual Sales

d. Accounts payable (AP) days: Conversely, this measures how long you take to pay your vendor invoices. You want to stretch your payables as long as possible without jeopardizing your good trade credit.

The formula: AP × 365 : Cost of Goods Sold

e. Inventory turnover: This tells you how often your inventory "turns over" in a year. You should have specific goals for inventory turns. Four times a year is a common inventory turn, but you can increase cash flow and profits without increasing sales by turning inventory faster.

The formula: Cost of Goods Sold / Inventory

7. Recognize the potential limitations of financial statements

Most companies in the twenty-first century (especially self-employed individuals and micro-businesses) are based more on intellectual capital than on manufacturing widgets, and their primary assets are intangibles—such as ideas, concepts, branding, and reputation—not equipment and hard assets. For them, traditional financial statement analysis doesn't capture the full picture of the company. These companies should focus primarily on their cash-flow statements.

Source: Don Sadler, vice president, editorial director, Media 3 Publications. Don Sadler is a business editor and writer with twenty years of experience in the business publishing arena. As the vice president and editorial director for Media 3 Publications, he directs editorial content for the company's various business publications. During his career, he has worked with the largest banks in the country to create custom publications targeted to their corporate customers. In addition, as a freelance writer, he has written dozens of articles published in a variety of national business periodicals, including *American Executive* and *Self-Employed America*. Contact him at *don@media3pub.com*.

Top Things to Look for in a Bank Reconciliation

You know the feeling. You're trying to balance your general ledger. You get down to the last line of the reconciliation and—you're out of balance. What now? Here is a list of things to look for to minimize the frustration, we hope.

1. Bank charges

These come in all shapes and sizes. Don't forget to record the normal monthly charges, as well as items such as check orders, minimum balance charges, excess check charges, and other nonrecurring fees.

2. Credit card fees

If you accept credit or debit cards, you will be incurring fees from your card processor. Different credit card companies charge their fees in different ways. For example, American Express typically deducts the fees from the charge, while Discover lumps its fees into one monthly amount. However they are recorded, make sure you pick them all up in your check register.

3. Debit cards

One of the easiest ways for your checkbook to be out of balance is using a debit card to pay for things. While debit cards are very convenient, you must remember to record the charge in your register. Otherwise, you may end up with a nasty surprise when the bank statement arrives.

4. Payroll

Payroll companies all offer the convenience of deducting amounts directly from your bank account. This may be for impounding of payroll taxes, direct deposit of employee checks, 401k contributions, or the payroll company's fee. Make sure that you enter the amount when the payroll arrives, so that you don't forget it.

5. Bounced checks, writing them

Occasionally, we all write checks, mistakenly thinking there is enough money to cover them. Some make this standard practice. In either case, make sure that you show the check as outstanding, unless it was redeposited. Also remember to record the associated fee.

6. Bounced checks, receiving them

Similarly, you may be on the receiving end of a check that does not have sufficient funds to cover it. This check will be deducted from your account along with a fee. If you redeposit the check, make sure that the income is not recorded twice.

7. Wire transfers

Depending on the type of business you transact, you may be required to wire money to your vendors. Again, this is a transaction without a clear paper trail, and sometimes, it slips through. Also remember to record the fee associated with the transfer.

8. Bank errors

Yes, sometimes the bank makes a mistake, too. Whether through vendor fraud or pure bank error, a check may clear twice. Most bank statements have the cleared checks listed in one section, and they usually use an asterisk to indicate a gap in check numbers or a duplicate number. Also, make sure that the check cleared for the proper amount. Keypunch errors can cause havoc with a bank reconciliation.

9. Duplicate check numbers

Some companies use the same bank account for regular checks and payroll, but each has a distinctive check number sequence. Invariably, since more of one type of check is written than the other, the check sequences will eventually overlap, causing two different checks with the same number to clear in the same month. If this should happen, make sure that you are clearing the correct check during the reconciliation process. This can be chaotic, but after a month or two, the situation will disappear.

10. Old outstanding checks

If you have outstanding checks that haven't cleared after several months, they should be investigated. The vendor may have lost the check, or you may have already written a replacement check. If you find that the check is no longer valid, make a journal entry to get rid of it. However, if you delete it too soon, it may clear, causing another difference in your reconciliation.

Source: David A. Caplan, CPA, MBA—David Caplan received his CPA in 1980, while working for a Big 10 public accounting firm. He was employed in various industries from 1981 to 1992, gaining insight on the inner workings of companies, and received his MBA from Temple University in 1986. In 1992, he purchased an accounting practice, which has quintupled in size since then. He handles all aspects of accounting, from personal income tax and advice to financial statements and corporate tax returns. He has

clients geographically located all over the United States. His Web site is *www.caplancpa.com*. He can be reached at PO Box 301, Lafayette Hill, PA 19444; (610) 834-5754; fax: (610) 834-1013.

Key Reports Used to Run a Business

Someone once said, "You can only expect what you inspect." Whatever you measure in a business will improve. Our expert, an MBA and experienced business consultant, offers these critical reports that every business owner and manager should be using to help run the company.

1. Daily sales contacts

The engine of sales is contacts (telephone, e-mail, face-to-face, proposals) made daily to prospects and customers.

2. Daily flash report

Ask accounting to provide a one-page report daily that shows the end-of-the-day balances in each banking account, line of credit, accounts receivable, and accounts payable.

3. Weekly pipeline report

Each salesperson should provide a Friday-night report naming new prospects, new proposals, and closed work for the week. That information should be used to update a sales forecast.

4. Accounts receivable

Finish the week by reviewing all accounts receivable and creating special instructions for following up on past-due accounts the following Monday morning.

5. Accounts payable

When you review accounts payable weekly (right after accounts receivable), then you will keep a profitable perspective on your business. You will not spend the new money coming in before you pay the bills in hand.

6. Back orders

New sales orders may not be good news if you have not delivered what you previously promised.

7. Employee overtime

Overtime affects morale and profit. By measuring overtime, you will keep better tabs on the performance level of employees and the need to add new positions.

8. Employee absenteeism

An employee who misses Monday one week and Friday the next averages four workdays a week. However, your perception may be much different. Track time off so that you always have numbers to match perceptions.

9. Productivity

Each business needs to create its own metrics of productivity. For service businesses, this could relate to the number of sales dollars per employee hours. For product businesses, it could be the number of products sold per employee hour.

10. Profit and loss statement and balance sheet

Review these financial statements by the tenth of the following month. Highly profitable companies practice fiscal fitness.

11. Return on advertising and marketing

Advertising and marketing are the "sexy, fun" part of business. However, they must achieve results. Every month, calculate the number of sales dollars generated from each dollar of advertising/marketing. For example, if you spend $300 on a postcard mailing that generates $3,000, you have a 10:1 return.

12. Performance evaluations

Keep a list of due dates for employee evaluations and check up twice a month to ensure that no one will receive a late evaluation. The surest way to kill morale is to delay evaluations.

13. Morale survey

Find a simple, one-page (or shorter) morale survey and administer it quarterly. Then, benchmark against yourself.

14. Annual business valuation

After you close out a fiscal year, ask your CPA or a financial consultant to run a valuation of your business. Then, benchmark against yourself from year-to-year.

Source: Pam Watson Korbel, MBA, is a business coach, trainer, speaker, and author specializing in entrepreneurial business growth. She is CEO and business synergist of SmartGrowth, Inc. (*www.smartgrowth.com*) and can be reached at (303) 790-9131 or *pam@smartgrowth.com*.

Most Common Financial Warning Signs

As a business owner or manager, you need to have the ability to recognize, acknowledge, and react quickly to financial warning signs that your business is headed for trouble. This could be the difference between keeping your business afloat or watching it go under. If you see any of these warning signs, you need to identify solutions and implement corrective actions immediately.

1. Losing market share and declining sales

It is a competitive market, and your customers are not ignorant about searching for the best products and services. Check often for declines in your product quality and/or customer service. Watch what your competitors may be doing to pull market share away. A seasonal decrease in sales can be common for certain kinds of businesses, but a steady downward curve for two or three quarters in a row may indicate trouble. Set reasonable sales goals and time frames for your firm. Then outline the specific steps you need to take to achieve those goals. Maybe it's time to design a new marketing strategy or expand geographically. Whatever you do, do not ignore this warning!

2. Sustained cash-flow problems

Many growing companies have cash-flow problems. An occasional crunch may not be a sign of an unhealthy business, but left unchecked, persistent cash-flow problems can mean major headaches ahead. Always be selective in granting credit. Remember to bill promptly and follow up when receivables pass the forty-five-day mark. In terms of accounts payable, focus on timing payments so they are received on or just before the due date. To improve cash flow, keep inventories low and take advantage of volume discounts only if you can use the entire amount purchased.

3. Too much business tied to one customer

Numerous experts advise that companies derive no more than one-third of their business from one customer. Spend some time each week on your marketing. If you don't have the time, consider hiring a marketing consultant, even part-time, who can help you expand your client list.

4. Poor financial recordkeeping

Keep good financial records. This is so valuable because it's difficult to manage what you can't measure. When a business is in trouble, financial paperwork often gets put off until the last minute or is forgotten altogether. This can give you problems with lenders, the Internal Revenue Service, and other government agencies. Take time each week to catch up on paperwork and consult regularly with your CPA to make certain that your company's legal and financial paperwork is in order.

5. Unwarranted increases in expenses

Increased expenses sometimes signify a lack of spending controls. Measure expenses against past months and also against the same period last year. Be sure that there is an approval process in place for expenses over a predetermined amount, and don't hesitate to question expenses periodically, especially those that don't support the production of income. Review workers' expenses. When you do this, they tend to become much more careful about how they spend the company's money. Another strategy is to shop around and get quotes from two or three vendors before purchasing supplies, inventory and services.

Source: Kentucky Society of Certified Public Accountants (*www. kycpa.org*)—The Kentucky Society of Certified Public Accountants is located at 1735 Alliant Avenue, Louisville, KY 40299; (502) 266-5272.

Top Ways to Manage Your Business to Maximize Its Value

Our expert, a business valuation consultant and author, provides a list of critical variables that contribute to the value of a business. He believes that the first two entries have the greatest impact on the value of your business.

1. Minimize the risk

The greatest risks to most small and medium-size businesses are, in descending order: overdependence on the owner and corresponding weak middle management; inadequate systems and organization, including computerization and backups; overdependence on one or a small number of customers, suppliers, or employees; and too much debt, which is financial risk.

2. Maximize the growth rate of cash flows

It is important to understand that growth in cash flows is not the same as growth in sales. Increasing sales growth may decrease net income if it is not carefully controlled. Start by making sure that net income is growing because net income is the engine that powers growth in cash flows. The rest is managing working capital, fixed assets, and debt optimally.

3. Manage your balance sheet

Changes in your balance sheet over time affect your cash flow. The object is always to achieve or at least move toward achieving the right balance. There is always a cost of having too much of each asset or liability, and there is a cost of having too little. If your business is large enough—probably at least $5 million in sales—it is likely that it is cost-effective to have a competent valuation professional or economist help you achieve the right balance.

4. Manage your net working capital

Net working capital (NWC) is current assets (typically cash, accounts receivable, and inventory) minus current liabilities. Having too much NWC is a drain on your cash flow and reduces the value of your business. Having too little NWC may cause you operational problems, which also can reduce the value of your business. For example, insufficient inventory will cause lost sales, while too much inventory drains cash and leads to obsolete inventory and write-downs. Insufficient accounts receivable means lost sales, while too much AR is a drain on cash.

5. Manage fixed assets

Expensive equipment and technology often saves time and makes a business more efficient, but it requires a sizable investment. In good times, the company with great equipment will tend to do very well, but in bad times, you can't lay off your equipment like you can lay off workers, and such a company will tend to do poorly. Thus, high fixed assets tend to accentuate the fluctuations from economic cycles, which creates operational risk. You should make sure that the payoff justifies the risk; it may or may not, depending on the specific numbers.

6. Use debt effectively

The government allows a tax deduction for interest payments. Used wisely, the "right" amount of debt will make your business more profitable in good times, as it can provide inexpensive capital to increase sales and profitability. Too much debt, though, is dangerous; in bad times, the fixed interest expense lowers profitability and increases your probability of bankruptcy. The greater the operational risks of your business are, the less financial risk (i.e., debt) you should have. Chief operational risks are overdependence on the founder/weak middle management, a highly cyclical business, and high fixed costs (i.e., much expensive equipment).

7. Balance all of these items

Achieving balance in all of these items is the greatest skill, because many of them are contradictory, as we have already discussed. For example, a high growth rate in sales may raise or lower profitability, and it may raise the risk of the business. Is faster growth causing greater fluctuations in net income and cash flow? Buyers prefer a steady growth of net income rather than much volatility. It is also important to consider the effects of high growth on the balance sheet items that we discussed, as they affect cash flow. The converse is also true. Policies that affect the balance sheet (like credit and inventory policy) affect cash flow, and therefore affect value.

Source: Jay B. Abrams (*www.abramsvaluation.com*)—The founder and CEO of Abrams Valuation Group, Inc. in North Hollywood, California, his firm specializes in business valuation, fractional interest discount studies, and litigation economics. His telephone number is (818)505-6008; his e-mail address is *jay@abramsvaluation.com*.

Signs Your Company Is Growing Too Fast

The paradox of business growth is that it can create more problems. Managed carefully, a business can grow and avoid these problems. But if things get out of control—watch out! How do you know if your business is growing too fast to keep up? Here is a list of some warning signs.

1. Not enough cash

Growth requires cash because generally you pay your employees and buy supplies before collecting a client receivable. You can calculate your optimal growth rate by using the sustainable growth equation (look at a business finance book), which factors in profit, available debt, and equity.

2. Consistently high levels of employee overtime

If your employees consistently work more than 20 percent overtime per week, their workload exceeds your capacity. This assumes that your employees are high performers. You should not add employees until the overtime pattern lasts four weeks or longer.

3. Low customer service

When you wish you had five more minutes for each customer in order to provide quality service, you have a problem. Remember that you can only sell more to your existing customers when their perceived value and service is high.

4. No prospect follow-up

Passing on requests for proposal/quotes and not following up on proposals creates a perception of poor quality service. One of the most frequent complaints from buyers is that prospective vendors never followed up.

5. Shortcuts around procedures

Employees will cut corners when there is not enough time to serve a customer, finish a report, file accurately, make a telephone call, complete a performance evaluation, and so on. In the long-run, shortcuts always hurt growth.

6. Tardy financial and administrative reports

Most companies prioritize according to the following system: customers are served first, then prospects, then internal requirements. However, companies that leave their internal reports on the bottom of the list eventually find declining business results.

7. Back orders

When production speed does not match selling speed, be sure to apprise customers of the timing that they can expect.

8. Missing deadlines

If you find yourself consistently asking for more time, you have reached the "red zone" of customer and employee service. No system has ever been created to borrow time.

9. Unclean and disorganized workspace

Although you may feel that you cannot devote the time to keep your paperwork organized and your office clean, you will actually lose the energy in an unkempt space.

10. No time for personal needs

You do not have enough time to go shopping (or attend to personal needs). The best companies create wealth for owners who do not have to be there every day. The business revolves around a system that runs without dependence on any individual, including the owner.

Source: Pam Watson Korbel, MBA, is a business coach, trainer, speaker and author specializing in entrepreneurial business growth. She is CEO and business synergist of SmartGrowth, Inc. (*www.smartgrowth.com*) and can be reached at (303) 790-9131 or *pam@smartgrowth.com*.

Best Ways to Reduce Inventories

Excess inventory hurts the company in several ways. It ties up cash, which could be used more productively in paying down debt or pursuing alternative opportunities. It takes up space, forcing you to add onto your facility, and uses unnecessary leased space. Excess inventory can increase your insurance and taxes. It exposes you to risks associated with shrinkage, obsolescence, and damage related to excess handling. Here are some of the steps you can take to get your inventory under control.

1. Evaluate your inventory control "infrastructure"

If you haven't already, is it time to automate inventory control? If you are using a management software package, is the inventory control module adequate for your needs? Do your processes support keeping accurate, timely inventory counts? Is your inventory layout conducive to administering "real-time" inventory control?

2. Perform a cost-benefits analysis on an increased commitment to inventory control

Can your staff take on the extra duties involved? While getting such a system going can require a lot of initial attention, inventory control systems save time in the longer run, by allowing you to know what's in stock without having to go to the warehouse, by quickly detecting any possible theft, and by lowering rates of stock-out (lost sales) and overstock.

3. Set a target for customer service level

Measures can include percentage of orders filled completely, or items delivered as a percentage of items ordered. The primary constraint on reducing inventory is, of course, the level of customer service. What's an acceptable service level for you—95 percent, 99.5 percent? Inventory control software generally uses such a figure to determine how much "safety stock" you need to meet this objective.

4. Implement cycle counting

To make a system work well, you have to be committed to keeping accurate inventory on a real-time basis, which necessitates "cycle counting." Cycle counting is an inventory management procedure in which a small subset of inventory is counted on any given day. Instead of taking a physical inventory once a year, for example, you can count 2 percent (one-fiftieth) of your inventory each week up to the fiftieth week of the year. Using this method, errors are caught more quickly, and extra counts can be performed on error-prone items.

5. Implement just-in-time

JIT includes a set of actions that work together to squeeze slack out of your processes. Do you enter received material as soon as it arrives? Can your key suppliers commit to shorter lead times?

6. Identify overstock items

Identify overstock items in your inventory control system. Sometimes the inventory may go straight to the trash heap, but some may be sent back to the manufacturer. You may want to think about having a garage sale and selling or donating the rest to a local housing agency.

7. Analyze the contribution of each item in the inventory

Take a hard look at the realistic contribution of every item in your inventory. You may need to keep some losers as "service items," but you will be amazed at how many of your items are break-even or worse.

8. Partner strategically

Can you narrow your number of suppliers by getting more items from the "majors?" You may currently split up orders to save a penny here and there, but the vendor left standing would probably meet or beat the other's prices for a greater share of your business. More from each vendor means more frequent replenishment, and more opportunities for just-in-time.

Source: Dr. John B. Vinturella, Vinturella and Associates, (*www.jbv. com*)—Dr. Vinturella has almost forty years' experience as a management and strategic consultant and entrepreneur, and fifteen of those years as an academic entrepreneur-in-residence and adjunct professor. Dr. Vinturella is coauthor of *Raising Entrepreneurial Capital*

(*Elsevier, 2004*) and author of *The Entrepreneur's Fieldbook* (*Prentice Hall, 1999*). He can reached at (504) 246-3999, and at *jbv@jbv. com*. His address is 11111 Winchester Park Drive, New Orleans, LA 70128.

Popular Ways to Turn Inventory into Cash

Inventory is money, and having it lying around your factory is not where your money belongs. Our expert believes that if you reduce inventory to just-in-time levels, then you can eliminate 85 percent or more of your inventory. But that's not all. You will also save more in annual inventory carrying costs. With less inventory, there are lower costs of holding inventory. Here's a list of methods to reduce inventory and increase cash.

1. Increase demand-forecasting accuracy

We only need enough inventory to satisfy demand, and that is where part of the problem exists. If demand can not be accurately forecasted, then we end up compensating for this unknown with inventory.

2. Increase manufacturing-cycle efficiency

How well manufacturing resources are used to produce a product determines the cycle efficiency. Defective product, product rework, and long lags between manufacturing cells cause inefficiency, which can be easily calculated. Raw materials should be converted into finished goods as quickly as possible. The speed at which this occurs defines your manufacturing cycle efficiency.

3. Increase supply-chain turns

Increasing the number of times purchases are made may increase acquisition costs and unit costs because of smaller order quantities. But you will benefit by increasing your cash flow and eliminating the carrying cost of the inventory (warehousing, material handling, taxes, insurance, depreciation, interest, and obsolescence totaling 25 percent to 35 percent).

4. Eliminate safety stock

Safety stock is really just a buffer for forecasting variance and supplier delivery time. While many levels are set arbitrarily in automated MRP systems, your safety stock levels will need to be reduced due to improvements in demand-forecasting accuracy, manufacturing-cycle efficiency and supply-chain turns.

5. Reduce purchasing errors

This can reduce overstocking and, more important, minimize stock-outs that result in expensive expedited purchases. Sell excess and obsolete inventory, or return it to your vendor.

6. Eliminate delivery variance

Do not allow vendors to deliver early or late, and make sure the delivered quantity does not vary from the order quantity. After all, delivery errors cause the need to carry more inventory. Instead, provide suppliers with forecasts of future needs.

7. Train purchasing personnel

Provide your purchasing and material management personnel with formal training. This will arm them with better negotiating skills that will result in better prices and terms.

Source: Chris Anderson, managing director of Bizmanualz, Inc. (*www.bizmanuals.com*) and coauthor of policies and procedures manuals, producing the layout, process design, and implementation to increase performance. Anderson has more than twenty years of sales, marketing, and business management experience working with small to large corporations and has worked with business process design, software, and systems engineering, consulting with companies large and small. Contact them at Bizmanualz, Inc., 7777 Bonhomme Avenue, Suite 2222, Clayton, MO 63105; toll-free: (800) 466-9953.

Ways to Increase Inventory Turnover

Are you looking for ways to increase your inventory turnover? Here are a few from our expert, the Ambassador of Selling.

1. Dating from vendors

"Vendor dating" means that the vendor will hold off billing for the goods delivered—for, say, sixty or ninety days—or they will make the invoice payable, with anticipation discount (i.e., 3 percent EOM) with a sixty- or ninety-day due date from date of delivery. You might say the goods are on consignment for that amount of time. However, the difference between vendor dating and consignment is that with the former, the bill has to be paid eventually. How does vendor dating increase turnover? Well, if the goods are ones that have been selling previously, most likely some or all of them will be sold before the bill has to be paid.

2. 80/20 rule

This is a method of a "horizontal" look at what and how much is selling when. Not only is business cyclical, but each product/service within a business is cyclical. Not everything sells well all the time, and some products/services sell less often or rarely. Possibly, however, these last two categories cannot be eliminated due to the 80/20 rule; that is, 80 percent of the products/services sold are done with 20 percent of the selection of products/services available. Most inventory systems show total on hand and sales for the previous month and to-date sales. But, to get a "horizontal picture," you would have to overlay each page of like items so it shows the relative changes month by month (or week by week if necessary) versus one month at a time. Since the 80/20 rule prevails with inventory, working on increasing the sales and rate of sale of slower selling items will help increase the sales of the better selling ones. It is also a better use of inventory.

3. Buy less more often

Try to buy less but more often even though buying more at one time may be less costly.

4. Consignment goods

Obtain consignment goods to back up current inventory or in addition to current inventory. The difference between vendor dating and consignment is that with the vendor dating, the bill has to be paid eventually. With consignment goods, only those goods sold have to be paid for. In addition, usually a consignment agreement says that unsold items may be returned as long as the goods and their packaging are still in salable condition.

5. Implement the "locker stock" program

Another way to increase inventory turnover that some vendors offer, is called a "locker stock" program. In this situation, the vendor puts goods in a store on consignment. However, the agreement says that the store and the vendor have to agree on what goods are on the display. Then, any goods sold will be replaced and the store pays for the replacement. The catch-22 of vendor dating, locker stock, or consignment is that often these goods are sold in lieu of selling goods the store already owns; hence, inventory turnover is not increased. Not only that, if sales of these special programs increase and sales of owned goods stay the same or decrease, inventory turn decreases. This is the merchandise version of Newton's law: For every force, there is an equal and opposite force.

6. Box-lotting

"Box-lotting" refers to taking slow(er) selling items/services with better selling ones at a combined special price.

7. Display changes

Change the display or manner of presentations or products/services so that the slower selling ones are more prominent.

8. Closeout sales

Have closeout sales to free money for better selling items.

Source: Alan J. Zell (*www.sellingselling.com*)—The Ambassador of Selling, he has become nationally recognized for his expertise in advising businesses, services, educational, governmental, and organizational entities. Clients seeking his services represent a wide spectrum including accountants, investors, educators, chambers of commerce, retailers, wholesalers, manufacturers, associations, and nonprofit organizations. Contact him at PO Box 69, Portland, OR 97207-0069; (503) 241-1988.

Key Issues in Corporate Social Responsibility (CSR)

Few corporate executives today believe that the only responsibilities of business are to be profitable and to act in accordance with the law. Corporations are now expected to address a wider range of stakeholders and mitigate the social and environmental harm generated by their operations. Following is a list of key issues that ought to be considered by today's "socially responsible" corporation. (Note: because social and environmental impacts vary among industries, not all issues are relevant to all companies.)

1. Corporate governance and transparency

Following a series of relatively recent corporate governance scandals, the issue of transparency has received greater attention by the business community. Sound corporate governance structures ensure the independence of board members, protect shareholder rights, and recognize the rights of company stakeholders. Good governance requires timely, accurate, and transparent reporting on the company's financial performance, company objectives, share ownership and voting rights, executive remuneration, related party transactions, and foreseeable risk factors.

2. Environment

At the 1992 Earth Summit in Rio, a coalition of 160 transnational corporations pledged to work toward more sustainable development by seeking innovative ways to protect the environment while sustaining economic growth. While some industries, such as oil and gas, inflict greater harm on the environment than others, most companies can help mitigate environmental damage by investing in energy-saving technology, reducing greenhouse gas emissions, developing environmentally friendly products, minimizing waste (for example, in packaging), and using natural resources more efficiently.

3. Employee relations

This category encompasses everything from labor relations to employee diversity. Responsible companies treat their employees well by paying fair wages, providing benefits packages, promoting work/life balance, supporting employee education and development, and recognizing workers' freedom of association and right to collective bargaining. In compliance with international labor standards, companies are expected to work to abolish child labor, eliminate all forms of forced labor, and refrain from discrimination in respect of employment and occupation.

4. Health and safety

Responsible companies demonstrate concern for the health and safety of their employees and their customers. Many companies now have formal occupational health and safety programs that aim to reduce the number of work-related injuries and fatalities, and improve employees' working conditions. Manufacturing companies, in particular, must work to eliminate the use of sweatshop labor and refrain from seeking regulatory exemptions regarding labor practices. Companies are also responsible for ensuring the safety of their products and should take the appropriate measures to ensure that their products do not pose a risk to consumer health or safety.

5. Human rights

In some cases, such as in the extractive industries, companies are forced to operate in countries with poor human rights records, or in conflict zones where the host country government is unwilling or unable to prevent human rights violations. In such cases, to avoid being complicit in human rights violations, responsible companies ought to consult regularly with nongovernment organizations to keep abreast of human rights issues in host countries. Companies should also develop a human rights policy that supports the articles of key documents such as the Universal Declaration of Human Rights and the United Nations Norms on Responsibilities of Transnational Corporations with regard to Human Rights.

6. Supply chain management

While many companies have been making great strides toward addressing social and environmental issues triggered by their own operations, they should also accept a degree of responsibility for their suppliers' actions. Companies should develop formalized policies to govern their supply chain and create monitoring mechanisms to ensure compliance. The challenge for large multinational corporations is to encourage the widespread adoption of appropriate CSR standards in global supply chains by facilitating their suppliers' implementation of industry best practices, rather than by discriminating against suppliers that may not be financially equipped to adopt CSR best practices on their own.

7. Community relations

Embedded in the doctrine of CSR is the idea of the social contract, which implies that corporations have a duty to give something back to the communities in which they operate. Increasingly, this is seen as requiring that corporations provide more than the products and employment traditionally expected of them. Corporations can make positive contributions to their communities through corporate donations, benefit-sharing, employee giving and volunteerism, and community development programs.

8. Stakeholder engagement

An extension of the notion of positive community relations, stakeholder engagement refers to disclosure, consultation, dialog, and sometimes partnership with a wide range of groups that can affect, or are affected by, the company's activities. Stakeholders generally include, but are not limited to, shareholders, customers, employees, financiers, communities, and nongovernment organizations. Also, as multinational corporations increasingly come into contact with aboriginal communities, special attention should be paid to aboriginal relations.

9. Curbing corruption

This category refers to measures taken to eliminate all forms of corruption, including extortion, bribery, and improper involvement with local political activities. Responsible companies should adhere to Transparency International's Business Principles for Countering Bribery regarding bribes, political and charitable contributions, facilitation payments, and gifts. Companies can work toward reducing corruption by establishing a corporate code of conduct that focuses on such issues, and by creating more transparent governance structures.

10. Monitoring and reporting

The integrity of a company is largely determined by its ability to put words into action; therefore, it is important for a company to monitor the progress of its CSR initiatives. While measuring social and environmental performance can pose real challenges, reporting can help communicate a company's commitment to society by describing the company's social and environmental initiatives. Reporting should be consistent and preferably verified by an independent third party.

Source: Melissa Whellams (*www.whellams.com*)—Whellams consults on issues related to corporate social responsibility and international development; past clients include multinational oil, mining, and biotech companies. She has a bachelor's in communication in international business, and at time of writing is pursuing a master's degree in international development. She can be contacted at *mwhellams@gmail.com*.

Considerations for Writing a Code of Ethics

Most major corporations, and many smaller companies, now have codes of ethics, along with a range of other, issue-specific ethics documents. Such a document embodies the ethical commitments of your organization; it tells the world who you are, what you stand for, and what to expect when conducting business with you. The content of a code, and the process for writing it, can vary quite a lot, but here's a list of some of the standard issues to consider.

1. Tailor your code

Ideally, a code of ethics should be custom-made for your organization. Ask yourself, what makes your code specific to your organization? Is there anything that differentiates it from similar documents devised by other firms in your field, or in other fields? If not, what makes it your code, other than the fact that your logo is at the top?

2. Get employees involved

The people who will be guided by the code should be actively involved in writing it. If your organization is too large to get everyone involved, consider selecting representatives from various departments or various business units. The document is bound to be more meaningful, and find higher levels of acceptance, if employees are part of the process.

3. Consult key stakeholders

It's a good idea to consult key stakeholders—including, for example, customers, suppliers, and local community groups—about what they think should be in your code. This will help reveal what important external constituencies see as your key obligations and will help make sure that the code you write deals with the full range of issues that might confront your organization.

4. Outsource the job carefully

Hiring a consultant to help write your code can be useful, but don't let them take over. A consultant can bring a wealth of knowledge and experience and can help you avoid a whole range of pitfalls, from lack of clarity to the inclusion of too little—or too much—detail. But at the end of the day, this code is still yours: it should reflect your organization's values, principles, and aspirations.

5. Seek out good examples

If you're writing your own code, begin by looking at relevant examples. There are lots of good codes out there (a quick Internet search can be very revealing). A code that is simply copied from another organization is unlikely to provide either effective guidance or inspiration—but there's also no point in reinventing the wheel.

6. Be clear about scope

Your code should make clear who within your organization will be governed by it. Does it cover everyone from the mailroom through to the boardroom? Only senior managers? Who has to sign off on it? Keep in mind that lower-level employees may not take very seriously a document that senior managers either aren't bound by or take lightly.

7. Be specific about implementation

How will the code be implemented? Once it's written, will it gather dust, or will it influence policy and practice? What procedures are in place to make sure that writing a code is more than just organizational navel-gazing? An effective implementation scheme (perhaps as an appendix to the code) will explain to all concerned how the values embodied in your code will be put into practice.

8. Plan for education

A key aspect of implementation has to be employee training and education. How will employees be educated about the code? A code can only be effective if your employees know about it. Will new employees receive training regarding the code's requirements? Will current employees receive refresher courses? Especially for large organizations, the steps required to train employees on the requirements of a code deserve special attention.

9. Be clear about enforcement

How, if at all, will the code be enforced? Are there specific penalties for violating the code, or is the code merely there to provide guidance? Who will decide when an employee has violated the code? Will that be up to the employees' immediate supervisor, or will that be the exclusive domain of senior managers?

10. Specify a sunset date

When will the code be reviewed and updated? Times change, and new issues come to light, so consider specifying a date for revising and refreshing your code.

Source: Chris MacDonald, PhD, teaches philosophy at Saint Mary's University in Halifax, Nova Scotia, Canada. He has published on a wide range of topics in ethics, ranging from business ethics and professional ethics through health care ethics and ethical issues in new technologies. He also runs the world's largest ethics bookstore, which can be found online at *www.ethicsweb.ca/books*, as well as a popular Web page on codes of ethics, at *www.ethic sweb.ca/codes*.

Maximizing Your Cash Flow

What to Look For in a Barter System

Nationally, over 250,000 businesses are involved in barter. It is estimated that 65 percent of the Fortune 500 companies engage in barter to one degree or another. Included on this list are Pepsi-Co, Inc., Pizza Hut, Casio, General Electric, IBM, Amoco, Caterpillar, 3M, Goodyear, Xerox, Pan-Am, Chrysler, and Hilton. There are many barter systems (sometimes called trade exchanges) out there, so here's what to look for.

1. Location

Just as in everything else in life, location, location, location should be a major consideration in choosing an exchange. It isn't important where the office of the exchange is; it's the location of the clients that counts. No matter how good a client list an exchange has, if all the goods and services you need are fifty miles away, what good are they?

2. Specialty and client list

The reality or joining an exchange is that your company is about to join an association of businesses that will work together and feed off of one another's excess (time, labor, goods, and services). Make sure the association fits your needs! Remember, no company will meet all your needs—that's not what barter is about—but they should be able to handle up to 10 percent of your business and then facilitate the spending of your trade dollars on things that will minimize cash expenses, or enhance your or your employees' lifestyle.

3. Style and methods of doing business

Each company works in its own way. Some work through assigned brokers, some work only online, some use a combination. Go with what is comfortable for you. If you like personal attention, the Web is not for you. If you like to trade at midnight, the Web is perfect. The choice is yours.

4. Longevity and track record of growth

They go hand-in-hand and should be looked at together. Sheer number of members alone does not make a good exchange. Ask these questions: How long has the exchange been in business? Does it continue to grow? How many members trade on a regular basis? What is the percentage of members *on hold*? Sometimes an exchange will contract in number of members, but the trade volume will increase due to the selectivity of the exchange in choosing its members. All of these factors are important.

5. Initiation, sign-up, or setup fee

No matter what they call it, most companies have some form of this fee, which pays all the startup costs, client training, and the salesperson who brought you in. Whatever the charge is, it should not be a deterrent or an incentive to join an exchange. Companies charge high amounts to join an exchange to show you how much they're worth, or to test your commitment, or because they are worth it. On the other hand, some companies charge next-to-nothing as an incentive during client recruitment drives, and some give you exactly what you are paying for.

6. Association or monthly fees

These fees vary, but they are charged on a monthly basis whether you trade that month or not. These fees pay for the company's ongoing costs.

7. Usage or transaction fees

These fees vary. Some companies charge when you buy, some when you sell, some split the fees and charge for both. The amount charged also varies from company to company, so pay attention.

Source: Empowered Barter (*www.empoweredbarter.com*)—Empowered Barter is a free reference and referral service for business owners. Empowered Barter aids business owners in learning about how and what to barter, in deciding whether barter or trade should be a part of their business, in choosing a trade or barter exchange in their area.

Typical Bills Paid First During a Cash Crunch

If you have a mountain of bills but are short on cash, which bills should get paid first? Our expert, who specializes in workouts and bankruptcy, offers what he thinks should be paid during a cash crunch. This list is geared more to consumers than businesses, but if you're running a struggling enterprise, you may find yourself in both categories.

1. The rent

Everyone has to live somewhere. You cannot risk being homeless. Therefore, pay the rent.

2. The squeakiest wheel

Some creditors will push harder than others. Most creditors will accept a partial payment and continue trying to collect rather than sue if payments are being made. Therefore, send something to the creditor(s) that is pushing the hardest.

3. Child support/alimony

In most states, the local district attorney is the official who helps collect past-due support. The result of not paying could be a few nights in jail. Jail is a bad place to try to pay your bills.

4. Utilities

Related to rent, it is a necessity of life and will be turned off by a computer if not paid. Reinstatement can also be costly; it may require a deposit and fees.

5. One credit card

Modern life requires that you have some form of plastic for everyday purchases. However, credit cards can be frozen if not paid. Therefore, you should have one card that is paid in full every month so that if a real emergency occurs, you have some amount of credit.

6. Debts to family

Although it may seem that debts owed to relatives can wait, they can also cause so much heartache that permanent damage can be done that can't be fixed when relatives have trouble over money. In the future, don't borrow from relatives.

7. Taxes

The penalties and interest on unpaid taxes can climb very fast. Also, taxing agencies have the ability to garnish wages and seize property. Even if your state does not currently offer tax amnesty, the IRS and most states will work out a payment plan. Try to stretch it out as long as possible. When things get better, pay it off.

8. Insurance

Driving uninsured is illegal in most states and can result in the loss of your license, making it even harder to earn a living. Maybe you can risk letting the homeowner's policy lapse if you are really tight and like Russian roulette, but you should not let the life insurance lapse. First, if you die, there is no time for reinstatement. If you get sick, you may not qualify for a new policy. If your policy has cash value, use it to make the premium payments. That will save cash in a pinch.

9. Highest interest debts

If you have any discretionary funds, pay the debt with the highest interest rate. That will reduce the ultimate amount you will pay.

10. Professionals

While most professionals, such as doctors, dentists, accountants, will want to try to keep you as a client, it would be a real problem for one of them to refuse service when you really need it.

Source: Howard M. Ehrenberg of SulmeyerKupetz, a professional corporation (www.sulmeyerlaw.com)—Ehrenberg is a member of the Chapter 7 Bankruptcy Panel of Trustees, appointed by the Office of the United States Trustee, and a state court receiver. He is certified as a Business Bankruptcy Law Specialist by the American Bankruptcy Board of Certification. He is also the author of several articles.

Contact him at 333 South Hope Street, Thirty-fifth Floor, Los Angeles, CA 90071; (213) 626-2311; e-mail: hehrenberg@sulmeyerlaw.com.

Popular Ways to Decrease Expenses

Every business, no matter how large or small, looks for ways to decrease expenses. Some are in financial crisis and need to do it to survive. Others would just like to have higher profit. Our expert, an experienced financial consultant, provides a few popular ways to accomplish the task. Here they are, in his words.

1. Employee layoffs

This is listed first because payroll is typically the largest single expense next to cost of goods sold, and it is the first place that employers look to cut. However, this can be a drastic step, and it can influence things such as employee morale, reputation, and unemployment costs. Before you take this course, make sure you have examined all of your other options.

2. Change health benefits

With health insurance soaring 20 percent per year, this is an area that gets expensive fast. Always make sure that the employee contributes something, even if it is a token amount. If not, there will be no incentive for the employee to be covered under the spouse's insurance, and you will end up footing the bill. Increasing deductibles and copays are small but effective ways to decrease health care costs.

3. Purchase in quantity

If you are in a manufacturing or distribution business, your suppliers normally have volume discounts. Even if you have no room to store the excess product, it is sometimes cheaper to rent a small warehouse, depending on the size of the discount. Also, try purchasing from a cooperative or a large consumer warehouse store.

4. Reduce credit card fees

If you sell to the public, it is almost imperative to accept credit and debit cards. The fees accompanying them can be overwhelming, but there is tremendous competition in the credit card–processing field. Have different companies give you quotes, but make sure you know *all* of their charges. Most important, ask them if there is a charge to cancel their contract.

5. Cut travel expenses

In the old days, the only way to have a meeting with someone in another town was to travel. Now, technology has provided teleconferencing, video conferencing, and Internet interfacing. These can be just as effective at a fraction of the cost. They also cut employee downtime and add productivity to existing staff, allowing you to decrease personnel.

6. Eliminate company cars

Change from a company car to a car allowance. This puts the onus of controlling auto expenses on the employee. It is a disincentive to using the company car for personal reasons, or scheduling unnecessary business trips. Unsafe drivers do not cause an increase in company insurance costs. If the employee exceeds his/her car allowance, the expenses are still potentially deductible, but the travel expenses for the business are capped.

7. Cut advertising costs

Do you really need that big Yellow Pages ad? Re-evaluating advertising efficiency could direct your budgeted dollars in a different direction, resulting in either increased revenues or reduced costs. Don't place ads just because everyone else does. Make sure they are working for you.

8. Evaluate telephone costs

With the advent of cell phones, pagers, and personal data assistants, communication costs have skyrocketed. Many companies offer group plans or service combinations that take advantage of economies of scale. In addition, re-examine your main switchboard setup to see if it is as efficient as possible.

9. Refinance loans

Start-up companies typically do not have the bargaining power to get the best loan terms from lending institutions. As your business matures, revisit your existing loans to see if refinancing can lower debt-service costs. It may even be possible for the business owner to take out an inexpensive home equity loan and lend the money to the company.

10. Relocate to smaller offices

As companies grow technologically, their space needs may actually decrease. Converting some employees to telecommuters can also decrease the amount of office space necessary. If your lease term is nearing an end, it may make sense to move to smaller quarters.

Source: David A. Caplan, CPA, MBA—David Caplan received his CPA in 1980, while working for a Big 10 public accounting firm. He was employed in various industries from 1981 to 1992, gaining insight on the inner workings of companies, and received his MBA from Temple University in 1986. In 1992, he purchased an accounting practice, which has since quintupled in size. He handles all aspects of accounting, from personal income tax and advice to financial statements and corporate tax returns. He has clients geographically located all over the United States. His Web site is *www.caplancpa.com*. He can be reached at PO Box 301, Lafayette Hill, PA 19444; (610) 834-5754; fax: (610) 834-1013.

Steps for Managing Your Petty Cash

Set up a petty cash fund if you need cash on hand to pay miscellaneous small business expenses. If yours is a retail business with cash on hand, you probably don't need a petty cash fund. Just be sure to carefully record all cash paid out of the cash register. Here's a list of steps for doing this properly.

1. Write a "petty cash" check

Write a check to start a petty cash fund, and then cash the check.

2. Place cash in a box

Physically place the cash in a petty cash drawer or box.

3. Keep an itemized list

As you pay for expenses out of petty cash, keep an itemized list of each expenditure.

4. Add up expenses

When the cash is almost depleted, add up the expenses on your itemized list.

5. Write another check for the total expenses

Write another check for the total of the expenses. That check should replenish the fund.

Source: CCH Business Owner's Toolkit: (*www.toolkit.cch.com*)—The Business Owner's Toolkit provides advice, guides, legal tools, business models, and other resources to small business owners.

Ideas for Hoarding Your Cash

Our expert wants us to remember: Cash flow and profitability are not the same thing. You can be profitable but not have a positive cash flow—and you can have a positive cash flow but not be profitable. Not understanding this difference is one of the surest paths to financial disaster. Here's a list of ideas for hoarding your cash for that rainy day.

1. Determine the answers to three key cash-flow questions

Optimizing cash flow starts with finding the answers to these three questions: First, where is your cash trapped? Cash can be tied up in various places in your business, such as uncollected accounts receivable, unrecognized costs and inventory, and fixed assets that aren't providing a return on your investment. Second, where does cash come from and where does it go? The best tool to help you answer this question is your cash-flow statement. If you're having cash-flow problems, look at the past three or four years of cash-flow statements to find out what's causing problems and what you can do to solve them. Third, can you improve your existing cash position and ongoing cash flow? Answering this question will help you devise specific strategies for improving your cash flow, including some of the strategies that follow.

2. Determine how much cash or liquidity your business needs

The answer will depend on many factors and vary from one company and industry to the next. For example, how fast do you sell your products or services? How fast do you collect from customers? How fast do you pay your suppliers? To find the right answer, you need to determine your cash conversion cycle—a guideline for liquidity that combines widely used financial ratios derived from your financial statements. It will tell you how much working capital you need to run your business without running out of cash.

3. Revamp your payables procedures to hold on to cash longer

Stretch your payables as long as possible without hurting your vendors, unless you're offered a discount for prompt payment. Take full advantage of your thirty days to pay if those are the agreed-on terms.

4. Reduce your investment in accounts receivable

Track your receivables carefully; be aware of what payments are due to you and when. State your payment terms clearly on your invoices and enforce them, and consider assessing penalties for late payments. Meanwhile, if you're offering extended payment terms, determine whether this is generating incremental sales and/or wider

margins. If not, they are reducing your profitability by tying up nonproductive cash.

5. Talk to your bank about using cash-management tools

You may be able to process receipts and collect receivables faster by using bank cash management services, like lockbox, concentration accounts and electronic funds transfer (EFT). Banks offer a broad range of cash-management tools that even small businesses can use to increase available cash.

6. Improve inventory management

Inventory likely represents one of your largest and most tangible investments, so it must be managed wisely. Compare your inventory levels and average inventory-turnover ratio with industry averages to see if you're in the ballpark. Can you shift a portion of the burden of carrying inventory to your suppliers by using just-in-time inventory-management processes? If you've accumulated excess inventory, can you liquidate it in a bulk sale? Also, make good use of one of the many inventory-management software products available.

7. Prioritize and negotiate when cash gets tight

If you find yourself in a cash-flow crunch, first prioritize your payment obligations. Legal obligations (like estimated quarterly tax payments) and payroll should come first, followed by at least minimum payments on corporate credit cards, bank loans and equity lines, insurance premiums, and auto or equipment leases. Also, don't be afraid to communicate and negotiate with suppliers about your cash position. You may be surprised at how cooperative they can be. Billing cycles usually aren't set in stone; most creditors and lenders will position bills in a cycle that's beneficial for you.

8. Make contingency plans for emergency cash

Before you find yourself in a cash-flow squeeze, make contingency plans for accessing emergency cash. Liquid cash reserves in a business savings, money market, or sweep account, of course, provide the best source of emergency funds. It's also a good idea to have a line of credit in place before you need to borrow funds, so that the money is available if and when you need it. Once you're approved, you can access funds up to your approved credit limit by writing a check or via the Internet or a phone call. The process of making such contingency plans can give you peace of mind—and help you sleep better.

Source: Don Sadler is a business editor and writer with twenty years of experience in the business publishing arena. As the vice president and editorial director for Media 3 Publications, he directs editorial content for the company's various business publications. During his career, he has worked with the largest banks in the country to create custom publications targeted to their corporate customers. In addition, as a freelance writer, he has written dozens of articles published in a variety of national business periodicals, including *American Executive* and *Self-Employed America*. Contact him at *don@media3pub.com*.

Typical Credit-Checking Procedures

A good credit-checking procedure before the sale will help keep you out of trouble after your customer has walked out the door. We're all anxious to make a sale, but it's not going to be a sale unless you collect the cash! Taking these few steps at the time of purchase may help you snag an uncreditworthy customer and save a lot of aggravation.

1. Credit cards

Accepting credit cards is a fairly safe credit risk because the risk is on the credit card company. That's one of the reasons you're paying them 2.5 to 5.5 percent of your credit sales. The company issuing the card takes responsibility for checking the cardholder's credit rating and for collecting the bills. As long as you follow the credit card company's procedures (checking the signature and expiration date on the card, for example), you should be able to eliminate your risk.

2. Make sure the check is signed and dated

Make sure that the check is signed and dated, that the amount is properly filled out in both places, and that the payee line is either filled in or left blank for you to fill in.

3. Ask for a driver's license, a phone number, and a credit card

If you don't know the person giving you the check, ask for a driver's license, a phone number, and a credit card. Take down the driver's license number; you might need it (and the phone number) if you have to track him or her down later. The credit card is just to satisfy yourself that the customer was able to establish credit somewhere. In fact, don't write the credit card number down on the back of the check—that's illegal.

4. Look for something out of order

Look for hints that something may be out of order. Is the customer's address preprinted on the check? Does the address on the check match the address on the driver's license? If you belong to a merchant's association or some other group that gives you access to a bad-check list, call to find out if the customer is on the list. (In fact, you might consider joining such an association for that very purpose.) If that isn't an option, ask questions until you're satisfied that everything is in order. If the customer's answers are insufficient, don't accept the check.

5. Call customer's bank to verify

If the check is for an unusually large amount, call the customer's bank to verify that sufficient funds are in the account.

6. Get a credit report

If you offer credit terms to an individual other than by check or by credit card—for example, lawyers and other professionals often send the bill after services are rendered—you can get a credit report on the individual that will give you information about his or her credit history. These reports can be obtained from any of the credit-reporting firms, such as TRW or Equifax. To find a credit firm, look in the Yellow Pages under "Credit Reporting Agencies," or similar listing. Before you can get a credit report, you must have permission from the customer. The permission does not have to be in writing; it can be verbal. There are, however, two exceptions to the rule that you have to get permission from the customer. If you already offer *open account* terms to the customer or if the customer owes you money, you don't have to get permission before you obtain the credit report.

7. Talk to others

While a credit report can be helpful, it is not infallible. It shouldn't, therefore, be your only source of information on the customer. If possible, you should try to talk to other businesses that may have extended credit to the customer. The amount of trouble you're willing to go to for information will depend on the amount of credit you're planning to give. If the customer's credit limit is to be, say, $100, you may find that it's not worth the trouble to track down more information.

Source: CCH Business Owner's Toolkit: (*www.toolkit.cch.com*)— The Business Owner's Toolkit provides advice, guides, legal tools, business models, and other resources to small business owners.

Key Receivables Collection Issues

Some things work and some things don't when collecting overdue accounts. The author of this list says that many of the most popular collection techniques are more bother than they're worth. Take a moment to consider whether these techniques are a good idea for you.

1. Late payment charges

Late payment charges are often ignored, they don't speed up collections, and they can be hard to enforce.

2. Early payment discounts

If early payment discounts are offered (such as 2 percent off for payment in 10 days), some customers take the discount and still pay in 30 to 60 days.

3. Collection agencies

Collection agencies should be considered a last resort. They take a big percentage and often alienate customers.

4. Going to court

Taking a deadbeat to court may result in a countersuit that costs much more to resolve than the delinquent bill.

5. Credit reports

Even the most reliable credit reports can be misinterpreted, resulting in doing business with bad credit risks or avoiding doing business with potentially good customers.

Source: Williams Babbit & Weisman, Inc. (*www.wbw-wwc.com*) is a commercial collection agency handling accounts in the United States and internationally. Contact them at World Wide Collections, 5255 N. Federal Highway, Third Floor, Boca Raton FL 33487; (800) 749-9990; Fax (561) 241-7305; e-mail: *contact@wbw-wwc.com*.

Popular Credit-Checking Firms

Business credit reporting agencies collect and sell information to help lenders and vendors evaluate potential business partners and borrowers. Our author, an expert at personal wealth and managing debt, provides here a list of her most favorite firms to use when checking business credit.

1. Dunn and Bradstreet

The "granddaddy" of business credit agencies, they supply a D-U-N-S number, which will be required for many small business loans—*www.dnb.com*

2. Experian

The same company that offers personal credit reports also has a division that prepares business credit reports—*www.Experian.com*

3. Business Credit USA

Offers a searchable database of over 14 million businesses in the U.S. and Canada—*http://Credit.net*

4. Equifax Business Solutions

Equifax Business Solutions is another one of the three major personal credit reporting agencies. Equifax also compiles and sells business credit reports—*www.Equifax.com*

5. Business Insight

Part of Factual Data Corporation, Business Insight provides verified information on businesses—*www.FactualData.com*

6. ClientChecker

ClientChecker is the "freelancers" credit bureau offering unlimited business credit reports on clients. Check before you agree to do work without upfront payment—*www.clientchecker.com*

Source: Gerri Detweiler (*www.BusinessCreditSuccess.com*) is Credit Expert for EverydayWealth.com and coauthor of Insider's Secrets for Business and Personal Credit.

Top Collection Agencies

Collection agencies are companies hired to collect debts that are owed. Per our expert, the following are some of the largest and most well known collection agencies in the country.

1. CardWorks LP

Delivers customized bankcard servicing, including customer service and collection solutions.

E-mail: *sales@cardworks.com*
www.cardworks.com

2. Tower Administrative Services

An administrator whose main function is to collect and remit client funds for insurance premiums and biweekly accelerated mortgage-reduction programs.

8 Marticville Road
Lancaster, PA 17603
www.toweradmin.com

3. AllianceOne Inc.

AllianceOne was formed in March 1999 through the simultaneous acquisition and merger of five established and well-regarded national, regional and market-specific receivables management companies. Although they are relatively new, their oldest legacy company has been in continuous operation since 1912.

Corporate Offices
717 Constitution Dr.
Exton, PA 19341
(484) 531-5000
Fax: (484) 531-5057
www.allianceoneinc.com

4. Risk Management Alternatives

Their services focus on helping clients' operating performance through improvements in cash flow, operating expenses, customer service, and retention.

2675 Breckinridge Boulevard
Duluth, GA 30096
(770) 925-5000
www.rmainc.net

5. Convergent Resources, Inc.

The company and its operating divisions employ more than 1,600 people in ten locations and offers a full range of ARM products and services, including bad debt recovery, receivables management outsourcing, and specialized recovery services.

Six Concourse Parkway, Suite 2920
Atlanta, GA 30328
E-mail: info@cri-usa-com
(770) 730-0015
www.cri-usa.com

6. JNR Adjustment Company

A national collection agency specializing in retail and commercial collections as well as check recoveries.

2905 Northwest Blvd., Suite 220
Minneapolis, MN 55441
(763) 519-2710
Toll-free: (800) 279-2567
Fax: (763) 519-2722
E-mail: *mailto:ron@jnrcollects.com*
www.jnrcollects.com

7. Arrow Financial Services LLC

Part of the Sallie Mae (NYSE: SLM) family of companies and a nationally recognized leader in the receivables management industry with more than $16 billion in consumer debt under management.

5996 W. Touhy Avenue
Niles, IL 60714
(847) 557-1100
Toll-free: (800) 279-0224
Fax: (847) 647-1215
www.arrow-financial.com

8. OSI Outsourcing Services Inc

One of the nation's leading providers of business process outsourcing services designed to boost client profitability through strategic receivables management.

390 S. Woods Mill Rd.
Chesterfield, MO 63017
(800) 487-2005
www.osioutsourcing.com

9. Greenberg Grant & Richards

Provides an end-to-end accounts receivable management solution, which reduces their daily sales outstanding and improves cash flow.

5858 Westheimer, 5th Floor
Houston, TX 77057
(713) 789-5893
Fax: (713) 789-0137
E-mail: *info@ggrinc.com*
www.ggrinc.com

10. GC Services LP

One of the largest private collection agencies in North America, serving money center banks, credit card companies, telecommunications giants, federal, state, and numerous municipal governments.

6330 Gulfton
Houston, TX 77081
www.gcserv.com

Source: America Data Management Corp (*www.adm-lists.com*)—A leading provider of direct marketing and data-processing services to thousands of clients, they provide the highest quality mailing, telemarketing, and opt-in e-mail lists available in the industry. Their clients include large Fortune 500 companies to small hometown marketers. They are committed to providing the highest quality data and the very best customer service. Contact them at (239) 573-1124; toll-free (800) 262-3637; fax: (239) 573-1154; or e-mail: *info@adm-lists.com*.

Criteria for Deducting Uncollectible Debt

You do not have to wait until a debt is due to determine whether it is worthless. A debt becomes worthless when there is no longer any chance the amount owed will be paid. You are allowed to write off that debt, for tax purposes, when you meet the following criteria.

1. Show that you took reasonable steps to collect debt

It is not necessary to go to court if you can show that a judgment from the court would be uncollectible. You must only show that you have taken reasonable steps to collect the debt.

2. Show that there is evidence of bankruptcy

Bankruptcy of your debtor is generally good evidence of the worthlessness of at least a part of an unsecured and unpreferred debt.

3. If you receive property, reduce debt by the fair market value of property

If you receive property in partial settlement of a debt, reduce the debt by the fair market value of the property received. You can deduct the remaining debt as a bad debt if and when it becomes worthless

Source: Internal Revenue Service (*www.irs.gov*).

Ways to Speed Up Cash Flow

Is your cash flowing out faster than it's flowing in? This can happen for a number of reasons and can be a sign that your business is growing at a faster speed than you are ready to handle. Without adequate operating capital, your ability to grow your business is limited. When this happens, you need a strategy that will either infuse your business with some quick cash or reduce your operating expenses. Here's a list of strategies to help you raise a few bucks.

1. Hold a sale

You reduce inventory while bringing in some quick cash. Offer a discount or other incentive to customers who pay now.

2. Ask for payment in advance for recurring services

If you are offering Web-hosting services, for example, offer one month free to customers who pay up front for twelve months' hosting.

3. Lease your equipment

Purchasing equipment ties up large sums of money. By leasing, your money is freed up for other purposes. Often it is possible to lease a variety of equipment, including office equipment, computers, software, telecommunications equipment, vehicles, and more.

4. Joint venture with another business

Find a business offering services or products that are compatible with yours and offer to promote each other's business. For example, if you are selling health food products, offer to cross-promote with a business selling fitness products. You'll both enjoy increased sales.

5. Obtain a line of credit

Bank credit is usually subject to standard ratios of debt to equity, working capital, and profitability.

6. Factor your accounts receivable

Sometimes known as "invoice discounting," factoring is the selling of your invoices (accounts receivable) for cash, instead of waiting thirty to sixty days to be paid by your customers. Businesses of all sizes use this tool, which is available through various specialized financial institutions. The funder buys your receivables at a discount, leaving you with enhanced cash flow. Not all invoices will be appropriate for factoring. The customer must be a low credit risk, there must be evidence of the transactions (such as a signed delivery waybill), and the customer must verify that the debt is owed.

7. Try an equipment sale leaseback

You can use equipment that you already own to secure financing. By transferring equipment assets onto an equipment lease, you can recover up to 100 percent of the equipment's value. The equipment remains in your own premises, and you can continue to use it. You must own the equipment free and clear to go this route.

8. Ask suppliers for credit

Or ask them to extend your credit. Another possibility is to discuss loan or consignment shipments from your suppliers.

9. Stop producing dated and low profit items

Stick with your core product until sales improve.

10. Cut back on stock or inventory

Ask suppliers to buy back stock at cost. You will have to allow them an administrative fee. Order supplies or inventory on an as-needed basis. Alternatively, you could contact other small businesses that stock the same inventory and discuss the possibility of bulk purchasing.

Source: June Campbell (*www.nightcats.com*) *who owns* Nightcats Multimedia Productions, a firm that provides writing services to businesses and organizations and provides content to print and electronic publications. Publications that have used June's work include *Entrepreneur International, Small Business Canada, The Home Business Report, Asian Entrepreneur, BC Business, Computoredge, Dance International, Mountain Living, Real Woman, Plant and Garden,* and *Income Opportunities.* Contact her at Nightcats Multimedia Productions, 103-145 West Keith Road, North Vancouver, BC, Canada V7M1L3; (604) 980-3261; e-mail: *campbelj@nightcats.com.*

Popular Credit Policies

Many small businesses do a good job delivering their goods and services but then find it difficult to collect payment, often causing a cash-flow crunch. This may be because the creditworthiness of a customer was not properly investigated in the beginning or because insufficient attention was paid to monitoring and collecting invoices due. Our expert feels that it behooves a business owner to establish reasonable credit policies, use proven techniques to optimize cash flow, and enforce terms in a diplomatic but firm manner because "the sale isn't complete until the money is in the bank." Here are some ways to strengthen your credit policies and reduce bad debt.

1. Optimize cash sales to avoid risk

There is no credit risk in cash. If your business allows for both cash payments and invoices, optimize the amount of cash, as a percentage of total sales, to the highest level possible for your industry or commercial sector.

2. Get deposits wherever possible

Larger sales orders, produce-to-order manufacturing, and, in particular, custom orders, should require a deposit of 10 to 50 percent of the final purchase price at order time. This will go a long way toward alleviating cash-flow shortages and assuring the customer's commitment to the order. Deposits of this nature should be nonrefundable.

3. Suggest credit cards to secure payment

Be sure you have the capability to accept major credit cards (Visa, MasterCard, American Express, and Discover). This is the next best thing to cash and reduces payment risk. In many instances, it also makes it easier for a customer to order. Customers who object to paying ahead of time may be assuaged by placing a "hold" on the amount of the sale against their card and processing the payment only after shipping the product or completing the service. This guarantees your payment (for a period, usually 30 days), yet doesn't appear as early payment to the customer. For credit card sales that are processed, your company account typically is credited by the credit card–processing company in one to three days for a service fee of 2 to 3.5 percent.

4. Require progress payments for work-in-progress orders or contract sales

If you manufacture a product or perform work over a long period—say, several months—include in your sales contract specific times when payments are due (for example: 10 percent at time of order, 40 percent at 60 days, balance at completion). This will go a long way to avoid cash tightness and provide funds for continuing the project. In many contract sales situations, the amount of the deposit is effectively the profit on the order and is obtained upfront; the balance or cost of the product is then transferred from customer to vendor at normal payment terms.

5. Develop and use a credit application form

Every business, large or small, that engages in invoiced sales should have a credit application. This can be as simple as a one-page, faxable form giving critical information such as the name and telephone number of the customer's accounts payable contact, department head, and chief executive. The form should also require a minimum of two trade references and a bank reference. A key administrative person (in smaller businesses, this is usually the office manager) is delegated responsibility for obtaining the information on the form, verifying the references, and suggesting a credit limit based on the findings.

6. Set a credit limit for every customer, large or small

After credit references have been checked, a credit limit should be set for every customer. For small customers, the credit limit should be set based on their midlevel to maximum demonstrated payment performance. For large companies, a credit limit should be set based on the amount of risk your company is willing to accept and is a direct reflection of the percentage of your business you are willing to devote to one customer. Typically, concentrating over 10 percent of your business in one customer begins to be a risk; 30 to 50 percent is very risky, and over 50 percent is potential disaster for your company. Bad things can happen to large companies as well.

7. Monitor receivables aging by total and by customer

At least weekly, calculate the average age of your outstanding invoices by customer and total. Assign responsibility (for example, the office manager) for generating and reporting on this information. Develop an "overdue" report that shows every invoice five days or more past your terms. Set specific, reasonable goals based on your industry for "average day's receivables" and tie one component of your office manager's compensation package to achieving the goal.

8. Develop standardized action procedures for overdue invoices

Develop a formal, written collection procedure including scripts or guidelines on contacting customers who have outstanding, overdue invoices. The approach taken is always courteous but increasingly firm as the overdue time increases. Typically, the first call is a courtesy inquiry only. At 60 days, they may be reminded of the company's terms and at their credit is in danger, at 90 days that their account will revert to COD, and at 100 days that litigation may proceed unless payment is received immediately. If the last stage is reached, be prepared to follow through promptly.

9. Avoid early dunning letters and use the telephone

Dunning letters, overdue notices, and account statements that indicate an overdue invoice usually do nothing but irritate a responsible customer who may have a reasonable explanation for a slow payment. Instead, have your person responsible for accounts receivable telephone the customer's accounts payable designee (found on the credit application) to ask if the invoice has been misplaced or if there is any other problem. Typically, 80 percent of slow payments are resolved in this manner, and a rapport is created between key personnel at both companies.

10. Use discount payment terms wisely, if at all

Offering an early-payment discount does not always produce the desired results. If your customer's problem is cash flow, they will be unable to take the discount. Often, customers who already pay on time will take advantage of the discount. You may properly rationalize this as an award to good customers, but you've just reduced your overall profitability as a result. Discounts that are attractive to customers most often do not produce a favorable offset in the time-value of money to your company. Better to poll your slow-pay customers first and individually to determine what the potential value of discounting might be to your cash flow.

11. Use your accounting system to help manage credit and accounts receivable

Many small businesses use simplified accounting systems such as QuickBooks or Peachtree, and these systems are capable of reducing the amount of time required for accounts receivable management. Credit limits can be set by customer, and the system will provide a warning message on entry of a new order should that order cause the limit to be exceeded. Aging reports by customer can be generated in a variety of formats. Data can be exported directly to an Excel spreadsheet and further analyzed if desired. Invoice data can also be directly exported to a customer via fax or e-mail, saving considerable time. Current customer contacts and telephone numbers are included in customer records and can be quickly extracted and used in screen reports to aid in collection calls. Be sure you are using all the features of your accounting system to help your effort in managing credit and accounts receivable.

Source: Robert A. Normand, executive director, Institute for Small Business Management (www.isbminc.com), and author of *Entreprenewal!, The Six Step Recovery Program for Small Business* (www.entreprenewal.com). He has served as a principal management consultant to more than 100 small businesses ranging from $500,000 to $50,000,000 in annual sales and has owned and operated several small businesses of his own in diverse industries. He can be reached at (941) 330-0889 or by using the contact links at the Web sites noted here. His mailing address is 3751 Almeria Avenue, Suite A4, Sarasota, FL 34239.

Most Effective Collection Techniques

For many firms or individuals, giving credit and then having to follow up to collect was not part of their original plan. Most folks would prefer a cash-only basis, but in order to do business at all or to expand, credit is often a necessity. Credit will be given and some individuals and firms just don't pay it back as agreed. These proven and successful techniques won't work with a professional credit criminal. Nothing will. In that situation, identify them, if it's appropriate, report them to a credit agency, perhaps assign it to a third party, and get on with your life. For all other situations, whether it is General Motors or your uncle Charlie, our expert says that you will be more successful when you know and use this list of top collection techniques.

1. Ask for the money

It appears obvious, but it is missed by those new to the business and sometimes not handled well by those who have been around longer and should know better. If a customer has not made their payment as agreed, call them up and ask them to pay. Ask for the full amount due, not just in generalities, but something specific like, "Will you mail me your check today for $X, please?" It may help you to keep Tom Cruise from *Jerry McGuire* in mind, "Show me the money!"

2. Never be short again

There will be some situations when the customer cannot make the full payment, despite your eloquent and assertive request. Don't make the mistake of asking them how much they can pay. That will make them think of the competition, other places they owe money, or want to spend "your money." It isn't any better to ask, "Can you pay half?" You may get half, but you'll often get less and you will *never* get more. What is better? Try this: "How much are you short of (full amount)?"

3. It ain't your money

In negotiating, the folks who tend to do well are those who want a deal, but don't need one. The same applies in collections. You are better to treat your collection activities like a game you care about, but not that much. If you treat it as if it is your money, then you're going to take it home with you at night, physically or mentally, and won't be able to see the bigger picture, when to press an advantage, and when to let one go.

4. Be prepared

It is the motto of the Scouts. Now it's your motto too! No matter what your business is, there are only about nine or ten excuses that you'll hear 90 percent of the time. Get ready for them! Work out the ten excuses, then figure out the most appropriate questions to ask based on the proven journalistic approach of *who, what, where, when,* and *why.* Think, too, of some statements that may be appropriate to use, some that have been successful.

5. Cool, calm, . . . and collected

Thomas Jefferson said that nothing gives you as much advantage over another as to remain cool and confident under any circumstances. At the same time, we've all got our hot buttons. We may not be able to change the buttons without years of therapy, but we can alter how we're going to react when somebody pushes one of them. If you are going to lose it, put them on hold or call them back later.

6. Candy from a baby

I'm thinking John Candy in the classic comedy movie *Planes, Trains, and Automobiles.* As Del Griffith, he was a shower curtain–ring salesperson. Late in the movie, John/Del was successfully selling his products to a number of different people, trying to raise money. But, he wasn't selling them as shower-curtain rings! He ensured they were something the customers wanted to buy. (In one case, it was earrings to some young girls who were about 12 years old. "They make you look fifteen," he said.) What is in it for *your* customers to make their payment?

7. Timing—timing—timing

In real estate, location is important. In collections, it is timing. When should you contact a customer who is past due? On most occasions, we'll give some folks a few days and the benefit of some extra time to get a check through the mail. But if a customer is new or has a history

of being late, change your timing and call them the day after the payment was due. "Mr. Harris, I'm just calling to confirm your payment was mailed to us yesterday." You could call them the day the payment is due or even the day before, "Will you be mailing that check tomorrow, Mr. Harris?" Don't let it slide just because they are a good customer. If they're that good, they'll pay you on time—or maybe even earlier!

8. Practice doesn't make perfect

Fred Astaire was one of the best classic dancers. Professionals make it look so easy. Of course, the audience never saw the hours Astaire put in on the sound stage before filming started or the days in his own studio with his choreographer before they even went to the sound stage. Be like Fred (or his partner Ginger, who had to do the same steps, backward *and* in high heels) and recognize that "perfect practice" is what makes perfect.

9. More power

In the original *Star Trek* series, Captain Kirk often said two things to Scotty the engineer: "Beam me up, Scotty" and "We need more power!" Scotty never said, "Aye, Captain," and turned up the power. There was always some reason they couldn't get more power; even so, Scotty was always able to deliver eventually. If a customer calls you with an offer to bring the account up-to-date or to clear the debt, he or she can almost always do better than the first offer.

10. Remember that spot

I remember a *Herman* cartoon in which a huge wooly mammoth is on its back with a tiny arrow sticking out of its belly. The caption between the two cavemen is "We've got to remember that spot!" Who knows where they come from, but sometimes a tiny arrow of a question or a statement works perfectly. If you don't notice it, it may be lost forever. Remember to take notes because the shortest pencil is better than the longest memory.

Source: Tim Paulsen, T. R. Paulsen and Associates (*www.trpaulsen.com*)—Tim Paulsen is an international specialist in the business of creative receivables management. He is the author of *Collect Those Debts* and *Paid in Full*. Mr. Paulsen has developed and led seminars and special programs for his clients across North America as well as in Barbados, China, India, Malaysia, Jamaica, Kuwait, the Philippines, and Singapore. His PaulZEN Method © for effective collection techniques is based on the philosophy of collecting a lot more money, quicker ... and still keeping your customers. He says, "The sale is not complete until the money is in the cash register *and the customer returns to deal with you again—paying on time!*"

Advantages of Accepting Credit Cards

According to one source, Americans carried 657 million bank credit cards, 228 million debit cards, and 550 million retail credit cards in their wallets at the end of 2004, and those numbers just keep increasing. Our expert feels that if your business doesn't accept credit cards, you are missing out on the following advantages.

1. Increased sales

Consumers are more likely to buy items if they can pay for them later. Credit cards can even be used for small impulse purchases today.

2. Easy financing

Your customers can buy high-ticket items without having to qualify for special financing. It is easier for them to "buy now, pay later."

3. Convenience

Most creditworthy adults carry at least one major credit card, and as long as the transaction is approved, you do not have to worry about verifying the consumer's ability to pay as you would with a check.

4. Worldwide acceptance

You can accept payment from customers anywhere in the world, as long as they use cards issued under the major brands you accept.

5. Go high tech

Credit and debit cards are commonly used to buy items for Internet purchases, and online merchant accounts make it easy and inexpensive to accept payment that way.

6. Better cash flow

In most cases, you will have access to funds from sales almost instantly. You do not have to wait for the check that is "in the mail."

7. Greater security

If your business operates a retail location, you will not have as much cash on hand if your customers pay by credit cards.

8. Continuity sales

With your customer's permission, you can charge their credit card periodically for a subscription or recurring purchase, without having to get their permission every time.

Source: Gerri Detweiler is a national credit expert and counsels entrepreneurs on business financing issues through *www.Business-CreditSuccess.com.*

The Downsides of Accepting Credit Cards

As a small business owner, it is imperative you carefully weigh the pros and the cons of every decision—especially when it comes to money. While accepting credit cards as a form of payment has many advantages, you may end up losing more money by not carefully considering and planning for these disadvantages.

1. Set-up costs

Budget both time and money to set up your system for accepting credit cards as payment. Set-up fees for face-to-face transactions run $50–$200. But if you choose to offer payments online, your time and fees can be significantly more costly. Your "time budget" includes the process of setting up your web site as well as time to enter data and content. Your "money budget" can be up to several thousand dollars for just a basic site, as well as the banks fees for online capabilities. You may find your budget doesn't allow for either the necessary time or money.

2. Fees

Expect to pay a wide variety of fees in addition to set-up fees. Following are some of the fees that you may incur. Equipment ranging in price from $30 to $1,000 (equipment can be leased), monthly statements costing $4 to $20 each, transaction fees of 5 to 50 cents each, the discount rate per transaction ranging from 1.5 percent to 3 percent, chargeback fees up to $30 for each return, costs for communicating

to the processor ranging from 5 to 12 cents per connection, cancellation fees for closing your account ranging from $300 to $800 (excessively high!), and other miscellaneous costs such as keeping a supply of charge slips and web-site hosting fees. Depending on your business the benefits may not outweigh the costs.

3. Waiting for money

It can take several days for funds to deposit in your bank account creating more time and money needed just to track transactions. Beyond the typical wait time, Merchant Account Providers can hold back your money if you have spikes in sales over your approved volume or typical order size.

4. Charge-backs

If a customer disputes a charge, funds can be refunded before you ever know or agree to the transaction, and even if goods are never returned. Most often charge-backs occur because of bank error, a misunderstanding by the customer, or fraud. However, you the merchant bear the burden of proof—you must present documentation showing goods or services were actually provided. Additionally, when the Merchant Account Provider requests documentation, you are usually charged a $10 fee in addition to the $30 charge-back fee.

5. Online security issues

Accepting online credit card payments comes with its own set of security issues. You'll need to make sure your customer's personal and credit card information is kept secure during transmission as well any information stored in a database, which is open to the threat of hackers if not secured properly. Security services cost additional fees increasing your overall budget.

6. Time learning new skills

Budgeting time for both you and your employees to learn the technology involved is critical, because if not processed correctly, a credit card payment can end up costing you money. In addition, accepting online payments requires additional time for learning how to update your web site—the best sites are updated frequently.

7. Fraud potential

The potential for fraud exists for both face-to-face transactions and online transactions; however, the risk is higher online. And you can still be held financially responsible even if you follow all the rules for obtaining proper authorization. For online transactions, be aware that consumers generally have more protection than merchants, who are more often than not stuck with the bill.

8. High-risk business issues

If you are considered a high-risk business, such as certain types of online businesses, you will find it more difficult (though not impossible) to gain merchant status. You will likely spend more time finding a provider; your fees may be higher; and you may have to deposit money into your account as security.

Source: Amy Arnold, Senior Reporter for CardRatings.com (*www .cardratings.com*)—Amy has been published by respected publications throughout the country. Publications include *Young Money Magazine, E/The Environmental Magazine,* and About.com. CardRatings.com fights credit card debt by providing consumers with ratings of credit cards. They are devoted to being the leading source of objective credit card rating information and currently offer approximately 20,000 credit card reviews.

Questions to Ask Your Credit Card Company

The questions that most often surface while processing credit cards are usually related to the interest rate and the transaction fee. However, there are other factors to take into consideration. Our expert, an experienced advisor and consultant, offers this list of questions to ask your credit card company.

1. Monthly fee

Are the fees for charges applied to the minimum monthly fee or is the monthly fee in addition to each transaction?

2. Statement fee

Is there a statement fee each month whether a charge is put through?

3. Minimum fee

Is there a minimum fee each month whether a charge is put through?

4. Transaction fee

Does the percentage or transaction fee go down if certain levels are reached and/or does the percentage or transaction fee go up if certain goals are not met? Does the percentage fee or transaction fee decrease as the average sale figure increases?

5. Software included

Is software or "swiper" unit included with signing up for credit card processing or are these one-time purchases or are they leased?

6. Additional costs

Are there additional costs for additional locations or does the average cost per location decrease with added locations?

Source: Alan J. Zell, the Ambassador of Selling, has become nationally recognized for his expertise in advising businesses, services, educational, governmental, and organizational entities. Clients seeking his services represent a wide spectrum including accountants, investors, educators, chambers of commerce, retailers, wholesalers, manufacturers, associations, and nonprofit organizations. Contact him at PO Box 69, Portland, OR 97207-0069; (503) 241-1988; Web site: www.sellingselling.com.

Popular Credit Card Equipment

As a business owner, you may want to accept credit cards from your customers. You will need to purchase credit card equipment and open a merchant account. We asked a leading provider of credit card equipment and merchant account services to recommend some of the more popular credit card–processing equipment they sell and here is their list.

1. VeriFone Omni 3200 SE

Integrated Printer. The VeriFone Omni 3200SE makes the bestselling payment terminal in VeriFone's history better. The terminal's fresh new look and customizable faceplates add branding power to the point of sale. The models also have a 30 percent smaller footprint than the original 3200/3210. An integrated printer with "clamshell" design provides drop-in paper loading to prevent jams and reduce calls to your help desk. Equally important, the enhanced processing performance, support for compressed application downloads, and 1MB memory trim transaction times and dramatically cutting phone-connect time and expenses. What's more, the Omni 3210SE includes a built-in PIN pad supporting 3DES security standards for debit and EBT transactions.

New: $295.

2. Hypercom T7 Plus

The Hypercom T7 Plus builds on the heritage of Hypercom's popular T7 family of terminals selling more than 3 million units. This latest model is designed for merchants requiring a compact countertop POS terminal accepting all magnetic-stripe cards and delivering fast online transaction authorizations.

New: $239.

3. Tranz 330

The most recognizable terminal in the credit card industry is the VeriFone 330. It is a proven terminal that offers the merchant the ability to accept all major credit cards and is supported by almost every processor in the world, so there is also no need to worry about compatibility. It handles the basic needs of a retail merchant flawlessly. The VeriFone Tranz 330 will support a printer, which can be added at any time. The terminal works perfectly with the Printer 220, 250, and 900. The terminal also offers you the ability to take debit cards with the addition of a PIN pad. Note: you must sign up for debit with your processor.

New: $229; refurbished: $89.

4. VeriFone Omni 3750

Sleek and stylish, VeriFone's Omni 3750 packs all the features and functions merchants could want into a single, stand-alone terminal. From smart-card capabilities and EMV certification, to secure support for multiple payment and value-added applications, to factory-installed memory configurations (1.5, 3 and 4 Mbytes), the Omni 3750 handles the most complex transactions and value-added applications.

New: $369; refurbished: $339.

5. Lipman Nurit 8010 Wireless Credit Card Machine

The Lipman Nurit 8010 Wireless Palmtop is the smallest and most flexible hand-held payment terminal available. It offers fast enabling and secure and error-free transactions. It is the perfect payment solution for retailers on the move who bring their products and services directly to their customers. With a global payment platform, the Nurit 8010 provides a host of operating advantages throughout the transaction process, bringing increased profits at lower operating costs. It doubles as a cellular phone by offering voice and data transfer in real time. The electronic signature capture providing an optional touch screen.

New: $789, Mobitex.

Or new: $759, GPRS.

6. Hypercom T7P Refurbished Thermal or Friction

The Hypercom T7P refurbished credit card machine is designed for upgrading authorization-only equipment and for merchants moving to data capture and debit applications. It features an integrated modular impact printer.

Refurbished friction: $189.

Refurbished thermal $199.

7. Lipman Nurit 2085

Do you need an affordable but highly flexible payment processing solution? Do you need to offer customers multiple payment options to enhance their in-store experience? The Nurit 2085 is a convenient, all-in-one solution, where terminal and printer, plus optional built-in PIN pad and smart card reader, are integrated into one compact design.

New: $249; refurbished: $229.

8. Lipman Nurit 3010 Wireless

The Lipman Nurit 3010 is the newest wireless offering from Lipman USA Inc. The culmination of many years' experience in both wireless processing and POS device manufacturing, this third-generation wireless product is a technological leader and an all-in-one solution. The self-contained unit includes an POS/EDC terminal, fast 12 line/sec thermal printer, internal pin pad, PCMCIA card slot (type I, II, and III), twelve-hour rechargeable battery, internal smart card reader (optional), LAN line and wireless modem all enclosed within an incredibly compact package.

Refurbished: $499.

9. VeriFone Omni 3200 Refurbished

The VeriFone OMNI 3200 has a user interface with screen addressable buttons that can display up to eight lines of text! It has a high-speed silent printer that prints a blazing 12.5 lines per second and is totally silent! The printhead life expectancy is more than 24 million lines! Refurbished: $199.

Source: Eagle Merchant Services (*www.eaglemerchantservices.com*) is a privately held company specializing in credit, debit, and EBT (electronic benefits transfer) card processing for retail and non-retail merchants. Contact them at 805 E. LaSalle St., Somonauk, IL 60552; (815) 498-9758; toll-free: (800) 255-0898; fax: (815) 498-9783; e-mail: *information@eaglemerchantservices.com*.

Best Ways to Protect Your Business from Credit Card Fraud

A quick look at all the details of a transaction should give you a good initial screening for red flags associated with credit card fraud. But even if everything in the initial screening looks good, remember that an authorization number received by the credit card means only that there is an account with that number and, at that moment, the funds are available. It does not mean that the transaction is valid. Therefore, you should take the following steps whenever possible.

1. Obtain the CVV2 number from the customer

Be sure you obtain the CVV2 number even if your system doesn't use it. This is the three-digit number to the right of the printed card number in the signature panel. If your customer provides a CVV2, it's an indicator that the card is good and they have the card in hand. If your system includes CVV2 service, use it but do *not* rely on it. Industry estimates are that it is effective less than 80 percent of the time.

2. Trace the IP number

If the order was placed online, then trace the IP (internet protocol) address. This can be one of your best tools, especially if the ship-to and bill-to addresses are different. Take a good look at origin of the order and compare it to the card-holder information. They should be similar. Visual route provides both an online demo and a PC version for download.

3. Cross-reference the cardholder's telephone number and address

Cross-referencing the card-holder's telephone number and address can give you an indication that the cardholder actually exists and lives where they say they do, but remember that if the cardholder has an unlisted number, the cross-reference will come back as no record found. Consider the cross-reference only as a verification. There are numerous cross-reference Web sites, including SmartPage, Langenberg.com, and others.

4. Verify the cardholder's address

Verifying the cardholder's address is the most difficult step, but remember that any address verification provided by your processor is probably not as current as the one at Visa/MC or the issuing bank, and CVV2 is not always working at all.

Source: Merchant911 (*www.merchant911.org*)—Merchant911 gives merchants the information they need to help themselves protect against online credit card fraud. They bring pressure on the credit card industry to change policies, procedures, and regulations so that *they* are responsible for their mistakes and poor fraud screening. Merchant911 acts as a clearinghouse for merchants to report credit card fraud and educate themselves about online payment–related problems and issues. Their e-mail is Contact@Merchant911.org.

Top Business Credit Cards

Our experts rate the top business credit cards around. Please note that some of the facts may have changed at the time of this printing, so you may want to double-check with the card issuers.

1. Citibusiness MasterCard

www.citi.com

Download transactions history with Quicken, Quickbooks, and Money. Free "Ask the Experts" business consulting program—ask specific business-related questions and within two business days, you'll receive a personalized answer that includes information, ideas, and suggestions.

2. Citibusiness MasterCard with Thank You Network

www.citi.com

Earn three reward points (ThankYou Points) for every dollar you spend on business purchases and professional services and one reward point (ThankYou Point) for every dollar you spend on all other purchases. 7,500 ThankYou Points after your first purchase.

3. Citibusiness Premierpass MasterCard

www.citi.com

One reward point for every $1 spent on purchases and one point for every mile flown on any airline. Three reward points for every $1 spent on certain business purchases.

4. Citibusiness/Aadvantage Visa

www.citi.com

Earn 1 AAdvantage Mile (American Airlines frequent flyer mile) for every dollar your business spends on purchases—up to 150,000 miles per year.

5. Advanta Platinum Business MasterCard

www.advanta.com

Special savings up to 25 percent or more on business products and services, such as Penny-Wise Office Products, Palo Alto Software, Ramada Inn, and IBM. Custom-design your card with your business name and obtain personalized business checks. Detailed expense management reports—Download into Quicken and Microsoft Money. Select your payment due date.

6. Business Cash Rebate Credit Card from American Express

www.amex.com

No minimum spending requirement and no cap to the amount of cash you can earn. Zero percent introductory APR on purchases with plastic only during your first six months of card membership. Free "ask an expert a question" business consultation service.

Source: CardRatings.com (*www.cardratings.com*)—CardRatings fights credit card debt by providing consumers with ratings of credit cards. They are devoted to being the leading source of objective credit card–rating information and currently offer consumer information regarding approximately 1000 unique credit card offerings, including two searchable databases containing approximately 1,100 credit card descriptions.

What to Look For When Shopping for a Business Credit Card

Small business owners frequently borrow funds and often use credit cards to get their business off the ground. The most frequently used kinds of credit were personal and business credit cards, lines of credit, and vehicle loans according to a study published in 2003 by the Small Business Administration. In fact, 46 percent of small firms used their personal credit cards and 34 percent used business credit cards to help in their business matters. While it is sometimes necessary to utilize personal credit cards during the start-up phase of a business, continuing to use a personal credit card may not be the wisest choice once a business is established. If you're looking for a business credit card, here's a list of things you should consider.

1. Annual percentage rate

It's a competitive market; make sure you are getting the best interest rate you can.

2. Fees

Are there annual fees or other types of fees? If so, will you gain enough incentives to justify the fees?

3. Perks

What kind of perks will benefit your company the most? If you travel a lot, then look for cards that earn miles with no blackout dates. If you make lots of business purchases, look for the cards that offer cash-back incentives or vendor discounts.

4. Ability to monitor spending

How often does the issuer send reports on spending and how detailed are the reports? Can you monitor individual employee expenditures? Can you view spending online? Can you download the reports into your accounting system? Are you able to code certain types of expenses and set limits on those expenses?

5. Flexibility

Can you set different credit limits for different employees? Can some employees have access to cash while others don't?

6. Card acceptance

If you travel a lot, make sure to get a card that is widely accepted such as MasterCard, Visa, Discover, or American Express.

7. ATM

Look for a national ATM network if you or your employees travel frequently.

Source: Rebecca Lindsey, senior staff writer for CardRatings.com (*www.cardratings.com*)—CardRatings fights credit card debt by providing consumers with ratings of credit cards. They are devoted to being the leading source of objective credit card–rating information and currently offer consumer information regarding approximately 1,000 unique credit card offerings, including two searchable databases containing approximately 1,100 credit card descriptions.

Top Questions to Ask Before Purchasing Credit Card Equipment

With so many different types of credit card–processing equipment on the market, choosing the correct type for your business can be a daunting task. Before you get started, there are a few questions you should ask.

1. Will I be "swiping" the cards through the terminal, or will I be manually keying in the information because the card is not present?

Most retail businesses have the ability to swipe the card because their customers are present at the time of the sale; these merchants should consider a traditional terminal and printer. However, some merchants will not have this luxury and may want a system that is more suited to their specific needs. For these businesses, PC software packages are available and most standard terminals will work fine for most applications.

2. How many transactions a month will I be doing?

Merchants who are doing more than a few transactions a day may want to consider a terminal with a thermal printer. Thermal printers are faster and quieter; they have fewer moving parts than a traditional dot-matrix printer, so are also less likely to fail. Thermal paper has come a long way in the last few years and is now much more resistant to fading and yellowing compared to old-fashioned thermal fax paper. Some older-model terminal and printer units now come in thermal versions for only a few more dollars.

3. Is there a phone line available at the business location?

Most businesses have at least one phone line at their business location, and a credit card terminal can share this line without much problem. However, consider how critical that phone line is to your business since it cannot be used while you are processing charges. If you get a high volume of calls or are going to process a high volume of charges, you may consider getting a second line. Also, some merchants, such as those selling products at trade shows, may find it cost prohibitive to have a phone line installed at each show. Merchants who may not have regular access to a phone line should consider either a wireless terminal that works over a cell phone, or similar networks, or one that can accept the card on premises and then process the actual transactions later (store and forward).

4. Do I need a printer?

Technically, merchants are not required to have a printer. However, considering there is usually only a small price difference between a stand-alone terminal and an integrated terminal and printer unit, it is a good idea to purchase a unit that has a built-in printer. Adding a printer after the fact is usually more costly and can take up more counter space. Check out the full price list and compare the prices of terminals to integrated units before buying.

5. Will I be accepting debit cards?

Merchants who accept debit cards should consider adding a PIN pad to give their customers additional payment options. Using a PIN pad may also lower the cost to the merchant for processing the transaction.

6. How many merchant accounts will I have?

For almost all businesses, the answer is one; but in some cases, a businesses may need more. Some examples of this are businesses that do a large volume of phone-order transactions and also a large volume of swiped transactions. For these merchants, there is a cost benefit to having a second merchant account. Also, some doctors and other professionals may share an office and run separate businesses out of the same space. These merchants may need an additional account for each business. There are now many terminal options for businesses needing more than one merchant account.

7. Which brand of terminal is right for me?

Your processor may work better with a particular brand, but typically, almost all of the major brands of credit card equipment will work with most major processors. If you've already decided on a particular brand of terminal, check out the latest models. Advancement in credit card terminals have been brisk over the last few years, and newer designs allow you to do more and are usually easier to work.

Source: MerchantWarehouse (*www.merchantwarehouse.com*) is a leading provider of merchant services, credit card services, and equipment on the Internet. Contact them at MerchantWarehouse.com, Inc., 55 Court Street, Third Floor, Boston, MA 02108; (800) 941-6557: fax: (617) 854-8923; e-mail: *info@merchantwarehouse.com*.

Questions to Ask When Interviewing a Money Manager

You can never ask a dumb question about your investments and the people who help you choose them, especially when it comes to how much you will be paying for any investment,

both in up-front costs and in ongoing management fees. To get you started, here are some of the most important questions to ask when choosing an investment professional or someone to help you, directly from the SEC.

1. Training
What training and experience do you have? How long have you been in business?

2. Investment philosophy
What is your investment philosophy? Do you take a lot of risks, or are you more concerned about the safety of my money?

3. References
Describe your typical client. Can you provide me with references, the names of people who have invested with you for a long time?

4. Compensation
How do you get paid? By commission? Based on a percentage of assets you manage? Another method? Do you get paid more for selling your own firm's products?

5. Their costs
How much will it cost me in total to do business with you?

Source: U.S. Securities and Exchange Commission (*www.sec.gov*), Office of Investor Education and Assistance (202) 551-6551; e-mail: *help@sec.gov*.

Outsourcing and Offshoring

Ways to Increase Revenues Through Outsourcing

Outsourcing—the practice of using different business partners to assist with different areas of your business—is far from being a new concept. In the past few years, though, outsourcing has become more popular than ever before as business owners start to realize the many ways in which outsourcing can help increase revenues. Here are just a few of the business processes you might want to consider outsourcing.

1. Information technology (IT) services

When you're running a small business, you have to become an expert very quickly on every aspect of that business. IT, however, is an area that requires specialist training and expertise, and unless you have that kind of skill, outsourcing to an IT partner can sometimes be the safest, and most effective, option.

2. Benefits administration services

Managing staff can be a real time-drain, especially when it comes to dealing with the paperwork related to defined benefits and contributions, worker's compensation, health and 401K plans, and absence management. Time spent on benefits administration is time that could be better spent on the core activity of your business. Outsourcing to a partner gives you that time back.

3. Finance and accounting services

Not everyone has what it takes to be an accountant. Quite apart from managing the day-to-day accounts, a good accountant can help you identify areas where you can reduce costs, thus increasing revenue.

4. Human resources and outsourcing services

It's estimated that around 40 percent of a small business owner's time is taken up with HR issues. That's a lot of time to spend on something that doesn't actually increase your revenue. Outsourcing these services to a partner enables employees and managers to access, update, and use HR information more efficiently and effectively.

5. Billing services

Document processing is another time-drain for many small businesses, and even more so now that customers are demanding instant access to information and ever-faster turnaround times. By outsourcing your billing services, you can meet that demand and free up your own time for more productive tasks.

6. Payroll services

As your business grows, so does your payroll—not to mention the time you'll spend administering it, as well as dealing with finance and tax-related activities. What's more, failure to manage these issues correctly can result in penalties from the IRS. What better reason to outsource?

7. Public relations outsourcing

PR can be a highly effective way of promoting your business. To do it right, though, you don't just need the ability to write a press release, you also need the knowledge and contacts to get it published. Often, that's the type of experience you can only get by outsourcing.

8. Marketing outsourcing

Marketing is an area that many small business owners struggle with. It's hard to know what kind of marketing will work best for your business, and how much to spend on your campaign. Partnering up with a marketing professional can help make sure you get the best possible return on your investment.

Source: Robert Moment, author, business strategist, and CEO of The Moment Group (*www.sellintegrity.com*)—The Moment Group is a small business coaching and consulting firm that shows entrepreneurs how to turn their ideas into wealth and start a successful business. Robert Moment can be reached at (703) 580-8002.

Top Risks of Employee Leasing

Many business owners will turn to employee-leasing companies, also known as professional employer organizations (PEOs), as a way to outsource the payroll and human resources functions of their businesses so they can concentrate on the core mission of their businesses. Employee-leasing companies also offer better benefits with their larger pool of employees than many small or medium-size businesses can offer employees by themselves. An additional attraction to employers is the outsourcing of liability for unemployment insurance and workers' compensation coverage and some of the liability for state and federal employment law violations. Unfortunately, for many unsuspecting employers and their employees, there have been severe problems. Here, our expert

lays out several risks that you must examine before committing these vital functions to another company.

1. Workers' compensation/unemployment insurance

Many leasing companies also run temporary staffing agencies, mixing the administration in order to conserve costs. The workers' compensation rates for employees classified as staffing may be lower than for those who are leased. Leased employees are considered long term and staffing agencies are mostly temporary. Employees must also be classified properly by the correct occupational payroll code in each state in which the company operates. If an employee is injured and is found to be in the wrong employee classification, he may not be covered by the carrier. Leased employees must also be reported to the PEO's state accounts as "leased," rather than "temporary staff." This distinction is where some PEOs have gotten into trouble with their insurance carriers. Also, if some employees are leased and other employees are on your direct payroll in the same state, some states will lump all of them under *your* unemployment insurance tax and workers' compensation accounts, which can be an accounting and liability nightmare.

2. Financial instability

Please ask for audited financial statements and have your CPA examine them in detail. In the rush to sign up clients, some PEO's underbid or take on risky businesses as clients, which can destabilize the leasing company's finances. Quality leasing companies are selective. Make sure that the PEO also has employment liability coverage to protect its assets against employment-related lawsuits. If a leasing company were to go bankrupt, employees could wait months to get paid while it is adjudicated. You may have to make them whole to keep them happy or to avoid being a party to a lawsuit. In the worst case, a state tax agency may hold your business responsible for any unpaid taxes or workers compensation payments as the coemployer.

3. Legal liability for employment law/tax issues—co-employership

One employee-leasing company's Web site states that by having them "hire your employees, and subsequently leasing them back to you through their PEO services, (it) enables your business or corporation to claim that it has no 'legal' employees." Although that may be true as long as things are going well, many state and federal jurisdictions will judge you as a "co-employer" and hold your business responsible if they find employment or tax laws are being broken and they cannot hold the leasing company accountable. The key to whether you are a co-employer is whether you control the activities of the employees of the business. Most business owners do not want to cede that control or authority to an outside company, so in effect, most clients of leasing companies are co-employers and share legal liability for the treatment and payroll handling of the client business.

4. Employee relations

Finally, the most important area of risk is the relationship that you have with your employees. If they have problems with the PEO's payroll and benefits administration, they will look to *you* for solutions, not the PEO, especially if the PEO is not quick to resolve problems. At that point, the PEO's problems become your problems. When you start such an arrangement, communicate carefully and deliberately with your employees; let them know the benefits for them with the assurance of your continued involvement with them to intervene and solve their problems if needed.

Source: Dan Curtin, principal and owner of Curtin Associates (*www.hrsolutions-socal.com*)—Mr. Curtin is a HRCI-certified, recognized consultant who advises small and medium-size businesses, manufacturers, and nonprofits on the West Coast about how to better manage their employees and stay in compliance with state and federal labor laws. He can be contacted at (800) 555-1212, or by e-mail at *consultant@socal.com*.

How Human Resource Outsourcing (HRO) Can Help Your Company

Need help managing employee-related matters such as health benefits, workers' compensation claims, payroll, payroll tax compliance, and unemployment insurance claims? You can contract with an HRO (also known as Professional Employer Organizations, or PEOs) to assume these responsibilities and provide expertise in human resources management. Here, our expert (a human resources outsourcer) provides a list of all the ways an HRO firm can help your company.

1. Primary responsibility is transferred to the HRO

By transferring primary responsibility for these time-consuming and unproductive tasks to a company that specializes in these areas, you will free up your time to focus on strategic functions, which can help you build your company and improve your bottom line. Businesses across America have discovered the incredible value of a HRO because they provide relief from the burden of employment administration.

2. Human resources won't be ignored

Business leaders realize that all duties performed within a given workday are not of equal impact on the company's bottom line. By focusing your time and energy on the "business of business" and not on the "business of employment," your time and energy is spent on areas that will have the highest impact on driving revenue. Expenses are reduced as you outsource noncore functions to an organization that specializes in managing employment costs. Employees benefit from the services of a professional human resources department and expanded benefits package.

3. If you desire, only certain services can be outsourced

Although over 90% of clients have recognized the full HRO/PEO program to be the ultimate value, there may be situations where it makes sense to utilize similar services under an Administrative Services Outsourcing (ASO) arrangement. This program includes payroll processing and tax filing under the tax I.D. number, benefits administration assistance and

human resource services. For those companies that do not wish to make a change with their payroll, but desire professional assistance with human resources management, help is available under a Human Resources Consulting (HRC) arrangement. Just as the name implies, this is a program of human resources consulting and training services, offered under an annual subscription.

4. You will retain control

You retain ownership of your company and you continue to make key business decisions and manage employees. As co-employers, the HRO and your company contractually share or assume employer responsibilities and liabilities. The HRO becomes responsible for payroll and employment taxes, human resource compliance, managing unemployment, maintaining employee records, and many of the other time-consuming and tedious chores associated with employment administration. Your company actually gains more command of the revenue-generating aspects of your business.

5. You'll get service from accredited firms

Look for an HRO that has been accredited by the Employer Services Assurance Corporation (ESAC). In order to attain and maintain accreditation, the HRO must subscribe to a strict code of ethics and undergo quarterly audits by an independent CPA firm to verify net worth, timely payment of payroll taxes and benefit premiums, adequate reserves for insurance claims, etc. The accreditation criteria are so stringent, that at the time of this printing, there are only 21 HROs in the U.S. who have been awarded accreditation (out of over 2,000 firms). In addition to the quarterly audit criteria, the ESAC provides clients of participating HROs with tangible protection through the Client Assurance Program, with Surety Bonds guaranteeing financial performance. To learn more, go to *www.esacorp.org.*

6. You may save a significant amount of money

Whether or not you will recognize a hard dollar cost savings will depend on your current costs of internal employment administration. Many companies are already outsourcing functions such as payroll, administration of their 401(k) plan, HR services and training, workers' compensation and unemployment claims management, Section 125 administration, insurance plans, COBRA administration, etc., and paying fees for these services as a small business to multiple vendors. With an HRO, you're able to consolidate these services through one vendor relationship and take advantage of the economies of scale that a larger group has to offer. Another consideration that contributes to cost savings are soft costs. These are the areas where you and other key staff are currently spending valuable time that, if you partnered with an HRO, would be freed up for more strategic functions. The HRO saves you the time that you would otherwise spend writing employment policies and producing employee handbooks, researching medical insurance plans, implementing a loss control program, providing HR and compliance training for managers and supervisors, processing payroll in-house,

administering benefits, tracking vacation and sick leave, responding to unemployment claims, records administration, etc.

7. Employees get more job security

Employees seek financial security, quality benefits, a safe working environment, and opportunities for retirement savings. When a company works with an HRO, job security is improved as the HRO implement efficiencies to lower employment costs. Job satisfaction and productivity increases when employees are provided professional human resource services, training, employee manuals, safety services and improved communications. And in many cases, a co-employment relationship with an HRO provides employees with an expanded employee benefits package, to include 401(k), life insurance, disability insurance, discount plans, etc.

8. You'll be part of a growing trend

The expertise required to manage the human resource elements of a small to midsized business has outgrown the experience and training of many entrepreneurs who started these small businesses. The HRO industry is growing at over 30 percent per year, as business owners seek solutions to the increasingly complex "business of employment."

Source: Timothy Doherty, Owner and CEO of Doherty Employment Group. Doherty Employment Group (*www.dohertyemployment.com*) provides a wide range of employment-related services including HR Outsourcing, payrolling, temporary, contract and full-time staffing. Doherty was twice listed in *Inc.* magazine's list of the 500 fastest growing companies and currently resides on the "Top 100 Private Owned Companies," "Top 25 Woman-Owned Companies," "Top

25 Employment Firms," and "Growth 50 Private Companies" lists by the Business Journal. Doherty Employment Group is a member of the Employer Services Assurance Corporation, ESAC (*www. esacorp.org*), the National Association of Professional Employer Organizations (*www.napeo.org*) and the American Staffing Association (*www.staffingtoday.net*). Tim can be contacted at *tdoherty@dohertyhro.com*.

Questions to Ask a Prospective Information Technology Consultant

You've decided to hire an IT consultant and are ready to start interviewing. But what do you ask them? Same questions you would ask any a prospective partner, but how do you determine the IT consultant's technical competence, assess whether you will get the level and quality of service you require, and decide if their values and yours make this a good long-term match? Including this list of questions in your discussion will help you select the best IT consultant for your business.

1. What are your core values?

Many companies have never considered their core values, but it's worth asking your prospective IT consultant this question. These core values should inform every decision made by the IT consultant's team members and will give you a good indication of the kind of service you should receive. Look for core values such as *Do what's right for the customer, Provide outstanding customer service, Provide value,* and *Maintain high integrity.* IT consultants with these kinds of values have thought about what it takes to provide excellent customer service

and are interested in establishing long-term relationships with their clients.

2. What services do you offer?

For the most part, you know what services you need. Can the vendor address your technology concerns and even suggest other services that you don't know that you need? Some IT consultants focus on a narrow range of services, such as creating and supporting computer networks. Others have elected to become a one-stop shop for a wide range of technology services including IT strategy, application selection, cabling, telephone systems, software development, Web site creation, and, of course, creating and supporting computer networks (which includes Internet access, firewalls, security, servers and workstations, backup, e-mail, virus and spyware protection, productivity applications). You need to decide if you prefer working with multiple specialized vendors, or with one vendor that can support most or all of your needs.

3. What if I need a technology service that you don't provide?

You will select a partner that matches your needs as closely as possible, but a time will come when you need a service that your IT consultant cannot provide. You could start looking for another IT consultant, but it would be much easier if your IT consultant has partnerships with a variety of technology companies and individuals who can provide additional services. For example, if you are mostly a PC shop but occasionally need Macintosh support, it's not important that your IT consultant have Mac experts, but it's very helpful if they have a partner who is a Mac expert, should the need arise.

4. What certifications have your company and your team members earned?

There are many different certifications in the IT world. The most important are the certifications bestowed on the *company* by manufacturers (i.e., Microsoft, Apple, Sonicwall, Cisco) and those earned by the vendor's *team members* from manufacturers (i.e., Microsoft MCSE, Cisco CCNA) or independent organizations (i.e., CompTIA A+, Server+, Network+, or Security+). Company and individual certifications show a commitment to partnering with manufacturers to earn higher levels of support and to gain deep knowledge of their products or of specialized areas in technology. Certifications are not the most important factor in selecting your IT consultant, and many excellent consultants do not elect to focus on them, but asking this question will lead to a useful discussion about why the IT consultant does or does not feel certifications are significant.

5. How do you handle on-site versus off-site support?

Most IT consultants will recommend some kind of remote support option, so that for certain problems they can log into your systems remotely and immediately fix the issue. Remote support can be much quicker than on-site support because travel isn't necessary, and often a technician can help you for a few minutes, even if they are at another client site. Many IT consultants have on-site minimums of one to four hours, but remote support minimums can be as little as fifteen minutes, if there is a minimum. Ask how fast, in general, the IT consultant can arrive at your location, if a problem cannot be quickly solved remotely. Some IT consultants offer service level agreements (SLAs) that guarantee either remote or on-site support within a specified period.

6. What is your business history in IT consulting?

As with many fields that don't *require* certifications, you will find IT consultants who are amateurs who decided to "go professional." Be wary of IT consultants with no technology-related university degrees or other certifications or those who have been in business a short time. One good way to confirm answers to this question is to ask for client references from similar businesses. Another is to review the company's Web site to verify its existence and that the answers provided in the interview match the information provided on the site.

7. What types of clients are your primary focus?

If you are a professional services firm, such as an accounting, law, or financial services firm, it is helpful if your IT consultant focuses on these types of companies, as opposed to, say, manufacturing or retail. Though there are some products that most companies use, every industry has products and applications that are specific to the industry, such as retail point-of-sale devices, legal billing software, and tax return programs. You have a better chance of receiving high-quality support with these tools and processes, if your IT consultant has previous experience with them.

8. Describe your team.

Some IT consultants are one-person shops, and others have one or more offices with larger teams. Depending on your business, either of these could be good options. This answer will give you a feeling for how responsive your vendor will be. You are looking for depth of resources and technical specialization. For example, if you have a Microsoft Exchange e-mail system, it's important that your vendor have an Exchange person on their team. If they are a one-person shop, ask how they handle the periods when they are on vacation.

9. Describe your pricing and any service agreements.

This is often the first question people ask, but it should usually be held to the end of the discussion to show the IT consultant that while pricing is important, a good match is more important. Pricing can be fixed, based on an ongoing maintenance agreement, or hourly, based on the services you request. Many IT consultants offer both options and may require service agreements with advanced payment. A service agreement lays out in detail the terms under which your IT consultant will provide services; a good agreement protects both you and the IT consultant from misunderstandings and poor memories. Look for clauses that cover payment terms, standards of care, liability, non-solicitation, and confidentiality. You may also be given a statement of work that covers individual

projects and that exists under the umbrella of a master agreement.

10. Final questions.

By this point, you should have a pretty good feeling for whether the IT consultant is a good fit for your company. If you have two or more companies that appear qualified, asking one of these final questions may give you that extra bit of information needed to make your selection: Why should I pick your company over any of your competitors? What was the last major problem you had with a client and how did you handle it? Do you have written samples of your documentation that I can review? What's in your trunk? (Many IT consultants have a box of spare parts so that they can get you up and running quickly.) What products or services will you be adding to your repertoire in the next year?

Source: David Oderberg, managing partner, TerraSage Technology Partners, LLC (*www.terrasage.com*)—TerraSage Technology Partners, LLC was established to help small and medium-size businesses capitalize on information technology. Contact him at 3313 Butler Avenue, Los Angeles, CA 90066-1305; (310) 439-2600; Fax: (310) 391-0076.

Largest Information Technology Consultants

IT consultants provide services such as business process outsourcing, security, networking implementation, and architecture overhaul. Many IT consultants are very small computer shops. Many others are large international organizations. Here are some of the largest IT consulting firms from our expert who helps IT people find jobs.

1. Booz Allen Hamilton

Number of offices: 100 worldwide; 2004 employees: 15,000 worldwide; 2004 revenue: $2,700 million

8283 Greensboro Drive
McLean, VA 22102
(703) 902-5000
Fax: (703) 902-3333
www.boozallen.com

2. Deloitte Consulting

2003 employees: 54,415 worldwide; 2003 revenue: $9,460 million

1633 Broadway
35th Floor
New York, NY 10019-6754
(212) 492-4500
Fax: (212) 492-4743
www.deloitte.com

3. IBM Global Services

Number of offices: 300; 2004 employees: 180,000 worldwide; 2004 revenue: $46,400 million

New Orchard Rd.
Armonk, NY 10504
(914) 499-1900
Fax: (914) 765-7382
www.ibm.com/services

4. Accenture

Number of offices: 110 worldwide; 2003 employees: 83,000 worldwide; 2003 revenue: $11,800 million

1345 Avenue of the Americas
New York, NY 10105
(917) 452-4400
www.accenture.com

5. BearingPoint

Number of offices: 162 worldwide; 2003 employees: 16,000 worldwide: 2003 revenue: $3,130 million

1676 International Drive
McLean, VA 22102
(703) 747-3000
Fax: (703) 747-8500
www.bearingpoint.com

6. Capgemini

2003 employees: 50,000 worldwide.

5 Times Square
New York, NY 10036
(917) 934-8000
Fax: (917) 934-8001
www.us.capgemini.com

7. HP Technology Solutions

2004 employees: 145,600; 2004 revenue: $79,900 million

3000 Hanover Street
Palo Alto, CA 94304-1185
(650) 857-1501
Fax: (650) 857-5518
www.hp.com

8. DiamondCluster International Inc.

Number of offices: 9 worldwide; 2004 employees: 500 worldwide; 2004 revenue: $155 million

875 North Michigan Avenue
Suite 3000
Chicago, IL 60611
(312) 255-5000
Fax: (312) 255-6000
www.diamondcluster.com

9. Telcordia Technologies

Number of offices: 36 worldwide; 2004 employees: 3,284

One Telcordia Dr.
Piscataway, NJ 08854-4157
(732) 699-2000
Fax: (732) 336-2320
www.telcordia.com

10. Keane

Number of offices: 72 worldwide; 2004 employees: 9,115; 2003 revenue: $805 million

100 City Sq.
Boston, MA 02129-3777
(617) 241-9200
Fax: (617) 241-9507
www.keane.com

Source: The Vault (*www.thevault.com*)—The Internet's ultimate destination for insider company information, advice, and career management services. Contact them at 150 West 22nd St., New York, NY 10011.

Considerations When Hiring a Foreign Distributor

One option for selling products internationally is appointing a foreign distributor. Like an export company, the distributor purchases the products and resells them. The seller is paid by the distributor, and the distributor usually bears the risk of nonpayment (although the risk can be shifted by conditioning payment on resale). The seller's only responsibility may be delivery of the products to a shipping company for redelivery to the distributor. If you're setting up an arrangement with a foreign distributor, definitely keep these issues in mind.

1. Terms

If sales will be made through a foreign distributor, have a written distribution agreement addressing issues such as the product lines covered by the appointment, sales territories and exclusivity, the initial term of the appointment, and renewal rights.

2. Financial implications

Other important terms relate to the price at which products will be sold to the distributor, the currency for payment and other payment terms, responsibility for sales taxes and import duties, product warranties, resale terms, and minimum performance requirements.

3. Intellectual property

The distribution agreement should also address ownership and protection of intellectual property and confidential information and restrictions on competition.

4. Termination

The distribution agreement will need to address grounds for termination, and the effect of termination on unsold inventory and ongoing obligations to customers, as well as determining the applicable law and the forum for resolving disputes.

5. Communications

Other issues include rights and responsibilities regarding translation of marketing materials supplied by the seller and the language in which communications will be conducted between the seller and the distributor.

6. Arbitration

If arbitration will be used, address the language in which the proceedings will be conducted and the responsibility for translation costs.

7. Controlling language

If the final contract is prepared in two languages, designate one of the versions as the controlling version if possible.

8. Antitrust laws

A disadvantage of selling through a distributor is that antitrust laws will limit the seller's ability to control the distributor's resale prices. Although the application of U.S. antitrust laws to export transactions is limited by the Foreign Trade Antitrust Improvements Act, many foreign jurisdictions have similar laws. Some countries limit maximum and minimum resale price restrictions, and some even prohibit nonbinding suggested retail prices.

9. Exclusive territories

Antitrust laws impact terms relating to exclusive sales territories. In the United States, agreements between competitors to allocate sales territories are per se illegal. In contrast, vertical agreements to allocate territories (e.g., an agreement between a supplier and a distributor) usually will not pose a significant risk of violating antitrust laws if the territorial restrictions are ancillary to a legitimate distribution contract and the overall effect and intent is not to harm competition.

10. European Union anticompetitive laws

In the European Union, a distribution agreement can generally limit the distributor's marketing efforts to a particular territory if the purpose and overall effect is not anticompetitive, but "absolute" territorial restrictions may violate competition laws. European Union antitrust laws have been extended by agreement to other European countries such as Norway, Iceland, and Liechtenstein. Exclusive dealing clauses raise similar antitrust issues.

11. Termination

It is important for a seller to clearly establish the basis on which a distribution agreement can be terminated. In the United States, as a general rule, distribution agreements can be terminated on any basis agreed to by the parties and set forth in the distribution agreement. There are many exceptions, however. Some states have distributor protection laws limiting termination for certain products. In addition, several states have restrictions on termination of distributor relationships that qualify as franchises.

12. Antitrust and termination

There are also antitrust limitations on termination. A termination motivated by anticompetitive intent (e.g., terminating a distributor because it refuses to follow informal minimum resale price requirements, may violate antitrust laws). As a general principle, termination provisions should be reasonable and termination rights should be exercised with due care to avoid legal challenges.

13. Foreign jurisdictions and termination

Many foreign jurisdictions have similar limitations on termination of distribution agreements. In addition, some foreign jurisdictions have special laws designed to protect local distributors by restricting termination. Generally, these laws require a certain minimum amount of notice and provide the distributor with a right to recover damages from the supplier if the notice requirements are not followed. In Belgium, distributors are entitled to receive "reasonable" notice of termination, which may vary from six months to two years. In addition, distributors in Belgium are entitled to termination payments if they are granted distribution rights for an indefinite term and the distributorship is terminated without cause. Even in countries that do not have specific distributor termination statutes, the courts have limited termination of distributors by applying related laws.

14. Termination restrictions

Restrictions on distributor termination are more likely to apply when the distributorship is exclusive. In addition to restrictions on termination, some countries will require the seller to continue to supply goods to a terminated distributor for a certain period after termination and repurchase the distributor's unsold inventory.

Source: *Guide to Doing Business Internationally*, a joint publication by the U.S. Department of Commerce, the Arizona Department of Commerce, and the Tempe Chamber of Commerce.

Issues to Consider Before Exporting Your Products

Is your company ready for exporting? Entering foreign markets can be a great way to boost sales. But what's your export strategy? Do you know how to get started? There was a time when exporting products to foreign countries was simply not practical for most small businesses. But today, exporting your products may be just the ticket for your company. Here our experts provide a list of some things to consider before you decide to send your products abroad.

1. Domestic sales

The first question you need to ask is whether your products are selling domestically. Exporting is not a panacea to boost sagging sales. If your products aren't selling here, then they probably won't sell anywhere else, either.

2. Exportability

Next, you'll need to decide if your products are exportable. Do your products fill a niche that is exclusive to the U.S. market? Are they packaged in a way that can be understood by non–English speaking consumers? Do they violate cultural taboos or contain ingredients that are prohibitive to their sale in a foreign context? These are all questions you will need to answer before you invest time and money in a costly export venture.

3. Foreign partnerships

Once you have decided that your products are both salable and exportable, you'll need to find foreign partners that are willing to either purchase or distribute your products. Unless you are planning to establish a retail operation on foreign soil, you are going to have to establish business-to-business sales relationships. You can either sell your products directly to foreign retailers or to foreign distributors that sell to those retailers. A secondary advantage of establishing foreign relationships is that your foreign partners will be able to provide you with valuable local insight about import regulations, product marketability, and local customs. Even though establishing foreign relationships can be difficult, you do have several resources at your disposal. The U.S. Commerce Department sponsors two Web sites—*www.export.gov* and *www.buyusa.com*—that contain directories of foreign buyers. Another resource is the U.S. embassy located in the country where you would like to sell your products. The embassy should be able to assist you in identifying indigenous companies that buy the kind of products your company sells.

4. Legal issues

The last step in establishing an export component for your business is to research the legal issues involved in exporting your products to certain parts of the world. Some products, such as technology and agricultural products, are subject to severe export limitations. There may also be import restrictions depending on the countries you are dealing with. Additionally, the post–September 11 world has created heightened sensitivities about exporting products that can be even remotely used in a military or terrorist capacity. Since you can't possibly be aware of all the restrictions and licensing

requirements you may or may not be facing, your best advice is to consult an attorney specializing in international law to make sure you are in compliance with the appropriate domestic and foreign regulations.

5. Market need

The very first question that needs to be asked is whether your product meets a need in the country in which you plan to sell it. A product may sell like hotcakes in the United States, but fail miserably abroad simply because it meets a market need that is specific to the States. In some cases, the product may meet a market need in regions of the target country but not the entire country as a whole. For example, if your product requires electricity, there may be a demand for it in urban areas, but not in rural ones because electricity is not readily available in many underdeveloped countries.

6. Possibility of modification to increase market demand abroad

Don't lose hope if you discover that demand for your product abroad does not exist at the same level as it does in the United States. Often, your product can be altered to make it more appealing to the global marketplace. Some modifications might not be cost effective enough to make them worth your while. Then again, an inexpensive and simple remedy might be enough to broaden your product's appeal to an acceptable level.

7. Foreign regulations governing sales

Don't assume that the regulations governing the domestic sale and distribution of your product will be the same when you take your product abroad. Chances are they won't be. The time to research applicable laws and regulations is now—before you invest precious time and resources in a product that can't legally be sold in your target market.

8. Packaging

Likewise, you'll need to do some advance research regarding the packaging of your product. Colors, designs, and packaging methods common in the United States don't necessarily translate in a foreign market. Consult with your international partners or conduct field research to learn what packaging is best for your product.

9. Product service and warranty options

One last item to consider is what happens after foreign consumers buy your product. Will you offer the same product service and warranty options to foreign buyers as you do for the buyers here? If so, how do you plan to deliver those services? Regardless of how you decide to answer these questions, just make sure you are prepared to deliver on the promises you make to buyers before you begin selling your product globally.

Source: Gaebler Ventures is a Chicago-based business incubator and holding company that develops and nurtures companies that are shaping the future. For additional information, visit *www.gaebler.com*.

Essential Components of a Service Level Agreement

Service level agreements, sometimes called SLAs, are an essential part of all outsourcing relationships. What are the key parts that need to be considered by both you and your outsourcing provider? Here are few to keep in mind.

1. Define the terms and performance levels

Definitions are essential to have in service level agreements. All technical and important terms should be defined in the agreement. Also include the metrics to be used to assess performance levels.

2. Include information on the people providing the service

Always have the names, locations, and contact information of the key people that will be providing the service to your company. Make sure the SLA can be updated in case these people change roles or leave the service provider.

3. The third party may be using other outsourcers

Remember that sometimes the outsourcers outsource. Your SLA should include information about whether the third party is using outsourcers to provide work for you.

4. Start and end dates

Your SLA should specify start and end dates. The agreement should explain how it can be renewed and the reasons that it may be terminated.

5. Managing your policies and problems

Always include how the services should be performed and what happens when problems arise. Include a penalty clause that explains what the alternative is if something goes wrong. The SLA should provide a procedure as well. Everyone involved should know who to call for help and what information they need so the service provider is able to fix the problem.

6. Accountability

The SLA should state who at your company and that the service provider is responsible for certain areas. The SLA should also include who has permission and who does not have permission to do certain things.

7. Where the service will be performed

Be clear about where the service will be performed and when the service provider will be available for service.

8. Escalation

Today, many service providers offer SLAs with different levels of classes. There are gold, silver, and platinum customers. These different levels will define how quickly you will get serviced. An SLA should state what conditions will prompt an escalation of an issue.

9. Needing answers quickly

If you have a problem, the SLA should state how fast you should get an answer The service provider may respond in one hour or in a day depending on the commitment. An emergency number should also be included in an SLA.

10. Backup plan

When all else fails and you have to turn to the backup plan, your SLA should state what the procedure will be if the primary service fails.

11. When to pay and when not to pay

If the service is not up to your satisfaction, your SLA needs to address your options.

12. When your plan changes

Scope creep happens when the initial definition of a project is expanded. It is one of the leading reasons projects fail. Does your SLA take plan changes into consideration?

13. Request credits

Sometimes you will have to pay up-front for future services. Get ready to get out your credit card. However, sometimes the services aren't good enough or something goes wrong. Because of this, your SLA will provide for service level credits. Outside providers should understand that they may make mistakes. Instead of getting into an argument, it's nice to know you have the ability to request credits for future services.

14. Payment

The SLA should always state how much the service is and when the payment is due. It should explain what services cost more and what services should be included.

15. Termination

The SLA needs to address what happens when one of the parties fails to hold up its end of the agreement. These failures could justify a termination. If an agreement ends, there needs to be an explanation that explains each party's liabilities and any amounts still due.

16. Measuring your SLA's success

You will need to have some sort of measurement in place to determine the success of your SLA. Make sure you find some way to quantifiably measure how well the service provider is doing. Your SLA should state what attributes will be evaluated and measured. In addition, include the measurement period.

17. Reporting

Your SLA agreement should state what reports the third party will be provide, what should be included in the reports, and how often you will receive a report.

Source: Gene Marks, author of *The Complete Idiot's Guide to Successful Outsourcing* (Alpha Books, 2005).

Advantages of Hiring a Subcontractor Instead of an Employee

When it comes to hiring an employee or outsourcing a job, there is no right or wrong answer. Each decision must be evaluated on its own business merits. Here's a list of some advantages of outsourcing the job to a subcontractor.

1. Costs less money

Hiring a subcontractor just costs less money. You don't have to cough up money for employer's taxes, health insurance, retirement plans, vacation time, sick days, and other overhead. Putting people on the payroll definitely has its downsides.

2. Helps avoid the infamous tax bite

If they are an employee, you've got taxes to worry about. Forget about the withholding taxes, because that's just a wash—you're taking in the money and giving it right back to the government. The real expenses are employer's taxes, the largest being FICA and Medicare. Whatever you're paying someone, multiply that by approximately 17 percent. That's your

additional cost that has to be paid into the system. Now add federal unemployment taxes and state/local employer taxes, and you're getting there. All told, you're probably going to pay close to 20 percent of a person's salary into the government right out of your pocket.

3. Reduces time and costs of paperwork and administration

It's bad enough you are going to have to spend extra money on taxes for your employees. With an employee, you also are going to incur even more costs to handle the necessary paperwork and administration. Each quarter you'll have to fill out required federal and state (and sometimes local) payroll tax returns. Additional returns are required by some taxing authorities monthly as well. If you make a mistake on the return, you'll drown in computer-generated nasty grams from the IRS (or municipality) before begging for mercy from the court.

4. Eliminates year-end reporting requirements

What about the year-end reporting requirements? As if the monthly and quarterly reports weren't enough, almost all taxing authorities want you to fill in year-end reconciliations. One of the biggest hassles is generating all those W-2s that report the wages and withholdings of every employee who received more than a dollar from your company during the past calendar year. Go ahead, do it all yourself. Or outsource it to a payroll company. Either way you'll be spending more money for the pleasure of having your new employee on board.

5. Eliminates paying for employees' R and R

In this country, a typical employee expects, at a minimum, two weeks' holiday and time off for sick days. Back in 1994, the Family Medical Leave Act became law, requiring employers to give an employee unpaid leave for certain medical issues. "Unpaid" means that the employer still has to fund their health insurance and other benefits, while leaving their job open. Never mind the cost of getting someone else in part-time to get the work done. That's not reimbursed to the business. Independent contractors do not get vacation. They do not get sick days. If they don't work, then they don't get paid. If there's not enough work, they may not get paid either! For some managers, this arrangement, as compared to hiring full-time employees, is much more attractive.

6. Eliminates paying for health coverage

Every employer knows how expensive health insurance is. The cost of providing adequate health coverage has been rising significantly year after year. Employees expect health insurance from their employers; it's one of the primary benefits provided to a work force. Some companies have been asking their employees to contribute more of their salaries to funding this expense than others. But getting health insurance through an employer is always less expensive than getting it on your own. Most employers contribute something and find themselves struggling to control these costs.

7. No retirement plan

When you hire an employee, you've got to think about retirement—the employee's retirement.

There's no law that says you have to put money away for them. But consider the reality: If Joe the warehouse manager starts slowing down after working his can off for your company over the past thirty years, what are you going to do . . . let him live off of welfare? There's an unspoken rule that employers look after their own. This is why so many managers and company owners implement retirement savings plans and give their employees incentives to contribute. Most companies now have some kind of retirement plan in place, and these plans almost always include contributions made by the employer. So expect that you will be paying some percentage of your employees' salaries into this plan. Obviously, this wouldn't be a consideration with outsourced help. You don't have to feel any kind of obligation for someone who's not on your payroll.

8. No family or personal problems

When you hire an employee, you're not just hiring a person. You're hiring that person's family too. If the employee's son has a drug problem, it could soon become your problem. If the employee has a disability, you're required, by law, to provide an acceptable working environment. If the employee is going through lifestyle changes, maybe a divorce or a family illness, your company is expected to do its part to help him get through it. This may mean giving paid time off or some other form of compensation.

9. No worries about employee protections under the law

Employees have many protections under the law that outsourced contractors do not enjoy.

Employees are protected by the Department of Labor. There are Employer Retirement Income Security Act (ERISA) laws that govern how their retirement plans are managed and to make sure that employers don't discriminate these plans in their favor. There's a federal minimum wage law. Contracts must be in compliance with the Fair Labor Standards Act. Safety and workplace rules, as required by the Occupational Safety and Health Administration must be in place. There are laws protecting employees against age, racial, and sexual discrimination. Hiring and terminating an employee is subject to strict guidelines that put employers into legal peril if violated. The Equal Employment Opportunity Commission oversees that employees get to play ball on a level field. If you employ union workers, you're going to have even more hoops to jump through! Few of these laws protect an outsourcer. An outsourcer is just a vendor, a third party.

10. No training

Training is extremely important for an employee to stay up-to-date. Each year companies spends millions training their employees how to better use their computer software, administer personnel plans, implement better safety procedures, as well as soft skills like negotiating and public speaking. Some companies pay for their employees to go back to school at night or even for a master's degree. This isn't cheap, but it could make for a loyal employee. An outsourced contractor, though, is on her own for training. A company expects that the outsourcer has done whatever she needs to do to make herself or her company qualified

for the task at hand. The employer is usually not expected to provide any training for an outsourcer as would be expected for an employee.

11. No overhead headache

There are a lot of overhead expenses related to employees that wouldn't be incurred if the work was outsourced. For example, a staff of fifty people needs voice-mail, e-mail, cubicles, office supplies, and other tools for their jobs. They'll also need extra administrative support to oversee payroll, benefits, problems, correspondence, and scheduling. Have you budgeted for these extras?

Source: Gene Marks, CPA (*www.marksgroup.net*), is a small business consultant and author of *The Small Business Desk Reference*, *The Complete Idiot's Guide to Successful Outsourcing*, and *Outfoxing the Small Business Owner*.

The Disadvantages of Hiring a Subcontractor Instead of an Employee

According to a recent survey by PriceWaterhouse, more than 80 percent of companies outsource some type of task or project each year. The survey concludes that "by farming out management of operations that are not mission-critical, (these companies) are better able to concentrate on growth, competitors and profitability." If you're not doing any outsourcing, you may be hurting your business. Of course, if outsourcing everything was always the solution, there'd be no employees at all. Obviously, this isn't the case. The billions of dollars that firms spend on outsourcing every year are dwarfed by the trillions spent on payroll. Here are some disadvantages of hiring an outsourcer instead of an employee.

1. The loyalty factor

What makes an employee sacrifice his paycheck for the good of the company? One word: commitment. When an owner or manager sticks out her hand and says, "Welcome aboard," you're not just being offered a job, you're being offered a commitment. The manager is hiring you as a permanent part of the family, so to speak. You're not being brought on to perform a task, and then let go. You are entering an age-old relationship between employer and employee. Both parties hope to be working with each other for a long time. Many of us desire job security. We want to be part of something. We want to succeed with a team. Working at a successful company makes us feel successful. An employee enjoys this security and doesn't want to lose it. There's a level of trust and dedication in this relationship that you'll probably never find in an outsourced arrangement.

2. Availability

If you outsource a project to an independent firm, then you'll be forced to deal with availability issues. The firm will be servicing other customers. They may have different priorities than yours. There may an extra layer of management that you'll have to navigate to get to the person you need. Maybe you want to know that you can reach the people working on your project, no matter who's doing the work, at nights or weekends if necessary. You don't want to hear that they're "unavailable" or "with a customer."

3. The control factor

You're not the outsourcer's boss. You're the customer. There's a difference. A service provider doesn't want to lose customers. But someone working for the service provider is more concerned with making his or her boss happy. As a customer, you're going to have to take your place in line with all the other customers served by the firm you've outsourced. You're going to be competing against other customers and priorities at the service provider's firm.

Outsourcing may force you to give up some control. If you want complete authority over your task or project, then you may not enjoy relinquishing it to an outside firm.

4. Not done in your industry

Maybe outsourcing isn't the right decision because it's generally not done in your industry. Would you be comfortable to learn that the pilot flying your plane is not an employee of the airline, but rather an independent contractor? Or that your airline is the only airline in the industry that has independent contractors flying their planes? Maybe you care; maybe you don't. But a clever competitor could certainly exploit this fact to its advantage, accusing a rival of sacrificing safety for cost and questioning the dedication to their employees and customers.

5. The (tax) rules

Hiring an independent contractor may also raise an eyebrow with the Internal Revenue Service. In fact, as we shall see later in this book, the IRS takes this so seriously that they've established specific guidelines for determining whether someone is an employee or a contractor. A classical employee-employer relationship may keep you off their radar screen. Tax exposures do worry owners and managers who hire independent contractors, so if you're the worrying kind, you be better off hiring.

6. Motivated by cash

Employees don't always need to be paid for all the work that they do. For example, sometimes it's about making partner, as was the case at an accounting firm I worked for. By dangling the carrot of partnership in front of the employees, the firm (and so many other accounting, law, and professional firms) extracted many hours of work well beyond a typical employment arrangement. Try getting that from an outsourced firm or independent contractor. Outsourcers are mostly motivated by cash. They work, they send you their bill, and you pay them. But with employees, the motivation can be perks other than cash. The prospect of a new title, a corner office, or a key to the executive washroom will entice an employee to work many more hours than someone from the outside.

7. Employees represent infrastructure

Having employees on your payroll tells the world that you've got enough work to employ all those people full-time. You're a real company. You have people's lives relying on your company's success. And this does a lot for your market value. If you're thinking of getting a bank loan, or going public, what do you think says "invest in me": fifty employees on staff or fifty subcontractors? If you're planning on selling your business one day, you'll be very interested in the value of goodwill that a potential buyer will want to pay over and above tangible assets. Goodwill includes customer lists, established processes, and your employees who will carry on the work for the new owner.

8. Government frowns on hiring outsourcers

Governments believe that hiring people is good for society. Outsourcing, especially in the current political environment, is not encouraged by our elected officials. To them, outsourcing means "taking jobs away from Americans," even though it might be the best choice for a business, allowing them to reinvest profits and expand. Since the days Caesar threw grain to the mob, politics is all about creating and holding on to jobs. People have to put food on the table, and they expect their government to help them if things get tough. The government wants people to have jobs.

Source: Gene Marks (*www.marksgroup.net*) is a small business consultant and author of *The Small Business Desk Reference, The Complete Idiot's Guide to Successful Outsourcing,* and *Outfoxing the Small Business Owner.*

Twenty Ways the IRS Distinguishes an Employee from a Subcontractor

Independent contractors are individuals who are in business for themselves and hire out their labor to clients. Be extremely careful not to misclassify a worker as an independent contractor because the tax consequences can be significant. When evaluating subcontractor/employee relationships, these are the typical factors that the IRS will notice.

1. Instructions

He or she is required to comply with an employer's instructions as to how to do the job. Independent contractors follow their own instructions.

2. Training

He or she is required to be trained by the employer on how to do the job. An independent contractor does not require training from the employer.

3. Integration

Services are fully integrated into the employer's business, which is significantly dependent on him. An independent contractor's services are not integrated into the employer's business.

4. Personal

He or she is required to perform services personally.

5. Assistants

He or she is hired, supervised, and paid by the employer. The IRS considers him independent when he generally hires his own assistants, required only to attain a particular result.

6. Continuity

There is a continuing economic relationship that may include work at recurring but irregular intervals. An independent contactor has no assumption of continuing relationship.

7. Hours of work

He or she is required to perform work within set hours of work specified by the employer. An independent contractor is free to establish her own hours of work.

8. Time required

He or she usually devotes full-time to the employer's business and may be restricted from performing work for others. An independent contractor can work at any time and for whomever he or she pleases.

9. Work location

He or she performs work on the employer's premises. An independent contractor's work may be performed anywhere, often at the worker's office or location.

10. Sequence of work

He or she follows orders or a sequence of work set by employer. An independent contractor is free to accomplish work in any sequence.

11. Reports

He or she generally makes regular or periodic, either oral or written, reports to the employer. An independent contractor is not necessarily required to submit regular reports.

12. Payment

He or she is generally paid by time (i.e., hour, week, or month). An independent contractor is generally paid by result (i.e., on completion of a project or by straight commission).

13. Expenses

He or she is generally reimbursed for business-related expenses, implying right of regulation and direction by the employer. An independent contractor generally covers his or her own expenses and her expenses may be included in her total payment.

14. Tools and materials

The tools and materials needed for the job are provided by the employer. An independent contractor uses his or her own tools and materials to accomplish work.

15. Facility investment

He or she generally has no investment in the facilities required to accomplish work, indicating dependence on the employer's facilities. An independent contractor has an investment in facilities, such as an office rented from third party.

16. Profit or loss

He or she cannot realize a profit or loss on his or her services. An independent contractor has exposure to economic gain or loss on accomplishment of work.

17. Simultaneous work

He or she performs work under a single financial arrangement. An independent contractor performs work simultaneously for multiple, unrelated persons or entities.

18. General public

He or she does not make services available to the general public. An independent contractor makes services available to the general public on regular basis.

19. Discharge

The employer can fire and thereby control the nature and pace of work through threat of firing. An independent contractor cannot be discharged so long as the result is satisfactory.

20. Termination

He or she can quit at any time without liability. An independent contractor can terminate only with risk of breach of contract liability.

Source: Small Business Administration (*www.sba.gov*).

Common Steps to Plan Your Outsourcing Relationship

After participating in and/or observing hundreds of outsourced relationships, here are a few steps to plan your outsourcing relationship to make sure the relationship goes as smoothly as possible from beginning to end.

1. Planning and analysis

This is the first step you will take to get your outsourcing arrangement underway.

2. Assignment of a dedicated project manager

Assign a strong project manager, or leader, right away. Make sure one person is responsible for the success (or failure) of the project.

3. Start your plan

In your contract, specify the deliverables of both you and your service provider. Always have a plan of action that documents your methodology for getting there. Sit down with your service provider as soon as you can and make sure you agree on the individual steps to be taken to get to your ultimate goal.

4. Visit the service provider's site

Meet the people with whom you will be working. Establish a personal connection. This will make it easier to work together, especially when problems arise.

5. Establish the stakeholders

The marketing manager may be acting as the project manager for the outside telemarketing relationship, but there are numerous others who should be held responsible if the relationship fails. The vice president of Marketing and Sales as well as individual sales managers and reps will all suffer if not enough leads are generated by the service provider. Be sure to identify all of the stakeholders before you start your project so you know who you're ultimate evaluators will be.

6. Know your risks and have a backup plan

If your plan is to outsource your human resource department, then what will your plan be if they fall down on the job, or your employees don't like them, or the cost savings they promised you hasn't come true yet? As you begin to plan your outsourcing relationship, think about the risks you may face and what you can do to minimize them. Always have a backup plan in case things don't go as you planned.

7. The design

This step is where you take the project plan and really perfect a good working document.

8. Nail down the details

Agree with the service provider on the timeline of your project. Now is the time to set milestones and more specific deliverables than what had been laid out in your contract. Here you should have a much more detailed list of tasks, responsibilities, and due dates. Put all of this into writing in your project plan and update

it as needed. Consider all of the service levels and measurement objectives included in your agreement here.

9. Build the internal team

Earlier in this list we talked about having a leader/project manager in place so you'll know who the stakeholders are. The outside firm you hire to help you implement the new manufacturing system will need Susan to assist them to gather data, Mike from IT to provide them with security codes and server access, and Bob from operations to help coordinate training. The project manager is going to need support from a team of people to make sure the relationship gets implemented successfully.

10. Provide resources

Your third party may need resources. There may be the need to reserve conference rooms, purchase computer equipment, and so on. During the design phase, you'll want to identify and secure all the resources needed and make sure they're available when they are needed.

11. Finalize your budget

Once your plan is set and the people and resources have been figured out, you should start to get an idea of the total costs involved. Hope that this amount is close to what you originally expected. Finalize the amounts, get additional approval if necessary, and prepare yourself to report on how well you're doing.

12. Set up strong reporting systems

Before you move forward, be certain your systems for reporting are in place. If your service provider will be measured on the reduction in time to close a complaint call, are you tracking these calls completely? If your outside telemarketer is being paid on the number of leads they generate, are you recording these leads in the right place? If you're budgeted to spend fifty thousand dollars on travel during the course of this relationship, are these travel costs documented?

13. Approve your plan

Now is the time to get your final plan approved by senior management. Always have it in writing and remember to include an executive summary. You want to be sure you have buy-in from the highest level possible. Circumstances can change from the time an agreement is signed to the time you're ready to execute your plan.

Source: Gene Marks (*www.marksgroup.net*) is a small business consultant and author of *The Small Business Desk Reference*, *The Complete Idiot's Guide to Successful Outsourcing*, and *Outfoxing the Small Business Owner*.

Items to Include in Your Request for Proposal

Any business that wants to sell their product or service to a governmental agency or foundation will need to respond to a request for proposal (RFP). RFPs for various agencies are published online and in a variety of publications. Although it is important to read each RFP carefully and respond specifically to the requested format, there are a number of standard items that must be included in your response.

1. Executive summary

Every proposal should start with a brief overview of the project. This is your opportunity to make a quick sales pitch for what you are going to produce. If this is not written well, the rest of your proposal may not be read.

2. Title page and table of contents

The title page should have a descriptive title, date, and contact information. The table of contents should list by page number the start of each section.

3. Introduction

The introduction provides an overview of the proposal. In it, you usually refer to the RFP and why you are the right business to complete this work.

4. Background

In this section, you demonstrate that you know the scope of work involved and how to make it happen. This is not the place to discuss your credentials. It is the place to show that you understand the problems that need to be addressed and how to handle them.

5. Description of the work to be performed

This is the "meat" of the proposal. Don't be afraid to be very specific about how you plan to accomplish the tasks necessary to respond to the RFP.

6. Output to be produced

What is the recipient going to receive from you? Include not only products that are requested in the RFP but also reports, quality evaluation of the products, and dissemination of products and reports.

7. Timeline

Provide a comprehensive schedule of when tasks will be accomplished.

8. Responsible parties and their qualifications

Here is where you brag about your credentials. Be certain to note who will be responsible for what. Tying this to the description of work to be performed gives a sense that you are organized and capable of completing the work required. Also note how much time each person will be devoting to the project.

9. Costs and resources needed

Include a detailed budget with hourly rates, projected hours, costs of equipment and supplies, and any external subcontracts. If you are subcontracting any of the work, add a description of the subcontractor.

10. Supporting documents

This section can include resumes, letters of reference, publications that are pertinent to the topic, or any other printed materials that might be important in indicating the knowledge and skills you bring to the project.

Source: Judith A. Kautz, PhD, MBA, owner of Small Business Notes (*www.smallbusinessnotes.com*)—Judith Kautz has worked in both the public and private sectors of business for more than thirty years. In private industry, she has been employed as a systems analyst and manager in computer consulting businesses, in addition to providing private consulting services in computer applications, statistics, and management. She can be contacted at *editor@smal lbusinessnotes.com*.

Steps to Selecting a Consultant

Small and midsize businesses often encounter business challenges that are beyond the experience of the owner or management team. One approach to addressing those challenges is to power through the issues and learn by experience. An approach that many companies use is to hire consultants who have the expertise and experience in addressing particular matters. The following list provides the means of supplementing your organization's know-how with that of experts, while ensuring that your time, and that of your direct reports, is used the most efficient and profitable way possible.

1. Identify the issue that needs solving

Consultants come from many different areas of expertise. Some are technical experts on a subject outside the core business of your company. These include lawyers, accountants, insurance brokers, and bankers. Others are technical experts on a piece of your business. These may include industry experts and information systems consultants. There is yet another category of consultants who work across industries and across functional areas of business. These include financial consultants, marketing consultants, and management consultants. Your first task is to identify whether the issue you want assistance with is a technical matter (how to deal with a tax dispute with the IRS, how to improve the organization and operation of your accounting functions) or a process matter (how to write your company's business plan, how to get your team working together more productively).

2. Establish what the cost of the issue is to your business

You need to establish an understanding of the cost to your business of not dealing with the issue: for example, lack of clear business direction or technical know-how, business liability, lost sales, uncoordinated marketing, or operational breakdowns. This will enable you to be clear about the amount you are willing to invest in consultant professional fees to resolve the problem, acquire the missing know-how, accelerate decision-making, change processes in your company, and so on.

3. Establish a general budget and time frame

The approach taken and the speed with which a consultant addresses your issue can vary based on your business circumstances. How quickly do you want this issue solved? How complex is it? How many of your resources may need to be involved in working with the consultant? How will consultant fees affect your cash flow? You need to have a sense of your answers to these questions before you speak with consultants.

4. Research your options

There are several ways to identify consultants who might assist you with your issue. If you have trusted business advisers (such as a CPA, business attorney, insurance broker), they are often well connected in the business community and can suggest reputable resources. Your trade association administrative office or members can be another source of introductions. Online searches may produce names and Web sites and published experts. Friends, family members, and other business owners and managers may well have had firsthand experience with consultants and be able to put you in direct contact with them.

5. Speak with the consultant by phone

This is the first step in interviewing consultants without overly disrupting your business day. Describe your business, your current challenges, and the issue you have identified that requires assistance. Ask the consultant to describe his area of expertise, how that addresses the issue at hand, and to describe clients for whom he has addressed similar issues in the past. This conversation can take from five to ten minutes per consultant. If you like both the content of the information you hear, the manner of the conversation, and the form of the consulting he describes, set up a time for a more detailed face-to-face interview.

6. Assess the consultant in person

Some consultants use a single repeated approach to their work for clients while others customize every engagement. Your conversation with prospective consultants should include how they work with clients on this type of issue, the general estimate of the amount of consulting time it will take, the amount of your time or your company's resources that will need to be involved in the effort, the time frame for the consulting effort they expect, and where the work will take place. Will they be doing the work or transferring the know-how to you or someone in your company? What resources will they need access to and what working space will they need on-site to accomplish their work?

They should be able to describe the consultant's professional fees, any expected expenses, charges for travel, telephone, and materials, invoicing and payment, and how often and by what means they will be updating you on the progress of their work. Depending on the level of complexity of the effort, the consultant may be able to give you a fixed fee or may need to break the effort up into phases of work. This means she can tell you what the first part of the effort will cost you, while each next phase will depend on the information uncovered, the solution suggested, and the recommendations you agree to for each next phase.

7. Select your consultant

Based on your conversations, ask your short list of preferred consultants to give you a written proposal. It may also be relevant to ask for and interview references. The document should summarize the discussion points and project scope, resources to be used and approach taken, project time frame, professional fees, and billing arrangements. Added to the personality fit you felt during your conversation, you will have enough information to select the expert you would like to have help you increase the value of your company.

Source: Linda Feinholz (*www.feinholz.com*) provides consulting and coaching services to business owners, managers, and professionals, helping them improve the effectiveness of their organization and their results. In addition to working with Avon, Walt Disney Imagineering, and the Los Angeles Metropolitan Transportation Authority, she assists small and midsize businesses in developing the plans, resources, capabilities, and systems to grow their businesses and increase their individual and organizational capabilities. Her work includes leadership and management development, business process redesign, and team development. She can be reached at *Linda@feinholz.com* or (818) 989-5989.

Common Ways for Measuring the Success of an Outsourcing Project

The aspect that is frequently underdeveloped in most outsourcing plans is quantifiable measures of success. Well-designed metrics help to ensure that the proposed outsourcing has a reasonable chance of returning a positive return on investment and after implantation, they help to ensure that outsourcing is reaching each of its goals. The types of metrics that our expert is recommending in this list have an added feature in that they also provide a standard against which you can compare your performance. As a result, you can more clearly see how you are doing because the metric includes a benchmark standard number, which allows you to compare your results to a standard.

1. Service level

Determining whether the types of services that were contracted are actually being provided and at least the minimum quantity level that is required. It is important to develop metrics that measure whether the types of services that were contracted for are actually being provided by the vendor. Service-level metrics generally measure whether each of the contracted services are being provided and at the volume or quantity level specified. Examples of typical service-level metrics include the number of service areas where employee benefits questions were answered, the hours of the week that calls were answered, the number of calls handled, and the cost per call (in the cases where the costs are not fixed in advance).

2. Service quality

Determine whether the quality of the service is up to contracted levels. Merely providing services is insufficient if the quality of the service is below acceptable levels. As a result, it is important to monitor the quality of the service provided by the vendor. Examples of typical quality of service measures include user satisfaction with the answers provided, user satisfaction with the way that the answers or provided, the average and maximum response time required to answer a call, the average accuracy of the answers provided (error rate), and that vendor services met all legal requirements.

3. Total cost reduction

The formula for assessing the total cost reduction is to start with the baseline costs that were incurred by running the process in-house prior to outsourcing. From the baseline costs, subtract the total cost of the vendor contract payments, and then subtract the internal costs of vendor management (for example, the salary of your internal vendor manager, related travel costs, the cost of communicating the shift to a vendor, the costs related to the RFP, accounting costs related to vendor transactions, and any software or equipment that was required to make the outsourcing arrangement possible). Next, subtract any actual employee head-count reduction (converted to salary dollars) as a result of the outsourcing. Assuming that the quality and amount of service provided by the vendor

is equal to or greater than the baseline services offered by internal HR, you can then compare the before and after costs of providing these services. If there is a net gain, then the next step is to determine if there are any unintended consequences as a result of the outsourcing initiative.

4. Unintended consequences

Have any other positive or negative impacts resulted from the outsourcing, and have those consequences added to the costs or the benefits? In addition to the traditional costs associated with outsourcing, assess any additional costs or benefits that might result from the initiative. This is because outsourcing traditional functions occasionally has some negative impacts that, in effect, increase the relative costs of outsourcing.

5. Better use of resources

Have the freed-up resources (as a result of the outsourcing) actually been put to better or more strategic use within the company? One of the primary goals of most outsourcing is to free up internal resources so that they can be redirected to areas where they are likely to have a higher strategic impact.

6. ROI of outsourcing

After these calculations have been completed, it is then possible to assess the overall return on investment of the outsourcing initiative. However, even if the ROI is low or negative, that does not automatically mean that you should drop the outsourcing effort. This is because the start cost of returning to internally based processes may be so high as to outweigh the benefits of dropping the outsourcing vendor. Other options may include selecting another vendor or using the metric data to refine and continually improve the outsourcing initiative.

Source: Dr. John Sullivan, Dr. John Sullivan and Associates (*www. drjohnsullivan.com*)—Dr. Sullivan has been described as one of the leading strategists in the field of human resources around the globe. Via his roles as an author, corporate adviser, and educator, he challenges the status quo and offers a bold forward-thinking look at what it takes to become a smarter, more powerful function. Dr. Sullivan has served as a professor of management at San Francisco State University for more than twenty years. He can be reached at 224 Palmetto Avenue, Pacifica, CA 94044; (650) 738-1922; fax: (408) 351-0153.

Typical Outsourcing Liability Issues

Most companies outsource for a variety of different reasons. It's a great way to bring resources and capabilities into a business that does not currently possess them. Companies may find outsourcing a good alternative to the costs of adding additional head count and all the extra costs associated with benefits, taxes, and so on. They may outsource certain functions in order to concentrate on their core competencies. Whatever the case, there are many potential liabilities associated with the practice of outsourcing.

1. Management buy-in

Unless there are clearly defined objectives and processes along with management criteria and expectations, a liability exists for misunderstandings and mismanagement of the outsourcing function. This may result in the loss of a real or perceived gain through the outsource function.

2. Finding the right outsource partner

In an ideal outsource relationship, the organization and the outsource provider share a similar vision, define realistic expectations, and work together to accomplish the venture in a positive manner. Unfortunately, this isn't always the case and problems may arise: the partners may find they cannot work together; one party may develop financial troubles; one party may feel it is not benefiting fairly from the relationship and become less motivated to live up to expectations; the outsource provider may not keep up with new technologies required to meet future expectations. It's critical that the company have a high confidence level that the right outsource partner has been chosen.

3. Determining the financial benefits of outsourcing

In evaluating the financial ramifications of outsourcing, many organizations employ a "straight dollar" methodology, comparing one bid against another. This method fails to consider more sophisticated and complete measures such as outsourcing's effect on cash flow, efficiency, and value creation.

4. Critical issues in the contract

It is important that the outsourcing contract correctly reflect all critical issues relating to scope, performance, and pricing. The key areas to consider are the terms of the agreement, the scope of services, confidentiality, service level agreements, force majeure, warranty, change management, pricing, and termination.

5. Scope of services

A well-defined scope of services will not require an outsource provider to build into its pricing a risk premium that would diminish the cost savings the company is looking to attain. The scope of services description needs to detail each category and subcategory of service expectation. This way any request for new services, performance failures, and so on are understood and dealt with accordingly.

6. Governance

There needs to be multiple levels of a company's governance to allow for issue escalation based on the urgency and importance of the issue. Lack of a consistent governing structure can end in a loss of the financial benefit of the outsourcing decision.

7. Start-ups

Many companies relying on start-up outsource projects encounter hidden costs, high staff turnover, and poor cross-cultural communications. In addition, projected start-up timing is subject to precise lead-time estimates, based more on guess and speculation than on historical accuracy.

8. Implementation

To ensure complete capture of all critical elements of the implementation process, the outsource provider needs to adhere to a formal project-management process. This includes assigning a dedicated project manager and the establishment of a project timeline with designated milestones and signoffs. Failure to control this process will result in potential delays or loss of productivity.

9. Training costs

Often, the training costs incurred at the beginning of an outsourcing project may delay the expected savings for at least a year to two into the engagement, precluding any benefit to the company for short-term contracts.

10. Operations and measurements

The key to the ongoing success of the outsourced project is the effective management of the relationship between the company and the outsource provider. The outsourcing provider's personnel should be trained to understand the company's business environment, culture, and goals.

Source: Randy C. Kravitz is president of Growth Management Partners LLC (GMP), a full service Chicago-based business advisory firm. The firm focuses its efforts on the continuing needs of small and midsize business owners and entrepreneurs. Kravitz, who spent more than twenty-eight years in international and domestic business development and senior management roles in three Fortune 500 companies, has a master's in marketing. He is an accredited Executive Associate of the Institute for Independent Business, an active and powerful network of over 3,000 successful senior executives and former business owners located in eighteen countries. GMP's other partners include All Covered, the only nationwide IT outsourcing services company that focuses on the unique computing, networking, and application needs of small and midsize businesses, and other local service providers of financial, operational, and selling services. He can be reached at 411 W. Ontario St., Suite 719, Chicago, IL 60610; (312) 573-1115; fax: (312) 573-1777; e-mail: randykravitz@iib.ws.The Law

The Law

Signs You Should File for Bankruptcy

Although it may seem like it to some of those who are impacted by bankruptcy, it is not necessarily an occurrence that sneaks up on people. There are warning signs for bankruptcy, and certain trends and factors in a business can indicate if bankruptcy could become a problem down the line. To help diagnose your business and potentially locate some bankruptcy-causing factors, the following is a list of warning signs for financial insolvency.

1. Continuous operating losses

A business that continually loses money will inevitably run into financial problems if they cannot turn that trend around. Eventually, losses will become too great and there will not be enough money on hand to pay off creditors, resulting in a need for bankruptcy.

2. Loss of key employees

If a company loses key employees, especially high-level managers or owners, it may suffer. The company may have relied heavily on the employee and as a result may struggle to perform as well financially as it had in the past. This can lead to insolvency, but it can be avoided by not relying too heavily on any one individual employee.

3. Use of out-of-date technology

Although it costs money to update technology, it is often a very worthwhile investment, especially if competitors are using the most recent technology. By trying to save money and operate with old technology, the company may lose productivity and efficiency, and in turn lose business to competitors, resulting in financial problems.

4. Overdependence on one partner

Similar to the loss of a key employee, the loss of a key partner (in the form of a supplier, lender, or customer) could have a negative impact on the company. Relying too heavily on any one associate like this could prove disastrous should that relationship ever end.

5. Undercapitalization

Simply enough, if the company does not have enough money, filing for bankruptcy will almost surely be inevitable. This is especially true if the company green-lights projects for which there is not enough money in an effort to get an edge over competition, or to just try to keep up.

6. Poor information systems

When the company is unable, as a result of poor information systems, to monitor costs, budgets, inventory, cash flows, or industry conditions, it will be unable to operate effectively. Without the ability to properly monitor and manage finances and operations, decision-making becomes difficult and problems will arise.

7. Hanging on to unproductive areas

If there are divisions or individual employees within a company that are especially unproductive, the company should be able to recognize this and eliminate them. Otherwise, these weak spots will eat up cash and company resources without bringing in any business or money, and this could eventually result in bankruptcy if let go for too long.

8. Poor accounts receivable management

To pay the bills, the company must have the incoming cash flow it deserves. This means that outstanding debts must be paid and no new products or services should be provided to people who still owe the company money. Without proper enforcement, the company will provide too many services without getting paid for its efforts, and this could lead to bankruptcy.

Source: Andrew J. Sherman is a partner in the Washington, D.C. office of Dickstein Shapiro Morin & Oshinsky LLP (*www.dsmo.com*), with more than 350 attorneys nationwide. Mr. Sherman is a recognized international authority on the legal and strategic issues affecting small and growing companies. He is an adjunct professor in the master's of Business Administration program at the University of Maryland and Georgetown University where he teaches courses on business growth, capital formation, and entrepreneurship. He the founder of Grow Fast Grow Right, an education and training company for executives of middle-market companies (*www.growfast-growright.com*) and the author of fourteen books on the legal and strategic aspects of business growth and capital formation. He can be reached at (202) 833-5000 or e-mail *ShermanA@dsmo.com*.

Top Reasons Businesses File for Bankruptcy

Ideally, you will never encounter financial problems large enough to require you to file for bankruptcy. Unfortunately, there is no way to predict absolutely whether bankruptcy will ever become necessary. You can, however, work to avoid bankruptcy by learning from the mistakes of other companies. To help with this, the following list contains the most common reasons businesses file for bankruptcy.

1. Industrywide problems

Deteriorating economic conditions across entire industries can often lead to individual companies becoming insolvent. For example, industrywide struggles have led to several individual airlines filing for bankruptcy and undoubtedly have a similar impact on other companies who rely on the strength of the industry to stay afloat.

2. Expansion problems

Companies can run into financial problems when making large strides to improve their business. A company that is overly aggressive in their expansion efforts may overpay for businesses it acquires along the way. This can lead to financial instability if the company borrows the money to purchase the other businesses and does not generate enough money to repay that debt.

3. Improved competition

The need to file bankruptcy may not have anything to do with the operations of the company but, instead, might result from an inability to keep up with competitors that are better capitalized and have better operations. This could result in customers switching to the better company and/or the weaker company trying to overcompensate for the differences, which can result in further financial problems.

Source: Robert Lapowsky, attorney and shareholder with the Philadelphia office of the firm of Stevens and Lee, is an American Board of Certification–certified business bankruptcy lawyer who has been practicing since 1979. He is a member of the American Bankruptcy Institute, Eastern District of Pennsylvania Bankruptcy Conference, Pennsylvania Bar Association, and American Bar Association. He can be reached at Stevens & Lee, 1818 Market Street, 29th Floor, Philadelphia, PA 19103; (215) 751-2866; e-mail: rl@stevenslee.com.

The Differences Between Chapters 7 and 11 Business Bankruptcies

The possibility of bankruptcy is an unfortunate reality of both business and personal life, and can often strike small businesses that run into financial problems. However, not all bankruptcy is the same, and there are different forms of bankruptcy filings within the business bankruptcy arena. Chapter 7 and Chapter 11 are the two most common forms of bankruptcy; the following is a guide to help us sort out the major differences between the two types of filings.

1. Court-appointed trustee versus existing management

In Chapter 7, a trustee is appointed by the court to take control of the company and guide it through the process of liquidating assets and repaying creditors. In Chapter 11, while under limited circumstances, the court may appoint a trustee; in most cases, the company's management and board of directors stay in place and control the company. One reason for this difference is that under Chapter 11, the company can continue to operate while reorganizing, hence the need for management that knows and understands the company and industry.

2. Liquidation versus reorganization

Chapter 7 forces the company to liquidate all of its assets to repay creditors. Chapter 11, however, allows the company to continue to operate and reorganize its debts, while having the option of liquidating some assets. As mentioned, the company's management usually stays in control to operate the company during the Chapter 11 process.

3. Distributions with or without plans of reorganization

In Chapter 7, the trustee makes distributions to creditors without a plan of reorganization, meaning the process of paying off debts can begin sooner and with less administrative work. On the other hand, in Chapter 11, a reorganization plan must be confirmed before distributions are made to creditors, and this can be a long and expensive process.

Source: Robert Lapowsky, attorney and shareholder with the Philadelphia office of the firm of Stevens and Lee, is an American Board of Certification–certified business bankruptcy lawyer who has been practicing since 1979. He is a member of the American Bankruptcy Institute, Eastern District of Pennsylvania Bankruptcy Conference, Pennsylvania Bar Association, and American Bar Association. He can be reached at Stevens & Lee, 1818 Market Street, 29th Floor, Philadelphia, PA 19103; (215) 751-2866; e-mail: rl@stevenslee.com.

Top Reasons for Businesses to File Chapter 7 Bankruptcy

Bankruptcy is something business owners seek to avoid, but unfortunately it is also something that becomes a reality for some businesses.

Should such a situation arise, there are different options for bankruptcy filings, with Chapter 7 (liquidation) and Chapter 11 (reorganization) being the most common forms of business bankruptcy. To help with the decision on which type of bankruptcy to file, here are the top reasons for a business to file Chapter 7.

1. Automatic stay of debts

Since there is an automatic freeze put on creditors from collecting on debts, the debtor is protected from lawsuits and their associated costs, as well as from aggressive creditors claiming a large number of assets. In Chapter 7, the automatic stay is designed to ensure that the business can liquidate itself without having to worry about creditors pounding down the doors.

2. Court-appointed trustee

The management and board of directors of a company are relieved of their decision-making duties, and a court-appointed trustee steps in to oversee the bankruptcy process. This could in some cases be viewed as a drawback, but it can also be a positive for management and a board that want to move on to other things.

3. Claims deadline

Creditors are required to file claims by a certain date in order to collect on their debts; claims disputes can be resolved quickly with an expedited process. This will force creditors to cooperate with the process in order to be repaid.

4. Distribution without reorganization

Under Chapter 7, the trustee makes distributions to creditors without a reorganization plan.

This allows debts to be paid off faster and the entire process becomes quicker and less complicated as less administrative work is required before debts can be repaid.

Source: Robert Lapowsky, attorney and shareholder with the Philadelphia office of the firm of Stevens and Lee, is an American Board of Certification–certified business bankruptcy lawyer who has been practicing since 1979. He is a member of the American Bankruptcy Institute, Eastern District of Pennsylvania Bankruptcy Conference, Pennsylvania Bar Association, and American Bar Association. He can be reached at Stevens & Lee, 1818 Market Street, 29th Floor, Philadelphia, PA 19103; (215) 751-2866; e-mail: rl@stevenslee .com.

Top Reasons for Businesses to File Chapter 11 Bankruptcy

Bankruptcy is something business owners seek to avoid, but unfortunately it is also something that becomes a reality for some businesses. Should such a situation arise, there are different options for bankruptcy filings, with Chapter 7 (liquidation) and Chapter 11 (reorganization) being the most common forms of business bankruptcy. To help with the decision on which type of bankruptcy to file, here are the top reasons for a business to file Chapter 11.

1. Business continuity

Chapter 11 allows the debtor to remain in business and attempt to reorganize debts. This, along with the automatic stay of debts, allows the company to maintain operations and thus gives it a chance to make the money necessary to pay off its debts.

2. Management remains in control

In Chapter 7, a court-appointed trustee takes over the debtor; in Chapter 11, the debtor's management stays in control of the business. This allows the people who know the company and the industry best to navigate their way through the bankruptcy process.

3. Automatic stay

Just as in Chapter 7 bankruptcy, there is an automatic stay on debts and creditors cannot bring lawsuits or collect large amounts of assets. This saves the debtor time and money that it can use to reorganize without pressure from creditors.

4. Claims deadline

Another benefit similar to that in Chapter 7, creditors must file a claim by a certain date, and disputes can be resolved quickly. This helps the process move smoothly and more quickly, since it reduces the amount of time spent waiting for creditors to file claims or for disputes to be resolved.

Source: Robert Lapowsky, attorney and shareholder with the Philadelphia office of the firm of Stevens and Lee, is an American Board of Certification–certified business bankruptcy lawyer who has been practicing since 1979. He is a member of the American Bankruptcy Institute, Eastern District of Pennsylvania Bankruptcy Conference, Pennsylvania Bar Association, and American Bar Association. He can be reached at Stevens & Lee, 1818 Market Street, 29th Floor, Philadelphia, PA 19103; (215) 751-2866; e-mail: *rl@stevenslee.com*.

Top Ways to Build a Better Board of Directors

A board of directors is a legal structure that protects and represents the interests of a company's shareholders. Choosing a good corporate board takes time and energy, but it's critical to your company's success. Picking the right team will increase opportunities and reduce problems. So how do you go about assembling the right group? Here's a list to show you the way.

1. Choose people with experience

Certainly, you want people who are well-connected, and you want people who make themselves available when you need help. But experience counts. Above all, you want people who have sold, acquired, and merged companies as well as taken them public. Recruit directors with expertise in the issues most likely to arise for your company.

2. Choose people with diverse skills

Recruit directors who have critical skill sets and who supplement your knowledge base. Finance and marketing usually fall into this category, but there are many other areas of expertise—such as e-commerce—that may be specifically crucial to your success. In addition, be aware that venture capitalists usually want a board seat in exchange for investing, in order to look after their interests. They can be of substantial value to your company.

3. Choose people who know your industry

You want professionals who can speak from experience and provide perspective on industry trends. These are not people who work for your competitors but rather ones who work in complementary or related fields.

4. Choose independent-minded directors

A common mistake that entrepreneurs make is to choose board members who are friendly to their cause. While it may be comforting to know these people are likely to side with you no matter how faulty your decision–making is, you deprive yourself of the opportunity for an honest, independent performance appraisal. An independent board that includes people who aren't insiders, major investors, company advisers, or golf buddies is in the best position to take an unbiased view of the company's performance and that of the CEO. This is exactly what you need if you're going to be successful.

5. Choose outsiders

Boards sometimes need to deal with such sensitive internal issues as the performance of key executives, including the CEO. Other issues they face may be directly related to the future of the company, such as succession, funding, or merger/acquisitions. These issues are best handled when the board is able to speak freely. A board with too many representatives from management has to contend with leaks to the staff, politicking, and people who have a vested interest in outcomes that may not necessarily be good for the company.

6. Choose people who are local

Make your life easier by picking board members who are easily accessible. There can be too many logistical problems if your directors have to get on a plane to attend your board

meetings: You have to worry about weather in other parts of the country and they have to allocate more time for travel.

7. Actively involve your board

Although CEOs sometimes view their directors as nuisances, the board is a strategic asset that plays a key role in corporate governance. Outside board members can be effective in evaluating the company's strategy, as no one else is in a position to question the CEO. In addition, qualified board members have a wealth of contacts that the CEO can tap into for potential customers, partners, management-team members, or additional investors. Don't hesitate to ask for—and insist on—directors' involvement in specific issues. The good ones do their homework before quarterly meetings, talk to managers and employees between meetings, and have a financial stake in the business so they truly represent shareholders' interests.

8. Communicate frequently with your board

A board functions best when it is prepared; ill-informed directors don't make the best decisions. Before any board meeting, call all directors and give them a brief overview of the major topics to be covered. If possible, provide all of them with necessary materials for review. There should be no surprises at a board meeting—especially bad news. Surprise forces members to react on the spot, without adequate time to reflect on appropriate alternatives. Directors need to know both the current state of company and any major pending issues, so they have time to think them through.

9. Listen to your board

Sometimes you are so close to an issue, you can't see it clearly. If the board disagrees with you, remember that they are not after your job. They are simply doing what, in their opinion, is best for the company and its shareholders. If you treat your board of directors as an adversary, you miss out on the value they can provide. But if you see them as an ally, you'll be able to tap into a significant resource that offers a tremendous payoff to you and your company.

10. Fire bad board members

Board members must be willing and able to spend the time necessary to help the company; otherwise, they shouldn't be on the board. If you realize you've made a bad choice, be prepared to fix the problem. You guessed it: fire him or her.

Source: Geri Stengel, president of Stengel Solutions (*www.stengel-solutions.com*), a business strategist. Stengel Solutions is a strategic planning and marketing firm specializing in solutions for industry leaders, growth businesses, and nonprofits. She can be reached at (212) 362-3088.

Reasons and Roles for a Board of Directors

If you have decided to incorporate, you may choose to have a board of directors, especially if the company is growing to the point where there are too many shareholders to effectively make important decisions. To get an idea of the key benefits of having a board of directors, we asked our experts to provide a list.

1. Connects owners and operators

When there are too many owners to effectively govern the company, power is given to the board of directors, who can then serve as an intermediary between the owners (shareholders) and those operating the company (senior management). This means the two sides will not be alienated and their respective authorities will work in conjunction. This is the central role of the board as an authoritative group.

2. Accountability/authority

The existence of the board allows for a recognized highest authority within the company. In addition to being the highest authority, the board, as a group, is also held accountable for all aspects of the company. This produces a structured design to the corporation where those in charge are clearly designated.

3. Security

The board of directors will monitor the operations of the company to ensure that things are running smoothly, that all necessary information is properly disclosed, and that investors are confident in the security and stability of the company. In doing so, the board assesses management's performance and implements changes, or even replaces management, when necessary.

4. Connections

Individual directors will almost inevitably have many contacts to key individuals and groups outside the corporation. At the behest of management, their connections to financial institutions, ability to conduct public relations activities, and ability to court potential customers could prove invaluable to the corporation.

5. Expert advice

The members of a board of directors will have knowledge, skills, and experience in the management of a corporation and can provide those running the operations of the company with advice on how to improve and strengthen the corporation, including the development of quality managers.. They can initiate offers to advise or can serve as a source of feedback for managers when asked. This is a nonauthoritative contribution of individual directors, so it must not be allowed to interfere with the board's authoritative role or the authority it has delegated to management.

Source: *Corporate Boards that Create Value*, by John Carver, with Caroline Oliver (Jossey-Bass, 2002). John Carver is the author or coauthor of five books on board leadership, the author of more than 150 journal articles on the topic, and is the coeditor of the bimonthly newsletter "Board Leadership." Caroline Oliver is the editor of *The Policy Governance Fieldbook* and is a founder and previous board chair of the International Policy Governance Association. More information on the authors is available at *www.carvergovernance.com* and *www.carolineoliver.com*, respectively.

Things to Include in a Noncompete Agreement

When hiring others to work on your team, it is a good business practice to require employees and consultants to sign noncompete agreements so that they won't leave and start a competing company, go to work for a competitor, solicit customers, or use and/or disclose company confidential information. Here is a list of essential components of a noncompete agreement.

1. Business interests being protected

Noncompete agreements are enforceable to the extent that they protect legitimate business interests. It is important to identify the specific business interests being protected (such as customer information, proprietary methods and tools, company confidential information including trade secrets).

2. Description of duties

The type of position and duties greatly influences the individual's access to company confidential information and the potential for harm to the company. Hence, post-employment restrictions are more appropriate for someone with access to key technologies or key customers than for an entry-level person. Using the same noncompete for all employees can backfire. The noncompete needs to be tailored to the specific situation. If the duties or position change (for example, an employee is promoted), a new noncompete may need to be prepared and signed.

3. Clear definition of restricted activities

The law favors allowing people to earn a living in their chosen profession. Overly broad restrictions are not enforceable. To make the agreement "reasonable" (and hence, more likely to be "enforceable"), consider focusing on specific restrictions such as restricting solicitation of customers or working for specific direct competitors, or limiting the applications/markets in which the person is restricted from working.

4. Duration of the restrictions

The length of the restrictions must also be reasonable. A reasonable term for a noncompete for a traditional company may be one year after termination of employment. For Internet companies, the reasonable term may be six months because the technologies and markets are changing so quickly.

5. Geography of restrictions

Reasonable geographic restrictions may be 15 miles from the current location for retail, or 50 to 100 miles depending on the business. For Internet-based businesses, geographic restrictions must be carefully defined since Web sites can be accessed from anywhere on the planet.

6. Allowable activities

Allowable activities probably include working for nonprofits or noncompeting companies. For consultants, who frequently work for a number of companies in the same industry, I recommend adding language that states that "the hiring company acknowledges that you perform similar work for other companies in the _____ industry and that nothing in this agreement precludes you from such work as long as the confidentiality of the hiring company's confidential information is preserved."

7. Disclosure of prior noncompetes

Previously signed noncompetes should be disclosed so that there are no surprises from a former employer seeking to enforce restrictions.

8. Assignment of rights

It's important to establish that the company owns the rights to inventions created by employees or contractors. This language can be included in a noncompete agreement or other documents related to the worker or project.

9. New employee or current employee

New employees can be asked to sign noncompetes. But, be cautious about forcing current employees to sign noncompetes. To be enforceable, a noncompete must be supported by "consideration." "Consideration" is a legal term for something of value. If the noncompete is signed prior to beginning employment, hiring is the "consideration." For existing employees, something of value (in addition to their current compensation) must be given.

10. Reasonableness

The noncompete should state that it is reasonable and that the employee/contractor acknowledges that it does not unduly restrict postemployment opportunities. In conclusion, reasonable noncompetes can protect an employer's interests without unduly restricting an individual's future options. Using a boilerplate agreement, "one size fits all situations" is not a good approach. You are better served by tailoring an agreement to the specific employee/contractor and identifying the specific business interests being protected. While enforcement varies from state to state, the basic rule is that noncompete agreements are enforceable if they: are fair and reasonable (in scope, duration, and geography); protect legitimate business interests; and do not impose substantial hardship (preclude a person from earning a living).

Source: Jean D. Sifleet, Esq., CPA, is an attorney whose career spans many years in large multinational corporations and includes three successful entrepreneurial ventures. Jean has extensive experience in dealing with noncompete agreements and intellectual property matters in the large and small companies and as a small business owner. She has authored numerous books and publications, including *Beyond 401(k)s for Small Business Owners—A Practical Guide to Incentive, Deferred Compensation and Retirement Plans* (John Wiley & Sons, 2004). This article is excerpted from her new book, *Advantage IP—Profit from Your Great Ideas* (Infinity, 2005). For more information, Jean's Web site is *www.smartfast.com*.

The Rights That Belong to a Copyright Owner

These are often referred to as "the bundle of rights." Your copyright gives you the right to stop others from the following actions.

1. Copying

Copying or reproducing your work directly.

2. Making

Making new works based on your work (these new works are called "derivative works").

3. Selling

Selling or distributing copies of the work.

4. Performing or displaying

Performing or displaying the work publicly.

5. Building

Building based on copyrighted plans (e.g., architectural drawings).

6. Destroying, altering, or removing

Destroying, altering, or removing copyrighted artwork built into buildings, under some circumstances. (This is not really copyright, as such, but it is a related protection under a different law.)

Source: Michael F. Brown (*www.bpmlegal.com*) is a partner in the Ithaca, New York, law firm Brown & Michaels PC. He has prosecuted many patent applications in a wide variety of fields, from animal vaccines to computer software, avionics and automotive products, household appliances to radio communications. Contact him at (607) 256-2000, ext. 11; e-mail: *brown@bpmlegal.com*.

Popular Types of Liens

A lien is a protection for a creditor that gives them the right to take control of property of a debtor if the debt is not paid. Liens are common, found in situations such as borrowing money from a bank for a car, in which case the bank would have a lien on the car until the loan is repaid. There are many situations in which a lien would come into play. The following is a list of common statutory liens.

1. Architect's lien

This is a lien on real property in favor of the architect who drew the plans and supervised the construction to insure payment of his or her fee.

2. Artisan/laborer's lien

This is a lien in favor of a person who is provided personal services that enhanced the value of an article of personal property at the request of the owner. The person has a lien on the article while it's in his or her possession and may retain possession until paid for services.

3. Carrier's lien

This lien ensures that a carrier has a right to hold cargo until payment is made for transporting it.

4. Garageman's lien

This is a lien in favor of a mechanic and against a motor vehicle, where the mechanic provided services to the motor vehicle at the request of the owner.

5. Judgment lien

This is a lien in favor of the holder of a judgment against property, both real and personal belonging to the judgment debtor.

6. Landlord lien

When provided for in a lease, this is a lien in favor of the landlord and against the personal property of the tenant located within the demised premises, as security for the payment of rent.

7. Maritime lien

This lien is a claim on a vessel for some service rendered to it to facilitate its use in navigation.

8. Mechanic's lien

This is a lien in favor of workers and suppliers of material for the value of work performed and materials furnished to construct or repair a structure. The lien attaches to the real property upon which the structure is located.

9. Tax lien

This is a lien in favor of taxing authority for payment of taxes.

10. Warehouseman's lien

This lien provides for the right of a warehouse to retain possession of goods until storage charges have been paid.

Source: Joseph Mitchell, an attorney with the firm of Harris Beach, of Rochester, New York (*www.harrisbeach.com*)—He is the leader of the firm's Collections Law practice group and focuses his practice on creditors' rights, collections, real estate, banking law, and regulation. He can be reached at Harris Beach PLLC, 99 Garnsey Road, Pittsford, NY 14534; (585) 419-8800; e-mail: *jmitchell@harrisbeach.com*.

Laws That Most Often Affect Business

As a business owner or manager, it is your responsibility to know what laws affect your business. Since every business, in every state, in every country is different, the laws that affect your business may be different than the laws that affect other businesses. Here our expert provides a list that will save you time, money, and grief by finding out what laws will affect your business ahead of time and keeping up-to-date on changes in the laws.

1. Business structure

If your business is a sole proprietorship, you may need a DBA (Doing Business As) certificate and a business license for the city in which you do business. Corporations have other requirements, which also vary from state to state. Find out what laws affect you based on your business structure.

2. Zoning laws

It is illegal to operate certain types of businesses in certain areas. Check with your local zoning commission to find out where you can operate the type of business that you have.

3. Licenses and permits

Different businesses may require specific licenses and permits. Make sure you have all the necessary licenses and permits specific to your business.

4. Laws specific to corporations

There are many tax laws and other laws that are specific to corporations. These laws vary from state to state, and generally affect how the corporation is set up and managed, and how stocks and securities are handled.

5. Environmental laws

If your business handles chemicals, hazardous wastes, or other materials that affect the environment, the Environmental Protection Agency will have laws that affect your business.

6. Employment laws

Employment laws will affect how you hire employees, how you pay them, and how you treat them. Failure to comply with employment laws will almost always result in a lawsuit, or an investigation by the Labor Board in your state.

7. Tax laws

There are too many tax laws for most business owners to keep up with—unless they are tax professionals. In order to comply with the tax laws, it is best to hire a tax professional.

8. Business and contract laws

Just as tax laws are complicated, contract laws are complicated as well. Protect yourself and your interests by hiring a business lawyer to help you comply with these laws, and to use these laws to protect yourself and your business.

9. Consumer protection laws

These laws are designed to protect consumers from fraud and from defective or dangerous products. A business lawyer can usually help you in this area as well.

10. Internet laws

If you conduct any portion of your business on the Internet, you must comply with specific laws. The biggest issue facing business owners conducting business on the Internet is the new SPAM laws.

Source: GlobalBX (*www.GlobalBX.com*) is a *free* business-for-sale listing exchange that provides a confidential forum to facilitate the buying and selling of businesses with thousands of businesses and franchises for sale as well as comprehensive business information for business buyers and sellers. Members can submit business, equipment and commercial real-estate loans to hundreds of direct lenders for *free*. Resources include buyer and seller's guides, franchise information, business loans, message boards, newsletter, business brokers, and advisers. View the Web site at *www.GlobalBX.com* or contact them at 5255 Stevens Creek Blvd., Suite 130, Santa Clara, CA 95051, or via e-mail at *service@globalbx.com*.

Things You Should Know about the Civil Rights Act

The Civil Rights Act prohibits employers with fifteen or more employees from discriminating against candidates and employees in all phases of employment. Many provisions of this act could directly affect you and your business. So here's a few things that you should know about this very important law.

1. Title VII of the Civil Rights Act

Title VII of the Civil Rights Act of 1964, also known as Equal Employment Opportunity (EEO) mandates, prohibits employers with fifteen or more employees from discriminating against applicants and employees in all aspects of employment—including recruiting, hiring, pay, promotion, training, and termination—on the basis of race, color, national origin, religion, or gender.

2. Employment decisions

Employment decisions, therefore, must be made on the basis of business necessity, not on an employee's or applicant's membership in a protected class.

3. Exceptions to Title VII

There are exceptions to Title VII that allow you to require that an applicant be a certain race, color, religion, or gender. These exceptions are known as bona fide occupational qualifications (BFOQs). BFOQs are rarely used because they are exceedingly difficult to justify.

4. Areas most affected

Areas most affected by Title VII include job advertisements, job qualifications, hiring decisions, job applications, interviews, discipline, and termination.

Source: CCH Business Owner's Toolkit (*www.toolkit.cch.com*)—The Business Owner's Toolkit provides advice, guides, legal tools, business models, and other resources to small business owners.

What to Do If You Are Accused of Patent Infringement

The time may come when you receive a letter saying you might be infringing someone else's patent or published application. Our expert, an experienced patent attorney, provides this list to help you cope with the accusation.

1. Don't panic! (with a tip of the hat to the Hitchhiker's Guide to the Galaxy)

Just because someone says you might be infringing on a patent (or a published application) does not mean that you are. In many cases, it turns out after investigation that the accused product does not infringe at all. Even if you are infringing, it's not the end of the world. Calm down, take a deep breath, and follow along.

2. Call a lawyer, immediately, and make an appointment.

Patent infringement accusations are not "do-it-yourself projects." You need professional advice, and you need it right away. Don't expect the lawyer who wrote your will or represented you when you bought your house to be of much help. You need a patent attorney, or a litigator with a patent attorney on call.

3. While you're waiting to see the lawyer, get your ducks in a row.

The infringement accusation should have listed the number of the patent you are accused of infringing. Go to the U.S. Patent and Trademark

Office Web site (*www.uspto.gov/patft/*) and download a copy of the patent.

4. Be prepared to discuss certain questions.

Have you made, used, or sold anything since the date of the patent that might be covered by the patent? Is there any part of the independent claims that your products clearly lack? When did you start selling your potentially infringing products? Was it more than a year before the filing date? Do you know of anything that was published more than a year before the filing date of the patent that describes the same device or method in the patent? Since the patentee's own sales are covered by the same one-year bar, do you know they were selling more than a year before they filed for their patent?

5. Do some research.

Look at old catalogs, advertisements, magazines, trade publications, even bid documents if you sell to government agencies. Do a worldwide Web search and see if you can find any Web pages that describe the patented invention and that might predate their filing.

6. Bring all of the documentation to your appointment with the attorney, and have him or her explain your situation.

You will probably have overreacted by this time—use this appointment as a reality check. Before you leave the attorney's office, make sure you understand exactly where you stand, as best as can be determined at that time. Know what you will need to do, what the risk is, and what your attorney will be doing.

7. Your attorney should contact the other side's attorney to let them know that they're not being ignored.

Whatever you do, don't try to handle the contact with the other side yourself. This situation needs to be handled by people who don't have an investment of ego, on either side.

8. Ask your attorney do an infringement analysis of your products and the patent.

This analysis will take some time and it will not be cheap, but you must have an infringement analysis (and maybe a validity study as well) if you are not simply going to go out of business at the first accusation. That's an option, of course, but if you were going to take it, you wouldn't be reading this list, would you? The attorney will probably have to order a copy of the prosecution history of the patent to properly interpret the claims. He or she may want to do a patent search to find invalidating art and will formally need to compare the claims in the patent to your product. If you are infringing the patent, your attorney may tell you informally. If not, your counsel should give you a formal written opinion that you can rely on if you are sued for infringement. The opinion won't insulate you from liability for infringement, but it will most likely keep the court from increasing damages for "willful" infringement.

9. Listen to the attorney's advice.

Your attorney is on your side, and you're paying for the advice. Listen to it.

Source: Michael F. Brown, patent attorney, chief operations officer, and partner in the Ithaca, New York, law firm Brown & Michaels PC (www.bpmlegal.com)—Mr. Brown was admitted to the New York State Bar in 1981 and is also admitted to practice in the U.S. District Court for the Eastern District of New York. He has prosecuted many patent applications in a wide variety of fields, from animal vaccines to computer software, avionics to automotive products, household appliances to radio communications. Contact him at (607) 256-2000, ext. 11, or at brown@bpmlegal.com.

Resources for Patent Searching

Because of the limitations of keyword searching (one person's screw is another's threaded fastener), it is best to use general keywords to find a related patent, and then use the patent classification system to find patents in that class and subclass. Here our expert provides a list of his best patent search resources.

1. United States Patent and Trademark Office (USPTO)

All issued U.S. patents and published U.S. patent applications are searchable by patent classification or number through this site. Keyword searching is possible on the full text of all U.S. patents issued in 1976 or later, and all published U.S. patent applications. A free plug-in is required to view patent drawings, and images of patents before 1976; follow the links on the Web site to download the plug-in.

www.uspto.gov/patft/

2. European Patent Office (EPO)

This site permits free keyword searching of titles and abstracts of millions of patents and published applications from around the world. Patents may also be searched by International Classification. Acrobat PDF Reader is required to view drawings.

http://ep.espacenet.com

3. Canadian Intellectual Property Office (CIPO)

Search the database for Canadian patents and published applications.

http://patents1.ic.gc.ca/intro-e.html

4. Japanese Patent Office (JPO)

Keyword or number searching of Japanese patents and published applications. Japanese patents, applications, and utility models (Kokai) may be retrieved by number.

www.ipdl.ncipi.go.jp/homepg_e.ipdl

5. Delphion

Formerly the IBM patent server, this for-pay subscription service allows searching U.S., European, Japanese, German and PCT applications by keyword or classification system. Adobe PDF Reader required.

www.delphion.com

6. Micropatent PatentWeb

Another for-pay subscription service. Offers full-text searching of all issued U.S. patents, as well as patents issued by other countries.

www.micropat.com

Source: Michael F. Brown (*www.bpmlegal.com*) is a partner in the Ithaca, New York, law firm Brown & Michaels PC. Brown has prosecuted many patent applications in a wide variety of fields, from animal vaccines to computer software, avionics and automotive products, household appliances to radio communications. Contact him at (607) 256-2000 ext. 11, or at *brown@bpmlegal.com*.

Typical Steps for Filing a Patent

Patent rights are granted by national patent offices, and so patent protection for an invention must be sought in each country individually. The procedure generally involves three steps. Our expert, an internationally renowned patent attorney, explains the process in this list.

1. Write a patent application

The first step in getting a patent on an invention is to write a patent application. In this application, you must disclose the invention in sufficient detail for the average skilled person to be able to reconstruct it. This way, anyone should be able to rebuild the invention and apply it once the patent rights run out. Writing a patent application is a tricky business, especially when it comes to claim writing. It is common for an inventor to write a detailed description and figures, while the claims and the brief description are written by a patent attorney based on the information in the detailed description.

2. A patent application is published

A patent application is published eighteen months after it has been filed (or 18 months after its priority application, if any, has been filed). This way, the world is informed about the fact that a patent can be expected on that particular invention. Someone else using the invention could then switch to a different technology or make reservations to pay for a license once the patent is granted. He or she could also start looking for relevant prior art (for example, documents on his or her use of the invention before the filing date) to get the patent annulled if it is granted eventually.

Once it has been published, the invention is there for all to see, and you, as the inventor, have lost control. If the patent application is subsequently rejected, you can't gain exclusivity through your patent nor through keeping the invention a trade secret. During the examination process, you have a chance to modify your claims and sometimes part of the description. This means that the patent as granted may differ substantially from the patent application as published. The patent as granted is also published, and the rights granted by a patent becomes effective upon publication.

3. Patent is compared to the state-of-the-art

To determine whether an invention is patentable, it must be compared against what was known at the day before the day of filing of the application. This is known as "the state-of-the-art" or the "prior art." Some countries, most notably the United States, have a so-called grace period. Publications by the inventor during the grace period, which can range to up to one year before the filing of the patent application, are also not considered to be part of the state-of-the-art. However, this only applies to the patent application for the countries in which such a grace period exists. Any publication of the invention makes that invention part of the state-of-the-art. Examples are publishing in journals, showing the invention at an exhibition, or giving a lecture about the invention. Almost always, the patent office will only consider databases containing printed publications because they are the easiest to search. In Europe, a separate search report is published next to the patent application. The applicant can then evaluate the search results and decide whether there is anything patentable left. If so, the patent application moves to the next stage: the examination. In the United States, no separate search report is published.

4. Patent is examined

After the state-of-the-art has been determined, the patent application is compared against the state-of-the-art by an examiner. The purpose is to determine whether the invention is novel and whether it involves an inventive step (is nonobvious). In order to accurately determine what the invention is, each patent application contains a number of claims at the end of the application. These claims define the invention and indicate for what patent protection is sought. So, the application may describe in very broad wording how the apparatus according to the invention to be constructed, but if the claims described only one specific example, then that specific example is considered to be the invention, regardless of the rest of the application.

Source: Arnoud Engelfriet, a European patent attorney who maintains a Web site called Ius mentis (*www.iusmentis.com*), which is Latin for "legal rights on mental things" (i.e., the rights granted by copyright, patent, or trademark law). The purpose of Ius mentis is to explain law and technology. The site has more than 250 articles on the subject. Engelfriet can be contacted through his Web site.

Reasons to Have a U.S. Patent

Before listing reasons you may want to file for a patent, it would be a good idea to review what a patent is, and is not: A patent is a grant by the U.S. Patent and Trademark Office of the right to stop others from making, using, or selling an invention in the United States for a limited period. A patent is not the right to practice your invention yourself; there might be other people with superior rights to yours who have "dominating patents" and can stop you from making, using, or selling until their patents expire. So, why might you want to have a patent?

1. Protecting your sales from competitors

This is the classic use of a patent: to stop others from making, using, or selling your invention.

2. Having something to license

If you don't intend to sell products, but do want to sell or license your rights in an invention, as an invention, then a patent or patent application gives you something to sell or license.

3. Advertising

There is some value to being able to advertise that your product is protected by a patent, or, if the patent hasn't issued (yet) that it is "patent pending." Many consumers will take this as a government endorsement of the product—"so wonderful, it's even got a patent!" Of course, while a patent isn't an endorsement, it is an indication that there was some novelty to the product, and that the genuine product can only be obtained from you or your licensees.

4. Raising money

Venture capitalists and banks like to see that a new company has patents, or at least patent applications filed, as an indication that the company has some intellectual assets and solidity. Most bankers and VCs can't actually read the patents or understand what they cover, but they are impressed by numbers.

5. Stopping others from getting patents that might interfere with your business

You cannot get a patent on something that was previously patented or disclosed in a publication. By filing an application on an invention, you make sure that no one who files after you will be able to get a patent that they could enforce against you. This applies equally well to published applications as to issued patents, so some people are filing applications they have no intention of actually paying to issue as patents, simply to get the subject matter on record. Of course, any publication will serve the same purpose; put up a Web page or an ad in a local newspaper, and your idea is published. However, such outside publications are difficult to search and will not be found by patent examiners. Published applications will be found by a patent search; thus, for patent purposes, they are more effective.

6. Getting in the way of competitors' ability to expand

This is called "patenting ahead of the competition." Some companies will try to figure out improvements to their competitors' products, and get patents on them as roadblocks for their competition. Of course, it takes fairly deep pockets to pull that off.

7. Trading material

If you've got a patent that is useful to a competitor, and they have one that you need,

you can trade patent rights. This is called "cross-licensing."

Source: Michael F. Brown is a partner in the Ithaca, New York, law firm Brown & Michaels PC(*www.bpmlegal.com*)—Brown has prosecuted many patent applications in a wide variety of fields, from animal vaccines to computer software, avionics and automotive products, household appliances to radio communications. Contact him at (607) 256-2000, ext. 11, or at *brown@bpmlegal.com*.

Ways to Protect Your Intellectual Property

Often the hardest part of figuring out how to protect your idea is to determine what kind of protection is most appropriate. This is complicated by the fact that ideas, as such, aren't really protected—what you can protect is the expression of an idea in the form of a product, a book or computer program, a painting or photograph, even a name for a product or service.

1. Patents

Patents are appropriate for "useful things" or methods of doing something. There are three main kinds of patents. Utility patents cover "inventions"—a machine, an article of manufacture, a method of doing something, a chemical or DNA sequence or the method of its use, products of genetic engineering, or improvements to any of these things. Plant patents may be granted to anyone who invents or discovers, and asexually reproduces, a new variety of certain kinds of plants. (Other kinds of plants, especially those altered by genetic engineering, may be protectable under utility patents.) Design patents cover the ornamental appearance of a useful device but not its function. For example, the "Swoosh" on the side of a Nike sneaker was the subject of a design patent.

2. Trademarks

Trademarks cover the name or some other symbol (logo) that represents the source of a product or service. Sometimes the appearance of a product or its packaging can be considered a trademark (often called "trade dress"). For example, the name *Coca-Cola*, or the shape of a Coke, bottle are registered trademarks. In rare instances, other things—such as sounds (Tarzan's yell or the MGM lion's roar), a sequence of notes (the NBC chimes), a piece of music (the Harlem Globetrotter's "Sweet Georgia Brown" or the Lone Ranger theme), colors (pink Fiberglas insulation), or even fragrances (a floral scent applied to Clarke thread)—may be registered as trademarks.

3. Copyrights

Copyrights protect works of authorship, composition, or artistry. Copyrights cover books, sculptures, paintings or photographs, computer programs, architectural works, movies and records, musical compositions, and so on. In the case of musical recordings, the copyright may extend to the music itself (tune and lyrics) and the recording of the performance.

4. Trade secrets

This protection is available, as the name suggests, for secrets used in business—the method of making a product or the ingredients that go into it, customer or prospect lists, any fact, which, if known, would give your competition an advantage. The inner workings (algorithms,

source code) of computer programs are often protected as trade secrets. The formula for Coca-Cola is a famous example of a trade secret.

Source: Michael F. Brown is a partner in the Ithaca, New York, law firm Brown & Michaels PC(*www.bpmlegal.com*)—He has prosecuted many patent applications in a wide variety of fields, from animal vaccines to computer software, avionics and automotive products, household appliances to radio communications. Contact him at (607) 256-2000, ext. 11, or at *brown@bpmlegal.com*.

How to Use Your Trademark Properly

Remember that your trademark is an indication of the source of goods or services. It is not the name or description of a specific thing, as such, nor is it necessarily the same as your company name. It is very important that a mark be used correctly, so that the mark's character is preserved. Here's a list of other ways to use your trademark properly.

1. Always use the generic description of the goods in combination with the mark

You can make copies on a "Xerox photocopier"; you do not "make a xerox."

2. Never use the mark as a verb

You can "copy" something on a Xerox copier; you cannot "xerox" it.

3. Capitalize the mark

Xerox, Craftsman, Kodak.

4. Use the word brand if necessary to clarify the status of your mark

"Kleenex Brand Facial Tissues," not "a Kleenex," and seal packages with "Scotch brand adhesive tape" not "scotch tape."

5. Never let your mark become "generic"

You cannot stop your competitors from talking about their products by pre-empting the name of the product. Thus, if a mark is not used correctly, there is a risk of it being declared generic. A generic mark is not really a trademark, but the only way to refer to a product. Some examples of marks that have become generic over the years are "yo-yo" (for "return tops"), "aspirin" (for "acetylsalicylic acid"), "escalator" (for "moving stairs"), "thermos" (for "vacuum flasks"), and "brassiere" (for "ladies' support garment").

6. Give the proper notice that you intend to reserve rights to a trademark

This is done by putting a trademark symbol (the r-in-a-circle symbol ® for federally registered trademarks, ™ or ℠ for unregistered marks) next to the mark when it is used. It isn't necessary to clutter every piece of text with the symbol every single time the mark is used; you just need to give "adequate notice" that you consider the word or phrase to be your mark. Certainly the symbol should be used the first time a mark is used in a document or label, and occasionally thereafter. Some manufacturers put a note on each label or document listing all of the marks on the label or document, and noting the trademark ownership ("Scotch® and

Magic Tape® are Registered Trademarks of 3M Corporation").

7. If you use someone else's trademark, acknowledge their rights

That is, if you talk about "Teflon® nonstick coating," be sure there's a disclaimer somewhere that "Teflon is a registered trademark of DuPont."

Source: Michael F. Brown is a partner in the Ithaca, New York, law firm Brown & Michaels PC (*www.bpmlegal.com*)—He has prosecuted many patent applications in a wide variety of fields, from animal vaccines to computer software, avionics and automotive products, household appliances to radio communications. Contact him at (607) 256-2000, ext. 11, or at *brown@bpmlegal.com*.

How to Choose a Trademark

A trademark search is a basic first step if you are considering adopting a new trademark or service mark. With today's computerized databases, a trademark search is relatively inexpensive and fast, and it is cheap insurance against having to change your mark or defend a lawsuit later. If you have a trademark search done by a service, be sure it includes Federal and State Registered Marks, at a minimum, and an opinion on the results.

1. Choose a mark carefully and be sure you're not infringing

Don't stop with registered marks—check out Web search engines and the Yellow Pages to find anyone using the mark who has not (yet) registered. You wouldn't want to spend a fortune adopting and promoting a mark nationwide, only to find out that a competitor has prior use rights. The test of a mark is "likelihood of confusion"—that is, is the proposed mark so close to an existing mark that it is likely to confuse the intended consumer as to the source of the goods? If there is any question, play it safe and try another mark (or consider contacting the prior user and getting her okay, if you really want to use a mark that might be a problem).

2. Choose the "strongest" mark possible

Marks vary in strength over a spectrum from a coined or invented mark, which can be very strong, through generic marks, which are not really trademarks at all. The stronger a mark is, the broader the protection it is afforded. Coined or Fanciful Marks have no meaning, outside the mark itself. Kodak or Xerox are good examples. Neither had any meaning in any language before they were invented to describe new products. Arbitrary marks use ordinary words, but the words are not associated with the product. For example, Shell for petroleum products, Wishbone for salad dressing, Amazon for a bookseller, Apple for computers. Suggestive marks are less broadly protected, since the words in the mark are associated with the product. They become stronger through use, as the mark acquires distinctiveness. Rent-a-Wreck for auto-renting services is suggestive. Descriptive marks convey an immediate idea of ingredients, qualities, or characteristics of the goods or services. "Very Best" might be a descriptive mark. Chapstick is descriptive, as it immediately suggests a stick for chapping. If the mark functions to identify the source of the goods, either when adopted or through use, it may be registrable, but it is

afforded less protection than coined, arbitrary, or suggestive marks. The division between suggestive and descriptive marks is not always easy to spot. Generic marks, as noted, are not registrable and convey no rights at all.

3. Sources of inspiration

Look in an encyclopedia or dictionary, or to mythology or geography or history for words whose connotations are positive and appropriate to your product. Midas implies wealth (for mufflers? Must be a connection somewhere), Hercules for strength (registered for rope since 1870, among 198 other things), Mercury for speed (FTD florist symbol or boat motors), the Rock of Gibraltar for permanence (used by Prudential Insurance), George Washington for honesty (broth, apples, many others), Obsession for emotional appeal (a perfume brand).

4. Make up your own words

Coined marks can be very strong and valuable, and you can make them sound as if they mean something when they do not. Consider "Häagen-Dazs" ice cream (an all-American product made in New Jersey, but it sounds ever so Scandinavian), or the Oldsmobile Achieva or Compaq Presario (sound elegantly European but are meaningless), or Exxon gasoline (a purely coined mark slightly reminiscent of their former Esso mark, and without the SO [Standard Oil] derivation). If you are planning for a line of products, consider choosing a mark that lends itself to becoming a "family" of marks. For example, Kodak has a wide variety of marks beginning with Kod-, as in Kodell for fabrics, Kodalux for processing, and Kodachrome for film.

5. Avoid these marks

Some marks, otherwise valid, are either prohibited by law or convey no rights. These marks should be avoided: geographic origin or primarily a surname; scandalous or disparaging marks; obscenities, racial or ethnic epithets; insignia of a government agency or of certain organizations protected by law; marks that identify a living individual or deceased president during the life of his widow without consent; famous marks; clever misspellings of otherwise unusable marks; And marks using elements that are protected under other laws.

6. Watch out for pitfalls . . .

Foreign words should be evaluated in terms of their English meanings. The popular "Pschitt soda" from France, or "Bimbo" doughnuts from Mexico are unlikely to make it big under those names in English-speaking countries. "Barberskum" is a Scandinavian word for shaving cream that probably would not be good choice in the United States. The Japanese Asse candy or B-M coffee are also not good bets for import, either. English words should be checked for their meaning in foreign languages, if international marketing is contemplated. Some Coca Cola bottlers found out that the Chinese characters they chose to represent the sounds *Coca Cola* meant "bite the wax tadpole,"not a connotation they would have chosen. Eventually they changed to characters that sounded the same, but meant "happiness in the mouth." Clairol's "Mist Stick" fell flat in Germany, where "mist" is slang for "manure." Consider regional variations in English, too. Other English-speaking countries may have problems with marks that are innocuous in American English. Although you can sell a "fanny pack" in American stores to American boys, British boys would find the suggestion laughable (they don't have "fannies," only girls do, and not in the same place). Most English speakers (other than Americans) would pronounce the letter *Z* as zed, while Americans use *zee*, so any mark depending on either pronunciation would fall flat in the other region (the many American E-Z product names just don't have the same connotation when pronounced "ee-zed"). In reverse, we've been approached by a number of foreign clients over the years who wanted to register English words that were innocuous in their countries but had unsavory or offensive connotations here.

Source: Michael F. Brown is a partner in the Ithaca, New York, law firm Brown & Michaels PC(*www.bpmlegal.com*)—He has prosecuted many patent applications in a wide variety of fields, from animal vaccines to computer software, avionics and automotive products, household appliances to radio communications. Contact him at (607) 256-2000, ext. 11, or at *brown@bpmlegal.com*.

Top Legal Web Sites

For both business owners and individuals, there are a number of legal issues that could pop up at any time. Most of these issues are innocuous and do not require the assistance of an attorney. For such matters, you may be best served by turning to a legal Web site to answer your questions. To provide a guide to which Web sites are the best for addressing certain legal issues, the following is a list of the top legal Web sites, based on internet traffic, from Alexa.com.

1. Internal Revenue Service—*www.irs.gov*

The site for the U.S. tax collecting agency provides tax information for individuals and businesses and also provides downloadable forms, instructions, and IRS publications.

2. U.S. Patent and Trademark Office—*www.uspto.gov*

The Web site of the USPTO provides users with information on applying for patents and trademarks and also provides free search access to patent and trademark databases.

3. Securities and Exchange Committee—*www.sec.gov*

The Web site for the U.S. agency in charge of federal securities laws provides information and electronic filing of forms for businesses and other professionals.

4. FindLaw—*www.findlaw.com*

This is a comprehensive legal information Web site providing information on cases, articles, law schools, bar associations and more for businesses, legal professionals, and the general public.

5. Federal Trade Commission—*www.ftc.gov*

The federal agency charged with protecting the U.S. consumer provides recent news on its Web site as well as information on consumer protection and antitrust law.

6. World Intellectual Property Commission—*www.wipo.int*

Promotes intellectual property throughout the world, and administrates various multilateral treaties.

7. Federal Communications Commission—*www.fcc.gov*

The federal agency that regulates all aspects of telecommunications provides forms, news, and information on communications law on its Web site.

8. Social Security Administration—*www.socialsecurity.gov*

The official site for the SSA provides news, trends, budget information, and publications, among other information, for the general public.

9. Legal Information Institute—*www.law.cornell.edu*

This award-winning site from the Cornell University Law School provides all kinds of legal information and is organized by topic.

10. Nolo—*www.nolo.com*

Nolo provides online legal information, along with sales of self-help books and software.

Source: Alexa.com, Most Popular Web sites in 'Legal Information.' Alexa.com is a search engine that ranks Web sites based on the amount of traffic the sites receive. Alexa provides rankings for Web sites in a wide variety of categories.

Most Prestigious Law Firms

A firm may be big, but are they really worth that high rate per hour? To get an idea of the most prestigious firms, based on the perceptions of other practicing attorneys across the country, our expert provides us with the following list of the top-rated law firms in the country, as rated by their annual Most Prestigious Law Firm survey.

1. Wachtell, Lipton, Rosen, and Katz
51 West 52nd Street
New York, NY 10019
(212) 403-1000
www.wlrk.com

2. Cravath, Swaine, and Moore
Worldwide Plaza
825 Eighth Avenue
New York, NY 10019
(212) 474-1000
www.cravath.com

3. Sullivan and Cromwell LLP
125 Broad St.
New York, NY 10004
(212) 558-4000
www.sullcrom.com

4. Skadden, Arps, Slate, Meagher, & Flom, LLP and Associates
4 Times Square
New York, NY 10036
(212) 735-3000
www.skadden.com

5. Davis, Polk, & Wardwell
450 Lexington Avenue
New York, NY 10017
(212) 450-4000
www.davispolk.com

6. Simpson, Thatcher, & Bartlett, LLP
425 Lexington Avenue
New York, NY 10017
(212) 455-2000

www.simpsonthatcher.com

7. Cleary, Gottlieb, Steen, & Hamilton
One Liberty Plaza
New York, NY 10006
(212) 225-2000
www.clearygottlieb.com

8. Latham & Watkins
633 West Fifth Street
Suite 4000
Los Angeles, CA 90071
(213) 485-1234
www.lw.com

9. Weil, Gotshal, & Manges, LLP
767 Fifth Avenue
New York, NY 10153
(212) 310-8000
www.weil.com

10. Covington & Burling
1201 Pennsylvania Avenue NW
Washington, D.C. 20044
(202) 662-6000
www.cov.com

Source: Vault.com (*www.vault.com*)—A career-information Web site that provides company information, job-seeker advice, and career management services. It was named by *Fortune* magazine as "the best place on the Web to prepare for a job search."

How to Survive Small-Claims Court

Every state has a system of small-claims courts that you can use to collect judgments for small amounts of money … if you have the nerve. Make no mistake, when you bring a suit in small-claims court, you do most of the work yourself, and pleading your own case before a real-life judge can be one of the scariest events of your life, even if you know you are 100 percent in the right. Yet sooner or later, if you run your own business, you will get into a situation where you have to bring an action in small-claims court to collect an overdue debt (or, God forbid, defend yourself against someone who thinks you owe them money). Here is a list of things to help you survive small claims court.

1. Get the pamphlet

The bar association in just about every state publishes a short guidebook, in pamphlet form, that takes you step-by-step through the small-claims court process in that state. This pamphlet, which is called something like "Guide to the Use of Our Small-Claims Courts," is usually available free of charge or for a small fee (less than $5) to cover postage. To find the address and telephone number of your state bar association, type *state bar associations* into your favorite Internet search engine or go to *www.findlaw.com/06associations/state.html*, a Web page that links to the home pages of virtually all state bar associations nationwide. Once you reach your state bar association, ask for their publications department.

2. Watch lots of television

I am absolutely serious about this. Here's a little secret. You know all of those courtroom television shows like *Judge Judy*, *Judge Joe Brown*, and *Judge Mills Lane*? They are all modeled on small-claims court proceedings! If you've never watched any of these shows before (I warn you that you are likely to get hooked on

them), check out the "television judge" Web site at *www.tvjudgeshows.com*, where the strengths and weaknesses of each show are thoroughly discussed. The judges in these TV shows are (or were), after all, real-life judges, and the judge in your small-claims court case is highly likely to behave the way the ones on TV do.

3. Prepare, prepare, prepare

I cannot say this enough—almost always, the victory in small claims court goes to the better-prepared party. If you claim that someone owes you money but (a) you never delivered a proper invoice stating when payment is due, (b) you failed to make a formal written demand for payment, and (c) the debtor has some serious objections to making payment (such as your products and services didn't work as you promised), your path to success in small-claims court will be rocky indeed. When you appear in court, be sure to bring copies of all relevant correspondence (contracts, invoices, purchase orders, warranty forms) that back up your case, in case the judge asks to look at them. Where your case is less than airtight, ask yourself where the weaknesses are, and be prepared to explain why those weaknesses occurred. Being organized, and having answers to the judge's questions, sends a strong signal to the judge that you really care about the outcome of the case, and that you are the one who deserves to win.

4. Stay away from lawyers

You can be *too* prepared for a small-claims court action, however. Although many attorneys will be happy to spend an hour or two with you to help you prepare for your case, small-claims courts and judges always frown upon parties who appear to have been overly prepared, or "horse-shedded," by their attorneys. If you do not normally use phrases like "May it please the court," "I object, Your Honor," and "Please let the record show" in your everyday speech, *do not* under any circumstances use them in a small-claims court.

5. Be on time

You must show up on time for your court date. In case of an emergency, if you cannot possibly attend your hearing, contact the court clerk's office and try to get a postponement, or "continuance," of the court date. Be sure to call your debtor as well. In most states, each party is entitled to one continuance if both parties agree. Otherwise, your request for a continuance will have to be approved by the court, and remember, you are not there to explain why you need the continuance. If you fail to get a postponement and do not show up for your trial, the judge or magistrate may dismiss your suit and you may be prevented from suing again for that money owed you.

6. Keep it simple

Now comes the stressful part. When you begin your presentation to the court, explain why the defendant owes you money. Answer any questions the judge or magistrate asks you as clearly and directly and possible, and *do not ramble.* Show him or her any bills, receipts, or letters that you have brought along as proof of your story (be sure to know in advance if you must bring originals, or whether copies will suffice). If you

have a witness, your witness will be allowed to tell what he or she knows after you speak. Next, the person you are suing will explain what his or her position is. Each party has a right to question a witness. If the other party fails to show up, ask the judge for a "default judgment"; in some states, the judge is not obligated to grant default judgments unless you request one.

7. Getting your money

If the case is decided in your favor, the party you sued will be ordered to pay. In most states, the judge has the power to order the defendant to pay in installments if it's clear the defendant cannot afford to pay the full amount in a lump sum. If the person who owed you money refuses to pay by the date ordered by the court, or if the payments are stopped later, apply to the court clerk's office for an "execution" to be issued against the party's wages, property, or bank account. Once the "execution" is issued, you will be required to give the execution to a sheriff, bailiff, or court officer who will serve the execution on the appropriate employer, banking institution, or other person who will have to pay the amount directly to the court officer. The court officer will then pay you.

Source: Cliff Ennico, a nationally recognized small business legal expert, is the author of the nationally syndicated newspaper column "Succeeding in Your Business" and the author of *Small Business Survival Guide* (Adams, $12.95). You can find out more about him at *www.cliffennico.com*. Contact him at 2490 Black Rock Turnpike, # 354, Fairfield, CT 06825-2400; (203) 254-1727; fax: (203) 254-8195; e-mail: *cennico@legalcareer.com*.

Chapter
one

Chapter
two

Chapter
three

Chapter
four

Chapter
five

Chapter
six

Chapter
seven

Chapter
eight

Your Taxes

Note: The information contained in this section was current at the time of publication. Please remember to check with your tax advisor.

Dealing with the IRS

Top Questions to Ask Your Tax Preparer

It's common knowledge that the wrong tax preparer can land you in a whole lot of hot water. Here is a list of questions that should test the abilities of a prospective tax preparer.

1. What are your qualifications?

A CPA (certified public accountant) or an enrolled agent are the best qualified to do taxes. Both of these designations regularly take classes and an exam for their designations. A CPA is more qualified, but if you have a simple or straightforward return, you need an enrolled agent.

2. Would you be willing to lie on my return?

If your preparer says yes, run as fast as you can. This action can get both of you in trouble, so think about why would he or she be willing to lie. Perhaps your preparer is not licensed. Licensed preparers can lose their designation if they are caught lying on a return.

3. How is your information protected in their office?

The computer and backup files should be secure after-hours. All paper files should be secured in locked cabinets, and located in a secure building. Identity theft is on the rise.

4. What are the fees?

Agree on a tax preparation cost before you hand over your information, so there are no surprises. There should be a flat fee for your tax return based on its complexity.

5. May I pay you extra to recheck my return against documents I have given you?

Ask your preparer to recheck your return. If you have the ability to check the return against your documents, that is fine. But you absolutely should check for the small things: correct spelling of your name, correct social security number, correct occupation, correct income, and any other minor items, which could turn major if entered incorrectly.

Source: Lois Center-Shabazz is the author of the award-winning book, *Let's Get Financial Savvy! From Debt-Free to Investing with Ease,* and is editor of the personal finance Web site: *www .MsFinancialSavvy.com.*

Least Expensive Tax Preparation Resources

Sometimes you, as a business owner, have a tax question that you consider small, and you don't want to bother your CPA. Some business owners want to do their tax return themselves. Here is a list of resources that may aid you without costing a lot of money.

1. The IRS

Usually thought of as the last people with whom you want to communicate, they may actually be the best. The IRS Web site (*www .irs.gov*) is very informative and easy to use. You can look up answers to questions and download forms and publications, as well as link to your state's Web site.

2. Other financial Web sites

Any competent search engine (Google, Yahoo) will pull up a large number of Web sites with tax preparation information. Usually, these sites are associated with accounting firms or brokerages, although some sites are independent. Always be wary of information found over the Web, however, since it may be wrong and will not hold up as evidence in an audit.

3. Tax guides

Every year around tax time, bookstores are filled with commercially published tax guides. Examples are books by Ernst & Young and J. K. Lasser, as well as the *Complete Idiot's Guide*, and they usually cost under $20. These books are divided into topical sections and are written on a level that can be easily comprehended by the average taxpayer.

4. Quickfinder

PPC publishes an excellent tax guide called *Quickfinder* that retails for around $45. It is categorized and indexed, and it is written in short paragraphs and bullet points. There are different versions for different types of tax, and it can be purchased at *www.quickfinder.com*.

5. Master Tax Guide

The *Master Tax Guide* is published by CCH and retails for around $55. It is geared toward professionals, making it quite difficult for the novice to understand. However, it is highly respected in the industry and provides specific references to the tax code.

6. Tax preparation software

Every year, more and more companies develop user-friendly tax software, such as TurboTax and TaxCut. These packages are written in an interview format, and they attempt to walk you through the preparation of your tax return. They also give you the ability to file your return electronically. However, they are not foolproof—as the old saying goes, "Garbage in, garbage out."

7. Internal Revenue Code

If you are the type who likes to know the nuts and bolts of things and wants information from the "horse's mouth," there is always the Internal Revenue Code. It is possibly the most complicated, technical writing that you will ever read, but it is available online, and it will certainly hold up in an audit (assuming that you interpreted it properly).

8. Your local library

In this technological age, we tend to forget that the public library exists. The bigger libraries usually have copies of various resources, including some of those mentioned here. In a pinch, this can work well, because they will normally be located in one specific area of the library.

9. Your accountant

Although doing it yourself is cheaper, don't forget your accountant. Having an accountant prepare a tax return is not always as expensive as you may think. In the long run, if it means fewer questions from the IRS, it may be well worth it.

Source: David A. Caplan, CPA, MBA—David Caplan received his CPA in 1980, while working for a Big 10 public accounting firm.

He was employed in various industries from 1981 to 1992, gaining insight on the inner workings of companies, and received his MBA from Temple University in 1986. In 1992, he purchased an accounting practice, which has quintupled in size since then. He handles all aspects of accounting, from personal income tax and advice to financial statements and corporate tax returns. He has clients located all over the United States. His Web site is *www.caplancpa.com*. He can be reached at PO Box 301, Lafayette Hill, PA 19444; (610) 834-5754; fax: (610) 834-1013.

How to Get More Information from the IRS and Other Federal Agencies

You can get help with unresolved tax issues, order free publications and forms, ask tax questions, and get more information from the IRS in several ways. By selecting one or some of the methods on this list, you will have quick and easy access to tax help.

1. Contact your taxpayer advocate

The taxpayer advocate independently represents your interests and concerns with the IRS by protecting your rights and resolving problems that have not been fixed through normal channels. While taxpayer advocates cannot change the law or make a technical design, they can clear up problems that resulted from previous contacts and ensure that your case is given a complete and impartial review. To contact your taxpayer advocate, call (877) 777-4778. Call (800) 829-4059 if you are a TTY/TDD user. Visit the Web site at *www.irs.gov/advocate*. For more information, see Publication 1546, The Tax-payer Advocate Services of the IRS—How to Get Help With Unresolved Tax Issues.

2. Small business tax education programs

Small business owners and other self-employed individuals can learn about business taxes through a unique partnership between the IRS and local organizations. Through workshops or in-depth tax courses, instructors provide training on starting a business, recordkeeping, preparing business tax returns, self-employment tax issues, and employment taxes. Some courses are offered free as a community service. Courses given by an educational facility may include costs for materials and tuition. Other courses may have a nominal fee to offset administrative costs of sponsoring organizations. For more information about this program, call the IRS Monday through Friday during regular business hours. Check your telephone book for the local number of the IRS office closest to you or call (800) 829-1040.

3. Free tax services

To find out what services are available, get Publication 910, IRS Guide to Free Tax Services. It contains a list of free tax publications and an index of tax topics. It also describes other free tax information services, including tax education and assistance programs and a list of Tele-Tax topics.

4. Internet

You can access the IRS Web site twenty-four hours a day, seven days a week, at *www.irs.gov* to *e-file* your return. Find out about commercial tax preparation and *e-file* services available free to eligible taxpayers. Check the status of your 2004 refund. Click on *Where's My Refund*. Be sure to wait at least six weeks from the date you filed your return (3 weeks if you filed electronically). Have your 2004 tax return available because you will need to know your filing status and the exact whole-dollar amount of your refund. Download forms, instructions, and publications. Order IRS products online. Research your tax questions online. Search publications online by topic or keyword. View Internal Revenue Bulletins (IRBs) published in the last few years. Figure your withholding allowances using the Form W-4 calculator. Sign up to receive local and national tax news by e-mail. Get information on starting and operating a small business.

5. Fax

You can get more than 100 of the most requested forms and instructions twenty-four hours a day, seven days a week, by fax. Just call (703) 368-9694 from the telephone connected to your fax. When you call, you will hear instructions on how to use the service. The items you request will be faxed to you. For help with transmission problems, call (703) 487-4608. Long-distance charges may apply.

6. Phone

Many services are available by phone. To *order forms, instructions, and publications,* call (800) 829-3676 for current-year forms, instructions, and publications and prior-year forms and instructions. You should receive your order within ten days. To *ask tax questions,* call (800) 829-1040. To *solve problems,* you can get face-to-face help every business day in IRS Taxpayer Assistance Centers. An employee can explain IRS letters, request adjustment to your account, or help you set up a payment plan. Call your local Taxpayer Assistance Center for an appointment.

To find the number, go to *www.irs.gov/localcontacts* or look in the phone book under *United States Government, Internal Revenue Service.* If you have access to TTY/TDD equipment, call (800) 829-4059 to ask tax or account questions or to order forms and publications. To receive information on *TeleTax topics,* call (800) 829-4477, and press 2 to listen to prerecorded messages. To receive *refund information,* call (800) 829-4477, and press 1 for automated refund information, or call (800) 829-1954. Be sure to wait at least six weeks from the date you filed your return (3 weeks if you filed electronically). Have your tax return available because you will need to know your filing status and the exact whole-dollar amount of your refund.

7. Walk in

Many products and services are available on a walk-in basis. You can walk in to many post offices, libraries, and IRS offices to pick up certain forms, instructions, and publications. Some IRS offices, libraries, grocery stores, copy centers, city and county governments, credit unions, and office-supply stores have a collection of products available to print from a CD-ROM or photocopy from reproducible proofs. Also, some IRS offices and libraries have the Internal Revenue Code, regulations, Internal Revenue Bulletins, and Cumulative Bulletins available for research purposes.

You can also walk in to your local Taxpayer Assistance Center any business day to ask tax questions or get help with a tax problem. An employee can explain IRS letters, request adjustments to your account, or help you set up a payment plan. You can set up an appointment by calling your local center and, at the prompt, leaving a message requesting Everyday Tax Solutions help. A representative will call you back within two business days to schedule an in-person appointment at your convenience. To find the number, go to *www.irs.gov/localcontacts* or look in the phone book under *United States Government, Internal Revenue Service.*

8. Mail

You can send your order for forms, instructions, and publications to the distribution center nearest you and receive a response within ten business days after your request is received. Use the address that applies to your part of the country.

Western United States:
Western Area Distribution Center
Rancho Cordova, CA 95743-0001
Central United States:
Central Area Distribution Center
PO Box 8903
Bloomington, IL 61702-8903
Eastern United States and foreign addresses:
Eastern Area Distribution Center
PO Box 85074
Richmond, VA 23261-5074

9. CD-ROM for tax products

You can order Publication 1796, IRS Federal Tax Products CD-ROM, and obtain current-year tax forms, instructions, and publications; prior-year forms and instructions; frequently requested tax forms that can be filled in electronically, printed out for submission, and saved for record-keeping; and Internal Revenue Bulletins. Buy the CD-ROM from National Technical Information Service (NTIS) at *www.irs.gov/cdorders* for $22 (no handling fee), or call 1-(877)-233-6767 toll-free to buy the CD-ROM for $22 (plus a $5 handling fee). The first release is available in early January and the final release is available in late February.

10. CD-ROM for small business

Publication 3207, The Small Business Resource Guide, CD-ROM, is a must for every small business owner or any taxpayer about to start a business. This handy, interactive CD contains all the business tax forms, instructions, and publications needed to manage a business successfully. In addition, the CD provides other helpful information, such as how to prepare a business plan, finding financing for your business, and much more. The design of the CD makes finding information easy and quick and incorporates file formats and browsers that can be run on virtually any desktop or laptop computer. It is available in early April. You can get a free copy by calling (800) 829-3676 or by visiting the Web site at *www.irs.gov/smallbiz.*

11. Comments on IRS enforcement actions

The Small Business and Agriculture Regulatory Enforcement Ombudsman and ten Regional Fairness Boards were established to receive comments from small business about federal agency enforcement actions. The Ombudsman will annually evaluate the enforcement activities of each agency and rate its responsiveness to small business. If you wish to comment on the enforcement actions of the IRS, call (888) REG-FAIR (1-888-734-3247);

e-mail *ombudsman@sba.gov*; or download the appraisal form at *www.sba.gov/ombudsman*.

12. Small Business Administration

The Small Business Administration (SBA) offers training and educational programs, counseling services, financial programs, and contract assistance for small business owners. The SBA also has publications and videos on a variety of business topics. You can access the SBA Web site at *www.sba.gov*. While visiting the SBA Web site, you can find a variety of information of interest to small business owners. Call the SBA Answer Desk at (800) UASK-SBA (800-827-5722) for general information about programs available to assist small business owners.

13. Small Business Development Centers (SBDCs)

SBDCs provide counseling, training, and technical services to current and prospective small business owners who cannot afford the services of a private consultant. Help is available when beginning, improving, or expanding a small business. You can walk in to a Small Business Development Center or Business Information Center to request assistance with your small business. To find the location nearest you, access the SBA on the Internet or call the SBA Answer Desk.

14. Business Information Centers (BICs)

BICs offer a small business reference library, management video tapes, and computer technology to help plan a business. BICs also offer one-on-one assistance. Individuals who are in business or are interested in starting a business can use BICs as often as they wish at no charge.

15. Service Corps of Retired Executives (SCORE)

SCORE provides small business counseling and training to current and prospective small business owners. SCORE is made up of current and former business people who offer their expertise and knowledge to help people start, manage, and expand a small business. SCORE also offers a variety of small business workshops.

16. Other federal agencies

You can access the GPO Web site at *www. access.gpo.gov*. Write to the GPO at the following address: Superintendent of Documents, U.S. Government Printing Office, PO Box 371954, Pittsburgh, PA 15250-7954; toll-free: (866) 512-1800; or, from the Washington, D.C., area, (202) 512-1800.

Source: Internal Revenue Service (*www.irs.gov*).

Most Common Tax Penalties

The law provides penalties for not filing returns or paying taxes as required. Criminal penalties may be imposed for willful failure to file, tax evasion, or making a false statement. The following lists the most common tax penalties identified by the IRS.

1. Failure to file tax returns

If you do not file your tax return by the due date, you may have to pay a penalty. The penalty is based on the tax not paid by the due date. See your tax return instructions for more information about this penalty.

2. Failure to pay tax

If you do not pay your taxes by the due date, you will have to pay a penalty for each month, or part of a month, that your taxes are not paid. For more information, see your tax return instructions.

3. Failure to withhold, deposit, or pay taxes

If you do not withhold income, social security, or Medicare taxes from employees, or if you withhold taxes but do not deposit them or pay them to the IRS, you may be subject to a penalty of the unpaid tax, plus interest. You may also be subject to penalties if you deposit the taxes late. For more information, see Publication 15.

4. Failure to file information reporting requirements

The following penalties apply if you are required to file information returns. For more information, see the general instructions for forms 1099, 1098, 5498, and W-2G.

5. Failure to file information returns

A penalty applies if you do not file information returns by the due date, if you do not include all required information, or if you report incorrect information. These penalties will not apply if you can show that the failures were due to reasonable cause and not willful neglect. In addition, there is no penalty for failure to include all the required information, or for including incorrect information on a de minimis number of information returns if you correct the errors by August 1 of the year the returns are due. (To be considered de minimis, the number of returns cannot exceed the greater of 10 or ½ of 1% of the total number of returns you are required to file for the year.)

6. Failure to furnish correct payee statements

A penalty applies if you do not furnish a required statement to a payee by the required date, if you do not include all required information, or if you report incorrect information. These penalties will not apply if you can show that the failures were due to reasonable cause and not willful neglect. In addition, there is no penalty for failure to include all the required information, or for including incorrect information on a de minimis number of information returns if you correct the errors by August 1 of the year the returns are due. (To be considered de minimis, the number of returns cannot exceed the greater of 10 or ½ of 1% of the total number of returns you are required to file for the year.)

7. Failure to supply taxpayer identification number

If you do not include your taxpayer identification number (SSN or EIN) or the taxpayer identification number of another person where required on the return, statement, or other document, you may be subject to a penalty of $50 for each failure. You may also be subject to the $50 penalty if you do not give your taxpayer identification number to another person when it is required on a return, statement, or other document.

Source: Internal Revenue Service (*www.irs.gov*).

Most Common Mistakes when Filing W-2 and W-3 Forms

By January 31, employers are required to send employees W-2 Wage and Income Forms to aid them in completing their individual taxes. Income tax and the amount of social security and Medicare taxes withheld from the employee's wages need to be on the form. In addition, employers must submit Copy A of the W-2 to the Social Security Administration (SSA) by the last day of February or the last day of March if filing electronically. W-2 forms are sent to the SSA along with the W-3 Form, Transmittal of Income and Tax Statements. Our expert, a leading national payroll service provides a list of the most common mistakes made when filing W-2 and W-3 forms.

1. Omitting numbers

Omitting/using invalid social security numbers (SSN) or employer identification numbers (EIN).

2. Inaccurate employee names

Omitting/using inaccurate employee names that do not match the name on their SSN cards.

3. Failing to report certain details

Failing to report any of the following: going out of business, employees who perform household work, employees earning less than $600.

4. Submitting wrong form

Submitting the wrong form to correct previously submitted information.

5. Submitting forms with wrong tax year

Submitting W-2 forms with the wrong tax year on them, or failing to enclose W-3 forms.

6. Sending forms to the wrong employees

Sending W-2 forms to incorrect employee addresses.

7. Preparing nonstandard forms

Preparing nonstandard forms.

8. Mismatching names and numbers

Mismatching employee names and social security numbers.

9. Inserting dollar signs

Inserting dollar signs in blank fields.

10. Using wrong font type

Using type fonts that are too large or too light (12-point Courier is recommended).

11. Excluding taxable income

Excluding taxable income (i.e., bonuses, use of a company vehicle)

Source: ADP Screening and Selection Services (*www.adphire. com*)—Founded in 1986 as Avert, Inc., ADP Screening and Selection Services continually leads the industry in background screening and human resources–related outsourcing solutions by providing dynamic online hiring technology. In 2001, Avert became a part of Automatic Data Processing, Inc. (ADP) and is now known as ADP Screening and Selection Services. Contact them at 301 Remington Street, Fort Collins, CO 80524; (800) 367-5933.

Most Common Tax Return Errors

Before filing your return, review it to make sure it is correct and complete. Be sure to review your entire return because any errors may delay the processing of your return. The IRS has identified the items on this list as the most common tax return errors. Use it as a checklist to help you avoid errors.

1. Incorrectly using the peel-off label and entering corrections

When you use the peel-off label and enter any corrections, make sure you've entered your social security number in the space provided.

2. Not having a label and having too many corrections

If you don't have a label or there are too many corrections, make sure you clearly print your name, social security number, and address, including Zip Code, directly on your return.

3. Incorrectly entering names and social security numbers

Make sure you enter the names and social security numbers for yourself, your spouse, your dependents, and qualifying children for earned income credit or child tax credit, exactly as they appear on your social security cards. If there have been any name changes, be sure to contact the *www.ssa.gov* or (800) 772-1213.

4. Selecting too many filing statuses

Make sure you didn't check too many filing statuses. Your return will get bounced.

5. Not checking the appropriate exemption boxes

Check the appropriate exemption boxes and enter the names and social security numbers exactly as they appear on the social security

cards for all the dependents claimed. Enter the total number of exemptions.

6. Not entering on the correct lines and not entering correct totals

Be sure to enter income, deductions, and credits on the correct lines. Always make sure the totals are correct.

7. Forgetting to put brackets around a negative on your return

When you have a negative on your return, remember to put brackets around it.

8. Not finding the correct standard to enter if you decide to take the standard deduction

If you decide to take the standard deduction and checked any box indicating either you or your spouse were sixty-five or older or blind, make sure you find the correct standard to enter on line 24 of Form 1040A or line 39 of Form 1040.

9. Not using the correct column when you use the tax table

When you use the tax table, make sure you use the correct column for your filing status.

10. Forgetting to sign and date the return

Remember to sign and date your return. When it is a joint return, make sure your spouse also signs and dates the return.

11. Forgetting to obtain a W-2 from all employees and not attaching Copy B to your return

Make sure you have a Form W-2 from all your employees. Don't forget to attach Copy B of each to your return. File only one return, even if you have more than one job. Combine the wages and withholding from all Form W–2s on one return.

12. Forgetting to attach any Form 1099-R that shows tax withheld

Attach any Form 1099-R that shows tax withheld.

13. Not attaching all other necessary schedules and forms

Attach all other necessary schedules and forms in the sequence number order given in the upper right–hand corner.

14. Forgetting to enclose a check or money order if you owe tax

If you owe tax, enclose a check or money order with the return and write your social security number, tax form, and tax year on the payment.

15. Not making a copy

Make a copy of the signed return and all schedules for your records.

16. Having incorrect or missing social security numbers

Be sure to not have any incorrect or missing social security numbers.

17. Entering incorrect tax

Check the tables and make sure you don't enter incorrect tax.

18. Having computation errors and having missing or incorrect identification numbers

Check for computation errors in figuring the child and dependent care credit or the earned income credit. Also, make sure you don't have missing or incorrect identification numbers for child-care providers.

19. Entering withholding and estimated tax payments on the wrong line

Make sure you don't have withholding and estimated tax payments entered on the wrong line.

20. Having math errors

Be careful of math errors. Check your addition and subtraction.

Source: Internal Revenue Service (*www.irs.gov*).

Top Benefits of Filing Taxes Electronically

EFTPS is the Electronic Federal Tax Payment System developed by the Internal Revenue Service and Financial Management Service (FMS) to enable taxpayers to pay their federal taxes electronically. The system allows taxpayers to use the Internet (www.eftps.gov), or phone to initiate tax payments. It's convenient, secure, and saves time. Here are some other great benefits.

1. Fast

You can make a tax payment in minutes.

2. Accurate

Because there are verification steps along the way, you are able to check and review your information before it is sent.

3. Convenient

EFTPS is available by Internet or phone—twenty-four hours a day, seven days a week—

and can be used to schedule payments in advance.

4. Easy to use

It's a step-by-step process that tells you what information you need to successfully complete your tax payment for any federal tax.

5. Secure

EFTPS offers the highest levels of security on the Internet.

6. Any business taxpayer can use EFTPS for any tax type

Any individual taxpayer, especially those making 1040ES payments or more than one tax payment a year, can use EFTPS.

7. No charge

EFTPS does not charge taxpayers for its services. However, if you choose to use a payment service offered by your financial institution, you may incur a fee from your financial institution. Please check with your financial institution directly to inquire about their fee structure.

Sources: Electronic Federal Tax Payment System (*www.eftps.com*) and the Internal Revenue Service (*www.irs.gov*).

Retention Time for Popular Business Documents

The art of effective record retention boils down to two standards: reason and risk. Some business owners fear risking adverse consequences and hang on to everything forever, an unreasonable behavior resulting in landfills. Others trash everything early and often, an unreasonably risky path to neatness. To guide you in minimizing your risks, here's a list of generally accepted, reasonable time periods recommended for retaining business records, which you may print out for future reference.

1. One year

Bank reconciliations
Duplicate deposit slips
I-9s (after termination)
Receiving sheets

2. Three years

Correspondence (general)
Employment applications
Insurance policies (expired)
Petty-cash vouchers

3. Four years

W-4 forms

4. Five years

OSHA logs

5. Seven years

Accident reports and claims (settled cases)
Accounts payable ledgers and schedules
Accounts receivable ledgers and schedules
Bank statements
Checks (canceled, with some exceptions noted below)
Contracts and leases (expired)
Contracts and leases still in effect
Electronic fund transfer documents
Employee personnel records (after termination)
Expense analyses and expense distribution schedules
Inventories of products, materials, supplies

Invoices to customers

Invoices from vendors

Leases (see Contracts)

Notes receivable ledgers and schedules

Payroll records and summaries, pensions, payroll taxes

Property records including costs, depreciation reserves, end-of-year trial balances

Purchase orders (purchasing department copy)

Sales records

Scrap and salvage records (inventories, sales, etc.)

Subsidiary ledgers

Time books/cards

Voucher register and schedules

Vouchers for payments to vendors, employees (including allowances and reimbursement of employees officers, etc., for travel and entertainment expenses)

6. Eleven years

Workers' compensation documents

7. Indefinitely

Audit reports of accountants

Cash books

Charts of accounts

Checks (canceled for important payments, i.e., taxes, purchases of property, special contracts)

Construction documents

Correspondence (important)

Deeds, mortgages, bills of sale, titles

Depreciation schedules

Financial statements (end-of-year, other months optional)

General and private ledgers (end-of-year trial balance)

Journals

Licenses

Loan documents, notes

Minute books of directors and stockholders, including by-laws and charter

Property appraisals by outside appraisers

Blueprints and plans

Tax returns and worksheets, agents' reports, any documents relating to income tax liability

Trademark registrations

Source: CCH Business Owner's Toolkit: (*www.toolkit.cch.com*)— The Business Owner's Toolkit provides advice, guides, legal tools, business models, and other resources to small business owners.

Most Common Tax Returns and Their Deadlines

Our expert, who calls herself the Tax Mama, loves to mother her clients. We asked her to share with us her list of common tax returns and deadlines that she issues to her client base every year. Although this list is for the 2006 tax year, you can certainly use it as guidance for years to come.

1. 01-03-2006

File Form 2290 - Heavy Highway Vehicles

2. 01-17-2006

4th Estimated Payment Due

Farmers and fishermen: Estimated Tax for 2005 Due

3. 01-17-2006

Employers make monthly Payroll Tax deposit

4. 01-31-2006

Furnish W-2s/1099/1098s to recipients

5. 01-31-2006

File Quarterly/Annual Payroll/Sales Tax Returns

6. 01-17-2006

Individuals: Filing personal return and pay all taxes without penalty if January 17, 2006 estimated payment missed

7. 02-15-2006

File new W-4 with Employer if you claimed exempt last year

8. 02-28-2006

Mortgage Interest: file Form 1098s with IRS

9. 02-28-2006

File W-2's with Social Security Administration

10. 02-28-2006

File 1099's with IRS

11. 03-01-2006

Farmers and fishermen: File and pay taxes due for 2005 and pay all tax due if estimated payments not made on 01.17.2006.

12. 03-15-2006

S-Corp Election Decision Due (if Applicable)

13. 03-15-2006

Corporate Returns or Extensions Due / Calendar Year Corps

14. 03-15-2006

Employers make monthly Payroll Tax deposit

15. 04-17-2006

Personal, Partnership Returns or Extensions are due

16. 04-17-2006

1st 2006 Estimated Payment Due

17. 04-17-2006

Employers make monthly Payroll Tax deposit

18. 05-01-2006

Quarterly Payroll Taxes Due

19. 05-01-2006

Quarterly Sales Taxes Due

20. 05-14-2006

Employers make monthly Payroll Tax deposit

21. 06-15-2006

2nd 2006 Estimated Payment Due

22. 06-16-2006

Employers make monthly Payroll Tax deposit

23. 06-15-2006

Personal Tax Returns due for U.S. Taxpayers overseas

24. 06-15-2006

or: File extensions for U.S. Taxpayers overseas with Form 4868

25. 07-17-2006
Partnership Returns Due

26. 07-17-2006
Or: File Partnership Extensions

27. 07-17-2006
Employers make monthly Payroll Tax deposit

28. 07-31-2006
2nd Quarter Payroll Taxes Due

29. 07-31-2006
2nd Quarter Sales Taxes Due

30. 08-15-2006
Employers make monthly Payroll Tax deposit

31. 09-15-2006
Employers make monthly Payroll Tax deposit

32. 09-15-2006
Corporate Returns Due—FINAL DEADLINE

33. 09-15-2006
3rd 2006 Estimated Payment Due

34. 10-02-2006
Last day to establish SIMPLE plans

35. 10-16-2006
Personal and Partnership Returns—FINAL DEADLINE

36. 10-16-2006
Employers make monthly Payroll Tax deposit

37. 10-31-2006
3rd Quarter Payroll Taxes Due

38. 10-31-2006
3rd Quarter Sales Taxes Due

39. 11-16-2006
Employers make monthly Payroll Tax deposit

40. 12-15-2006
Employers make monthly Payroll Tax deposit

41. 01-01-2007
Last Day to Open KEOGH account for 2006 deposits

42. 01-15-2007
4th Estimated Payment for 2006 Due

43. 01-15-2007
Employers make monthly Payroll Tax deposit

44. 01-31-2007
Send W-2s/1099s to recipients

45. 01-31-2007
File Quarterly/Annual Payroll/Sales Tax Returns

Source: Eva Rosenberg, MBA, EA (*www.taxmama.com*)—Eva has degrees in Accounting and International Business, several years in national and local CPA firms, lots of years of freelance and consulting work with companies of all sizes, and across many industries. She also has had a tax preparation, consulting, and writing practice of more than 20 years; she teaches all over the country, and has authored and coauthored many books and articles. She can be contacted at *TaxMama.com*, or c/o TaxAnxiety, Inc. P.O.

Box 280549, Northridge, CA 91328; e-mail: *taxmama@taxmama. com*. You can find this calendar updated annually at *www.tax-mama.com/taxcalendar.html*.

Ways to Avoid an Audit

There is no guarantee against an audit. Not only is the federal government looking for money, but the states and local governments are struggling as well to meet budgets. Even when every item on a return is reported correctly, an audit can still result. This is due to random audit testing for statistical purposes. However, there are certainly things to focus on that will minimize the chances of an audit. Here's a list to keep you out of trouble!

1. Be average

The IRS scans tax returns for reasonability. The reasonability test is based on the results of random tax audits and statistics gathered from prior year tax return filings. Should amounts on a tax return fall outside the reasonability area, the return may be manually reviewed to determine if an audit is warranted. An example would be a large charitable contribution compared to the amount of income earned. It is important to retain documents to support deductions claimed, especially if the amount is large. The statistics from the prior tax year can be found on the IRS Web site at *www.irs.gov,* Statistics of Income Bulletin.

2. Attach an explanation of unusual items

The IRS insists that they do not want documents or receipts attached to returns. However, a short explanation of an unusual item may help prevent an auditor from pursuing the issue further.

3. Avoid high audit risk areas

Certain areas by their nature attract the eyes of the IRS. Examinations of business expenses have historically resulted in more changes than other areas. Therefore, a return that includes business expenses may have a higher risk of being audited than other returns. Avoiding high-risk areas is easier said than done. If you are entitled to claim the deductions, do so. However, it is important to ensure that proper substantiation is maintained.

4. Avoid seesaw issues

There are often items on one return that impact another return—for example, alimony or exemptions. If one spouse deducts alimony and the other spouse does not report the income, or reports a different amount, an audit is almost certain. If an individual is claimed by two people, as is often the case when parents are separated and both are contributing to the child's support, the IRS will question both returns. For business returns, an example is a buy-and-sell agreement where one party treats a payment as goodwill while the other treats it as a covenant not to compete. The tax treatment is different for each, and the IRS is looking for consistency. It is important that both parties agree to the tax treatment before filing returns.

5. "Non tax" returns are not exempt from audit

Charitable organizations are required to file annual returns. Even though no tax is due (unless there is unrelated business income), the IRS may choose to audit these returns for compliance purposes. Is the charity functioning for the purpose for which they became exempt? Are disbursements appropriate? Often times these "non tax" returns are audited because information requested on the return has not been provided. Once a return is selected for audit, any items on the return can be examined. Therefore, make sure all questions are properly answered and no items are left blank before the return is filed.

6. Avoid tax shelter items

If it is too good to be true, the IRS thinks so, too. Some very appealing investment tax shelters are constantly being developed by creative investment counselors. They may be legal, but when the government is looking for ways to collect more taxes, these investment vehicles will be scrutinized very carefully.

7. Business returns: Focus on the balance sheet

Make sure that the beginning balance-sheet amounts tie in with the prior year–ending balance-sheet amounts. It is a simple task for the IRS to scan these two items and a mismatch will almost certainly generate a question.

8. Ensure that S corporations pay salaries to shareholders

One way to avoid paying social security taxes is not to allocate any of the profits of an S corporation to officer's salaries when salaries would normally have been paid for the services provided. The IRS wants to make sure that

social security taxes are paid when applicable and, therefore, makes a point of verifying that a reasonable salary is paid to shareholders. This is an easy item for the IRS to scan, and if they find no salary or a small salary deducted on the return, an audit is more likely.

9. Focus further on the balance sheet

Unusual items would raise the eyebrows of an experienced IRS auditor. Examples are negative cash accounts, large shareholder loans, little or no inventory for a business that should normally maintain an inventory.

10. Keep proper documentation for items reported on the return

If you are audited and the audit results in a no change, the chances of an audit in the subsequent year are slim, assuming the income and expense items are similar. Alternatively, an audit that resulted in changes will in most instances result in the expansion of the audit to the next year.

Source: Marcia Geltman, CPA, principal with Nisivoccia & Co LLP. She has eighteen years of public experience specializing in income tax, and estate and gift tax. Her prior experience includes fifteen years as a revenue agent with the Internal Revenue Service auditing business tax returns, and working as an IRS instructor and a member of the IRS Speaker's Panel.

Common Steps to Take if You're Audited

An audit from the IRS can be a frightening experience for any business owner. When you receive a notice from the IRS that they want to examine your return, remember there are steps you can take that can make the experience easier to deal with.

1. Calm down

Receiving a notice from IRS informing you that they want to examine your return is something like those nightmares where you show up for a final exam in school and realize you've forgotten to read the book or attend any of the classes. Definitely not a joyful occasion. But most people overreact and go into panic mode. This is not the best frame of mind to be in, as you're getting ready for an audit. Audits don't have to be nightmares if you're properly prepared.

2. Decide whether to get help or tackle the job yourself

You'd want to get help from a CPA, attorney, or Enrolled Agent if you suspect you've done something wrong. Even if you're pretty sure you did everything right, it's a good idea to hire a professional if you're not sure you understand the tax law, especially if there is a significant amount of money at stake. If you paid a professional to prepare your return, it would make sense to get this person to represent you in the audit, since he or she would already be familiar with your business.

3. Organize your records for the year or years being audited

You want to be able to tie your documentation in with the numbers shown on your tax return. Make sure to maintain consistency. For example, the IRS frequently examines travel and entertainment. Typical evidence to support these deductions would include your appoint-

ment calendar, as well as invoices and receipts. If you have invoices showing you were in San Francisco from May 2 through May 5, you want your calendar to reflect that you had appointments with business contacts in San Francisco on those days, or that you attended a conference in San Francisco during that period. This would seem to be common sense (and it should not be a problem at all for people who keep good records as they go along).

4. Look at your records from the IRS agent's point of view

The IRS revenue agent who examines your tax return is a human being trying to get through his or her workday, just like everyone else. Naturally, the agent will look more favorably on someone who makes his or her job easier. What would you rather be handed: a grocery bag full of crumpled receipts or a neat stack of receipts stapled together with a calculator tape on the front, with a total that exactly matches the amount shown on the tax return? Who would you be more likely to believe: a person who has to dig around through a pile of papers for five or ten minutes to find something, or a person who can immediately produce well-organized documentation?

5. Remember whom you're dealing with and what you need to prove

The IRS revenue agent's job description includes determining the correct amount of tax owed. But you, the taxpayer, have the burden of proof with respect to the items reported on your tax return. The revenue agent will disallow deductions unless you have convincing proof that the numbers you have reported are "real"—that is, you actually paid it, and it was a legitimate business expense. Back up your numbers with convincing documentation. You need to supplement with invoices and canceled checks or electronic records of payment. If the expense is unusual, you need to be able to justify it as a business expense.

6. Always be prepared

The ideal time to get ready for a tax audit is when you're preparing your tax return. The kind of records you want to keep for at least three years after filing your return include: bank statements; receipts (preferably arranged in neat categories with calculator tapes that tie to the numbers shown on the tax return for each account); appointment calendars; mileage logs; records of attendance at business conferences or continuing education events; entertainment records, including names of people entertained and an explanation of how the entertainment was related to your business; electronic copies and backups and/or printouts of your accounting records, including income statement, balance sheet, and general ledger; payroll records, including quarterly and year-end payroll tax returns; and copies of lease agreements. Records related to depreciable assets should be maintained for as long as you own the assets. Sometimes a photograph is worth more than 1,000 receipts.

Source: Barbara Lamar, attorney/CPA, specializing in advising closely held businesses and their owners on how to maximize after tax profits. She can be contacted at (512) 470-8225, or at BLamar@lamarlaw.net.

Top Tax Schemes Identified by the IRS

The "Dirty Dozen" tax schemes are a list of typical tax scams identified by the IRS and updated each year. Involvement with tax schemes can lead to imprisonment and fines. The IRS routinely pursues and shuts down promoters of these scams. But remember that anyone pulled into these schemes can face repayment of taxes plus interest and penalties. Here they are.

1. Trust misuse

Unscrupulous promoters for years have urged taxpayers to transfer assets into trusts. They promise reduction of income subject to tax, deductions for personal expenses, and reduced estate or gift taxes. However, some trusts do not deliver the promised tax benefits, and the IRS is actively examining these arrangements. As with other arrangements, seek the advice of a trusted professional before entering into a trust.

2. Frivolous arguments

Promoters have been known to make the following outlandish claims: the Sixteenth Amendment concerning congressional power to lay and collect income taxes was never ratified; that wages are not income; filing a return and paying taxes are merely voluntary; and being required to file Form 1040 violates the Fifth Amendment right against self-incrimination or the Fourth Amendment right to privacy. Don't believe these or other similar claims. Such arguments are false and have been thrown out of court. While you have the right to contest your tax liabilities in court, no one has the right to disobey the law.

3. Return preparer fraud

Dishonest return preparers can cause many headaches for taxpayers who fall victim to their ploys. Such preparers derive financial gain by skimming a portion of their clients' refunds and charging inflated fees for return preparation services. They attract new clients by promising large refunds. Choose carefully when hiring a tax preparer. As the saying goes, if it sounds too good to be true, it probably is. No matter who prepares the return, you are ultimately responsible for its accuracy.

4. Credit-counseling agencies

Be careful with credit-counseling organizations that claim they can fix credit ratings, push debt payment agreements or charge high fees, monthly service charges, or mandatory "contributions" that may add to debt. The IRS Tax Exempt and Government Entities Division has made auditing credit-counseling organizations a priority because some of these tax-exempt organizations, which are intended to provide education to low-income customers with debt problems, are charging debtors large fees, while providing little or no counseling.

5. "Claim of right" doctrine

In this scheme, a taxpayer files a return and attempts to take a deduction equal to the entire amount of his or her wages. The promoter advises the taxpayer to label the deduction as "a necessary expense for the production of income" or "compensation for personal services actually rendered." This so-called deduction is based on a misinterpretation of the Internal Revenue Code and has no basis in law.

6. "No gain" deduction

Similar to the "claim of right," filers attempt to eliminate their entire adjusted gross income (AGI) by deducting it on Schedule A. The filer lists his or her AGI under the Schedule A section labeled "Other Miscellaneous Deductions" and attaches a statement to the return, referring to court documents and including the words "No Gain Realized."

7. Corporation sole

Participants apply for incorporation under the pretext of being a "bishop" or "overseer" of a one-person, phony religious organization or society with the idea that this entitles the individual to exemption from federal income taxes as a nonprofit, religious organization. When used as intended, corporation sole statutes enable religious leaders to separate themselves legally from the control and ownership of church assets. But the rules have been twisted at seminars where taxpayers are charged fees of $1,000 or more and incorrectly told that these laws provide a "legal" way to escape paying federal income taxes, child support, and other personal debts.

8. Identity theft

It pays to be choosy when disclosing personal information. Identity thieves have used stolen personal data to access financial accounts, run up charges on credit cards, and apply for new loans. The IRS is aware of several identity theft scams involving taxes. Sometimes scammers pose as the IRS itself. Last year the IRS shut down a scheme in which perpetrators used e-mail to announce to unsuspecting taxpayers that they were "under audit" and could set matters right by divulging sensitive financial information on an official-looking Web site. The IRS does not use e-mail to contact taxpayers about issues related to their accounts.

9. Abuse of charitable organizations and deductions

The IRS has observed an increase in the use of tax-exempt organizations to improperly shield income or assets from taxation. This can occur, for example, when a taxpayer moves assets or income to a tax-exempt supporting organization or donor-advised fund but maintains control over the assets or income, thereby obtaining a tax deduction without transferring a commensurate benefit to charity. A "contribution" of a historic facade easement to a tax-exempt conservation organization is another example. In many cases, local historic preservation laws already prohibit alteration of the home's facade, making the contributed easement superfluous. Even if the facade could be altered, the deduction claimed for the easement contribution may far exceed the easement's impact on the value of the property.

10. Offshore transactions

Despite a crackdown on the practice by the IRS and state tax agencies, individuals continue to try to avoid U.S. taxes by illegally hiding income in offshore bank and brokerage accounts or using offshore credit cards, wire transfers, foreign trusts, employee leasing schemes, private annuities, or life insurance to do so. The IRS, along with the tax agencies of U.S. states and possessions, continues to aggressively pursue taxpayers and promoters involved in such abusive transactions.

11. Zero return

Promoters instruct taxpayers to enter all zeros on their federal income tax filings. In a twist on this scheme, filers enter zero income, report their withholding, and then write *nunc pro tunc*—Latin for "now for then—on the return.

12. Employment tax evasion

The IRS has seen a number of illegal schemes that instruct employers not to withhold federal income tax or other employment taxes from wages paid to their employees. Such advice is based on an incorrect interpretation of Section 861 and other parts of the tax law and has been refuted in court. Recent cases have resulted in criminal convictions, and the courts have issued injunctions against more than a dozen persons ordering them to stop promoting the scheme. Employer participants can also be held responsible for back payments of employment taxes, plus penalties and interest. It is worth noting that employees who have nothing withheld from their wages are still responsible for payment of their personal taxes.

Source: Internal Revenue Service (*www.irs.gov*).

Lowering Your Taxes

Typical Things to Do to Prepare for Your Accountant

Most small business owners have at least a yearly meeting with their accountant, if not quarterly or more frequent. The more prepared you are for these meetings, the less your accountant will need to charge. Here is a list of things to get ready to keep your costs down.

1. Prepare a general ledger or trial balance

If you use accounting software, it should be fairly easy to print out a general ledger. This is a great starting point for the accountant, since it shows a broad overview of your transactions, as well as the detail behind them. If the general ledger is too cumbersome, a trial balance will normally suffice.

2. Gather all of your bank statements

Let's hope that your bank accounts have been reconciled. If not, the accountant can use the bank statements to pick up items such as bank charges, bounced checks, and debit card usage. Make sure that you also have copies or printouts of the canceled checks.

3. Calculate an end-of-period inventory number.

Many businesses, especially wholesale and retail trade, have inventories that are material to the financial statements. Don't expect your accountant to make up the number. Do a physical count at the end of the reporting period, and cost it out based on your inventory method.

Make sure you reconcile it for items in transit, if necessary.

4. Provide all payroll records

Payroll is a critical part of most businesses. If you do not have a payroll service filing your payroll tax returns, chances are your accountant will need to do that. Make sure you have check registers for all pay periods, and that you have records of all payroll tax deposits made, including any made after the end of the period that relate back to the period in question. Also, verify that all employees have accurate addresses and social security numbers. If you have received payroll tax forms in the mail, provide them as well.

5. Provide a detailed list of accounts receivable

Your accountant will want to verify that the number for accounts receivable on your trial balance is accurate. An aged accounts receivable trial balance is the best way to do that. In addition, it will show if any accounts are seriously delinquent, which may be able to be written off. Make sure you include items that were shipped during the period, but were not billed yet.

6. Calculate outstanding accounts payable

Provide your accountant with a list of outstanding bills, in detail or by vendor, that relate to the reporting period. If necessary, categorize them by expense account, so that a proper accounts payable accrual can be made. Make sure you include amounts, or at least an estimate, for items received during the period but not billed yet.

7. Detail all purchases of fixed assets

For any major purchases of equipment, furniture, fixtures, or improvements, provide invoices, or at least a list of dates, descriptions, and amounts. This is critical for the accountant to calculate depreciation and amortization. Also, provide a list of fixed assets that were either retired or sold, along with the sales price and date, if any.

8. Provide end-of-period loan balances

If you have outstanding bank or other loans, make sure that you know the principal balance at the end of the period. This can be attained by looking at the latest loan invoice or an amortization table. If neither is available, contact the lender. Amortization tables are important for the accountant also, so that a determination can be made as to how much of the principal is current (due during the next twelve months) versus long term.

9. Keep track of your estimated tax payments

If your company needs to make estimated payments, your accountant should know how much was recommended for you to pay each quarter. However, only you know how much you actually paid. Sometimes companies skip a payment, due to lack of money, a change in circumstance, or just plain forgetfulness. Also, provide the date of payment, in the event that it was remitted late.

Source: David A. Caplan, CPA, MBA—David Caplan received his CPA in 1980, while working for a Big 10 public accounting firm. He was employed in various industries from 1981 to 1992, gaining insight into the inner workings of companies, and received his MBA from Temple University in 1986. In 1992, he purchased an accounting practice, which has quintupled in size since then. He handles all aspects of accounting, from personal income tax and advice to financial statements and corporate tax returns. He has clients located all over the United States. His Web site is www.caplancpa.com. He can be reached at PO Box 301, Lafayette Hill, PA 19444; (610) 834-5754; fax: (610) 834-1013.

Most Prestigious Accounting Firms

The 2005 Vault accounting employer prestige rankings are here. This year, they surveyed accounting professionals in order to rank the top firms in accounting.

1. PricewaterhouseCoopers LLC
300 Madison Avenue
New York, NY 10019
(646) 471-3000
Fax: (813) 286-6000
www.pwcglobal.com/us

2. Deloitte
1633 Broadway
New York, NY 10015
(212) 492-4000
Fax: (212) 492-4154
www.Deloitte.com

3. Ernst & Young LLC
5 Times Square
14th Floor
New York, NY 10036-6530

(212) 773-3000

Fax: (212) 773-6350

www.ey.com

4. KPMG LLC

345 Park Avenue

New York, NY 10154-0102

(212) 758-9700

Fax: (212) 758-9819

www.us.kpmg.com

5. Grant Thornton LLP

175 West Jackson Blvd

20th Floor

Chicago, IL 60604

(312) 856-0001

Fax: (312) 565-4719

www.grantthornton.com

6. BDO Seidman

130 E. Randolph St.

Suite 2800

Chicago, IL 60601

(312) 240-1236

Fax: (312) 240-3329

www.bdo.com

7. McGladrey & Pullen, LLP

3600 American Blvd West

3rd Floor

Bloomington, MN 55431-4502

(952) 835-9930

Fax: (952) 921-7702

www.mcgladrey.com

Source: Accounting Firm Rankings at Vault (*www.vault.com*)—Vault is one of the Internet's most popular destinations for employers, hiring managers, and HR professionals.

Top Ways to Write Off an Asset in Its First Year

Normally, you can't take a current business deduction for the entire cost of a capital asset in the year you purchase it, because the asset's usefulness to your business will extend beyond the year in which it was purchased. However, there are exceptions to this rule. Here are some considerations that you can run by your accountant from our small business expert.

1. Use special tax provisions

A special tax provision allows small businesses the option of claiming a deduction in the first year for the entire cost of such qualifying business assets, up to $102,000 in 2004 (originally $100,000 in 2003 and indexed further for inflation in 2005 through 2007). The 2002 limit was only $24,000, and the substantial increase is due to the enactment of the Jobs and Growth Tax Relief Reconciliation Act of 2003.

2. Look for areas in the country with special exemptions

Businesses in the New York City Liberty Zone (essentially southern Manhattan) continue to get an additional first-year deduction of $35,000. The Liberty Zone was established by the Job Creation and Worker Assistance Act of 2002 to help the area recover after the September 11 terrorist attacks. This deduction is available for qualified business property purchased and placed in service in the Liberty Zone after September 10, 2001, and before 2006. If you want to make use of this election, you must do so on your original tax return for the period, on Form 4562, Depreciation and Amortization, or on an amended tax return filed before the due date for your original return (including any extensions). If you don't claim it, you cannot change your mind later by filing an amended tax return after the due date.

3. Meet certain qualifications

What qualifies for the election? To qualify for this expensing election, the property that you purchase must be tangible personal property, that you actively use in your business, for which a depreciation deduction would be allowed. The property must be newly purchased new or used property, rather than property you previously owned but recently converted to business use. Also, property you acquired by gift or inheritance does not qualify, nor does property you acquired from related persons such as your spouse, child, parent, or other ancestor or descendent, or another business with common ownership.

4. Property must be eligible

Eligible types of property include property that is not a building or a structural component of a building but is an integral part of manufacturing, production, or extraction, or of furnishing transportation, communications, electricity, gas, water, or sewage disposal services; or a research or storage facility used in connection with any of these processes. It can also be a single-purpose livestock or horticultural structure, or a petroleum-products storage facility that is not a building. Beginning in 2003, off-the-shelf computer software is eligible for the expensing election, too. An air-conditioning or heating unit doesn't qualify, however. Neither

does intangible property such as a patent, contract right, stock, or bond.

5. Property must be used more than 50 percent for business

The property must be used more than 50 percent for business. If you want to expense property that will be used partly for personal or family reasons (e.g., a home computer that you use for business about 75 percent of the time, and for personal use the other 25 percent of the time), you can expense only the portion of the property's tax basis that corresponds to its percentage of business use.

Source: ItsSimple.biz (*www.itssimple.biz*) is a very popular free Internet resource center that assists small business owners by providing valuable information, guidance, and business-development tools. ItsSimple.biz is a free Internet resource center to assist small business owners. Contact them at ItsSimple.biz, 316 California Ave., Suite 433, Reno, NV 89509; (775) 324-2900.

Typical Tax Consequences of Buying a Vehicle

For every business owner, there comes a time when the old vehicle will no longer suffice. Or, perhaps this is the year that you need a special purpose vehicle such as a delivery truck or van. At some point, nearly every business owner will have to consider purchasing, leasing, or otherwise obtaining a vehicle. Before you purchase a vehicle, becoming familiar with the following tax matters may help you save money.

1. Excise taxes

You need to be aware that purchasing certain vehicles may subject you to various excise taxes. The excise taxes may be related to the whole vehicle or only to certain vehicle components (e.g., tires). These taxes may be hidden costs that could influence your decision in terms of choosing a vehicle. As such, it is well worth your time to discover if there are any applicable excise taxes before you commit to making a purchase.

2. The "gas guzzler" tax

This tax is imposed on new cars that fail to meet federal fuel economy standards. Although this tax is imposed on the manufacturer, it becomes part of the retail price. Before computing the depreciation deduction for a business car, you must reduce the basis of the car by the amount of the gas guzzler tax you paid. So, you can't recover the tax through depreciation.

3. Tax deduction for clean-fuel vehicles

To encourage the use of vehicles powered by cleaner-burning fuels, a deduction from gross income is permitted for a portion of the cost of certain "clean-fuel" vehicles placed in service after June 30, 1993, and before January 1, 2007. Examples of "clean fuels" are natural gas and hydrogen and fuels that are composed of at least 85 percent methanol, ethanol, alcohol, or ether. For 2004 and 2005, the maximum clean fuel deduction for cars and light trucks is $2,000. For some trucks and vans with a gross weight of more than 10,000 pounds but not more than 26,000 pounds, the maximum deduction is $5,000. For trucks and vans with gross weight of more than 26,000 pounds, the maximum deduction is $50,000. The $50,000 maximum also applies to buses that can seat 20 adult passengers. Under the phase-out provisions for this deduction, the dollar limits above are reduced by 75 percent for property placed in service in 2006. The deduction will be eliminated entirely in 2007 (unless Congress extends it once again). If you file Schedule C for your business, this deduction should be claimed as an "other expense." If the vehicle is used only partly for business, the portion of the deduction that applies to personal use would be claimed on Line 33 of Form 1040, entering your deduction and "Clean Fuel" on the dotted line.

4. Tax credit for electric vehicles

A 10 percent tax credit (based on your purchase price) is allowed for certain electric vehicles placed in service after June 30, 1993, and before January 1, 2007. The maximum credit may not exceed $4,000 in 2004 and 2005. The credit will be reduced by 75 percent in 2006 and eliminated entirely in 2007 (unless it, too, is saved from extinction by Congress). Until then, the allowable credit is claimed on IRS Form 8834, Qualified Electric Vehicle Credit.

Source: ItsSimple.biz (*www.itssimple.biz*) is a very popular free Internet resource center which assists small business owners by providing valuable information, guidance and business-development tools. ItsSimple.biz is a free Internet resource center to assist small business owners. Contact information: ItsSimple.biz, 316 California Ave., Suite 433, Reno, NV 89509, Tel: (775) 324-2900.

Most Common Nondeductible Expenses

As a small business owner, you may be thinking about the things you want to deduct when tax time comes. However, there are certain expenses that are always nondeductible. Here are some expenses that the IRS says you cannot deduct.

1. Adoption expenses

You cannot deduct the expenses of adopting a child, but you may be able to take a credit for those expenses.

2. Campaign expenses

You cannot deduct campaign expenses of a candidate for any office, even if the candidate is running for re-election. These expenses include qualification and registration fees for primary elections.

3. Capital expense

You cannot currently deduct amounts paid to buy property that has a useful life substantially beyond the tax year or amounts paid to increase the value or prolong the life of property. If you use such property in your work, you may be able to take a depreciation deduction.

4. Check-writing fees on a personal account

If you have a personal checking account, you cannot deduct fees charged by the bank for the privilege of writing checks, even if the account pays interest.

5. Club dues

Generally, you cannot deduct the cost of membership in any club organized for business, pleasure, recreation, or other social purposes. This includes business, social, athletic, luncheon, sporting, airline, hotel, golf, and country clubs.

6. Commuting expenses

You cannot deduct commuting expenses (the cost of transportation between your home and your main or regular place of work). If you haul tools, instruments, or other items in your car to and from work, you can deduct only the additional costs of hauling the items, such as the rent on a trailer to carry the items.

7. Fines or penalties

You cannot deduct fines or penalties you pay to the governmental unit for violating a law. This includes an amount paid in settlement of your actual or potential liability for a fine or penalty (civil or criminal). Fines or penalties include parking tickets, tax penalties, and penalties deducted from teachers' paychecks after an illegal strike.

8. Health and spa expenses

You cannot deduct health spa expenses, even if there is a job requirement to stay in excellent physical condition, such as might be required of a law enforcement officer.

9. Home security system

You cannot deduct the cost of a home security system as a miscellaneous deduction. However, you may be able to claim a deduction for a home security system as a business expense if you have a home office.

10. Homeowner's insurance premiums

You cannot deduct premiums that you pay or that are placed in escrow for insurance on your home, such as fire and liability or mortgage insurance.

11. Investment-related seminars

You cannot deduct any expenses for attending a convention, seminar, or similar meeting for investment purposes.

12. Life insurance premiums

You cannot deduct premiums you pay on your life insurance. You may be able to deduct, as alimony, premiums you pay on life insurance policies assigned to your former spouse.

13. Lobbying expenses

You generally cannot deduct amounts paid or incurred for lobbying expenses. These include expenses to influence legislation; participate, or intervene, in any political campaign for or against any candidate for public office; attempt to influence the general public, or segments of the general public, about elections, legislative matters, or referendums and to communicate directly with covered executive branch officials in any attempt to influence the official actions or positions of those officials.

14. Lost or mislaid cash or property

You cannot deduct a loss based on the mere disappearance of money or property. However, accidental loss or disappearance of property can qualify as a casualty if it results from an identifiable event that is sudden, unexpected, or unusual.

15. Lunches with coworkers

You cannot deduct the expenses of lunches with coworkers, except while traveling away from home on business.

16. Meals while working late

You cannot deduct the cost of meals while working late. However, you may be able to claim a deduction if the cost of the meals is a deductible entertainment expense, or if you are traveling away from home.

17. Personal legal expenses

You cannot deduct personal legal expenses such as those for the following: custody of children, breach of promise (to marry) suit, civil or criminal charges resulting from a personal relationship, damages for personal injury, preparation of title (or defense or perfection of a title), preparation of a will, and property claims or property settlement in a divorce. You cannot deduct these expenses even if a result of the legal proceedings is the loss of income-producing property.

18. Political contributions

You cannot deduct contributions made to a political candidate, a campaign committee, or a newsletter fund. Advertisements in convention bulletins and admissions to dinners or programs that benefit a political party or political candidate are not deductible.

19. Professional accreditation fees

You cannot deduct professional accreditation fees such as the following: accounting certificate fees paid for the initial right to practice accounting, bar exam fees and incidental expenses in securing admission to the bar;

medical and dental license fees paid to get the initial licensing.

20. Professional reputation

You cannot deduct expenses of radio and TV appearances to increase your personal prestige or establish your professional reputation.

21. Relief fund contributions

You cannot deduct contributions paid to a private plan that pays benefits to any covered employee who cannot work because of any injury or illness not related to the job.

22. Residential telephone service

You cannot deduct any charge (including taxes) for basic local telephone service for the first telephone line to your residence, even if it is used in a trade or business.

23. Stockholders' meetings

You cannot deduct transportation and other expenses you pay to attend stockholders' meetings of companies in which you own stock but have no other interest. You cannot deduct these expenses even if you are attending the meeting to get information that would be useful in making further investments.

24. Tax-exempt income expenses

You cannot deduct expenses to produce tax-exempt income. You cannot deduct interest on a debt incurred or continued to buy or carry tax-exempt securities. If you have expenses to produce both taxable and tax-exempt income, but you cannot identify the expenses that produce each type of income, you must divide the expenses based on the amount of each type of income to determine the amount that you can deduct.

25. Travel expenses for another individual

You generally cannot deduct travel expenses you pay or incur for a spouse, dependent, or other individual who accompanies you (or your employee) on business travel.

26. Voluntary unemployment benefit contributions

You cannot deduct voluntary unemployment benefit fund contributions you make to a union fund or a private fund. However, you can deduct contributions as taxes if state law requires you to make them to a state unemployment fund that covers you for the loss of wages from unemployment caused by business conditions.

27. Wristwatches

You cannot deduct the cost of a wristwatch, even if there is a job requirement that you know the correct time to properly perform your duties.

Source: Internal Revenue Service (*www.irs.gov*).

Ways to Identify Meal and Entertainment Expenses

Can't we all have a little fun? You can, but according to the IRS, you won't be able to deduct it all. Entertainment includes any activity generally considered to provide entertainment, amusement, or recreation. Generally, only 50 percent of meal and entertainment expenses are allowed as a deduction. The following are ways to identify meal and entertainment expenses, directly from those party-poopers themselves.

1. Expect benefits

To meet the directly related test under the general rule, you must show that you had more than a general expectation of getting income or some other specific business benefit at some future time.

2. Show that you engaged in business

To meet the directly related test under the general rule, you must show that you engaged in business with the person being entertained during the entertainment period.

3. Active conduct of business

To meet the directly related test under the general rule, you must show that the main purpose of the entertainment was the active conduct of business.

4. Show that expenditure was allocable

To meet the directly related test under the general rule, you must show that the expenditure was allocable to you and a person with whom you conducted business during the entertainment or with whom you would have conducted business (if it were not for circumstances beyond your control).

5. Clear business setting

You may also meet the directly related test by showing that the expenditure was for entertainment occurring in a clear business setting directly in furtherance of your trade or business.

6. Compensation for services

You may also meet the directly related test by showing that the expenditure was made directly or indirectly to someone (other than an employee) as compensation for services.

7. Prize or reward payment

The expenditure was paid as a prize or award that is required to be included in the recipient's gross income.

8. Active conduct of business and bona fide discussion

For entertainment to meet the associated test, you must show that the entertainment was associated with the active conduct of your trade or business and directly preceded or followed a substantial and bona fide business discussion.

Source: Internal Revenue Service (*www.irs.gov*).

Top Deductions for Compensation Expenses

You can generally deduct the pay you give your employees for the services they perform. What qualifies as a deductible compensation expense? Here's a list from the IRS.

1. Awards

You can generally deduct amounts you pay to your employees as awards, whether paid in cash or property. If you give property to an employee as an employee achievement award, your deduction may be limited.

2. Achievement awards

An achievement award is an item of tangible personal property that meets all the following requirements. It is given to an employee for length of service or safety achievement. It is awarded as part of a meaningful presentation. It is awarded under conditions and circumstances that do not create a significant likelihood of disguised pay.

3. Length-of-service award

An award will qualify as a length-of-service award if either of the following applies. The employee receives the award after his or her first five years of employment. The employee did not receive another length-of-service award (other than one of very small value) during the same year or in any of the prior four years.

4. Safety achievement award

An award for safety achievement will qualify as an achievement award unless one of the following applies. It is given to a manager, administrator, clerical employee, or other professional employee. Or, during the tax year, more than 10 percent of your employees have already received a safety achievement award (other than one of very small value).

5. Bonuses

You can generally deduct a bonus paid to an employee if you intended the bonus as additional pay for services, not as a gift, and if the services were performed. However, the total bonuses, salaries, and other pay must be reasonable for the services performed. If the bonus is paid in property, see entry 16.

6. Gifts of nominal value

If, to promote employee goodwill, you distribute turkeys, hams, or other merchandise of nominal value to your employees at holidays, you can deduct the cost of these items as a nonwage business expense. Your deduction for de minimus gifts of food or drink are not subject to the 50 percent deduction limit that generally applies to meals. For more information on this deduction limit, see entry 12, meals and lodging.

7. Education expenses

If you pay or reimburse education expenses for an employee, you can deduct the payments. Deduct them on the "employee benefit programs" or other appropriate line of your tax return if they are part of a qualified educational assistance program. (For information on educational assistance programs, see Educational Assistance in section 2 of Publication 15-B.)

8. Fringe benefits

A fringe benefit is a form of pay for the performance of services. You can generally deduct the cost of fringe benefits you provide in whatever category you would otherwise include the cost. For example, if you allow an employee to use a car or other property you lease, deduct the cost as a rent or lease expense. You may be able to exclude all or part of the value of some fringe benefits from your employees' pay. You also may not owe employment taxes on the value of the fringe benefits. (See Table 2-1 in Publication 15-B for details.) The following are examples of fringe benefits: benefits under employee benefit programs (defined in entry 9), meals and lodging, use of a car, flights on airplanes, discounts on property or services, memberships in country clubs or other social clubs, and tickets to entertainment or sporting events.

9. Employee benefit programs

These programs include accident and health plans, adoption assistance, cafeteria plans, dependent care assistance, educational assistance, life insurance coverage, and welfare benefit funds. You can generally deduct amounts you spend on employee benefit programs on the "employee benefit programs" or other applicable line of your tax return. For example, if you provide dependent care by operating a dependent care facility for your employees, deduct your costs in whatever categories they fall (utilities, salaries, etc.).

10. Life insurance coverage

You cannot deduct the cost of life insurance coverage for you, an employee, or any person with a financial interest in your business, if you are directly or indirectly the beneficiary of the policy. (See Regulations section 1.264-1 for more information.)

11. Welfare benefit funds

A welfare benefit fund is a funded plan (or a funded arrangement having the effect of a plan) that provides welfare benefits to your employees, independent contractors, or their beneficiaries. Welfare benefits are any benefits other than deferred compensation or transfers of restricted property. Your deduction for contributions to a welfare benefit fund is limited to the fund's qualified cost for the tax year. If your contributions to the fund are more than its qualified cost, you can carry the excess over to the next tax year. Generally, the fund's "qualified cost" is the total of the following amounts, reduced by the after-tax income of the fund: the cost you would have been able to deduct using the cash method of accounting if you had paid for the benefits directly, And the contributions added to a reserve account that are needed to fund claims incurred but not paid as of the end of the year. These claims can be for supplemental unemployment benefits, severance pay, or disability, medical, or life insurance benefits. (For more information, see sections 419c and 419A of the Internal Revenue Code and the related regulations.)

12. Meals and lodging

You can usually deduct the cost of furnishing meals and lodging to your employees. Deduct the cost in whatever category the expense falls. For example, if you operate a restaurant, deduct the cost of the meals you furnish to employees as part of the cost of goods sold. If you operate a nursing home, motel, or rental property, deduct the cost of furnishing lodging to an employee as expenses for utilities, linen service, salaries, depreciation, and so on.

13. Deduction limit on meals

You can generally deduct only 50 percent of the cost of furnishing meals to your employees. However, you can deduct the full cost of the following meals. Meals whose value you include in an employee's wages (for more information, see section 2 in Publication 15-B). Meals that qualify as a de minimus fringe benefit as discussed in section 2 of Publication 15-B (this generally includes meals you furnish to employees at your place of business if more than half of these employees are provided the meals for your convenience). Meals you furnish to your employees at the work site when you operate a restaurant or catering service. Meals you furnish to your employees as part of the expense of providing recreational or social activities, such as a company picnic. Meals you are required by federal law to furnish to crew members of certain commercial vessels (or would be required to furnish if the vessels were operated at sea); this does not include meals you furnish on vessels primarily providing luxury water transportation. Meals you furnish on an oil or gas platform or drilling rig located offshore or in Alaska (This includes meals you furnish at a support camp that is near and integral to an oil or gas drilling rig located in Alaska).

14. Loans or advances

You generally can deduct as wages an advance you make to an employee for services performed if you do not expect the employee to repay the advance. However, if the employee performs no services, treat the amount you advanced as a loan. If the employee does not repay the loan, it may be deductible as a bad debt. If someone owes you money you cannot collect, you have a bad debt. There are two kinds of bad debts—business and nonbusiness. Generally, a business bad debt is one that comes from operating your trade or business. You can deduct business bad debts on your business tax return.

All other bad debts are nonbusiness bad debts and are deductible only as short-term capital losses on Schedule D (Form 1040). For more information on nonbusiness bad debts, see Publication 550.

15. Below-market interest rate loans

A below-market loan is a loan on which no interest is charged or on which interest is charged at a rate below the applicable federal rate. On certain loans you make to an employee or shareholder, you are treated as having received interest income and as having paid compensation or dividends equal to that interest.

16. Property

If you transfer property (including your company's stock) to an employee as payment for services, you can generally deduct it as wages. The amount you can deduct is the property's fair market value on the date of the transfer less any amount the employee paid for the property. You can claim the deduction only for the tax year in which your employee includes the property's value in income. Your employee is deemed to have included the value in income if you report it on Form W-2 in a timely manner. You treat the deductible amount as received in exchange for the property, and you must recognize any gain or loss realized on the transfer. Your gain or loss is the difference between the fair market value of the property and its adjusted basis on the date of transfer.

17. Reimbursements for business expenses

You can generally deduct the amount you pay or reimburse employees for business expenses they incur for your business for items such as travel and entertainment. However, your deduction for meal and entertainment expenses is usually limited to 50 percent of the amount paid. If you make the payment under an accountable plan, deduct it in the category of the expense paid. For example, if you pay an employee for travel expenses incurred on your behalf, deduct this payment as a travel expense. If you make the payment under a nonaccountable plan, deduct it as wages.

18. Sick and vacation pay

You can deduct amounts you pay to your employees for sickness and injury, including lump-sum amounts, as wages. However, your deduction is limited to amounts not compensated by insurance or other means. Vacation pay is an employee benefit. It includes amounts paid for unused vacation leave. You can deduct vacation pay only in the tax year in which the employee actually receives it. This rule applies regardless of whether you use the cash or accrual method of accounting.

Source: Internal Revenue Service (*www.irs.gov*).

Most Common Capital Expenditures

Businesses spend money on various things such as purchases of goods, overhead, payroll. Sometimes a question arises about whether an expenditure is an expense or a capitalizable item. This list will give examples of typical purchases that should be capitalized.

1. Land

If you purchase a piece of property, it must be capitalized and normally will not be depreciated. Expenses such as real-estate taxes and investment interest are also usually added to the basis of the property, instead of being expensed.

2. Buildings

Real estate that is owned is always capitalized. The building must be owned by the company *not* by the owners of the company. The cost of land should be separated from the cost of the building, since land is not depreciable.

3. Improvements

The cost of major improvements to a building are capitalized, whether the company owns the building or just rents, as long as the improvements are paid for by the company. The threshold for determining a major expense varies from business to business, depending on the size of the company. Also, if an improvement extends the life of the building (e.g., a roof), it should be capitalized, as opposed to cosmetics, such as painting.

4. Heavy machinery

Major industrial equipment used in the manufacture of goods must be capitalized. Small tools and supplies are usually expensed.

5. Furniture and fixtures

Major furniture purchases and fixtures, such as display cases or shelving, are capitalized. Again, which purchases are major depends on the size of the company. Normally, small chairs or low-cost items are expensed. Carpeting may or may not be capitalized, depending on characteristics such as removability and frequency of replacement.

6. Office equipment

Computers, fax machines, copiers, telephone systems, and other office equipment not purchased for resale are capitalized unless the purchases are minor. For example, if a printer is purchased apart from an entire computer system, it is normally expensed as office supplies.

7. Autos and trucks

Trucks used for the transport of company materials (construction, inventory, etc.) are capitalized, as well as company autos for employees. The percentage of the cost of company autos that relates to personal business should be added to the employee's W-2 at the end of the year.

8. Leased equipment

Certain equipment under lease must be capitalized. The decision is usually dictated by the buyout terms at the end of the lease. If there is a 10 percent or $1 buyout, it is usually a capital lease, as opposed to a fair market buyout, which is an operating lease. Operating lease costs are expensed as incurred.

9. Signs

Company signage may or may not be capitalized. Some factors in the decision are the magnitude of the expense, portability of the sign, and ownership of the sign.

10. Intangibles

Intangibles include items such as liquor licenses, patents, copyrights, trademarks, non-compete agreements, and goodwill. These are usually capitalized and depreciated over fifteen years.

Source: David A. Caplan, CPA, MBA (www.caplancpa.com)— He received his CPA in 1980, while working for a Big 10 public accounting firm. He was employed in various industries from 1981 to 1992, gaining insight on the inner workings of companies, and received his MBA from Temple University in 1986. In 1992, he purchased an accounting practice, which has quintupled in size since then. He handles all aspects of accounting, from personal income tax and advice to financial statements and corporate tax returns. He has clients geographically located all over the United States. He can be reached at PO Box 301, Lafayette Hill, PA 19444; (610) 834-5754; fax: (610) 834-1013.

Most Common Deductible Travel Expenses

Once you have determined that you are traveling away from your tax home, you can determine what travel expenses are deductible. You can deduct ordinary and necessary expenses you have when you travel away from home on business. The type of expense you can deduct depends on the facts and your circumstances. When you travel away from home on business, you should keep records of all the expenses you have and any advances you receive from your employer. You can use a log, diary, notebook, or any other written record to keep track of your expenses. The types of expenses you need to record, along with supporting documentation are listed here.

1. Transportation

If you have expenses for transportation, you can deduct the cost of travel by airplane, train, bus, or car between your home and your business destination. If you were provided with a ticket or you are riding free as a result of a frequent traveler or similar program, your cost is zero.

2. Taxi, commuter bus, and airport limousine

If you have expenses for taxis, commuter buses, and airport limousines, you can deduct the cost of fares for these and other types of transportation that take you between the airport or station and your hotel, and the hotel and the work location of your customers or clients, your business meeting place, or your temporary work location.

3. Baggage and shipping

If you have expenses for baggage and shipping, you can deduct the cost of sending baggage and sample or display material between your regular and temporary work locations.

4. Car

If you have expenses for cars, you can deduct the cost of operating and maintaining your car when traveling away from home on business. You can deduct actual expenses or the standard mileage rate, as well as business-related tolls and parking. If you rent a car while away from home on business, you can deduct only the business-use portion of the expenses.

5. Lodging and meals

If you have expenses for lodging and meals, you can deduct the cost of your lodging and meals if your business trip is overnight or long enough that you need to stop for sleep or rest to perform your duties properly. Meals include amounts spent for food, beverages, taxes, and related tips. You can deduct the cost of meals in either of the following two situations: It is necessary for you to stop for substantial sleep or rest to perform your duties properly while traveling away from home on business, or the meal is business-related entertainment.

6. Cleaning

If you have expenses for cleaning, you can deduct the cost of dry cleaning and laundry.

7. Telephone

If you have expenses for the telephone, you can deduct costs of business calls while on your business trip. This includes business communication by fax machine or other communication devices.

8. Tips

If you have expenses for tips, you can deduct the cost of tips you pay for any expenses in this list.

9. Other

If you have other expenses, you can deduct the cost of other similar ordinary and necessary expenses related to your business travel. These expenses might include transportation to or from a business meal, public stenographer's fees, computer rental fees, and operating and maintaining a house trailer.

10. Incidental expenses

The term *incidental expenses* means fees and tips given to porters, baggage carriers, bellhops, hotel maids, stewards or stewardesses and others on ships, and hotel servants in foreign countries, transportation between places of lodging or business and places where meals are taken, if suitable meals cannot be obtained at the temporary duty site, and mailing costs associated with filing travel vouchers and payment of employer-sponsored charge card billings. Incidental expenses do not include expenses for laundry, cleaning and pressing of clothing, lodging taxes, or the costs of telegrams or telephone calls.

Source: Internal Revenue Service (*www.irs.gov*).

Brilliant Deductions for the Self-Employed

The big corporations know that business success hinges on tax and financial savvy. Here are some tax deduction tips that will help guide independent professionals through the maze of tax laws written not for indies but for the corporate world and the employees who inhabit that world.

1. Give the old clunker a break

Maximize your auto expense deductions by using both your cars for your business driving. If you have been using only the old clunker to cart around your supplies or to drive from your office to meet with clients, put some business miles on the new Volvo as well. If, for instance, 3,000 of the Volvo's 10,000 miles per year are for business, you will get a deduction of 30 percent of all Volvo costs. That means 30 percent of the $40,000 purchase price as well as things like insurance, gas, and so on. If you've used the old clunker almost totally for business—let's say 90 percent—you can still deduct 90 percent of its costs as well.

2. Work at home and deduct more business transportation costs

The IRS has liberalized the rules on office-in-the-home. At one time, you couldn't take a deduction for home office or studio if you also worked at another location. Now you are allowed a home-office deduction even if the space is used

only for administrative tasks like calls, recordkeeping, or billing, as long as the office area of your home is used exclusively and regularly for your business. So, how does sitting at a desk in your home increase transportation expenses? Well, the IRS does not allow a deduction for the costs of commuting from home to work and back. But it does allow a deduction for getting from one workplace to another. So if you start your workday in your home office by answering e-mails or working on a presentation and then commute to your other office, you are now going "from one workplace to another." You can then deduct your transportation costs, whether it's business miles in your car or subway or bus fare. Bonus: the extra tax benefits of home-office and transportation deductions come with not one extra penny out of your pocket.

3. Come one, come all

So you're planning a big bash to show off your new product or service, by invitation only. Wait a minute, before you mail those invitations, think about this. If your exhibit or presentation is open to the public (such as a grand opening), you get to deduct the entire cost of food and liquor served. If the exhibit welcomes invited guests only, sorry, but you can deduct only 50 percent of those costs.

4. Reach for it

When you pick up the check at a business lunch or dinner, get a business card from your companion(s) and staple the card(s) to your copy of the restaurant receipt. You need to document meals and entertainment expenses, including date, amount, name of restaurant, business relationship of those present, and business purpose. The business card is a quick documentation aid.

5. Keep it clean

Spill red wine on your white silk blouse while attending a business conference? Dry cleaning and laundry while on your business trip are deductible business expenses. You may also deduct the costs of the first dry cleaning bill after you return home from a business trip. Careful: Don't get too creative and save all your winter's dirty clothes for cleaning the day after you return from a three-day business trip.

6. Hire your child

Are you grooming your twelve-year-old to take over your business? Do you put her to work in your office every Saturday? If you do, and you're a sole proprietor or a husband-and-wife partnership, hire your child. The wages are taxable to your child at her tax bracket, not yours. You reduce your profit by paying out a wage expense, and, if your child is under eighteen, you will pay no social security or federal unemployment taxes on her wages (often no state payroll taxes either). Your child must have a real job (not $200 per week to empty wastebaskets). You will also have to file payroll forms, but the additional paperwork and cost is usually worth it.

7. Hire your spouse

You can give him liberal employee benefits and deduct all the costs from your gross income. Give him a comprehensive medical plan that covers him and his entire family (that includes you and the kids). That means all medical costs including insurance, hospitals, doctors, prescriptions, eyeglasses, dental—all of which can be deducted from your business income. If you want to be really nice to the guy you can provide long-term-care insurance for him and his spouse (that's you), as well as term-life insurance. Careful: He must actually perform duties for your business. Companies like BizPlan (*www.tasconline.com*) will handle the paperwork for you for about $200 per year and, if you comply with the rules, they guarantee their work should there be an audit.

8. Fund your spouse's pension

While you have your honey working for you, why not give him a pension? In effect, you'll be funding your own retirement plan as well. What you contribute to his pension is deductible from your gross business income. You won't pay taxes on this money until it is withdrawn from the pension—years down the road. If you have other employees, what you provide to your spouse may have to be provided to them as well.

9. Be late to be smart

It's often to your advantage to file your tax return well after April 15. With extensions you may file your return and contribute to most self-employed pensions as late as October 15. You—and your tax pro—have choices on how different items on your tax return may be treated. Events this year may help determine which choice is most advantageous for last year. For instance, an upmarket may mean you have enough money to fully fund last year's pension, or a bad year may mean that you should fully deduct your equipment purchases last year. Careful: An extension means more time to file. To avoid penalty and interest, you must have all your taxes paid by April 15.

10. Don't hide income

We've all run across examples of the underground economy: They run on cash and are probably not reporting their income. For the most part, they are marginal businesses that will never amount to anything. The people who use their services can treat them any way they choose, and these illegal businesses are without recourse because they can't come out of hiding. Being a member of the business community is good for your enterprise. When indies go legit, they never regret it. They sleep better, too.

Source: June Walker (*www.junewalkeronline.com*) has been a financial and tax consultant to the self-employed for twenty-five years. Her clients are worldwide and include psychologists, carpenters, IT consultants, attorneys. June is the author of *Self-Employed Tax Solutions: Quick, Simple, Money-Saving, Audit-Proof Tax and Recordkeeping Basics for the Independent Professional* (The Globe Pequot Press, 2005). For more information, e-mail her at *june@junewalkeronline*, or call (888) 219-7771.

Top Federal Tax Credits Utilized

The federal tax laws contains some fairly generous tax credits for those who are lucky enough (or smart enough) to be able to take advantage of them. The credits can generally be divided into these four categories: credits for certain taxes, credits for activities that benefit disadvantaged or low-income persons, credits for activities that benefit the environment, and credits for certain other investments. Here's a list of popular federal tax credits that you might be able to take advantage of.

1. Credit for FICA tax on tips

Under current law, employees who get $20 or more in tips in a single month must report their tips to their employers. If you have tipped employees, you have to pay social security and Medicare (FICA) taxes to the tune of 7.65 percent on tips that are reported to you, even though you don't have any control over the amounts. The purpose of the rule is to make sure that tipped employees are adequately covered by social security pension, disability, and survivors' benefits. However, the rule was seen to place a particularly heavy burden on the restaurant industry. So, if your business is one that provides food or beverages for customers to consume on or off the premises, and if your waiters, waitresses, or delivery personnel are customarily tipped by your patrons, you're entitled to a tax credit for any FICA taxes you pay on the tips, whether or not your employee reports the tips. Before 1997, tips for food not consumed on the premises (for example, tips for pizza delivery) did not count toward this credit. The upshot of all this? Your workers receive social security credits toward their future benefits on account of the tips, but you don't have to pay for these benefits. There is an exception to the general credit rule: if you pay your employees below the minimum wage, with the expectation that tips will bring them up to the minimum, you can't claim the credit for FICA on the portion of the tips that is used to bring them up to the minimum wage.

2. Gasoline tax credit

You can claim a credit for any federal excise taxes you pay on gasoline and special fuels (like undyed diesel, heating oil, liquefied petroleum gas, and compressed natural gas), when you use the fuel for certain purposes: farming; nonhighway purposes of your trade or business; intercity, local, or school buses; or export or foreign trade. You can't claim this credit for any personal (nonbusiness) use, so forget about claiming it for your snowmobile or pleasure boat! The credit is claimed on Form 4136, Credit for Federal Tax Paid on Fuels. It is refundable, meaning that the IRS will pay it to you even if you have no tax liability for the year.

3. Foreign tax credit

You can claim a credit for foreign income taxes, or taxes imposed by possessions of the United States, that you paid or accrued during the tax year. For example, you might have become liable for foreign taxes on profits from overseas operations or investments. You can elect to deduct these taxes instead of taking the credit, if you prefer, although claiming the credit will generally save you more money. The credit is claimed on Form 1116, Foreign Tax Credit. Like most credits, it can't be used to reduce your alternative minimum tax (AMT).

4. Employee retention credit

The Katrina Emergency Tax Relief Act of 2005 offers a new tax credit to encourage small employers to keep employees on their payrolls. The credit is 40 percent of the first $6,000 in wages paid to each eligible employee after August 28, 2005, and before January 1, 2006, by employers located in a core disaster area (i.e., the president declares a disaster area), for the period the business is rendered inoperable as a result of damage caused by Hurricane Katrina. This credit is only available to small employers, defined as a business that employed an average of no more than 200 employees during the tax year.

5. Work opportunity tax credit

This credit was designed to provide an incentive to hire persons from certain disadvantaged groups that have a particularly high unemployment rate (including urban youths, government assistance recipients, ex-convicts, veterans, and vocational rehabilitation referrals). It was created in 1996 to replace the expired targeted jobs credit. The work opportunity tax credit has been extended a number of times and currently applies to the wages of employees who begin working for the employer through December 31, 2005.

6. Credit for qualified electric vehicles

If you purchase a new electric vehicle and place it in service before 2006, you can receive a tax credit for 10 percent of the purchase price (up to $4,000). In 2006, the maximum credit is reduced by 75 percent. The credit is eliminated entirely in 2007. Any part of the cost that you elect to expense under Section 179 is not eligible for the credit, and the credit amount reduces the tax basis of the vehicle. The credit is claimed on Form 8834, Qualified Electric Vehicle Credit.

7. Energy credit

An energy credit is allowed for 10 percent of the cost of the following types of property placed in service during the year: (a) equipment that uses solar energy to generate electricity, heat or cool a structure, provide hot water, or provide solar process heat; or (b) equipment used to produce, distribute, or use geothermal energy stored in rocks, water, or steam. The property must be depreciable (i.e., used in your business). The energy credit is part of the investment tax credit and can be recaptured (paid back to the IRS) if the qualifying property is sold or disposed of before the end of its recovery period. It is claimed on Form 3468, Investment Tax Credit.

8. Reforestation credit

For those in timber production, the 10 percent reforestation credit applies to up to $10,000 of the expenses you incur each year to forest or reforest your property. Eligible expenses include the costs of site preparation, seeds or seedlings, labor, and tools, including depreciation on machinery and equipment. The property must be held for growing trees for sale or use in the commercial production of timber products. The reforestation credit is part of the investment tax credit and is claimed on Form 3468, Investment Tax Credit.

9. Alcohol fuels credit

Producers of alcohol fuels or mixtures such as gasohol or ethanol can receive a tax credit for any sale or use of such fuels. The credit was scheduled to expire after September 30, 2005. No carryforward of the credit is permitted for any tax year beginning after 1994. The alcohol fuels credit is part of the general business credit. It's claimed on Form 6478, Credit for Alcohol Used as Fuel.

10. Enhanced oil recovery credit

If you begin or significantly expand a domestic oil recovery project that uses certain tertiary recovery methods—such as the injection of liquids, gases, or other matter—to increase crude oil production, you can take a credit for 15 percent of your qualified enhanced oil recovery costs for the tax year. The enhanced oil recovery credit is part of the general business credit. It's claimed on Form 8830, Enhanced Oil Recovery Credit.

11. Renewable resources electricity-production credit

This credit is based on electricity that is produced before 2006 from wind, closed-loop biomass (organic material grown exclusively for electricity production), or poultry waste facilities and sold to third parties. The credit for calendar year 2004 is 1.8 cents per kilowatt hour of such electricity sold (1.9 cents for 2005). The credit is part of the general business credit. It is claimed on Form 8835, Renewable Electricity Production Credit.

12. Research and development (R & D) credit

The R & D credit is designed to encourage businesses to increase the amounts they spend on research and experimental activities. The credit applies for qualified research paid or incurred on or before December 31, 2005. This credit is one that has expired and been retroactively reinstated several times (most recently by the Working Families Tax Act of 2004), so it's likely that it will continue to be extended in the future. The R & D credit is generally 20 percent of the amount by which your research expenses for the year are higher than your "base period amount." To qualify for the credit, the research must be technological in nature (not research in the social sciences, arts, or humanities) and must be intended to be useful in the development of a new or improved business component. Further, it must relate to a new or improved function, performance, reliability, or quality. Qualified research expenses includes in-house research, 65 percent of the cost of research done by a person other than an employee of the taxpayer, and 75 percent of the costs paid to a qualified scientific research consortium. The R & D credit is claimed on Form 6765, Credit for Increasing Research Activities, and is part of the general business credit.

13. Orphan drug credit

The orphan drug credit is designed to encourage development of drugs for rare diseases and conditions, the occurrences of which are so infrequent that drug development would otherwise be economically unfeasible. The credit expired at the end of 1994 but was permanently reinstated for qualified testing expenses paid or incurred after July 1, 1996. The credit is equal to 50 percent of the qualified clinical testing expenses for the year. The orphan drug credit operates in much the same fashion as the R & D credit, except that there is no requirement that expenses exceed a base amount. Where the same expenses would qualify for both the orphan drug credit and the R

& D credit, you must choose between them—the same expenses can't be claimed as a credit twice. The orphan drug credit is claimed on Form 8820, Orphan Drug Credit.

14. Rehabilitation credit

This tax credit is designed to encourage the rehabilitation of older real estate or certified historic buildings. It allows you to take a tax credit for the expenses you have for renovating, restoring, or rehabilitating (but not enlarging or adding new construction to) certain structures. The percentage of expenses you can take as a credit is 10 percent for buildings originally placed in service before 1936, and 20 percent for buildings listed in the National Register of Historic Places. The credit is further limited to the tax paid on $25,000 and is phased out for taxpayers with adjusted gross incomes between $200,000 and $250,000. If a project involves both rehabilitation and enlargement, only the costs allocated toward rehabilitation are eligible for the credit. If you claim this credit, you must reduce the depreciable tax basis of the property by the amount of the credit. To be eligible for the credit, the rehabilitation expenditures must be for nonresidential real property. An exception to this rule applies to certified historic structures, which may be used as residential rental property. The building must be "substantially rehabilitated"; that is, the expenses in some twenty-four-month period must be more than the greater of $5,000 or your adjusted basis in the building. Also, unless the building is a certified historic structure, at least 75 percent of the external walls must be retained, with 50 percent or more kept in place as external walls, and at least 75 percent of the existing internal structural framework of the building retained in place. The rehabilitation credit is part of the investment tax credit and can be recaptured (paid back to the IRS) if the qualifying property is sold or disposed of within five years of the time it is placed in service. The credit is claimed on Form 3468, Investment Tax Credit.

15. Retirement plan start-up credit

To stimulate greater retirement saving, small employers who establish new retirement plans are now entitled to a tax credit for doing so. The credit is only available to employers with 100 employees or fewer who have not maintained a qualified retirement plan during the three-year period immediately before the first effective year of the new plan. This credit is set to expire for tax years beginning after 2010. The credit amounts to 50 percent of the costs incurred in creating or maintaining a new qualified plan, up to a maximum of $500 in each of the first three years the plan is effective. Essentially, this means that you have to spend at least $1,000 per year to get the full credit. Any setup and administration costs not offset by the tax credit (i.e., those above $1,000 in the first three years and those incurred after the first three years) are deductible as ordinary and necessary business expenses.

16. Employer-provided child-care credit

For tax years beginning before 2011, small, as well as middle-size, businesses will be eligible for a tax credit of 25 percent of the qualified child-care expenses they provide and 10 percent of the cost of qualified child-care resource and referral services they offer. The employer-provided credit is capped at $150,000 per tax year. Expenses eligible for the credit include payments under a contract with a qualified child-care facility to provide child-care services to the business' employees. Qualified child-care expenses also include the amounts paid or incurred by the employer to acquire, construct, establish, and operate a qualified child-care facility for employees. The facility itself must meet any state and local government laws and regulations, like licensing requirements, that may apply for its location.

Source: CCH Business Owner's Toolkit (*www.toolkit.cch.com*)—The Business Owner's Toolkit provides advice, guides, legal tools, business models, and other resources to small business owners.

Most Visited Tax Web Sites

As a business owner, questions may arise about your taxes throughout the year. We interviewed an expert, who is a certified public accountant, and asked her which tax-related Web sites she visits the most. These are Web sites she uses on a daily basis.

1. Internal Revenue Service

The Internal Revenue Service offers America's taxpayers top-quality service by helping them understand and meet their tax responsibilities. The IRS is a bureau of the Department of the Treasury and one of the world's most efficient tax administrators. As one of the most often visited sites in America, tax professionals and the public use this Web site as their primary source for tax forms and publications, for tax research, and for authoritative information related to federal tax laws and changes.

www.irs.gov

2. State Franchise Tax Board

The Franchise Tax Board is the department that administers state personal income taxes, corporation taxes and sales tax for the expert's home state of California. Other states have similar entities. The Franchise Tax Board also collects debts on behalf of other agencies and certain counties and local entities. This Web site offers everything there is to know about California law and legislation, forms and publications, tax amnesty, and other current issues affecting California taxpayers. Forms and publications are also available in Spanish, and a section in Spanish is devoted to answering general tax questions. The Web site also has a very comprehensive site index.

www.ftb.ca.gov

3. CCH Tax Research Products

CCH Tax and Accounting, a WoltersKluwer Company, provides tax research knowledge, integrated with powerful software and advanced tools for tax professionals to maximize their productivity. Each morning I check my e-mail for the latest tax law news. Keep up with the most current federal and state tax law changes by subscribing to their daily e-mail service. Go to Sign Up for CCH Tax News Headlines at the bottom of the page.

http://tax.cchgroup.com/default

4. Spidell Publishing Inc.

To keep up-to-date on state tax changes visit Caltax.com. At Caltax.com, tax professionals can also learn about and order from Spidell Publishing's host of products and services geared to California tax professionals. Spidell Publishing is widely known by California tax professionals as being the leading authority in matters for California taxation. Caltax.com's Breaking Tax News section provides up-to-the minute news about California taxes, including issues of Spidell's California Taxletter, FAQs, statutes, regulations, government manuals, notices, rulings, cases, and a comprehensive tax library to meet your research needs.

www.caltax.com

5. American Institute of Certified Public Accountants

The American Institute of Certified Public Accountants (AICPA) has been serving the accounting profession since 1887. The AICPA and its members are committed to serving the public good. Member services include professional guidance on topics ranging from professional standards and ethics to personal financial planning to financial literacy. The AICPA facilitates continuing education standards and course material. They sell books and other materials used by the members of the profession. Membership in the AICPA is not required, but it is the authoritative body recognized by all CPAs.

www.aicpa.org

6. California Society of Certified Public Accountants

The California Society of Certified Public Accountants has fourteen chapters serving the 28,000 members of the society. The chapters have local forums where CPAs get together to talk about issues of common interest. They also have speakers that talk about topics of interest to members and provide continuing education opportunities at the same time.

www.calcpaweb.org/

7. The Wall Street Journal Online

The Wall Street Journal Online can provide your business with many useful resources. An online subscription to the Wall Street Journal Online gets you research tools, portfolio tracking, personalized news, and much more. Glancing through the Wall Street Journal Online is a great way to start the day.

www.wsj.com

8. Treasury Direct

TreasuryDirect's Web site allows you to buy and redeem securities directly from the U.S. Department of the Treasury in paperless electronic form. It gives you the flexibility to manage your savings portfolio online as your needs and financial circumstances change. This is a vital money management tool for individuals and for companies.

www.treasurydirect.gov/

Source: Marilyn Ziemann, CPA (*www.ziemanncpa.com*), is a sole practitioner who has offered personalized tax and consulting services to her clients since 1970. She is an independent consulting specialist for individuals and small businesses. Ziemann is also a personal financial planner, writer of articles on tax and personal finance, and was an investment adviser for ten years. You can contact her at PO Box 665, Altadena, CA 91003-0665; (626) 794-9621; e-mail: *marilyn@ziemanncpa.com*.

Popular Tax Books for Small Business

With so many tax books out there, how do you know which is the right one for you? We asked our experts, who specialize in small business matters, to recommend some great tax books for small business owners and managers. Here they are.

1. *Creating Your Own Retirement Plan: A Guide to Keoghs & IRAs for the Self-Employed, 2nd edition,* by Twila Slesnick, John C. Suttle, Amy Delpo, Nolo Press (February 2002).

Straightforward information you need to select, establish, and operate a retirement plan. The book covers simple IRAs, SEP IRAs, traditional IRAs, Roth IRAs, profit-sharing plans, defined benefit plans, and 401k plans. It explains how to select the best plan, set it up, make contributions, administer the plan, and then—finally—receive distributions.

2. *The Ernst & Young Tax Saver's Guide, revised edition,* by Ernst & Young LLP (Editor), Margaret Milner Richardson (Editor), Peter W. Bernstein, Wiley (October 2002).

Offers advice and techniques that will help you lower taxes. It is packed with hundreds of unique, money-saving tips, and gives you the lowdown on the new tax law and the best year-round strategies to save more money on your taxes.

3. *J. K. Lasser's Taxes Made Easy for Your Home Based Business, 5th edition,* by Gary W. Carter, Wiley (November 2002).

Clarifies the current tax environment with regard to home-based businesses and shows you how to make the most of the new tax laws.

4. *Minding Her Own Business: The Self-Employed Woman's Guide to Taxes and Recordkeeping, 3rd edition,* by Jan Zobel, Adams Media Corporation (February 2000).

A good year-round guide to reducing taxes and avoiding audits for anyone, not just women.

5. *Retirement Bible,* by Lynn O'Shaughnessy, Wiley (January 2001).

A complete guide to the personal finance issues surrounding retirement, from 401ks to estate planning and trusts. It features information on saving money on taxes, calculating how much money will be needed for a comfortable retirement, and the essentials of IRAs, stocks, bonds, mutual funds, and other investments.

6. The *Small Business Survival Guide: How to Manage Your Cash, Profits and Taxes, 3rd revised edition,* by Robert E. Fleury, Sourcebooks (September 1996).

Bookkeeping, cash flow, accounting statements, and taxes.

7. *Small Time Operator: How to Start Your Own Business, Keep Your Books, Pay Your Taxes, and Stay Out of Trouble, 27th edition,* by Bernard B. Kamoroff, Bell Springs Publishing (August 31 2000).

Detailed advice on everything people need to know to take control of their business and be a success. This latest edition includes a new section on doing business on the Internet.

8. *Tax Savvy for Small Business: Year-Round Tax Strategies to Save You Money, 6th edition,* Frederick W. Daily, Nolo.com (July 2002).

Tells business owners what they need to know about federal taxes, and shows them how to make the best tax decisions for their business, maximize their profits, and stay out of trouble with the IRS.

9. *Working for Yourself: Law and Taxes for Independent Contractors, Freelancers and Consultants, 4th edition,* by Stephen Fishman, Nolo Press (August 2002).

How to successfully meet business start-up requirements, comply with IRS rules, draft consulting and independent contractor agreements, and get paid in full and on time.

Source: Small Business Notes (*www.smallbusinessnotes.com*)—Provides information and resources for other businesses struggling to provide that same quality in a challenging economic environment. Their purpose is to provide the resources for all the information that a small business person needs to operate his or her business. Contact editor Judith Kautz by sending e-mail to: *info@smallbusinessnotes.com.*

Top Criteria to Distinguish a Business from a Hobby

Since hobby expenses are deductible only to the extent of hobby income, it is important to distinguish hobby expenses from expenses incurred in an activity engaged in for profit. In making this distinction, all facts and circumstances with respect to the activity are taken into account and no one factor is determinative. Here is a list of the factors that should normally be taken into account.

1. Businesslike manner

Whether you carry on the activity in a businesslike manner.

2. Time and effort

Whether the time and effort you put into the activity indicate you intend to make it profitable.

3. Dependence on income

Whether you depend on income from the activity for your livelihood.

4. Losses

Whether your losses are due to circumstances beyond your control (or are normal in the start-up phase of your type of business).

5. Methods of operation

Whether you change your methods of operation in an attempt to improve profitability.

6. Knowledge

Whether you, or your advisers, have the knowledge needed to carry on the activity as a successful business.

7. Profit

Whether you were successful in making a profit in similar activities in the past.

8. When did you make a profit and how much

Whether the activity makes a profit in some years, and how much profit it makes.

9. Future profit

Whether you can expect to make a future profit from the appreciation of the assets used in the activity.

Source: Internal Revenue Service (*www.irs.gov*).

Reasons Your Business May Be Required to Use a Calendar Tax Year

There are two kinds of tax years. The most popular is a calendar year that is twelve consecutive months beginning January 1 and ending December 31. The other alternative is a fiscal year that is twelve consecutive months ending on the last day of any month except December. Sometimes you are required to use a calendar year for tax purposes. Here's why.

1. Recordkeeping

You keep no books.

2. Period

You have no annual accounting period.

3. Present tax year

Your present tax year does not qualify as a fiscal year.

4. Required

You are required to use a calendar year by a provision of the Internal Revenue Code or the Income Tax Regulations.

Source: Internal Revenue Service (*www.irs.gov*).

Most Important Year-End Tax-Planning Steps

As the end of calendar year approaches, it'll be time to think about what can be done to minimize the amount of taxes paid to the IRS by your business. Although tax planning should be a year-round process, there are several year-end strategies you can take, particularly if you are an S corporation. Our expert provides this list of things to think about before the year ends.

1. Keep inventory as low as possible

Try to keep your inventory as low as possible on December 31. Since you are taxed based on the value of your goods in stock, it makes sense to minimize your inventory.

2. If you are an accrual-based taxpayer, delay end-of-December billing until January

Since income is recognized when it is billed and shipped, you can delay the tax effects from one year to the next.

3. Book all tax-deductible expenses and account payable before the end of the year

For the same reason, it makes sense to book all tax-deductible expenses and accounts payable before the end of the year, rather than waiting until next year. This includes your personal expense report for December. Cash-based taxpayers must pay these expenses, while accrual-based taxpayers need only receive and enter the bills and pay the first of the following year.

4. Set up a qualified retirement plan

There may be time to set up a qualified retirement plan. A defined-benefit plan can be a good way to reduce taxes while preparing for your retirement.

5. Start thinking about next year

If you expect a big change in your next year's income, you should consult with an accountant now to minimize the tax impact. If you are a subchapter S corporation, you should plan to have the annual meeting of your board of directors as close to the new year as possible.

Source: HIS CPA (*www.hiscpa.com*) provides accounting and tax services to businesses and individuals. As certified public accountants, their goal is to provide sound financial, accounting, and tax advice to their clients. For more than twenty-five years, the firm has worked with companies and individuals in the Atlanta metro and Gwinnett County areas, ranging from start-up entrepreneurs to multimillion-dollar businesses. Their firm can be contacted at 1940 Woods River Lane, Duluth, GA 30097; (779) 814-9304.

Differences Between a Loan and a Dividend

A dividend is a transfer of money or other assets from a corporation to a shareholder of the corporation. A loan does not imply a relationship between the two parties, other than the relationship of debtor to borrower. The differences given here, supplied by our tax expert, could mean a big difference to your tax bill if not handled correctly.

1. General versus specific

A *Loan* is a generic term that doesn't imply any sort of relationship between the parties, other than the relationship of debtor and borrower. A *Dividend* is a specific term for the transfer of money or other assets from a corporation to a shareholder of the corporation, at a time when the corporation has positive earnings and profits.

2. Repaid versus for keeps

A loan must be repaid, usually with the addition of interest. A dividend is for keeps.

3. Nontaxable versus taxable

Loan proceeds are not taxable to the borrower, whereas dividends are subject to income tax. When loans are paid back, only the interest portion of the payment is taxable.

4. Asset, an account, or note receivable versus shareholder's equity account

A loan is shown on the lender's financial books as an asset—an account or note receivable. Interest received is shown as income, while the principal portion of a note payment is a nontaxable return of capital. A dividend appears on the corporation's balance sheet among the equity accounts.

5. Liability, account, or note payable versus income

A loan is shown on the borrower's financial books as a liability—an account or note payable. A dividend is shown on the recipient's income statement as income.

6. No relation to stock ownership versus relation to stock ownership

Dividends are paid equally to all shareholders of a certain class of stock, whereas loans generally do not bear any relationship to stock ownership. Whereas a shareholder of a closely held C corporation will prefer to characterize a distribution as nontaxable repayment of a loan, the IRS may challenge the shareholder's position and try to recharacterize the distributions as a taxable dividend.

Source: Barbara Lamar, attorney/CPA, specializes in advising closely held businesses and their owners how to maximize after tax profits. She can be contacted at (512) 470-8225 or at *BLamar@lamarlaw.net.*

Common Differences Between Cash and Accrual Accounting

Your accounting method includes not only the overall method of the accounting use, but also the accounting treatment you use for any material item. You choose an accounting method for your business when you file your first income tax return. After that, if you want to change your accounting method, you must generally get IRS approval. The two most popular methods are cash and accrual. Here's a summary of the differences between the two.

1. No inventory versus inventory

Most individuals and many sole proprietors with no inventory use the cash method because they find it easier to keep cash method records. However, if an inventory is necessary to account for your income, you must generally use an accrual method of accounting for sales and purchases.

2. Gross income

Under the cash method, include in your gross income all items of income you actually or constructively receive during the tax year. If you receive property or services, you must include their fair market value in the income. Under an accrual method, you generally include an amount in your gross income for the tax year in which all events that fix your right to receive the income have occurred and you can determine the amount with reasonable accuracy.

3. Deducting expenses

Under the cash method, you generally deduct expenses in the tax year in which you actually pay them. This includes business expenses for which you contest liability. However you may not be able to deduct an expense paid in advance or you may be required to capitalize certain costs, as explained under the Uniform Capitalization Rules. Under an accrual method of accounting, you generally deduct or capitalize a business expense when both the following apply. The all-events test has been met. The test has been met when all events have occurred that fix the fact of liability and the liability can be determined with reasonable accuracy. Economic performance has occurred.

Source: Internal Revenue Service (*www.irs.gov*).

Most Common Abusive Foreign Tax Schemes

There's a difference between tax avoidance and tax evasion. Some advisors may want you to put money into a 'foreign trust' to avoid taxes. Tax evasion using foreign jurisdictions is accomplished using many different methods. Some can be as simple as taking unreported cash receipts and personally traveling to a tax haven country and depositing the cash into a bank account. Others are more elaborate involving numerous domestic and foreign trusts, partnerships, nominees, etc. The following schemes are not all-inclusive, but just a sample of some of the more abusive tax schemes provided by the IRS.

1. Abusive foreign trust schemes

The foreign trust schemes usually start off as a series of domestic trusts layered upon one another. This set up is used to give the appearance that the taxpayer has turned his/her business and assets over to a trust and is no longer in control of the business or its assets. Once transferred to the domestic trust, the income and expenses are passed to one or more foreign trusts, typically in tax haven countries. Once the assets are in foreign trust, a bank account is opened either under the trust name or an International Business Corporation (IBC). The trust documentation and business records of this scheme all make it appear that the taxpayer is no longer in control of his/her business or its assets. The reality is that nothing ever changed. The taxpayer still exercises full control over his/her business and assets. There can be many different variations to the scheme.

2. International Business Corporations (IBC)

The taxpayer establishes an IBC with the exact name as that of his/her business. The IBC also has a bank account in the foreign country. As the taxpayer receives checks from customers, he sends them to the bank in the foreign country. The foreign bank then uses its correspondent account in the to process the checks so that it never would appear to the customer, upon reviewing the canceled check that the payment was sent offshore. Once the checks clear, the taxpayer's IBC account is credited for the check payments. Here the taxpayer has, again, transferred the unreported income offshore to a tax-haven jurisdiction.

3. False billing schemes

A taxpayer sets up an International Business Corporation (IBC) in a tax-haven country with a nominee as the owner (usually the promoter). A bank account is then opened under the IBC. On the bank's records the taxpayer would be listed as a signatory on the account. The promoter then issues invoices to the taxpayer's business for goods allegedly purchased by the taxpayer. The taxpayer then sends payment to the IBC that gets deposited into the joint account held by the IBC and taxpayer. The taxpayer takes a business deduction for the payment to the IBC thereby reducing his/her taxable income and has safely placed the unreported income into the foreign bank account.

Source: Internal Revenue Service (*www.irs.gov*)

Popular Strategies for Reducing Tax Liabilities

Nothing in life is certain except death and taxes, the old saying goes. But while there may be no getting around paying taxes, there's nothing that says you have to pay more than your fair share. Here is a list of a few strategies for reducing your business' tax bill.

1. Hire your children

Find something in your business that your children can do—maybe over the Christmas holidays—and pay them for it. If they're under eighteen, their wages aren't subject to FICA, unemployment, or Medicare taxes. If they earn less than $5,000 during the year, they don't have to file a return. You may be giving your kids this much money anyway, so this is one way to get up to a $5,000 business deduction for it.

2. Establish a Section 105 health reimbursement arrangement (or HRA)

You can reimburse and deduct your medical expenses and those of your employees when you set up an HRA. You may elect to make deposits (that are excludable for income and FICA tax purposes) to covered employees' HRA accounts each month, and there are no maximum contribution amounts.

3. Look into all opportunities for contributing to retirement plans

Most contributions to qualified retirement plans are tax deductible, up to the annual contribution limits. The Simplified Employee Pension plan (or SEP) is the most popular plan among the self-employed, due to its simplicity and low cost. It's very easy and inexpensive to set up a prototype SEP plan with your financial institution. Other good options are traditional and Roth IRAs and 401k's, including the new "single K," which is a 401k designed for sole proprietors.

4. Take the home-office deduction

If you use a portion of your home regularly and exclusively for your business, then you can deduct a portion of those expenses on your federal income tax return. In the past, many self-employed people were hesitant to take the home-office deduction for fear that it might trigger IRS scrutiny, but anyone who is self-employed and works out of his or her home should try to find a way to qualify and take the deduction.

5. Plan for the Section 179 expensing deduction

Section 179 of the Internal Revenue Code allows you to deduct immediately (rather than depreciate) up to $25,000 of capital purchases (such as those for equipment, computers, and office furniture) for your business. Plan your equipment and capital purchases throughout the year to take maximum advantage of this deduction. For example, if you're planning a major capital expenditure during the first part of next year, you could buy this year and accelerate the deduction.

6. Make shrewd year-end tax moves

When it comes to year-end tax planning, the basic premise is to try to defer as much income into next year and accelerate as many expenses (i.e., deductions) into this year as you can, thus delaying some amount of tax payment for a year. However, if you anticipate that you or your business will be in a higher tax bracket next year, you might do the opposite: accelerate income and defer expenses. This could increase your tax bill for the current year but lower your overall tax liability. To defer income (for cash-basis companies), hold invoices until after December 31, and use the installment method (if available) for sales of noninventory property. For accrual-basis companies, hold off on shipping products or providing services (if it's feasible) until after December 31, and ship FOB destination, rather than FOB shipping point, to delay passing of title and realization of income.

7. Consider these additional moves for deductions before the end of the year

Buy supplies that you will need early next year. Donate excess inventory and make charitable contributions to qualified nonprofit organizations. As long as you pledge the donations and contributions before year-end, you have until March 15 of next year to actually make them. Declare employee bonuses (accrual-basis companies only) that you plan to pay early next year. Like charitable donations and contributions, the bonuses don't actually have to be paid until March 15. Declare vested vacation pay that you will pay out in the first two and a half months of next year (accrual-basis companies only).

Source: Don Sadler, vice president and editorial director, Media 3 Publication—He is a business editor and writer with twenty years of experience in the business publishing arena. For Media 3 Publications, he directs editorial content for the company's various business publications. He has worked with the largest banks in the country to create custom publications targeted to their corporate customers. In addition, as a freelance writer, he has written dozens of articles published in a variety of national business periodicals, including *American Executive* and *Self-Employed America*. Contact him at don@media3pub.com.

Top Ways to Reduce Your Tax Rate

The rates used to calculate your company's tax liabilities are based on those set by the IRS. No matter how hard you try, you're not going to change the rate! However, there are three main ways that you can take advantage of a lower tax rate. Here's how.

1. Change your form of organization

Choose the optimal *form of organization* for your business (such as sole proprietorship, partnership, or corporation).

2. Structure transactions as capital gains payments

Structure a transaction so that payments you receive are classified as *capital gains*. Long-term capital gains earned by noncorporate taxpayers are subject to *lower tax rates* than other income.

3. Shift income from high-tax-bracket taxpayer to a low-tax-bracket taxpayer

Shift income from a high-tax-bracket taxpayer (such as yourself) to a lower-bracket taxpayer (such as your child). One fairly simple way to do this is by *hiring your children*. Another possibility is to make one or more children part-owners of your business, so that net profits of the business are shared among a larger group. The tax laws limit the usefulness of this strategy for shifting unearned income to children under age fourteen, but some tax-saving opportunities still exist.

Source: CCH Business Owner's Toolkit: (*www.toolkit.cch.com*)—
The Business Owner's Toolkit provides advice, guides, legal tools,
business models, and other resources to small business owners.

Payroll, Estate, and Other Taxes

The Most Important Questions to Ask Your Estate Lawyer

As a business owner, it will be important for you to have an estate lawyer, at least if you want to avoid family squabbles after you've moved on to the next world. The following are important questions you should ask your estate lawyer.

1. Does a will avoid probate?

If there are assets in your individual name when you die, your will generally must be probated. If probate avoidance is important, consider a "funded" revocable, living trust. *Funded* means you've transferred your assets to your trust during your lifetime. Ask your lawyer, if you decide against such a trust, or do not get all of your assets into your trust during your lifetime, does she have a simplified probate procedure that significantly minimizes time and expense?

2. What is the difference between a will and a trust?

A will directs the distribution of your estate after you die and must be probated. A trust also directs the distribution of your estate after you die (usually) but does not need to be probated. With a will, you still own your assets in your name. With a funded trust, assets you have transferred to your trust are owned by the trustee of your trust, typically you or you and your spouse, as long as you are competent. Assets you have placed in your trust during your lifetime will still be owned by the trustee

of your trust after you die, usually a "successor" trustee, such as your spouse, a bank, or an adult child. A trust can be used to continue the investment and management of assets after your death, for the benefit of your children, or for anyone who may be dependent on you. A trust can be used for the lifetime management of your property and investments if you're disabled, but so can a durable power of attorney in most cases.

3. What is a living will?

Some states do not have a living will per se. Instead, some states authorize the power of attorney for health care, which allows you to state your desires regarding life-sustaining treatment (like a living will) and has the added advantage of allowing you to name a surrogate, called a *patient advocate*, to make medical and health care decisions for you if you can't.

4. Why should I have a durable power of attorney?

If you become disabled so that you can no longer handle financial and legal matters, it is important for you to have named someone to take your place in handling these things. With a durable power of attorney, you name an agent to act for you if you're disabled, usually a spouse, then an adult child, sometimes a bank. Otherwise, a loved one may need to ask the probate court to be appointed the conservator of your estate. This is embarrassing, expensive, and time-consuming, at least relative to signing a power of attorney. Married persons commonly assume that either spouse can act as to jointly held property; this is not true of jointly held real estate, stocks, bonds, and a power of attorney is essential for married couples as well as single adults.

5. How do I protect my minor children if my husband or wife and I both die?

You'll want to name guardians for your children, which you can only do if you make a will. In addition, you'll want someone responsible to hold and distribute your estate for your children, to make sure your children are provided for as they grow up, and have the benefits of a good education. This is the purpose of a contingent family trust, in which you name a trustee and give the trustee directions for holding, investing, and disbursing money for your children. Without a trust, your estate is divided into equal shares for your children at your death, regardless of your children's ages; each of your children is entitled to receive his or her share of your estate outright at age eighteen. Most parents are uncomfortable with leaving large sums of money to children at a young age and without any controls. Except in large estates, most parents prefer a single trust for all of their children until each child has grown up and received a basic education, to make sure there is enough money and to treat all children equally. Also, a child may turn out to have special needs; if the estate has been divided into shares at the parent's death, such a child may literally use up his or her share, without any

legal right to invade a sister's or brother's trust for the needed funds.

6. What about life insurance and retirement plans?

Often, people have much of their wealth in life insurance and retirement accounts, so it is extremely important to make sure payments from these policies and accounts will be made properly. Your estate planning should include the review of the beneficiary designations for your life insurance, retirement accounts, annuities, and deferred compensation plans, so that the payouts from these plans and accounts are properly coordinated with the rest of your estate plan. Special drafting may be required for the beneficiary designations for your retirement accounts, for example, to avoid estate tax or for the recipients to enjoy tax-deferred growth for as long as possible.

7. How do I know if I need to update my estate plan?

It's a good idea to look at your estate-planning documents about once a year to see if anything might need changing or updating. Also check with your estate lawyer every couple of years or so, or whenever you've experienced a birth, marriage, disability, or death in the family, or significant change in the size of your estate. Your lawyer should also try to keep you informed about any major changes in the laws that might affect your particular plan.

Source: Klute Miller, PLC (*www.klutemiller.com*)—A Michigan-based firm, Klute Miller offers legal services in business law and banking, estate and tax planning, litigation, and real estate. Contact them at

Court Place—Suite 101, 728 Pleasant Street, St. Joseph, MI 49085; (269) 983-1000.

Steps to Take When Creating an Estate Plan

Planning an estate is a project many people think about but cannot get motivated enough to do. A well-planned estate is of great importance especially in light of today's booming stock market, the constant changes in the tax laws, and the ever-increasing number of dual-income families. It can also significantly reduce the tax due at your death, thereby increasing the amount passing to your beneficiaries. Here is a list of steps to get you started on your estate plan.

1. Obtain an understanding of your financial value

A rough estimate of the value of your assets is necessary to explore the options available to you and to determine how complex or how simple your estate plan should be. Threshold estate planners look at the applicable credit amount (as defined in the Internal Revenue Code), which is the amount that can pass free of any federal estate and gift tax. Obtaining an understanding of your financial value can be accomplished by compiling a list of your assets. Once you have determined the value of your assets, subtract the total of any liabilities such as mortgages and car loans. This will give your "net estate."

2. Know how your assets are titled

How an asset is titled is just as important as knowing what it is worth. To plan your estate, you must know how much of the asset you own and who will receive it on your passing.

Although numerous forms of ownership exist, property owned by two or more individuals is usually titled under one of three methods: (a) tenants in common, (b) joint tenants, and (c) tenants by the entireties. In all three forms of ownership, each tenant owns an undivided one-half interest (or one-third interest if there are three tenants, etc.). The right of survivorship causes ownership of a deceased tenant to pass automatically to the surviving tenant; this does not occur between tenants in common. On the death of a joint owner, the property passes to the surviving tenant irrespective of the provisions in your will. On the other hand, property held as tenants in common will pass under provisions of your will or according to the laws of your state if you do not have a will. These rules may vary from state to state.

3. Execute a will

Perhaps the best argument for a will is to explain what might happen if you pass away without one. Dying without a will means it is left to the state intestacy laws to determine who will administer the estate and who will receive your assets. These laws might be inconsistent with your intentions.

The law will not take into consideration your wish to donate your estate to charity or that you felt strongly about giving a sentimental item to a friend. Although the intestacy law differs from state to state, it generally distributes property to your relatives in order of their family relationship to you. For example, your children would inherit before your grandchildren.

4. Consider a "living" will

A will takes care of your assets when you pass away. A living will, also called an *advance directive for health care*, makes provisions for you physically if you are in a terminal condition and unable to make your own medical decisions. The purpose of a living will is to allow you to control what medical procedures you want performed or withheld in the event of a terminal condition and a state of permanent unconsciousness. This document has become so popular that often as a matter of routine office procedure a doctor will ask if you have one.

5. Consider a "durable" power of attorney

A durable power of attorney allows another individual (agent or attorney in fact) to make decisions for you in the event that you are mentally or physically unable to tend to your affairs. Generally, the power given to the agent allows him or her to pay your bills, sign your checks, and engage in other banking transactions. The bottom line is your agent must be someone you trust to act in your best interest.

Source: Adapted from *A Simple Approach to Developing Your Estate Plan* by BPW/USA member Leslie Heffernen, *Business-Woman Magazine* (Winter 2000).

Key Rules to Know If Employing Your Parents

When considering hiring a parent, you should consider many factors. A parent employee may be treated as nonparent employees in some instances and not in others. The following information lists just a few of the considerations involved in employing your parent.

1. Paperwork

A parent employee is required to file the same employee forms upon hiring as any other employee. These forms can include an I-9 (a Social Security Administration form) and a W-4 (an Internal Revenue Service form), as well as the corresponding state requirements for a new hire. File these forms with the appropriate governing authorities where applicable, and keep copies in an employee file. This file should be kept and retained according to the same regulations that surround nonparent employees. It is also prudent to maintain a written job description for any parent employee, also retained in the employee file. A job description will define the expectations of the employee's role as well as aid in dispelling possible tax avoidance questions presupposed by the governing authorities.

2. Payroll taxes

Many business owners are misinformed about a parent employee not being responsible for most of the payroll taxes for which other employees are liable. Unfortunately, this is not the case. A parent employee is responsible for the federal income tax withholding and the social security/Medicare taxes (FICA). However, you are not liable for the federal unemployment tax (FUTA) when hiring a parent. Many states agree with the FUTA regulations and follow the parent exemption; however, some do not and may still require payment of the state unemployment tax for parent employees. Consult your state unemployment tax agency before assuming an exemption.

3. Qualifying compensation

A parent employee is subject to the same compensation regulations to which nonparent employees are subject. Qualifying compensation include salaries, nonqualified deferred compensation recognized under section 409A of the Internal Revenue Code, vacation allowances, tips, unreturned reimbursements for expenses in excess of the value of the expenses, nonaccountable plan reimbursements for business expenses, wages not paid in monies, bonuses, commissions, and taxable fringe benefits. Simply stated, any compensation for services that are not specifically exempt from payroll taxes are taxable (refer to IRS Publications 15, 15-A, and 15-B for a listing of the specific forms of compensation that are exempt).

4. Taxable services

Compensation paid for services rendered in a trade or business are considered qualifying wages for the federal income tax withholding, FUTA, and FICA. Most domestic services like child care are not subject to these taxes for parent employees. However, there are special rules when mental or physical conditions require that the parent be employed for domestic care. In these cases, the parent's wages are taxable in the same manner as trade or business services are.

5. Available benefits

In some business organizations, a parent employee is able to enjoy the same fringe benefits offered to other business employees under the same taxable regulations. However, in the case of the S corporation, a 2 percent shareholder has many restrictions regarding the eligibility of participation in employee benefit programs. Under current legislation, parents are considered a 2 percent shareholder if their child-owner is a 2 percent shareholder of the S corporation. Therefore, the parent employee is also restricted in their participation of certain fringe benefits.

6. The family factor

When you hire a relative, especially a parent, it can be a wonderful experience. You are able to utilize a reliable and well-known resource with whom you have already built a rapport. However, it is all too easy to fall back into a parent-child relationship on the job. This is not productive or advantageous. Many business owners cannot criticize or direct their parent employees as they would other employees, and this can lead to friction and animosity either between the employer and the parent or among the other employees. Be sure your business needs the skills your parent can offer, and before hiring your parent, consider the history of your relationship.

Source: Michelle Neumeier, EA, owner of Home Business Tax Solutions (*www.hbtsinc.com*), assists small and home-based business with their income, sales and payroll tax responsibilities. She can be reached at W181 N9022 Melanie La., Menomonee Falls, WI 53051; (262) 844-1067; e-mail: *www.michelle@hbtsinc.com*.

Key Rules to Know If Employing Your Child

When considering hiring a child, there are many factors to consider. The most prominent advantage in hiring your child is the savings realized in payroll and income tax liabilities. However, this is not the only advantage. There are many regulations governing the child employee that will come from both state and federal authorities. Thoroughly research these regulations before hiring any child employee. The following information lists just a few of these considerations involved when employing your child.

1. Paperwork

A child employee is required to file the same employee forms upon hiring as any other employee. These forms will include a I-9 (a Social Security Administration form) and a W-4 (an Internal Revenue Service form), as well as the corresponding state requirements for a new hire. File these forms with the appropriate governing authorities where applicable, and keep copies in an employee file. This file should be kept and retained according to the same regulations that surround nonchild employees. It is also prudent to maintain a written job description for any child employee, to be retained in the employee's file. A job description will define the expectations of the child's role and help dispel possible tax avoidance questions presupposed by the governing authorities. When constructing a job description, keep in mind the child's age and abilities. Also research state regulations to guard against hiring a child who is too young or for a role specifically disallowed by state law.

2. Payroll taxes

Child employees under the age of eighteen are not liable for the Medicare/social security tax (FICA) or the federal unemployment tax (FUTA) in a sole-proprietor business organization. A child's wages are subject to the FICA and FUTA taxes if the child is employed by a parent's corporation, S corporation, or partnership (unless both partners are the child's parents, then the treatment is like that of the sole proprietor), regardless of age. The federal income tax withholding is required where applicable wage limits have been reached, regardless of the business' organization. When a child is between eighteen and twenty-one years of age, the wages are subject to FICA but not FUTA in the sole proprietorship and the partnership where both partners are the child's parents. Once the child has reached twenty-one, the qualifying wages are subject to payroll tax liabilities as are nonchild employees.

3. Qualifying compensation

A child employee is subject to the same compensation definitions to which nonchild employees are subject. Qualifying compensation include salaries, nonqualified deferred compensation recognized under section 409A, vacation allowances, tips, unreturned reimbursements for expenses in excess of the value of the expenses, nonaccountable plan reimbursements for business expenses, wages not paid in monies, bonuses, commissions, and taxable fringe benefits. Simply stated, any compensation for services that are not specifically exempt from payroll taxes are taxable (refer to IRS Publications 15, 15-A and 15-B for a listing of the specific forms of compensation that are exempt). Taxable forms of compensation are subject to the federal income tax withholding, FICA, and FUTA for the child employee, where applicable according to age.

4. Taxable services

Compensation paid for services rendered in a trade or business are considered qualifying wages for the federal income tax withholding, FUTA, and FICA taxes for child employees, where applicable according to age regulations. Most domestic services provided in the parent's home, like child care, are not subject to these taxes.

5. Benefits available to your child

In some business organizations, a child employee is able to enjoy the same fringe benefits offered to other business employees under the same taxable regulations. However, in the case of the S corporation, a 2 percent shareholder has many restrictions regarding the eligibility of participation in employee benefit programs. Under current legislation, a child is considered a 2 percent shareholder if the parent-owner is a 2 percent shareholder of the S-Corporation. Therefore, the child employee is also restricted in participation of certain fringe benefits.

6. The family factor

When you hire a relative, especially a child, it can be a wonderful experience. Typically you are able to share income from a higher income-tax bracket (that of the parent or business) to a lower income-tax bracket (that of the child). You are also able to save on payroll tax liabilities where the business organization and the age of the child warrant it. However, employers often fall into pitfalls, such as illegally employing young children or employing children to undertake tasks that are specifically restricted, such as in the case of young children working directly with dangerous machinery. Age restrictions and employment restrictions are left to the state authorities to regulate and determine. Be sure to research your state's regulations before hiring your child. Strict adherence to these regulations will ensure a more beneficial employment experience.

Source: Michelle Neumeier, EA, owner of Home Business Tax Solutions (www.hbtsinc.com), assists small and home-based business with their income, sales and payroll tax responsibilities. She can be reached at W181 N9022 Melanie La., Menomonee Falls, WI 53051; (262) 844-1067; e-mail: www.michelle@hbtsinc.com.

Most Important Payroll Tax Rules

Even if you're the do-it-yourself type, it's a good idea to get a professional to help with payroll taxes. Why? Because payroll taxes are the most frequent cause of trouble between small businesses and the IRS. Once the penalties and interest start mounting up, it can be very difficult to catch up. According to our expert, the following represents some of the most important payroll tax rules that you should know, at a minimum.

1. When an employer withholds income tax and FICA amounts from an employee's paycheck, the employer is, in effect, a trustee.

A trustee has a fiduciary duty to make sure withheld amounts are deposited with IRS on a timely basis on the employee's behalf. A fiduciary duty is a higher level of duty than ordinary care, and the payroll tax rules take this into account.

2. Having a fiduciary duty means tougher penalties.

According to the IRS, payroll taxes are the most frequent cause of trouble between the IRS and small businesses. Common problems include miscalculating, withholding, and failure to make timely tax deposits. It's ironic that the most frequent problems occur where the employer has the highest level of duty to comply with the rules.

3. Tough penalties are imposed when payroll tax deposits are not made on time.

It's frighteningly easy to get behind on payroll tax deposits, since they are due more frequently than other taxes. Also, there is not just one due date for all taxpayers. Deposits must be made either monthly or semiweekly, depending on the amount of tax owed in the "look-back" period (see entry 4).

4. Employers are classified into two groups: monthly or semiweekly.

At the beginning of each calendar year, the employer must determine which schedule should be used by looking at the total taxes reported on Form 942, line 11, from July 1 two years back to June 30 of the previous year. For example, for 2005, you would look at Forms 941 starting with the one covering the period July–September 2003 and ending with the form covering the period April–June 2004. If the amount deposited during this period is $50,000 or less, your deposits will be due monthly. If the amount deposited is more than $50,000, your deposits will be due semiweekly.

New employers are automatically classified as monthly depositors.

5. Make sure you follow the monthly deposit schedule deadlines.

If you are a monthly depositor, your payroll tax deposits must be made by the fifteenth day of each month following any month during which you paid employees (or on the next business day if August 15 falls on a weekend or bank holiday). For example, for the month of July 2006, your deposit is due by August 15, 2006.

6. The semiweekly deposit schedules depend on paydays.

For paydays falling on Wednesday, Thursday, and Friday, payroll tax deposits are due the following Wednesday. For paydays falling on Saturday, Sunday, Monday, or Tuesday, payroll tax deposits are due on Friday. If the due date falls on a weekend or bank holiday, the payment is due on the next banking day. If a bank holiday falls during the three days after the end of the semiweekly period, you will have an additional banking day to deposit. For example, your employees are paid on Friday, and Monday is a bank holiday. Your deposit is not due until Thursday. This allows three banking days to make the deposit. However, if your payday is on Thursday and Monday is a banking holiday, your deposit will be due at its normal time, Wednesday.

7. Be aware of the $100,000 next-day rule.

As if the rules were not already complicated enough, there is an exception. The good news is that it would be highly unusual for this rule to apply to a small business. If you should ever have a tax liability of $100,000 or more on any single day during a deposit period, you must deposit the tax by the next banking day, regardless of what deposit schedule you normally use—and you automatically become a semiweekly depositor on the next day. You will remain a semiweekly depositor for the remainder of the current year and also for the following year.

8. You may be required to make electronic deposits.

If the total of all federal tax liabilities (including payroll taxes, corporate income tax, and excise taxes) exceeded $200,000 during any year, you must make electronic deposits. The Electronic Federal Tax Payment System (EFTPS) must be used to make electronic deposits. If you are required to make electronic deposits and fail to do so, you may be subject to a 10 percent penalty. Deposits made electronically must be initiated at least one business day in advance of the due date. If deposits are initiated on the day they are due, they will be considered late.

9. There are penalties for failure to make timely payroll tax deposits.

A 2 percent penalty applies for deposits made one to five days late. A 5 percent penalty applies if deposits are made six to fifteen days late. The penalty is 10 percent for deposits made sixteen days late or more. This also applies to amounts paid within ten days of the date of the first notice the IRS sent asking for the tax due. A 10 percent penalty also applies to deposits made at an unauthorized financial institution,

deposits paid directly to the IRS or paid with your tax return (see Publication 15, section 11 for exceptions for payments with returns). A 10 percent penalty applies on amounts subject to electronic deposit requirements but not deposited using EFTPS. A 15 percent penalty applies on amounts still unpaid more than ten days after the date of the first notice the IRS sent asking for the tax due or the day on which you receive notice and demand for immediate payment, whichever is earlier.

Source: Barbara Lamar, attorney/CPA, specializes in advising closely held businesses and their owners how to maximize after tax profits. She can be contacted at (512) 470-8225 or at BLamar@lamarlaw.net.

Top Types of Payroll Taxes

Every employer should know about there four main types of federal payroll taxes. Typically, a state will also have two types of payroll taxes. Each state has the ability to set and maintain their own rates, filing requirements, and wage caps and floors. Both the federal and the state payroll tax liabilities are based upon the qualifying wages paid to an employer's employees. Here our expert advises us on the top types of payroll taxes that every business owner and manager should know.

1. Medicare tax

The Medicare tax is a federal tax whose funds are accumulated for medical benefits paid to qualifying individuals when they reach a specified age (this age can change according to federal design). Employees, those retired and still employed, and their spouses are eligible to receive Medicare benefits on reaching the predetermined age. An employer is responsible to deposit 1.45 percent of an employee's qualifying gross wages, for their portion of an employee's Medicare liability. The employer is also responsible for withholding a matching 1.45 percent of the employee's qualifying gross wages as the employee's portion of the Medicare tax liability. This tax is deposited according to the size of the company and reported quarterly. The reports are filed using federal form 941 and are due April 30, July 31, October 31, and January 31 (of the following year).

2. Social security tax

The social security tax is a federal tax that funds employee's social security benefits. It is a program that is based upon the employee's wages and not based upon the needs of the recipient. Together the Medicare and the social security tax were formed under the Federal Insurance Contribution Act and may be better known as the FICA tax. For this tax, the employer deposits 6.2 percent and withholds a matching 6.2 percent of the employee's qualifying gross wages up to a predetermined wage cap. This cap is adjusted for inflation. Once the qualifying gross wages have exceeded the cap for an employee, the employer no longer withholds or deposits funds for the social security tax on that particular employee. The tax is also deposited and reported along with the Medicare tax on federal Form 941, under the same reporting regulations.

3. Federal income tax withholding

The federal income tax is withheld in its entirety from the employee's gross wages. The employer does not match or pay for this tax. It is determined through either a mathematical calculation or through the use of a set table (the tables can be found in the Internal Revenue Service Publication 505). In determining an employee's withholding, an employer must maintain a current W-4 for their employees, showing the number of allowances, marital status and additional withholding requests. This tax is also reported quarterly on Form 941 along with the FICA tax.

4. Federal unemployment tax (FUTA)

The Federal unemployment tax (FUTA) is a tax on the first $7,000 in qualifying wages that an employer pays an employee. The employer pays this tax in full and does not withhold it from the employee's wages. If an employer's state requires a state unemployment tax (SUTA), a credit is available to the employer for the FUTA liability. The FUTA is reported annually on a Form 940; however, it may be deposited quarterly or annually, depending on the current limit regulations and the employer's payroll.

5. State income tax withholding

There are only a handful of states that do not have a state income tax. For those states, the state income tax withholding rules will not apply. For those states that do hold employers liable for the state income tax withholding for their employees, the regulations are often similar to those of the Internal Revenue Service's. Generally, the reports are filed quarterly with the funds deposited quarterly, monthly, or annually, depending on the size of a company's payroll. The amount to be withheld is subtracted in full from the employee's wages. It is calculated either through a formula or table method and often uses the information provided on the federal Form W-4, although many states do require a new-hire reporting form of their own. An employer should always notify and research the state withholding requirements, even if he or she lives in a state that does not require a state income tax, simply to ensure proper reporting.

6. State unemployment tax

Similar to the FUTA, states have ensured a means to provide for their residents if they become unemployed. Each employer is liable for this tax either when the total payroll reaches a specific floor or when they have employed qualifying employees for a specific duration of time. Again, each state has the ability to regulate the rate, wage levels, and employee qualification for this tax. If an employer resides in a state that does not have a state income tax, they may still be held liable for a state unemployment tax. For this reason it is wise to notify the appropriate authorities of an employer's employment status. Typically, this information can be discovered through a state department of revenue or similar governing authority.

Source: Michelle Neumeier, EA, owner of Home Business Tax Solutions (*www.hbtsinc.com*), assists small and home-based business with their income, sales, and payroll tax responsibilities. She can be reached at W181 N9022 Melanie La., Menomonee Falls, WI 53051; (262) 844-1067; e-mail: *www.michelle@hbtsinc.com*.

Most Common Sales Tax Exemptions

In every state that imposes a sales tax, the general rule is that each retail sale of tangible personal property is presumed to be taxable. In other words, if you happen to make retail sales, you generally must collect or pay sales tax with respect to each sale unless you can show that the sale was somehow exempt from tax. Each state offers its own unique set of exemptions from its sales tax. In general, exemptions are provided on the basis of the type of property being sold, the identity of the purchaser, or the use to which the property will be put. The following are the most common sales tax exemptions. Do you qualify?

1. Property-based exemptions

Every state recognizes that there are certain commodities that individuals must purchase to subsist. Accordingly, most states offer product-specific exemptions for items such as food, clothing, prescription medicines, and medical (prosthetic) devices.

2. Purchaser-based exemptions

Under federal law, states are prohibited from taxing sales that are made to the federal government or its various agencies. Similar exemptions exist in each state, with the exception of California, for sales to the state and its agencies and to cities, counties, and other local jurisdictions in the state. Also common are exemptions for sales to nonprofit charitable, religious, and educational organizations.

3. Use-based exemptions

The exemptions that fall into this category are those provided to support certain industries (such as agriculture, manufacturing, or industrial processing) or to encourage certain activities for the public good (such as industrial development or expansion or pollution control). For example, many farming states offer exemptions for sales of products or equipment used to produce food for human or animal consumption. Similarly, most states offer exemptions for sales of materials or supplies used in manufacturing a product for sale.

Source: ItsSimple.biz (*www.itssimple.biz*) is a very popular, free Internet resource center that assists small business owners by providing valuable information, guidance, and business-development tools. ItsSimple.biz is a free Internet resource center to assist small business owners. Contact them at ItsSimple.biz, 316 California Ave., Suite 433, Reno, NV 89509; (775) 324-2900.

States That Have Flat Corporate Income Tax Rates

When you have a flat-tax system, all income is taxed at the same rate. Some states have flat-tax rates and some state tax rates vary depending on your income. In states with flat-tax rates, no matter how much you earn in income, you will pay one fixed tax rate. Depending on how much your business earns, it may benefit to choose a state with a flat-tax rate. In states without a flat rate, businesses with higher incomes pay tax at a higher rate than those with lower income. The following is a list of states that have flat corporate income tax rates.

1. Alabama
Flat income tax rate of 6.5%

2. Arizona
Flat income tax rate of 6.96%

3. California
Flat income tax rate of 8.84%

4. Colorado
Flat income tax rate of 4.63%

5. Connecticut
Flat income tax rate of 7.5%

6. Delaware
Flat income tax rate of 8.7%

7. Florida
Flat income tax rate of 5.5%

8. Georgia
Flat income tax rate of 6.0%

9. Idaho
Flat income tax rate of 7.6%

10. Illinois
Flat income tax rate of 7.3%

11. Indiana
Flat income tax rate of 8.5%

12. Kansas
Flat income tax rate of 4.0%

13. Maryland
Flat income tax rate of 7.0%

14. Massachusetts
Flat income tax rate of 9.5%

15. Minnesota
Flat income tax rate of 9.8%

16. Missouri

Flat income tax rate of 6.25%

17. Montana

Flat income tax rate of 6.75%

18. New Hampshire

Flat income tax rate of 8.5%

19. New Jersey

Flat income tax rate of 9.0%

20. New York

Flat income tax rate of 7.5%

21. North Carolina

Flat income tax rate of 6.9%

22. Oklahoma

Flat income tax rate of 6.0%

23. Oregon

Flat income tax rate of 6.6%

24. Pennsylvania

Flat income tax rate of 9.99%

25. Rhode Island

Flat income tax rate of 9.0%

26. South Carolina

Flat income tax rate of 5.0%

27. Tennessee

Flat income tax rate of 6.5%

28. Utah

Flat income tax rate of 5.0%

29. Virginia

Flat income tax rate of 6.0%

30. West Virginia

Flat income tax rate of 9.0%

31. Wisconsin

Flat income tax rate of 7.9%

32. District of Columbia

Flat tax rate of 9.975%

Source: Federation of Tax Administrators (*www.taxadmin.org*)

Most Common State and Local Taxes

Taxes are a continuing challenge for all small businesses. In addition to federal taxes, states and local governments also ask for a share of your hard-earned income. Each locality has its own method for generating revenue. Here are some of the most common.

1. Sales tax

Sales taxes are levied on the sales of goods and services. These can be assessed in two ways. The vendor can be taxed on the amount of goods and services sold. This is also called, in some states, an excise tax. A consumer tax taxes a retail sale. The vendor at the retail establishment collects the money and sends it to the state.

2. Unemployment tax

Employers with one or more workers must pay a payroll tax on wages paid to employees. This tax often does not apply to agricultural and domestic workers or to family members. If an employee is terminated, the unemployment tax will provide a limited amount of support while he or she is seeking other employment.

3. Workers' compensation

Employers with one or more employees must pay premiums. In some states you are allowed to self-insure. This protects the employee and employer when a work-related injury occurs.

4. Property tax

Not only do most states tax any real estate that you own, but many states tax any tangible property, such as machinery, equipment, inventory, furniture, and fixtures.

5. Personal income tax

States introduced the personal income tax into America. Not all states have this tax.

6. Use tax

Many states tax for the use of certain items such as roads or public facilities. Additionally, a use tax may be levied on out-of-state purchases or sales, including Internet sales.

7. Fuel tax

Every state imposes a liquid fuel tax on gasoline and diesel fuel purchased within the state.

8. Corporate income tax

If you are incorporated, there is often a state corporate tax imposed on the income of the corporation. A number of states provide tax exemptions or lower corporate income tax rates to certain types of businesses as an incentive for businesses to locate within their state.

9. Estate tax

Estate and/or inheritance taxes are primarily an issue for family-owned businesses, where the family wishes to retain a controlling interest in the business on the death of one of the owners. Not all states have this tax.

Source: Small Business Notes (*www.smallbusinessnotes.com*)— They provide information and resources for other businesses struggling to provide that same quality in a challenging economic environment. Their purpose is to provide the resources for all the information that a small business person needs to operate his or her business. Contact editor Judith Kautz by sending e-mail to *info@smallbusinessnotes.com*.

Note: The information contained in this section was current at the time of publication. Please remember to check with your tax advisor.

Communications

Things to Consider Before Hiring an Answering Service

Is your receptionist slacking? Or maybe you operate a virtual office. Answering services provide all of the capabilities of a full-time receptionist (and phone system) and have become a popular form of outsourcing. Our expert, a communications trade industry group, provides these thoughts on hiring an answering service.

1. Training

How is their staff trained? A standardized training program helps ensure that your callers will receive consistent service. Do the company's employees attend national or regional educational and technical programs? This assures you that the company will have the latest information and training to provide you with a service plan designed to meet your needs.

2. Staffing

How does the company ensure that enough staff is available to minimize long rings or hold times? What type of notice will they need from you if your call volume should increase due to special promotions or a change in office hours?

3. Compliance

Does the company comply with local, state, and federal regulations and carry business insurance, including errors and omissions coverage?

4. Stability

How many years has the company been in business? What is the average tenure of the staff with this company? Is the company active in the local business community?

5. Reliability

Does the company have backup power and redundancy of critical system components?

6. Available services

Are customer service representatives available twenty-four hours a day, seven days a week, including holidays? Does the company offer a combination of automation and customer service agents, if appropriate for your business? The use of a personalized announcement to give office hours combined with an option to access a customer service agent is one way to reduce expenses. Does the company offer a variety of message notification methods, such as e-mail, fax, alpha paging, voice mail, and phone calls, to meet your current and future needs? Do the customer service agents have the ability to access the Internet? If your company relies heavily on this technology, be sure to ask about this. Ask what other business support services they offer. Many services now have the capability to schedule appointments and make reservations, provide help desk and dealer-locate services, and take product orders and track employee attendance. They may also offer telephone and videoconferencing services.

7. Pricing

Make sure you understand how charges are computed. Charges can be based on time or calls. The company should work with you to design a service package that offers your company the best value for its needs; ask for a written proposal. Request references and call them.

Source: The foregoing is u   ¹ with the permission of the Association of TeleServices Inte   onal, Inc., an international trade association established by a.   or professionals in the teleservices business. This includes telep!   e answering services, voice-mail services, call center services a. J any other business that provides enhanced communication services. Contact them at 12 Academy Avenue, Atkinson, NH 03811; toll-free: (866) 896-2874; fax: 603-362-9486; Web site: www.atsi.org.

Popular Videoconferencing Services

Videoconferencing is the integration of video, audio, and peripherals that enable two or more people to communicate simultaneously over telecommunications lines. During videoconferencing, you can transmit synchronized images and verbal communications between two or more locations. Our expert, who tracks the videoconferencing marketplace, provides this list of the more popular services available today.

1. 1stWorks Corporation

The 1stWorks network architecture uses highly efficient compression technology that leverages the power of the Internet to deliver multimedia presentations anywhere to anyone. All data streams are encrypted so your videoconference is secure from end-point to end-point.

30 Noon Hill Ave.
Norfolk, MA 02056
(508) 541-6781

E-mail: *info@1stWorks.com*
Web site: *www.botcomm.com*

2. Arel Communications and Software, Inc.

Arel Communications and Software, a technology leader in interactive Web communications, develops, markets, and sells a universal conferencing software solution for enterprise-wide deployment of integrated voice, video, and data Web conferencing/collaboration and training applications.

1200 Ashwood Parkway, Suite 550
Atlanta, GA 30338
(770) 396-8105
E-mail: *sales@arelcom.com*
Web site: *www.arelcom.com*

3. Citizens Conferencing

Citizens Conferencing, a wholly owned subsidiary of Citizens Communications, is a full-line conferencing service bureau, offering audio, video, and Web conferencing.

1349 South Wabash Avenue
Chicago, IL 60605
(800) 530-6342
Fax: (312) 765-6772
E-mail: *sales@citizensconferencing.com*
Web site: *www.citizensconferencing.com*

4. ConferencePlus

Since 1988, ConferencePlus has been providing a full portfolio of advanced audio, video, and Web conferencing solutions with unparalleled customer service.

1051 E. Woodfield Road
Schaumburg, IL 60173
(866) 571-PLUS (7587)

E-mail: *getinfo@conferenceplus.com*
Web site: *www.conferenceplus.com*

5. InterCall

InterCall, a division of West Corporation, is the largest service provider in the world specializing in conference communications. InterCall's services include audio, event, video, and Web conferencing solutions.

8420 W. Bryn Mawr, Suite 400
Chicago, IL 60631
(773) 399-1600
Web site: *www.intercall.com*

6. LiveOffice Corporation

IMConferencing provides high-quality desktop videoconferencing services featuring MPEG4 technology. IMC requires no up-front hardware investment and getting started is simple with just a basic Web cam and PC.

23133 Hawthorne Blvd. #200
Torrance, CA 90505
(800) 251-3863
E-mail: *sales@imconferencing.com*
Web site: *www.imconferencing.com*

7. MCI Conferencing

MCI Conferencing is the world's largest and most experienced provider of conferencing services.

8750 West Bryn Mawr Avenue
Chicago, IL 60631
(800) 480-3600; (773) 399-1700
E-mail: *Conferencing-info@mci.com*
Web site: *http://e-meetings.mci.com*

8. NTT-IT Corporation

MeetingPlaza provides a total solution for remote conference and distance education needs. Its highly scalable video, reliable audio, and versatile functions for collaborative works show you a new horizon of multiuser communication environment.

Kannai-Waizu Bldg 2F
2-9-1 Naka-ku, Furo-cho Yokohama 231-0032 Japan
+81 45 651 7555
E-mail: *isg@meetingplaza.com*
Web site: *www.meetingplaza.com*

Source: ConferZone (*www.conferzone.com*)—The first objective e-conferencing resource that tracks the latest technology and trends in the marketplace, ConferZone provides comprehensive, objective content so businesses can make educated and sound decisions when purchasing e-conferencing services or products. Contact them at 1555 California, Suite 615, Denver, CO 80202; (303) 316-0175; fax: (303) 265-966, *editor@conferzone.com*.

Popular Web Meeting Services

Want to start up a meeting over the Web and share your presentation out to desktops in real time? There are a number of companies providing this service. Most of these products regrettably now only support Internet Explorer and Windows configurations, although the more enlightened are finally embracing Firefox and other Mozilla browsers.

1. Brainshark

www.brainshark.com

2. Centra Conference
www.centra.com

3. ConferenceHub
www.conferencehub.com

4. Easy WebPresenter
www.easywp.com

5. eBoardroom Suite
www.e-boardroom.net/en/

6. e/pop Web Conferencing
www.wiredred.com

7. Egenda
www.encounter.net

8. GatherPlace
www.gatherplace.net

9. Genesys Meeting Center
www.genesys.com

10. Glance
www.glance.net

11. HostPresentation
www.hostpresentation.com

12. iSession
www.instantservice.com

13. Meeting Place
www.cisco.com

14. mShow
www.mshow.com

15. MS Live Meeting
http://main.livemeeting.com

16. NetTogether Presenter
www.nettogether.com

17. Raindance Meeting
www.raindance.com

18. The Switchboard
http://theswitchboard.ca/

19. TopClass
www.wbtsystems.com

20. ttcGlobalTalk
www.ttcglobaltalk.com

21. Web Conferencing Central
www.web-conferencing-central.com

22. Webex
www.webex.com

23. WebTrain Communicator
www.webtrain.com

Source: David Strom (*www.strom.com*)—One of the leading experts on network and Internet technologies, Strom has written extensively on the topic for more than seventeen years for a wide variety of publications, including holding several editorial management positions for both print and online properties. He presently is editor-in-chief for Tom's Hardware where he is responsible for managing a technical staff of seven full-time writers and several freelancers who produce a series of technical Web properties, newsletters, and other content involving computer enthusiast, gaming, and IT industries. Contact David at *david@strom.com* or at (818) 991-0282, ext. 204.

Things to Consider Before Buying a Fax Machine

Ready to replace that old fax machine with a new one? Before driving out to the office superstore, take a look at this list first. Then you'll be prepared to ask the right questions.

1. Printing technology

Nearly all machines use plain office paper. Less expensive models generally use thermal-printing technology, and printouts don't have the same longevity as ink-jet faxes. Ink-jet faxes can usually print, copy, and fax in color. Laser fax machines are also available, although most are monochrome units. Laser fax machines usually print sharper text.

2. Speed

Transmission speed ranges from about fifteen seconds per page (for less expensive models like the Brother 575) up to about three seconds per page (for the Brother 1940CN and Canon L80). If you only need to send the occasional fax, you can save money by going with a slower model.

3. Memory

Fax machines store incoming and outgoing pages in memory. This lets the machine save an incoming fax in memory if it runs out of paper, and then print the fax when you reload the paper tray. Try for at least 512KB of memory, although some newer models have 8 to 16MB (up to 480 pages).

4. Other features

Besides speaker phones and digital answering machines, some faxes include such telephony features as caller ID, a distinctive ring that enables it to distinguish between a human or fax machine call, auto redial, fax forwarding, polling, and speed dialing.

Source: ConsumerSearch (*www.consumersearch.com*) is a Web site that ranks, describes, and analyzes top reviews of consumer products, along with lists of top-rated products. Contact Derek Drew (CEO and editor-in-chief) at 5467 31st Street NW, Washington, DC 20015; (202) 966-7907; e-mail: *derekdrew@consumersearch.com*.

Things to Consider Before Buying a Multifunction Printer/Fax

You need to print, scan, copy, and fax, and you have a small office space. Or maybe you have a limited budget and don't want to invest in a bunch of hardware devices. Or maybe you do one thing a lot—like fax, or print or scan or copy—and want a device that does that one thing well and the others okay. A multifunction device in your home office could be a great investment, a timesaver, and an inexpensive (or expensive if you invest in one of the higher-end machines!) backup to a primary laser printer or fax machine scanner. This list give you some things to consider before buying this device.

1. Cost

The cost is not just the purchase price, but the cost of printing each page (toner cartridges, fuser rollers, etc.).

2. Speed

Copying, printing, and faxing.

3. Technology

Ink jet versus laser and the quality differences in print output that each technology offers.

4. Resolution

For printing *and* scanning, the bigger the numbers are, the better it is (in "dots" per inch).

5. Software

Especially for Optical Character Recognition (OCR) that is required for the scanning part of the device to function.

6. Memory

More is better here (improves speed in all areas, especially for large or image-intense documents).

7. Interfaces

Interfaces for your PC, your network, or both.

8. Compatibility

Windows, Macintosh, Linux, and more.

9. Media handling

The amount of paper you can put in the trays and feeders and types of paper (including envelopes, transparencies, and size varieties).

10. Service and support

Always "big." The warranty, service strategy, and contact capabilities.

Source: Home Office Reports (*www.homeofficereports.com*)—Home Office Reports supplies comprehensive, information on a wide variety of technologies, from PCs to networking, telephones and telephone services to digital cameras and accounting. Contact them at 2102 Clematis Ct., McKinney, TX 75070; (972) 529-9719; fax: (972) 540-1674; e-mail: *dmielke@homeofficereports.com*.

Popular Internet Fax Services

Who needs a fax machine nowadays anyway? Internet fax services have several benefits in addition to not requiring a phone line. You can send or receive faxes anywhere there's Internet access. You also have a fax that is always on and that never runs out of paper or ink. All faxes received are then e-mailed to you so you can store them electronically. Not bad. If you're looking into Web-based faxing, then take a look at these popular services, recommended by an expert in the field.

1. Efax

The undisputed leader in the field of Internet faxing. Offers free version, though free version doesn't provide you with a local number. Regular service is expensive. Offers many other products—remote control of computer, etc. Requires proprietary fax viewer software to view faxes. The most local area code numbers available in the U.S.

6922 Hollywood Blvd., 5th floor
Los Angeles, CA 90028
Phone: (800) 958-2983
www.efax.com

2. Fax-away

Competitive regular service. Web faxing not supported. Many customizable features and options for sending. The personal fax number they assign you is not local; they are all in some location where the area code is not local to you—just like the free eFax service—which is not too useful for your customers.

417 Second Avenue West
Seattle, WA 98119 USA
www.faxaway.com

3. Internet Fax Provider

Offers toll-free numbers which can be used anywhere in the U.S. with the first 200 received and 100 sent faxes per month included in the monthly rate. This is very convenient for the people sending faxes to you, as they will not pay any additional long distance charges. Best rate for Internet faxing. Many customizable features and options for sending. Comprehensive Web faxing features.

4708 Yorkshire Dr.
Macungie, PA 18062
Phone: (800) 437-3297
Fax: (866) 262-1612
www.internetfaxprovider.com

4. MaxEmail

Offers local numbers in the U.S. However, you will find that only the major cities are covered. Good receiving plans.

www.maxemail.com

5. CallWave

Installable software helps consumers and businesses get more out of their wireless phone, home phone, and Internet-connected PC by 'bridging' calls between these devices.

P.O. Box 549
Santa Barbara, CA 93102
www.callwave.com

6. Data On Call

The company offers a comprehensive suite of fax services including electronic faxing (inbound and outbound), web/fax integrations, developer APIs, fax broadcasting, fax on demand, and custom applications.

4849 Ronson Court, Suite 102
San Diego, CA 92111
Phone: (888) 429-4615
Fax: (858) 712-3600
www.dataoncall.com

7. Digital Mail

E-mail to fax and fax to e-mail services. Users receive a unique phone number, accepting voice mail and faxes.

70-74 City Road
London
EC1Y 2BJ
www.digitalmail.com

8. EasyLink

Small Business Integrated Desktop Messaging, E-mail to fax, fax to email and desktop faxing. The service was previously named FaxSav.

33 Knightsbridge Rd.
Piscataway, NJ 08854
Phone: (800) 828-7115
Fax: (732) 652-3810
www.easylink.com

9. FaxMate

E-mail to fax, desktop to fax, broadcast fax, and fax to fax via the Internet. Its U800 service allows users a personal toll-free number, which automatically forwards faxes and voice mail to e-mail.

Betteroff Networks Pty Ltd
Suite 239, 421 Brunswick Street
Fortitude Valley Queensland Australia 4006

Phone: 1300 76 4455

Fax: 1300 55 1201

Phone: (61) 500 844 111 (outside Australia)

10. IntelliFax

Allows you to send and receive Internet faxes. Provides middleware for other Internet fax vendors.

GreenFax

2935 Byberry Road

Hatboro, PA 19040

Phone: (215) 293-0919

Fax: (215) 701-8714

www.intellifax.com

Source: Vincent Lynn (*www.faxiq.com*) is a former telecommunications engineer in telecom who has reviewed many telecommunications products for large and small business. He has worked with large telecom service providers in marketing and development. He currently reviews technology for business development in the Northeastern United States. Contact him at *vlynn@faxiq.com*.

Reliable Long-Distance Suppliers

We asked our telecommunication expert to provide us with a list of those companies that, in his opinion, provide the most reliable service to their customers. Here they are, in alphabetical order.

1. Airespring

Airespring provides a very reliable nationwide network that offers discount rates for a small, medium, or large business.

(888) 389-2899

www.airespring.com

2. AT&T (Formerly SBC)

AT&T offers numerous business plans in the majority of the country, including international locations. Note that SBC and AT&T have merged to create the new AT&T.

(800) 750-2355

www.att.com or *www.sbc.com*

3. BellSouth

BellSouth covers a large footprint of the southern and southeastern areas of the country. They offer a variety of business plans for both small and large operations.

(866) 620-6000

www.bellsouth.com

4. Qwest Communications

Qwest provides a large service area across the country. For a business located in the northeastern part of the country, Qwest offers an unlimited business long-distance plan to those with Qwest as the local provider.

(800) 603-6000

www.qwest.com

5. Verizon

Verizon offers a robust selection of business plans that cover the entire country. In addition, Verizon offers a business owner the opportunity to bundle local, long-distance, and wireless service on one bill.

(800) 483-5000

www.verizon.com

Source: David Wood is the author of *Dialing For Deals: How to Cut Your Phone Bill in Half!* widely recognized as the bible of how to lower your monthly phone bill. He has been featured on more than seventy TV and radio shows as well as numerous magazines.

His book is full of tips on how to shop for service and where to find unadvertised bargains. His Web site is *www.DialingForDeals.com*.

Things to Consider Before Buying Long-Distance Services

Just about everyone has followed the advertising campaigns on television that promise the "right long-distance plan for you." However, with all the companies and so many plans available to choose from, it's not exactly an easy choice to make. Take a look at this list for some professional tips from the experts at the Telecommunications Research and Action Center.

1. Conduct a long-distance checkup

Conducting a checkup is easy. The first step is to call your carrier's toll-free customer service number and ask if you're on their least expensive calling plan. Make sure that when they look at your records, they examine a typical calling month. If you decide you are not satisfied with your current situation, this is a great time to shop around.

2. Determine your calling patterns

Take a look at your long-distance bills for the past three months. Determine when you make the greatest number of calls, and the average length of your conversations. Determine whether there is a pattern to your calls, such as frequently dialing the same number or area code, or making the bulk of your calls during a certain time of day.

3. Identify your user characteristics

A user that makes calls throughout the day, evening, night, and weekend is along the lines of an average long-distance user. Find the calling

pattern that best resembles the time and money you spend on the phone in a typical month.

4. Compare plans

Read each plan's description to ensure that you meet the requirements to receive discounted rates, and also to ensure that the plan includes all the features and services you desire.

5. Do your research

Once you are interested in some plans, follow up with additional research. Call the carriers to confirm that these would, indeed, be the best plans for you, that the rates are still the same, and the features and services you want are still offered with those calling plans. Remember, plans change frequently and competition results in even more frequent rate and service changes.

Source: Telecommunications Research & Action Center (TRAC—*www.trac.org*)—Founded in 1983 to promote and advocate for the interests of residential telecommunications customers, TRAC has, for almost twenty years, been conducting studies and publishing charts to aid consumers in choosing the correct and most efficient service for their calling needs. TRAC can be contacted at PO Box 27279, Washington, DC 20005; (202) 263-2950. Questions can be sent to *trac@trac.org*.

Ways to Reduce Long-Distance Costs

Choosing the best long-distance service is an extremely important aspect of running your business, because every penny that you save can be applied elsewhere to your business operation. The problem is that many dread the thought of switching long-distance service because of a bad experience or confusion over how to choose the best calling plan for your budget and calling patterns. Now's the time to learn that lowering your phone bill is easier than you think, and our expert has these ideas.

1. Where to start

Know your own needs. You cannot begin to save money until you have at least a basic idea of your own needs and calling patterns. Where are the majority of your calls going: in-state, state-to-state, or international? One plan that has a low state-to-state rate might have lousy in-state rates, and it can sometimes be tough to find a "one-size-fits-all" plan. Long-distance providers make a fortune from business owners who don't know their own calling patterns.

2. Read the small print

Now that's a commonsense tip, isn't it? However, I know of business owners who were so focused on seeing a low rate that the fine print was only an afterthought. If you enjoy living with regrets, go ahead and skip the small print! For those of you who already have enough regrets in life, check the fine print for terminology concerning contracts, monthly or minimum fees, and what the monthly charge will be for the PICC fee.

3. PICC fee (sounds like pick C)

A PICC (presubscribed interexchange carrier charge) is charged to a business that has more than one business line. Note the words *business line*; this means that if you run a home-based business and are using a residential line, you never have to pay the PICC. For business lines, a carrier shouldn't charge the PICC if you have only one line, and many companies won't charge it on the first line if you have a multiline account. Expect to pay anywhere from $1.50 to $4.31 per line, per month. If you use a Centrex system, the PICC should be much lower.

4. Monthly or minimum fees

A monthly fee is typically a fee you will pay every month, no matter how much long-distance you have used. Watch for the letters MRC (monthly recurring charge). In addition, note any minimum usage requirements. Some plans will require you to spend a certain amount each month (monthly minimum); other plans will charge a small fee if you don't hit a certain spending level each month (minimum usage fee).

5. Long-distance rates

I know business owners who pay twenty-eight cents per minute for a state-to-state (interstate) call. In fact, anything above five cents is too much. As for in-state long-distance (intrastate), the rates will vary widely based on your state. International rates can also vary greatly, and many carriers make a fortune from naive business owners. Especially for international and in-state calls, it does pay to shop around because many carriers offer extremely discounted rates for these calls.

6. Billing increment

Many residential plans bill in sixty-second increments, meaning that each call is rounded up to the next minute. For business long-distance, your goal is six-second increments. A common plan is six-second increments with an eighteen-second minimum. Simply put: Any call between one and eighteen seconds will bill at an eighteen-second call and then will bill in six-second increments. This can save you money compared to every call billing in one-minute increments, especially on toll-free service.

7. Toll-free numbers

Unless you have no business outside your local calling area, a toll-free number invites new customers to contact you with no cost to them. It will also show your current customers that you care enough about their business to cover the cost of the call. If you're asked to pay a monthly fee per toll free number, never pay more than $2 per number. In addition, never pay more than five cents per minute for a long-distance call from outside your state.

8. Using a bundled plan

Many business owners will bundle their local service with long-distance service. A few things to keep in mind: (a) If you don't make many long-distance calls, a bundled plan will waste your money; (b) the price quoted to you will not include taxes and fees; and (c) if you make thousands of minutes of long-distance calls each month, a carrier might still cut you off even if that plan is advertised as including "unlimited long-distance." Read the small print!

9. VoIP (computer-to-computer)

The last two tips will deal with VoIP (Voice over Internet Protocol), also known as Internet phone service. While the old version of computer-to-computer calls included echos, delays, and garbled sounds, the VoIP of today can be clearer than a land-line phone. Consider computer-to-computer VoIP if you make long-distance calls between offices. Here's an example: a business was spending a fortune on long-distance calls between their offices located within one state and to a few office locations out of state. This business began using computer-to-computer VoIP for all of these calls and saved almost $2000 per month!

10. VoIP (Using your touchtone phone)

Many business owners are now turning to this type of VoIP, which uses your high-speed Internet (DSL, Cable, T-1), an adaptor, and a regular touchtone phone. A small business VoIP plan might offer all local calls, long-distance, and numerous calling features for $20 to $40 per month, per line. Although this can be an excellent way to cut your long-distance bill, you must do your homework on the potential problems of VoIP. Just one example: Lose your power and you've lost your service.

Source: David Wood is the author of Dialing For *Deals: How to Cut Your Phone Bill in Half!* widely recognized as the bible of how to lower your monthly phone bill. He has been featured on more than seventy TV and radio shows as well as numerous magazines. His book is full of tips on how to shop for service and where to find unadvertised bargains. His Web site is *www.DialingForDeals.com*.

Reliable Phone System Manufacturers

Communication in any organization is the driving force to be successful in your business; that's why the telecommunications infrastructure is the key that provides effective connections to the outside world. There are many phone systems available for businesses to buy. We asked our expert, a company that sells and services many popular phone systems, to list the most reliable manufacturers of phone systems. Here's who made the cut.

1. Iwatsu
8001 Jetstar Drive
Irving, TX 75063
(972) 929-0242
Fax: (972) 929-8919
www.iwatsu.com

2. Northern Telecom
Nortel Networks
2221 Lakeside Boulevard
Richardson, TX 75082-4399
 (972) 684-1000
www.northerntelecom.com

3. Panasonic
Panasonic Corporation of North America
One Panasonic Way
Secaucus, NJ 07094
www.panasonic.com

4. Samsung 816 Plus
Samsung Telecommunications America Inc.
1301 East Lookout Drive
Richardson, TX 75082
(972) 761-7000
www.samsung.com

Source: AEX Communications, Inc. (*www.aexcom.com*)—They sell, service, and install telephone and voicemail systems. Contact them at 4445 West 77th St., Suite 102, Edina, MN 55424; (952) 224-5500: fax: (952) 224-5501; e-mail: *aex@aexcom.com.*

Things to Consider Before Buying a Phone System

Getting a corporate phone system? Don't go any further before reading this list. We consulted a leading provider of phone systems and asked them what their customers should be thinking about before purchasing from them. Here's what they had to say.

1. Ease of use
Keep in mind that most small businesses are small for that reason; they don't have a large technical department to tinker around with a huge, complicated phone system. So, unless you have a bunch of technically gifted people lying around your office, why invest in a system that is so complicated to use that you have to be an expert to do so?

2. Expandability
Small business usually means a small number of employees. If you purchase a system that can be easily expanded, you are setting yourself up for the chance to add to the existing system without having to throw away the original system-smart investment.

3. Upgradability
When you are first buying a system, start out basic. Once you have mastered the existing system and understand all the components, then you can upgrade as needed.

4. Find a system that will work with you
As your system grows and expands, make sure that you have made the initial purchase of a system with components that are upgradable.

For example, get phones that won't have to be replaced with extremely expensive phone units.

5. Size

Yes, believe it or not, some systems are so large they take up an entire closet. Chances are, as a small business, you have a small office, and in that case you are probably using the closet for other things. Smaller systems are designed to fit under a desk, not in a room.

6. Cost

A very important factor: the smaller systems start as low as $695, while the larger ones can sell over $30,000! Wow, big difference, so find one that works for you in both size and price.

7. No use waiting for a deal

The last point to make about phone systems is that unlike other electronics that tend to drop in price over the years, phone systems have shown to be pretty consistent. So if you think that by waiting a few years that your ideal phone system will be more affordable—think again!

Source: We spoke to Chris Brennan at Centrepoint Technologies (*www.talkswitch.com*), a designer, developer, and manufacturer of award-winning telephone systems. You can contact Chris at *cbrennan@talkswitch*.com, or at (613) 725-2980, ext. 136.

Popular Telephone System Resellers

Need a new phone system but don't know where to start? TelephonyWorld.com is an independent resource that serves the telecommunications industry. When your business needs a new telephone system, this list of resellers can provide you telephone products and solutions.

1. AHERN Communications

A worldwide distributor of telephone headsets, PC headsets, cordless telephone headsets, cordless phones, caller ID, surge protectors, conference phones, music on hold, agent monitoring software, and other telecom products.

60 Washington Court
Quincy, MA 02169
(800) 451-5067
(617) 471-1100
Fax: (617) 328-9070
E-mail: *info@aherncorp.com*

2. Alliance Datacom

Provides corporate end-users fast delivery of new, used, refurbished, as well as remanufactured WAN (data communication) products worldwide.

10455 Markison Road
Dallas, TX 75238
(888) 872-5619
(214) 550-6201
Fax: (214) 503-8660
www.alliancedatacom.com

3. Automated Power Technologies

Manufactures and sells a wide range of standard and custom power protection products for industrial and telecommunication markets.

24 Rancho Parkway
Lake Forest, CA 92630
(800) 908-7655
Fax: (949) 768-5959
www.automatedpower.com

4. Bizfon

Leading edge telephony solutions. Company dedicated to improving the communication systems of small businesses.

50 Stiles Rd.
Salem, NH 03079
www.bizfon.com

5. Business Voice Systems

New emerging voice and data systems integrators.

5005 Raintree Drive
West Des Moines, IA 50265
(515) 225-7732
Fax: (515) 225-8561

6. Capernaum, Inc.

Computer Telephony Solutions Provider
6320 St. Augustine Road. Suite 3
Jacksonville, FL 32217
(904) 224-4406
www.capernaum.com

7. Comtech Group

Premier IBM Business Partner and the largest AS/400 Solution Provider in the Central Region.

555 Skokie Blvd., Suite 340
Northbrook, IL 60062
(847) 480-3100
Fax: (847) 480-3560
www.comtech-group.com

8. Komtel Inc.

Well-regarded telephony solutions provider.
30 Main Street, Suite 501
Danbury, CT 06810
(203) 790-9989

Fax: (203) 790-9995
www.komtel.com

9. Loredec Corp.

Exclusive distributors of telephony solutions.

95 Shaker Road
East Longmeadow, MA 01029
(413) 525-3316
Fax: (413) 525-3319
www.loredec.com

10. Sundance Communications

New and refurbished telephone equipment for most telephone systems.

9447 S. 2950 W.
S. Jordan, UT 84095
(801) 253-4454
www.Telbroker.com

Source: TelephonyWorld (*www.telephonyworld.com*)—An on-line information resource and interactive buyer's guide for the computer telephony and telecommunication industry. At this site, visitors can find information on computer telephony and telecommunications companies, products, solutions, and relevant industry news. Contact them at 299 Rues Lane, East Brunswick, NJ 08816; (732) 432-0375.

Popular Voice Mail Systems

The majority of voice mail systems available today have the ability to forward messages to another voice mailbox, send messages to multiple voice mailboxes, add voice notes to a message, store messages for future delivery, make calls to a telephone or paging service when a message is received (outbound notification), transfer callers to another phone for personal assistance, and play different message greetings to different callers. Our expert, a reseller of well-known voice mail systems, has provided us with this listing of their most popular voice mail systems. This information was current at the time of printing, but please make sure you double-check with the vendors for any changes.

1. Panasonic Voice Mail Systems

Add voice mail to your KX-TA824, Hybrid, or Digital Hybrid phone system. Four different systems are available, starting at less than $500. Each is expandable to support heavier call loads and additional message storage capacity.

2. Partner Messaging R7 Voice Mail System

PARTNER Messaging products deliver powerful, yet easy-to-use, voice-messaging capabilities that simply plug into your new or existing PARTNER system.

3. Samsung Flashmail Voice Mail

The new Samsung voice mail systems store data on compact flash media. These systems have no moving parts, so they'll never miss or skip a part of a message.

4. Amanda Voice Mail Systems

Amanda voice mail systems are available to support many different phone systems. The base model (SOHO) supports four simultaneous callers with up to seventeen hours of message capacity for less than $900.

5. Comdial DX-80 8 Port Voice Mail System

For higher call volumes, the "in-skin" voice mail card may be installed in any Comdial DX-80 system to support up to eight simultaneous callers. Available in a flash memory or 150-hour message capacity hard-drive version.

6. Aleen VME 4000 Small Voice Mail System

For small two-port or four-port voice mail systems, the Aleen is a perfect solution.

7. NEC IntraMail Voice Mail Systems

NEC's legendary reliability and quality standards are evident with the introduction of the new, fully integrated, flash memory–based IntraMail voice mail systems for use with either a DS1000 or DS2000 telephone system.

8. Samsung StarmaiL

Samsung's StarmaiL, designed for use with Prostar and DCS Compact telephone systems, offers the ultimate combination of simplicity and sophistication in a voice mail system. Use it to answer all incoming calls, as a backup to an operator, or simply as a voice-messaging system.

Source: TWAcomm.com, Inc. (*www.twacomm.com*), a leading provider of phone systems specializing in business phones and business phone systems for small to large companies with phone systems for any application. TWAcomm.com is located at Ocean-view Promenade, 101 Main St. 3rd floor, Huntington Beach, CA 92648; toll–free: (877) TWAcomm or (877) 892-2666.

Popular Voice–over-Internet Protocol (VoIP) Providers for Small Business

Voice-over-Internet Protocol (VoIP) is a system that allows making telephone calls using a computer network and standard software over the Internet. VoIP digitizes and compresses the voice signal from your telephone into a digital signal that travels over the Internet and then converts it back at the other end so you can speak to anyone with a regular phone number. Our expert, an industry watchdog, provides this list of the more popular providers.

1. Sunrocket

Sunrocket offers voice mail, caller ID, call waiting, three-way calling, and keeps your number and 911.

www.sunrocket.com

2. Vonage

Vonage offers voice mail, caller ID, call waiting, three-way calling, keeps your number and 911.

www.vonage.com

3. My phonecompany

My phonecompany offers voice mail, caller ID, call waiting, three-way calling, and keeps your number and 911.

www.myphonecompany.com

4. Packet8

One of the first providers, Packet8 offers voice mail, caller ID, call waiting, three-way calling, and keeps your number and 911.

www.packet8.net

5. BBTelSys

BBTelSys offers voice mail, caller ID, call waiting, three-way calling, and keeps your number and 911.

www.BBTelSys.com

6. NetZero

NetZero offers PC–based calling that includes voice mail, caller ID, and call waiting. Free calls to other NetZero users.

www.netzero.net

7. SpeakEasy

SpeakEasy offers voice mail, caller ID, call waiting, three-way calling, and keeps your number. You may also get business-class phone service and Internet access.

www.SpeakEasy.net

8. IConnectHere.com

IConnectHere, one of the first providers, offers voice mail, caller ID, call waiting, three-way calling, and keeps your number. No 911 is currently offered.

www.IConnectHere.com

9. AOL TotalTalk

AOL TotalTalk offers voice mail, caller ID, call waiting, three-way calling, and keeps your number.

www.totaltalk.com

10. AT&T CallVantage

AT&T CallVantage offers voice mail, caller ID, call waiting, three-way calling, and keeps your number and 911.

www.callvantage.att.com

Source: VoipReview.org (*www.voipreview.org*) is an information place for consumer VoIP providers and small business VoIP providers. Contact them at Voipreview.org LLC, 4830 S. Zinnia Way, Morrison, CO 80465; (303) 374-1329; fax: (503) 961-0931.

Popular Reasons to Get VoIP

Are you considering a Voice-Over-Internet Protocol (VoIP) phone system? It's important to view the advantages that other consumers see as the "upsides" to the service.

1. Cost savings

Most VoIP providers charge a monthly fee of about $20 to $40 with unlimited local and long distance minutes. Those who make a lot of long distance calls should see substantial savings.

2. Enhanced phone features

Because of the technology VoIP utilizes, in addition to the standard features on regular phone such as Caller ID and Call Waiting, VoIP users will have access to voice activated dialing, video conferencing, voice mails in written form, and spoken e-mails. In fact, many VoIP systems use "soft phones," which are special software programs that are used in conjunction with the voice board in your laptop or PC, and a headset and microphone act as an extension to your VoIP platform anywhere there is a high-speed internet connection.

3. Phone number and location flexibility

VoIP subscribers can have multiple area codes across the country. For example, a VoIP subscriber located in Washington, DC, can have a VoIP phone number with a Florida area code in addition to their DC VoIP phone number. So, if you move, all you need to do is take your VoIP adapter with you and VoIP should work the same as from your home or business.

4. Taxes and fees

Currently, VoIP providers do not have to pay taxes and regulatory fees that standard phone service providers have to pay when the calls are completed over the Internet. Therefore, these costs are not included on your VoIP bill. This is subject to change if federal and state regulators change their policy concerning VoIP providers.

5. Converged Network

End to end IP telephony by using one network for the transport of voice, integrated data and video. Seamless to all users in your company connected with high speed proper bandwidth broadband to the internet. There is no need for legacy PBXs due to the integration into your network while remote users can act like they are at the office no matter where they are in the internet world.

6. Implementation

It's important to have a vendor experienced in installation, training, and support for your VoIP platform. The convergence of all this stuff into your network is going to require some expertise in making sure you have the right network gear to accomplish a smooth transition to VoIP. Also, moving forward with your converged system is going to require ongoing support and training to help you and your employees take advantage of the features and network access now available to you with voice over internet protocol.

7. Hosted application versus full cost of ownership

There are several companies today that offer a monthly service for equipment and software to implement your VoIP data and voice communication system. They provide broadband connections to the internet, hardware and software necessary to get the VoIP PBX deployed throughout your company, and ongoing training and support for a monthly fee versus a capital or lease purchase by your company. This cost-effective solution may provide an easy transition to a VoIP system without the high cost of entry. It also gives you the ability to insure your purchase does not become obsolete because most companies provide hardware and software upgrades in their monthly fees.

Source: Gary Ritacco is President of eComm (*www.askecomm.com*), a communications solution provider of voice, data and video convergence tools. Gary can be reached at 800-372-4600 or through e-mail at *gsr@askecomm.com*.

Gadgets and Gizmos

Questions to Ask Before Buying a PDA

Are you in the market for a new personal data assistant (PDA)? Or maybe this is your first time purchasing a PDA. Our expert devotes his very soul to the topic of PDAs. We asked him what questions a prospective buyer should ask before buying a new unit. Here's his list.

1. What factors should I consider when buying a PDA?

Two things you should think about first are what you want to do with the PDA and how much you are willing to spend. Both of these factors can immediately lead you in a direction toward certain products, and in many cases these two factors will actually work together to help you find a device. Also consider if you want or will need phone functionality built in. If you do, you will likely have to purchase a device from a wireless carrier or online, as opposed to in-store (which is where you will find more general function PDAs). But the most important thing you must consider is the feel of the device, and the only way to see if a PDA is right for your hand, pocket, and usage is to try it out at a local store.

2. What effect does the processor have on my device?

The processor speed really only comes into play when you want a device for more than just a calendar and address book. When you start using more advanced applications such as media programs (video and audio), GPS, and graphical games, processor speed is more important. Faster processors are not always better; often, a processor with a higher speed (measured most often in MHz) consumes more power and either drains your battery faster or requires a more powerful battery. Don't look for Intel Pentium and AMD Athlon here, processors in mobile devices include the Intel XScale and TI OMAP. Find out more about processors and which devices use which processors in the hardware section of *www.davespda.com*.

3. How much memory (RAM/ROM) do I need?

RAM and ROM are very important considerations. In many mobile devices, RAM does not work exactly as it does in your desktop or laptop computer. RAM can often be written to and data can be saved there, although it is lost if the battery ever dies. Most manufacturers are now including more ROM than RAM because it is not lost when the device loses power. If a device has 128 MB of ROM, part of that is shared by the operating system, so you will have 32 to 64 MB less than that available than you might expect. Memory is really only a minor consideration when it comes to address books and contacts; most people won't fill up 32 MB, let alone 128 MB or 256 MB. Most of all, consider memory as space for additional programs and larger files like documents. Find out how much memory a device has in the hardware section of *www.davespda.com* and compare devices with the PDA Comparison tool.

4. Is it possible to upgrade my processor or internal memory?

Neither of these can be physically changed by you as the user, as in a desktop computer. The processor simply cannot be upgraded at this point. No companies provide a service for upgrading it. But on the memory side of things, you may have one option. Pocket PC Techs (*www.ppctechs.com*) can upgrade the internal memory of some devices.

5. What can I do to expand my PDA?

While you might not be able to add memory as you could a hard drive or RAM to your computer, you can add more memory and other functionality through expansion cards. CompactFlash (CF) and Secure Digital (SD) are often the expansion card types found in PDAs. Expansion cards can add over 4 GB of memory to a device (like a CF microdrive, which is actually a miniature hard drive), Wi-Fi, Bluetooth, a camera, GPS, barcode scanner, and more.

6. What is the difference between MMC and SD? MiniSD? What about CF?

MMC and SD are two different types of the same style card. While it used to matter more which you used, the difference is minor for the most part, and most devices now use SD as opposed to MMC. An added benefit to SD is SDIO, which is found on most PDAs with SD slots. SDIO allows for the use of expansions like Wi-Fi and Bluetooth cards. MiniSD is simply a smaller SD card mostly found in phones. CF was one of the original PDA expansion types and is much larger than SD, but often expansions are cheaper in the CF form factor and are released earlier.

7. Does using SD instead of CF limit my expandability?

In some ways, it does. If you have a device with only an SD slot, there might be functionality that is not available, though as technology progresses, more functionality is "smashed" into the small form factor. Most often, new technology is put into CF cards first and later comes to SD cards. CF cards will likely always be first to offer greater amounts of memory, again due to the size and the ability to fit a spinning hard drive inside the card.

8. What is Wi-Fi? Bluetooth? Cellular Wireless?

The easiest way to think of Bluetooth and its uses is to relate it to USB. Bluetooth is, in essence, a wireless version of USB. Especially in the case of getting your device connected to your desktop/laptop machine, Bluetooth wireless will replace your USB connection. But more than just that connectivity, Bluetooth will also allow you to connect to other Bluetooth devices such as headsets and cell phones. To make a local area network with wireless, Wi-Fi is the way to do it. Wi-Fi is also known by its IEEE standard name, 802.11. The most common form of Wi-Fi is 802.11b, but recently 802.11g was introduced into the PDA market allowing for faster connection speeds. Wi-Fi is, in essence, a wireless version of the Ethernet in the form of a local area network. The only way to connect from anywhere is to use a cellular data wireless connection. Cellular data wireless (often just referred to as wireless) comes in two forms: GSM/GPRS and CDMA (sometimes also referred to as 1xRTT). Both forms are similar and are decided on by networks. In the United States, T-Mobile and Cingular are GSM/GPRS based, and Verizon and Sprint networks use CDMA.

9. If I buy a device that was just released, how long will it be new?

The eternal question when it comes to computers. Some would say it is out-of-date as soon as you get it. That might be true, but I think your question is probably "how long until I have to upgrade?" The big upgrade factor is a new version of the operating system on the device as well as new hardware. Operating systems can come out as often as every year, and new technologies pop up all over the place. The best plan for finding out what is going on is to check the news at sites like *www.davespda.com* and follow what is new in the market.

10. Palm OS versus Windows Mobile

The best way to gauge which operating system is right for you is to consider how you plan to use a PDA. If you plan to use a PDA primarily as an organizer (or as an upgrade from an organizer/planner), then Palm OS is likely a better choice because it is more structured for this use. You may like a Windows Mobile device better if you are a strong Outlook user and want something similar. In that case, the functionality of Windows Mobile is similar to Outlook, compared to that of the Palm OS.

Similarly, if you are an Office user and want pocket versions of Word and Excel, then Windows Mobile would again be a stronger option because it comes with built-in software for Word and Excel document creation and manipulation. If your focus is more on using a PDA for media functionality, either operating system could be a good option, but older versions of the Palm OS are not as strong as Windows Mobile in dealing with media. In either case, the best way to make a decision is to try out devices running each operating system.

11. Is it possible to move my data from a Palm OS device to a Windows Mobile device?

Yes, quite possible. One option is to sync calendar and contacts data through Outlook, which is very easy to do. There are also software solutions available to help. As for the software, you pretty much have to find similar software for the new operating system. Consider the differences between using software on different mobile device operating systems to be similar to the Windows versus Mac situation.

12. What happens when the device's batteries die?

PDAs include backup batteries. While the device cannot be turned with the backup battery, it will hold the charge to keep anything in RAM intact. If you are using ROM space for storage or a memory card, the device losing power only limits you from using the device until power is found. If you find that your battery is dying often, there are backup power options available. Visit *www.davespda.com* for more information.

13. Do I really have to initially charge my PDA for as long as the manual says?

Yes. Do not risk not fully charging your battery; it is possible it will not be able to hold a full charge after the first time if it is not fully charged initially.

14. When should I charge my PDA?

This is one of those eternal questions when it comes to batteries. Most PDAs now use lithium-based batteries. Lithium batteries do not have the memory effect like NiMH. It used to be that if you charged batteries that weren't dead, you eventually wouldn't be able to charge them fully. With lithium, the opposite is true. Charge your device as often as possible. Every night is a good option, even if you didn't use it during the day. Topping of a lithium battery is okay.

15. How do I protect my screen?

Screen protectors are a must-have, although some kind of case is a very good first line of defense. Screens are built to be used by a stylus, so there is some level of protection built in, but screens are rather fragile when it comes to having the device in your pocket or purse. If you want to protect your screen from more normal wear and tear (which I highly recommend), do not skimp on the price tag of screen protectors. One high-quality screen protector will last much longer and do a much better job than a set of cheap ones. Consider the ClearTouch Screen Protector or get a JavoEdge JAVOSkin Bundle, which includes not only a case but a good screen protector.

16. Where can I find my device's serial number?

Device serial numbers are often listed under the battery of a device. You must remove the battery to find the serial number of the device. The device model number is also listed here. Usually the model number is also on the front of the device; you can also find model numbers in the hardware section of *www.davespda.com*.

Source: David Conger(*www.davespda.com*)—Dave's PDA Place believes it is important to identify products in all sides of the market to inform users about what is available to them and what would be the best product for them. The site provides updated hardware specifications, updated news, new interactive ways of looking for PDA information, advice for new PDA users and perspective PDA users, and help so that more people understand PDAs. Dave's PDA Place is not about selling devices or making a profit, but it is about finding a PDA that can benefit the end-user best. Contact him at *dave@davespda.com*.

Questions to Ask Before Buying a Digital Camera

Before plunking down your hard-earned cash to buy a digital camera, check out this multi-question list. It covers key questions about camera features, image storage capacity, power source, accessories, warranty, return policy, and repair service.

1. Return policies

What is your policy if I decide to return the camera? Is there a restocking fee?

2. Megapixels

How many megapixels does the camera have? Will it be enough for the *maximum* size photos I plan to print?

3. Features

Are there any features that set this camera apart from others? Does it have auto features for focus, exposure, and white balance?

4. Shooting capabilities

Does the camera have both point-and-shoot and advanced shooting capabilities? Does it have manual controls?

5. Focal length

What is the focal length of the zoom lens? What is the 35mm equivalent?

6. Zoom

Is the zoom optical (a true zoom)? Does the camera have a digital zoom (a simulated zoom); if so, can it be turned off?

7. Modes

Does the camera have a macro mode for close-up photos? What are the other scene modes?

8. Memory

How does the camera store photos? Is the storage built-in, removable, or both? What type of memory card is used? Does the manufacturer recommend using a high-speed memory card?

9. Image storage capabilities

Is a memory card included in the purchase? If so, what is the capacity? How many images can be stored at the highest resolution; at the lowest?

10. Battery type and cost

What types of batteries are used in the camera? Are they standard or proprietary? If proprietary, what is the cost to purchase an extra battery and where can I purchase it? Can the camera also use standard alkaline or lithium batteries?

11. Included accessories

What cables are included with the camera? What other accessories are included in the price?

12. Software

What software comes with the camera? Does it include an image-editing program?

13. Gray market

Is the camera gray market? If so, does it have a warranty and is it eligible for authorized repair in my country? Are camera drivers and video and electrical components compatible in my country?

14. Warranty

What type of warranty does the camera have? How long is it? Does it cover both parts and labor for the entire time?

15. Extended warranty

Does the warranty cover parts and labor? Does it cover anything beyond mechanical and electrical failures and defects in workmanship and/or materials? Can it be renewed or transferred to a new owner? Does it have a "no lemon" policy? Can it be canceled and, if so, will I receive a prorated refund?

16. Service and support

If the camera ever needs repair, can I have it done locally or must I mail it? Will service be done by an authorized repair service center? What is the typical turn-around time? Does the manufacturer offer phone or online technical support for the camera?

Source: Digicamhelp (*www.digicamhelp.com*) started as a small subweb of another site. Digicamhelp consists of hundreds of pages of information about digital cameras and photography. Many hours are spent researching and distilling complex digital photography-related topics into a few paragraphs, so they can be more easily understood by new and intermediate digital camera users. Contact them at *info@digicamhelp.com*.

Top Considerations when Purchasing a Projector

A good projector can cost you thousands, so it's not a purchase that should be taken lightly. We consulted our experts, who sell business projectors nationwide and asked them what a typical buyer should consider before purchasing a projector. Here's some of the questions they recommended you should ask.

1. How bright should my projector be?

Projector brightness is measured in ANSI lumens. Though manufacturer measurement standards vary, there are some basic guidelines you can follow to help ensure that the projector you choose is bright enough for your application. Audience size and ambient light will all affect the amount of brightness needed. Here are some brightness recommendations:

- 1,000—1,500 lumens low ambient light, presentations (small audiences)
- 2,000—2,500 lumens with some ambient light (medium audiences)
- 2,500—3,000 lumens with bright ambient light (medium to large audiences)
- 3,000—5,000 lumens with bright light (large audiences)

2. How do I get the best image?

Higher resolution (or more pixels) generally equals a better picture. However, the computer or alternate data or video source also factors into the equation. If possible, match your projector resolution to your computer resolution pixel for pixel (e.g., 1024 ×768) for best results. If that's not possible, higher-resolution projectors are more future proof and will most likely still create the best looking image. Common projector resolutions for business projectors are SVGA (800 × 600) 480,000 pixels or XGA (1024 × 768) 786,432 pixels.

3. What about contrast ratio?

Projectors with higher contrast ratios show better detail and subtlety in colors and, in particular, more shades of gray. For business applications such as PowerPoint presentations, contrast ratios are not important considerations. However, if the projector is used to display video in dark rooms, and color depth is a concern, consider a projector with a contrast ratio of 2000:1 or higher. For general business applications, 400:1 or better will do the job.

4. How portable should the projector be?

Thanks to advancing technology, presentation projectors have become more portable than ever. Portable projectors weigh in around two to eight pounds and have footprints that are smaller than a laptop computer. A good travel case that carries both a projector and a laptop is a convenient accessory for road warrior presenters.

5. Which features make a projector easy to use?

Most of today's portable projectors are very easy to use. They come with about as much hardware as a laptop. Usually just two to three cords (power, PS II mouse, and audio/video cables) and the projector itself pack into a bag small enough to carry on the plane, or place in the backseat.

6. Is there more to consider?

Many projectors have added features that can make your presenting life easier and more successful. Wireless projectors for easy setup, network ability for control, from remote location and added security, component video inputs for better quality video, digital keystone correction for versatility in projector placement, wireless mouse control, for freedom to move while you present, lens shift for more convenient setup and built-in audio.

7. What about short throw lenses?

A common throw distance is one foot of screen for every two feet of space between projector and screen. That is a general rule for projectors with a standard lens. Projectors with short throw lenses are able to create larger images with less distance between projector and screen.

8. When is a short throw lens beneficial?

A short throw lens allows users to create the big picture they want in a tight space. Short throw lenses are commonly used in environments such as small conference rooms, small classrooms, tradeshow booths, and small home theaters.

9. Who makes short throw lenses?

Many manufacturers have short throw lenses as an option on selected projectors. However, some manufacturers include short throw lenses as a standard feature on specially designed projectors.

10. What is the difference between a short throw and long throw lens?

Short throw lenses help create larger pictures from shorter distances; long throw lenses help create smaller, more viewable images from greater distances. A long throw lens is advantageous in large venues, particularly in fixed installations. Churches often require long throw lenses for worship spaces, because the projector is often mounted far away from the screen, behind the congregation. Without a long throw lens, the image would be too large.

11. What are zoom lenses?

Manual or digital zoom is a feature on many standard, long, or short throw lenses. The zoom feature allows for larger or smaller images from the same distance, much like a zoom lens on a 35mm camera.

12. Do short and long throw lenses cost more than standard lenses?

If a short or zoom lens is not standard on the projector you choose, and you need one, an external lens may be an option. The cost of external lenses varies and is typically expensive, depending on the type of lens you need and the projector model. Not all projectors can use external lenses, and in some cases, adding one may void the manufacturer's warranty.

Source: Projector People (*www.projectorpeople.com*) represent all the major manufacturers of business and home projectors, For twenty years, they have sold, serviced, and educated their customers on the use of projection equipment around the world. Contact them at 6313 Benjamin Rd., Suite 106, Tampa, FL 33634.

Manufacturers of Reliable Photo Printers

Your business may make use of photo printers so you're probably familiar with the names of the major manufacturers of these devices. Our technology experts, homeofficereports.com, has reviewed them all. We asked them to list out their thoughts on which manufacturers provide the best photo printers and here they are, in alphabetical order.

1. Canon

Canon makes competitively priced products, but consumable costs are not cheap. They have solid printers, competitive pricing, and good technical support strategy.

2. Dell

Dell's first product in this space is competitively priced with good functionality—and weighs in at only 3.61 pounds (but you'll be surprised how heavy that can be if you have to carry it around for a while). It's worth a look.

3. Epson

Epson has solid printers, competitive consumables costs, and high print resolutions for the price. Our biggest complaint is their lack of telephone support for their photo ink-jet printer line.

4. HP

HP and printers have gone together for a long time. They still do. HP's photo ink jets are solidly built and well priced, and the long-term cost of operating the printers is competitive as well. HP is always a safe, innovative buy.

5. Kodak

If you own a Kodak camera and don't plan on printing photos larger than four by six inches—and you can put up with a cost of around sixty-two cents per print—it's a great solution.

6. Lexmark

Lexmark's photo printers are competitively priced, but the selection is small and their connectivity is limited.

7. Olympus

If you don't want to hassle with your PC or Macintosh to print your photos, then the Olympus photo printers are for you. Also, if you are willing to pay for high-quality output, these printers have some of the best print quality available.

8. Polaroid

A good photo printer, however, if you want to print a photo in any size other than four by six inches, choose a printer from another manufacturer.

9. Samsung

Inexpensively priced, the "gotcha" is in the print packs. Better quality, however, than the standard inkjet output. We like the SPP-2040 with 2-inch color LCD and 7-in-1 media card reader.

10. Sony

If you don't want to hassle with your PC to print your photos, then the Sony photo printer is for you. Also, if you are willing to pay for high-quality output, this printer has some of the best print quality available.

Source: Home Office Reports (*www.homeofficereports.com*)—They supply comprehensive information on a wide variety of technologies from PCs to networking, telephones and telephone services to digital cameras and accounting. Contact them at 2102 Clematis Ct., McKinney, TX 75070; (972) 529-9719; fax: (972) 540-1674; e-mail: *dmielke@homeofficereports.com*.

Manufacturers of Popular Color Laser Printers

Color lasers are wonderful business tools. They can save you money if you want to print your own high-quality business cards, brochures, and other marketing materials in small quantities and are much faster and have significantly better quality than color ink jets. Here is a list of the top manufacturers of color laser printers.

1. Brother

Brother laser printers have easy-to-install print drivers and are straightforward to set up for use. Brother lasers are very simple to configure. You'll be printing in no time.
www.brother.com

2. Dell

Dell's color laser printers have easy-to-install drivers and are very simple to set up for use. Dell's color lasers deliver print speeds between twenty-five and thirty-five pages per minute for black and white and five to twenty-five pages per minute for color printing. Plenty of speed for most home business needs.
www.dell.com

3. Genicom/Tally

The Genicom/Tally laser printer drivers are easy to install and the printers are straightforward to set up and begin to use. Genicom/Tally's color lasers produce color prints at speeds between six and twenty-six pages per minute. The T8024 offers twenty-six pages per minute in both black-and-white and color printing modes.
www.tallygenicom.com

4. HP

HP's color LaserJet drivers are easy to install and the printers are simple to set up and begin using. HP printers for the home-business market print at black and white speeds of eight to twenty-two pages per minute and color speeds of four pages per minute—based on your needs, they can help you and your business save lots of time.
www.hp.com

5. IBM

IBM's software drivers and color laser printers are straightforward to install and set up for use. IBM printers produce color documents at speeds from twenty to twenty-eight pages per minute—you can choose the printer that best meets your production and productivity needs.

www.ibm.com

6. KyoceraMita

KyoceraMita's color laser printer drivers are easy to install and the printers are simple to set up for use. KyoceraMita makes fairly high-end "workgroup" color printers. They have competitive performance—thirty-one pages per minute for black and white and seventeen pages per minute color.

7. Lexmark

Lexmark's color laser print drivers and printers are easy to install and set up for use. Lexmark printers can accommodate the needs of most home-based businesses for speed and performance. Their printers range in speed from twenty to thirty-six pages per minute in black-and-white and eight to thirty-two pages per minute for color printing.

www.lexmark.com

8. Minolta-QMS

The Minolta-QMS color laser print drivers and printers are easy to install and set up for use. Minolta-QMS makes laser printers with color print speeds of four to twenty-five pages per minute. In most cases, more than enough speed and performance for the home-based business owner.

www.minolta-qms.com

9. Okidata

The Okidata printers are easy to set up and use. Okidata makes eight color laser printers in fourteen models with monochrome print speeds of twenty to forty pages per minute and color print speeds of twelve to thirty pages per minute. In most cases, more than enough speed and performance for the home-based business owner.

www.okidata.com

10. Ricoh

The print drivers for the Ricoh laser printers as well as the printers themselves are easy to set up and use. Ricoh makes laser printers with black-and-white print speeds of almost seventeen to thirty-eight pages per minute and color print speeds of eight to thirty-five pages per minute.

www.ricoh-usa.com

11. Xante

Xante's print drivers and printers and straightforward to install and set up for use. Xante makes printers with black-and-white print speeds of thirty-seven to forty pages per minute and color print speeds that range from thirty to forty pages per minute.

www.xante.com

12. Xerox

Xerox's print drivers and printers are straightforward to install and set up for use. Xerox makes color lasers that can meet the requirements of any home-based business—with very high page-per-minute speeds (especially for the price at the low end) of twenty-one to forty pages per minute in black-and-white and five to thirty-six pages per minute in color.

www.xerox.com

Source: Home Office Reports (*www.homeofficereports.com*) supplies comprehensive, information on a wide variety of technologies from PCs to networking, telephones and telephone services to digital cameras and accounting. Contact them at 2102 Clematis Ct., McKinney, TX 75070; (972) 529-9719; fax: (972) 540-1674; e-mail: *dmielke@homeofficereports.com*.

Things to Consider Before Buying a Printer

Our IT expert has purchased countless printers for himself and his clients over the course of his career. We wanted to know his thoughts on what should be considered before buying our next printer and here's his list.

1. First consider an ink-jet printer

Ink-jet printers have one or more replaceable ink cartridges that store the color and/or black ink. The ink is actually sprayed onto the paper by a tiny nozzle. These printers produce high-quality documents, including text, graphics, and even photographs in color or black and white. Ink jets are the most popular printers for home use, primarily because of their relatively low cost. Many offices use ink-jet printers as well for the same reason. If initial cost is your primary concern, you can pick up a decent ink-jet printer for around $50.

2. Look at the benefits of laser printers

Laser printers are used primarily in office and corporate settings. They use a toner cartridge and drum (similar to a copier) to place the content on the paper. These "consumables" are rather expensive, but they last longer than an ink cartridge. Large offices often use a high-speed network laser printer that is shared by everyone. Of course, when there is an issue with the printer, everyone is affected. The initial cost of a quality laser printer can be considerably higher than the other types of printers.

3. Don't rule out dot-matrix printers

Dot-matrix printers use old-fashioned ribbons and printheads to place the content on the paper. Once common in homes as well as offices, these printers are now used almost exclusively in offices where printing on continuous forms is necessary. The initial cost is typically somewhere between the other two printer types, but the ribbons are fairly inexpensive and they tend to last a long time.

4. Budget for the cost of the ink cartridges

Cartridge prices vary a great deal from one printer model to another. One printer might require a $30 cartridge while the printer next to it uses a $17 cartridge. Toner cartridges and drums vary widely in price. A less expensive printer may well end up costing more over the course of a year if you purchase a model that uses more expensive consumables.

5. Think about speed

For home use, even the slowest ink-jet printers will probably be acceptable, but if you prefer a faster printer, be prepared to pay more.

6. How important is reliability

Since these printers are used primarily in an office setting, they usually get a lot of use. This goes double for a networked printer. You'll probably want to consider reliability over price when comparing laser printers.

Source: Rick Rouse is an IT expert, respected author, and the owner of RLROUSE Directory & Informational Resources (*www.rlrouse.com*), one of the Web's busiest directories and informational reference sites. His highly popular SEO Toolkit has helped thousands of Web masters and business owners achieve top search engine rankings and lots of targeted traffic for their Web sites. You can reach Rick at his Web site: www.rlrouse.com or via e-mail: *rick@rlrouse.com*.

Reliable Ink-Jet Printers

The following are the top-rated ink-jet printers from ConsumerSearch.com. Of course, these units and prices are current at the time of printing and new models (and prices) will quickly take their place. However, if you stick with the model's product line you'll find that our expert's recommendations will continue to hold true.

1. Canon Pixma iP4000

Best ink-jet printer. Along with separate cartridges for cyan, magenta, yellow, and black, this Canon inkjet printer uses a different dye-based black ink for better photo output. Reviews say this produces great photos for the price. In its class, the Pixma posts the fastest text printing speeds and lowest ink costs, making it an excellent multiuse printer. There's direct printing from compatible cameras, and an automatic duplexer for two-sided printing. Although the Canon ink-jet printer is initially more expensive than the budget HP Deskjet, it's faster, prints better and costs less in the long run because of cheaper replacement ink. Price: $100 (estimate).

2. Canon Pixma iP6000D

Best ink-jet printer with LCD. The Canon Pixma iP6000D is an upgrade to the top-rated Pixma iP4000. Extra features include memory card slots and a 2.5-inch color LCD preview screen for printing photos without a computer. Two extra ink tanks—one for photo cyan and one for photo magenta—give photos a boost in quality. Reviews say the Canon is a good all-around printer, but its photo output can't compete with the pricier Canon iP9900 or the HP PhotoSmart. Price: $115 (estimate).

3. HP Deskjet 3930

Budget ink-jet printer. Reviews say ink-jet printers as cheap as the HP Deskjet 3930 aren't worth it in the long run, since replacing the ink cartridges almost equals the price of the printer. The HP is slower and doesn't print as well as more expensive models. It has no PictBridge support or memory-card slots for direct printing from a digital camera. Despite the low price, the HP has a one-year warranty and is a good choice if you plan to print only occasionally. Price: $40 (estimate).

4. HP PhotoSmart 8450

Photo ink-jet printer. Reviews say the HP PhotoSmart has every feature you'd want in a full-size photo printer: memory card slots, PictBridge compatibility, a 2.5-inch LCD preview screen, eight ink colors, an Ethernet port for networking, and the ability to print on 44-inch-long banner paper. Reviews say photos are beautiful; text print-quality is outstanding and sharp. Though the HP is inexpensive compared to other photo printers, its ink costs are higher. Price: $175 (estimate).

5. Canon i9900

A 13-by-19-inch photo ink-jet printer. Reviews say the Canon i9900 satisfies those who want larger prints than the HP or Canon and want them fast. The i9900 can print a borderless 13-by-19-inch photo in less than three minutes. The Canon uses eight ink cartridges to achieve dynamic, rich color and 2-picoliter droplets to achieve smoother tones. Reviews say photo output can easily pass for a lab print. There's a PictBridge port for direct printing from a digital camera, but unlike the HP, the Canon ink-jet doesn't have an LCD preview screen. Price: $400 (estimate).

6. Canon Pixma iP90

Portable ink-jet printer. The Canon iP90 measures just twelve-by-seven-by-two inches and weighs just four pounds, so it's a good choice if you need to print documents on the road. The Canon iP90 has a PictBridge port and iRDA, so you can wirelessly beam print jobs from a PDA or smartphone. Text and photo output are good, say reviews, but you'll pay a price for portability. Extras like a battery (est. $110) or Bluetooth adapter (est. $80) are expensive. Price: $215 (estimate).

Source: ConsumerSearch (*www.consumersearch.com*) is a Web site that ranks, describes, and analyzes top reviews of consumer products, along with lists of top-rated products. Contact Derek Drew, CEO and editor-in-chief, at ConsumerSearch, Inc., 5467 31st Street NW, Washington, DC 20015; (202) 966-7907; or e-mail: *derekdrew@consumersearch.com*.

The Internet and Your Business

Top Questions To Ask Your Prospective E-commerce Consultant

Are you simply looking for a brochure site? Will you be selling products or services online? What type of products or services? Will you be capturing information in a database? Do you intend to host the site or are you going to outsource hosting? Once clear about what you need, it will be easier to find the right match for an e-commerce consultant. The answers to this list of questions should help you determine if there is a fit.

1. How long have they been in this business?

As with any business relationship, knowing how long a consultant has been doing this type of work indicates their level of experience. Although newcomers may have much to offer, you should know which level of the experience spectrum your consultant falls into.

2. How large is their organization?

A small organization may be able to offer better pricing because of lower overhead, but a larger organization offers depth. That knowledge may influence your final decision.

3. How many e-commerce sites have they set up?

You may find someone who has experience designing brochure sites but not with e-commerce sites. You need someone who understands the intricacies of e-commerce and is familiar with databases.

4. Have they developed any sites similar to yours? What did those sites cost?

Review those sites. Although no two sites are identical, experience with similar sites makes it unlikely that you will be paying for a learning curve. The consultant should be able to explain any differences in cost between your site and others.

5. What do they consider their "sweet spot"?

In a perfect world, your need would fit within that sweet spot. Both larger and smaller targeted consultants may be able to do the project, but the closer you come to that sweet spot, the greater the likelihood for success.

6. Do they have a business background?

If you require reporting or accounting from your site, a consultant with a business background will more easily understand your needs.

7. Do they have a technical background?

Subtle technical and engineering issues often arise, such as integrating third-party software, licensing, and platform dependencies. There may be difficult decisions that require tradeoffs between the budget, the feature list, and the delivery schedule. A strong technical background can help sort through these issues and assist in deciding where the best value lies.

8. What is their record for on-time delivery?

Projects do run over for a number of reasons, on the part of the developer and the client. However, overall, an experienced consultant should be able to anticipate and minimize time and cost overruns.

9. How much of your time do they think this will require? What will be required of you?

Developing any Web site is not an issue of simply hiring someone else to do it. This will be representative of your business. There will be many decisions to be made. There will be content to be written. Ask the consultant what client resources have been required for similar projects.

10. Can they describe the Web site development process they follow?

Check to see if their process includes steps such as discovery and planning, branding and interface concepts, page development, database programming and quality assurance/testing.

11. What about ongoing changes? Do you expect to manage your own site, or do you want your Web developer to manage the site?

Consider both the look and feel of the site as well as content management. Someone on your staff must, at a minimum, be able to manage the product database.

12. Will they arrange for Secure Sockets Layer (SSL) encryption?

If you are going to accept credit cards or other customer information online, the security of your customer data should be a top concern. There will be a cost associated with this.

13. Do they offer search engine optimization?

Unless you intend to use your site as a brochure site only and are not expecting people to find you on the Web, but only through referral to your site, you must be listed in search engines. If your consultant does not do this, ask for a referral to someone who specializes in search engine optimization.

14. Do they offer Web hosting, or do they have a Web-hosting partner they work with regularly?

If not, make certain that the tools they use are compatible with the host you choose. Ask to see multiple examples of their work. You want to make certain that their graphic approach appeals to you.

15. Do they create the site, or do they outsource development? If they outsource, is it done locally or offshore?

There is no right answer here, but you should know how your site will be developed. If it is outsourced offshore, the specification must be highly detailed before being handed to the developers.

16. How does their personal style fit with your internal staff?

This is a relationship that you hope will continue over time. You want someone who works smoothly within your organization.

17. What type of project management do they use?

Their style needs to match yours for you to understand what is happening and how the project is progressing.

18. Last, but not least, what questions do they have for you?

This is a significant question. You can tell a great deal about a firm by the depth and scope of questions they ask you. The right consultant can help make the process easier and refine your approach to result in a top-notch site.

Source: Sheri Syler Adams, CEO, Adams Consultants (*www*
.adamsconsultants.com)—They help small to midsize businesses and divisions of large corporations take advantage of the opportunities in their marketplace. They enhance (or if needed, create) innovative business systems and leverage technology to optimize information flow to executives, line managers, and staff. Contact her at (818) 990-4020, or e-mail: *sheri@adamsconsultants.com*.

Typical Costs to Set Up an E-commerce Site

There really is no "typical cost" for setting up an e-commerce site. These sites can range from several hundred dollars to hundreds of thousands of dollars. The more functionality, the more bells and whistles, the higher the cost. At the low end, you can purchase a template for as little as $95 and simply add your products. At the high end, a custom development for a sophisticated site with lots of features and functionality can cost upward of $100,000. However, in any case you will need to include the following.

1. SSL Certificate

Customers are wary of the web. They want to be certain that you are who you say you are. An SSL Certificate provides this assurance. SSL Certificates range from $29.95 per year to $995.00 for a high assurance SSL certificate.

Price varies with the number of points authenticated and the level of encryption offered.

2. Domain name registration fee

Ranges from $3.95 to $34.95 per year. If you are hosting externally, your host can register your domain name for you.

3. Account set-up fee charged by the online Credit Card processor

These fees vary from processor to processor.

4. Hosting externally

The initial setup fee ranges greatly from hosting company to hosting company and is affected by the sophistication of your application and infrastructure. Monthly hosting fees range from under $10 for a brochure site to over several hundred dollars a month for a sophisticated setup; backups are generally included. A mirrored site is optional, but recommended. What happens if your site goes down and how much of an impact will this have on your business? If your site is critical to your success, you will want a mirrored site. This will require the involvement of your hosting company's staff for an additional fee, plus the cost of hosting the second site. Check with your hosting company for this cost.

5. Hosting the site internally

You must budget for servers, firewalls, backups, mirrored site (cost of hosting a copy of the site somewhere) and system administrators (staff who keep the site up and running.)

6. Marketing

The cost for marketing is dependent on the level of marketing you choose to do. At the least, you must register with the various search engines. Optimally, you would engage a SEO (search engine optimization) specialist to continually make certain that you come close to the top of listings.

Source: Sheri Syler Adams, CEO, Adams Consultants (*www .adamsconsultants.com*)—Adams Consultants helps small to midsize businesses and divisions of large corporations take advantage of the opportunities in their marketplace. They enhance (or if needed, create) innovative business systems and leverage technology to optimize information flow to executives, line managers, and staff. Contact her at (818) 990-4020. Sheri's e-mail address is *sheri@adamsconsultants.com*.

Top E-commerce Payment Providers

Payment gateways are credit card–processing services that allow you to authorize and process credit card orders online in real time. There are a large number of companies that offer payment gateway services but not all will suit your needs. The following list includes our expert's preferred payment providers for conducting E-commerce transactions.

1. ViaKlix
www.viaklix.com

2. Verisign
www.verisign.com

3. AuthorizeNet
www.authorizenet.com

4. Card Service International
www.cardservice.com

5. Link Point
www.linkpoint.com

6. CyberSource
www.cybersource.com

Source: Sheri Syler Adams, CEO, Adams Consultants (*www.adam sconsultants.com*)—Helps small to midsize businesses and divisions of large corporations take advantage of the opportunities in their marketplace. They focus on business systems—repeatable processes that have a clear purpose, are accountable, and well documented so they are easily repeatable. To maximize growth and profit, they enhance (or if needed, create) innovative business systems and leverage technology to optimize information flow to executives, line managers, and staff. Contact them at (818) 990-4020 or by e-mail at *sheri@adamsconsultants.com*

Ways to Run a Successful E-commerce Site

Just because you've built your e-commerce Web site doesn't mean the customers will begin to come. You need to bring in the visitors, showcase your products, convince them to buy, and bring them back yet again to make any significant gains. The customers need to be wooed by the unique customer experience that will bring them back, and have them sing your praises to their friends, spreading your name. This may seem like a tall order, but it isn't. Listed here are some great ways to build, manage, and profit from your e-commerce Web site.

1. Organize your catalog around product categories

Many sites either provide a long list of products or lump them behind a search button, making it difficult to find them. Arrange your products into logical categories and sub-categories, but do not overdo it. Research says that most people get overwhelmed with more than seven categories. The customer must be able to search any product easily without help. Your product should have a clear, high-quality picture and short, detailed specifications. If necessary add video or pictures of different viewpoints (top angle, side view) along with the product specification.

2. Provide multiple payment options

Keep all kinds of payment options available to your customers. Not everyone feels comfortable buying through a credit card or has one. Allow for debit cards, fax, telephone, snail mail, paper, and electronic checks. Sign up for the fraud-checking facility, without which you could easily end up losing entire day's sales within minutes. Provide a currency converter if you offer products or payment in other currencies. Including a telephone number for customer support on the order is a must. It gives the buyers some extra feelings of security that they can always talk to a live person if anything goes wrong in the buying process.

3. List clearly outlined privacy policies

Make your privacy policy public. Keep it in a prominent place, and link it to the home, products, and checkout pages, so that customers who are wary of providing personal and credit card details feel comforted. Tell them if you plan to share their e-mail address with others, or plan to send in promotional mail or newsletters. Further, allow them to unsubscribe or opt out of such e-mail if they want. Never

sell the customer's personal particulars unless they have agreed; this is a sure way to lose credibility doubly fast.

4. List clearly outlined security policies

If you plan to collect sensitive information from your customers, you should use security systems like SSL (Secure Socket Layer). This guarantees that the data provided by your customer will not fall into the hand of a malicious hacker while transferring from his computer to the Web server. This also will reassure your customers that you are truly concerned about the security of their personal information.

5. List clearly outlined terms and conditions

Write clearly and prominently all the sales and after-sales support terms to avoid confusion. The Internet is worldwide, and your customer can come from any country. List your shipping and handling costs up-front, and be ready to ship anywhere on Earth. Publish your returns policy, support hours, and even the approximate time taken to deliver the goods. Send a confirmation note thanking the customer, and listing all the products, prices, and key terms of the purchase in an e-mail. Keep the customer updated of the order status at all times by e-mail or by providing a link in your shopping page where they can check the status of their order anytime.

6. Build a newsletter around your products

To snag new customers and keep the old ones remembering you vividly, seriously plan to launch a newsletter, and send it to all prospects and customers on a regular basis. Apart from the credibility of being a serious player in the market, dazzle them with your commitment by releasing the newsletter on fixed days—like the fifteenth of every month, or every Monday. You can also show your expertise in your field by writing regular, in-depth articles, covering the latest trends in the industry, and reviews of new products. Your customers, distributors, and partners will start to await your newsletter eagerly. Sprinkle your promotions and products among the contents of the newsletter, and be ready to receive an increase in Web traffic and order bookings every time you send out the newsletter.

7. Promote your site everyday

Strong marketing is the most important aspect of having a successful Web site. The best of sites won't make money if people don't come in hordes. Launch promotions, and get the word to everyone possible within your target audience. Do promotions using direct mail to your existing customer, in your newsletter, and fliers. All the methods of traditional marketing apply here. Don't leave any technique untried. Remember the old adage—Market, market, market.

8. Measure results and reorganize

Measure the results you are getting from each promotion religiously, and note what works and what doesn't. Experiment. Study. Fine-tune. This is the only way to know how effective your campaigns and promotions are. You can also bring in some external people to visit your site and give you sincere feedback about each page. The more critical they are, the more changes you will make, and eventually

it will benefit you and your customers. Keep making changes and test what works and what doesn't on a continuous basis. What works today may not work tomorrow.

9. Keep a simple, yet effective, Web design

There is intense competition on the Web. Make a compelling Web site that showcases your USP (unique selling proposition) and brings the customer back to your site. Differentiate from the rest by using your imagination to make your site stand out from the rest. A cool, catchy, easy-to-remember name could definitely help. Make a simple site, with plain HTML, and a consistent look and feel on all pages. Use an easy-to-read font, at least a size 10 size, preferably an 11. Do not load with graphics and huge pictures that may slow down your page. Keep the catalog simple, and with a consistent design with handy links to Home, Checkout page, Privacy Policy, Terms and Conditions, Customer Profile pages and at the same, consistent place on each page. Make it easy to browse the store and mark products for later purchase.

10. Make the login process a breeze

The fewer clicks needed to order, the better. Amazon patented their One-Click method that minimized the clicks, making the checkout process simpler and easier. Try to make the registration or login process minimal, and only keep the most relevant fields mandatory.

11. Reduce pop-up messages

Too many pop-ups distract and disgust the customer. Especially after the visitor closes your Web site window, if you start to pop up other windows with more promotions, it leaves a feeling of being chased. It is also the signature of most of the adult sites, so steer away from such insensitive practices. Show your professionalism and respect the customer's privacy and time. It will help to build your image as a serious and professional site and enhance your credibility.

12. Use a reliable hosting service

Use a service that is good and reliable, and can provide you with customer support at all hours. Web hosting is getting less expensive, but it is better to pay a little more and get a fast and reliable service. Nothing loses a customer faster than a slow site or a site that is down frequently. Compare a few hosting services, and ask around before signing up for one. You won't regret it.

13. Deliver more than what the customer is expecting

Customer expectations are a sure way of winning them over. Let them feel that they really are lucky, that they made the right decision by selecting to order from you. Give them something for free—such as free gift wrapping, a free report, a free coupon for discount on their next purchase, or a free personalization of the product they chose. Getting a product or service for free, or getting premium service by paying only standard fare, will delight the customer and open doors for future sales.

Source: Vinai Prakash is a successful e-commerce consultant who has been providing sage advice to small and medium businesses in building, managing, and profiting from e-commerce Web sites for the past six years. He is a sought-after author and speaker. Vinai

can be contacted at *vinai@intellisoft.com.sg* for speaking engagements, as well as for consultancy engagements and advice on profiting from e-commerce.

Top Questions to Ask Your E-commerce Payment Provider

Accepting credit cards over the Internet can be a dangerous business. You're taking responsibility for not only collecting your customer's money, but also ensuring their privacy too. Any lapses and you could be in trouble. We asked one of our E-commerce experts to provide us a list of questions to ask your payment provider and here they are.

1. Who is the acquiring bank?

This is the bank that provides our merchant account and into which your online payments are deposited. Ever heard of them?

2. What is an Internet merchant account?

This is a special account with your acquiring bank that allows you to accept credit cards over the Internet. There is typically a processing fee for each transaction. Where is this account and how much are the fees?

3. Who is the credit card association?

This is the financial institution that provides credit card services through participating banks. Examples include Visa and MasterCard. Are they accredited and reliable?

4. Who is the customer issuing bank?

This is the financial institution that provides your customers with their credit card. Is this a well known and insured financial institution?

5. What is a customer gateway?

This service provides connectivity among the various participants to process authorizations and payments. This is usually the entity referred to as the e-commerce payment provider. What type of controls do they have in place?

6. What is a processor?

The data center that processes transactions and settles funds is called a processor. They are connected to your site on behalf of your acquiring bank via a payment gateway. How is this data secured?

7. Ask these critical questions of your provider.

Do they work with your merchant bank? What is the monthly service fee? How much per transaction? Is there a minimum transaction fee per month? Is there a setup fee? How much is it? How long will it take to get approval? What must the provider see to get approved? Ask to see a demonstration user interface that will be used by your staff to review transactions, enter refunds, and so on. What programming languages does the online interface support? Do they have payment sample pages? What credit cards and payment types do they support? Are the fees different for each? Do they have any type of online skeleton catalog that you can use/interface with if you need that type of application?

Source: Sheri Syler Adams, CEO, Adams Consultants (*www.adam sconsultants.com*)—They help small to midsize businesses and divisions of large corporations take advantage of the opportunities in their marketplace. They enhance (or if needed, create) innovative business systems and leverage technology to optimize information flow to executives, line managers, and staff. Contact her at (818) 990-4020 or e-mail at *sheri@adamsconsultants.com*.

Considerations When Choosing an Internet Service Provider

Many people don't put a lot of thought into their choice of Internet Service Provider (ISP). As a result, if you ask three people what they think of their current ISP, you may get three rather colorful responses. Even though there are a number of ISPs to choose from, getting a reliable Internet connection and good technical support isn't necessarily easy. Here are expert provides a list of questions you should pose to your Internet Service Provider before signing on with them.

1. What do you want to do?

The first question you need to ask is: what do you want to do with your Internet access? If all you need is a simple service to send e-mail to your Aunt Emily, you can probably get by with the bottom of the line standard dial-up account. However, if you are a Web developer, you are probably going to want very different bandwidth and services.

2. Where are you calling from?

In many areas, local access is a key issue. For those in metropolitan areas, finding local access numbers, DSL, or cable modem service won't be a problem. However, if you live in a small town, you may discover that your choices are more limited. Along the same lines, if you travel a lot, check out local access numbers for other areas, since dialing in on 800 numbers can incur extra costs that get expensive quickly.

3. What speed do you want?

Where you are connecting from and your bandwidth requirements narrow down your choices. For example, in some areas of rural North Idaho, getting DSL or cable access isn't likely to happen. So those of us out in the sticks who need high bandwidth are looking at satellite service. But two-way satellite is expensive and service has been bad in many cases, so many people still opt to remain with dial-up accounts. DSL coverage is spotty in many areas and may involve calls to both the phone company and an ISP. If you are considering an always-on connection like DSL, don't forget to include extra costs such as a new modem and firewall software in your budget. Be sure to understand exactly what new hardware and software you'll need before you sign up with an ISP.

4. Can you connect reliably?

A related issue for dial-up users is how often you can get through to your favorite access number. With always-on connections such as DSL or satellite, how often does the service "go down"? A dirty little secret is that some ISPs have more accounts than their bandwidth can really handle. If all their users were to log on at the same time, service would drag to a crawl or be completely unavailable. (What good is unlimited access if you can never log on?)

5. What are the limitations?

Be sure to compare any limitations that the service imposes. Some ISPs limit how much data you can transfer or how much time you can spend on line. Also compare how much server space an ISP gives you for a Web page. If you have ambitious plans, you may also want to see if the provider lets you run CGI scripts or Front Page extensions on your Web pages. (Note that many services don't allow any type of programming to run behind personal web pages.)

6. What features and support do they offer?

Different ISPs offer an array of features, which may or may not be important to you. Some ISPs let you access your e-mail through a remote account or let you have more than one e-mail address at the same account. Also find out if they have a real human on the other end of the tech support line and what the hours are. Verify that the support number is either a local call or an 800 number. Before you select an ISP, it's a good idea to call the tech support line. If you can never get through, find a different ISP.

7. What equipment and connections do they have?

Ask prospective ISPs a lot of questions about their equipment setup. Find out what hardware they are using and if they are using the latest versions of communications software. You don't want to deal with some guy that's got a row of creepy old modems in his back bedroom. Don't be intimidated; if they can't or aren't willing to explain their system so you can understand it, move on. Talk to the prospective ISP about the technology they are using for their connections and make them explain it to you in real English.

8. How do your friends like it?

Ask your friends what they think about their current provider. This type of anecdotal information—while not exactly scientific—is important. Find out what kind of connection speed they are getting, whether they get busy signals, and any experiences they've had with tech support.

9. How much does it cost?

Note that price is the last question on the list. Saving $2 a month is not a bargain if you never get a decent connection. Only after an ISP has answered your other questions should you compare prices. Be sure to include any start-up fees and prepayment discounts into the equation. When you select an ISP, a little up-front research can save you a lot of aggravation in the long run. Remember that the only thing worse than choosing an ISP is having to go back and start all over again when you discover that the choice you made in haste didn't work out.

Source: Susan C. Daffron is the President of Logical Expressions, Inc., (*www.logicalexpressions.com*), a company that helps small businesses create, manage, and distribute content. Logical Expressions specializes in fusing high-quality unique content with search-engine and human-friendly Web sites. They offer writing, editing, programming, and design services and publish a free computer magazine called Computor Companion (*www.computorcompanion.com*). The magazine is targeted toward business owners/managers, computer professionals, and home PC computer users. It includes easy-to-understand articles designed to help readers use their computers more effectively to accomplish everyday tasks.

Largest Internet Services Providers

Looking to get online? The following list ranks some of the top ten U.S. ISPs by subscriber in 2005 by an online industry expert.

1. America Online
All U.S. AOL brand accounts
Subscribers: 21.8 million; market share: 23.2 percent
www.aol.com

2. Comcast
Cable broadband
Subscribers: 7.7 million; market share: 8.2 percent
www.comcast.com

3. SBC
DSL only
Subscribers: 6.0 million; market share: 6.4 percent
www.sbc.com

4. EarthLink
DSL, dial-up, cable, satellite, PLC, and Web hosting
Subscribers: 5.4 million; market share: 5.7 percent
www.earthlink.com

5. Road Runner
Cable broadband
Subscribers: 4.5 million; market share: 4.8 percent
www.roadrunner.com

6. Verizon
DSL only

Subscribers: 4.1 million; market share: 4.4 percent

www.verizon.com

7. United Online

Counting paid dial-up only

Subscribers: 3.1 million; market share: 3.3 percent

www.unitedonline.com

8. Cox

Cable broadband

Subscribers: 2.8 million; market share: 3.0 percent

www.cox.com

9. BellSouth

DSL only

Subscribers: 2.4 million; market share: 2.6 percent

www.bellsouth.com

10. Charter

Cable broadband

Subscribers: 2.0 million; market share: 2.2 percent

www.charter.com

Source: ISP-Planet (*www.isp-planet.com*)—A resource and information site for Internet service providers.

Popular Web-Hosting Companies

If you've got a Web site, then you're going to need a web hosting company. There are lots of companies to choose from. We consulted our expert, a company that ranks and reviews other hosting companies and asked them to provide us with some of the more popular web-hosting companies and here's their list.

1. LunarPages

Disk space: 3000 MB

Data transfer: 400 GB

Offer: Host four Web sites on one account

Founded in 2000

Hosted accounts: 90,000

www.lunarpages.com

2. Apollo Hosting

Disk space: 1.5 GB

Data transfer: 70 GB

Offer: Multiple domains/free Miva Merchant

Founded in 1999

Hosted accounts: 165,000

www.apollohosting.com

3. IPOWER

Disk space: 10,000 MB

Data transfer: 250 GB

Offer: $7.95/month; host six domains in one, thirty-day guarantee

Founded in 2001

Hosted accounts: 400,000

www.ipowerweb.com

4. Gate.com (Affinity Internet)

Disk space: 2000 MB

Data transfer: 200 GB

Offer: Three months free; free setup

Founded in 1996

Hosted accounts: 500,000

www.gate.com

5. HostGator

Disk space: 3500 MB

Data transfer: 50 GB

Offer: Unlimited databases and domains; 24/7 support; $6.95/month

Founded in 2002

Hosted accounts: 250,000

www.hostgator.com

6. Web siteSource

Disk space: 5,000 MB

Data transfer: 50 GB

Offer: Host four Web sites on one account, unlimited sub domains

Founded in 1998

Hosted accounts: 100,000

www.Web sitesource.com

7. GoDaddy

Disk space: 4000 MB

Data transfer: 25 GB

Offer: Free domain/setup; thirty-day guarantee; $6.95

Founded in 1997

Hosted accounts: 9,566,367 *Domains

www.godaddy.com

8. PowWeb

Disk space: 12, 000 MB

Data transfer: 300 GB

Offer: Two years free; free setup and domain name

Founded in 1999

Hosted accounts: 100,000

www.powweb.com

9. HostMySite

Disk space: 1 GB

Data transfer: 50 GB

Offer: Free two months hosting and free setup

Founded in 1997

Hosted accounts: 40,000

www.hostmysite.com

10. BlueHost

Disk space: 10,000 MB

Data transfer: 250 GB

Offer: Free site builder, domain, setup; $6.95/month

Founded in 2003

Hosted accounts: 85,000

www.bluehost.com

Source: Web site HostDirectory.com (*www.websitehostdirectory .com*)—Companies are selected based on rank in customer service, support, offers, and plan details, not just the number of hosted accounts. We know each of these companies personally and have worked with many of them for years.

Considerations when Choosing a Web-Hosting Company

With very few exceptions, if you have a business, you probably have, or should have, a Web site in your marketing strategy. But in the wide-open market of Web-hosting services, the quality, costs, and features vary wildly. This list will help you research and consider the elements that matter in a small business Web host, if you decide to make the decision yourself and without professional assistance.

1. Size

Most of the early Web-hosting companies started out in someone's basement or living room.

After all, who could tell? As long as you had the right equipment, connectivity, and knowledge, you, too, could be in business selling space on your Web server. Only you know if you're comfortable trusting your business site to a small or one-person hosting company, or if you prefer a large corporate institution or media company as your host. Size doesn't matter nearly as much as the considerations still to come.

2. Customer service

Look at their Web site and determine what your options are for customer service. Do they provide availability twenty-four hours a day, seven days a week? Do they have a toll-free number? On the other hand, do they charge for service calls? Is e-mail the only way to reach them? Check their site to see if they have a customer forum; you might find some clues about how they respond to questions, and if their customers are satisfied. Get on Google.com and search for uncensored reviews and complaints that others might have registered about them.

3. Technical support

In the same vein, what kind of additional resources and help do they provide on their Web site for technical support? Some of the best hosts provide a "knowledge base" of searchable articles, tutorials, and how-to tips on utilizing the features they provide. Whether you or someone else is actually administering the site, the availability of a good knowledge base is invaluable.

4. Reliability

Try to find out what their server uptime is. Ask if they have any guarantees—but be aware that some of the best hosting providers won't even go this far—they know there will be periodic outages and instead make statements about their staffing and ability to respond quickly to technical problems. Depending on the site you want to host, you will need to determine if this is a satisfactory guarantee.

5. Backups

Do they provide daily tape backups of the server? If not, how often? Will they restore your site in the event of a problem? And, do they charge for this service? A good Web host will never need to use those backups, but the peace of mind, knowing your site is backed up daily, is invaluable.

6. Server environment

The type of server your site requires will hinge on the elements of your site that require programs, such as shopping carts, affiliate programs, and content management. What you use on your site will drive what server you can use (and vice versa). For example, if your site is written in ASP, you'll need a Windows-based server, instead of UNIX. If you are unsure, you might want to ask the more technical people involved in your site development, if any.

7. E-mail accounts

Web hosting usually includes a mail server, and every package provides number of POP3 and alias accounts. You will need to ask yourself in advance, how many e-mail accounts you will need (this is typically equal to how many people will have their own e-mail account in your organization). Another thing to determine is whether

Web-based e-mail is available. If you travel at all, or ever need to access your e-mail outside your own office (i.e., at home), this is an incredibly useful feature to have because all you need is an Internet connection and Web browser, anywhere in the world, to get your mail.

8. Security

Different hosting companies provide different levels of security, just as different site owners have different needs and expectations. Ask what is provided, and how they secure your hosted site, and protect visitors to your site. If you plan to use the hosting for mail service, look for a host that provides spam controls and anti-virus scanning within their mail-server environment. Another security feature you might also need is password protection. Will your hosting allow you to password-protect a section of your Web site? If you plan to do any e-commerce on your site, you should ask what features, such as a shared security certificate, are available.

9. Statistics

One of the most valuable aspects of marketing online is that you can gather all sorts of information about the visitors to your site, and tweak the user experience accordingly. But this benefit is lost if your hosting company doesn't provide good statistics. There are a dozen different statistical applications available through Web hosts; some much more full featured and useful than others. Some sites have screen shots of sample statistics, or if they tell you what they use, you can always go to the Web site of the statistics package and look for information on what kind of data you'll see. The best packages, like WebTrends and SmarterStats, let you customize the data views and reports, automatically send yourself periodic reports by e-mail, get any date range in the history of the site, and provide graphical charts for at-a-glance understanding.

10. Ease of use

The best hosting packages provide a simple-to-navigate control panel that lets you maintain your site, or have someone else maintain it. It provides menu access to things like adding/editing e-mail addresses and aliases, accessing the statistics, billing information, and in some cases, editing your Web site or checking your e-mail. You might also verify the mechanisms for uploading your files to the Web server, and be sure that it conforms to whatever Web-design or file-upload software you use. For example, if you are building a site in Front Page, make sure that Front Page extensions are included.

11. Special features

Some of the larger hosting companies also offer extras in their hosting packages. Planning for your business, you'll want to figure out if these extras are worth any additional costs, or if you should go with a less full-featured hosting and use other outside services. For example, some hosting comes with e-mail list management, shopping-cart programs, and basic Web-site builders. While most professionals will advise you not to "eat where you sleep," many Web hosts also provide domain name registration services under a single control panel, too.

12. Cost

Last, what does the hosting cost? Can you get a better deal by paying a year in advance? What are your contractual commitments—can you leave when you want to, without a hassle? Hosting is relatively cheap now, and a great many hosting companies provide extraordinary service and features for very little per month. Likewise, there are others that charge way too much for the same features! That said, approach the raft of free and advertising-based hosts with tremendous caution, when hosting a business Web site. Considering the reasonably priced hosts that provide high-quality services, it is better to invest in a well-known host than try to go the free-hosting route.

Source: Eileen Parzek (*www.sohoitgoes.com*)—An award-winning graphic designer and writer providing digital and print graphic design and Web-design services. Always found at the intersection of information, creativity and technology, her business, SOHO It Goes! Business Design Studio helps small businesses make a big impression, increase their reach, and grow. You can reach her at (518) 729-4453 or by e-mail at *turtle@sohoitgoes.com*.

Most Visited Web Sites—Overall

Our expert ranks Web sites based on their popularity. They also provide categories of their rankings too. We figured any small business owners would like to know which Web sites are most frequently visited by other small business owners. Here is their list, based on number of hits.

1. *www.yahoo.com*
Yahoo! offers personalized content and search options; chat rooms, free e-mail, clubs, and pages.

2. *www.msn.com*
This site offers dial-up access and content provider.

3. *www.google.com*
Google enables users to search the Web, Usenet, and images. Features: PageRank, caching and translation of results, and an option to find similar pages.

4. *www.passport.net*
This is Microsoft's bill-paying electronic wallet.

5. *www.ebay.com*
Ebay offers international person-to-person auction site, with products sorted into categories.

6. *www.microsoft.com*
This is the official homepage of Microsoft Corporation.

7. *www.amazon.com*
Amazon is the bookseller and Internet pioneer.

8. *www.fastclick.com*
This is an online advertising agent that provides products, such as Ad Network and AdServer, to ensure optimal output and performance for its clients.

9. *www.aol.com*

America On Line's portal, offers search, shopping, channels, chat, and mail.

10. *www.go.com*

This site offers a searchable directory, news, stocks, sports, and free e-mail.

Source: Alexa.com—Founded in April 1996, Alexa Internet grew out of a vision of Web navigation that is intelligent and constantly improving with the participation of its users. Alexa Related Links and Traffic Rankings are the embodiment of this vision, growing and getting better as more people join the Alexa community of smart Web surfers.

Popular Web Sites for Small Businesses

Whether starting out as an entrepreneur or searching for ideas to improve your existing small business, there are a number of online resources for business owners. However, some are more helpful than others, and some are more popular among those interested in small business information. The following list includes the top ten Web sites, based on traffic, as ranked by search engine Alexa.com in their Resources for Entrepreneurs category.

1. Constant Contact - Do-It-Yourself Email Marketing

Do-it-yourself email marketing solution for small businesses and associations. Create, send, and instantly track professional html email newsletters and promotions. Free 60-Day Trial.
www.constantcontact.com

2. Entrepreneur.com

Online and print small business publication. Information to help start, grow or manage a small business.
www.entrepreneur.com

3. AllBusiness.com

AllBusiness.com provides entrepreneurs, small and growing businesses, consultants and business professionals everything they need to start, manage and grow their companies.
www.allbusiness.com

4. U.S. Small Business Administration

An electronic gateway of procurement information for and about small businesses. Search engine for contracting officers, marketing tool for small firms, and link to procurement opportunities and important information.
www.sba.gov

5. Internal Revenue Service

Provides tax information and forms for U.S. businesses.
www.irs.gov/businesses/index.html

6. Inc.com

Magazine focused on business resources for the entrepreneur.
www.inc.com

7. Quicken Web Site

Financial planning software for personal finance, small business finance, debt management. Track and manage financial information.
www.quicken.com

8. Internal Revenue Service: Small Businesses and Self-Employed

Tax resources for U.S. small businesses.
www.irs.gov/businesses/small

9. WAHM

Newsletter and online magazine for moms working from home.
www.wahm.com

10. Division of Corporations - Florida Department of State

Offering forms, information and online filing.
www.sunbiz.org

Source: Alexa rankings of Web sites for entrepreneur resources (*www.alexa.com*). Alexa is a search engine service that ranks the top 500 Web sites, based on traffic, in a variety of different categories. In addition to rankings, Alexa provides an information profile of each Web site and a listing of related Web sites.

Popular Ways to Get Your Web Site on a Search Engine

That major advantage search-engine positioning has over other methods of producing revenue online is that once high rankings are attained and provided that the tactics used were ethical and that continued efforts are made to keep them, they can essentially hold and provide targeted traffic indefinitely. Here are the ten steps to higher search-engine positioning from an expert in the field:

1. Choose keywords

You first must choose your keywords. This is perhaps the most important step of the process as incorrectly targeting phrases can result in traffic that is not interested in your product. Look through the potential keyword phrases and think, "Who would be searching using that phrase?" If the answer is "a student looking for information," then chances are it won't result in a sale. If the answer is "someone who is looking specifically for a product I offer," then this is a prime candidate as a targeted keyword phrase.

2. Site content

Get a good deal of new content down in order to ensure that you know exactly where you are going and exactly what you need to do to get there. Creating some of the new content before starting the optimization process can be doubly helpful because it can reveal potential additions to your Web site that you may not have considered (a forum or blog for example). If you already have a site, perhaps simply sit on your back deck, sip on a coffee, and imagine what you would do if your whole site was lost and you had to start again (other than launch into a very colorful discussion with your hosting company).

3. Site structure

A solid site structure is very important. Creating a site that is easily spidered by the search engines yet attractive to visitors can be a daunting and yet entirely rewarding endeavor. To adequately structure your Web site, you must think like a "spider," which is not as difficult as it may sound. A search-engine spider reads your Web page as you would read a book. It starts at the top left, reads across, and then moves down. So, you must give priority to what you place near the top of your page.

4. Optimization

Once you have created your keyword targets and your content, and established your site structure, you must now move on to the most obvious step: the optimization of your content. As noted, a spider places importance on what it reads highest on the page; so, beginning with a sentence that includes your targeted phrase only makes sense. That said, stuffing in keywords to add weight to your page generally doesn't work. Make sure to use your keywords in the heading, but don't shy away from also adding additional words (though not too many).

5. Internal linking

To ensure that your Web site gets fully indexed, you have to make sure that the spiders have an easy pathway. There are two main ways to insure that your site gets well spidered *and* that the relevancy is added. The first is to place text links on the bottom of your homepage to your main internal pages (not *every* page, that just looks odd). The second is to create a site map to all your internal pages and link to it from your homepage. Both methods have advantages and disadvantages, but that's a whole list unto itself.

6. Human testing

Put the site past someone who has never seen it before (and preferably who won't know how much work you've put in and tell you it's great even if it's not). Ask her to find specific information and see how long it takes. Ask someone else to just surf your site and watch which links he clicks and ask him why he chose those ones. Most important, find out how the content reads. You've spent hours working through the content at this point and are probably not the least biased on its readers. Find out how it reads to someone who has no invested interest in the site and correct any issues he may bring up.

7. Submissions

Submit to directories (both general and topic-specific) and to a few topical search engines, but for the most part submitting to Google, Yahoo!, MSN, and the other major engines has proven to be a bit of a waste of time. The major search engines are spidering search engines, which means they will follow links wherever they go. Simply having sites that are spidered by the major search engines linking to you will get your site found. They should get picked up in about a week. When you simply skipped this step and sought out reputable directories and other sites to get links from, the homepage of the site can get indexed in as little as two days. Neither will hurt your rankings, but to make the best use of your time, seek out directories and other Web sites to get links from and leave the spiders to find you on their own.

8. Link building

All of the major search engines give credit to sites that have quality links pointing to them. How many is enough depends on your industry and targeted phrases. Running a search on Google that reads *www.yourcompetition.com* will reveal approximately how many links a competitor has. The first place to seek links is with general and topic-specific directories. After that, you may want to move into reciprocal link building. Reciprocal link building is the exchange of links between two Web sites. Some Web masters will simply link to any Web site that links back to them. I highly recommend being more particular than that. Find Web sites that you believe your site visitors would genuinely be interested in. You want to find links from sites that are related to yours. There are obviously many more methods to building links than directories and reciprocal link building.

9. Monitoring

You will have to monitor the major search engines for your targeted phrases. Also, you will need to review your stats to see where your traffic is coming from and what search terms are being used to find you. If a month passes and you don't see any changes, then you need to do more work. I'm not saying take a month off. A solid search engine–positioning strategy involves constantly adding content, building links, and ensuring that your visitors are getting the information they want to have and finding it as easily as possible.

Source: Beanstalk Search Engine Positioning, Inc. (*www.beanstalk-inc.com*)—Beanstalk Search Engine Positioning was founded out of the need for ethical yet effective search engine–positioning firms. Contact them at 192 St. Charles Street, Victoria, BC Canada, V8S 3M7; (250) 370-9750; e-mail: *mary@beanstalk-inc.com* or *dave@beanstalk-inc.com*.

Your Business Software

Popular Software Distributors

A software distributor acts as an intermediary between manufacturers and the end user. Many of these companies sell software by the bulk to their own reseller channel. Many also sell direct to end users. Here are some of the largest, and most popular software distributors in the country.

1. D&H
Nationwide software distributor serving most industries.

2525 North Seventh Street
PO Box 5967
Harrisburg, PA 17110-0967
(800) 877-1200
www.dandh.com

2. ASI
Wholesale commercial distributors of computer hardware and software.

48289 Fremont Blvd.
Fremont, CA 94538
(510) 226-8000
Fax: (510) 226-8858
Toll-free: (800) 2000-ASI
www.asipartner.com

3. Infotel Distribution
Distributes software and other computer products.

6910 State Route 36
Fletcher, OH 45326
(888) 528-4504
www.infoteldistributors.com

4. SuperCom Canada
Primarily a hardware distributor, an established Canadian company, specializing in the distribution of computer products and consumer electronic products and the production of personal computers.

Supercom Toronto
4011 14th Avenue
Markham, Ontario, L3R 0Z9
(905) 415-1166
Fax: (905) 415-1177
www.pub.supercom.ca

5. Ingram Micro

One of the world's largest distributor of technology products and services.

1759 Wehrle Drive
Williamsville, NY 14221-7887
(716) 633-3600
www.ingrammicro.com

6. Gates/Arrow Distribution

Full-line technical distributor of computer systems, peripherals, and software to value-added resellers in North America.

Arrow Electronics, Inc.
50 Marcus Drive
Melville, NY 11747-4210
(631) 847-2000
www.arrow.com

7. Graybar

Primarily electronics and communications distributor.

34 N. Meramec Avenue
St. Louis, MO 63105
(800) 825-5517; (7 A.M.–5 P.M. CT)
www.graybar.com

8. Tech Data

Serves technology resellers in United States, Canada, Caribbean, Latin America, Europe, and Middle East.

Tech Data Corporation

5350 Tech Data Drive
Clearwater, FL 33760
(727) 539-7429
Sales: (800) 237-8931
Customer Service: (800) 237-8931
www.techdata.com

9. AVUS

Grew from local distributor to a respectable nationwide distributor and integrator of computer hardware, software, and systems.

12851 Reservoir St.
Chino, CA 91710
(800) 978-eSys (800-978-3797)
Local: (909) 464-9886
Fax: (909) 464-9655
www.avus.com

10. EMJ

Canadian-owned distributor of computer hardware and software.

EMJ, a division of SYNNEX Corporation
PO Box 1012 STN Main
Guelph Ontario N1H 6N1
(519) 837-2444
Fax: (519) 836-1914
www.emj.ca

Source: BumperSoft.com (*http://developers.bumpersoft.com/ resources/distributors.htm*)—An up-to-date, useful resource on the Internet for free digital downloading of software. Bumper-Soft.com enables IT professionals, developers, home and business users to have a hands-on evaluation of products they're considering for purchase.

Popular Accounting Software: Midmarket

As your business grows, choosing the right accounting software becomes more and more critical. You can't just go to Staples anymore and buy a shrink-wrapped package. You now need to evaluate more robust systems. Here are a few of the top accounting-software programs for the midmarket.

1. ACCPAC Advantage Series Corporation Edition (Now Sage)

ACCPAC Advantage Series Corporate Edition is a completely Web-based, affordable, and expandable business management solution for medium-size accounting environments. It offers powerful analysis and reporting tools and a robust accounting feature set complete with operations management capabilities.

(800) 253-1372
www.accpac.com

2. ACCPAC Pro Series

ACCPAC Pro Series is specifically designed for the growing company that requires a complete suite of accounting and operations modules. This scalable solution provides you with the financial management power you need—at a price you can afford.

(800) 253-1372
www.accpac.com

3. Accountmate

Accountmate is an award-winning solution that fulfills the needs of small to midsize companies. It can be customized quickly and easily to fit the way you do business.

(415) 883-8873
www.accountmate.com

4. BusinessVision 32

Affordable, expandable, and remarkably flexible, BusinessVision 32 is the most powerful system in its price range. It is available in four different versions, each a complete integrated and scalable solution designed to grow as your company grows.

(800) 945-8007
E-mail: *sales@businessvision.com*
www.businessvision.com

5. Great Plains

Microsoft Great Plains is a comprehensive business-management solution built on the highly scalable and affordable platform of Microsoft technologies. It offers a cost-effective solution for managing and integrating finances, e-commerce, supply chain, manufacturing, project accounting, field service, customer relationships, and human resources.

(888) 477-7989
www.microsoft.com

6. MAS 90 & MAS 200

MAS 90 & MAS 200 are both widely recognized for their ease of use and ability to empower customers with insightful information. The company offers software to midsize and small businesses to improve workflow and enhance sales performance.

(866) 308-2378
www.bestsoftware.com

7. Navision

Microsoft Business Solutions–Navision is a cost-effective and fully customizable business-management solution designed to meet the specific needs of small and midsize companies. It includes integrated functionality for financial management, supply-chain collaboration, CRM, and e-commerce.

(888) 477-7989

www.microsoft.com

8. Solomon

Microsoft Business Solutions–Solomon offers a full range of business applications. Microsoft Solomon can be customized for your needs, easily integrated into current systems, and adapted over time as your needs change.

(888) 477-7989

www.microsoft.com

9. SouthWare Excellence Series

SouthWare is the provider of an integrated family of financial and management information software for all size organizations and a wide variety of industries. The SouthWare Excellence Series focuses on placing power in the user's hands to tailor a system that meets their unique requirements. Using the portable technology, the SouthWare Excellence Series supports more than 600 hardware/operating system combinations, including Windows NT/2000/98/95, Unix, Linux, AIX, and networks such as Novell.

(312) 821-1146

www.southware.com

10. SYSPRO

SYSPRO enterprise software is the foundation of successful supply-chain management. SYSPRO meets the comprehensive information technology needs of emerging companies with a totally integrated solution that encompasses: ERP, APS, CRM, and e-commerce. The software enables companies in a variety of industries to maximize the planning and management of business processes to better position themselves in their respective markets, ensure customer fulfillment, and ultimately, improve bottom-line results.

(714) 437-1000

www.syspro.com

Source: Accounting Software Advisor (*www.accountingsoftwareadvisor.com*)—The company's mission is to deliver useful information about technology and accounting systems to the CPA community and business community through lectures and published Web sites. They strive to deliver up-to-date and accurate information regarding the top accounting-software products and technologies in an unbiased manner. Their mailing address is The Willford Building, 4989 Peachtree Parkway, Norcross, GA 30092; (770) 734-0950.

Popular Accounting Software: Entry Level

There are thousands of accounting-software packages in the marketplace today. Each one offers unique features and capabilities that are to be commended, admired, and sometimes applauded. However, on close inspection, most suffer from obvious problems such as older technology, proprietary technology, lack of support, lack of an adequate size customer base, lack of a distribution channel, poor performance on a local area network, bugs, missing modules, missing key features, lack of capital, and so on. Here are some of the most popular entry-level accounting-software programs as selected by our expert. This list is not in any particular order.

1. BusinessVision 32

Affordable, expandable, and remarkably flexible, BusinessVision 32 is the most powerful system in its price range. It is available in four different versions, each a complete integrated and scalable solution designed to grow as your company grows.

(800) 945-8007

E-mail: *sales@businessvision.com*

www.businessvision.com

2. Small Business Accounting

This solution is Microsoft's answer to Quick-Books. Released in September 2005, Small Business Accounting is designed to provide all of the functionality of QuickBooks on a better technology platform and for a 80 percent lower price tag.

(800) 426-9400

www.microsoft.com/smallbusiness

3. Small Business Financials

This solution, produced by Microsoft, can import QuickBooks data, which may be very important for business owners converting to a new system.

(800) 426-9400

www.microsoft.com/smallbusiness

4. M.Y.O.B.

M.Y.O.B. offers small business solutions that include accounting and small business management tools. Enjoy a complete suite of small business software and tools that will help you mind your own business smarter, whether your accounting needs are basic or more complex.

(973) 586-2229

www.myob/us/products/new_win.htm

5. Peachtree Complete Accounting

Peachtree Complete Accounting offers the essentials, such as invoicing and bill paying, as well as more advanced features, such as powerful reporting, basic inventory, and analysis elements.

(770) 724-4000

www.peachtree.com/PeachtreeAccounting Line/Complete/

6. QuickBooks

QuickBooks have all the financial management features, plus improved tools and customization options to help you work more efficiently.

(888) 729-1996

www.quickbooks.intuit.com

7. Simply Accounting

Simply Accounting 2005 Basic was designed for fast-moving businesses. It's easy to learn and use, yet powerful enough to keep up with all accounting needs. Whether you sell products or services, Simply Accounting Basic has all you need to run your business. It automates everything from making purchases to making sales and everything in between. It's even flexible enough to meet the most demanding payroll requirements.

(800) 773-5445

www.simplyaccounting.com

8. Vision Point

This software is designed for the small to midsize business. ACCPAC Accounting Systems'

VisionPoint 10.0 is a feature-rich application that delivers big business functionality. VisionPoint 10.0 can accommodate growth and change as your business moves forward. It has the features you need now, plus the ones you'll want in the future.

(800) 253-1372

www.accpac.com

Source: The Accounting Software Advisor (*www.accountingsoftwareadvisor.com*)—The company's mission is to deliver useful information about technology and accounting systems to the CPA community and business community through lectures and published Web sites. They strive to deliver up-to-date and accurate information regarding the top accounting-software products and technologies in an unbiased manner. Contact them at Willford Building, 4989 Peachtree Parkway, Norcross, GA 30092; (770) 734-0950.

Steps for Evaluating Accounting Software

There are more than 4,400 common features found in today's top accounting-software products; however, attempting to evaluate all of these features is a daunting proposition. Here is a simplified process for selecting accounting software.

1. Print a financial statement to the screen

This process can be very revealing. To start with, it allows you to see how many default financial-statement formats come standard with the system. Some products provide a balance sheet and income statement while others provide numerous standard reports including a statement of cash flows. This process also allows you to see the flexibility of reporting options prior to printing. This gives you the chance to answer questions: Can I define the desired date range? Can the reports be printed to someone's e-mail address or fax machine?

2. Customize a data-input screen

It is important to evaluate the ability to edit, change, and add to the data-input screens. Ask the reseller to demonstrate the process of inserting a new data field and rearranging that field on the screen. You might also ask the reseller to relabel the data field and establish default settings for that new field. Some products provide full control over the data-input screen design while others do not.

3. Enter an inventory item

The simple process of setting up a single inventory item is very telling. This process allows the user to explore the look and feel of the accounting system, gain an understanding of the depth of features within an advance core module, and in general, take the system for a ride. As you begin the task of setting up a new inventory item, determine how intuitively the system is laid out. Is the starting menu obvious? Can you easily find the correct screen on which to begin this process? After finding the inventory item setup screen, click the help button. Does the help screen offer step-by-step instructions?

4. Process a sales order

You can tell a great deal about an accounting-software package by entering a simple order into the system. This will allow you to gain insights into the look and feel of the system, the way it navigates, the speed, the ease of use, the breadth of features.

5. Evaluate the account number structure

An important feature that you should always evaluate early on is the size and segmentation of the product's account number structure. Often you can eliminate many inadequate products by first checking this feature. If that structure is inadequate—no matter how superior the product in every other way—reject the software. It's important to understand what's behind that statement.

6. Drill down and around

The best accounting-software products in the land offer strong "drill down and drill around" capabilities. This helps you answer questions about your data. The next time you evaluate an accounting-software system, put it to the test. See if you can drill from the customer setup screen to that customer's invoices to the items included on those customer invoices and then to pictures and statistics related to those items.

7. Integrate to popular add-on report writers and tools

The best accounting-software products have taken great efforts to integrate their products with the most popular report writers, tools, and other add-on applications in the marketplace. As you evaluate your accounting-software candidates, determine whether the proposed system works with the following proven add-on solutions: FRx, Crystal Reports, Best! Fixed Assets, Microsoft Excel via ODBC, and ACT! or Goldmine.

Source: Accounting Software Advisor (*www.accountingsoftwareadvisor.com*)—The company's mission is to deliver useful information about technology and accounting systems to the CPA community and business community through lectures and published Web sites. They strive to deliver up-to-date and accurate information regarding the top accounting-software products and technologies in an unbiased manner. Their mailing address is The Willford Building, 4989 Peachtree Parkway, Norcross, GA 30092; (770) 734-0950.

Popular External Backup Devices

Growing needs in both enterprise data storage and data protection have accelerated the enterprise storage spending worldwide. If a computer system fails, data may be lost; and the extent to which this creates a problem is largely dependent on the quality of your data backups. Backing up is one thing; restoration is another. The choice of a backup device will generally depend on the quantity of data, the backup frequency, the ability to store several copies offsite easily, and the speed at which restoration is required. Our expert provides these options.

1. Tape backup kits (Network Server)

Tape drives are a legacy device, in that they used to be more popular than they are today. However, they are still the best option for large server environments. They offer large capacity (up to 800 GB compressed on a single LTO3 tape, and you can combine several tapes in one tape library, achieving exponential amounts of capacity). They also offer the flexibility of being able to store many tapes offsite, an important component to data protection.

2. External hard disk drives (Network Server)

While the data transfer rate for an external hard disk drive (via USB or Firewire) is not as great as that for an internal (removable) drive, this is a very convenient way to quickly set up a large capacity backup device. The Iomega range of drives is supplied with excellent backup software. Capacity ranges from 40 GB to 400 GB. A challenge to using disk drives is that you typically do not use as many drives as you would tapes, thereby limiting your flexibility of storing drives offsite, as they tend to be much more expensive than tapes and have limited expandability options, as you would have in a tape library. These devices are often used for servers and for computers.

3. CD/DVD burners (Computer Workstation)

Compact Disk Burners (CD Burners) are also known as CD-Recordable or CD-RW drives. DVD Burners are also available. The capacity of a standard CD-Recordable disk is 700 MB; a DVD-Recordable disk is 4.7 GB. These devices are fast becoming the most popular form of backup device in modern computers; in fact, our recommended computer packages include a CD Burner as the standard drive. Backup disks can be read by virtually any normal CD-ROM drive which makes this a very portable backup format. This is a low-cost solution that is reusable, allows for quick data restoration but has low capacity and is most appropriate for individual computers.

4. Floppy drives (Computer Workstation)

Almost no one backs up to floppy drives these days, but they are still a convenient device for storing smaller files. The capacity of a 3½-inch floppy drive is 1.44 MB.

5. Zip drives (Computer Workstation)

Zip drives are a longstanding favorite and work just like a floppy disk drive, albeit with much greater capacity. To read a zip disk, any given computer must have a zip drive installed or an external zip drive as well. Capacity of zip disk is in the range of 250 MB to 750 MB.

6. Removable hard disk drives (Computer Workstation)

If you need to preserve a complete copy of your computer together with the operating system, all programs and data, you will need a hard disk drive of a similar capacity to that which is installed in your computer. If the backup drive is fitted to a removable frame, then you can store this backup off-site; in fact it makes sense to have a couple of drives to rotate weekly or thereabouts. Capacity ranges from 40 GB to 250 GB.

Source: KPInterface, Inc.—An IT consulting firm focused on providing fixed fee annual services to the small business market throughout the Philadelphia metropolitan area. Contact Matthew Kirby, Owner, at *mkirby@kpinterface.com*.

Top Things to Ask an Off-Site Backup Company

An off-site backup company is a subscription service that can provide a safe and reliable online backup solution. We asked our experts, who specializes in data backup services to provide us a list of what questions a prospective customer should consider when creating off-site backups, and here's what they said.

1. Restoration

Will the data backup service be able to restore the customer's data after hard drive failure, catastrophe, or human error?

2. Data encryption

Is the data encrypted before, during, and after transmission to the remote location? What level of encryption is used during remote backup activities?

3. Confidentiality and billing

Can the confidentiality of the customer's data be fully guaranteed? Is billing based upon the compressed size of the customer's data?

4. Growth, contracts, and support

Will the data backup service be scalable if the business should grow from 5 users to 500 users? Is there an annual contract for the backup service, and if so, are there any early termination fees? Are there round-the-clock support services and monitoring of the facility? How secure is the remote facility?

5. Storing and intrusions

Is the data stored on hard drives or a tape drive, and how many copies of the data are maintained at the remote location at all times? Does the remote backup service actively monitor for intrusion attempts, and if so, are these attempts logged and is there a protocol for response?

6. Network redundancy and remote access

How many levels of network redundancy support the service? Does the customer have remote access to stored files?

7. Replication, mirroring, and alternate versions

What are the replication and mirroring policies for data storage? Are alternate versions of user documents stored, and if so, for how long?

8. Remote and failed backups

Does the remote backup service manage open files such as Outlook or QuickBooks? Are there notification systems for failed backups?

9. Service and scheduled backups

Is the service intended for archival or data backup, and are the scheduled backups incremental? If so, how are files changes transmitted?

10. Data backup program

Will the data backup program access network drives, and are files compressed before sending to the server?

Source: Keith H. Christoffers, owner of SyncCom—Data Management Group (*www.synccom.com*)—He specializes in data backup services for the home user, small business, corporate enterprise, and many others. Contact them at PO Box 1814, Bloomfield, NJ 07003; (877) 850-7339.

Considerations Before Choosing a Database

A "database" is software used to input, organize, manipulate, retrieve and analyze information. It also refers to the data—and its structure—stored by such software (sometimes called the "back-end"). Sometimes you need a piece of software (called a "front-end") to input, view, and report the information in the database. The type of database package you choose depends on the type of business you run, how many people need to access your data, and what your data is used for. Here's a list of things to think about before choosing the database for your next system.

1. Do I need a basic database?

Some basic packages include the front-end and back-end capabilities of a database rolled into one package. These include packages like Microsoft Windows Cardfile. These small and inexpensive programs (some are free) are great for the single user or small business with simple data requirements like customer lists or inventory. Where all the data is in a single file, it is called a "flat file" database. These packages often include templates for simple input forms, searches, and reports.

2. Do I need a relational database?

The next level of database is the relational database. Relational databases allow for more efficient storage of data by "pointing" data in different databases to each other, instead of duplicating information. An invoice database might point to a customer database and an inventory database to avoid having to store basic (and repetitive) customer and product data with each invoice. A relational database helps redundant storage of information and makes it easier to define and perform searches. When working with large volumes of data, a relational database is a must for speed and data integrity. Imagine in the invoicing and customer database discussed above if a client moved and only the customer

database was changed . . . you might not be able to find old invoices for that particular client any more. Also, when creating new invoices, users don't have to re-enter the customer information: just the customer number. Of course, relational databases come with a price: professional help is needed, and it takes more time for planning and programming (particularly for designing the most efficient storage of data, called "normalization"). Programs such as Microsoft Access and Claris FileMaker Pro are great mid-level database packages, and include a programmable front-end and report generators that most experienced users can work with.

3. Do I need a client/server relational database?

The "elite" of databases today are client/server relational databases. The client/server architecture allows for multiple people on different computers to access the same data at the same time. The data resides on the "server," and the users access the data on other machines called "clients." The sheer complexity of these systems demands professional and experienced development engineers to create a totally client-custom solution. Leading vendors like Progress, Oracle, and Microsoft SQL Server provide software to manage data in such complex environments. Some of these packages require customized front-end applications so users can enter or view the data itself. Front-end software can be created using tools like Borland's Delphi, Microsoft Visual Basic, and C++. Of course, the new generation of databases will have varying degrees of Web-enabling, allowing the database to be updated or queried using HTML Web forms, and have information displayed as standard HTML Web pages. Look forward to dramatic changes in database functionality in the coming year(s).

Source: FoundLocally (*www.FoundLocally.com*) develops high-traffic city-based community portals used by both locals and visitors for twenty different communities across Canada. FoundLocally was founded in 1999 to give the public access to broad community information, and to provide local businesses and community groups a way to reach their local on-line audience to communicate about their organizations, their events, jobs, news and coupon offers at an affordable price. Contact them at their Web site.

Best Free E-mail Services

Getting free e-mail is pretty easy nowadays. But who offers the best service? Our internet security expert provided this list of their favorites.

1. GMail

Gmail is a free, search-based Web mail service that includes more than 2,000 MB of storage and offers POP/SMTP access to its e-mail.
http://gmail.google.com

2. Yahoo!

There's more in store with Yahoo! Mail. All free Yahoo! Mail users will now receive an e-mail storage increase to a whopping 1 GB, removed its SMTP service in the past but now added it again.
http://mail.yahoo.com/

3. GMX

A reliable e-mail provider, GMX is the biggest provider of free e-mail in Germany, so it is here to stay. Unfortunately, GMX discontinued their English language service lately. They now only maintain the German user interface.
www.gmx.co.uk

4. HotPOP

It has an easy setup and works okay, and that is more than you can expect with most free e-mail services. Note that the free account has a 500 KB size limit for e-mail messages.
www.HotPOP.com

Source: iOpus (*www.iopus.com*)—A maker of security and Internet applications for both developers and end users. Contact them at their Web site or by email at *info2@iOpus.com*.

Popular Instant Messaging Services

Teenagers aren't the only ones instant messaging these days. Instant messaging has become a very popular way of corporate communication, too. We asked our expert, who tracks the way people use the Internet, to list the most popular instant messaging services and here's what they found.

1. AIM.COM/AIM (App)

www.aim.com
Unique visitors: 30,164,000

2. MSN Messenger Service

www.msn.com
Unique visitors: 24,013,000

3. Yahoo!

www.yahoo.com
Unique visitors: 23,311,000

4. ICQ

www.icq.com
Unique visitors: 1,950,000

5. Google Talk (App)

www.google.com/talk
Unique visitors: 719,000

6. PalTalk

www.paltalk.com
Unique visitors: 652,000

7. Trillian (App)

www.trillian.com
Unique visitors: 547,000

8. XFire

Unique visitors: 123,000
www.xfire.com

Source: ComScore Media Metrix, December 2006—A service of comScore Networks, comScore Networks (*www.comscore.com*) is a global information provider and consultancy to which leading companies turn for consumer behavior insight that drives successful marketing, sales and trading strategies. Contact them at 11465 Sunset Hills Road, Suite 200, Reston, VA 20190; (703) 438-2000; fax: (703) 438-2051.

Popular E-mail Applications

Not everything is free, and the better e-mail systems are no different. Here's a list of the most popular e-mail applications used by businesses today and our expert's thoughts on each. It's easy to find more information about these products keying in the product or vendor name on any major search engine.

1. Apple

.Mac Mail is part of the .MAC software/service provided by Apple. It is easy to install and set up for use. .Mac is priced at $99.95 for one year of service and the software. It has lots of capabilities, including Web hosting, calendar integration, offsite storage, and 125 MB space to keep your e-mail "online" if you wish. This is a comprehensive, simple to use and inexpensive service/software for the Mac user. It is a no-brainer to add on to a new Macintosh.

2. Chaos Software

Chaos Software's Express Plus 2 is straightforward to install and set up for use. Express Plus 2 is priced at $35.00. A basic business e-mail client designed for use with Chaos Software's Time and Chaos contact manager. A solid e-mail client that is at its best when used with Cahos software's Time and Chaos Contact Manager.

3. KDE

KMail comes with the KDE 3.3.2 Unix/Linux desktop environment, And it comes along with any Unix/Linux software OS that includes the KDE 3.3.2 desktop environment. The strength of KMail is not only its basic e-mail and address book features and functions but also its strong integration of security and security protocols—SSL/TLS, Open PGP. Overall, it's an easy choice for Linux/Unix users.

4. KMT Software

KMT Software High Impact e-mail Basic and Professional are straightforward to install and set up for use with your messaging or contact management application. High Impact e-mail 3.0 basic is priced at $49.95, Professional at $99.95. Nice-looking, professional templates for the home-business owner who doesn't have time to create everything from scratch. Real time-savers—and great looking as well. Easy, professional looking e-mail—and fast too.

5. LesTec Pty Ltd.

LesTec's Mailer is simple to install and begin using. Les Tec ML Mailer is priced at $41.80. Its best features are those that allow you to view e-mail headers before downloading (and delete them as well!) and standard replies and filters for suspect e-mail. There are many other nice features such as the ability to share and/or password-protect mail folders as well as the HTML mail templates. If you just need an e-mail package and want some antispam features and functions included, LesTecML Mailer is a good solution. However, for U.S.-based users, the fact that you'll have to get support from Australia could be problematic.

6. Microsoft

Outlook Express is especially simple; Outlook offers more features and functionality and adds complexity. However, both are easy to use and are straightforward in their implementations. Cost effectiveness depends on whether you are using the Microsoft suite of products. Outlook Express comes standard with Windows operating systems, Outlook with the Microsoft Office desktop suite. You can also purchase Outlook separately for $109. The integrated approach of Outlook provides lots of features and functions to make you more productive, especially if you

use it in combination with Microsoft Office. Again, the robust calendaring, contact management, and task management included are big pluses and set Outlook apart from most of the competition.

7. Mozilla

Thunderbird is easy to download, install, and set up for use. What's better than free? If you want a CD, it will cost you $6.00. Thunderbird's key attributes (beyond being a basic e-mail client) are security (S/MIME, digital signing, message encryption, and certificate support) and junk mail filtering. For folks who just can't stand the thought of using anything that Microsoft makes or who love open-source software, then Mozilla's Thunderbird is a terrific option. Good software and you can't beat the price!

8. Netscape

Netscape is easy to install and starts you off with a wizard to set up your e-mail services. It is a decent mail interface with junk mail controls and Palm integration. A good alternative if you do not want to use Microsoft Internet Explorer's Outlook Express.

9. Outspring Software

QuickMail has been used by Macintosh owners almost since the first Macintosh was built in the 1980s. It installs quickly and easily and has the standard, easy-to-use Macintosh and now a sleek Windows interface as well. It has everything you'll need to do e-mail and manage your contacts but no calendar, task, and other integration that we believe is a necessary part of today's e-mail packages. QuickMail is nice for Macintosh users, but unless you have both Windows and Macintosh computers (with Mac's being the prevalent technology), there are better options for Windows PCs. This is a package that has a long history, and it will work and work well.

___

Source: Home Office Reports (*www.homeofficereports.com*)—They supply comprehensive information on a wide variety of technologies from PCs to networking, telephones and telephone services to digital cameras and accounting. Contact them at 2102 Clematis Ct., McKinney, TX 75070; (972) 529-9719; fax: (972) 540-1674; e-mail: *dmielke@homeofficereports.com*.

Popular Law Firm Software

Law firms have the same business issues as everyone else. There's a large industry of technology specific to law firm management. This lists shows us some of the more popular applications that law firms utilize to manage their practice. This information was current at the time of printing, but please make sure you double-check with the vendors for any changes.

1. AbacusLaw

Time, billing, trust accounting, general ledger, payroll, accounts payable & receivable, check writing, financial statements, etc. Comes fully integrated with calendars, court rules, cases, conflicts, contacts, dockets, docs, emails, files, instant messages and more. Enter data once and use it everywhere. No more duplicate entries or needing to use multiple systems. Data is fully linked for clients and cases.

5230 Carroll Canyon Rd, Suite 306

San Diego, CA 92121
Phone: (800) 726-3339
E-mail: *sales@abacuslaw.com*
Web site: *www.abacuslaw.com*

2. Tabs3

Reliable billing software that helps you get your bills out faster and increase your productivity. Used by law firms for over 25 years, Tabs3 is recommended by 95% of firms that use it. Includes a free copy of PracticeMaster Basic. Integrates with Tabs3 Financial Software, QuickBooks® and PracticeMaster.

1621 Cushman Drive
Lincoln, NE 68512
Phone: (402) 423-1440
E-mail: *sales@tabs3.com*
Web site: *www.tabs3.com/findlawt*

3. PCLAW

Since 1982 over 30,000 law firms have depended on PCLaw for integrated time billing, accounting and practice management. PCLaw also includes check writing, trust accounting and general ledger. PCLaw is designed for firms with up to ten timekeepers and for larger firms they offer PCLawPro. To help new users get started, PCLaw offers a free Timeslips or QuickBooks conversion and a 30-day money-back guarantee.

300 Pearl St., Box 2000
Buffalo, NY 14202
Phone: (800) 387-9785
E-mail: *sales@pclaw.com*
Web site: *www.pclaw.com*

4. Omega

From timekeeping to billing to reporting, Omega's software includes everything a firm needs to take care of business. The company has been a leader in integrated financial and practice management systems for mid-size and larger law firms for over 30 years. Contact them at

1875 N. 44th St.
Suite 200
Phoenix, AZ 85018
Phone: (800) 356-1339
E-mail: *info@omegalegal.com*
Web site: *www.omegalegal.com*

5. The Tussman Program

Tussman Programs, Inc. has been a leader in developing legal billing, accounting, and docket calendar software for over 20 years.

Tussman Programs, Inc.
2308 6th Street
Berkeley, CA 94710
Contact: Richard Zerga
Phone: (800)228-6589
E-mail: *rjz@tussman.com*
Web site: *www.tussman.com*

6. The Plaintiff Law Office Software

Has been providing software specifically designed for Plaintiff Firms for 20 years: Case Management, Document Management, Scheduler/Calendar, Accounting, Interest Allocation, Cost Recovery, Time & Billing. You can purchase only the modules you need. Interfaces with QuickBooks®, Word®, WordPerfect®, Palm®, and more. Output info to Adobe PDF® format.

713 St. Clair Avenue, Suite B
Huntsville, Alabama 35801
Phone: 1-877-202-0235 ext. 101
E-mail: *info@theplaintiff.com*
Web site: *www.theplaintiff.com*

7. FindLaw

Thomson FindLaw's FirmSite provides law firms with web sites to generate lucrative new business through the web and use technology to systematically build stronger, more profitable relationships with existing clients. Attorneys can also be prominently listed on their web portal, Findlaw.com, the world's most visited legal information site.

610 Opperman Drive
Eagan, Minnesota 55123
Phone: 1-866-44FindLaw
Web site: *www.lawyermarketing.com*

8. Elite®

The Elite software suite enables professional services firms to streamline all of the essential tasks involved in running a successful practice. Functionality includes financial and practice management; business intelligence; business development; embedded workflow and collaboration and more.

Thomson Elite
5100 W. Goldleaf Circle
Suite 100
Los Angeles, CA 90056
Phone: (323) 642-5200
E-mail: *salesinfo@elite.com*
Web site: *www.thomsonelite.com*

9. ProLaw®

Designed specifically for small- and mid-size law firms, corporate legal departments and government agencies, ProLaw integrates with Microsoft Outlook, Word, and Westlaw research.

Thomson Elite
5100 Goldleaf Circle
Suite 100
Los Angeles, CA 90056
Phone: (800) 977-6529
E-mail: *prolawinfo@thomson.com*
Web site: *www.thomsonelite.com*

Source: FindLaw (*www.findlaw.com*), a highly trafficked legal Web site, provides the most comprehensive set of legal resources on the Internet for legal professionals, businesses, students and individuals. These resources include Web search utilities, cases and codes, legal news, an online career center, and community-oriented tools, such as a secure document management utility, mailing lists, message boards and free e-mail. Contact them at: (Corporate Headquarters) 610 Opperman Drive, Eagan, MN 55123, Phone: (651) 687-7000, Fax: (800) 392-6206.

Popular Utilities Software

What software utilities are most businesses using? We asked our expert, a consultant and technology specialist, to give us her thoughts. This list of utility programs can help you make some of your common tasks easier. And the best news is that many of them are inexpensive or even free!

1. Adobe Acrobat Reader

Most people who have spent any time surfing the Internet have encountered Adobe Acrobat files. A PDF file looks just like you designed it even when displayed on other systems. All the fonts, pictures, and layout look just like they do on your system. To open a PDF file, you need the free Acrobat Reader. You can download it from Adobe's Web site at *www.adobe.com/products/acrobat/main.html*. Once you have installed the Reader, you can look at any PDF file.

2. WinZip

Because file sizes seem to get larger every day, WinZip *(www.winzip.com)* is a program no computer user should be without. With WinZip, you can compress one file or many files into an archive. Then the recipient uses their copy of WinZip to extract your archive. WinZip gives you an easy way to get a lot of files where you need them to go.

3. Symantec Norton Anti-Virus/System Works

If you don't have anti-virus software, your data is at risk. Norton AntiVirus comes alone or packaged with Norton System Works (*www.symantec.com*). The cost of buying or upgrading existing anti-virus software is small compared to the cost of getting a virus. If you think you may already have a virus, you also can scan your system and remove viruses for free using Symantec Security Check at *www.symantec.com/securitycheck*.

4. Spybot Search and Destroy

Unfortunately, spyware is one of the realities of computing today. Although no tool is perfect for removing spyware, Spybot Search and Destroy *(www.spybot.info/en/index.html)* is good and, since it is freeware, the price is right.

5. Short Keys

Short Keys *(www.shortkeys.com)* is one of those tiny utility programs that has been around forever and is too useful to give up. Using it, you can set up replacement text or paragraphs for particular keystrokes. It works a lot like the AutoText feature in Microsoft Word, except it works in any program. You type a keystroke combination, and ShortKeys replaces it with the text you specify. The full version costs $19.95; the more limited "light" version is free.

6. Ahead Nero CD/DVD Burning Software

Although Windows XP has CD burning features built-in, it can be helpful to have a more full featured CD and DVD burning program. Nero *(www.nero.com)* has a lot of useful features and lets you set options, so you can burn disks that are compatible with other operating systems, such as those for the Macintosh.

7. Power Toys/Tweak UI

Microsoft has a free suite of utility programs called Power Toys, which includes many handy items including Tweak UI, which lets you access many elements of the user interface (UI) without the need to edit the registry. Power Toys is technically not supported by Microsoft, but a new updated version appears shortly after each version of Windows is released. The current one for Windows XP is located here: *www.microsoft .com/windowsxp/pro/downloads/powertoys.asp*

8. G-Lock Spam Combat

If you are overrun with spam in your e-mail inbox, you may have become confused by the array of spam-stopping tools out there. Many of them force you to reconfigure your mail settings. However, G-Lock takes a different approach with its Spam Combat program *(www.glocksoft .com)*. Unlike most mail software, it downloads only the e-mail headers, instead of the entire e-mail. It color codes the headers, so you can tell the good stuff from the bad stuff easily. And you can delete what you don't want while it is still on the server so nothing nasty accidentally ends up on your hard disk to cause trouble.

9. OmniPage Pro

If you need to get text off of a printed page and get it into a word processor, and unless you like typing, you might want to look into optical character recognition or OCR. This process translates printed text characters into type that can be edited and otherwise manipulated on a computer using a standard word processor. OmniPage Pro *(www.nuance.com)* works with most popular scanners and is easy to use.

Source: Susan C. Daffron is the President of Logical Expressions, Inc., (*www.logicalexpressions.com*), a company that helps small businesses create, manage, and distribute content. Logical Expressions specializes in fusing high-quality unique content with search-engine and human-friendly Web sites. They offer writing, editing, programming, and design services and publish a free computer magazine called Computor Companion (*www.computorcompanion.com*). The magazine is targeted toward business owners/managers, computer professionals, and home PC computer users. It includes easy-to-understand articles designed to help readers use their computers more effectively to accomplish everyday tasks.

Most Visited Freeware Web Sites

Want to get some free software? Our techno-geek expert provides some highly recommended sites that you can use in your business.

1. ZDNet and CNet Downloads

These two sites are just different faces of the same site. That site, however, offers the biggest collection of software on the Web. Finding what you want is easy because they have best file search engine of them all.

www.zdnet.com

2. No-Nags

This is simply the best freeware download site on the Web. The shareware side is slowly being added and is not yet as impressive.

www.nonags.com

3. SnapFiles/WebAttack

This site offers a huge collection, great organization, and a refreshingly clean presentation let down by a somewhat-unhelpful file search facility.

www.snapfiles.com

4. MajorGeeks

This site only carries tech tools and utilities, and there's not a lot of guidance to help you select wisely. However, if you are looking for tech tools, this is *the* place to go.

www.majorgeeks.com

5. FileForum-Betanews

Not the largest download collection, but if you are looking for very latest products, you'll find them here long before other download sites.

www.fileforum.betanews.com

6. Tucows

This is a huge collection with worldwide mirrors for fast downloading. The Classic "cow ratings" for products are as reliable as ever. This once class-leading site has lost its way a little in recent times.

www.tucows.com

7. ServerFiles.com

This is the old 32bit.com site relaunched as a specialist site for server software for network administrators and IT professionals. Quite a few products have ratings, some with full reviews. It's a unique offering and highly recommended if you fit the target market.

www.serverfiles.com

8. SoftPedia

This large commercial site has a good collection of user reviews but is marred by lots of ads and general screen clutter.

www.softpedia.com

9. 5 star shareware

This quality UK site claims to feature only the best products in each category—and it does . . . almost.

www.5star-shareware.com

10. VoodooFiles

This is a specialist download site for gaming, multimedia, and performance tweaking with lots of quality reviews.

www.voodoofiles.com

11. Topshareware.com

This good general interest download site is competent enough but fails to offer anything to distinguish itself from similar sites.

www.topshareware.com

12. Shareware junkies

Every product here is independently reviewed, although many of the reviews are becoming dated. It can be helpful when you are trying to decide what you need.

www.sharewarejunkies.com

13. Allen's WinApps

List A is a fast and well-organized site with a huge selection of software, but the search engine is woeful and there is little in the way of guidance.

www.winappslist.com

14. WinPlanet

This is the aging remnant of the once-excellent Stroud's CWS Apps site. It's now part of the Internet.com megasite and is still a useful site with many products rated and some reviewed. Overall though, it is but a pale shadow of its former self.

www.winplanet.com

15. Pass the shareware

A limited and somewhat aging collection, it is refreshingly free of advertising.

www.passtheshareware.com

Source: Gizmo Richards' Techsupportalert.com (*www.techsupport alert.com*) You'll find Gizmo's top picks of hundreds of great Web sites and software programs all independently reviewed and rated by category. Contact them by *e-mail at gizmo@techsupportalert .com or editor@*techsupportalert.com.

Popular Label-Design Software

Label-design software provides your company the opportunity to design and print labels for your business. These are the most popular options for your company.

1. Teklynx Label Matrix

Bar code label-design and integration software combines advanced bar code label design and printing with unrivaled ease of use. Starting at: $338.

5300 N. 118th Court
Building F
Milwaukee WI 53225
(414) 535-6200
Fax: (414) 535-6201
www.teklynx.com

2. Teklynx Label View

Bar code label software can design bar code labels and integrate your bar code label software and printing system with existing systems with unmatched power and flexibility. Starting at: $185.

5300 N. 118th Court
Building F
Milwaukee WI 53225
(414) 535-6200
Fax: (414) 535-6201
www.teklynx.com

3. Number Five Label 5

Professional label-design and printing software. Starting at: $240.

2045 Royal Ave., Suite 126

Simi Valley, CA 93065

(805) 522-9906

Sales: (805) 522-9907

www.nfive.com

4. Zebra Create-A-Label

This powerful utility provides Create-A-Label 3 v3.04 support for Windows XP. Starting at: $150.

International Headquarters

333 Corporate Woods Parkway

Vernon Hills, Il 60061-3109

(847) 634-6700

Toll-free: (866) 230-9494

Fax: (847) 913-8766

www.zebra.com

5. Zebra Bar One

Bar code label software. Starting at: $335.

International Headquarters

333 Corporate Woods Parkway

Vernon Hills, IL 60061-3109

(847) 634-6700

Toll-free: (866) 230-9494

Fax: (847) 913-8766

www.zebra.com

Source: POS Global (*www.posglobal.com*)—A leading global source for affordable point-of-sale and auto identification products. Contact them at 4004 W. Plano Parkway, Plano, TX 75093; (972) 769-7300.

Popular Microsoft PowerPoint Add-Ons

So many people rely on Microsoft PowerPoint for their presentations, that it's a part of the vernacular in the business world. If you use this presentation tool frequently, you can radically improve the effectiveness of your PowerPoint presentations. Here is a list of resources to get you started from a PowerPoint aficionado.

1. Beyond bullets

This is a great Web site on how to use PowerPoint more effectively. The content is very stimulating—and will challenge your presuppositions. This is not a collection of more templates and clip art. Instead, it presents serious thinking about the way you use PowerPoint and how to improve your effectiveness. *http://sociablemedia.typepad.com/beyond_bullets/*

2. Crystal graphics

This is a great source for PowerPoint add-ins that enhances the basic program. Television-like transitions, 3D titles, supershapes, and custom templates are some of the more popular add-ins. There is one caution: Some of the effects, particularly the television-like transitions, require some serious hardware horsepower.

www.crystalgraphics.com

3. DesignSense

This company advertises itself as "graphic design training for businesspeople." It contains a series of design lessons for people (like me!) who have no formal graphic design training. They claim that the training you receive on the site is equivalent to a forty-hour graphic design course. However, it is condensed into twelve hours of computer-based training.

www.designsense-cd.com.

4. Excelsius

Excelsius is a charting program. It essentially creates animated flash movies, based on Excel data. It is highly customizable and very sophisticated. This also makes for a somewhat steep learning curve. However, if you want your charts to have the "wow" factor, no other charting program comes close.

www.infommersion.com/products.html

5. Masterviews

This site is actually a blog. It offers a large collection of very specific and very practical PowerPoint tips. Comments from readers further enhance the value of the content. The site also offers news related to new PowerPoint add-ins and related hardware (like wireless pointers and mice).

www.masterviews.com.

6. Microsoft clip gallery live

This is Microsoft's clip art site. It is a good resource and it's free. However, some prefer JupiterImages.com. It's probably worth checking here first to see if you can find what you need. If you find that it just doesn't have enough horsepower, then you can join JupiterImages.com or some other subscription site.

http://office.microsoft.com/clipart/default .aspx?lc=en-us&cag=1

7. MindManager X5

This is one of the five most-used pieces of software on my computer. It will change forever the way you plan and prepare your presentations. It is essentially a brainstorming tool that allows you to create "mental maps" of your presentations. It will help you quickly get all your ideas out of your head and then organize them. This tool provides a much faster path to the final result. When you are done with your map, you can export it directly to PowerPoint. Best of all, MindJet, the software developer, offers a free thirty-day trial.

www.mindjet.com/us/

8. PowerPoint add-ins

This is a collection of mostly useful add-ins written by PowerPoint Guru, Shyam Pillai. Some favorites are the "Handout Wizard for PowerPoint," which allows you to create customized layouts; "Rename Shape/Slide Add-in," which enables you to rename slides and shapes by clicking on them; and "Toolbox for Power-Point," which provides a collection of Shyam's VBA code snippets for PowerPoint.

http://skp.mvps.org/download.htm

9. PowerPoint ImageObjects

This site offers a collection of what others call "floating objects." These are graphic objects with transparent backgrounds that appear to float on top of the slide. The site offers collections of symbols and shapes, metaphor objects, numbers, bullets, and other objects. These objects are very cool and very professional.

www.creativemindsinc.com/image_objects .htm

10. PowerPoint templates pro

This is yet another collection of professionally produced PowerPoint templates. You can purchase single templates or a collection of templates. The site's customers include an impressive roster of Fortune 100 companies. *www.powerpointtemplatespro.com.*

Source: Michael Hyatt's blog, Working Smart (*http://michaelhyatt. blogs.com*)—Hyatt is the president and chief executive officer of Thomas Nelson Publishers, the largest Christian publishing company in the world and the ninth largest publishing company of any kind. Contact him at *michael.hyatt@gmail.com.*

Popular Graphic Design Software Applications

Graphic Designers create visual communication by applying text and graphics together for print or electronic media. Designers achieve visual messages through logos, brochures, annual reports, posters, newsletters, web sites, signs, ads and more. The most important tool a graphic designer has within his or her toolbox is a computer and design software. Depending on what type of design or project a designer is creating will decide what applications are used. It is very common that designers use multiple design software applications to create a finished product. The following software applications are the most commonly found in the Graphic Design and Visual Communication field.

1. Adobe Software Family

Adobe Software Family has many different design software applications. Software applications range from image editing software, computer illustration, page layout, web graphics and Web site development. Adobe software family titles are: Photoshop, Illustrator, InDesign, Acrobat, GoLive, Livemotion, Dimensions, Framemaker, and Streamline. You can purchase the applications individually or design application bundles. To learn more about specific Adobe software titles go to *www.adobe.com.* The estimated price ranges from $100.00 to $2000.00. Adobe software is compatible with PC platform and Macintosh computers.

2. Corel Software Family

Corel Software Family is very similar to the Adobe software family. Software applications range from image editing software, computer illustration, page layout, web graphics and Web site development. Software titles are: CorelDraw, Painter, and PaintShop Pro. You can purchase the applications individually or design application bundles. To learn more about Corel Software titles go to *www.corel.com.* The estimated price ranges from $30.00 to $2000.00. Corel software is compatible with PC platform and Macintosh computers.

3. Macromedia

Macromedia is the creator of web site design software titled Dreamweaver. This design software allows graphic designers and web designers to design and edit HTML computer code. HTML stands for Hypertext Markup Language and is the computer language used to design web pages. To learn more about Macromedia Dreamweaver design software go to *www.macromedia.com.* The estimated price for this software ranges from $400.00 to $1500.00. Macromedia software is compatible with PC platform and Macintosh computers.

4. Quark Xpress

Quark Xpress is a desktop publishing design software application. Designers that use this type of design software create media output for magazines, newspapers and book publishers. Quark Xpress allows the designer to incorporate graphics with text to create an effective visual communication. To learn more about Quark Xpress go to *www.quark.com*. The estimated price for this software ranges from $700.00 to $800.00. Quark Xpress software is compatible with PC platform and Macintosh computers.

Source: Joe Stern (Stern Photography and Design) is a Graphic Designer: 304 Sterling Lake Drive, Ocoee, FL 34761

Popular Business-Planning Software

A well-conceived business plan can serve as a management tool to settle major policy issues, identify "keys to success," establish goals and checkpoints, and consider long-term prospects. While this may seem a daunting task to first-time entrepreneurs, many "veterans" have found that there are software packages that can help to organize and format the material required for a comprehensive plan. Here's a list of popular business planning software from our expert.

1. Business Plan Pro (BPP)

The sales leader in "plan-ware" is Palo Alto Software's Business Plan Pro. Business Plan Pro includes more than 500 sample business plans, built-in market research, two expert business books included, step-by-step financial guidance, legal tools and reference library, import from Excel collaboration features, cash pilot for "what-if" cash-flow scenarios.
www.paloalto.com

2. Business Resource Software's Plan Write

Business Resource Software's Plan Write includes features such as a library of sample business plans, Business Plan Wizard to guide you, complete financials and charts, and expert system support for your strategy. Step-by-step instructions, hundreds of examples to save time, automatic 3D color charts, complete financials, interface with QuickBooks from Intuit, format preferred by banks/investors/SBA, customized for your business, export to Word, Excel, PowerPoint, HTML, expert analysis plan review.
www.brs-inc.com

3. Planware's PlanWrite

Planware's software packages for business and financial planning and development are easy to download, install, and use. Business Plan Write's major strength is its simplicity. Business Plan Write presents a structured outline for the business plan with a concept explanation and checklist of details. The outline can be easily edited to tailor the business plan to special requirements.
www.planware.org

4. PlanMagic's Business

PlanMagic business plan, marketing plan, and financial plan software is used worldwide for start-up, growth, and expansion planning. Plan, analyze, and monitor any business anywhere, with ease.
www.planmagic.com

5. SmartOnline

Smart Business Plan is a powerful Web-based application where business plans can be downloaded for printing or conveniently published online so potential partners and investors can view the plan at any time from any Web-enabled computer.

www.smartonline.com

6. Fundable Plans

Fundable Plans is another online service. Using Acrobat (pdf), it provides a "clickable" outline for quick and easy navigation through your plan. Other features include a sample business plan, easy e-mail for instantaneous (and free) delivery, and the de facto standard for portable documents.

www.fundableplans.com

Source: Dr. John B. Vinturella, Vinturella and Associates, (*www.jbv.com*)—A management consulting firm specializing in entrepreneurs and small business. Dr. Vinturella, company principal, has almost forty years of experience as a management and strategic consultant and entrepreneur, and fifteen of those years as an academic Entrepreneur-in-Residence and adjunct professor. He can be reached at (504) 246-3999, and at *jbv@jbv.com*. His address is 11111 Winchester Park Drive, New Orleans, LA 70128.

Your Computers and Security

Top PC Manufacturers Worldwide

We thought about providing a list of the top selling computers, but this information changes weekly. Instead, we turned to one of our technology experts and asked him to give us his thoughts on the top computer manufacturers. Because what's really important is the company behind the product. Here's what he had to say.

1. Dell

Dell has clearly established itself as the major market force in the industry. Building its reputation for delivering quality made-to-order systems available only directly from the manufacturer, Dell commands a 16.4 percent worldwide market share and a whopping 30.3 percent U.S. market share. Their worldwide market share grew 23.1 percent in 2004, shipping almost 31 million units. When mainframe computers ruled, many IT professionals jokingly said that "no one ever lost their job by choosing IBM." They apply the same reasoning today to Dell—it's considered the "safe" choice.

2. Hewlett-Packard

Ranked at number 2 on both the worldwide and U.S. market share lists at 14.6 percent and 18.4 percent, respectively, Hewlett-Packard delivered approximately 27 million units in 2004. However, Hewlett-Packard's market share increased by 12.0 percent in 2004, a lower figure than any other manufacturer on the top five list. Time will tell, of course, but this may spell trouble for Hewlett-Packard as smaller companies like Acer gain momentum in the corporate world.

3. IBM

Virtually nonexistent in the consumer market, IBM has long supplied its corporate clients with PCs and mobile computers with a reputation for quality (although somewhat pricey) systems. With the sale of its Personal Computing Division (PCD) in 2004 to Lenovo, IBM exits this competitive market to focus on its server and consulting businesses. In 2004, IBM had a 5.5 percent worldwide market share and a 4.7 percent U.S. market share with an overall 16.3 percent growth, shipping 10.3 million units.

4. Fujitsu/Siemens

Almost unheard of in the U.S. market, Fujitsu/Siemens remains a key player in Europe and Asia, having been a major supplier of mainframes dating back to the earliest days of computing. Fujitsu's worldwide market share currently stands at 3.8 percent with a 13.7 percent growth from 2003. Most notably, they are not present on any U.S. lists, yet they have increased their market share in Europe, the Middle East, and Africa by a whopping 46.9 percent.

5. Acer

Making major inroads for the second consecutive year, Taiwan-headquartered Acer had a 3.4 percent market share in 2004 selling 6.4 million units but, more significantly, saw a 29.6 percent growth from last year, propelling it to the top five list and surpassing all other manufacturers in growth rate. Clearly a rising force in the PC market, Acer has been focusing its marketing efforts on the corporate customers, providing a wide range of servers and storage devices in addition to traditional PCs and mobile computers.

Source: Tom Greendyk—A principal of Tech Logic Associates LLC, an IT consulting services firm located in Wayne, Pennsylvania. Tech Logic Associates provides a broad range of computer support and networking services to small businesses in the greater Philadelphia area. Tech Logic Associate's Web site is *www.tech-logic.biz*; they can be reached by telephone at (610) 687-9197 or by fax at (610) 225-0440.

Top Laptop Manufacturers

More and more people are looking into buying a laptop either as a primary computer or for travel. The machines are so feature-rich these days that it's easy to find a laptop that's at least as powerful as most desktop machines. The world of computers changes quickly, so it's worth sticking with established brands that have a good track record like the companies listed below.

1. Dell

The old commercial says, "Dude, you're getting a Dell" and apparently a lot of laptop owners heeded the call. Dell *(www.dell.com)* laptops are inexpensive and generally reliable. As with all Dell computers, you can customize your new laptop, depending on your needs. They offer everything from high-end corporate laptops to ultra-lightweight notebooks.

2. Toshiba

Toshiba *(www.toshibadirect.com)* has a long history of designing laptops that are smaller, lighter, and thinner than the competition. Recent Toshiba laptops also include its EasyGuard technology to address the various security, reliability and connection issues of mobile users.

3. Sony

Although Sony *(www.sonystyle.com)* might be better known for TVs than laptops, the company has been making its Vaio laptops for quite some time. Many of them feature wide screens and high-end video components for multimedia users.

4. Lenovo

When IBM sold off its PC business, the company's ThinkPad laptops went too. Now ThinkPad notebooks are a product of Lenovo *(www. lenovo.com)*. ThinkPads were the first laptops to have the "eraser" pointing device and current ThinkPads still have them in addition to a touchpad. Recently, Lenovo started offering widescreen versions of ThinkPads as well.

5. Acer

Acer *(http://global.acer.com)* is one of the top five PC vendors in the world so it should come as no surprise that the company offers several lines of notebook computers. The company even offers a Ferrari laptop that was created in conjunction with the car company. Its red and black carbon fiber casing even features the Ferrari prancing horse logo.

6. Apple

It's no secret that Mac enthusiasts love their PowerBooks. And Apple *(www.apple.com)* must have some deal with Hollywood because almost every laptop you see in the movies or on TV has a little Apple logo on it. The laptops aren't just nice to look at. They also have been rated well for quality and Apple has received accolades for its after-sale technical support.

Source: Susan C. Daffron is the President of Logical Expressions, Inc., (*www.logicalexpressions.com*), a company that helps small businesses create, manage, and distribute content. Logical Expressions specializes in fusing high-quality unique content with search-engine and human-friendly Web sites. They offer writing, editing, programming, and design services and publish a free computer magazine called Computor Companion (*www.computorcompanion.com*). The magazine is targeted toward business owners/managers, computer professionals, and home PC computer users. It includes easy-to-understand articles designed to help readers use their computers more effectively to accomplish everyday tasks.

Top Questions To Ask Before Buying A Laptop Computer

Buying a laptop can be a frustrating business. Standards change, new technology gets introduced and, even for experienced buyers, we do it infrequently enough to forget everything we learned the last time we bought. We asked our expert, a technology specialist, to provide us a list of the top questions to ask before buying a laptop computer. He intentionally left any particularly specifications or numbers out, because they change constantly.

1. How much does it weigh?

You may not think weight is the most important issue on Day 1 of ownership, but on Day 243, after hauling that 8-pound brick around airports and parking lots, you'll understand its significance. For first time laptop buyers especially, you can't know how you'll use your new toy. Lighter is better and try before you buy.

2. What's the form factor?

Form factor goes along with weight. How big is the screen? If you're planning on collaborating with others (or watching a lot of DVDs in your hotel room), you'll want a bigger screen. Of course, a 17-inch laptop doesn't fit on an airplane seat-back tray very well.

3. Should I buy Windows or Apple?

The days of OS lock-in are largely over. I have an Apple laptop and a PC desktop and they rarely cause compatibility issues. I prefer the Apple PowerBooks because they're durable, sexy and commodified. By commodified, I mean that there's a limited number of choices to be made, so you don't waste your time considering a hundred permutations.

4. Is it wifi-enabled?

Increasingly, wireless internet cards come standard on laptops. Still, make sure yours has one and that it uses current technology. Even if you don't see yourself as a work-in-a-cafe kind of person, people change and wifi-cards are incredibly cheap. Also, if you need to connect to the Web using your mobile phone, ensure your laptop is Bluetooth-enabled.

5. How long does the battery last?

Battery life is influenced by many factors, but the longer the battery, the better. Consider buying an extra battery, particularly if you're going with a smaller, lightweight laptop with a small battery. Additionally, spend some time learning how to optimize your battery usage.

6. Which drives does it have?

DVD drives are now pretty much standard on all laptops, but make sure yours has one. As for a hard drive, bigger is always better. Hard drives also have a revolutions per minute rating (RPM). Faster is better here, and business users will notice the difference.

7. How much RAM does it have?

Buy as much RAM as you can reasonably afford. It's more important than processor speed, particularly if you like to have multiple applications open at the same time (and who doesn't?).

8. How many ports does it have?

By ports, I mean all those little slots and berths along the side and back of the computer. In particular, you want to count the USB ports. You might, for example, want to plug in a mouse, keyboard and external printer simultaneously, which would require three USB ports.

Source: Darren Barefoot is a technologist and writer from Vancouver, BC. His company, Capulet Communications (*www.capulet .com*) provides professional writing, marketing and public relations services designed specifically for high-tech companies. This list was compiled with the generous help of his readers at DarrenBarefoot.com

Popular Servers

A server is a computer that is connected to several less powerful computers and that can utilize the databases and applications that your business needs to operate efficiently. These are some of the most popular servers at the time of publication as provided by our friends at the National Federation Of Independent Business's *My Business* magazine. Of course, these units and prices are current at the time of printing and new models (and prices) will quickly take their place. However, if you stick with the model's product line you'll find that our expert's recommendations will continue to hold true.

1. Sun Microsystems Sunfire V20z

Perfect for: Expanding businesses that need practical flexibility
Cost: From $1,500
www.sun.com

2. IBM xSeries 206

Perfect for: Small business owners who don't know much about computers
Cost: From $500
www.ibm.com

3. Dell PowerEdge 400SC

Perfect for: First-time server buyers with simple IT needs
Cost: From $350
www.dell.com

4. Dell PowerEdge 2650

Perfect for: Businesses running out of room
Cost: From $1,600

www.dell.com

5. HP ProLiant ML 350G3

Perfect for: Growing businesses running sophisticated applications

Cost: From $2,340

www.hp.com

Source: *My Business* magazine, the member publication of the National Federation of Independent Business (NFIB) (*www.nfib .com*)—NFIB is the largest advocacy organization representing small and independent businesses in Washington, D.C., and all fifty state capitals. NFIB was ranked the most influential business organization (and third overall), in "Washington's Power 25" survey conducted by *Fortune* magazine. Contact them at 53 Century Blvd., Suite 250, Nashville, TN 37214; (800) NFIB-NOW or (615) 872-5800.

Issues to Consider Before Buying a Server

Ready to buy a new server for your network? Our experts know all about these things. They tell us that buying a server is not the same as buying any old PC. Here is a list of a few issues to consider before purchasing a server.

1. Case/rack

When looking at the case or rack, look at the expandability as well as the accessibility of hardware. Determine how may drive bays, if any, are available as far as what type of drive bays (5.25 inches vs. 3.5 inches) or available hard drive bays in the computer.

2. Drives

The server has a hard drive, CD-ROM, and provides backup; this is the most important consideration.

3. Memory

Memory is and has always been an important consideration when looking at purchasing a server or any computer. Determine the amount of memory included in the server as well as verify if that memory can be upgraded in the future. At least 512 megabytes of memory should be installed into the network or file server.

4. Network card

Network cards allow users to connect to other computers and have small networks in their home or office. This allows for data transfer, file sharing, Internet connection sharing, printer sharing and various other helpful uses.

5. Operating system

When setting up a new network, verify which operating system or networking software is included with the server. If no operating system is included with the computer, verify which operating systems—for example Novell, Windows NT, Windows 2000, Unix, Solaris, Linux, SCO—have been tested with the computer.

6. Power

For large networks or servers, power may be an important consideration. Look at the available amount of power supplies as well as the capacity of each of the power supplies. Additionally, if you believe power may be an issue in the future, look at the availability of upgrading or adding additional power supplies to the server.

7. Processor

The computer processor and the amount of processors the computer can support is one of the most important considerations when looking at a server. Consider the following: What type of processor is included (Intel Pentium, Intel Xeon, Digital, or other)? How many processors can the server support (2, 4, 8, or more)?

Source: Computer Hope (*www.computerhope.com*)—A collection of free services that allows any user to access its database of extensive free computer-related information. With these resources available, Computer Hope has become a popular destination for end users as well as computer support facilities for answering computer-related questions. Contact them at PO Box 1118, West Jordan UT 84084.

Top Reasons to Buy a Tablet PC Instead of a Laptop

Using a Tablet PC during a typical management meeting is totally different from using a laptop. According to our expert, a heavy technology user, it's the difference between night and day and the difference between success and failure. Wow. Here's a list explaining why.

1. Discretion

Nothing is more distracting during a management-style meeting than having a participant typing away on a laptop. In contrast, working with a Tablet PC in your lap appears no different from what you would be doing with a pen and notepad in your lap. This is particularly true if you use, as recommended later, an executive-style portfolio case that makes your Tablet PC resemble an executive notepad portfolio.

2. Communication barriers

Placing a laptop with the screen flipped up in front of you on a conference room table creates a physical barrier between you and others in the room. This is literally a barrier to communication. The Tablet PC is normally on your lap, and out of sight. Or it is flat on the desk like a writing pad.

3. Personal effectiveness

Research shows that if you use both hands to accomplish a task, a much larger percentage of your brain becomes engaged in that operation. Typing with both hands tends to totally engage your brain in the typing activity and makes you less visibly tuned in to the meeting. In contrast, writing with one hand during a meeting is second-nature to most of us. The brain stays mostly engaged in the meeting activities. We can take notes and participate in a meeting at the same time. Using a Tablet PC in a meeting is little different from this.

4. Eye contact

Related to number 3, and for the same reasons, many users have reported that it is much easier to maintain periodic and consistent eye contact with others in a meeting when using a Tablet PC versus using a laptop. This has a dramatic effect on the perception of others that you are engaged and personable. Lack of eye contact also limits your ability to read body language of others, adding to your distance from the meeting.

5. Taking notes in ink

It facilitates creativity in your note taking, communicates more about the meaning of your notes, integrates better with sketches and expressive marks on the note-taking page, is a better way to represent information copied from whiteboards and presentations, is a faster way to record notes, faster than even the most speedy and accurate handwriting recognition.

Source: Michael Hyatt's Working Smart blog (*http://michaelhyatt .blogs.com*)—He is president and chief executive officer of Thomas Nelson Publishers, the largest Christian publishing company in the world and the ninth largest publishing company of any kind. The company is publicly traded on the New York Stock Exchange. Contact him by e-mail at *michael.hyatt@gmail.com*.

Top Questions to Ask Before Buying a Tablet PC

A powerful hybrid of the notebook and PDA, tablets combine "pen-based" computing with large LCDs, and notebook-level processors. However, since tablets are still fairly new, it will be more important than ever to carefully consider your choices before you buy. Following are a list of some basic things to think about before you rush out and purchase that sparkling new, highly functional, and very cool tablet.

1. Cost

The bigger and brighter the LCD, the greater the processing power, memory, disk space, are, the more expensive the system.

2. Weight

If you need your tablet to be your primary computing platform, you'll probably end up carrying around a computer that is a few pounds heavier than if you have a desktop computer as well to act as your "primary" system. Make sure the system you buy is compatible with your ability/willingness to carry it!

3. Speed

Think about the combination of processor, memory, graphics, video, audio cards/memory, operating system—well, you get the picture; a lot of factors go into "speed."

4. Configuration

Sounds vague, but what is important here is how many drives and ports are "in the box" versus having to be changed in and out. In other words, do you have to change out a drive to go from floppy to CD? How many USB ports are available on the box itself?

5. Display

The display might be the single biggest issue with a tablet. How large a screen do you require to comfortably enter data and view documents? Do you work with graphics, so staring at a tiny screen with low resolution will make you go blind? Make sure your tablet's display meets your personal working requirements.

6. Battery life

Always a big issue, especially if you have a large display like the ones in almost all tablets. Make sure you can get enough life out of the system's battery to make it useful when you're on the road. And by the way, if the spec says two hours, plan on ninety minutes or less!

7. Hard drive

The bigger the better—especially if you are working with multimedia or other large file types.

8. Memory

More is better, but you knew that already.

9. Connectivity

For your printer, your network (wireless is big for travelers!), your external storage devices, keyboards, mice, camera, PDA, phone, and so on.

10. Drive options

CD, DVD, CD R/W, DVD R/W and their speeds.

11. Extras

What comes in the package—travel accessories, microphone, earphones, software, and much more.

12. Service and support

Always "big" with us—the warranty, service strategy, and contact capabilities.

13. Carrying and case

Finally, we highly recommend that you decide *how* you want to carry around your tablet? Backpack, case? Our recommendation is to use the smallest case you can that you can fit your travel *essentials* into. What do we mean? If your bag is too comfortably roomy, you'll soon find yourself filling it with papers and accessories you don't really need—and bearing the load along with it!

Source: Home Office Reports (*www.homeofficereports.com*)—They supply comprehensive information on a wide variety of technologies from PCs to networking, telephones and telephone services to digital cameras and accounting Contact them at 2102 Clematis Ct., McKinney, TX 75070; (972) 529-9719; fax: (972) 540-1674; e-mail: *dmielke@homeofficereports.com*.

Popular Tablet PCs

To organize a consumer friendly list of popular Tablet PCs, our expert felt compelled to categorize the various models into three groups. Just like making the right choice in an automobile purchase, you should consider the best class of Tablet PC models to suit your individual needs. The list of three categories and the descriptions provided should give you an idea of what type or class of Tablet PC will best suit your needs. Of course, these units are current at the time of printing and new models will quickly take their place. However, if you stick with the model's product line you'll find that our expert's recommendations will continue to hold true.

Category 1 (Slates)

The slate-design Tablet PC has the full power of a thin, light notebook computer sans the keyboard. With a very thin profile and unique form factor, the slate Tablet PC is especially easy to carry. The slate never ceases to impress as a substitute for pen and paper at a board meeting or the local Starbucks.

1. Fujitsu Stylistic ST5000 series

The Fujitsu ST5000 Tablet PC has long battery life and exceptional security features. An indoor/outdoor screen option is available for custom orders. The built-in "Trusted Platform Module" and biometric scanner ensure security for the traveling professional.

www.fujitsu.com

2. Electrovaya Scribbler SC3000 series

The Electrovaya SC3000 Tablet PC offers a wide viewing-angle display. This series also features the best in advanced biometric security and an innovative "keyboard" that snaps on the display as a protective cover.

www.electrovaya.com

3. Motion LE1600 from Motion Computing

Motion Computing is an industry recognized name in the manufacturing of outstanding Tablet PCs. The award-winning LE1600 has received high praise from a variety of reviewers.

www.motioncomputing.com

4. The HP TC1100 (Hewlett-Packard)

The TC1100 Tablet PC from HP is one of the smallest and lightest slates on the market. This model can fit in most any briefcase or bag and won't weigh you down. A small keyboard that attaches to the unit is included.

www.hp.com

Category 2 (Thin and Light Convertibles)

A "convertible" Tablet PC offers the best of standard notebook and Tablet PC features combined. This design is perfect for the notebook user who also needs Tablet PC functionality. Listed here are the best convertibles in the "thin and light" class, offering a good balance of portability and power.

1. IBM/Lenovo ThinkPad X41 Tablet PC

Weighing in at less than three pounds, the ThinkPad X41 Tablet PC exudes the essence of portability. This tablet will please business users who are already familiar with the ThinkPad features and quality that has made IBM/Lenovo a first choice for the mobile professional.

www.lenovo.com

2. HP TC4200 Tablet PC

The HP TC4200 is one of the sturdiest, well-built Tablet PCs on the market. In addition to its powerful processor and fast hard drive, the TC4200 looks sharp and professional for the user who wants to "dress to impress."

www.hp.com

3. Fujitsu Lifebook T4000 series Tablet PC

The T4000 convertible Tablet PC from Fujitsu may be configured to order. Consumers may choose the advanced Atheros or common Intel Centrino wireless from Intel. Fujitsu's exceptional support ensures trouble-free operation for the end-user.

www.fujitsu.com

4. The Toshiba Portégé M400 Tablet PC

The Toshiba M400 stands out since it is the first Tablet PC to feature Intel's new "Core Duo" technology. Although there is a "core solo" configuration available, the dual-core model is an absolute powerhouse in a small package. This model is a perfect fit for the user who wants

to travel light, but needs the extra performance and speed that a multi-core processor delivers.
www.toshiba.com

Category 3 (Desktop Replacement Convertibles)

Tablet PC models in this category are perfect for users seeking a Tablet PC to be their "only" computer. These models typically offer larger displays, powerful dedicated graphics, and larger hard drives. Desktop replacement models are heavier and have shorter battery life, so there are compromises to be made when choosing a model in this category.

1. Toshiba Tecra M4 Tablet PC

The Toshiba M4 is the only Tablet PC to date that offers a 14.1 inch high-resolution display. The M4 may be custom-ordered with the features needed. This machine is literally a portable powerhouse that can handle just about any demanding computing task with ease.
www.toshiba.com

2. Acer TravelMate C314 Tablet PC

The Acer C314 features a large 14.1 inch display and a unique ergonomic keyboard design. The sturdy build and hefty power make this model a good bet for the student or professional who needs to take their Tablet PC out on the road.
www.acer.com

Source: Barry Doyle is the editor-in-chief of TabletPCReviewSpot.com. TabletPCReviewSpot.com features unbiased reviews of Tablet PC hardware, software, and more. Engage in discussion and share tips with a friendly community in the forums. Original content is updated regularly to keep up with news, hardware, and relevant Tablet PC–related updates.

Reasons to Own an Apple

Some business owners are diehard Apple users, and others swear by Windows-based computers. Which system is right for you? In order to settle the debate of whether you are a good candidate to purchase an Apple platform, consider this list when making your purchase.

1. Considered more secure

A nice thing about Apple platforms is that since most viruses are written for PCs, the Macs don't pick up viruses like PCs do.

2. Have lots of freeware

Compared to the typical PC that you have to purchase additional software for both home and office to run, the Apples are equipped and ready to run with free software.

3. Seem to crash less

Apple computers spend a lot less time being repaired compared to PCS. In fact, Apple made number one on the most reliable desktop list. Written with UNIX, the Apple rarely crashes like PCs. Unlike PCs where the people designing the hard drive aren't the same people designing the software, Apple does all the work—and it is evident in the stability of the system.

4. Will work with PCs

Although many argue that the Apple isn't compatible with PCs, many offices are now networked with both types.

5. Better built for the Internet

Mac advertises that Apples are the easiest way to get on the Internet. Since each Mac comes with a built-in modem and Internet Explorer, and Ethernet, you can hook right up to DSL or cable broadband in no time.

6. Have great office applications

Mac's version of Office actually runs better than Microsoft's version of the program. In addition, you can share files between the two platforms because Mac software is written for both systems.

7. Better suited for videos

Mac computers are known for their built-in tools that allow you to create your own movies; with iMovie and FireWire, importing video from a digital recorder is fast and easy. You can edit your input by adding titles, transitions, and special effects.

8. Easily create your own DVDs

Using iDVD, you can create masterpieces by dragging your movies and digital photos into the program, click the burn button, and you're done.

9. Used by more creative types

Apples are best for creative projects such as video, audio, and photos. And with the built in freeware, it is easy to create all this without purchasing additional software.

10. Are popular for consumers

Because of their ease of use and freeware, Apples are perfect for the first-time buyer or for someone who knows little about computers.

Source: Eric Good, manager of the video division at Sunrise Electronics & Computers (*www.digitalsunrise.com*), 1048 Lincoln Way East, Chambersburg, PA 17201. You can reach Eric at *egood@digitalsunrise.com* or at (717) 267-1340.

Things You'll Need to Access Your Computer Remotely

Nowadays, being out of the office doesn't mean you can't be in touch. There's been a proliferation of easy to use tools that can help you access your computer through the internet. This way you can get your email, revise documents, update spreadsheets all through the web without bringing anything with you. To access your computer remotely though, you'll need to take certain things into consideration. Our technology expert here gives us his list of things to keep in mind.

1. Security

If your machine is the only device connected to the network (i.e., a dial-up connection or a PC directly connected to a cable modem or DSL modem), then a PC-based firewall and remote access solution will be sufficient. If there are other devices connected to the network, a security solution at the point of access (e.g., a router or VPN switch) will help to protect the other devices from being hacked. What type of data am I keeping on this machine? Is it confidential to myself, my company, or my clients? Is it something that I would want to see in the morning paper? Maintaining a secure wall around this data will protect you from identity theft, which is a major problem for Internet users today.

2. Connectivity

The type of connectivity required to your machine should be driven by the type of access that is required. If you are accessing small text files on an infrequent basis, a dial-up solution could be sufficient for your needs. If you need to upload and/or download large files, such as presentations, video, or graphic files, or accessing large databases for searches or updates, a broadband solution is going to provide a much more usable solution.

3. Type of access required

One of the major considerations in setting up a remote connectivity solution is to determine the type of access that you require. A user that requires access only to files stored on the PC will need a different solution than the user who wants to be able to remotely control the machine, which allows you to work on that machine as if you were sitting in front of it. Access to only data files stored on the machine can be handled quite easily through most of the newer versions of Microsoft Windows, such as Windows 2000 and Windows XP.

4. Access software

Once you have determined your security solution and your connectivity, you are ready to look at the actual access software for your PC. Again, there are several things to keep in mind while going through this process: Security—does the program have additional security measures that force me to log in, or does it just grant direct access? Can I see what is happening on my machine when it is being controlled, and can I cancel that remote access from my machine if someone who was not authorized to access my PC were to gain control? Usability—can I utilize all of the features of my PC while controlling it remotely, or is there some functionality that doesn't work? Is there a chat feature to allow me to send text messages to someone who may be sitting in front of my PC while I am controlling it? Does the display show in true colors or am I limited to the number of colors available in the remote control?

Source: Andrew Armstrong, independent consultant with ten years' industry experience, in desktop, server, and remote connectivity solutions. Phone him at (907) 301-8491 or e-mail *armstran@hotmail .com*.

Top Ways to Protect Your Computer from Hackers

For sure, the internet is a great thing and your employees are using it every day to help them do their jobs. But you've also opened up your computer network to potential harm from malicious hackers. Our expert, an online security consultant, has provided us with this list that of suggestions that each of your employees should follow to minimize this risk.

1. Protect your personal information

If you're asked for your personal information—your name, e-mail or home address, phone number, account numbers, or social security number—find out how it's going to be used and how it will be protected before you share it. If you get an e-mail or pop-up message asking for personal information, don't reply or click on the link in the message. The safest course of action is not to respond to requests for your personal or financial information. If you believe there may be a need for such information by a company with whom you have an account or have placed an order, contact that company directly in a way you know to be genuine. In any case, don't send your personal information via e-mail because e-mail is not a secure transmission method.

2. Know with whom you're dealing

It's remarkably simple for online scammers to impersonate a legitimate business, so you need to know with whom you're dealing. If you're shopping online, check out the seller before you buy. A legitimate business or individual seller should give you a physical address and a working telephone number at which they can be contacted in case you have problems.

3. Know about phishing

Phishers send spam or pop-up messages claiming to be from a business or organization that you might deal with—for example, an Internet service provider (ISP), bank, online payment service, or even a government agency. The message usually says that you need to "update" or "validate" your account information. It might threaten some dire consequence if you don't respond. The message directs you to a Web site that looks just like a legitimate organization's but isn't. The purpose of the bogus site is to trick you into divulging your personal information so the operators can steal your identity and run up bills or commit crimes in your name. Don't take the bait: Never reply

to or click on links in email or pop-ups that ask for personal information.

4. Be careful when file-sharing

File-sharing can give people access to a wealth of information, including music, games, and software. But file-sharing can have a number of risks. If you don't check the proper settings, you could allow access not just to the files you intend to share but also to other information on your hard drive, such as your tax returns, e-mail messages, medical records, photos, or other personal documents. Take the time to read the End User Licensing Agreement to be sure you understand and are willing to tolerate the side effects of any free downloads.

5. Be careful of free downloads

To avoid spyware, resist the urge to install any software unless you know exactly what it is. Your antivirus software may include antispyware capability that you can activate, but if it doesn't, you can install separate antispyware software, and then use it regularly to scan for and delete any spyware programs that may sneak onto your computer.

6. Be careful when opening e-mail attachments and links

Don't open an e-mail or attachment—even if it appears to be from a friend or coworker—unless you are expecting it or know what it contains. You can help others trust your attachments by including a text message explaining what you're attaching.

7. Use antivirus software and a firewall, and update both regularly

Antivirus software protects your computer from viruses that can destroy your data, slow your computer's performance, cause a crash, or even allow spammers to send e-mail through your account. It works by scanning your computer and your incoming e-mail for viruses, and then deleting them. To be effective, your antivirus software should update routinely with antidotes to the latest "bugs" circulating through the Internet. Most commercial antivirus software includes a feature to download updates automatically when you are on the Internet.

8. Know what a firewall does and why you need it

Firewalls help keep hackers from using your computer to send out your personal information without your permission. While antivirus software scans incoming e-mail and files, a firewall is like a guard, watching for outside attempts to access your system and blocking communications to and from sources you don't permit. If your operating system doesn't include a firewall, get a separate software firewall that runs in the background while you work, or install a hardware firewall—an external device that includes firewall software.

9. Be careful of Zombie Drones

Some spammers search the Internet for unprotected computers they can control and use anonymously to send unwanted spam e-mails. If you don't have up-to-date antivirus protection and a firewall, spammers may try to install software that lets them route e-mail through your computer, often to thousands of recipients, so that it appears to have come from your account. If this happens, you may receive an overwhelming number of complaints from recipients, and your e-mail account could be shut down by your Internet Service Provider (ISP).

10. Be sure to set up your operating system and Web browser software properly, and update them regularly

Hackers also take advantage of Web browsers (like Internet Explorer or Netscape) and operating system software (like Windows or Linux) that are unsecured. Lessen your risk by changing the settings in your browser or operating system and increasing your online security. Updating can be as simple as one click. If you're not using your computer for an extended period, turn it off or unplug it from the phone or cable line. When it's off, the computer doesn't send or receive information from the Internet and isn't vulnerable to hackers.

11. Protect your passwords

Keep your passwords in a secure place, and out of plain view. Don't share your passwords on the Internet, over e-mail, or on the phone. Use passwords that have at least eight characters and include numbers or symbols. Avoid common words; some hackers use programs that can try every word in the dictionary. Do not use your personal information, your login name, or adjacent keys on the keyboard as passwords. Change your passwords regularly (at a minimum, every 90 days). Do not use the same password for each online account you access.

12. Back up important files

If you follow these tips, you're more likely to be more secure online, free of interference from hackers, viruses, and spammers. But no system is completely secure. If you have important files stored on your computer, copy them onto a removable disc, and store them in a safe place.

13. Learn whom to contact if something goes wrong online

If your computer gets hacked or infected by a virus: Immediately unplug the phone or cable line from your machine. Then scan your entire computer with fully updated antivirus software, and update your firewall. Take steps to minimize the chances of another incident. Alert the appropriate authorities by contacting your ISP and the hacker's ISP (if you can tell what it is).

14. Be aware of Internet fraud

If a scammer takes advantage of you through an Internet auction, when you're shopping online, or in any other way, report it to the Federal Trade Commission, at ftc.gov. The FTC enters Internet, identity theft, and other fraud-related complaints into Consumer Sentinel, a secure, online database available to hundreds of civil and criminal law enforcement agencies in the United States and abroad.

15. Be careful of deceptive spam

If you get deceptive spam, including email phishing for your information, forward it to *spam@uce.gov*. Be sure to include the full header of the e-mail, including all routing information. You also may report phishing e-mail to *reportphishing@antiphishing.org*. The Anti-Phishing Working Group, a consortium of ISPs, security vendors, financial institutions, and law enforcement agencies, uses these reports to fight phishing.

16. Know what to do if you mistakenly give your personal information

If you believe you have mistakenly given your personal information to a fraudster, file a complaint at ftc.gov, and then visit the Federal Trade Commission's Identity Theft Web site at *www.consumer.gov/idtheft* to learn how to minimize your risk of damage from a potential theft of your identity.

Source: OnGuardOnline (*http://onguardonline.gov/*)—Provides practical tips from the federal government and the technology industry to help you be on guard against Internet fraud, secure your computer, and protect your personal information.

Issues to Consider Before Purchasing a Firewall

Do you worry that your DSL, cable modem, or T1 connection to the Internet makes your computer network vulnerable to attack? If not, you should! The bad guys have become increasingly sophisticated about hacking into underprotected computer networks. Small and medium-size businesses (SMB) are particularly vulnerable because they are less likely to have the focus on security that larger and public companies have as a result of federal legislation Buying a firewall is one very important component of your security program. Here is a list of issues to consider before making your purchase.

1. What are the threats?

Simply stated, you are trying to protect against unauthorized or unintended access to systems or information, unauthorized disclosure of information, and denial of service (overwhelming systems with attacks to prevent authorized users from gaining access). Hackers have automated programs that can launch thousands of attacks per hour. Every system attached to the Internet is at risk.

2. What am I protecting?

Do you have just a few PCs, or do you have hundreds of devices on your network? Do you have one server or many? Are your Web site and/or e-mail systems inside your network or hosted outside? Do you have many applications running or just a few? Do you have one department or several departments whose data needs to be kept separate? Do you have people using laptops, remote users, or wireless access? Today's firewalls have features that can help protect your information in all of these scenarios.

3. Firewall certifications

Security product vendors have the option to submit their products to independent government-certified laboratories and/or commercial security certification bodies (such as ICSA or Checkmark) for certification. Buying a product that has passed evaluation and certification provides a higher level of confidence that the product will perform as specified.

4. Software versus hardware firewalls

Firewalls can be separate hardware devices (hardware firewalls) or can be software installed on a server (software firewalls). Hardware firewalls are typically preferred in a network environment because they are higher-quality, hardened devices that are very difficult to modify by hackers and are optimized to provide the best performance for traffic moving through them. Servers running software firewalls are vulnerable to the same attacks as your other servers and to performance limitations. Software firewall can also be used on workstations to protect each individual machine against attacks and against propagating viruses if they get infected.

5. Packet filtering and intrusion detection and prevention

Packets are units of information that travel across the Internet. Firewalls use a technique called "packet filtering" to examine network traffic. With packet filtering, network traffic source and destination addresses can be determined as well as whether the packet originated on the Internet or was a response to a request made by a PC inside your network (AKA stateful packet inspection or SPI). At minimum, your firewall should support SPI. Deep packet inspection (DPI) looks deeper into the packet and defends against attacks targeting applications and network protocols. DPI firewalls are a must for protecting financial or otherwise sensitive information.

6. Antivirus/antispam

The newest generation of firewalls can include features that generally had been performed by devices or software outside the firewall. This expansion of capabilities is known as unified threat management (UTM) and comes in many different forms. One form is the inclusion of antivirus and antispam features in one or two flavors: with gateway antivirus, the firewall can scan incoming traffic for viruses and spam and prevent it from entering your network; and with network antivirus, the firewall can also check your servers and workstations when they try to access the Internet, and prevent access unless virus protection software is in place (which the firewall then provides to the PC or server).

7. Content filtering

Another unified threat management feature is content filtering. Content filtering is used to monitor all Web sites viewed by your users, and if anything objectionable is requested, it is blocked with a message stating that the content violates company policy. This feature is helpful if you are worried about team members viewing unauthorized Web sites. It may also limit downstream liability in cases of sexual harassment because you have taken a concrete step toward preventing objectionable material from being downloaded.

8. Virtual private networks (VPNs)

VPNs are used to provide a secure, encrypted channel across the Internet. For example, if you have two offices, you can connect them with a VPN and allow traffic to pass securely, even though it is on the Internet. Many telecommuters use VPNs to securely access the resources in the office from home or from the road. If either of these situations applies to you, then look for a VPN feature on your firewall.

9. Logging, alerting, and reporting

In addition to the features used to configure your firewall, there should be management features for logging and viewing logged threats; alerting you, your system administrator, or IT consultant that attacks have occurred; and for reporting that shows how your Internet connection has been used, varying from a list of Web sites visited to which users are using most bandwidth.

10. Wireless features

If you desire a wireless network, many vendors provide wireless versions of their firewalls, so you don't have to buy a separate device to add wireless features to your wired network. Wireless features include the ability to support a VPN between the PC and the firewall, so that all wireless traffic is secure. The VPN would typically require you to enter a VPN username and password to gain access to the network. This is the most secure approach.

11. Other features

Redundancy is the ability to have your firewall on two different Internet connections so that if one connection fails the other takes over. You can use two DSL connections, or some firewalls let you connect to one DSL and one dial-up connection if that is fast enough during a DSL failure. Adaptability is the ability to upload new firmware (the software that runs on a firewall) and to apply patches that mitigate new threats.

12. Installation and support

Having a professional install and configure your firewall will provide greater assurance that its full capabilities are being used, and that it is configured correctly. Excellent manufacturer support is also critical as threats are discovered or problems found that impair your firewall's ability to operate.

Source: David Oderberg, managing partner, TerraSage Technology Partners, LLC (*www.terrasage.com*)—TerraSage Technology Partners, LLC is, an IT Consultancy that advises business owners on technology issues; designs, builds, and supports computer networks; and builds effective Web presences. Mr. Oderberg can be reached at *doderberg@terrasage.com* or at (310) 439-2600.

Effective Firewall Software

The central piece of Internet security software is a firewall to protect your computer from intrusion threats—programs looking to steal data from your computer, possibly even hijacking your identity. Although you can get separate firewall and antivirus software, combining them in a suite, along with additional security features, can save you some money and ensure that your software works together to thwart threats. Here is a list of some of the best firewalls. This information was current at the time of printing, but please make sure you double-check with the vendors for any changes.

1. Trend Micro PC-cillin

Security suite. Trend Micro PC-cillin receives high scores in reviews for its excellent antivirus protection, and while most experts agree its firewall is also good, it takes some knocks in reviews, where it misses a few threats. Experts say ZoneAlarm's firewall is better. Trend Micro includes a spam filter, parental controls, and a spyware scanner, but reviews say these components can't match standalone software. PC-cillin is less expensive than other security suites, and reviews say it does have great antivirus protection. It also does not cause as much system drag as Norton Internet Security.
www.trendmicro.com/en/

2. ZoneAlarm

Free firewall. The basic version of Zone-Alarm's firewall is a free download. The free version doesn't block pop-ups, scan e-mail, or protect against phishing scams, but if you already have other security software, this may be all you need. The free ZoneAlarm takes more manual configuration than ZoneAlarm Pro, but reviews say it provides an excellent defense against intrusion from potential hackers.
www.zonelabs.com

3. Agnitum Outpost Firewall Pro Firewall

Outpost Pro is better known in Europe than in the United States, but several reviews here recommend it. Outpost Pro passes all tests with flying colors and is easy to set up. Running more in the background than ZoneAlarm's firewall, Outpost Pro's multiple configurations can be customized for the same computer. Outpost offers some spyware protection, and includes plug-ins that filter content—so Flash banners are blocked, for example. Although ZoneAlarm is still recommended the most, the up-and-coming Outpost is a unique alternative.
www.agnitum.com

4. Norton Internet Security 2005 Security suite

Although Norton's suite is still the most widely sold package, it gets poor reports from users and professional reviewers alike. Reviews say the Norton suite seems to be slowly losing even longtime fans because of its heavy use of system resources, which slow down computing performance. *PC Magazine*'s latest evaluation notes that the slowdown is often so annoying that users disable Norton entirely. Both ZoneAlarm and Trend security create less system drag, and are better choices. Price: $65 (estimate).

www.symantec.com

Source: ConsumerSearch (*www.consumersearch.com*)—A Web site that ranks, describes, and analyzes top reviews of consumer products, along with lists of top-rated products. Contact Derek Drew, CEO and editor-in-chief, 5467 31st Street NW, Washington, DC 20015; (202) 966-7907; e-mail: *derekdrew@consumersearch.com*.

Effective Antispy Software

This software helps users combat an ever-growing number of programs designed to gather system information from the infected computer and send it back to advertisers—or worse—keyloggers looking to steal passwords and other sensitive data. The following lists some of the best antispy software on the market. This information was current at the time of printing, but please make sure you double-check with the vendors for any changes.

1. Webroot Software Spy Sweeper

In reviews, Spy Sweeper gets better detection and spyware removal rates than other anti-spyware software; in some tests, it finds, eliminates, and blocks almost 100 percent of threats. Other reviews report a success rate of between 80–95 percent, adding that no anti-spyware can detect every threat. The user interface is clear and concise, and Spy Sweeper includes real-time scanning.

www.webroot.com

2. PC Tools Spyware Doctor

In the very latest testing, Spy Sweeper is slightly better at removing spyware from your system. But in many reviews, Spyware Doctor finishes almost dead even with Spy Sweeper. Reviews say Spyware Doctor is a sophisticated spyware removal tool with an excellent user interface.

www.pctools.com

3. Lavasoft Ad-Aware SE Personal

Free anti-spyware software isn't as robust or effective as Spy Sweeper. But free software is a good backup, since reviews say no single spyware removal tool can catch all threats. The well-respected Ad-Aware SE Personal beats the competing Spybot Search & Destroy in tests. Ad-Aware Personal doesn't offer real-time protection or scheduled system scans, but it makes an excellent supplement to your primary anti-spyware software program.

www.lavasoft.com

4. Microsoft Windows Defender beta 2

Formally called Microsoft Anit-Spyware, Windows Defender is still in testing phases, though it is available to anyone for free. Although reviews say it isn't yet perfect, Windows Defender does have real-time scanning (Ad-Aware SE Personal does not). The user interface is excellent and easy to use. Although reviews say Windows Defender missed some spyware in tests, it's a good free product to use in conjunction with Ad-Aware SE Personal, Spy Sweeper or Spyware Doctor.

www.microsoft.com

5. CWShredder

If you are plagued by a persistent spyware toolbar called CoolWebSearch, you need CWShredder. This free download doesn't do anything else. It has a singular purpose—to adapt to and exterminate the ever-mutating CoolWebSearch, which hijacks your Web browser and leads you to its advertisers' sites. Experts say no other spyware remover is as effective at removing CoolWebSearch.

www.cwshredder.net

Source: ConsumerSearch (*www.consumersearch.com*)—A Web site that ranks, describes, and analyzes top reviews of consumer products, along with lists of top-rated products. Contact Derek Drew, CEO and editor-in-chief, 5467 31st Street NW, Washington, DC 20015; (202) 966-7907; e-mail: *derekdrew@consumersearch.com*.

Popular Antivirus Software

The following is a list of the most popular antivirus software and some thoughts from our experts, specialists at home office technology. This information was current at the time of printing, but please make sure you double-check with the vendors for any changes.

1. BitDefender

BitDefender's antivirus products are straightforward to install and set up for use. Solid features and functions, competitive pricing, and a good technical support strategy means they should definitely be on your purchasing short list.

2. Boomerang

Good software at a competitive price. Our biggest concern regarding a Boomerang purchase continues to be the "lite" technical and customer support capabilities the company offers.

3. Broderbund

Broderbund's ZoneAlarm applications are easy to install and implement. We like the software but hate the support strategy. Especially when it comes to security software, which affects the very basics of your system—its ability to function on a network—we believe that technical support needs to be more than an e-mail! However, with that said, we also reiterate that if you are a confident techie, what the heck, you'll figure it out anyway, and probably enjoy doing it.

4. Bullguard

Not only do you get a well-thought-through antivirus and firewall software package with everything you'll need to protect your system from intruders, you also get 100 MB of storage on Bullguard servers to back up critical data/files that can be expanded to 5 GB to back up your entire system. Bullguard has also done a good job with their support strategy with lots of online information and twenty-four-hour live chat to handle their business outside Europe.

5. CA

eTrust EZ Anti-virus and eTrust Security Suite are simple to install and set up for use. Solid anti-virus software with real-time scanning, automatic updates, e-mail scanning and neuristic scanning. The eTrust Security Suite rolls four CA software packages into one for a lower cost–anti-virus, firewall, anti-spyware and anti-spam system.

6. Intego

Offers standard virus protection for the Macintosh environment. Intego makes good software for the Macintosh environment.

7. Kaspersky

Kaspersky's Anti-Virus, Personal Security Suite and Security for PDAs are both simple to install and set up for use on your system or PDA. Solid Anti-rivus software backed by a good tech support strategy. Well worth your consideration.

8. McAfee

This software is considered one of the industry "benchmarks" for functionality and reliability. We also like McAfee's robust support strategy and organization. You probably can't go wrong with a McAfee purchase.

9. Norman

Norman's Virus Control is simple to install on your system. Virus Control includes Norman's Sand Box technology that can detect viruses that are "unknown" through creation of an emulator where possible viruses "run" as they would in a real system. When execution stops the Sand Box is analyzed for changes. The software is "tuned" to look for new e-mail, network, or peer-to-peer worms. strong antivirus technology at a competitive price.

10. Novatix

Its best asset is the ability to view "quarantined" files to ensure their safety before launching them on your system—and infecting it. Useful software at a competitive price.

Source: Home Office Reports (*www.homeofficereports.com*)—They supply comprehensive information on a wide variety of technologies from PCs to networking, telephones and telephone services to digital cameras and accounting Contact them at 2102 Clematis Ct., McKinney, TX 75070; (972) 529-9719; fax: (972) 540-1674; email: *dmielke@homeofficereports.com*.

Typical Ways to Avoid Spamming

Spam always finds a way to get into your computer, even with the help of cleaning programs. Here are some ways to avoid spam, from an expert who creates technologies that protect computer users from ever-increasing cyber threats.

1. Maintain at least two e-mail addresses

You should use your private address only for personal correspondence. The public address should be the one you use to register on public forums, in chat rooms, and to subscribe to mailing lists.

2. Don't publish your address

Never publish your private address on publicly accessible resources.

3. Your private address should be difficult to spoof

Spammers use combinations of obvious names, words, and numbers to build possible addresses. Your private address should not simply be your first and last name. Be creative and personalize your e-mail address.

4. Mask your private address

If you have to publish your private address electronically, mask it to avoid having it harvested by spammers. *Joe.Smith@yahoo.com* is easy to harvest, as is Joe.Smith at yahoo.com. Try writing Joe-dot-Smith-at-yahoo-dot-com instead. If you need to publish your private address on a Web site, do this as a graphics file rather than as a link.

5. Treat your public address as a temporary one

Chances are high that spammers will harvest your public address fairly quickly. Don't be afraid to change it often.

6. Use public addresses

Always use your public address to register in forums, chat rooms, and to subscribe to mailing lists and promotions. You might even consider using a number of public addresses in order to trace which services are selling addresses to spammers.

7. Never respond to spam

Most spammers verify receipt and log responses. The more you respond, the more spam you will receive.

8. Do not click on unsubscribe links from questionable sources

Spammers send fake unsubscribe letters in an attempt to collect active addresses. You certainly don't want to have your address tagged as active, do you? It will just increase the amount of spam you receive.

9. Change your address

If your private address is discovered by spammers—change it. This can be inconvenient, but changing your e-mail address does help you avoid spam—at least for a while!

10. Make sure that your mail is filtered by an antispam solution

Consider installing a personal antispam solution. Only open e-mail accounts with providers who offer spam filtration prior to mail delivery.

Source: Kaspersky Labs, Inc. (*www.kaspersky.com*)—Founded in 1997, Kaspersky Labs rapidly became a world leader in information security software including expertise to provide cutting-edge protection against all major cyber threats: viruses, hackers, and spam. The company has eight regional offices and partners in more than fifty countries creating a global network. Contact them at 300 Unicorn Park, Woburn, MA 01801; (781) 503-1800; fax: (781) 503-1818; or e-mail: *info@us.kaspersky.com*.

Most Popular Antispam Software/Filter

E-mail spam has become a large productivity drain on businesses worldwide. Our expert knows all about spam. She's a hacker herself. Here is her list of the most popular antispam software/filters around.

1. Thunderbird

If your company is small and struggling with cash flow, and your e-mail address is new, free can be beautiful. Thunderbird, the free e-mail client from http://mozilla.org, lets you tag incoming e-mails as spam. It uses these to "learn" what is spam and what isn't, and saves them to a junk file. You can check that file to see if important correspondence was accidentally diverted into it. However, you want to be sure to back up your spam detection files. If the flood of spam is several hundred per day, this technique can take months and require that you manually tag tens of thousands of e-mails before you can make headway.

2. Eudora

If you have had an e-mail address for ten years or so, you might be getting over a thousand junk messages every day. If your company only has one or two of these magnet addresses, and a broadband connection, Eudora might be an ideal solution. The paid version has a filter that automatically recognizes spam and filters it on the desktop. You can set it to whatever level you find does the best job. As with Thunderbird, all spam goes into a junk folder, so you can make sure the junk threshold is right.

3. Fastwires

If broadband or even just dial-up is enough bandwidth for you, Fastwires, *www.fastwires .net*, blocks spam automatically, for all customers, without accidentally blocking good e-mail. The way their antispam technician does it is to set up honeypot e-mail addresses—for example, by listing them on Web sites where spam harvest engines pick them up. Then every day he uses sophisticated hacker tools to tell where spam is really originating (the return address always lies). Then he blocks those addresses so they never reach your computer. Unless you expect to get e-mail direct from the computer of some notorious spammer, this should never cost you a vital message. Tech support is great, via both e-mail and phone. This may be the best solution for the mom-and-pop business under siege.

4. Mail-Filters

If you have too many e-mail addresses getting too much spam, you pay a fortune for the bandwidth that incoming junk hogs. Mail-Filters. com, Inc., *http://mail-filters.com*, offers several solutions. A company that has just one Internet gateway and that uses a DNS server outside its network can arrange for its MX records to point company e-mail to one of the Mail-Filters servers. They filter out spam and just send you the good stuff. If you want to check to make certain they aren't throwing away vital correspondence, they can oblige you any time. If you have a larger company, it may work best to install Mail-Filters.com server software on your network and have your IT staff manage the spam washing. Users say the tech support is great, by both e-mail and phone.

Source: Carolyn Meinel, computer technology consultant, author of *The Happy Hacker, a Guide to Mostly Harmless Computer Hacking* (American Eagle Publications, 1998, 1999, 2002) and other articles. Carolyn is also a computer security volunteer at AllExperts (*www.allexperts.com*).

7

Your Customers and Prospects

Customer Service Topics

Popular CRM Vendors for Enterprises

CRM (customer relationship management) software is instrumental in helping you retain your customers and grow your company. The following is a list of popular vendors who specialize in managing relationships with your customers, in alphabetical order. These vendors primarily focus on larger companies with more than 50 to 100 users.

1. Amdocs Limited—Amdocs Clarify CRM
75 Federal Street, Suite 300
Boston, MA 02110
(617) 526-1227
www.amdocs.com

2. Clear Technologies, Inc.—C2 CRM
1199 South Beltline Road, Suite 120
Coppell, TX 75019
(972) 906-7500
www.cleartechnologies.net

3. Epiphany, Inc.—Epiphany E6
475 Concar Drive
San Mateo, CA 94402
(650) 578-7200
www.epiphany.com

4. Firstwave Technologies, Inc.—Firstwave CRM 2004
Overlook III, Suite 1000
2859 Paces Ferry Road
Atlanta, GA 30339
(770) 431-1200
www.firstwave.com

5. OnContact Software Corporation—CMS
W67 N222 Evergreen Blvd., Suite 212
Cedarburg, WI 53012
(262) 375-6555
www.oncontact.com

6. Onyx Software—Onyx Enterprise CRM
1100–112th Avenue NE, Suite 100
Bellevue, WA 98004
(425) 451-8060
www.onyx.com

7. Optima Technologies, Inc.—ExSellence
1110 Northchase Parkway, Suite 250
Marietta, GA 30067
(770) 951-1161
www.optima-tech.com

8. Oracle/PeopleSoft, Inc.—PeopleSoft CRM
500 Oracle Parkway
Redwood Shores, CA 94065
(650) 506-7000
www.peoplesoft.com

9. Pivotal Corporation—Pivotal CRM Suite
700–858 Beatty Street
Vancouver, BC
Canada V6B 1C1
(604) 699-8000
www.pivotal.com

10. SAP America Inc.—mySAP CRM
SAP America Inc. Strategic Planning & Support
3999 West Chester Pike
Newtown Square, PA 19073
(610) 661-1000
www.sap.com

Source: Barton Goldenberg, president, ISM, Inc. (*www.ismguide* *.com*)—A nationally recognized CRM consulting firm. He is a regular columnist and member of the editorial board for CRM Magazine. Contact him at 6900 Wisconsin Avenue, Suite 505 Bethesda, MD 20815-6111; (877) ISM-GUIDE or (301) 656-8448; fax: (301) 656-8005; or at *bgoldenberg@ismguide.com*.

Typical CRM Mistakes

Customer relationship management (CRM) can add significant value to an organization, but many implementations fail due to a few basic mistakes. Here are some of the most common pitfalls companies face.

1. No project team

A diverse team consisting of various people from the company from different departments such as sales, marketing, customer support, and management should be assembled to support CRM implementation.

2. Lack of strategic vision

Throughout the process, business objectives and goals should be discussed with the project team to ensure that needs are met.

3. No success metrics

Quantify specific success objectives. For example, identify the top five lead sources or reduce customer service calls by 30 percent.

4. No business process review

Think about what information you want to know about your leads, accounts, contacts. What information can you not track? What do you want to track? Get your project team together to outline your business processes.

5. Complexity prohibits productivity

Clear, well-defined fields in your CRM system will make it easier when searching for information. All information and fields in the system should have a purpose and be an integral part of the business process.

6. Cannot easily share and report

Users should not be highly restricted when using the system. An open sharing model and a simple hierarchy to encourage collaboration are best when using a CRM system.

7. Inadequate training

Take advantage of your CRM supplier's training courses. It is very important that all information is entered in a consistent fashion and data is relevant to your business.

8. Not managing to the application

A very common mistake is that the users do not fully switch over to the new CRM system. Critical, pertinent information is in the system, and there are a number of great ways you can use the application to manage your business, rather than relying on legacy reporting tools.

9. No change management process

This is an issue for the CRM project team. The procedure for changes to the system should be decided on, so there is no confusion or misinformation.

Source: The Marks Group PC (*www.marksgroup.net*) is a certified Microsoft CRM and GoldMine partner. They can be reached at 45 E. City Avenue #342, Bala Cynwyd, PA 19004; (888) 224-0649.

Popular CRM Vendors for Small and Medium Businesses

Customer relationship management software is instrumental in helping you retain your customers and grow your company. The following list includes popular CRM vendors, in alphabetical order, that specialize in managing relationships with your customers, especially for small and medium businesses, and their software.

1. ACCPAC International—ACCPAC CRM (Now Sage CRM)
7775 The Bluffs Northwest
Austell, GA 30168
(770) 261-1000
www.accpac.com

2. Ardexus, Inc.—Ardexus MODE
6300 Northwest Drive
Mississauga, ON
Canada L4V 1J7
(905) 673-5668
www.ardexus.com

3. Axonom, Inc.—Powertrak
10860 Nesbitt Avenue South
Minneapolis, MN 55437
(952) 653-0400
www.axonom.com

4. Best Software—SalesLogix
ACT! and SalesLogix
8800 N. Gainey Center Drive, Suite 200
Scottsdale, AZ 85258
(888) 855-5222
www.bestsoftware.com

5. Clear Technologies, Inc.—C2 CRM

1199 South Beltline Road, Suite 120
Coppell, TX 75019
(972) 906-7500
www.cleartechnologies.net

6. FrontRange Solutions, Inc.—GoldMine & HEAT
4120 Dublin Blvd., Suite 200
Dublin, CA 94568
(925) 404-1800
www.frontrange.com

7. iETSolutions, LLC—iETSolutions Enterprise
959 Concord St.
Framingham, MA 01701
(508) 416-9010
www.iet-solutions.com

8. Interchange Solutions, Inc.—Salesplace
19 Allstate Parkway, Suite 120
Markham, ON
Canada L3R 5A4
(877) 377-6687
www.me4n.com

9. Maximizer Software, Inc.—Maximizer Enterprise
1090 West Pender Street, 10th Floor
Vancouver, BC
Canada V6E 2N7
(604) 601-8000
www.maximizer.com

10. NetSuite, Inc.—NetCRM & NetSuiteNet-Suite, Inc.

2955 Campus Drive, Suite 100
San Mateo, CA 94403-2511
(650) 627-1000
www.netsuite.com

Source: Barton Goldenberg, president of ISM, Inc. (*www.ismguide* *.com*)—A nationally recognized CRM consulting firm. He is a regular columnist and member of the editorial board for CRM Magazine. Contact him at 6900 Wisconsin Avenue, Suite 505, Bethesda, MD 20815-6111; (877) ISM-GUIDE or (301) 656-8448; fax: (301) 656-8005; or at *bgoldenberg@ismguide.com.*

Steps to a Successful CRM Initiative

A clear vision backed by good planning and execution are critical to a Customer Relationship Management (CRM) project's success. Here our expert provides us with advice on how to achieve CRM success for your business.

1. Business executives must "own" CRM projects

From identifying goals and objectives to defining and supporting business processes and metrics to ensuring adequate funding for implementation and support. Upper management buy-in and leadership is critical to the success of any CRM initiative.

2. CRM projects need governance—not command and control

Recognize the dynamic and interdepartmental nature of marketing campaigns, sales interactions, and service calls, and manage CRM deployments accordingly—by a representative team or governing body. Get input from all major areas that make up a CRM initiative, including sales, marketing, and customer care, early in the process.

3. Organize your culture

Establish a customer-focused culture throughout the entire organization.

4. Get a full view of your customer

Ensure seamless integration with your back-office applications, so critical elements of other third-party applications help provide a true 360-degree view of the customer.

5. Look into other successful businesses

Get expert advice from technologists who have mastered the art of successful CRM implementations.

6. Get your team involved

Design and implement employee buy-in programs that help your team understand the value of CRM.

7. Build reports

Review, update, and implement automated business rules throughout the organization and report on the efficiencies and effectiveness of their use.

8. Implement a system

Design a system that is highly open, robust, and scalable as the amount of information you gather and manage will grow with the organization and increase over time. Make sure your corporate IT is responsible for the integration strategy, maintenance of master data, and adherence to technology standards in connecting these new applications.

9. Identify

Recognize your most profitable customers and provide products, services, and promotions that keep them as happy, loyal customers.

10. Recognize your performance

Identify tangible and measurable links to business performance before implementing a CRM project. First, identify the processes that require change, the current level of performance achieved, and ongoing improvements.

Source: Sundip R. Doshi, CEO, Surado Solutions, Inc. This White Paper was originally published in *Defying the Limits*, by Montgomery Research, Inc. It is reprinted with permission of Surado Solutions, Inc.

Popular Features of CRM Software

If you're looking to keep a close eye on your prospects and customers, then you're going to want a good customer relationship management (CRM) application. This is a billion-dollar industry, made up of hundreds of software products, resellers, vendors, and consultants. What should a typical company look for in a quality CRM program? Our expert, a veteran CRM reseller and consultant (and your humble editor), provides some of the more popular features used by his clients.

1. Calendar

A good CRM application should have full calendaring capability for each individual and for the workgroup. Users with the right privileges should be able to view their own and others' calendars by date range and activity.

2. Communications

CRM applications either have built-in e-mail capability or seamless integration with Microsoft Outlook. Users should be able send e-mail templates, mass e-mails, and mass mailings to their customer base with a simple point-and-click interface.

3. Integration

CRM applications need to speak directly with Microsoft Office, accounting applications, Web sites, and other databases in order to make their users fully productive. In addition, the CRM program should come with tools that a developer can use to integrate its database with other like databases and systems.

4. Marketing campaigns

CRM users should be allowed to classify their contacts and complete an unlimited number of profile fields so that marketers can use this data to create and implement marketing campaigns. These campaigns would include mass mailings, e-mailings, telemarketing calls, and integration with Web sites.

5. Forecasting and opportunity management

CRM applications should have good sales-force automation capabilities. This includes the ability to forecast individual sales and also track larger-scale opportunities. Forecasted sales and opportunities should then be linked to individual contacts.

6. Automation

Speeding up workflow is a key feature of the best-of-breed CRM applications.

Automation capabilities should allow escalation, auto scheduling, alerting, and accomplishing multiple tasks at once. These capabilities should be easily configured by CRM users or the system administrator.

7. Service management

CRM applications should have service management modules that allow for the creation of call tickets, assigning tickets, searching assets, and using a knowledge base. Service modules would be shared by sales users, too, so they can see what kind of work is being done with their customers. This assures that both sales and service employees are on the same page.

8. Reporting

The ability to report from your data is a critical part of any CRM application. Most applications come with their own report writers, or even the very popular Crystal Reports. At the very least, a CRM application should have connectivity to its database using Microsoft Excel or Microsoft Access.

9. Lead management

Leads come in to a company in many different ways: on the phone, through the Web, at a trade show are just a few ways. Your CRM application should be able to identify leads, perform certain follow-up actions, and then escalate them to a higher status as they become warmed up.

10. Remote access

Nowadays, every sales or service person needs to get to the data from different locations. CRM applications should not only synchronize to remote databases but should also synchronize data between itself, Outlook, and most popular hand-held devices. In addition, the application should have the capability of being accessed online through most computers.

Source: Gene Marks, president of the Marks Group PC (*www.marksgroup.net*)—An information technology consulting firm specializing in customer relationship management, accounting, and service management technology.

Reasons a CRM System Is Critical for Sales

Customer relationship management packages can be very effective for you and your business. It is important to learn which packages best fit your organizational structure and culture. CRM systems can improve marketing, sales, and support of your business. Here are some reasons you should purchase a CRM system.

1. Marketing automation

A CRM package can help you maintain a database of current and prospective customers and automate marketing tasks to reach them.

2. Sales force automation

Your sales force can use a CRM package to get customer information when they need it, track customers through the sales funnel, and help manage their time so they can concentrate on what they are good at. This includes giving mobile salespeople access to the CRM package through hand-held devices.

3. Customer service/support

Customer service and after-sales support staff can benefit from a CRM package that helps them address customer questions, problems, and issues, as well as managing follow-up calls or e-mails. Increasingly, this includes handling, Web queries and Web-based customer self-service support areas.

4. Field service management

Your CRM package can help your field service staff manage and process onsite customer service calls. This includes giving field service staff remote access to the CRM package through hand-held devices.

5. Help desk

A CRM package can give your help desk the ability to tightly manage your important assets (IT or physical), as well as reacting to and sometimes even predicting customer issues quickly and effectively. The provision of Web-based customer self-service help tools is also a feature of some CRM packages.

6. Partner relationship management

If channel partners are an important part of your business, your CRM package can help administer and report on your channel program, manage training and knowledge bases, and manage joint marketing initiatives.

7. Sales-effectiveness systems

Your CRM package can also help improve the effectiveness of your sales force through interactive sales coaching, presentation/proposal development tools, and configuration

tools that let your sales force configure the customer's solution at the time of sale.

Source: The Marks Group PC (*www.marksgroup.net*) is a certified Microsoft CRM and GoldMine partner. They can be reached at 45 E City Avenue, #342, Bala Cynwyd, PA 19004; (888) 224-0649.

Popular Customer Loyalty Programs

Customer loyalty programs can be expensive and may backfire in some cases. It is very important to understand what type of loyalty program you want to launch for your business. Our expert shares with us his favorite ways to keep customers loyal.

1. A membership program

Membership programs are one of the best ways to keep customers coming back. Most programs provide special incentives to members as part of their membership. A good example of a membership program is the YMCA!

2. A rewards program

Rewards programs provide gifts and perks that are "earned" according to the amount of business your customers do with you. In the hot tub retail industry, many manufacturers have an annual trip that only their most successful dealers get to enjoy. The dealers who get to attend have "earned" their way by selling a preset number of hot tubs throughout the year.

3. Create a community

Every human has a deep inner need to belong to a community. "Belonging" gives us security and helps us to understand our place in life. How do you create a community? Participate in local events. An example would be a shoe store sponsoring a local marathon or charity race.

4. Create intertwined business processes

Basically, this method consists of positioning your business processes so deep in your client's or customer's business processes that it would financially hurt their business if they were to stop doing business with you. For example, if you run all your Web service using a certain tool, it would literally rip the guts out of your business if you were to decide to move to another service. That's guaranteed customer loyalty.

Source: David Frey, owner of marketingbestpractices.com and the author of the bestselling manual *The Small Business Marketing Bible* and the senior editor of the *Small Business Marketing Best Practices* Newsletter. Contact him at *david@marketingbestpractices.com*.

Popular Customer-Retention Strategies

A reward program is great customer-retention strategy. You entice people to transact again with your company based on a reward or an incentive. Often these strategies can be very effective. Here's a list of retention strategies to consider implementing in your business.

1. Continuous reinforcement

Continuous reinforcement is a reward that always occurs. Every time the mouse presses the lever, food comes. In the business world, a reward like this is "free shipping with every order" or "everyday low prices."

2. Fixed ratio/variable ratio

Ratio rewards are based on repetition. With fixed ratio, the reward occurs precisely every x

times. So every tenth time the mouse presses the lever, food comes down the chute. This is akin to Subway's "buy twelve feet, get one foot free" or similar punch cards. The variable ratio version is similar, but x isn't a constant number (though it averages to a constant number). A lottery might give winning odds of one in a million. It isn't exactly one in a million every time, but it is on average. You may never win. But you keep playing because you have an equal chance of winning each time.

3. Fixed interval/variable interval

Interval rewards are based on time. In the fixed version, no matter how many times the mouse presses the lever; food comes out only at a specific interval, such as once every ten minutes. In the variable version of our example, food comes out approximately every ten minutes but not exactly. Sometimes it's nine minutes, sometimes eleven, but it always averages to ten. GNC Foods has a special members' discount the first week of every month. This is a fixed interval reward, as are a store's annual sale and a daily lunch special from 11 A.M. to 2 P.M. The variable version includes radio contests that grant prizes "sometime this hour." You don't know exactly when, but basically it's every hour.

4. Token economy

A related reward schedule is the token economy, which is also commonly used for rewards or incentives. In a token economy, points (or something similar) are accrued and then traded for goods. Think arcades that give you tickets that can be exchanged for a number of prizes. Or airlines' point programs. Token economies exhibit traits similar to fixed ratio rewards, though rewards can vary based on the number of points used. Because you can buy different rewards based on varying number of points, there's always the potential of getting a reward.

Source: Jack Aaronson, CEO of the Aaronson Group (*www.aar onsongroup.com*), as well as a corporate lecturer. The Aaronson Group's expertise includes multichannel user experience and user-centric design. As a corporate lecturer, Jack also travels around the world teaching companies how to effectively implement personalization, loyalty programs and multichannel CRM. Jack writes the CRM column for ClickZ.com, and has his own newsletter about personalization and multichannel marketing.

Top Reasons Customers Leave

When it comes to figuring out why your business loses customers, you need to understand a number of important factors in order to keep your customers happy. According to a study of all types of small businesses by the Small Business Administration, there are six reasons that customers may leave your business.

1. Perception that the business doesn't care about the customer

You need to let the customer know that they are important to you and your business, because what binds relationship buyers to your company is the totality of the relationship which includes recognition, service, information, helpfulness and overall friendly employees. These customers are relationship buyers and are by far the most important to your business.

2. Dissatisfaction with the product

Not much can be done once a customer is dissatisfied with your product. The key here is to provide the customer with quality, brand identity, and a product that meets their needs.

3. Price

If your product is too expensive, customers will have a tendency to leave and look elsewhere. If your product is too inexpensive, your customer may think it of poor quality. Make sure you look at your competitors, and make sure you let your customers know why your product is better then the competitor. If they know and believe in the advantages, they will be willing to pay more for your product.

4. Recommendations of friends or family

Never underestimate the impact of your customers' friends or family; their opinions may weigh heavily on customers' buying decisions. Your customers will trust and agree more with someone with whom they have a personal relationship. So, having a good relationship with your customer may help you overcome this factor.

5. Customer moves away or moves out of your buying category

Customers may unexpectedly move to another area or even no longer fit into your buying category. For example, a customer may decide to no longer sell a product for which they purchased supplies from your company. Thus, they would no longer be in need of your services.

6. Death

This was the smallest and most obvious reason that a customer would no longer purchase from your business.

Source: Small Business Association (*www.sba.gov*).

The Benefits of an Extranet

An extranet is a portion of the Internet that, with security access, you make available to your customers, suppliers, and employees. An extranet can offer a range of benefits to your business. Of course these can depend to a large degree upon your original reasons for introducing the extranet in the first place. However, here are a few of the benefits that organizations using extranets typically experience.

1. Brings your suppliers together

An extranet will help join up the supply chain through the use of online ordering, order tracking, and inventory management.

2. Reduces documentation costs

You will reduce costs by making manuals and technical documentation available online to trading partners and customers.

3. Enables collaboration

You will enable collaboration between business partners—perhaps members of a project team—by enabling them to work on common documentation online, so speeding up the development and approval processes and reducing the need for meetings.

4. Improves relationships

An extranet will help to improve business relationships with key trading partners because of the close collaborative working that extranets support.

5. Improves customer service

You'll see improved customer service by giving customers direct access to information and enabling them to resolve their own queries.

6. Provides a single interface to your company

An extranet will provide a single user interface between you and your business partners.

7. Enables better and more secure communications

You will improve the security of communications between you and your business partners, since exchanges can take place under a controlled and secure environment such as a virtual private network.

8. Disseminates news to your users

An extranet will share news of product development exclusively with partner companies.

9. Provides flexible working tools for your staff

You will assist in the move toward flexible working for your own staff because an extranet allows remote and mobile staff to access core business information on an as-required basis, irrespective of location.

Source: Business Link (*www.businesslink.gov.uk*)—An easy-to-use business support, advice, and information service managed by the United Kingdom government. The service is uniquely placed to identify business support services from across the government, voluntary, and private sectors.

Elements to Consider when Preparing Customer Surveys

Since all businesses depend on customers to survive, a customer survey is an invaluable tool to gain critical feedback and insight. However, a survey program is only valuable if this effort is properly designed, implemented, interpreted, and updated. Although there are no scientific principles to guarantee outcomes, here are some elements to consider when preparing customer surveys.

1. Specify the purpose

There are endless possibilities for using a customer survey. For example, surveys can be used for market segmentation, developing consumer profiles, product image or positioning, price or service perception analysis, testing a marketing campaign, benchmarking against the competition, or new product development. Without outlining clear objectives, a customer survey will accomplish very little.

2. Target audience

Although surveying every customer may sound ideal, most businesses find that constructing an appropriate sample size and using a targeted approach is more practical. A business may want to develop different surveys to target questions to specific customer groups. Defining the target audience will allow for development of tailored survey questions.

3. Frequency and duration

While a survey that measures customer satisfaction may be an ongoing time series designed to track customer perceptions over time, other surveys could be developed for a set duration. Generally, surveys should be changed or updated when they are not accomplishing the original objectives, there is a better technique or method, or there is a new variable to explore. Finding an appropriate balance with survey frequency and duration will avoid underutilization or overutilization of survey data. Furthermore, deciding on frequency and duration before implementing a survey program will help influence the means of administration.

4. Mode of administration

This decision may be narrowed based simply on available customer contact information. For instance, some frames have only customer addresses, telephone numbers, or e-mail addresses, while some businesses may not have any formal customer contact information and therefore rely on personal interaction. Cost may be a limiting factor as each method requires resources in terms of additional equipment or staff. Methods may be combined to enhance the quality of data in a cost-effective manner. Overall, customer survey quality is a complex mix of these and other salient features connected to the mode of administration.

5. Accuracy and reliability

Survey questions can be unstructured—that is, open-ended or free response—or structured that specify the set of responses as well as their format. Structured questions can be framed as multiple choice, branching, dichotomous, ranking, or scales. Questions should be designed in a logical order and organized around topic areas. Those methods that rely on visual or automated techniques must concentrate more on form and design development. If survey questions and administration are not accurate and reliable, costly mistakes can be made when interpreting and applying the results.

6. Response rates

There are many variables that influence why a respondent may or may not complete a customer survey or specific questions. The effort required by the respondent may influence willingness to participate. Regardless of the customer survey method used, the business should attempt to improve response rates. This can be done by proper timing, prior notification, incentives, follow-up, and other facilitators. Low response rates or incomplete surveys can lead to misleading and tainted survey results.

7. Pretest

Before using a customer survey, pretest it to identify and eliminate potential problems. All aspects of the survey should be explored, including question content, wording, misinterpretations, sequence, form and layout, nonresponses, difficulty, instructions, and administration. Even the most carefully designed question or process can be improved. Pretesting can be done with personal interviews, focus groups, and a small-scale real-world testing.

8. Reporting and using data

The one thing that all customer satisfaction surveys have in common is that they solicit opinions. Once a survey is completed, the responses need to be placed in a format useful for analysis and reporting. Usually, survey answers are coded or grouped into categories for data processing. If a business is not adequately prepared to use customer survey data, it should not implement the program in the first place. Reports of survey results must be timely because the value of survey data is time sensitive. Everyone, including upper management, must fully understand the survey results and be committed to continual improvement.

Source: Brian R. Tromans, director of Client Relations, Tully, Rinckey & Associates, PLLC (www.tullylegal.com)—The firm was recently named one of the Top 50 law firms and one of the Great Places to Work by the Business Review. Tromans can be contacted at 3 Wembley Court, Albany, NY 12205; (518) 218-7100; e-mail: btromans@tullylegal.com.

Popular Customer Survey Companies

Some businesses hire market research firms to survey their customers or target customers. For new or smaller businesses, this can be an expensive proposition, and it's helpful to have resources in your toolbox that offer the option of conducting your own surveys. Here are some great online resources you can use for surveys.

1. Survey Monkey

If you have a large mailing list or want to send a lot of surveys, the best deal here is the professional subscription. For $19.95 month, you can send an unlimited number of surveys and receive up to 1,000 responses per month.

www.SurveyMonkey.com

2. Zoomerang

I love their slogan, "Easiest way to ask, fastest way to know." Offers a basic product (free) plus paid packages geared to education, nonprofit, and a professional version, which can send surveys in several languages and has no limit on the number of responses you can receive.

www.zoomerang.com

3. SnapPoll

Simple site which offers you an easy way to put a one-question survey on your Web site and receive results. Requires no sign-up, allows you to customize colors for the form, and prevent multiple "votes" from the same person. Free—supported by what they call "nonobtrusive advertising."

www.SnapPoll.com

4. PHP Form Generator

This is a free survey generator that is open-source code. You can choose as many questions as you'd like—in any format (check, text, drop-downs, etc.). You do have to create your own stats, but it's a fairly simple procedure for smaller surveys.

http://phpformgen.sourceforge.net/

5. OneMinutePoll

Software—available at a yearly subscription price—that teaches you how to write surveys correctly to find out what your customers want, so you can provide it. Software automates your polls, generates code for your Web page, and allows you to see results in real time.

www.OneMinutePoll.com

6. Advanced Survey

Free and paid services that offer both Web page surveys and e-mail surveys (where you invite participants—via e-mail—to take a survey). You can ask multiple questions in one survey, and can ask yes/no questions, open-ended text questions, customizable number scales (Pick a number from 1 to 10 with 10 being best, for example …), and multiple choice.

www.advancedsurvey.com

7. Question Pro

A very sophisticated system for surveying customers, it has predesigned templates for common surveys: Customer Satisfaction, New Product/Concept Testing, Product Surveys, Conference Feedback, and more. These surveys can also be designed with "branching," where the answer to one question is used in a subsequent question. No free options here, but there is a thirty-day free trial.

www.questionpro.com

8. Relevant Tools

This company offers custom Web forms with automatic email response for as little as $10/month for a basic membership, which includes up to 500 database records and up to 500 e-mail messages/month.

www.relevanttools.com

9. HotScripts

A great resource for programmers and Web masters. It has a host of scripts in various programming languages and is constantly being updated by programmers from around the world. If you search on "surveys," you'll find lots of scripts in lots of programming languages you can use.

www.hotscripts.com

10. NetReflector

This company offers a very sophisticated self-serve solution for the do-it-yourselfer, and assisted and automated solutions for companies that need to survey customers and/or employees worldwide on a regular basis. They offer Webinars, articles, and other resources on creating the invitation, the importance of regular surveys, and using online technologies for surveys.

www.netreflector.com

Source: Maria Marsala (*www.ElevatingYourBusiness.com*)—A former Wall Street trader, she is a nationally known trainer, author, and consultant. Since 1998, she has helped more than 1,000 business owners to make more money in less time by creating SIMPLE systems that work.

Improving Your Sales

Questions to Ask a Sales Manager Before Hiring

So, now you are ready to hire a sales manager. You have developed the job description so that you know exactly what you want the person to be able to do. You have also created a list of qualities that you want the right person to possess. And you're all set when it comes to the salary, compensation, and benefits package. Now all you have to do is find some candidates, interview them, and hire someone. Here are a few of the most crucial questions to ask a potential sales manager.

1. How did you get started in this business?

2. How long had you been in the business before you realized what it took to be successful?

3. Why did you leave your last position?

4. What is your formal education? Do you have an informal "school of hard knocks" education?

5. Do you think people can be trained to be successful?

6. What influences from the past have been continuing motivators in your life?

7. Do you have a guiding philosophy in your life?

8. What were your original goals?

9. Was there a turning point in your life when you could have gone another way? Why did you pick this route?

10. Have you ever had a significant failure in business? What did you learn from that?

11. How many hours do you work a week?

12. How do you use your leisure time?

13. When and how do you plan your day?

14. Do you follow a system when making decisions? If so, what is it?

15. What do you look for in a person who wants to join your company?

16. What do you feel is an individual's main hindrance to achieving full potential?

17. How have you helped your employees overcome this hindrance?

18. Which of your accomplishments is the most satisfying?

19. What would you regret not accomplishing before you die?

20. Do you have any questions for me?

Source: Dan Beaulieu, founding partner, D.B. Management Group (*www.dbmpcb.com*)—A consulting firm entirely dedicated to the Printed Circuit Board Industry. The company advises its clients on marketing, sales, management, engineering, quality, Web pages, brochures, and managing, measuring and motivating a sales force. Contact him at (207) 873-0793 or via e-mail at *danbeaulieu@aol*

.com. His recently published book, *Printed Circuit Basics*, is available from UP Media Group.

Important Questions to Ask Before Hiring a New Salesperson

When sitting in the employer's chair, you should see the questions being asked of a prospective salesperson as a form of "selling the company." The questions asked tell the interviewee what the culture of your firm is and how you differ from other firms that the prospect may have worked for or interviewed with. Our expert, a nationally recognized sales consultant, provides his thoughts on some of the more important questions to be asked of a prospective salesperson.

1. Before applying for this job, what have you done to learn about our business and/or our industry?

The reason for this question is to show how interested or creative the person is; this gives an inkling of his or her self-motivation.

2. What experience have you had with the industry we are in or serve? If little or none, what will you do to learn about the industry, and how much time and effort will you take to learn about it?

You want to know if this person has taken the time and effort to learn as much as possible about selling the firm's products and services and how these fit into the industry and the firm's customers' use of what they buy.

3. How familiar are you with our business and the products and/or services we sell? If little or none, what will you do to learn about

the industry and how much time and effort will you take to learn about it?

If the answer(s) to the first two question are negative, it is important that the salesperson be open to taking the time to learn as much as possible about selling the firm's products and services and how these fit into the industry and the firm's customers use of what they buy.

4. What did you like and dislike about your old job (without giving names, use only situations)?

Such a question will give insights into whether these same negatives or positives are applicable to the situations the prospective employee would be facing.

5. What would you like for a base salary now and what do you want it to be in [RL] (6 months, a year, etc.)?

Negotiating for a salary is very stressful. You want to know what prospective employees are thinking. By asking them to name what they want to reach in terms of salary places the onus on them to accomplish many of the tasks the previous questions asked.

6. How long can you survive on that base salary before you are out selling to our customers and those in the industry(s) that would be able to generate commissions?

Very likely, the base salary will be lower than what the salesperson had been getting even if she were doing less than what was expected. Yet, you have to know what the prospect needs to live on lest the starting base salary is not enough and that would make her disgruntled from the start.

7. Here is a list of the types of firms that are customers. How familiar are you with any of these types of firms and, possibly, are there any firms you can name? In the latter case, what do you know about them?

Even if the prospective salesperson was coming from a different industry, there may be some crossover that would give him a step up with these firms. In same cases, the buyers may be the same person(s).

8. What will you do to drop some of the techniques you used in your prior sales position in order to adapt to the culture of our business and industry?

Changing from one culture to another, even if the old and new firms are/were competitors is a big step for both the new employee and the firm's staff. If the staff or customers did not like what the previous firm was doing, it will be harder for them to accept the new salesperson.

9. If you call on a customer/client and no sale is made, what do you do?

Not making a sale is not a catastrophe., but not learning from it is. Being able to accept no and making the changes to move toward yes is an important function of being in sales.

10. Would you be willing to make suggestions or complaints concerning things that are not working for you without the fear of job security, stepping on someone's toes, or being seen as blaming others for your failure?

Of course, the success of this question falls on management, but asking it shows the prospective salesperson that the company is open to input.

Source: Alan J. Zell, Ambassador of Selling (*www.sellingselling*
.com)—He has become nationally recognized for his expertise in advising businesses, services, educational, governmental, and organizational entities. Clients seeking his services represent a wide spectrum including accountants, investors, educators, chambers of commerce, retailers, wholesalers, manufacturers, associations, and nonprofit organizations. Contact him at PO Box 69, Portland, OR 97207-0069; (503) 241-1988.

Top Reasons to Use a Broad-Based Sales-Recruiting Firm

People are a company's more important assets. They can make or break the fortunes of a business. Professional recruiters can deliver the right people for today's highly competitive business environment. If you are looking to hire new employees, here are some of the reasons you may want to look into using a broad-based sales-recruiting firm.

1. Observe strict confidentiality

If your company has a key opening, it can be vulnerable. Confidentiality can keep competitors from being tipped off to management shake-ups, new product and market initiatives, and can protect against employee and supplier apprehension. Recruiters value the sensitive information they become aware of during the search process and respect your vulnerability.

2. Tap into a global network of contacts

Most often, the best candidates are already employed, and many of them will deal only with a recruiter. They appreciate the worth of third-party representation, confidentiality, and professional mediation. Recruiting superior candidates can be a complex process and is best performed by a professional.

3. Cost effective

The benefit of using a recruiter can be weighed against the cost of preparing and executing an advertisement campaign, screening and qualifying candidates, and operating without a needed employee for an extended time, compared to the relative insurance of getting the right person for the job. The use of recruiters is an investment in improving the quality of an organization's staff. But even beyond that, the risk in not using recruiters can be great. For smaller companies—where one hiring mistake can have disastrous results—using recruiters is sometimes even more important than for very large companies.

4. Cover a wide geographical area

Generally, when recruiting on your own, you will only have access to local candidates. Recruiters, on the other hand, have access to a national internal database. Highly organized and detailed information on hundreds of thousands of candidates can be easily accessed. Therefore, recruiters can reach candidates from all over the world, in turn increasing the chance of finding the most qualified candidates.

5. Provide a guarantee

For example, should you make a wrong decision when hiring a candidate, or should your candidate quit, most sales recruiting firms will give a thirty- to ninety-day guarantee to replace the candidate should anything go wrong. This is a very valuable tool because it is as if you are getting insurance on your employees, saving you valuable time and money.

Source: Vincent Albrecht, president, Management Recruiters of Hillsborough (*www.mrhillsborough.com*) A full-service, professional recruiting and placement organization, serving clients locally and nationally on a contingent, retained, and interim basis. More information is available at 971 Route 202 North, Suite 7, Branchburg, NJ 08876; (908) 722-3252; fax: (908) 722-3253; or e-mail: *vincea@mrhillsborough.com*.

Most Common Sales Mistakes

Even the most seasoned sales professional makes mistakes from time to time. Our experts here know all about mistakes; they've certainly seen enough of them over the years. In their opinion, here are the eight most common sales mistakes.

1. Allowing a prospect to lead the sales process

The best way to control the sales interaction is to ask questions. This is also the best way to learn whether your product or service meets the needs of your prospect. Quality questions that uncover specific issues, problems, or corporate objectives are essential in helping you establish yourself as an expert.

2. Not being prepared

When you make a cold call or attend a meeting with a prospect, it is critical that you are prepared. This means having all relevant information at your fingertips, including pricing, testimonials, samples, and a list of questions you need to ask. Create a checklist of the vital information you will need and review this list before you make your call. You have exactly one opportunity to make a great first impression, and you will not make it if you are not prepared.

3. Talking too much

Too many salespeople talk too much during the sales interaction. They espouse about their product, its features, their service, and so on. Stress key points about your product and then let the client do the talking, by asking questions.

4. Lacking a focused sales structure

The structure of a sales force consists of elements such as the way sales territories are defined, the way markets and customers are targeted, the training and development system of the company, and the sales tools that are used. A highly focused, well-designed sales structure can be one of your company's greatest assets, as it ultimately shapes the behavior of the sales force.

5. Giving the prospect information that is irrelevant

Don't present your client with useless information that they don't need. Make the most of your presentation by telling them how they will benefit from your product or service and how your product or service relates to their specific situation.

6. Neglecting to ask for the sale

If you sell a product or service, you have the obligation to ask the customer for a commitment, particularly if you have invested time assessing their needs and know that your product or service will solve a problem. Many people are concerned with coming across as pushy, but as long as you ask for the sale in a nonthreatening, confident manner, people will usually respond favorably.

7. Failing to prospect

When business is good many people stop prospecting, thinking that the flow of business will continue. However, the most successful salespeople prospect all the time. They schedule prospecting time in their agenda every week. Even the most seasoned sales professional makes mistakes from time to time.

8. Not knowing your customer

Some customers have been called on for years, and yet the salesperson doesn't know any more about them today then he/she did after the second sales call. The ultimate sales skill is the ability to know the customer deeper and in a more detailed way than your competitors do. And outselling the rest depends on understanding the customer better than anyone else.

Sources: *The Five Most Common Mistakes Sales People Make*, by David Kahle (*www.davekahle.com*); and *Small Business, Increase Your Sales by Avoiding These Mistakes*, by Kelley Robertson, president, Robertson Training Group (*Kelley@RobertsonTrainingGroup.com*).

Popular Ways to Dig Up Information on Your Competitors

Nowadays there are more ways than ever to dig up information about your competition. Our expert, who's associated with the Canadian government, give us these ideas.

1. Call

Call your competitors and ask for product brochures and other marketing materials.

2. Buy

Buy your competitors' products/services and analyze them.

3. Visit

Visit their stores. Talk to their employees.

4. Attend seminars

Attend their seminars and any other events open to the public.

5. Download

Download information from their Web sites.

6. Read their annual reports

If your competitor is a public company, buy some shares so you will receive annual reports and other corporate notices.

7. Ask your customers

Ask them how your products and services compare with others they have heard about.

8. Ask about information your customers have received

Ask what information they have received from any of your competitors who have approached them.

9. Take note if a customer complains, compliments, or makes other comments about competition

When customers call your company, make sure the employee answering the phone takes notes if customers complain, compliment, or make any comment about the competition.

10. Ask suppliers

Ask them to pass along information they receive from any of their other customers in your industry.

11. Check their Web sites

Check your competitors' Web sites and other corporate information for lists of customers.

12. Attend events

Attend their corporate events and subscribe to their publications.

13. Attend conferences, for industry information

Attend conferences. Attend presentations and visit booths of your competitors and other organizations that affect the direction of your industry. Collect brochures.

14. Join associations

Join industry associations.

15. Find information on the Web

Learn about searching and using keywords to find information on the Web.

16. Have information delivered

Get on the mailing/e-mail lists for newsletters and other notices from your competitors, customers, and suppliers.

17. Subscribe to various publications

Subscribe to local newspapers and publications of business associations where your competitors, customers, and suppliers are located.

18. Subscribe to government publications

Subscribe to publications of government departments, regulatory bodies, and standards-setting organizations involved with your industry.

19. Investigate media-monitoring services

Media-monitoring services are probably the oldest method for automating competitive intelligence. Services are available to track print, broadcast, and/or online media by defined geographic area, for keywords, or other identifiers specified by the client. Any instances where the keywords appear are recorded and delivered to the client, on paper or via the Internet. Media monitoring is a relatively inexpensive and time-saving form of gathering information, though not as fast or comprehensive as some other methods.

20. Investigate outsourced consulting and research services.

For small and medium enterprises willing and able to hire outside help, expert competitive-intelligence services are available to either conduct searches for you, show you how to do it—or both.

21. Use automated technologies

Investigate the use of software to gather information automatically from the Web. Whatever methods you use to gather information, they should not stand alone. You need to incorporate them into an enterprise-wide competitive-intelligence function, which includes analysis and is designed to help you make better decisions within your competitive strategy.

Source: Ebiz.enable, Industry Canada (*http://strategis.ic.gc.ca*)—A Canadian government–run site that provides information, advice, and statistics for both consumers and businesses. Reproduced with

the permission of the Minister of Public Works and Government Services, 2005.

Typical Mistakes when Producing a Catalog

Ever wonder what kind of work went into that product catalog you received in the mail or downloaded from a supplier's Web site? Would you like to produce a catalog for your customers too? We asked our expert, who specializes in creating product catalogs to create a list of typical mistakes that companies make in this process and here are the results.

1. Similar covers

Typically, catalog customers will toss any book they think they've seen, or any catalog that's not different or interesting looking enough to hold onto. Catalogers that create the same-looking cover book after book are probably trying to execute a campaign or create a recognizable look. Neither is a bad objective, but you have to differentiate the execution of each catalog edition. To correct this creative error, consider planning a campaign of covers at the beginning of the year or season. Use marketing information such as mailing dates, seasons, events, holidays, and other relevant facts to shape a cover strategy that supports positioning and builds the desired brand identity.

2. Hard-to-read logos

A logo should act as a masthead, whether it is on the top, on the bottom, or in a corner, so that it is instantly recognizable. Never use a logo that is too small or difficult to read from a distance. You also don't want to use cover type that is larger and more prominent than the catalog's name. The logo should be the first thing, beyond the art, that the reader sees. As long as a logo is prominent and readable, go in the direction of simplicity. Let's face it, some of the most successful catalogers—L.L. Bean, J. Crew, Lands' End—have the simplest and easiest logos to read.

3. Copycat creative

Copycat creative is the use of recognizable creative strategies that are "owned" by other catalogers that developed them or that use them dramatically and consistently to support their positioning and build brand image. Catalogers that don't have enough of a differentiated positioning or are hesitant about taking creative risks are most likely to "borrow" other mailers' creative execution. But replicating a creative look that is associated with another catalog company will not support your brand image, and it's unproductive in the long run. The originators of strong design concepts usually maintain the recognition and credit; they also typically have the insight and talent to stay in front of the competition with continually evolving creativity.

4. Disorganized or confusing spreads

Some catalogers need to clean up their act—literally. There's no excuse for tough-to-read, tough-to-follow layouts, which can turn off the customer, make a catalog difficult to shop from, and most certainly depress response rates. If your creative look displays a lack of space, type, photography, or overall design sense, it's time for a new art director. Some catalogers shoot without layouts and then expect to put together a cohesive, flowing catalog. That's like building a house without a blueprint. Layouts help plan the elements that affect the overall look of the book when it's put together. Feature shots, models, backgrounds and locations, lighting, and numerous other factors can look disjointed if not planned out prior to photography.

5. Voiceless copy

It's a backhanded compliment when a copywriter is labeled a "catalog writer." The complimentary part is that his or her name may be passed along as someone who can pull cryptic information off a fact sheet to create copy blocks and write a seventy-two-page catalog in four days. The not-so-complimentary part is that "catalog writers" can also have a reputation for cranking out boring, uninspiring, and sometimes fluffy copy. It's hard to find inspired, refreshing, and marketing-oriented people who can write copy that sells products and promotes a brand. When trying new people, have them write sample editorial and selling copy based on information you provide. This allows you to compare copywriting candidates on a level playing field.

6. Unreadable type

Hard-to-read type is a top complaint among consumers, yet many art directors keep selecting small type sizes and hard-to-read fonts, or using reverse type and surprint (type over photographs or other artwork) onto busy backgrounds. Yes, sometimes hard-to-read type looks better, but what's the use if you can't read it? There's no point in selecting type for the sake of design—not when you're selling.

7. Inappropriate or poorly cast models

Models can improve sales and bolster a brand presentation—if they are approachable, relevant, and aspiring to the target audience. The selection of models is important, as is the way they are styled and made up. For instance, an upscale audience may be more attracted to high fashion, glamour, and an aloof feeling, while customers of more moderately priced catalogers may prefer to see happier faces and more lifestyle poses. A big creative mistake that many catalogers make is not having enough ethnic diversity among the models in their books. A cross-ethnic presentation can be more appropriate—plus the increased use of African-American, Hispanic, and Asian models in particular improve catalog performance.

8. Missing keys

One of the jobs as a cataloger is to make shopping as easy as possible. The process of taking in information involves (a) seeing a product photograph of interest; (b) finding the product name and price; and (c) reading the copy block that describes it. Keying a product with the copy block is one of the best techniques for making the connection between the photograph and the copy block, especially if the copy does not appear right next to or below the product's photograph. A common and effective approach is to use the letters of the alphabet, in an easy-to-read font, as the keys. Place a letter clearly in the artwork, in a consistent place among the various photos, and then place the same letter immediately before the copy that refers to the product.

9. Lack of feature shots and hero spreads

The easiest and quickest way to add vitality and excitement to a catalog is to make sure that every spread contains a feature product and a subfeature. These products, which are normally identified by the merchandising team as bestsellers or the most expensive or profitable items, warrant special treatment. Use some sort of specialty presentation—greater space allocation, a background tint, outlining—to make these products stand out and create excitement, interest, and pacing in a catalog.

10. Complicated backgrounds

One of the most destructive things a cataloger can do is overcomplicate product shots. Unfortunately, in an effort to upgrade overall presentation or enhance the merchandise, some catalogers end up creating shots that detract from the product. Backgrounds can also be a problem in the photography studio, when in the course of creating a location, a feeling, or a season, the propping gets overcomplicated. There are all different levels of prop stylists who work on catalogs. Often the most talented know how to show merchandise off by using less.

Source: Glenda Shasho Jones, president of Shasho Jones (*www.sjdirect.com*)—A New York–based catalog consulting firm, the company is located at 267 West 25th Street in New York City. She is a frequent speaker on catalog marketing and creative, a regular contributor to *Catalog Age*, has appeared on CNBC, CNN, and MSNBC and is a bona fide catalog shopper. Her book *The Identity Trinity; Brand Image and Positioning for Catalogs* was published in 1997 by *Catalog Age*.

Top Steps to Close the Sale

Every good salesperson wants to know the quickest way to close that next sale. According to our expert, a highly regarded sales and customer service consultant, salespeople must first understand what the buying decisions are. Prospects will make value judgments about the salesperson, the company, the product or service, the price, and the time to buy. It's crucial to understand how these decisions are made, so you can most positively present each one. Our expert says there are seven steps that parallel the customer's buying decisions, which he provides in this list.

1. Approach

In this first step, you are selling yourself—your professionalism, your integrity, your good judgment and your trustworthiness. It will be easier to accomplish this if you can establish and maintain rapport with the prospect by continually selling yourself throughout the entire sales cycle. People buy because they like you, so wear a sincere smile, use positive language, develop a genuine interest in your prospects, use their name, compliment them, listen to their needs, and make them feel important.

2. Qualify

During step two, you will work to maintain the positive rapport established in the approach step as you shift your focus to the specific business reason for your sales call. This is your information-gathering period. During this time you will determine if the prospects have a genuine need for your product or service, if they have buying authority, and if there are adequate funds available for the purchase.

You will qualify them as genuine prospects by asking open-ended questions to uncover their problems and needs.

3. Agreement on need

Moving into step three, you will summarize the information you gathered in steps one and two to verify these facts and ensure that you and your prospect are in agreement. Your prospects will buy not because they understand your product or service but because you understand them. Therefore, you must determine their specific needs and effectively demonstrate that you fully grasp and appreciate them.

4. Sell the company

You will sell the company in step four. Your prospects' second buying decision is about your company. Does it operate with integrity? Does it have the competence and capability to perform as promised? Focus on the key points that distinguish your company from the competition. Familiarize your prospects with your firm, its products, its customers, and its reputation. Supply your prospects with the information necessary to make this decision positively.

5. Fill the need

Now you can fill the need. The next two buying decisions are about the product or service you sell and the price. In step five, you will show your prospects how your product or service solves their problems or fills their needs precisely, as well as the value they will receive for their investment. Ask questions to uncover what fears, uncertainties, or doubts your prospects might have and prepare ahead of time to address each one as it comes up. It is crucial that you unearth all of the concerns prior to discussing price. Should objections surface unexpectedly later in the sales cycle, they could threaten your sale.

6. Ask for the order

The only buying decision left is when to buy. During step six, the act of commitment, it is time to ask for the order. If the prospect is qualified, summarize the features and the benefits you agreed on, quote the investment or price and ask for the order. If an objection arises, acknowledge it with a neutralizing statement, such as "I see," "I understand," or "I can appreciate that." Then, re-establish areas of agreement by citing three features they liked, add an additional feature-benefit reaction, and then ask for the order.

7. Cement the sale

Finally, in step seven, you will cement the sale. Salespeople often mistakenly think their job ends when they close the sale. Really, it's only the beginning. Each sale you close represents an opportunity for new business—either from referrals or repeat business. Since people buy emotionally and then justify their buying decisions logically, it is important to take time with each of your customers to cement the sale. Develop a summary statement you can use to review the wise, sound, and intelligent reasons for the purchase.

Source: Roy Chitwood is an author and consultant on sales and customer service. He is the former president and chairman of Sales & Marketing Executives International and is president of Max Sacks International, Seattle, (800) 488-4629, www.maxsacks.com. If you would like to subscribe to his free Tip of the Week, "You're on Track," please e-mail contact@maxsacks.com.

Key Things You Should Know about the National Do Not Call Registry

Thinking of telemarketing to consumers? Be very, very careful! With the new National Do Not Call Registry, anyone who registers should not be called by you. Violations will come with steep fines. Here are a few key things every telemarketer should know about this legislation.

1. The FTC is in charge.

The National Do Not Call Registry is managed by the Federal Trade Commission (FTC), the nation's consumer protection agency. It is enforced by the FTC, the Federal Communications Commission (FCC), and state law enforcement officials.

2. The registry was created to offer consumers a choice regarding telemarketing calls.

The FTC's decision to create the National Do Not Call Registry was the culmination of a comprehensive, three-year review of the Telemarketing Sales Rule (TSR), as well as the commission's extensive experience enforcing the TSR over seven years. The FTC held numerous workshops, meetings, and briefings to solicit feedback from interested parties and considered more than 64,000 public comments, most of which favored creating the registry. You can review the entire record of the Rule review at *www.ftc.gov/bcp/rulemaking/tsr/tsrrulemaking/index.htm.*

3. The time frame is short.

As of January 1, 2005, telemarketers covered by the National Do Not Call Registry have up to thirty-one days from the date a consumer registers to stop calling.

4. Telemarketing to businesses is still okay.

The National Do Not Call Registry is only for personal phone numbers. Business-to-business calls and faxes are not covered by the National Do Not Call Registry.

5. There are limits to the FTC's jurisdiction.

Placing a number on the National Do Not Call Registry will stop most telemarketing calls but not all. Because of limitations in the jurisdiction of the FTC and FCC, calls from or on behalf of political organizations, charities, and telephone surveyors would still be permitted, as would calls from companies with which the consumer has an existing business relationship, or those to whom they've provided express agreement in writing to receive their calls.

6. Political calls and charities aren't covered.

Political solicitations are not covered by the TSR, since they are not included in its definition of telemarketing. Charities are not covered by the requirements of the national registry. However, if a third-party telemarketer is calling on behalf of a charity, a consumer may ask not to receive any more calls from, or on behalf of, that specific charity. If a third-party telemarketer calls again on behalf of that charity, the telemarketer may be subject to a fine of up to $11,000.

7. Surveys are okay.

If the call is really for the sole purpose of conducting a survey, it is not covered. Only telemarketing calls are covered—that is, calls that solicit sales of goods or services. Callers purporting to take a survey, but also offering to sell goods or services, must comply with the National Do Not Call Registry.

8. Your customers are excluded.

By purchasing something from the company, a customer established a business relationship with the company. As a result, even if they put their number on the National Do Not Call Registry, that company may call them for up to eighteen months after their last purchase or delivery from it, or their last payment to it, unless they ask the company not to call again. In that case, the company must honor the request not to call.

9. Overseas telemarketing calls are covered.

Any telemarketers calling U.S. consumers are covered, regardless of where they are calling from. If a company within the United States solicits sales through an overseas professional telemarketer, that U.S. company may be liable for any violations by the telemarketer. The FTC can initiate enforcement actions against such companies.

10. Consumers can choose to speak to you.

If a consumer gives a company written permission to call, they may do so even if the consumer has placed their number on the National Do Not Call Registry.

11. State requirements also prevail.

The National Do Not Call Registry requirements are at least as stringent as most state laws.

Most unwanted telemarketing calls will be covered by the National Do Not Call Registry. States also can continue to enforce their laws, which will not be limited by the FTC. However, the FCC's requirements impact some state laws.

12. Complaints are handled by the FTC.

Do not call complaints will be entered into the FTC's Consumer Sentinel system, a secure, online database available to more than 1,000 civil and criminal law enforcement agencies. While the FTC does not resolve individual consumer problems, a complaint will help them investigate the company and could lead to law enforcement action.

Source: Federal Trade Commission (*www.ftc.com*).

Popular Techniques for Getting Referrals

The typical business turns over 20 percent of its customers every year because of errors, changes in customers' buying influence or personnel, customers moving or going out of business, customers being acquired and local purchasing eliminated, customers' need becoming obsolescent, or customers going out of business. Prospecting new accounts is crucial to the survival and growth of businesses, and many companies spend countless dollars on cold calling via direct salespeople or telemarketing. Referrals are readily accepted but often not solicited and, therefore, not realized as an exceptionally good and rewarding source of new business. Here are some ways for taking full advantage of this excellent lead source.

1. Become the expert using referrals

A referral takes you out of the realm of purveyor and into the mode of being a problem-solver. When you need a new lawn service, do you look in the Yellow Pages or ask a few friends for their advice? When referred, you already have an idea that this person has successfully solved your friend's problem (often the friend describes the referred in glowing terms). When a new contact is referred to you, you can get to the solutions quicker with a shorter sales pitch.

2. Get referrals from existing customers

Sales personnel need to be trained and required to ask for referrals. Satisfied customers are more than willing to suggest potentials if asked. Every customer meeting should end with a request for a referral to companies or people your satisfied customer knows. Add a component of the sales compensation plan that pays on the number of referrals. Pay a higher commission rate on new customers for a period of time. Offer a reward program (that meets corporate governance criteria) to customers who refer new business.

3. Get referrals from brand-new customers

You just completed your first order and determined your new customer is very happy with your service. "That's great. I'm really happy we did the right thing by you. You know, our success depends on growing our business with great customers like you. Can you think of any of your colleagues, friends or business acquaintances that could use our services?" Ask about the business you noticed down the street. Have a telemarketer call and audit the first sale and ask the same question.

4. Get referrals from potential customers who have not yet bought from you

"Well, Mr. Smith, it doesn't appear as if there is any business that we can do together at the present time, but I'm sure that you have many business acquaintances in the area. Would you know of any other business in the area that could use our products or services?" The point is whether or not you do business, ask for referrals.

5. Get referrals from employees

Most people know at least 200 people by acquaintance or friendship, and employees also know who might use your product or service. If you have ten employees, that's 2,000 potentials and a 1 percent conversion would produce twenty new customers. Encourage employees to refer. Make it a topic at regular employee meetings. Set up a quarterly reward program (dinner, concert or game tickets for 2, a microwave, $100 cash). This not only produces additional business but increases team spirit, morale, and pride in the company.

6. Get referrals from suppliers

Who knows your business better or is more willing to help you (and themselves) grow than the people who provide your raw materials, resale product, or services. Make it a point to interview supplier reps and ask for referrals. If you're big enough to have a purchasing department, train your purchasing people to ask for referrals and reward them for successful leads. Don't forget to ask your referrer if you can use their name.

7. Get referrals from your delivery service personnel

UPS, FedEx, Roadway, and other delivery services visit a myriad of accounts regularly. Ask them who might use your products and services. It is amazing how much you can learn by asking questions of delivery people (including competitive information or whether a customer's operation has any problems). Give a UPS driver a brief, clear description of a type of business that you're looking for, and it's likely he or she has been to several of them in the vicinity.

8. Get referrals from new hire training

Consider some real world training when you hire a new sales or administrative person. Have the new hire call some of your existing customers and set an objective to learn about various products and why they use them. In the process, they can also ask for referrals that can lead to new business. This exercise also provides input for after-sales quality control and can be a very valuable source of market research.

9. Get referrals by networking

Other business owners who are your friends or acquaintances are constantly in contact with still other business owners, friends, relatives, and acquaintances who could provide suggestions and new business possibilities. Describe your business to them and ask for suggestions. Start a brain trust, disguised as a breakfast group and include your banker, lawyer, and other small business owners. Talk about what's happening in the area and what new businesses are developing or moving in. It is not unreasonable to expect that more than 50 percent of your new customers will result from diligently practicing the solicitation of referrals, reducing the cost of acquiring customers, and providing an ample supply of new business to reach your growth goals.

Source: Robert A. Normand, executive director, Institute for Small Business Management (*www.isbminc.com*) and author of *Entreprenewal!*, *The Six Step Recovery Program for Small Business* (*www.entreprenewal.com*). Normand has served as a principal management consultant to more than 100 small businesses ranging from $500,000 to $50,000,000 in annual sales and has owned and operated several small businesses of his own in diverse industries. He can be reached through the Web sites, by telephone at (941) 330-0889, or at 3751 Almeria Avenue, Suite A4, Sarasota, FL 34239.

Popular Cold-Calling Techniques

Cold calling can be a very difficult task to master. However, a well-managed cold-calling system can be a fantastic source of qualified leads for your business. So, if you decide to make cold calling part of your lead-generating system, here are some ideas to do it as productively as possible.

1. Have a lot of leads

The more people you have to talk with, the less important any one of them will be to you. What's important is finding those people who want to do business with you. The disappointment of hearing no from someone is a lot easier to take when you know you have a long list of other people to talk with.

2. Qualify (or prequalify) your leads

Before you start calling people, make sure they meet your criteria for a qualified lead. Or at least make sure they meet as many criteria as possible. Focus your calls on people who appear to have a need for what you do. Forget the rest. Your time is valuable, so don't waste it on people who don't fit your profile.

3. Persistence is painful not profitable

Speaking of not wasting time, don't waste too much time pursuing any one lead. Make no more than two to three calls to a cold lead; if you do not connect with them, forget them. Or, put them back at the bottom of the list, so you don't spend your precious time on people who simply are not reachable. They might become reachable in the future. Or they might not. Either way, understand and accept they are not reachable right now, so don't spend your precious time on them.

4. Have a goal for your cold-calling program

Before you even start your calling, know what your goal is. Are you calling to obtain or confirm information? To further qualify them? To schedule a meeting? To close a sale? Whatever your specific goals are, they should be about moving your leads through your sales cycle.

5. Don't waste time

If the person you're calling says he's not interested right now, don't waste your time or his trying to "overcome his objection." We are taught to push through the first couple of objections to get a close, but that tactic is best left for a face-to-face meeting. On a cold phone call, it's okay for the person to say no, because he probably does not have a need or interest right now. However, if you can get a person talking about her business as it relates to your product or service, you stand a better chance of breaking through her defenses and getting her to commit to a meeting or whatever the next step is in your sales cycle.

6. Remember why you're calling

When you're cold calling, it's easy to get distracted by rejection or by people who want to talk about things that do not help you reach your goal. Remember, you're calling for a reason. Stay focused on that reason. Write it down and keep it in front of you if that helps. Don't allow yourself to get distracted.

7. Schedule your calling

Set aside a block of time when you'll make your calls. This helps get you started and not get sidetracked by other things that come up during the day. You might vary the time from day to day to see what works best. Also, it's best to not take incoming calls while cold calling (if you can arrange this).

8. Manage your activities and monitor your outcomes

Because cold calling often yields a low-percentage return, it's easy to lose motivation and feel as though you're not getting anywhere. Instead, focus on your inputs, your activities. Then observe the results of those activities, but don't get too tied up with them. A good way to do this is to simply set an activity goal for each time you cold call. Maybe your goal is twenty-five outgoing calls a day. Do that for a week or two and see what your results are. If the results are what you want, keep doing that activity at that level. If the results are not what you want, then change your activities or your activity level.

9. Warm up first

If the very thought of cold calling sends chills up and down your spine, make your first call to a friend or customer with whom you already have a good relationship. This will relax you and get you used to talking on the phone. You can practice using your script to guide your words and your delivery. But don't read any script word for word. If you do, you'll sound like a robot, not an intelligent professional.

10. Ask for a commitment

Finally, the most important part of your call: asking for a commitment. One of the worst time-wasters for salespeople is when leads say they're interested, but they really are not. An effective way to prevent this is to get them to commit to something. If they're willing to commit something, it's much more likely they are interested in working with you. You might ask to schedule a meeting. Or maybe you're asking them to commit to a call back at a specific day and time. Some people even ask for a commitment before they send information. Your goal is to move the person on the other end of the phone line forward in your sales cycle or to a lower priority in your database (or get rid of them).

Source: Kevin Stirtz, author of *How To Make Cold Calling Work For Your Business* (*www.kevinstirtz.com*)—Stirtz has spent most of his career growing small businesses. He is a professional speaker, consultant, and writer. You can reach Kevin via e-mail at *kevin@kevinstirtz.com* or by calling (952) 212-4681.

Marketing Your Products and Services

Biggest Direct-Mailing Mistakes

Successful direct mailing can depend on avoiding the big mistakes. It is important for you and your business to understand where direct mailing can go wrong. Here is a list of the biggest mistakes a direct-mailing expert and copywriter with over twenty-five years of experience has made.

1. Ignoring the most important factor in direct-mail success: the mailing list

A great mailing package, with superior copy and scintillating design, might pull double the response of a poorly conceived mailing. But the best list can pull a response ten times more than the worst list for the identical mailing piece. The most common direct-mail mistake is not spending enough time and effort up-front, when you select—and then test—the right lists. Remember: In direct marketing, a mailing list is not just a way of reaching your market. It is the market.

2. Not testing

Big consumer mailers test all the time. Publisher's Clearinghouse tests just about everything . . . even the slant of the indicia on the outer envelope. Business-to-business marketers, on the other hand, seldom track response or test one mailing piece or list against another. As a result, they repeat their failures and have no idea of what works in direct mail—and what doesn't. In direct mail, do *not* assume you know what will work. Test to find out.

3. Not using a letter in your mailing package

The sales letter is the most important part of your direct-mail package. A package with a letter will nearly always out pull a postcard, a self-mailer, or a brochure or ad reprint mailed without a letter.

4. Stressing features versus benefits

Perhaps the oldest and most widely embraced rule for writing direct-mail copy is "stress benefits, not features." But in business-to-business marketing, that doesn't always hold true. In certain situations, features must be given equal (if not top) billing over benefits.

5. Not having an offer

An offer is what the reader gets when he responds to your mailing. To be successful, a direct-mail package should sell the offer not the product itself. For example, if someone mails a letter describing a new mainframe computer, the letter is not going to do the whole job of convincing people to buy the computer. But the letter is capable of swaying some people to at least show interest by requesting a free brochure about the computer. Make sure you have a well-thought-out offer in every mailing. If you think the offer and the way you describe it are unimportant, you are wrong.

6. Using superficial copy

Nothing kills the selling power of a business-to-business mailing faster than lack of content. The equivalent in industrial literature is called the "art director's brochure." You've seen them: showcase pieces destined to win awards for graphic excellence. The brochures that are so gorgeous that everybody falls in love with them—until they wake up and realize that people send for information not pretty pictures. This is why typewritten, non-illustrated sales brochures can often pull double the response of expensive, four-color work. One of the quickest ways to kill that response is to be superficial. Talking in vague generalities, rather than specifics, or rambling without authority on a subject, rather than showing customers that you understand their problems, their industries, and their needs.

7. Saving the best for last

Some copywriters save their strongest sales pitch for last, starting slow in their sales letters and hoping to build to a climactic conclusion. Leo Bott, Jr., a Chicago-based mail-order writer, says that the typical prospect reads for five seconds before she decides whether to continue reading or throw your mailing in the trash. The letter must grab her attention immediately. So start your letter with your strongest sales point. Know the "hot spots" of your direct-mail package,—the places that get the most readership: the first paragraphs of the letter, its subheads, its last paragraph, and the postscript (80% of readers look at the PS); the brochure cover, its subheads, and the headline of its inside spread; picture captions; and the headline and copy on the order form or reply card. Put your strongest selling copy in those spots.

8. Failing to follow up

Hot leads rapidly turn ice cold when not followed up quickly. Slow fulfillment, poor marketing literature, and inept telemarketing can destroy the initial interest that you worked so hard to build. Don't put 100 percent of your time and effort into lead-generating mailing and nothing into the follow-up, as so many mailers do. You have to keep selling, every step of the way.

9. Forgetting the magic words

This mistake is not using the magic words that can dramatically increase the response to your mailing. General advertisers, operating under the mistaken notion that the mission of the copywriter is to be creative, avoid the magic words of direct mail, because they think those magic phrases are clichés. But just because a word or phrase is used frequently doesn't mean that it has lost its power to achieve your communications objective. In conversation, for example, "please" and "thank you" never go out of style.

10. Starting with the product—not the prospect

You and your products are not important to the prospect. The reader opening your sales letter only wants to know: "What's in it for me? How will I come out ahead by doing business with you versus someone else?" Read, talk, and listen to find out what's going on with your customers. Talk to your customers. Good direct mail—or any ad copy—should tell them what they want to hear. Not what you think is important.

11. Failing to appeal to all five senses

Unlike an ad, which is two-dimensional, direct mail is three-dimensional and can appeal to all five senses: sight, hearing, touch, smell, taste. Yet most users of direct mail fail to take advantage of the medium's added dimension. Don't plan a mailing without at least thinking about whether you can make it more powerful by adding a solid object, fragrance, or even a sound. You ultimately may reject such enhancements because of time and budget constraints.

12. Creating and reviewing direct mail by committee

Perhaps the biggest problem today is direct mail being reviewed by committees made up of people who have no idea (a) what direct mail is, (b) how it works, or (c) what it can and cannot do.

Source: Robert W. Bly (*www.bly.com*)—He can be contacted at 22 East Quackenbush Avenue, 3rd floor, Dumont, NJ 07628; (201) 385-1220; fax (201) 385-1138. An independent copywriter and consultant with over twenty-five years' experience in business-to-business, high-tech, industrial, and direct marketing, he writes sales letters, direct-mail packages, inserts, Internet direct mail, ads, brochures, articles, press releases, newsletters, Web pages, white papers, and other marketing materials clients need to sell their products and services to business and direct-response buyers. He also consults with clients on marketing strategy, mail-order selling, e-marketing, and lead-generation programs.

Considerations for Creating a Great Direct-Mail Letter

If your letter has made it this far, don't lose in the bottom of the ninth inning. This is arguably the most critical part of the direct mailing. You got the right target companies, you've found the name and title of the correct decision-maker for your product or service, the envelope has made it past the gatekeeper, and the letter has been removed from the envelope. Now your letter needs to be good! Our expert, a very experienced marketing firm, offers these things to keep in mind.

1. Ensure the message matches the target audience's needs

Make sure the offer of your products or services matches the needs of the recipient of the mailing. Don't make your pitch to a company president if your message only applies to the engineering staff.

2. Get to the point quickly

If you begin your letter with general information and do not make your point, you will lose the reader. It is critical you make your point in the first few lines of the letter, at least in the first five.

3. Be clear and concise

John Wayne once said, "Talk low, talk slow, and don't say too much." That is darn good advice, Pilgrim! Enough said.

4. Sell benefits—please

Many manufacturers, especially those founded and run by entrepreneurial engineers, love to list and discuss product features. Don't ignore potential buyers. They want to know how using your product or service will benefit them. Go ahead and list your features if you must, but make sure you include the end-user benefits. If your drill offers X, Y, and Z-axis control, make sure you indicate this speeds up the drilling process by 22 percent, saving time and labor costs and increasing accuracy and reducing scrap by 8 percent. Now the recipients know your product can improve their operation.

5. Sell—don't tell

This isn't easy because we all aren't comfortable selling. Look at your words. "Koch Group has been in existence for 30+ years." That's a statement that tells. What if we said, "Koch Group has been assisting small and mid-size manufacturers to profit from our industrial marketing services since the mid-'60s." Now we are selling.

6. Keep it personal and conversational

With today's access to current data, there is no excuse for sending out a form letter. Personalize each letter you send out in your direct-mail campaign. Write as though you're talking to the recipient of your letter. Be conversational, but make sure you clean up all the dirty language!

7. Use letters to generate leads not sales

A one-page letter is an excellent tool to generate leads and interest, but it is far too short to effectively sell products or services. Your goal is to generate a response, whether it is a return mail card, a fax, an e-mail, phone call, or fax. You just want an opportunity; you can't get the sale from a single direct-mail letter.

8. Hand-sign it—make it personal

If you are sending out a mass mailing, it is easy to have an administrative staff person sign your name, or get a machine to do it. Make your letter look as personal as possible and sign it yourself with blue ink.

9. Write to eighth-grade readers

Write as though you are writing a letter to your son or daughter in eighth grade. Regardless of the education or IQ of the recipient, most of us read at an eighth-grade level. Don't use big fancy words; make the letter easily understandable. Use technical descriptions when you have to, but simplify your language as much as possible.

10. Use a PS (postscript)

Response rate testing indicates that the typical letter recipient's eye moves down the page to the PS before they read everything in the letter! If possible, restate your selling proposition in the PS.

11. Use white space

It is hard for the reader to wade through lots of endless text. Use short paragraphs. Use bulleted or numbered lists to make points. Give the reader a break. Make it easy to get through the whole letter.

12. Keep it to one page

Most presidents, purchasing agents, plant engineers, or other targets are busy. Make your point, sell the benefits, make it easy to read, and keep it to one page. The readers don't have a lot of time.

13. Use the active tense

Active is always more powerful than passive. Say "Call our toll-free number now, (800) 470-7845, to receive a free copy of our article 'Working With Reps, 10 Ways to Improve

Success,' and improve your manufacturers' reps' efforts" rather than "If you'd like to improve your manufacturers' reps' efforts, contact us at (800) 470-7845 for a free copy of our article 'Working With Reps, 10 Ways to Improve Success.'"

14. Make a no-risk offer

Offer the recipient something—and make it no risk. Offer free information, an article, some industry tips, a free tutorial, or a product sample. Make sure it is clear there is no risk or obligation on their part. Use this as a "door opener" not a "sales closer."

15. Create a deadline

Whether there is a real deadline or one you create, make one. Usually, the imposition of a deadline increases the rate of responses because the recipients understand they have only a limited time to act.

16. Call to action

You have got to ask for the order. "Call our toll-free number, (800) 470-7845, for a free industrial marketing needs consultation." Don't just end your letter with a whimper and go away.

17. Use postage reply mail

Include a business reply card or reply envelope if you want a mailed response. Make sure it is postage paid. Don't lose a legitimate inquiry for the cost of a stamp! Even in today's high-tech communications age and the World Wide Web, direct-mail research studies indicate a good percentage of responses come by mail.

18. Include a guarantee

If you can offer a guarantee, do it. Some products or services do not easily lend themselves to the offer of a guarantee. Then guarantee your follow-up, your delivery, your customer service, or the best pricing. By offering a guarantee, you offer credibility to your manufacturing products or services.

19. Include testimonials

Nothing speaks better for your product or services than an end-user who is totally pleased. If you use names and companies, make sure you get a signed release. You don't want the beneficiary of your marketing piece to be a former customer's attorney!

20. Include all your contact information

Include your name, your phone number, your toll-free number, your fax number, and your e-mail address. People respond in different ways—give them options.

21. Follow the rules

Direct mail has been effectively used for decades and decades. It has generated rules based on success. If you follow the rules, your likelihood of success will increase.

Source: Koch Group, Inc. (*www.kochgroup.com*) is a second-generation consulting firm offering industrial marketing solutions for manufacturers. They offer practical solutions to the unique marketing problems faced by manufacturers and industrial service providers. Contact them at 240 East Lake Street, Suite 300, Addison, IL 60101; (630) 941-1100; e-mail: *info@kochgroup.com*.

Tips for Creating Your Direct-Mail List

Before you launch into your direct-mail campaign, make sure your database is as good as possible. Here are some tips for creating the best direct-mailing list.

1. Set your criteria for recipients

Criteria can include company size, types of products it manufactures or distributes, their SIC code, number of years in business, and other key criteria. Don't use a "shotgun approach." Make sure your list mailing employs a targeted approach.

2. Get an appropriate list

Direct mail marketers often cite the 60-30-10 Rule. Translated that means 60 percent of your mail success depends on the list, 30 percent on the offer, and only 10 percent on the creativity. It is critical to obtain, or generate, a mail list with the correct target companies or audience for your products, services, and the most important first step. Consider using a list broker to identify the list that meets your needs most concisely.

3. Make sure the list is current

If it is twelve to eighteen months old, and many are, up to 30 percent of the information may be inaccurate!

4. Eliminate the duplicates

Don't send the same letter to the same company unless it is to different locations or different names identified with titles that make them likely decision-makers for your product, service, or offer.

5. Always mail to a person not to a title

Obtain accurate first and last names, with correct spelling, and the titles of the intended recipients. If you have questions about the data obtained, verify through state, regional, or local manufacturer's directories, association lists, trade publication lists, or simply call the company to get the correct information. Misspelled names, company names, or addresses can doom your mailing to the trash without a second thought on the part of the recipient.

6. Clean up truncations

Many lists are sold with truncated company names: Co, Corp, Mfgs, Mfrs, and many others. Others have truncated titles. Don't send out a letter to "John Smith, Treas," or "John Smith, Pres." This will likely send your envelope or mail piece direct to the trash.

7. Don't allow your list to be used until these truncations are cleaned up and expanded

If you get more motivated, make sure you clean up all the address truncations: Dr, St, Ct, Trl, Blvd. Clean them up to ensure your envelope address looks as much like a personalized letter as possible.

8. Mind your customer list

Your best potential for new sales lies with companies you have already produced for or serviced. Make sure past and current customers know about all the services or products you offer, not just the ones they have taken advantage before.

9. Check existing customers for the right contact

Look at the titles of those you usually work with at your existing customers. Determine the titles of those you deal with most often. Then target those titles when you seek list data for your contacts with your new mailing campaign.

Source: Koch Group, Inc. (*www.kochgroup.com*) is a second-generation consulting firm offering industrial marketing solutions for manufacturers. They offer practical solutions to the unique marketing problems faced by manufacturers and industrial service providers. Contact them at 240 East Lake Street, Suite 300, Addison, IL 60101; (630) 941-1100; e-mail: *info@kochgroup.com*.

How to Get the Most from Your Mailhouse

There are ways to mail smarter and get more bang for the buck when working with a mailhouse. Take advantage of their knowledge in optimizing all of the ingredients for a successful mailing. Mailhouses are experts on postal rules and regulations, presorting, and postage discounts, so you'll get the best possible mailing rates. They use USPS-certified CASS address-standardization software to provide significant postal rate discounts and maximize delivery efficiency. Here are some of the ways you can get the most out of working with a mailhouse.

1. A clean list saves money

One of the first things to look at is your mailing list. A clean list is very important; people move, change jobs. Bulk mail sent to the wrong address will not be delivered and will not be returned, leaving you wondering why the response rate wasn't higher. It's a good idea to have your mailhouse check lists for duplicate names, especially when merging multiple lists, and run all lists through postal CASS certification to add ZIP+4 codes and correct misspelled addresses, all of which speeds delivery times.

2. Have the mailhouse help increase your deliverability rates

Mailhouses use tools such as the NCOA (National Change of Address) service, which you should use at least twice a year to reduce undeliverable mail by providing the most current address data.

3. Target smart

You will get the best results when the characteristics of the people on your list match the profile of your "ideal customer." Analyze your product and your present customer. Understand who would benefit from your product or service. Study your competitors and how they market the product. Then have the mailhouse try to find a list that matches these definable characteristics closely.

4. Design for discounts

Next, consider the physical characteristics of the piece you are mailing. Has it been designed to take advantage of the maximum postage discounts? Automation rates are available for pieces that meet Postal Service specs for "machineable" mail. Use the mailhouse design, team design, or review your mailer to make sure you are able to get the best postal rates.

5. Design for results

Use the design team of a mailhouse as a resource to boost your response rate. Does your mail piece still have the same basic look that it did two years ago? Maybe it's time to consider some design changes that will bring more prospects in the front door. After all, the name of the game is still return on investment, so if the cost is higher, more sales will also be needed.

Source: PrintMailers, Inc. (*www.pminet.com*)—A mailing house firm that specializes in managing and producing their customers' projects from consultation, design, list acquisition, offset and laser printing, and complete lettershop and fulfillment services. Contact them at (800) 656–8883: e-mail: *marketing@pminet.com*.

Questions to Ask an Outside Printer Before Hiring Them

Looking to do a large printing job? There are lots of printing firms around, but how can you separate the good from the fair? We asked our expert, a production manager responsible for the printing facility of Chubb and Son Insurance. His job involves printing many company materials. Here are the questions he would ask an outside printing firm.

1. Where are you located?

Location makes it easier to move product between places. Additionally, when you are designing, you will want to check it throughout the process. It is important when designing a new piece to do a press check.

2. Do you have free pickup and delivery to and from my office?

Delivery can get expensive. Free pickup and delivery is cost and time efficient and very helpful to your organization.

3. Do you have the ability to distribute (mail) my products once you have printed them?

Having your printer mail your products ensures that your project is completed in one location. Otherwise, you will have to deal with mailing your products on your own and add another step in your project's process!

4. Do you use digital printers or quick presses for short-run jobs?

Digital printers and quick presses are typically less expensive when running fewer than 5,000 prints.

5. How many colors can you print in one pass?

Small presses can only print two to four colors in a pass. High-end color pieces can require six to eight colors. To achieve a high-end piece on a small press requires two or more passes, creating a higher expense.

6. Can you apply coatings/varnishes?

Coatings or varnishes add dimension to the look and feel of the piece as well as providing a protective layer to those pieces that are going to be handled a lot (i.e., brochures).

7. What kind of finishing equipment do you have?

You will want to know if they can cut paper, fold paper, staple, and put binding on your finished pieces.

8. Are any of your services contracted through another vendor?

If so, ask them to explain. If your product has to leave their facility for more work by another vendor, it will run your cost up more than if they could do it themselves.

9. Do you print business cards, stationery, and letterhead as well as high-end multi-color marketing pieces?

You need to know their full range of printing capabilities. The more your printer does for your company, the less you have to allocate to other organizations.

10. What are the turnaround times for your most common jobs?

The shorter the turnaround time is, the quicker your job is done; which increases your time to market.

11. Do you have the ability to provide creative design services?

You want to know if your printer has the ability to design your products. Designing is not an easy thing to do, which means you may have to find a designer through another service. If your printer can include design, it will be worth your money spent.

12. How are your print/design jobs priced?

You need to know if you are getting a good price for the job they are doing. Shop around and see what kind of package or deal you can get from various printers.

13. Is the sales representative knowledgeable and responsive?

You may know more about what you want than the printer. Make sure that when you are talking to the sales representative, they are a pleasure to do business with and they know

exactly what kind of job you need completed. Low cost can mean low quality; do not be tempted by price!

14. What is the required file format for electronic job submission?

Can jobs be submitted via the Internet? You will want to know how you can get your submissions to your printer so you are aware of all processes in your project.

15. Do you have large-format printers/presses to allow for multiple pieces to be printed on one sheet of paper?

By putting one piece of paper through the press, you can get multiple pieces printed that only need to be cut to the appropriate size. This is a big money saver!

Source: William J. Stickle, assistant vice president/production manager, Chubb and Son Insurance Company (*www.chubb.com*)— Contact him at 145 Chubb Way, Branchburg, NJ 08876; (908) 704-6200; e-mail: *BStickle@chubb.com*.

Ways to Increase the Effectiveness of Your Company's Newsletter

A handy way to maintain ongoing contact with your customers is your newsletter, and it's one of the easiest and most effective sales generators you can use. It arrives in your customers' mailbox on a regular basis. If written well, it is informative and appreciated. Customers begin to look forward to this regular message from their supplier. It serves as a reminder, even an incentive, for them to buy from you. Here are seven ways to increase the effectiveness of your company's newsletter.

1. Keep it objective

This is not the place for advertising slogans or bombast. If you are having a sale, announce it as if it were a news event. Avoid superlatives. If the newsletter looks to the reader like just another advertisement, you lose your credibility, and your customer's attention.

2. Use four-color

It looks better, and it doesn't have to cost a lot. Print a year's supply of just the masthead in four-color. Then, each month or each quarter, simply print the articles in black ink and have a four-color newsletter for little more than the price of one.

3. Keep it simple

Four pages works best (single sheet of 11 by 17 inches folded once). Make it easy and fun to read, with lots of brief (four- or five-paragraph) articles, photos, cartoons, charts, and graphs.

4. Make it look like a newspaper

Divide the pages into columns. Use a standard newsprint typestyle below a masthead with a clever name. If possible, use the name of your firm in the masthead.

5. Speak directly to your customers

Feature a column from the president of your company. In the column, summarize each of the articles that appear in the newsletter, perhaps a paragraph on each.

6. Create testimonials from satisfied customers

Use Case Studies—for example, how your company solved a particularly sticky problem. They help to build your image and credibility, and your customers will enjoy seeing their name in print.

7. Make it fun

Page two of your newsletter should be your fun page. Use a joke box (keep them clean), a silly quote, or a "Did You Know" column with fun facts of trivial information. Things like celebrity birthdays, the population of Katmandu, the cost of a Big Mac in Moscow, or unusual world records. Buried among the four or five factoids is one pertaining to your business (e.g., "Did You Know ABC Company has the only fully digital gimcrack in town?").

Source: Robert Grede, founder, The Grede Company, marketing and strategic planning consultants (*www.thegredecompany.com*)—Clients range from start-up operations to Fortune 500 firms. He taught marketing and entrepreneurial management at Marquette University for many years and is a syndicated columnist and frequent contributor to magazines and author of the bestselling *Naked Marketing—The Bare Essentials* (Prentice Hall) and *5 Kick-Ass Strategies (to Reach the Next Level)* (SourceBooks). A familiar face on television and radio talk shows, he speaks on the subject of marketing and strategic thinking at civic organizations and corporate venues.

Ways to Maximize E-mail Response Rates

Internet direct mail typically generates a response rate between 1 and 20 percent, although some do better and a few do worse. The copy in your e-mail plays a big role in whether your e-marketing message ends up at the bottom or the top of that range. Here are some proven techniques for maximizing the number of e-mail recipients who click-through to your Web site or other response mechanism.

1. At the beginning of the e-mail, put a from line and a subject line

The subject line should be constructed like a short attention-grabbing, curiosity-arousing outer-envelope teaser, compelling recipients to read further—without being so blatantly promotional it turns them off. Example: "Come on back to Idea Forum!"

2. The from line identifies you as the sender if you're e-mailing to your house file

If you're e-mailing to a rented list, the line might identify the list owner as the sender. This is especially effective with opt-in lists where the list owner (e.g., a Web site) has a good relationship with its users.

3. Avoid free in your subject line

Despite the fact that the word free is a proven, powerful response-booster in traditional direct marketing, and that the Internet culture has a bias in favor of free offers rather than paid offers, some e-marketers avoid FREE in the subject line. The reason is the "spam filter" software some Internet users have installed to screen their e-mail. These filters eliminate incoming e-mail, and many identify any message with FREE in the subject line as promotional.

4. Lead off the message copy with a killer headline or lead-in sentence

You need to get a terrific benefit right upfront. Pretend you're writing envelope teaser copy or are writing a headline for a sales letter.

5. In the first paragraph, deliver a mini-version of you're the complete message

State the offer and provide an immediate response mechanism, such as clicking on a link connected to a Web page. This appeals to Internet prospects with short attention spans.

6. Expand after the first paragraph

After the first paragraph, present expanded copy that covers the features, benefits, proof, and other information the buyer needs to make a decision. This appeals to the prospect who needs more details than a short paragraph can provide.

7. Use the offer-and-response mechanism at the beginning and at the end

The offer-and-response mechanism should be repeated in the close of the e-mail, as in a traditional direct-mail letter. But they should almost always appear at the very beginning, too. That way, busy Internet users who don't have time to read and give each e-mail only a second or two get the whole story.

8. Use wide margins

You don't want to have weird wraps or breaks. Limit yourself to about fifty-five to sixty characters per line. If you think a line is going to be too long, insert a character return. Internet copywriter Joe Vitale sets his margins at 20 and 80, keeping sentence length to sixty characters, and ensuring the whole line gets displayed on the screen without odd text breaks.

9. Take it easy on the all-caps

You can use WORDS IN ALL CAPS but do so carefully. They can be a little hard to read—

and in the world of e-mail, all caps give the impression that you're shouting.

10. In general, short is better

This is not the case in classic mail-order selling where as a general principle, "the more you tell, the more you sell." E-mail is a unique environment. Readers are quickly sorting through a bunch of messages and aren't disposed to stick with you for a long time.

11. Regardless of length, get the important points across quickly

If you want to give a lot of product information, add it lower down in your e-mail message. You might also consider an attachment, such as a Word document, PDF file, or html page. People who need more information can always scroll down or click for it. The key benefits and deal should be communicated in the first screen, or very soon afterward.

12. Use a helpful, friendly, informative, and educational tone, not promotional or hard-sell

Trying to sell readers with a traditional hyped-up sales letter won't work. People online want information and lots of it. You'll have to add solid material to your puffed-up sales letter to make it work online, Refrain from saying your service is "the best" or that you offer "quality." Those are empty, meaningless phrases. Be specific. How are you the best? What exactly do you mean by quality? Who says it besides you? Even though information is the gold, readers don't want to be bored. They seek, like all of us, excitement. Give it to them.

13. Include opt-out options

Including an opt-out statement prevents flaming from recipients who feel they have been spammed by stating that your intention is to respect their privacy, and making it easy for them to prevent further promotional e-mails from being sent to them. All they have to do is click on Reply and type UNSUBSCRIBE or REMOVE in the subject line. Example: "We respect your online time and privacy, and pledge not to abuse this medium. If you prefer not to receive further e-mails from us of this type, please reply to this e-mail and type 'Remove' in the subject line."

Source: Robert W. Bly (*www.bly.com*)—An independent copywriter and consultant with over twenty-five years' experience in business-to-business, high-tech, industrial, and direct marketing, he writes sales letters, direct-mail packages, inserts, Internet direct mail, ads, brochures, articles, press releases, newsletters, Web pages, white papers, and other marketing materials clients need to sell their products and services to business and direct-response buyers. He also consults with clients on marketing strategy, mail-order selling, e-marketing, and lead-generation programs. He can be contacted at 22 East Quackenbush Avenue, 3rd floor, Dumont, NJ 07628; (201) 385-1220; fax: (201) 385-1138.

Ways to Make Your Web Site Stand Out

It is important for you and your business to have features on a Web site that are popular, appealing, and effective. This will retain your customer's interest while on your Web site and can promote sales and future traffic. Our expert specializes in Web-site design—so here are a few ways to make your Web site stand out.

1. Easy to read

If you use background colors or images, the text on top of the background should be in a color that can easily be seen. Use a color scheme that complements and is pleasing to the eye. White space between images and sections of text make a page easier to view.

2. Easy to navigate

A visitor should be able to find the information they are looking for without hassle and frustration. Group navigation buttons together. If you use image links, provide text links for visitors who have images turned off on their browser or are using an older browser that doesn't support images.

3. Easy to view

A Web site should be easily viewable in all screen sizes without a visitor having to scroll horizontally (left to right).

4. Quick to download

Graphics and sounds add download time to a Web page. Use them sparingly. Don't make your visitors wait too long for your site to download, or they will click away and probably won't return. It is a good idea to find out what the approximate download times are for people who are using 28K and 56K telephone modems. Not everyone has DSL or cable Internet.

5. Avoid dead links

Make sure that links on all your pages are working, whether they are internal links to pages within your site, or links to external Web sites.

6. Keep the content fresh

People are more apt to return to your Web site if they find new and interesting material. Post articles on your site, offer a newly updated "Internet Special," or provide fresh, helpful links. All these things cause visitors to bookmark your site as a reference tool.

7. Clear and to the point

Visitors should have a clear understanding of what your Web site is about when they visit. Studies have shown that people do not like to read computer screens, so keep your Web site copy interesting to read and to the point.

8. Keep your target audience in mind

Think about the people who would be interested in visiting your Web site. If you are designing a Web site about razor blades and shaving cream for men, the site should have a masculine feel. Decorating with pink hearts and roses may not be a good idea.

9. Provide a form for visitors to contact you

Visitors are more likely to fill out a form to contact you than click on an e-mail link. Always make things easy for your visitors ... especially when it comes to contacting you.

10. Browser compatible

Check your Web site in the most popular browsers to make sure everything is displayed properly. The top two browsers used are Internet Explorer and Netscape Navigator, but there are others such as the AOL browser, Mosaic, Opera, and Web TV. Various versions of the same browser also display differently. It is a good idea to have a program on your computer that checks browser and version compatibility.

Source: Mount Evans Designs (*www.mountevansdesigns.com*)— A Web-design consulting firm located at 243 Ridge View Trail, Idaho Springs, CO 80452.

Popular Internet-Marketing Methods

Internet marketing is important to you and your business in order to increase Web-site traffic and prospective clients or customers. The list here, created by an Internet-marketing expert, will help you and your company increase your business by using the Web.

1. Track and analyze your Web-site traffic

Most Web hosts offer traffic analysis data to their clients, and it is arguably the most important tool at your disposal in measuring the effectiveness of your Internet-marketing techniques and overall Web-site performance. By taking the time to understand this data, you can begin to understand the motivations and interests of your audience. Are many of them leaving on one particular page? Perhaps you should make some changes to keep their interest. Are most of them looking at one particular part of your site? Perhaps you should make it a more featured area. Since this data updates on a regular basis, you are also able to gauge the effectiveness of any changes that you make. These are the most basic examples; there are many more useful bits of information available—what search terms your visitors are using to find you, what sites are bringing you the most traffic, how long your visitors are staying, and so on. Maintaining a successful Web site is an ongoing process, and visitor data is crucial to getting optimum results.

2. Exchange links with noncompeting, quality companies related to your industry

This is a simple but effective piece of Internet-marketing advice. Link exchanges allow you to get quality traffic while increasing the prestige of your business. Visitors who enter your site from a link they find on another site are predisposed to believe that they will find something of value there (if not, why would the site take the time and effort to link to it?). By making sure that the companies you exchange links with are not direct competitors, you are unlikely to lose business. The added benefit to link-building Internet-marketing techniques is that they can give a tremendous boost to your link popularity, which is a major factor in determining how your site gets ranked in search engines.

3. Write informative articles about your business or products and make them available to online publications and Web masters

Numerous sites will allow you to offer original informational articles for others to publish. Such an exchange benefits you in several ways. First, all of these sites require anyone who is reprinting your article to provide a link back to your site, which can provide highly targeted visitors (visitors who most likely already have a good impression of you from your article). This is also another way to boost your link popularity, which is vitally important to your search engine rankings. Moreover, if you offer a service, a reputation is your most valuable asset. Widely distributed articles can help to establish you as an expert in your field and help you to gain credibility with your future clients. Although Internet-marketing techniques such as these may require a considerable time investment, the payoff can be well worth the trouble.

4. Give your Web-site visitors a clear call to action

If your site isn't intended to sell a product or gain a customer, then what is it for? Your Internet-marketing techniques should have a clear purpose, meaning that every page on your site should focus on getting the visitor to take an action. This could be purchasing something online, filling out a form or sending an e-mail, making a phone call, or even simply moving on to the next step in the process. Your Web site should be more than a static billboard proclaiming that you are open for business; it should compel your visitors to follow a specific path that leads to a sale. The answer can be as simple as placing a prominent offer on your pages.

5. Don't overlook the obvious

This might fall better into the category of Internet-marketing advice, rather than Internet-marketing techniques. However, it is important that you compare your Web site to an actual store. Is everything clean and organized, or is everything messy and cluttered? Many Web sites give bad first impressions with issues that could easily be avoided. Broken links are a sign of sloppiness that are fairly common. To combat this, there are several Web sites that will automatically scan your site and identify any broken links. Seeing little red *x*s where a graphic or photo should

appear is another common problem that is easily addressed. Does your site maintain its look and functionality with most browsers? People are sometimes dismayed to learn that their site (which looks great in Internet Explorer) doesn't maintain its look or functionality with other popular browsers such as Netscape. The time and resources required to fix these problems are small when compared with the cost of tarnishing your professional image.

Source: Medium Blue, Internet-marketing specialists (*www.medium blue.com*)—Contact them at 670 Eleventh Street NW, Atlanta, GA 30318; toll-free: (888) 213-2531; e-mail: *info@mediumblue.com*.

Popular Ways to Find Customers

What's the hardest thing about starting a business? For many new business owners, the answer is "finding customers." Having a great product or service that you are sure many people will need isn't good enough. Customers won't find you or your Web site just because you have started selling a product or service. Indeed, most business owners have to go on regular and frequent fishing trips to find customers and keep new business coming in their doors. But how do you do that? Here's a list of suggestions to get you started.

1. Develop a plan

Consider who would make the ideal customer. If you sell to businesses, consider what department is most likely to buy your products or services, and what individual (what level of responsibility) would be the one to determine the specific purchase requirements. (Make some calls if you don't know!) Then consider how that individual would normally find products or services like yours. What circles do they travel in? Who are they likely to listen to, or where do they look when they want to buy a product or service? Find a way to put your information, or yourself, in their path.

2. Realize there is no one path to success

Sales often happen because prospective customers hear about your products and services in several different ways and from several different sources. The more often they hear about you, the more likely they are to consider what you have to offer when they are ready to buy.

3. Work your local newspapers

Daily and weekly newspapers are an incredible source of contact information and leads to potential customers. Watch for names of people who have been promoted, who have won awards, who have opened new businesses, or who in any way may be potential customers. Send those people personalized mailings letting them know the benefits of what you sell. Try to attend meetings they will be at, as well. When you meet them or send mail, let them know you read about them and congratulate them on their success or mention how interesting the article about them was.

4. Watch for events that may bring your potential market together

Contact the organizers of the event and offer to give away your product or service as a prize during the event in exchange for having the group promote you in their promotions.

5. Attend meetings and seminars that your prospects might attend

If you've been doing that and haven't made contacts that could lead to sales, look in the newspapers to see what other organizations hold events that might attract your target market and attend some of those meetings.

6. Follow up after meetings

Contact the people you've met to see if they may be prospects. If they say they don't need your services now, ask when a good time to call them back would be, or if they have business associates who could use what you sell now.

7. Give a little to get a lot

Give away free samples of your product, and ask the recipients to tell their friends if they are pleased. Or, if you are a consultant, give away some free advice. This could be in the form of a newsletter that contains news or tips and hints, or it could be a free consultation during which you provide just enough information to help the client scope out their project and know that you have the ability to handle it.

8. Work your personal network

Ask your friends if they know people who can use your services, or people who may know others who could use your services. If your pricing structure will allow it, offer friends and business associates a finders' fee for referrals that turn into jobs.

9. Study your competition

Advertise where they do. Promote yourself where your competition promotes themselves.

10. Use multiple small ads instead of one big one

If most people in your type of business advertise to bring in customers, do the same. But don't plan on making a big splash with one large ad. Plan smaller ads to run over a long time in the same publications that your competitors use. The repetition will build name recognition. If you advertise in the Yellow Pages, consider taking out ads in multiple category headings. If you provide office support services, you might want to advertise under the Word Processing and the Typing headings.

11. Ask for feedback when prospects don't buy

Did they find a product that better served their needs? Did they decide they don't need the product at all? Did they just postpone their buying decision? Did they find it difficult to place an order on your Web site? Use what you learn to make needed changes and watch your sales start to grow.

Source: Janet Attard, owner, Attard Communications, Inc. (*www .businessknowhow.com*)—Her firm provides editorial content, online community, and Web-development services. She is the founder of the award-winning Business Know-How small business Web site and information resource. She is also the author of *The Home Office and Small Business Answer Book and of Business Know-How: An Operational Guide For Home-Based and Micro-Sized Businesses with Limited Budgets.* Contact her at (631) 467-6826 or by e-mail at *attard@businessknowhow.com.*

Top Technology-Based Marketing Tools

Today's incredible technology can do the work of thousands in a click of a button. It is important that you look into marketing tools that are sure to be a success for your business! This list has been made by a small business expert and marketing consultant.

1. Electronic newsletters

One of the most effective follow-up marketing tools available is the humble newsletter. Electronic newsletters are much like paper-based newsletters in that they inform, entertain, and make product or service recommendations. The difference is that you can send an electronic newsletter instantly to thousands of people with the simple push of a button for almost no cost whatsoever. The key to making electronic newsletters work is to write, in a personal voice, as though you were talking to your prospect or customer face-to-face.

2. E-mail autoresponders

An autoresponder service automatically sends multiple e-mail messages that you create on a scheduled basis that you define. Your autoresponder service will automatically send customers one e-mail containing the content that you are offering to give out. Perhaps you send a useful tip or technique in a field they would like to know more about, without any manual intervention from you. Included in each day's tip could be an offer to visit your Web site to take advantage of a special offer or to visit your store to receive a personalized educational session.

3. Self-produced audio/video CDs

When prospects make a decision to buy, they often know very little about your product or service and are crying out for knowledge and advice so they make the right decision. The first small business owner who takes the time to educate the prospect is usually the one who gets the sale. The problem is that it takes a lot of time and effort to educate prospects on a face-to-face basis (or over the telephone). Using educational audio and video products, you can create a relationship of trust and admiration without having to physically be there to do the work.

4. Telephone hot lines

How would you like to capture the name and address of all your lead sources and know exactly where they all came from? Capturing this information would allow you to do follow-up marketing with your prospects and compute the exact return-on-investment of each of your marketing and advertising campaigns. Telephone hotlines allow you to do just that … and more. At the end of the month you go online, click a button, and a report spits out the exact source of each of your leads and when they came in. Now you have some powerful information that will allow you to track the return on each marketing campaign precisely.

5. Internet-based pay-per-click advertising

More and more people are going to the Internet to search for information before they call any small business. It's critical to be the first business that your prospects finds in their search. Pay-per-click advertising allows you to do that in a low-risk way. Pay-per-click adver-

tising programs such as Overture and Google's Adwords program allow you to bid for search engine placement. With Google AdWords or Overture you create your own ads, choose keywords to match your ads to your audience and pay only when someone clicks on them. You may only have to pay five cents per click to be at the top of the search engines. In less than one hour, any retailer or small business owner can launch their own pay-per-click Internet-advertising program.

6. Voice broadcasting

Voice broadcasting allows you to send personalized reminders, invitations, and/or verbal coupons to existing customers. The message is sent out via a broadcaster directly to your customer's voice-mail machine for only pennies per delivered message. Imagine the impact of sending out a voice message before your direct-mail campaign to your customers, letting them know that they will be receiving a great offer from you and that it's going to be delivered in the next day or so and to be on the lookout for it. You simply record your message, upload it to the voice broadcasting service along with your customer's phone numbers, and tell the service the date and time you want the message delivered.

7. Online direct-mail systems

With the click of a mouse, you can now send out postcards and greeting cards. The days of printing letters and postcards, stuffing envelopes, and licking stamps are over. Postcards and greeting cards make excellent follow-up marketing relationship-building tools. Imagine being able to send not one but an entire series of fully customized postcards or greeting cards to your prospect over a specified time, with just a couple clicks of a mouse. Follow-up marketing will never be the same.

Source: David Frey, owner of MarketingBestPractices.com and the author of the bestselling manual, *The Small Business Marketing Bible*, and the senior editor of the *Small Business Marketing Best Practices* Newsletter. Contact him at *david@MarketingBestPractices.com*.

Things to Include in a Marketing Budget

Some people feel that marketing is all about money. Even bad products can sell well if they're marketed effectively. Even though your product or service is a quality one, that's no guarantee of success. You'll need to market, and this will be expensive. Here is a list of things to include in your marketing budget created by Small Business Administration, which helps at every stage of developing and expanding a successful business.

1. Marketing communications

An umbrella term used to describe activities that deliver marketing messages to *target audiences*. In other words, all the activities you undertake to "talk" with customers, prospects, and other important audiences. Marketing communications is one component of the marketing discipline that includes market research, product development, and selling.

2. Market research

A systematic, objective collection and analysis of data about your target market, competition, and/or environment with the goal being increased understanding. Through the *market research process*, you can take data—a variety of related or unrelated facts—and create useful information to guide your business decisions. Market research is not an activity conducted only once; it is an ongoing study.

3. Promotion plan

A promotion plan outlines the promotional tools or tactics you plan to use to accomplish your marketing objectives. To the new or inexperienced marketer, the promotion plan might be mistaken as the entire marketing plan because it outlines where the majority of the marketing budget will be spent. It is, however, just one component of the marketing plan; there are additional strategy and planning components described in a marketing plan.

4. Advertising

It may be critical to the existence of your business. Hardly any business, particularly a retail operation, can stay alive without it. Companies that don't advertise may have their sales and profits swallowed up by other companies that do advertise regularly.

5. Community involvement and special events

Because your community supports your business, it's a good business practice to support your community. (But first, a quick word about community. Community is more than a location, such as a town or city. Community also refers to groups of people, such as the Hispanic community in a city, the small business community in a county, etc.) The great thing about participating in community events and programs is that it's a win-win for both you and your community.

6. Press kits

A press kit is a set of materials designed to communicate your message in detail to reporters and media directors. It is used to help reporters and directors gain an understanding of your company, product, or service so they will write about it.

Source: Office of Women's Business Ownership Small Business Administration (*www.sba.gov*)—Contact them at 409 Third Street SW, Fourth Floor, Washington, DC 20416; (202) 205-6673; e-mail: *owbo@sba.gov*.

Ways to Do Your Own Market Research

Getting information from your customers and prospects is easy! Here are a few of the many possible techniques that you can try on your own, from an expert on doing things cheaply.

1. Ask

If you bring people to an event, ask for a show of hands about how they all learned about it (don't forget "from a friend"); if you book clients for appointments, ask at the time they make the appointment; if you run a retail store, let each cashier keep a tally of what brought the customer in, and how much was purchased (an easy way to do this: preprint some index cards on which the cashiers can check off the source and write the dollar amount).

2. Join a group

Join online discussion groups where your customers hang out. Post to the list that you want feedback on a new product or packaging idea.

3. Get feedback online

Set up a Web page on your own site to collect feedback.

4. Use survey tools

Use tools like *www.HostedSurvey.com*—which allows you to set up your survey online, hook it to your Web site, or e-mail invitations to your customer list, collect responses, view reports, and download the data to your own computer—and that don't cost you an arm and a leg.

5. Try a real-life test

For instance, offer a choice of free reports on the same topic. The one that gets the most responses should be the name of your next product.

6. Use codes

In any direct-mail campaign, advertisement, or online medium, you can know exactly what caused your customer to respond. For instance, an ad would specify a response to PO Box 1164-B1, while a particular rented list might be directed to PO Box 1164-N17. Web pages can have tracking codes built right into the URL, so you can analyze them later in your statistics package.

7. Check out what others are doing

Years ago, I considered leading specialized tours of certain New York City neighborhoods. I contacted the NYC Convention & Visitors Bureau to find out about tours that already existed, and quickly decided this was not a market I could afford to enter, because I live three hours out and there were dozens of fascinating tours already, at rock-bottom prices. As a result of my early research, when I abandoned the business idea, I was out only about two hours of my time and the cost of a phone call to the visitor center.

Source: Shel Horowitz (www.frugalmarketing.com)—Internationally known marketing consultant, copywriter, and speaker, he specializes in affordable, effective marketing for small businesses, entrepreneurs, and nonprofits. He also wrote the award-winning books, *Principled Profit: Marketing That Puts People First, Grassroots Marketing: Getting Noticed in a Noisy World*, and four other books. Contact him at shel@principledprofits.com or by phone at (413) 586-2388.

Questions to Ask Before Starting a Marketing Campaign

A marketing campaign can be a big waste of money, time, and effort. Make sure you and your business are starting off on the right foot. Here is a list of questions to ask before starting your campaign created by our expert, a director for the Florida Gulf Coast Office of KSR, a full-service marketing agency.

1. Are you using enough disciplines?

The most effective marketing programs comprise several disciplines. Ads, press releases, media events, article placements all work together in synthesis, sometimes toward different goals. One may be better for building awareness, another for gaining credibility, still another for generating leads. Putting all of your eggs in one marketing basket narrows your playing field and minimizes your effectiveness.

2. When should you start your campaign?

Marketing is a continual endeavor, one that needs to be exercised in the boom seasons as well as the dry. If you stop marketing when business is good, where will customers come from when it starts to taper off? In a similar vein, don't depend on residual results from one public relations event or one ad or one media placement. People who read an article about you in the paper will patronize your business at least for a week or two. Then the slump will hit. You need a supporting marketing program so that customer activity doesn't die out as soon as the spike is over.

3. How do you attract customers and keep them interested?

It's great to have ads, publicity pieces, and direct-marketing campaigns that are on target when it comes to attracting the interest of potential customers. But too many leave those same potential customers high and dry. You don't snag a game fish and neglect to reel it in because it's hooked! Customers are looking for direction. Give it to them. Make your offer compelling . . . then make it easy for your customer to take the next step in the buying process.

4. How do you get loyalty from your customers?

You've got to turn purchasers into loyal customers. Authors and marketing experts Ben McConnell and Jackie Huba advocate the development of "customer evangelists"—people who are so pleased with your product or service, they go out and tell the world. "This group of satisfied believers can be converted into a potent marketing force to grow your universe of customers," they claim. The number of loyal customers will increase when they find your product and/or service to be the best around.

5. What do the customers want?

Consumers want two things from you: to recognize (or make them aware of) a problem or need that they have, and to offer them the means to solve or satisfy it. Provide compelling evidence that your business is the obvious and only logical choice to solve that problem, and your results should go through the roof.

Source: Bob Massey has won state and national awards for Excellence in Business Writing, and is the account services director for the Florida Gulf Coast Office of KSR, a full-service marketing agency. You can contact him at (941) 255-1055, or e-mail bob@ksrteam.com.

Top Telemarketing Firms

Is your business looking for a telemarketing firm? The following firms are some of the best in the industry.

1. Vertrue Incorporated

Vertrue is an integrated marketing services company that gives consumers unrivaled opportunities to improve their lives through exclusive access to significant discounts and unique services.

750 Washington Boulevard
Stamford, CT 06901
and 680 Washington Boulevard
Stamford, CT 06901
www.vertrue.com

2. DialAmerica Marketing Inc.

DialAmerica has been in the telemarketing business for over forty-seven years, longer than any other telemarketers in business today. Today, DialAmerica is the largest, privately owned telemarketing company in the United States with annual revenues of $220 million.

960 Macarthur Boulevard
Mahwah, NJ 07495
www.dialamerica.com

3. ICT Group Inc.

ICT Group offers a full range of services to support the sales, service, and marketing needs of clients within major industry segments.

100 Brandywine Boulevard
Newtown, PA 18940
(800) 799-6880
(800) 201-1085
www.ictgroup.com

4. RMH Teleservices Inc.

Founded in 1983, RMH has grown steadily to become the highest quality, most innovative, and committed provider of outsourced customer relationship management services.

507 Prudential Road
Horsham, PA 19044
(215) 441-3000
(800) 220-2274
www.rmh.com

5. Telespectrum Worldwide Inc.

Telespectrum is a full-service, multichannel provider of Consultative Customer Contact (C3) solutions. Their expertise includes incubation and rollout in acquisition, customer care, retention, win-back, or complete lifecycle management solutions.

1000 Chesterbrook Blvd
Berwyn, PA 19312
(888) 878-7400

Fax: (610) 699-5700
www.telespectrum.com

6. InfoCision Management Corp.

InfoCision's goal is to provide commercial marketing clients with the highest quality inbound teleservices, outbound teleservices, and e-services . . . period. The staff, from account staff and call center management to communicators, are experts in key industries and applications.

325 Springside Dr.
Akron, OH 44333
(330) 668-1400
www.infocision.com

7. Convergys Customer MGT Group

Convergys' billing, customer care, and human resources solutions combine skilled customer service representatives with advanced customer and information management technologies and state-of-the-art processes.

201 East Fourth Street
Cincinnati, OH 45202
(513) 723-7000
www.convergys.com

8. Sitel Corporation

Their vision is to "build lasting partnerships with their clients by enhancing the value of their customer contacts, relationships, and information.

7277 World Communications Drive
Omaha, NE 68122
(402) 963-6810
Toll-free: (800) 25-SITEL
www.sitel.com

9. West Corporation

Founded in January 1986, West Corporation has evolved from an inbound telemarketing service bureau to one of the nation's leading providers of customized contact solutions.

11808 Miracle Hills Dr.
Omaha, NE 68154
Administration: (800) 762-3800 or (402) 963-1200
Sales: (800) 841-9000
www.west.com

10. TeleTech Services Corporation

Founded in 1982, TeleTech provides proven services for every stage of the customer lifecycle, through a strategic platform that encompasses people, process, technology, and infrastructure. TeleTech interacts with 2 million customers every day using the phone, Web, e-mail, and automated solutions.

9197 South Peoria Street
Englewood, CO 80112-5833
(800) TELETECH
Outside the United States: (303) 397-8100
Fax: (303) 397-8199
E-mail: *info@teletech.com*
www.teletech.com

Source: America Data Management Corp (*www.adm-lists.com*)— A leading provider of direct-marketing and data-processing services to thousands of clients. They provide the highest-quality mailing, tele-marketing, and opt-in e-mail lists available in the industry. Their clients include large Fortune 500 companies and small hometown marketers. They are committed to providing the highest quality data and the very best customer service. Contact them at (239) 573-1124; toll-free: (800) 262-3637; fax: (239) 573-1154; e-mail: *info@adm-lists.com*.

Reasons to Attend a Trade Show

Trade shows can be very expensive. Sometimes it's worth the investment; many times it's not. Before attending a trade show, first decide why you will attend, and then what you will do before, during, and after the show. This will take some organization and time initially, but it will pay off in the long term. The following are some important benefits of attending trade shows.

1. Conduct market research

Trade shows offer a great variety of information. You will have the opportunity to sample products and services from hundreds of different vendors in a short time.

2. Meet existing suppliers and customers

It will depend on your business, but you can make weeks or months worth of sales calls or meetings in a very short period.

3. Investigate new suppliers

If you are not happy with your current supplier or products, this is the perfect opportunity to interview new companies quickly and efficiently.

4. Conduct business meetings

You can meet colleagues and customers over coffee or after an educational session. To do this same thing without the show would cost you money and time.

5. Correct a problem

If you have a problem with a current product, take this opportunity at the show to visit that supplier's exhibit and ask if they can help you solve the problem.

6. Network with colleagues

If you cannot afford to be there as an exhibitor, being a delegate is the next best thing. It will give you the opportunity to be seen in the industry and remain current.

7. Attend educational sessions

Some trade shows offer breakout seminars and lectures. Again, in just a few days you can obtain information that would take you months without the show.

Source: GFTC, Guelph Food Technology Center (*www.gftc.ca*)—Canada's only not-for-profit, unsubsidized food technology center. GFTC provides creative, confidential technical solutions, training, consulting, and auditing to the Canadian agrifood industry in the areas of R & D, product development, packaging, shelf life, food safety, quality, and productivity improvement. Each year, GFTC assists more than 500 companies and organizations and provides training to more than 3,600 people—and they attend a lot of trade shows! Contact them at 88 McGilvray Street, Guelph, Ontario, N1G 2W1, Canada; (519) 821-1246; fax: (519) 836-1281; e-mail: *gftc@gftc.ca*.

Things Your Staff Will Need to Know at a Trade Show Booth

Just because you spent a bunch of dough on a flashy trade show booth doesn't mean you'll succeed at the next show. Your staff are a critical part of how you'll fare. They need training and direction. Here are a few things your staff should know before entering a trade show booth, provided by our expert, a trade show coach who works with companies to improve their meeting and event success through coaching, consulting, and training.

1. Reason

Ask your booth staff why your company exhibits at any particular show, and their answers may surprise you. Tradition and because the competition is exhibiting at the show are among the most often cited reasons booth staff give when asked this question, yet these reasons seldom appear in the company's list of motivations. Explain to your staff the role trade show participation plays in the company's marketing strategy, including items such as timed product launches or establishing a competitive presence. Once the staff understands the role of the trade show, outline the goals you have for show participation in general, and specific benchmarks for each particular show. This will allow your staff time to think about how they can contribute to the team's success.

2. Response

Small talk is easy. Gathering valuable customer information in a casual manner is difficult. Train your booth staff to elicit the desired responses by asking engaging, open-ended questions. Using how, what, when, and why questions encourages attendees to share their business concerns and presents your staff with an opportunity to offer solutions. Role-playing exercises may feel awkward at first, but they often help staff develop the confidence needed to work the show floor effectively. Actually practicing conversations also gives the opportunity to discuss nonverbal communication cues, including posture, physical space, gestures, and eye contact.

3. Route

What happens to all the leads your staff gathers after the show? If you've recently finished a show season, ask your staffers what happened to all those business leads. If they're scratching their heads and looking puzzled, you've got a problem. Leads have an extremely short shelf life. The longer they aren't pursued, the more likely they are to prove fruitless, mediocre, or they went to the competition.

4. System

Staff should be trained to gather all possible contact information and to make relevant, specific notes on the lead form. Having a system in place to distribute and follow up with leads immediately after the show will capitalize on all the time, effort, and resources you put into your trade show participation. There is often a disconnection between trade show leads and the sales staff. Stress to your sales staff that creating new business relationships based on trade show leads is a company priority. Make them accountable for any leads that they were given to avoid having the new leads getting lost in the shuffle.

5. Recess

A very important part of forming a strong trade show team is recess. Schedule some fun training exercises, both to reinforce the educational aspects of your day and for teambuilding purposes. Trade show days are very long, and a team that not only works well together but enjoys each other's company will have a tremendous edge over the competition.

Source: Susan Friedmann, CSP (Certified Speaking Professional), The Tradeshow Coach (*www.thetradeshowcoach.com*)—A Lake Placid, New York, speaker, author, and consultant who works with exhibitors, show organizers, and meeting planners to create more valuable results from their events nationally and internationally. She is the author of *Meeting & Event Planning for Dummies* and many other titles.

Tips to Use Trade Show Giveaways Effectively

Walk around any trade or consumer show and you will be able to collect a bag full of advertising specialties or giveaway items all designed to promote. But look a little more closely. How many really do an effective job? How clearly do they get a message across? Is the message sufficiently visible? Is the giveaway useful or unique enough that you would want to keep and use it? All these questions, and more, need to be considered before jumping into the giveaway game. When thinking about advertising specialties for your next show, consider this list of questions.

1. What do you want to achieve by giving away a premium item?

Design your giveaway items to increase your memorability, communicate, motivate, promote, or increase recognition. It is important not only that the message have an impact, but also the premium itself.

2. How will you select your premium item?

There are a multitude of different items you could consider as a premium. However, which one will best suit your purpose? To select the right item, you need to decide your objective. Do you want it to enhance a theme, convey a specific message, or educate your target audience? A

clear purpose should help make your selection process easier. A promotional specialist can also help you make an effective selection. Remember that your company image is reflected in whatever you choose to give away.

3. Whom do you want to receive your premium?

Having a clear objective for your premium item will also help you decide who should receive it. You may consider having different gifts for different types of visitors. You might have different quality gifts for your key customers, prospects, and general passersby.

4. How does your giveaway tie into your marketing theme?

Is there an item that naturally complements your marketing message? Have the message imprinted on the item and make sure that your company name, logo, and phone number appear clearly. An important aspect of any gift is to remember where it came from long after the fact.

5. What is your budget?

The price range for premium items is enormous. Quality, quantity, and special orders all impact the price. Establish a budget as part of your exhibit marketing plan. Consider ordering the same item for several different shows. The greater the quantity of your order is, the lower the individual unit price is.

6. What must visitors do to qualify for a gift item?

There are several ways to use your premium effectively—for example, as a reward for visitors participating in a demonstration, presentation, or contest; as a token of your appreciation when visitors have given you qualifying information about their specific needs; as a thank-you for stopping at the booth. Avoid leaving items out for anyone to take; this diminishes their value and has little or no memorability factor.

7. Will your giveaway directly help your future sales?

Consider handing out a discount coupon or a gift certificate that requires future contact with your company for redemption. Consider premiums that will help generate frequent visits to customers and prospects, such as calling you for free refills.

8. How does your premium item complement your exhibiting goals?

Premiums can be used to prequalify your prospects. One company uses playing cards. Prior to the show, they send "kings" to their key customers, "queens" to suppliers, "jacks" to new or hot prospects. They request that the cards are brought to the booth in exchange for a special gift. When the cards are presented, the booth staff already knows certain information about the visitor. They can then act on their previous knowledge and use time with the visitor more productively.

9. How will you inform your target audience about your giveaway item?

A sufficiently novel or useful giveaway can actively help to draw prospects to your booth. So make sure your prospects know about it. Send a "tickler" invitation with details of the giveaway or create a two-piece premium, sending one part out to key prospects prior to the show and telling them to collect the other half at your booth.

10. How will you measure the effectiveness of your premium?

Establish a tracking mechanism to measure the success of your giveaway. If it is a redemption item, code it so that you know it resulted from the show. Postshow follow-up could include a question about the premium: Did visitors remember receiving it and how useful was the item? After the show, critique your giveaway with your exhibit team: Did it draw specific prospects to the booth? Was it eye-catching enough to persuade passersby to stop? Did your customers find it useful? Did it project the right corporate image? There are plenty of exciting premiums for you to choose from so that you can avoid the usual pens, pencils, and key chains. Make your premium work for you and it will be money well invested.

Source: Susan Friedmann, CSP (Certified Speaking Professional), The Tradeshow Coach (*www.thetradeshowcoach.com*)—Lake Placid, New York, author of Meeting & Event Planning for Dummies, she also works with exhibitors, show organizers, and meeting planners to create more valuable results from their events nationally and internationally.

Common Trade Show–Exhibiting Mistakes

We all make mistakes; however, if we are aware of the pitfalls that can occur, there is a better chance we can avoid errors that, more often than not, can be fairly costly. The following is a list of some of the most common mistakes exhibitors make preshow, at-show and postshow:

1. Failing to set exhibiting goals

Goals, or the purpose for exhibiting, are the essence of the whole trade show experience. Knowing what you want to accomplish at a show will help plan every other aspect: your theme, the booth layout and display, graphics, product displays, premiums, literature. Exhibiting goals should complement your corporate marketing objectives and help accomplish them.

2. Forgetting to read the exhibitor manual

The exhibitor manual is your complete reference guide to every aspect of the show and your key to saving money. Admittedly, some show management make these easier to read than others. Albeit, everything you need to know about the show you are participating in, should be contained in the manual: show schedules, contractor information, registration, service order forms, electrical service, floor plans and exhibit specifications, shipping and freight services, housing information, advertising, and promotion. Remember that the floor price for show services is normally 10 to 20 percent higher, so signing up early will always give you a significant savings.

3. Leaving graphics to the last minute

Rush, change, and overtime charges will add significantly to your bottom line. Planning your graphics in plenty of time—six to eight weeks before the show—will be less stressful for everyone concerned and avoids many blunders that occur under time pressures.

4. Neglecting booth staff preparation

Enormous time, energy, and money are put into organizing show participation, such as display, graphics, literature, and premiums. However, the people chosen to represent the entire image of the organization are often left to fend for themselves. They are just told to show up. Your people are your ambassadors and should be briefed beforehand about why you are exhibiting, what you are exhibiting, and what you expect from them. Exhibit staff training is essential for a unified and professional image.

5. Ignoring visitors' needs

Often staff members feel compelled to give the visitor as much information as possible. They fail to ask about real needs and interest in the product/service. They lack questioning skills and often miss important qualifying information. Preshow preparation and training are key.

6. Handing out literature and premiums

Staff members, who are unsure of what to do in the booth environment or feel uncomfortable talking to strangers, end up handing out literature or giveaway items just to keep occupied. Literature acts as a barrier to conversation, and chances are that it will be discarded at the first opportunity. It is vital that the people you choose to represent the organization enjoy interacting with strangers and know what is expected of them in the booth environment.

7. Being unfamiliar with demonstrations

Many times staffers show up for duty only to discover they are totally unfamiliar with booth demonstrations. Communicate with your team members before the show and ensure that demonstrators know what is being presented, are familiar with the equipment, and how to conduct the assigned demonstrations.

8. Overcrowding the booth with company representatives

Companies often send several representatives to major industry shows to gather competitive, general, and specific industry information. These people feel compelled to gather at the company booth. They not only outnumber visitors, but they also monopolize staff time and restrict visitor interaction. Have strict rules regarding employees visiting the show and insist staffers not scheduled for booth duty stay away until their assigned time. Company executives are often the worst offenders. Assign specific tasks to avoid them fumbling around the booth.

9. Ignoring lead follow-up

Show leads often take second place to other management activities that occur after being out of the office for several days. The longer leads are left unattended, the colder and more mediocre they become. Prior to the show, establish how leads will be handled, set timelines for follow-up, and make sales representatives accountable for leads given to them.

10. Overlooking show evaluation

The more you know and understand about your performance at shows, the more improvement and fine-tuning can take place for future shows. No two shows are alike. Each has it own idiosyncrasies and obstacles. There is always room for improvement. Invest the time with your

staff immediately after each show to evaluate your performance. It pays enormous dividends.

Source: Susan Friedmann, CSP (Certified Speaking Professional), The Tradeshow Coach (*www.thetradeshowcoach.com*)—Lake Placid, New York, author of *Meeting & Event Planning for Dummies*, she works with exhibitors, show organizers, and meeting planners to create more valuable results from their events nationally and internationally.

Questions to Ask When Interviewing an Event Planner

Planning a corporate event? If it's a certain size, then you'll probably want to get help from an event planner. Here are some questions you should ask an event planner before hiring them. This list is provided by our expert, a Philadelphia-based meeting and event planner.

1. What kind of meeting management is offered through the service?

There are many aspects of meeting management such as site sourcing, contract negotiation, attendee registration and communication, database management, travel coordination, onsite meeting operation, budget and expense reconciliation, supplier negotiations, management of outside activities, entertainment or speaker acquisition, food and beverage management, reporting, and accurate invoicing/billing. All of these are examples of the service your event planner should be able to provide.

2. Do you adhere to a timeline for program planning and management?

Program and timeline management will indicate that they will be ready for every phase of your event and have completed an idea of how your event should be managed. There should be regular communication to update the timeline or tasks, redefine needs, and assure adherence to the plan—for you and the planning company.

3. Do you provide purchasing or program development?

An example of this would be site sourcing and selection, hotel negotiations for rooms and food, preferred vendor programs, independent contractor management, and coordination of third-party service providers such as audio-visual, printing, and transportation. This way you don't have to spend time worrying about smaller details when your planner service should encompass it within their scope of services.

4. How do you handle attendee management and registration?

Do they have the ability to manage attendee registration via traditional means, such as fax and mail? Do they have a Web-based system and automated means of registering attendees? Let your service provider be aware of who your audience encompasses and that you would like everyone attending the event to be accounted for, so you can use it as benchmarking data and for future program planning.

5. What type of service is provided in a dinner meeting/event?

Dinner events also need to be well communicated and thought through. Make sure they can provide site sourcing of a variety of venues, food and beverage management, the knowledge of the space so that it is conducive to your

program, attendee communications and tracking, expense reconciliation, and reporting.

6. Do you coordinate travel needs for all events?

You want to make sure that everyone has a means for getting to and from, where to go, or how to get there! This includes air, ground, airport transfers, and so on.

7. What kind of wrap-up tasks do you include?

Comprehensive reporting including cost savings, attendee surveying for quality assessment, and accurate and timely billing reconciliation are three areas that should be covered at the finish of an event. You can learn a lot through what others thought about the event that can help in future planning. Having a postconference debrief meeting with your planner will help allay any problems from recurring and solidify the relationship and your expectations for future.

Source: Gray Consulting (*www.gcimi.com*)—A Philadelphia-based corporation whose business is focused solely on all aspects of meeting and event management, including program development and planning, site selection, negotiation and contracting, database and attendee management, financial/budget management, and onsite services. Contact them at 833 Chestnut East, 12th floor, Philadelphia, PA 19107; (215) 413-2034.

Best Books about Marketing

To grow your knowledge and awareness about grass-roots marketing methodologies and other effective business-building practices, our customer service experts highly recommend this reading list. These books have helped influence their thinking and as a result, they champion and evangelize them to their colleagues and friends.

1. *Influence: The Psychology of Persuasion* by Robert B. Cialdini
Collins, 1998.

2. *The Experience Economy* by B. Joseph Pine and James H. Gilmore
Harvard Business School Press, April 1999.

3. *The Anatomy of Buzz* by Emanuel Rosen
Currency, April 16, 2002.

4. *Selling the Dream* by Guy Kawasaki
Collins, August 3, 1992.

5. *Purple Cow: Transform Your Business by Being Remarkable* by Seth Godin
Portfolio Hardcover, May 2003.

6. *The Republic of Tea* by Mel Ziegler, Patricia Ziegler, and Bill Rosenzweig
Currency Doubleday, 1992.

7. *Secret Service* by John DiJulius
American Management Association, January 2003.

8. *Diffusion of Innovations* by Everett M. Rogers
Free Press, 1962.

9. *The Secrets of Word-of-Mouth Marketing: How to Trigger Exponential Sales Through Runaway Word of Mouth* by George Silverman
American Management Association, April 2001.

10. *Creating Customer Evangelists: How Loyal Customers Become a Volunteer Sales Force* by Ben McConnell and Jackie Huba
Dearborn, January 2003.

Source: Ben McConnell and Jackie Huba—consultants, speakers, and authors of *Creating Customer Evangelists: How Loyal Customers Become a Volunteer Sales Force.* Read their blog at *www.churchofthecustomer.com.*

Promoting Your Company

Typical Advertising Mistakes

Spending all your money on advertising but getting no results? Find out whether you're guilty of committing one of these huge blunders.

1. The quest for instant gratification

The ad that creates enough urgency to cause people to respond immediately is the ad most likely to be forgotten immediately once the offer expires. It is of little use in establishing the advertiser's identity in the mind of the consumer.

2. Trying to reach more people than the budget will allow

For a media mix to be effective, each element in the mix must have enough repetition to establish retention in the mind of the prospect. Too often, however, the result of a media mix is too much reach and not enough frequency. Will you reach 100 percent of the people and persuade them 10 percent of the way? Or will you reach 10 percent of the people and persuade them 100 percent of the way? The cost is the same.

3. Assuming the business owner knows best

The business owner is uniquely unqualified to see his company or product objectively. Too much product knowledge leads him to answer questions no one is asking. He's on the inside looking out, trying to describe himself to a person on the outside looking in. It's hard to read the label when you're inside the bottle.

4. Unsubstantiated claims

Advertisers often claim to have what the customer wants, such as "highest quality at the lowest price," but fail to offer any evidence. An unsubstantiated claim is nothing more than a cliché the prospect is tired of hearing. You must prove what you say in every ad. Do your ads give the prospect new information? Do they provide a new perspective? If not, prepare to be disappointed with the results.

5. Improper use of passive media

Nonintrusive media, such as newspapers and Yellow Pages, tend to reach only buyers who are looking for the product. They are poor at reaching prospects before their need arises, so they're not much use for creating a predisposition toward your company. The patient, consistent use of intrusive media, such as radio and TV, will win the hearts of relational customers long before they're in the market for your product.

6. Creating ads instead of campaigns

It is foolish to believe a single ad can ever tell the entire story. The most effective, persuasive and memorable ads are those most like a rhinoceros: They make a single point, powerfully. An advertiser with 17 different things to say should commit to a campaign of at least 17 different ads, repeating each ad enough to stick in the prospect's mind.

7. Obedience to unwritten rules

For some insane reason, advertisers want their ads to look and sound like ads. Why?

8. Late-week schedules

Advertisers justify their obsession with Thursday and Friday advertising by saying "We need to reach the customer just before she goes shopping." Why do these advertisers choose to compete for the customer's attention each Thursday and Friday when they could have a nice, quiet chat all alone with her on Sunday, Monday and Tuesday?

9. Overconfidence in qualitative targeting

Many advertisers and media professionals grossly overestimate the importance of audience quality. In reality, saying the wrong thing has killed far more ad campaigns than reaching the wrong people. It's amazing how many people become "the right people" when you're saying the right thing.

10. Event-driven marketing

A special event should be judged only by its ability to help you more clearly define your market position and substantiate your claims. If 1 percent of the people who hear your ad for a special event choose to come, you will be in desperate need of a traffic cop and a bus to shuttle people from distant parking lots. Yet your real investment will be in the 99 percent who did not come! What did your ad say to them?

11. Great production without great copy

Too many ads today are creative without being persuasive. Slick, clever, funny, creative and different are poor substitutes for informative, believable, memorable and persuasive.

12. Confusing response with results

The goal of advertising is to create a clear awareness of your company and its unique selling proposition. Unfortunately, most advertisers evaluate their ads by the comments they hear from the people around them. The slickest, cleverest, funniest, most creative and most distinctive ads are the ones most likely to generate these comments. See the problem? When we confuse response with results, we create attention-getting ads that say absolutely nothing.

Source: Reprinted with permission from Entrepreneur.com. Copyright © 2005. All rights reserved. Advertising expert Roy Williams (aka the "Wizard of Ads") is the author of *The Wizard of Ads, Secret Formulas of the Wizard of Ads, Magical Worlds of the Wizard of Ads, Accidental Magic,* and *Free the Beagle.*

Ways to Stretch Your Advertising Dollars

We all know that to succeed, you must spread the word about your business. But how? If traditional advertising media are too expensive, how do you deliver a marketing message to your customers and potential customers? Our expert believes in the power of what he calls Tightwad Media: cheap, frequently overlooked ways to communicate with that target market. It's important to note that these Tightwad Media Alternatives don't replace traditional advertising media. You still need to advertise to a mass audience to bring in new customers and generate broad awareness. These ideas are marketing-smart, low- or no-cost supplements to your existing advertising media plan.

1. Your after-hours answering machine message

Buying airtime on a radio station is expensive, and your radio commercial will reach a lot of people who are not interested in your products or services. But, with your answering machine message, you can speak directly to customers and potential customers—people who are interested, because they called you! If your after-hours callers are customers, they probably just want to know your hours. If they're potential customers, they probably want more information about your business. So, provide that information!

2. Your vehicle

Billboards are expensive. Bus-bench advertising is expensive. However, you have a ready source of outdoor advertising: your business vehicle. It's well worth putting signs on your business vehicle's doors or back and side panels. A basic sign should have your business name, a marketing message, and phone number or Web site URL. Having your logo on the sign is generally worth the added cost because it looks more customized and helps extend your graphic identity. Even the most-expensive vehicle sign option is considerably cheaper than the smallest outdoor media buy using billboards or bus benches. And, they direct your marketing message to people in or around your existing jobs, clientele, or customers—a very targeted market indeed.

3. Your business cards

You could spend a fortune on brochures, handing out thousands to people who may not be interested enough to read through it. Also, brochures tend to get tossed aside for later reference. Business cards, on the other hand, are cheap, small, and tend to be kept. Here's the Tightwad Marketing secret: All business cards identify the business but very few market the business. Think of your business card as a "storefront.

4. Great customer service

Door-to-door sales are expensive. But, how about when the customer comes to your door? A cheerful tone of voice when you answer the phone, a smile for every customer, prompt handling of customer inquiries—these things sound almost trite, but you wouldn't believe how many small businesses don't make the effort. This is by far your most cost-effective marketing tool. After all, it markets your business on a personal level to the people who are most inclined to be customers—because they already are. No other marketing tool is so targeted. And, it costs you nothing!

5. Your receipt

Imprinted pencils, pens, and other promotional giveaways work because they find their way into your customer's home. Yet, your customer takes something home with every sale: a receipt. Most cash registers and receipt terminals can imprint a message on the receipt tape. Your business name should be prominent, of course, and also your phone number and a marketing message. If your cash register can't imprint a customized message, or if you use generic receipt pads, then buy an inexpensive self-inking rubber stamp for about $25.

6. Invoices

Direct mail is one of the most forms of effective media. However, direct-mail programs are expensive. Yet, think about this: You're probably already sending mail to your customers—mail that is almost always opened and looked at—your invoice. Like a receipt, an invoice should be a marketing piece. If you mail a one-page invoice, you can add another piece of paper without changing your postage costs. In fact, if you're using a U.S. first-class stamp, you can mail up to three sheets of standard-weight (8½ by 11 inch) paper in a number 9 or number 10 envelope. A flyer with special offers or event information is good. Even better is an evaluation form and request for referrals. Customers can return the forms with their payments, and you get valuable feedback plus qualified sales leads.

Source: John Kuraoka (*www.kuraoka.com*)—A freelance advertising copywriter, he can be contacted at 6877 Barker Way, San Diego, CA 92119-1301: Telephone/fax: (619) 465-6100; or e-mail him at *john@kuraoka.com*.

Popular Forms of Advertising

Advertising is an obvious necessity for any business owner or manager. You and your business need to grab the attention of prospective clients or customers, and to do that, you will need a variety of methods to reach different audiences. Here is a list of the most popular forms of advertising your business can choose from.

1. Brochures or flyers

Many desktop publishing and word-processing software packages can produce highly attractive tri-fold (an 8½ by 11 sheet folded in thirds) brochures. Brochures can contain a great deal of information if designed well and are becoming a common method of advertising.

2. Direct mail

Mail sent directly from you to your customers can be highly customized to suit their nature and needs. You may want to build a mailing list of your current and desired customers. Collect addresses from customers by noticing addresses on their checks, asking them to fill out information cards, and so on. Keep the list online and up-to-date. Mailing lists can quickly become out-of-date. Notice mailings that are returned. This method should be used carefully because it can incur substantial cost. You don't want to inundate your stakeholders with information so make the most of your message.

3. E-mail messages

These can be wonderful means to getting the word out about your business. Design your e-mail software to include a "signature line" at the end of each of your messages. Many e-mail software packages will automatically attach this signature line to your e-mail, if you prefer.

4. Magazines

Magazine ads can get quite expensive. Find out if there's a magazine that focuses on your particular industry. It can be very useful because it already focuses on your market and potential customers. Consider placing an ad or writing a short article for the magazine. Contact a reporter to introduce yourself. Reporters are often on the look out for new stories and sources from which to collect quotes.

5. Newsletters

This can be powerful means to conveying the nature of your organization and its services. Consider using a consultant for the initial design and layout. Today's desktop publishing tools can generate very interesting newsletters quite inexpensively.

6. Newspapers (major)

Almost everyone reads the local, major newspaper(s). You can get your business in the newspaper by placing ads, writing a letter to the editor, or working with a reporter to get a story written about your business. Advertising can get quite expensive. Newspapers are often quite useful in giving advice about what and how to advertise. Know when to advertise—this depends on the buying habits of your customers.

7. Newspapers (neighborhood)

Ironically, these are often forgotten in lieu of major newspapers, yet the neighborhood newspapers are often closest to the interests of the organization's stakeholders.

8. Online discussion groups and chat groups

As with e-mail, you can gain frequent exposure to yourself and your business by participating in online discussion groups and chat groups. Note, however, that many groups have strong ground rules against blatant advertising.

When you join a group, always check with the moderator to understand what is appropriate.

9. Posters and bulletin boards

Posters can be very powerful when placed where your customers will actually notice them. But think of how often you've actually noticed posters and bulletin boards. Your best bet is to place the posters on bulletin boards and other places that your customers frequent, and always refresh your posters with new and colorful posters that will appear new to passersby. Note that some businesses and municipalities have regulations about the number or size of posters that can be placed in their areas.

10. Radio announcements

A major advantage of radio ads is they are usually cheaper than television ads, and many people still listen to the radio, for example, when in their cars. Ads are usually sold on a package basis that considers the number of ads, the length of ads, and when they are put on the air. A major consideration with radio ads is to get them announced at the times that your potential customers are listening to the radio.

11. Telemarketing

The use of telemarketing is on the rise. Telemarketing reaches a variety of audiences so you do not have to target a specific demographic.

12. Television ads

Many people don't even consider television ads because of the impression that the ads are very expensive. They are more expensive than most of major forms of advertising. However, with the increasing number of television networks and stations, businesses might find good deals for placing commercials or other forms of advertisements. Television ads usually are priced with similar considerations to radio ads—that is, the number of ads, the length of ads, and when they are put on the air.

13. Web pages

You probably would not have seen this means of advertising on a list of advertising methods if you had read a list even two years ago. Now, advertising and promotions on the World Wide Web are almost commonplace. Businesses are developing Web pages sometimes just to appear up-to-date. Using the Web for advertising requires certain equipment and expertise, including getting a computer, getting an Internet service provider, buying (usually renting) a Web site name, designing and installing the Web site graphics and other functions as needed (for example, an online store for e-commerce), promoting the Web site (via various search engines, directories, etc.), and maintaining the Web site.

14. Yellow Pages

The Yellow Pages can be very effective advertising if your ads are well placed in the directory's categories of services, and the name of your business is descriptive of your services and/or your ad stands out (for example, is bolded, in a large box on the page, etc.). The phone company will offer free advice about placing your ad in the Yellow Pages. They usually have special packages where you get a business phone line along with a certain number of ads.

Source: Carter McNamara, cofounder of Authenticity Consulting, LLC (www.authenticityconsulting.com)—McNamara is an internationally known expert in nonprofit capacity building, and his firm provides nonprofit capacity building and nonprofit business development services throughout the United States. He can be reached at 4008 Lake Drive Avenue, North Minneapolis, MN 55422-1508; (800) 971-2250.

What an Advertising Agency Can Do for You

Good ad agencies provide a service that can alleviate most of your marketing needs and problems. Here is a list of services that an agency can provide for your company. Our expert is an association of advertising agencies that serves both local and national businesses.

1. Determine your customers

Ad agency personnel are skilled in assisting companies determine just who their customers really are and what makes them tick. Such insight is invaluable when it comes to creating a message that will be meaningful to them and encourage them to buy your product.

2. Expertise

While it's often said that "everyone is an advertising expert," the professional creative talents required to write, design, and produce compelling print and broadcast sales messages are found mostly in advertising agencies.

3. Media

Planning the optimum mix of media space, time, location, and frequency is both an art and a science. Delivering your creatively designed message to as many of your potential customers as possible, with minimal waste, and for the fewest dollars is a skill that media professionals are trained to achieve.

4. Internet

The Internet is an important part of advertising campaigns today. Ad agency professionals understand the value of a strong Web presence, and in addition to translating your brand image onto the Web, can help you use it as an interactive sales, marketing, and consumer research tool.

5. More dollars for your company

By outsourcing advertising and communications activities, your company can devote needed internal resources to keeping the rest of your business running smoothly—finance, R & D, product development, the factory, and administration.

Source: Advertising Agency Association of British Columbia (*www .aaabc.ca*)—The AAABC is a nonprofit advertising industry association dedicated to improving the quality of advertising.

Questions to Ask an Advertising Agency Before Hiring Them

An advertising agency can handle any or even all of the marketing for your business if that's what you want. This is important to your business because then all of your advertising and marketing is under one agency and one cost. However, selecting the right agency for your company is hard to determine. Here is a list of steps and questions you should ask before hiring an agency for your company.

1. How much?

It doesn't matter what you want to do in the way of marketing if you can't afford it. Your marketing plan (and your business advisers) should be the guides for determining the dollar amount you can put into promotion. This determination is always a balancing act: Too little put into advertising could mean slower growth than desired; too much could drain other areas of your business.

2. Full service or freelance?

Based on your budget, determine if you should use a full-service agency or freelance advertising professionals. Ad agencies usually like to handle a wide variety of promotional activities for a company (although some are flexible enough to focus on specific areas such as PR, brochure creation, etc.). Top-quality freelancers, on the other hand, will readily work on projects you specify. It's a given that working with an agency requires a higher initial budget than working with freelancers, but it's not a given that the quality of work will be higher. Many freelancers once worked with agencies. If you require an array of services (such as coordinated newspaper, TV and radio marketing), an ad agency may be your best bet.

3. Which industry?

Assuming that you decide to hire an ad agency, it's best to locate agencies that are familiar with your industry. Too many small businesses hire agencies based on work done for other types of businesses. While it's usually not a great idea to use an agency that works for your chief competitor, you should ask an agency about previous work done in your field.

4. What tasks?

Before talking with agency representatives, perform the following activities within your own company: select a review committee, if you will not be acting alone throughout the selection process; meet with the committee and determine specific types of marketing you will be requiring; go over budgets to make sure they are realistic; set a timetable for selecting an agency; assign to an individual within the committee the task of contacting agencies. This individual should inform the agencies about what services you will require and what your budget is.

5. Who else?

Using references from colleagues, your own past use of agencies, Yellow Page advertising, and so on, select a list of agencies. If your budget is small, invite only two or three agencies to meet with your review committee. If you have a large budget and will require extensive services, contact more. Prior to the agency interviews, ask each agency to provide you with information about the agency's employees who will be working on your projects, examples of former work for companies in your industry, and hourly or per-project charges. Ask to be shown personally through each agency's office before the formal interview with your committee. This will help you get a feel for how the agency works. Also, ask to speak with several clients of each agency; find out how efficient, timely, and flexible the agency is. Don't hesitate to ask if the clients feel that the agency has helped boost their business.

6. At the interview

During an interview, focus on the agency's experience with your industry and size of account, specific examples of previous work, degree of innovation or creativity in suggesting types of ad campaigns, availability of key personnel within the agency to work on your account, and the "chemistry" between the agency and your selection committee. Ask the agencies questions such as "Why do you feel that you will be able to promote our specific type of business successfully? What are some of your particular strengths—and weaknesses? Do you see any potential difficulties in our choices for media ·selection? Can you achieve what we need with the budget we're proposing? Do you have other suggestions for marketing?"

7. Sign Here

Select an agency and put in writing all financial agreements, timelines for creation of ads, responsibilities of the agency and your company, and ownership of creative work. The agreement with the agency you select is as important as any other business contract you write, so consult with your attorney and business adviser throughout the process.

Source: National Federation of Independent Business (*www.nfib.com*)—NFIB is the largest advocacy organization representing small and independent businesses in Washington, D.C., and all fifty state capitals. NFIB was ranked the most influential business organization (and third overall), in "Washington's Power 25" survey conducted by *Fortune* magazine.

Reasons Classified Ads Are Better than Other Ads

Our expert says that classifieds can have some real advantages over display ads or other media buys. Here's a list of reasons why.

1. They're cheaper.

Even at $5 a word, a twenty-word classified is only $100—but a one-eighth page display ad may run many times that. Some classifieds are as little as a nickel a word, or even free.

2. They're targeted.

People looking in that section want exactly the sort of thing you're advertising, especially if you choose a niche publication to start with—and then you're paying for a lot fewer non-prospects.

3. They have a good working relationship with the reader.

People aren't afraid to ruin their magazine by marking up pages. In the classified section, a few tick marks won't matter.

4. You can easily track responses.

As a direct-response medium, they're easy to test (with a code that tracks the magazine, the specific issue, and the offer).

5. You can use it as an introduction.

In today's world, the small canvas is no longer a problem—because even if you only have twenty words, one of them can be a Web site address—and that Web site can provide unlimited information. From a marketing point of view, including a Web site is far superior to a toll-free number or having to write for more information.

Source: Shel Horowitz (*www.frugalmarketing.com*)—Internationally known marketing consultant, copywriter, and speaker, he specializes in affordable, effective marketing for small businesses, entrepreneurs, and nonprofits. The author of the award-winning books, *Principled Profit: Marketing That Puts People First, Grassroots Marketing: Getting Noticed in a Noisy World*, and four other books. Contact him at *shel@principledprofits.com* or by phone at (413) 586-2388.

Tips for Writing More Effective Industrial Copy

Writing industrial-oriented copy is quite different from writing consumer-oriented copy. The major difference is that technical people want technical information. The industrial copywriter is selling to engineers, managers, purchasing agents, and other technical people whose understanding of and interest in complex product information is inherently far greater than the average consumer's. Here are ten time-tested tips for writing industrial copy that sells. Apply them to your next ad, mailer, or catalog, and watch the reply cards come pouring in.

1. Be technically accurate

Industrial marketers sell systems to solve specific problems. Copy must accurately describe what the product can and cannot do. Being accurate means being truthful. Industrial buyers are among the most sophisticated of audiences. Technical know-how is their forte, and they'll be likely to spot any exaggerations, omissions, or "white lies" you make. Being accurate also means being specific. Writing that a piece of equipment "can handle your toughest injection molding jobs" is vague and meaningless to a technician; but saying that the machine "can handle pressures of up to 12,000 pounds" is honest, concrete, and useful.

2. Check the numbers

Many of us became writers just to get away from having to deal with numbers; all the math whizzes in our class went on to become computer programmers, accountants, and media buyers. But to write effective industrial copy, you've got to approach members with a newfound respect. Just think of the disaster that would result if a misplaced decimal in a sales letter offered a one-year magazine subscription at $169.50, ten times the actual price of $16.95. You can see why this would stop sales cold. Get it wrong, and you've lost a sale. All numbers in industrial promotional literature should be checked and double-checked by the writer, by the agency, and by technical people on the client side.

3. Be concise

Engineers and managers are busy people. They don't have the time to read all the papers that cross their desks, so make your message brief and to the point. Take a look at some industrial direct mail. Letters are seldom more than a page long; you almost never see a four-page letter in industrial selling. As Strunk and White point out in *The Elements of Style*, conciseness "requires not that the writer . . . avoid all detail and treat his subjects only in outline, but that every word tell." In other words, cram your industrial promotions full of product information and strong sales arguments. But avoid redundancies, run-on sentences, wordy phrases, and other poor stylistic habits that take up space but add little to meaning or clarity.

4. Simplify

The key to successful industrial copywriting is to explain complex concepts and products clearly and directly. Avoid overly complicated narratives; write in plain, simple English. One way to achieve simplicity in your industrial writing is to avoid the overuse of technical jargon. Never write that a manufacturer's new dental splint "stabilizes mobile dentition" when its function is to keep loose teeth in place. When you're deciding whether to use a particular technical term, remember Susanne K. Langer's definition of jargon as "language more technical than the ideas it serves to express." Never let your language make things more complex than they already are.

5. Talk to the users to determine their needs

Elaborate marketing research is often unnecessary in industrial selling. By talking with a few knowledgeable engineers, you can quickly grasp what makes a technical product useful to industrial buyers. Because the products are highly technical, you can't rely on your own feelings and intuition to select the key selling points. The benefits of buying a kitchen appliance or joining a record club are obvious, but how can a layman say which features of a multistage distillation system are important to the buyer, and which are trivial? By speaking with technical and marketing people on the client side, you can find out which product features should be highlighted in the copy and why they appeal to the buyer. Then, apply your usual skill in persuasive writing to turn these features into sales-oriented "reason-they-should-buy" copy. The kind of copy that generates leads, goodwill, orders, and money.

6. Understand how the promotion fits into the buying process

The sale of an industrial product can require many lengthy steps; machinery is seldom marketed by mail order. Sometimes your package can be used to generate the lead. Or it may help qualify prospects. Many industrial marketers use sales letters to distribute catalogs, remind customers of their products, or answer inquiries. Know where your copy fits into the buying process so you can write copy to generate the appropriate response.

7. Know how much to tell

Different buyers seek different levels of technical information. If you're writing for top management, keep it short and simple, and pile on the benefits. If you're pitching to technicians, be sure to include plenty of meaty technical information.

8. Don't forget the features

By all means, stress customer benefits in your copy. But don't forget to include technical features as well. In the industrial marketplace, a pressure rating or the availability of certain materials of construction often means the difference between a buy or no-buy decision. Although these features may seem boring or meaningless to you, they are important to the technical buyer. Direct-response copywriters often work up a list of product features and the benefits that these features offer the consumer. Then, the benefits are worked into the sales letter. In industrial copywriting, we do the same thing, except we include the features in the copy.

9. Use graphs, tables, charts, and diagrams to explain and summarize technical information quickly

Put strong "sell copy" in your headlines, subheads, and body copy; relegate duller "catalog information" to tables, sidebars, charts, and inserts. And don't hesitate to use visuals; photographs add believability, and drawings help readers visualize complex products and processes.

10. Include case histories to demonstrate proven performance

Industrial buyers want to know that your product has proven its performance in real-life applications. Case histories—concise "product success stories"—are a sure-fire way to put the buyer's mind at ease. The case history approach is one area where industrial and consumer writers agree. After all, every direct-response writer knows that the best advertising is a satisfied customer.

Source: Robert W. Bly (*www.bly.com*)—An independent copywriter and consultant with over twenty-five years' experience in business-to-business, high-tech, industrial, and direct marketing, he writes sales letters, direct-mail packages, inserts, Internet direct mail, ads, brochures, articles, press releases, newsletters, Web pages, white papers, and other marketing materials clients need to sell their products and services to business and direct-response buyers. He also consults with clients on marketing strategy, mail-order selling, e-marketing, and lead-generation programs. Contact him at 22 East Quackenbush Avenue, 3rd floor, Dumont, NJ 07628; (201) 385-1220; fax: (201) 385-1138.

Ways to Improve Your Marketing Materials Immediately

Our expert believes that most promotional literature is banal and indistinguishable from the crowd. This is because many people don't place themselves in their prospects' shoes. Read your literature from the viewpoint of a prospective buyer, and critically ask if it passes the "So What?" test. You have to put yourself in the buyer's shoes. No one drives down the highway to read billboards, and no one goes through mail or searches the Web to read promotional material. People are in search of value for themselves and their organizations. According to our expert, here are some things to do tomorrow—immediately—that will enhance your written promotions and help you stand out in the crowd:

1. Use results, not features

Don't talk about how well you construct your sales training programs, talk about the degree of increased new business generated by graduates of your sales programs. Don't emphasize greater cooperation from your team building work, but rather focus on less duplication from competing activities and reduced costs from that decreased duplication.

2. Use third-party testimonials

Everyone expects you to claim that you're the best. It's far more credible to have someone else proclaim that you're the best. Obtain specific testimonials from people willing to provide their names and titles from as recognizable sources as you can find. "Did a great job!—vice president at major financial institution" isn't one-tenth as powerful as, "Summit Consulting Group's analysis and redesign of our mortgage lending operation increased our market share by 7 percent in the first year alone.—Jane C. Powers, Senior Vice President, Mortgage Lending, Fleet Bank."

3. Use bullets, not text

People don't like to read, and a good promotional piece can't be too long in any case (forget those pages of promotion from the "Sell real estate and make a billion from your home" nut cases—we're in the consulting profession). Use bulleted items to make your points about your results, your client engagements, your products, etc.

4. Use a very wide net

Do not be specific. In fact, be as broad as your comfort level allows. Most people use promotional literature to "deselect," looking for evidence that they don't or can't use the service. The more specific you are, the more deselection ammunition you're providing. No brochure ever sold a client, but most of them turn away prospects. You want the prospect to be at least open to a next step, which may be trying to find out more specifics. Don't listen to the people advising you to place yourself in a "niche." Niches are too easily covered up or overlooked.

5. Use your client list

Well-known clients are important because their very existence provides a certain comfort level to prospects, and supplies instant credibility. Unless clients have specifically forbidden you to do so, you may cite the names of organizations which have engaged your services. (You may not be able to use their logos, but you can use their names.) Don't allow your greatest asset to be your greatest secret.

Source: © Alan Weiss 2005 All rights reserved. Alan Weiss of Summit Consulting Group (*www.summitconsulting.com*). He is an experienced consultant, a prolific speaker, and the author of more than 500 articles and twenty-three books worldwide, including the bestselling *Million Dollar Consulting* (McGraw-Hill). He can be contacted at PO Box 1009, East Greenwich, RI 02818-0964; (401) 884-2778; e-mail: *info@summitconsulting.com*.

Ways to Make Your Product Unique

Sometimes it is not one attribute but a combination of attributes that makes the product different. Uniqueness is the key to differentiating your product from all the others that are focused on your target market. Here are some ideas on making a product stand out from all the others.

1. Largest selection

One way you can make your product or service stand out is to offer the largest selection of products, services, or programs—for example, Home Depot, E-Bay, Staples, Amazon.com

2. Innovative product

If you have a new product with a patent covering it or a service that others don't offer, you will have something that no one else can offer—for example, Windows, Viagra, Value Program.

3. Multiple uses

Once you have a product or service to offer, look for other ways that the customer can use the same product or service—for example, a baby carrier that has a carriage base, an electric can opener with knife sharpener, aspirin used to relieve pain and prevent heart attacks, a cell phone that is also a camera.

4. Superior customer service

Keep reminding your customers that you are eager to help them by giving extraordinary support on your product or service—for example, Nordstrom, doctors who make house calls, a mobile lawyer's office, and a glass company that comes to your workplace to change the glass in your automobile.

5. Convenient location

Make it easy for customers to do business with you by providing them access in exactly the place where they will need your product or service—for example, a bank in the supermarket, an ATM in airport, setting up a stand to sell umbrellas on a busy street corner on a rainy day.

6. Expert consulting

If you have deep knowledge of your product or service, you can be useful in helping your customers before and after the sale is made—for example, a computer salesperson who understands connectivity issues and can help you integrate your equipment with the new computer, a real-estate agent who has a huge Rolodex and provides referrals to other vendors that a new home owner would need.

7. Price

If you have a product or service with a high price, you offer prestige. If you offer the lowest price, the thrifty customer will be attracted to your product or service—for example, high price, Lexus, Canyon Ranch; low price, Target, Wal-Mart.

8. Lasting effect

The product or service you offer have a longer lasting effect than any others—for example, Extra Strength Tylenol, a bike lock that cannot be opened, a car battery that lasts five years, long-lasting car tires.

9. Guarantee

Offer a guarantee with your product or service—for example, money back if not satisfied, free conversion back to a previous vendor if unsatisfied.

10. Packaging

Offer a package that is different from others (prettier, stronger, environmentally friendly, easier to open, child-proof)—for example, packaging material that dissolves in water, free gift wrapping for all purchases, child-proof aspirin bottles, juice drinks with a straw.

Source: Parker Associates (*www.asparker.com*)—A business and career coaching firm started and managed by Alvah Parker who specializes in career and business coaching for individuals. She has fifteen years of sales, marketing, coaching, and management experience with AT&T. As a SCORE* Business Counselor, she has helped many new business owners to start or grow their businesses. As sole proprietor of Parker Associates, she coaches entrepreneurs, small business owners, lawyers, managers, and people in transition to find work that is fun, fulfilling, and profitable. Contact her at PO Box 562, Swampscott, MA 01907; (781) 598-0388.

Ways to Get Free Publicity

Getting your company noticed will help generate interest in what you do. You could retain a public relations firm or, like our expert suggests, you could be doing a lot of other things to generate some free publicity yourself. Here's his list of ideas.

1. Writing articles

Articles don't have to be long; they just need to be informative. Share your experience. Cite your wisdom. Tell a story. Make a list. These are all things you can write an article about. Everyone is more of an expert in one particular area than another. Writing about how to do something is always of value to readers. Writing articles gives you instant credibility, too. Submitting online, as well as offline, provides another good chance to get your name in *print* at no cost. Be sure to put your contact information in a contact resource box at the end of the article.

2. Newsletters

Writing a newsletter is another way to keep your name top-of-mind. This can be online or offline. Online newsletters are often referred to as e-zines; offline newsletters are printed and mailed. Both contain content valuable to your target market and many times advertise your products and services. It's always been said that your best prospect is a current customer. Advertising to current customers is your best bet to get more business. E-zines are e-mails to your permission-based e-mail database. The cost of this is nothing, yet the return potential is infinite.

3. Public speaking

Speaking in front of an audience usually makes you an expert. People like to buy from experts. If they're in your audience, then they'll remember your expertise and come to you when they need your product or service. Chambers of commerce are also good targets but so are all the service clubs that need luncheon speakers. Speaking is free, and it's just like making a sales call to many people at one time.

4. Free reports

Offering a free report online is a good way to get an e-mail from prospects you can market to later. This is the whole basis of permission-based marketing, or opt-in lists. You can do the same thing offline. If you're doing a postcard campaign and you offer a free report, you can get an instant appointment from the postcard or at least a phone call. You can increase the response of a direct-mail program from 1 percent to double-digit percentage returns. The free reports can be a dressed-up article, a list, a survey that you've done, or some research-based information. Use your imagination here.

5. Radio

Radio is expensive, you say? Not if you are being interviewed or calling in on a talk show. Getting interviewed is free, except for your continual follow-up with producers. Calling in is free, but sometimes it's hard to relay contact information. Both of these work, especially when supplemented with other marketing strategies.

6. Online forum participation

There are many online newsgroups or forums for a particular subject area. Participating in these is another way to get your name out. Advertising is not usually permitted. Participating by answering and asking questions will position you as an expert and a resource for others. Many online forums will let you put an e-mail signature with a link to your site or message with another site linked. Take full advantage of this; these links get clicked often when of interest to the forum participants.

7. Letters to the editor

A little-known secret that's a good follow-up to a press release is a letter to an editor. This is free PR. Many times a letter to the editor has a better chance of getting published than the actual press release. Sometimes you'll get a press release published with editorial comments from the editor. The letter to the editor is a great place to respond to editorial comments as well as to further state a position. You'd be surprised how many people read this column in publications. This is also another way to become friends with the editor. If they see you enough and match you with a newsworthy press release, then your chances of getting a press release in print increases.

Source: Alfred J. Lautenslager, an award-winning marketing, public relations consultant and direct-mail promotion specialist from Entrepreneur magazine (*www.entrepreneur.com*). Visit him at *www.market-for-profits.com*.

Things a Public Relations Firm Can Do for You

PR agencies can perform many different services for your business. Even small businesses can compete against the big guys if they're got the right public relations team. Many companies don't understand the value of what a good

PR firm can do for them. So we asked our PR expert to tell us all the things that they do.

1. Public relations strategy and branding

A good PR firm integrates and aligns public relations with other branding efforts and overall company goals. This develops a comprehensive, customized program that integrates and aligns PR with other branding efforts and overall company goals. PR firms develop and execute a strategic plan, message development, and tactical campaigns that build on their clients' positioning initiatives to generate constant, wide-ranging media coverage.

2. Media relations

They will achieve a constant flow of outstanding, on-target, on-message media coverage. The cornerstone of all client programs should be a comprehensive and prioritized media program that promotes a story to all appropriate and agreed-on print, broadcast, and online media, from industry verticals to key trade press to major national business outlets. The account team should be proactively and creatively pitching their client's story to reporters every day. The team should develop all necessary PR background materials as well as press releases. Regular contact with key reporters will ensure placement in trend stories, features, and news reports. The media relations program should also include media training for their clients' corporate spokespeople.

3. Industry analyst relations

A good PR firm will establish and maintain regular communication with key industry analysts to stay on the radar screen and get into the right quadrant. Analysts also play a key role with the media, providing critical outside validation and market commentary. Public relation firms secure meetings with these contacts around major news and strategy developments and prepare clients for these briefings with guidance on messaging and presentation content. In addition, they should maintain ongoing contact with regular e-mail update memos to all relevant analysts with technology, product, and customer updates from their clients. Available services should also include creating presentations for use with industry analysts and preparing detailed scripts for use in analyst meetings.

4. Speakers bureau

A good PR firm will position their clients' executives as industry/issue experts. They will arrange speaking engagements at key industry conferences to establish their clients' executives as subject matter experts. Public relations firms develop a comprehensive target list of conferences, trade shows, and other appropriate opportunities for speeches and presentations by the client's executives. They draft presentation abstracts and proposals for all appropriate speaking opportunities. Once a speaking opportunity is secured, they act as liaison between the conference organizers and the client to manage the presentation details.

5. Crisis communications

They should be prepared for any crisis. The golden rule of any crisis communications situation is tell the truth, tell it all, and tell it quickly. Because no one can anticipate when a crisis will hit, it is important to be prepared for myriad situations. Public relation firms develop comprehensive crisis planning and communications programs that prepare their clients' and spokespeople to respond to internal and external corporate crises and adverse events. A crisis communications management program includes creation of a comprehensive crisis communications plan, crisis communications workshops on-site, and media training for designated crisis spokespeople.

6. Government relations

Your firm should also conduct strategic, effective public affairs campaigns. As government policy strengthens its play within the private sector, it is becoming essential for businesses to build a presence on Capitol Hill. Public relations–trained professionals can book multiday meetings in Washington, D.C., with influential members of Congress and government officials, coordinate radio and television appearances to draw the national spotlight on clients' current affairs insight, and facilitate multimedia Webcasts to position clients as experts. From national Capitol Hill legislators to state, city, or town political figures, a targeted government relations program should be in place to build lasting relationships and deliver an edge on the competition in the government arena.

Source: Schwartz Communications (*www.schwartz-pr.com*)—A top honor public relations firm located in Boston and San Francisco. Contact them at Prospect Place, 230 Third Avenue, Waltham, MA 02451; (781) 684-0770; fax: (781) 684-6500; e-mail *info-web@schwartz-pr.com*.

Questions to Ask a Public Relations Firm Before Hiring Them

Finding the right public relations firm is important because there could be some areas of public relations that you may not need. Our expert, the owner of her own public relations firm, gives us a list of questions that will help you choose a firm that best suits your company.

1. What are some examples of campaign tactics?

Seeing previous campaign tactics allows you to assess what their plan will be with your company.

2. Can you provide examples of print and media coverage from other clients?

See what type of work they have done and assess their performance.

3. How often will we get media coverage?

Get a reasonable estimate of frequency of media coverage. You need to know what you are paying for.

4. What markets will be pursued?

Know the markets that will be pursued and make sure they are practice-appropriate.

5. May I see previous press releases for other clients?

This will help you see what you are paying for and see how successful those releases turned out to be.

6. May I see a list of references?

Look into who is supporting them and see what they have to say about them.

7. What is the account executive-to-client ratio, and how much time will be devoted to the account within a given week or month?

Let them know that you want dedication and make sure they spend the amount of time they committed to.

8. Are there any additional expenses, such as monthly disbursements?

Don't let them hit you with any additional costs. Ask about what they charge beforehand.

9. Do you provide weekly reports?

Weekly reports show dedication and organization. This will help you and your business see the progress the PR firm has made with your organization.

10. Can you provide an outline of your campaign strategy and explain company policy?

Try to see what they have planned for you and your business. If you don't like something, let them know and make sure you are getting what you want. Have them explain company policy so you know what you are dealing with.

Source: Katherine M. Rothman, president, KMR Communications (www.kmrcommunications.com)—A public relations firm located at 114 East 32nd Street, Suite 1200, New York, NY 10016; (212) 213-6444.

Top Rules for Sending E-mail to the Media

Looking to get some free PR? One way is to get your company mentioned in the press. More and more journalists are accepting pitches and story ideas by e-mail. Here's some advice to turn more of those contacts into press coverage.

1. Choose your subject line very carefully

Interesting and informative, but not hard-sell. Be as descriptive as possible without sounding like a spammer—and focus on the news peg. Aim for fifty characters or fewer, sixty tops. Here's an example I just wrote for a client: Pro-Anorexia Sites "Danger to Children," Says Expert (News Release). Fifty-two characters not counting the parenthetical at the end—and it's at the end so that if something is cut off, I don't lose the important words *Anorexia, Danger, Children, Expert*.

2. Responding to a published query by a journalist, put the name of the service and then the subject, e.g., Profnet: Small Biz Money Savers

If you'd like an affordable source of journalist queries, matching the keywords you select and coming directly into your inbox, visit *www.frugalmarketing.com/prleads.shtml*.

3. Be interesting

Write in the most interesting way possible (again, without going off the edge into sales/spam).

4. Keep it short

One screen is best; three paragraphs is a comfortable maximum. (Include a Web page for more info--the full URL—so they don't have to poke around on your site.)

5. Send to the specific journalist's direct e-mail address

You can usually find contact info on the publication's Web site or examine the staff box and learn the pattern—for instance, *asmith@yourpaper.com*.

6. Send only to people who directly cover the subject of the release

Otherwise, you're spamming—and contributing to the big problem of journalists who refuse to read e-mail.

7. Know about the journalist

If possible, reference a previous story or the journalist's "beat" (subject area).

8. Don't send attachments

Never send an attachment—but offer to send one on request, if that's appropriate.

9. Remember, they are busy

Remember that journalists are extremely busy and always on deadline. They need you as much as you need them, but the easier you make their job, the more likely that they'll call you rather than someone else.

Source: Shel Horowitz (*www.frugalmarketing.com*)—Internationally known marketing consultant, copywriter, and speaker, specializes in affordable, effective marketing for small businesses, entrepreneurs, and nonprofits, he is the author of the award-winning books *Principled Profit: Marketing That Puts People First, Grassroots Marketing: Getting Noticed in a Noisy World*, and four other books. Contact him at *shel@principledprofit.com* or at (413) 586-2388.

Typical Items to Include in a Press Kit

There are many items that can go into a press kit, depending on the situation, the audience, or the use. A press kit for potential investors is much different than a press kit for potential clients. Although a press kit should be comprehensive, do not include every promotional item or piece of marketing collateral ever produced by your company. Only put information that is current and most relevant to your target reader. We asked our expert, an award winning public relations professional, to list for us the typical things a company should include in their press kit.

1. Letter of introduction

Sometimes referred to as the pitch letter, this first-impression item is where you will grab or lose the reader's interest. Tell them up-front why they should care about what you're telling them. Provide a table of contents or a brief description of the items enclosed in the actual press kit. Let them know you are available for follow-up interviews and questions. Also make sure to include your contact information in this letter.

2. Information on the company

This includes your company's history, a company profile, and profiles of the chief officers, senior management, and ownership. Include bio sheets, if appropriate.

3. Product and service information, including a product, service, or performance review

This will let editors see what others are saying about you or help the editor write his or her own review. Support it with product or service fact sheets, sell sheets, or company brochures that are specific to your product or service.

4. Recent press publications and articles

Copies of recent press coverage are very appropriate for a press kit. After all, what other media have done will be of interest to current media targets. This can include article reprints and printouts of online press that a company might have received.

5. Press releases

Many times, these are what instigated and caused the printing of the articles.

6. Audio and video files of radio or TV interviews, speeches, performances, and any other media-covered event

Hard copies will suffice if the actual media are not available. Today, some companies are putting online audio clips on their Web pages and in online media kits.

7. A sample news story

This is your chance to guide the media or your reader. Some editors will even print it verbatim because they view ready-to-print articles as an easy way to fill up space with little effort on their part. They do, of course, usually edit these stories, so be prepared.

8. Financial data

Since many media kits are put together for investors, any news related to the industry, financial statements, or any other investor-related news are very appropriate for the press kit.

9. List of frequently asked questions

This helps the reader determine what questions to ask you in an interview or what to include in the article.

10. Other items

You may also consider including nonprofit and community-service involvement; recent awards; photos (if appropriate); factual background material and/or white papers; specific information and schedules of upcoming promotions and events; significant statistics specific to your industry, demographics, and target audiences; feature article material, such as articles written by company officers or senior management; missions, goals, and objectives; samples or examples; camera-ready logo art; giveaway information; and an order form.

Source: Alfred J. Lautenslager, an award-winning marketing and PR consultant, direct-mail promotion specialist, principal of marketing consulting firm Marketing Now, and president and owner of The Ink Well, a commercial printing and mailing company in Wheaton, Illinois. Contact him at www.1-800-inkwell.com, or e-mail him at al@market-for-profits.com.

Typical Components of a Press Release

Interested in issuing a press release to promote your company's products or services? Most press releases nowadays follow a pretty standard format. We asked the experts at PR Newswire how a press release should look and here's what they said.

1. FOR IMMEDIATE RELEASE

These words should appear in the upper left-hand margin with all letters capitalized.

2. Headline

This should be a sentence that gives the essence of what the press release is about.

Articles, prepositions, and conjunctions of three letter words or fewer should be lowercased.

3. Dateline
This should be the city your press release is issued from and the date you are mailing your release.

4. Lead paragraph
A strong introductory paragraph should grasp the reader's attention and should contain the information most relevant to your message such as the five Ws (who, what, when, where, why). This paragraph should summarize the press release and include a hook to get your audience interested in reading more.

5. Body
The main body of your press release is where your message should fully develop. Many companies choose to use a strategy called the inverted pyramid, which is written with the most important information and quotes first.

6. Company boilerplate
Your press release should end with a short paragraph that describes your company, products, service, and a short company history. If you are filing a joint press release, include a boilerplate for both companies.

7. Contact information
Always include the name, phone, and e-mail address of a key contact person.

Source: PR Newswire (*www.prnewswire.com*)—A global leader in news and information distribution services for professional communicators. Contact Rachel Meranus, director, Public Relations, at (212) 282-1929.

Top Recipients of Corporate Promotional Items
Ever wonder who actually gets those T-shirts, coffee mugs, golf balls and pens with corporate logos? Should you be giving away these promotional items, too? We went to a our expert, who sells this stuff across the country and asked them who typically receives the stuff that they sell and here's their list.

1. Business and executive gifts
2. Dealers' distributor program rewards
3. Employee relations and events
4. Trade shows
5. Brand awareness
6. Employee service awards
7. Public relations
8. New product/service introduction
9. New customer accounts
10. Internal promotions

Source: Promopeddler.com (*www.promopeddler.com*)—A one-stop online source for volume pricing on the world's largest selection of top-quality Logo Imprinted Items. Contact them at Sherwood West Bldg, 20015 SW Pacific Hwy. 99, Floor 3, Sherwood, OR 97140; (800) 455-1350.

Popular Corporate Promotional Items

Thinking of giving away some stuff with your company name on it? Looking to generate some attention and increase market awareness? This list is from a 2002 study of sales by one of the country's leading providers of corporate promotional items.

1. Clothing

2. Pens and writing utensils

3. Calendars

4. Desk supplies

5. Bags

6. Glassware

7. Recognition awards

8. Sporting goods

9. Buttons

10. Automotive gear

Source: Promopeddler.com (*www.promopeddler.com*)—A one-stop online source for volume pricing on the world's largest selection of top-quality Logo Imprinted Items. Contact them at Sherwood West Bldg, 20015 SW Pacific Hwy 99, Floor 3, Sherwood, OR 97140; (800) 455-1350.

Popular Promotion Ideas

Knowing how to promote your business or product is something every business needs. All businesses fund some form of promotion because it greatly increases sales and popularity within the market. Here are some great ways to promote your business.

1. Games and contests

Mass-marketers frequently run games and contests on a nationwide scale. People look under bottle caps, collect game pieces, or submit entries in an effort to win prizes. Games and contests can be conducted on a smaller scale. Your promotions must be designed to get people to buy from you; the market research you can conduct is just a secondary benefit. Whatever games you devise, play fair with your customers. Don't charge them to enter, and be sure to state how and when the winners will be selected, say that the offer is void outside of a certain area and after a certain date, and that any taxes are the responsibility of the winner. And be sure to check out the local laws with your attorney before you start any contest, game, or drawing.

2. Premiums and gifts

Premiums and gifts, sometimes called "ad specialties," have been around a long time. The modern version of this free gift idea is aimed at name awareness: magnets, calendars, luggage tags, T-shirts, pens, pencils, or coffee mugs that carry your name, logo, and perhaps phone number or Internet address. Anything that lasts and will be used by your prospective buyer can be effective. The key question, as it is for any promotional activity, is whether the cost of the premiums or gifts will be recovered through increased business.

3. Coupons

Many small businesses use coupons as part of their promotional programs. The more common ones entitle the bearer to some benefit, such as a price reduction on a particular product or service. Others reward frequent customers for their loyalty. Be sure that your pricing supports the cost of this type of promotion. Don't forget that only a small percentage of coupons are actually used. One good thing about coupons is that it's easy to monitor the results: you'll see every one that comes in. Do not forget an expiration date!

4. Rebates

A rebate is similar to a coupon, except that it is not honored at the time and point of purchase. Instead, the customer must complete and submit the rebate form, generally by mail. Rebates on automobiles are not, in fact, true rebates in this sense of the term. If you had to send a proof of purchase form to the auto manufacturer to get the $600 "rebate," that would be a true rebate. Rebates are a good form of promotion because you receive a lot of information about your customer, and in order for your customer to get a discount, they must remember as well.

5. Product or service demonstrations

For a small business, a demonstration is often the most effective and cost-efficient selling tool. Demonstrations are often more expensive per sampled target buyer when compared to advertising costs per target reached. However, demonstrations are many times more effective than single advertising ad exposures in any medium. Demonstrations should be conducted at point-of-purchase whenever possible to maximize the opportunity for a buyer or end user to purchase immediately. A promotion demonstration often takes the form of a free product sample or free

trial service. Also, demonstrations of products and services are the foundation for potentially free, word-of-mouth advertising, the most effective form of advertising known.

Source: CCH Business Owner's Toolkit (*www.toolkit.cch.com*) They provide advice, guides, legal tools, business models, and other resources to small business owners.

Questions to Ask a Graphic Design Firm Before Hiring Them

One of the earliest mistakes a small business can make is to assess inaccurately their ability to create professional marketing materials and, if lacking, not to hire a competent graphic designer to help in the process. Not sure where to begin? Good designers often have a following and a reputation in their community. Here are some questions you can ask to ensure choosing a design firm that will fit well with your business and your needs and deliver to your expectations.

1. May I see your portfolio?

Most graphic design firms today have a portfolio online. While this is usually sufficient, you should feel comfortable asking print designers to send or show you examples of their work if you are hiring them for that kind of work. It is very important that you look at a broad selection of the designer's work. This might be an online portfolio or a presentation in person. Review at least three of their past projects or Web sites, and ask questions about what their involvement was, if it is not clear. A smart designer will provide case studies so you can tell what the goal was and see how they achieved it. Good design is subjective, but if you don't find work in their portfolio that you would be proud to have represent your business, move on.

2. May I call on your past clients?

Once you have some designers in mind, contact some of their past clients for input and testimonials—don't ever rely on just what the designer gives you! If they have a problem with you choosing which clients you can contact from their portfolio, without an explanation, you should be concerned.

3. What are your credentials?

Some amount of formal design education is generally better than none, although there are certainly exceptions. Similarly, the more experience, the better—it takes about three to five years working in the trenches to get a full grasp of the industry, although this might include time spent in school. Even the greatest natural talents needs real-world experience to hit their stride. That said, if you are comfortable working with a relatively inexperienced designer, that is okay—just make sure you know what you are getting.

4. What are your areas of expertise?

The "right" designer is often more than a graphic designer. If you are hiring a design firm, you need to know what talents and services are available. Depending on your needs, having a graphic designer who is competent in both Web and print might be ideal. If you're hiring a designer to develop marketing materials, a strong background in marketing strategy is essential. If you are hiring a Web designer, find one who can execute the technology for your site, not just cre-

ate pretty pictures on the Web. If you are hiring a designer for logo design, ask about their experience with branding and corporate identity.

5. How do you price your services?

Price is one of the tricky variables in hiring a design firm. Beware of drastically low "deals," even with seemingly good designers who are offering cut rates to be competitive. The problem is they often can't stay in business that way and are forced to go get a job, which might leave you in a lurch. There are certainly different levels of designers for different levels of clients. For example, a large ad agency might be out of the range of a micro business, but a solo designer with agency experience and low overhead working at a home office might be just the solution. The important thing is to shop around and give an identical scope to multiple firms that you've qualified as credible and reputable and then compare.

6. How will we work together?

It is a good idea to find out how they manage the workflow between you, to make sure it aligns with your preferences. From your first contact with a designer, you should be observing her communication style. Make sure you establish communication the way you expect to conduct business—whether by phone or e-mail. Note whether she is able to clearly articulate what you will be purchasing, how quickly she responds to your requests, and how accessible she seems to be. This is an early way to see if a designer is overextended and too busy to provide timely services to you. Bearing in mind that people always move quicker when there is a job on the table, this period can provide important clues about how well she can meet your needs. Although it might seem that graphic design is ideally suited for virtual business, this is completely dependent on both the client and the designer. It *is* completely possible to manage this relationship online, but if you are not comfortable working virtually, you really should hire someone who can meet you face-to-face. Similarly, don't assume all graphic designers who are set up on the Web can truly manage a virtual relationship—this is where your background research and impromptu calls to their customers will provide input.

7. What is your business background?

Being an artist is no excuse for being a poor businessperson. You need to find a graphic designer who has a strong, organized practice with a defined customer relationship/project management system in place to manage his business. Without this, you will find your projects falling through the cracks, your phone calls not being answered, and your billing erratic. While it is hard to see "inside" a business at first, the process of asking other companies for referrals and communicating with the designer will illuminate these issues. Even more important, a seasoned businessperson will likely tell you if he is not the best person for the job and offer alternatives.

8. What are our contractual agreements?

Before you commit to work with a design firm, be very sure you know what you are going to be getting for your money. This is where the real questioning begins. What is the detailed scope of the project? What is considered "out of scope"? What will you owe them and when is it due? Who is responsible for acquiring raw materials and intellectual property rights? Who exactly will be servicing your account? What happens if you are not happy? How many revisions will you have? What are the final deliverables? When can you expect them? Who owns the final product? How will the project be delivered? These are the primary considerations—but suffice it to say, if the design firm is *not* offering you a detailed proposal and legal agreement, you should not proceed at all.

9. Ask yourself …

After all this, intuition is possibly the most important test in choosing a design firm. Your business is your passion, and maybe even your lifeblood. You need to ask yourself if the designer you will work with "gets" what you are doing and feels some ownership and partnership in representing your business to the world. While some concerns can be alleviated with good communication, if you feel a vague sense of unease, wait and find the right designer. For such an important and often costly investment, it will be worth it in the long run.

Source: Eileen Parzek is an award-winning graphic designer and writer providing digital and print graphic design and Web-design services. Always found at the intersection of information, creativity, and technology, her business, SOHO It Goes! Business Design Studio (*www.sohoitgoes.com*) helps small businesses make a big impression, increase their reach, and grow. You can reach Eileen at (518) 729-4453 or by e-mail at *turtle@sohoitgoes.com*.

Chapter
one

Chapter
two

Chapter
three

Chapter
four

Chapter
five

Chapter
six

Chapter
seven

Chapter
eight

8

Your People

Hiring and Firing

Steps to Select the Best People for Your Business

Most business owners want to hire quickly so as to not divert their attention from other business concerns demanding their time. The most successful businesses, large and small, succeed as a result of the efforts of the staff. Therefore, one of the most valuable uses of your time is in hiring the right people to accomplish the company's work. The following list provides the means of ensuring that your time, and that of anyone else you involve in the hiring process, leads to people who raise the capabilities and skills and results of your company.

1. Use every avenue available to find candidates

In addition to the obvious sources of newspapers, Internet job listing sites, and headhunters, tell everyone you know, in every walk of your life what position you are looking to have filled. Nearly 65 percent of all jobs are found through word of mouth and friend or acquaintance connections. If you want the widest pool of qualified candidates to draw from, you need to stir them up from many different sources.

2. Review resumes before speaking with a candidate

Resumes can provide information on many fronts regarding the candidate, beyond actual job experience. Reviewing the document before ever speaking with a candidate will allow you to compare several resumes at the same time,

and get an early idea about each candidate's appropriateness for the role you want filled without any pressure of having someone watch you read and come up with questions. In particular, how much attention to detail did the candidate pay to laying out the information in a readable fashion? And to spelling and grammar? How clearly did he explain the work he has done in the past?

3. Prioritize the resumes

Separate the best resumes from the rest of the stack. Write out a list of the questions you have about each person that could be answered by phone.

4. Conduct phone interviews

Many resumes are written with the assistance of friends and professionals. Before you spend valuable time face-to-face with candidates, screen them by phone. Whether you or someone you assign conducts the phone interview, call and let the person know you have a few questions. Begin the interview by describing the company and the open job's role in the organization. Describe one or two of the challenges that position faces in relationship to others in the company, and even in dealing with vendors, customers, advisors. With the resume and list of questions in front of you, this is your opportunity to listen to how the candidate presents herself and addresses your questions. You will find you are able to trim your list of candidates based on the answers you get over the phone. Thank her for her time and let her know someone will get back to her.

5. Schedule face-to-face interviews during business hours

If the candidate is not a fit, provide him with immediate notice so he can get on with his job search. This can be done by phone or in writing. If the candidate's resume matches your impression over the phone, and you liked what you heard in your conversation, schedule an interview in person with her at your place of business. This is your opportunity to observe how she conducts herself in unfamiliar surroundings. Is she prompt? How does she interact with the other people in your company before and after she meets with you? How does she behave with you?

6. Include "case" questions and unusual questions in your meeting

Interviewing is your opportunity to see more detail about the person behind the resume. Many guidelines for interviewing propose questions such as "What are your strengths and weaknesses?" The answers to these questions are well practiced by most candidates. To get closer to the real person, you need to see how he thinks, communicates, takes responsibility, collaborates to solve problems. Whether your candidate is coming to discuss a position as a clerk or as a manager, prepare at least three questions along the lines of challenges and conflicts that position faces. One at a time, ask the candidate to describe how he might see himself addressing that issue when it comes up. There are no correct answers to case questions,

so the candidate cannot prepare neat answers. As a result you will be able to watch him think, listen to how he would approach an issue, how far his experience would help, and the attitude with which he faces conflicts. In reaction to the responses you get to your case question, you may pose additional complications to see how he deals with complex situations.

7. Conduct group interviews

One of the most valuable and rarely used techniques for interviewing is a group interview before the senior person ever meets with the candidate. Have several people team up for the face-to-face interviews. To conduct group interviews, the interviewing team needs to sit down with the list of questions for about a half-hour to refine the case questions, decide who is going to lead areas of the conversation, and so on. The purpose is not to intimidate the candidate but rather to allow several people to conduct a conversation, each trading off asking questions and listening to the answers being given and probing for different information in a very efficient way. The best candidates can usually be clearly identified by the way they conduct themselves in this unusual format, and when an offer is generally made, the others who participated in the interviews know who they will have as a new teammate.

8. Probe the candidate

In addition to seeing how candidates respond to your questions, this is your opportunity to see how they initiate gathering the information they need to make decisions. Ask them what questions they have for you. The questions they pose will demonstrate whether they are actually interested in the job, the company, the people they will be working with, or just want any job. A candidate who has no questions for you may not be bringing the quality of thinking you need in your company.

9. Select the best candidate for the job

Whenever possible, select the most highly qualified, most experienced candidate you can for the job. Your company's value increases as you hire experience and maturity, so the business depends less on your capabilities. The experience you hire will allow you to focus on critical business decisions while capable staff take competent care of the daily challenges of your company.

10. Conduct the final interview

When you believe you have identified the candidate you prefer for the job, conduct a final interview to probe the questions that the candidate has as a result of the conversations you and your team have now had. This series of conversations will enable you to refine the job responsibilities you want the candidate to take on, and your expectations of how quickly her performance should get up to speed once she is hired. You are now ready to make her an offer.

Source: Linda Feinholz, president of Feinholz & Associates, provides consulting and coaching services to business owners, managers, and professionals, helping them improve the effectiveness of their organization and their results. In addition to working with Avon, Walt Disney Imagineering, and the Los Angeles Metropolitan Transportation Authority, she assists small and midsize businesses in developing the plans, resources, capabilities, and systems to grow their businesses and increase their individual and organizational capabilities. Her work includes leadership and management development, business process redesign, and team development. Information on her services can be found at *www.feinholz.com*. She can be reached at *Linda@feinholz.com* or (818) 989-5989.

No-Cost Staffing Ideas

Any business can benefit by bringing in an extra pair of hands to help out. No-cost staffing solutions are essential when a business is growing, and helpful at other times. The work can range from data entry or reception duties to event planning. The secret to a successful experience is to be clear what the company needs. This list will provide you with some ideas for getting extra hands in the office, without losing an arm and a leg.

1. Contact a local high school

Most high school programs have a co-op or mentor program that will place a student who is interested into a specific company to get an understanding of what is involved in that industry. Discuss your needs with the teacher in charge of that program.

2. Private English language school

Speak to the principal or director of the school to find out if volunteer placement is part of their program. If not, he or she may be willing to circulate a volunteer posting to students to find someone suitable for your company. This is a particularly good match for technical or computer work.

3. Government agency that works with new immigrants

There are agencies that find volunteer placements for immigrants to gain some valuable work experience in their new homeland. This gives them a better chance to find a job that is in their industry of choice. There may be a follow-up program that subsidizes their wage for a couple of months.

4. Church bulletin

Place a request for a volunteer for a specific project in the local church bulletin. There may be an executive in transition or a retired person who would derive pleasure from taking on an interesting project.

5. College or university placement

There is a little more effort involved in securing a college or university placement student. The supervising teacher needs to meet with the employer to discuss the student and get regular progress reports. The benefit is that he or she can often help with advanced-level work. Your company may need a draftsperson or a new designer. Find the program that is training students in the field you require and discuss what's possible. Many of these student placements are so successful that the new graduates end up being hired by the company.

Source: Elizabeth Verwey, Small Office Mentors, has tried each one of these no-cost staffing solutions. They have helped the business in specific and important ways. Her book, *The Mentors' Circle*, will be released in 2006. Check *www.officementors.com* to learn more about how to grow your business with a group of peers, using The Mentors' Circle Model. Contact her at *Elizabeth@officementors.com*.

Required Documentation for a New Employee

Hiring someone new requires paperwork. We went to the IRS and found out the forms that you should know about when hiring someone. Here they are.

1. Form I-9

You must verify that each new employee is legally eligible to work in the United States. Both you and the employee must complete the U.S. Citizenship and Immigration Services (USCIS) Form I-9, Employment Eligibility Verification. You can get the form from USCIS offices or from the USCIS Web site at *http://uscis.gov*. Call the USCIS at (800) 375-5283 for more information about your responsibilities.

2. Form W-4

Each employee must fill out Form W-4, Employee's Withholding Allowance Certificate. You will use the filing status and withholding allowances shown on this form to figure the amount of income tax to withhold from your employee's wages. In certain circumstances, you may be required to send a copy of an employee's Form W-4 to the IRS. If you have an employee who submits a Form W-4 claiming more than ten withholding allowances, or claiming an exemption from withholding when the employee's wages are normally more than $200 a week, see Publication 15.

3. Form W-5

An eligible employee who has a qualifying child is entitled to receive advance earned income credit (EIC) payments with his or her pay during the year. To get these payments, the employee must give you a properly completed Form W-5, Earned Income Credit Advance Payment Certificate. You are required to make advance EIC payments to employees who give you a completed and signed Form W-5. For more information, see Publication 15.

4. Form W-2, Wage Reporting

After the calendar year is over, you must furnish copies of Form W-2, Wage and Tax Statement, to each employee to whom you paid wages during the year. You must also send copies to the Social Security Administration.

Source: Internal Revenue Service (*www.irs.gov*).

Items to Include in a Job Description

Think of a job description as a "snapshot" of a job. The job description needs to communicate clearly and concisely what responsibilities and tasks the job entails and to indicate, as well, the key qualifications of the job—the basic requirements (specific credentials or skills)—and, if possible, the attributes that underlie superior performance. Our expert, a human resources consulting firm, provides for us here a quick look at the categories that make up a well-written job description.

1. Title of the position

List the title of the position, such as senior mailroom clerk.

2. Department

List the department the person will work in such. For a mailroom clerk, the department may be the operations department.

3. Direct reports

This section explains to whom the person will directly report. An example would be the building services supervisor.

4. Overall responsibility

This part explains the overall responsibility of the position, such as to supervise mailroom staff and interface with all levels of management, regarding mail and supply deliveries.

5. Key areas of responsibility

This section explains the person's responsibility in more detail. Clarify the actual tasks and responsibilities before you start thinking about what special attributes will be needed by the person who will be fulfilling those responsibilities. For example, maintain established shipping/receiving procedures; sort and distribute mail on a timely basis; maintain all photocopiers, fax machines, and postage meters; order, store, and distribute supplies; facilitate all off-site storage; inventory and record management requests; document current policies and procedures in the COS department as well as implement new procedures for improvement; oversee the use of a company van when needed; and ensure that water and paper are available for customers on a continuous basis.

6. Coworkers

The section explains whom you will work with on a regular basis. An example for this job may be the building services supervisor, mailroom staff, all levels of management.

7. Term of employment

This section explains the length of employment. For example, the term of employment may be twelve months.

8. Qualifications

Qualifications are the skills, attributes, or credentials a person needs to perform each task. Some examples of qualifications would be a strong sense of customer service, good organizational skills, ability to lift a minimum of twenty-five pounds, supervisory experience in a corporate mailroom environment, good driving record.

Source: Judith G. Lindenberger, president, Lindenberger Group (*www.lindenbergergroup.com*), a human resources consulting firm. Contact her at (609) 730-1049 or e-mail at *info@lindenbergergroup.com*.

Key Questions to Ask During an Interview

Asking key questions that require well-thought-out and concise answers will allow you to see how prepared the individual is and if the candidate can think on his or her feet. Our expert, a national staffing firm, provided us with this list of key questions to ask a prospective employee.

1. What do you consider your most significant accomplishment?

The candidate should be able to provide a detailed example of her involvement in a situation or project that includes factors such as long hours, attention to detail, a tight deadline, or hard work that resulted in a successful outcome.

2. What do you consider your most significant strength?

The candidate should be able to provide specific examples of five or six strengths—ones most compatible for the available position.

3. Why do you believe you are qualified for this job?

Look for the candidate to name two or three main factors about himself that relate to the job he is interviewing for. The candidate should be specific and include a technical skill, management skill, or personal success story.

4. How have you grown or changed over the past few years?

Maturity, increased skills, and increased self-confidence are important developmental aspects. Being able to discuss these aspects effectively is indicative of a well-balanced, intelligent individual. Overcoming personal obstacles or recognizing manageable weaknesses demonstrates that the candidate is an approachable and desirable employee.

Source: Kelly Services, Inc. (*www.kellyservices.com*)—A Fortune 500 company headquartered in Troy, Michigan, that offers staffing solutions that include temporary services, staff leasing, outsourcing, vendor on-site, and full-time placement. Kelly serves 200,000 customers through 2,600 company owned and operated offices in thirty countries and territories. Kelly provides employment for nearly 700,000 employees annually, with skills including office services, accounting, engineering, information technology, law, science, marketing, light industrial, education, health care, and home care. Visit *www.kellyservices.com*.

What to Look for when Interviewing a Job Candidate

First impressions really do count. As soon as the candidate walks into your office for an interview, you make your first judgment. What should you look for during the interview, besides knowledge, skill, and ability? There's a lot of subtle things that you should be considering. Our expert, a national staffing firm that interviews and places thousands of people in jobs every day, offers the following tips when screening and evaluating job applicants.

1. Did you feel comfortable shaking the person's hand?

A firm grip still sends the strongest, most positive message.

2. What kind of facial expressions does the applicant exhibit?

Is the job seeker smiling, frowning, twitching, sweating . . . terrified?

3. What about posture?

Posture is often a good indicator of an individual's degree of interest and ability to listen and react.

4. Does the candidate emanate confidence or does he/she appear timid or withdrawn?

It's pretty obvious that the person who is self-assured has a big advantage.

5. How are the candidate's verbal skills?

Look for someone who speaks in full sentences, with attention to grammar. This individual may well be representing you and your company in the near future.

6. What about the tone of voice?

A candidate who mumbles or speaks in a whisper is at a distinct disadvantage to someone who speaks in a well-modulated, clear voice. Watch the pauses during or between sentences. They can serve as your guide to the candidate's thought processes.

7. Is there proper eye contact?

Direct eye contact is important and indicates the person is giving you full attention.

8. Does the candidate have the ability to listen, rather than just to talk?

In the interview process, you're looking for answers. If the candidate doesn't pay attention to what you are saying, he or she is just presenting a monologue. This could be an indication of the individual's inability to concentrate, take direction, or be a team player.

9. What about the individual's attitude?

It's praiseworthy to show ambition. On the other hand, look out for a candidate who blames others for past failings, or "bad mouths" his old employer.

10. Look for confidence without arrogance.

Both of these traits come naturally, and indicate what you can expect later in interpersonal and professional relationships. The candidate's body language can tell you a lot, also. Is the applicant slouching in his or her chair? Does he or she look away from you all the time?

11. Look for a strong candidate.

Strong candidates are sure of their abilities and have come to the interview well prepared.

You've already read the resume. It was good enough to warrant a personal interview. Now you'll want to hear much more about an individual's work history, with examples of accomplishments. It is important to note what candidates say, and their substantiation of the events.

12. You're not just looking for a new person; you should aim to improve your organization.

Every candidate brings along special work and leadership skills.

13. Find out how the individual's background translates to your industry.

The candidate's education, training, and experience can be a big bonus to your organization.

14. In the candidate's tone of voice, you should hear the implied "you need me because I bring these things."

A positive attitude is the applicant's strongest selling tool. Listen for it.

15. As you and the applicant talk, try to measure how this person will relate to you, your boss, and your boss's boss.

The "winning" candidate will interact with all sorts of people. You will be judged on how well he or she does as an employee. Because you helped bring the candidate into the company, his or her performance reflects on your managerial ability. Go for the gold. That's how you create a win-win.

16. Don't look for "yes" people.

Try to find people who will bring something fresh and new to the organization, who are not afraid to speak up when they have a point of view.

17. For the good of your company, keep this motto in mind: "I want to hire my replacement."

As a successful manager, you plan to move up the organizational ladder. Don't you want to have good people following in your footsteps?

Source: Kelly Services, Inc. (*www.kellyservices.com*)—A Fortune 500 company headquartered in Troy, Michigan, that offers staffing solutions that include temporary services, staff leasing, outsourcing, vendor on-site and full-time placement. Kelly serves 200,000 customers through 2,600 company owned and operated offices in thirty countries and territories. Kelly provides employment for nearly 700,000 employees annually, with skills including office services, accounting, engineering, information technology, law, science, marketing, light industrial, education, health care, and home care.

Top No-No Questions in an Interview

Don't go there! The following list is comprised of subject matter that is widely regarded as off-limits for discussion in an interview by employment experts. Most of these subjects relate directly to federal and state employment laws. Legislation covering equal employment opportunity is extensive and complex. Check not only federal laws, but also your own state's laws and guidelines. Remember, state laws vary! So before you get into more trouble, here's a list of questions to avoid.

1. Questions pertaining to age

Do not ask the candidate questions about their age. Also, be careful using the word *overqualified* with older candidates.

2. Questions about an arrest record

Never ask candidates questions about their arrest record (this is different from convictions—in most states; it is permissible to ask if the candidate has ever been convicted of a crime).

3. Questions about race or ethnicity

During the interview, avoid all questions pertaining to the candidates' race and ethnicity.

4. Questions concerning the candidate's citizenship prior to hiring

Do not ask questions concerning the candidates citizenship before you hire them. (It is permissible to ask, "Will you be able to provide proof of eligibility to work in the United States if hired?")

5. Questions concerning the candidate's ancestry, birthplace, or native language

Never ask the candidate questions about their ancestry, birthplace, and native language; however, it is permissible to ask about their ability to speak English or a foreign language if required for the job.

6. Questions about the candidate's religion

Avoid questions pertaining to their religion or religious customs or holidays.

7. Questions about the candidate's height and weight

Never ask questions concerning the candidate's height and weight if it does not affect ability to perform the job.

8. Questions about relatives

Do not ask the candidate questions concerning the names and addresses of relatives (only those relatives employed by the organization are permitted).

9. Questions about home and with whom they live

Avoid questions about whether the candidate owns or rents his/her home and who lives with them (asking for their address for future contact is acceptable).

10. Questions that deal with financial situation

During the interview, do not ask questions concerning the candidate's credit history or financial situation. In some cases, credit history may be considered job-related, but proceed with extreme caution.

11. Questions about education and training

Stay away from questions concerning education or training that is not required to perform the job.

12. Questions about sex and gender

Never ask questions concerning sex or gender. Avoid any language or behavior that may be found inappropriate by the candidate. It's his/her standard of conduct that must be met.

13. Questions about pregnancy or medical history

Avoid questions concerning pregnancy or medical history. Attendance records at a previous employer may be discussed in most situations as long as you don't refer to illness or disability.

14. Questions about their family, marital status, or child care

Do not ask questions concerning the candidate's family or marital status or child-care arrangements (it is permissible to if the candidate will be able to work the required hours for the job).

15. Questions about memberships in organizations

If it is not related to the job, never ask questions concerning the candidate's membership in a nonprofessional organization or club.

16. Questions about physical or mental disabilities

Always avoid questions concerning physical or mental disabilities (asking whether the candidate can perform the essential job duties is permitted). The ADA allows you to ask the applicant to describe or demonstrate how they would perform an essential function(s) when certain specific conditions are met. Check the law or consult with an attorney before moving forward.

Source: Small Business Administration (*www.sba.gov*).

Ways to Limit Your Employee Reference Risks

Employers can have risk in several ways with employment references of their ex-employees. They can have legal risk in giving them to potential employers, obtaining them from other employers or not checking them at all. In all cases, they may find themselves being sued for defamation or similar claims, discrimination, or invasion of privacy. Due to these risks, many employers have adopted policies of not giving out references at all or of giving out only basic employment data such as dates of employment, job titles, and wage rates. Here's how you can minimize the risk of giving out references.

1. Always do reference checks on the final applicants for any open position for your business

Resume fraud is rampant and you want to know that the person you hired is whom you think you hired and their background and credentials are factual. You also want to know that he is in the country legally, not under a false identity and has no criminal record or tendencies that could harm your business or your employees. A comprehensive reference program should verify all past employment, college degrees, and criminal history at the very least. For sensitive positions, credit checking is also advised. Past behavior can sometimes predict future behavior. Calling past supervisors can give you information on the applicant's work habits or inclinations or bring up issues that could be critical to aspects of your business. An example would be that an applicant was fired for embezzlement or theft, and you were considering them for an accounting position. You do not want to find these things out after you become a victim.

2. Hire the professionals to do your reference checking

You must comply with federal and state laws regarding how employment background investigations are handled. In some states, applicants are entitled to a copy of any reports, especially if a negative action is taken against their candidacy. In other states, they must get a copy of the report regardless of what is turned up. Federal law requires disclosures to employees regarding credit reports. Hire a professional reference check company for this purpose that also has the ability to verify criminal records in state and federal jurisdictions, education, social security number, credit reports, and, if necessary, driving records. A professional service will make sure they comply with all federal and state laws and proper disclosures. They will ensure that they do not ask applicants' references inappropriate questions nor will they record inappropriate information in their background reports.

3. Have a consistent policy on giving references on your past employees

If you make exceptions to a policy of not giving references by giving references for deserving employees, you may open the door to claims of discrimination. It is usually in your best interests to have a policy that permits some limited disclosure about an employee's work performance if you get a written release from the ex-employee. You can get more information from your fellow employers if you give disclose more to those same employers in your community. More and more states are beginning to require that references be given by law in the interest of public safety. They are requiring this to expose potential criminal behavior prior to a new employer hiring an applicant, particularly with respect to child care and fiduciary issues.

4. If you decide to allow information to be disclosed in references, take some precautions

Limit who in your organization can give references to those properly trained in the policy and the laws governing references. Usually the HR department or payroll department is assigned such duties. *Do not* allow supervisors to give references. They are too hard to control and may say the wrong thing. Make sure they know the policy that they are not to give references under any circumstances. Educate yourself with the general types of information that you can safely disclose and with the circumstances under which the disclosure is proper. Make sure you make no defamatory statements that are not completely backed up by facts. Keep comments limited to job-related information and follow a prescribed list of allowed information that can be released. Get a written release from your ex-employee that authorizes your disclosure of information in employment references. This is your best protection against reference-related litigation. You can save yourself a lot of potential problems if you make this a practice. It is good to ask the inquiring agency or employer for the release before any information is disclosed. If they cannot provide one, confine the information you disclose to name, title, and dates of employment only. If they produce a signed, written reference release, check the employees' signature to match what you have on file. If it does, you can also release the reasons for discharge, salary, and whether you would rehire them or not. Avoid any prolonged discussions and be sparing in your comments, limited to these areas.

5. Keep references out of personnel files of people who are hired

By keeping reference files away from personnel files, you protect the reference contact's identity. You can also avoid embarrassing problems later if negative statements are read by the employee or a supervisor reviewing the personnel file that could lead to employment or promotional discrimination. It can also prevent defamation if written references are not accurate and people who review the personnel files do not see them and disclose the information to others. Reference checking is an important part of the hiring process and should be handled carefully, for the applicant's and your protection. Be aware of all regulations for your states before developing a policy or contracting with a company to handle this on your behalf.

Source: Dan Curtin, principal and owner of Curtin Associates (*www.hrsolutions-socal.com*)—He is an HRCI certified, recognized consultant who advises small and medium-size businesses, manufacturers, and nonprofits on the West Coast about how to better manage their employees and stay in compliance with state and federal labor laws. Curtin Associates is a consultancy affiliated with TR Anton Inc., a national firm in business since 1983. Mr. Curtin can be contacted at (323) 937-02612 or by e-mail at *consultant@socal.com*.

Common Interviewing Steps to Evaluate a Prospective Employee

As a business owner, you may feel a bit anxious about interviewing candidates, especially if it is your first time. This list should help you evaluate the candidate in a short period and let you know if this is the right person for your business.

1. Work experience

A discussion of work experience should vary widely based on how long the applicant has been employed. Questions appropriate for a recent high school or college graduate will make little sense when interviewing a professional with fifteen years of experience. For an applicant with substantial experience, a reasonable starting point would be a discussion of the most recent position. In addition to focusing on the jobs themselves, it might also be helpful to discuss why the applicant has changed jobs in the past, the duration of each prior employment, and chronological gaps in employment. When interviewing someone who has not been working long, ask about the jobs held, the duties and responsibilities, likes and dislikes, and what he or she has gained from them. Ask about work experiences during school or the summer and then concentrate on the more recent jobs in detail.

2. Education

As in the case of the work-experience portion of the interview, the education discussion must be tailored to suit the applicant's educational level. When interviewing for a professional position, the focus would shift to the professional education. For recent graduates, discuss high school and the subjects they preferred, their grades, extracurricular activities, and anything else of importance such as on-the-job training they may have had. Ask a question such as, "What was high school like for you?" Select specific follow-up questions for each educational experience and move forward chronologically. Don't necessarily accept answers at face value. Chronology reveals patterns. Take the information and the patterns of the behavior that you're being told and analyze them in terms of the performance skills you determined that you needed before the interview began.

3. Activities and interests

Turn to the present, and tell them that you would like to give them the opportunity to mention some of their interests and activities outside of work—hobbies, what they do for fun and relaxation, community activities, professional associations, and anything else they would like to mention that might be relevant to the job. Ask them, "What would you like to mention?" Again, select specific follow-up questions. Show interest and attention and respect for the applicants. Don't talk down to them. Don't use an inappropriate language level.

4. Self-assessment

At this point of the interview, tell them it is time to summarize the conversation. Ask them to list some of their strengths—qualities both personally and professionally that make them a good prospect for any employer. Select specific follow-up questions as needed.

5. Transition to the information-giving phase

If you are still interested in the applicant, proceed to this phase of the interview. On the other hand, if you have already decided that the applicant isn't suitable, there isn't much point in describing a position that the applicant won't be filling. Tell the applicant that he has given you a good review of his background and experience and that you have enjoyed talking with him. Before you turn to talk about your business, ask if there is anything else he wants to tell you about his background that wasn't covered. Then ask the applicant if he has any specific questions or concerns before you give him the information about the job and opportunities. Then give the applicant information about your company including the job, benefits, location, and so on. Remember to tailor your presentation as appropriate to the interest in the candidate.

6. Closing

Ask the applicant, "Do you have any other questions about the company, the job, or anything else?" If you have already decided not to offer the applicant a job, you can let him know at this point. Do so cordially and uncritically; you needn't be specific about why you have rejected the candidate. Tell him, "I've enjoyed talking with you today, but we won't be able to offer you this position." If you think that you would consider the applicant for another position in the future, say so. If pressed for a reason why an applicant won't be offered a job, you always have the option of saying that you do not discuss the reasons for your hiring decisions. Or you may explain that, for example, you have already interviewed other, more qualified applicants. Use your judgment, realizing that it can create a very awkward situation if you merely tell the applicant that he is unqualified or lacking experience. If you have found a promising candidate, you can continue. Ask her, "What is your level of interest at this point?" Let the applicant know what steps are likely to happen next, whether another interview will be needed, and how long it will be before a decision is made.

Source: ItsSimple.biz (*www.itssimple.biz*)—A very popular free Internet resource center that assists small business owners by providing valuable information, guidance and business-development tools. ItsSimple.biz is a free Internet resource center to assist small business owners. Contact them at 316 California Ave., Suite 433, Reno, NV 89509; (775) 324-2900.

Typical Legal Considerations Before Hiring a New Employee

Hiring a new employee isn't a simple as you think. Here's a list of some typical legal considerations to take into account before hiring a new employee, from an expert specializing in small business matters.

1. Hiring contractors

Do you want a contractor or a real employee to join your team? Both options offer advantages and disadvantages. If the contractor isn't operating as a company, you will want him to fill out the IRS 1099 form. The contractor is responsible for paying his own taxes—not you.

2. Hiring employees

Employees get the W-2 form instead at the end of each year to report their income. You are responsible for deducting the tax from the employee's paycheck and sending it to the IRS. You are most likely also responsible for paying money for the social security, workers' compensation, and unemployment. Check with an accountant or lawyer and eventually consider hiring a payroll company to take of everything for you.

3. Benefits

What benefits do you have to offer? What extra benefits are you going to offer employees (health insurance, etc)?

4. Job requirements

What are the job requirements/responsibilities?

5. Probationary period

Are you going to have a probationary period for employees?

6. Nondisclosure agreement or noncompete clause

Are you going to offer a noncompete clause? (Check with a lawyer to make sure it is legal in your area.)

7. Contract

You will need a very clear and detailed contract that specifies what is required from the employee and what is expected from you. The contract should list everything that might need to be regulated this way. Check with a lawyer and also do your research. Every state might have different requirements. Your local SBA office will eventually be able to help you.

8. Term of contract

What kind of contract do you want to offer? Is it going to be open or limited time (e.g., 3 months)?

Source: SmallBusinessLand (*www.SmallBusinessLand.com*)—Offers free knowledge for the small business community.

Common Hiring Mistakes

Hiring the wrong person for a key job can really kill a small business. We asked our expert who provides assessment services, what hiring mistakes are most commonly made. If you learn to eliminate these mistakes from your hiring procedures then you really should improve your chances of hiring more talented candidates with the right skills.

1. Relying only on interviews to evaluate a candidate

A recent study by the International Personnel Management Association found that the typical interview only increases your chance of choosing the best candidate by 2 percent over the flip of a coin. While interviews are the most common selection method, managers often don't receive proper training or tools to identify the skills of the candidate. An interview, however, can be used by managers to evaluate how well a candidate might work with others.

2. Using successful people as models

Even though duplicating success might seem like a good idea; evaluating the characteristics of top performers alone does not provide clear reasons why people succeed. Often winners and weaker performers share the same characteristics. Finding factors that distinguish the winners from the weaker performers is more important than understanding common characteristics.

3. Too many criteria

To hire winners, decide on six to eight factors that separate them from weaker candidates. Through a method called "validation" you can make better hiring decisions. This process identifies critical job success factors and weighs each factor's importance. The government originally used validation research to prove that employment selection practices predicted job success and were not discriminatory.

4. Evaluating "personality" instead of job skills

High energy, honesty and a solid work ethic are personality traits that seem to practically guarantee success. However, objective statistical research shows little correlation between any personality factor and any specific job. Only tests of job skills or knowledge are proven to predict job success consistently.

5. Using yourself as an example

While your own success might lead you to believe that you can instinctively identify candidates with potential, don't count on it. When you use yourself as a model, unconsciously your ego often interferes and can bias your objectivity in judging others.

6. Failure to use statistically validated testing to predict skills critical for job success

In some companies brainstorming is used to identify candidate selection criteria. This technique tends to focus on theories instead of facts, theories that suggest that high self-esteem guarantees a better employee. Often the emphasis is placed on attitude and experience rather than ability and skills. Validated skills provide a more significant and consistent indicator of success potential.

7. Not researching why people have failed

Research has shown that people fail in a job for reasons different from the criteria used to select and hire them. Many managers can list the reasons why people fail, but will seldom use this information for future hiring decisions. By incorporating these "failure points" into the selection process can reduce mistakes by as much as 25 percent.

8. Relying on "Good Guy" criteria

Generally, people like others who look and act like them. People who appear to be like you frequently are considered to be "good guys". We all want to hire good people, but being a good person on its own does not ensure success on the job. Skills are a much more consist and significant indicator of a person's success potential.

9. Bypassing the reference check

Recruiting and placement agencies report as many as 15 to 20 percent of candidates submit false information on resumes and job applications. An individual who twists the facts to get a job will probably bend the rules on the job. Checking references may seem to be tedious, but it beats having to fire someone in two weeks. To err in hiring talent is human, but when you are willing to revamp your standard hiring process, you have an opportunity to lead your company in a new and more profitable direction.

Source: Mel Payne, MBA, CCP, RCC President, Knowledge & Success, Inc. (*www.knowledgeandsuccess.com*)—Knowledge & Success, Inc is an assessment, training and development company that assist clients with building successful organizations using World Class standards and tools. He can be contacted at (215) 230-4128 or *mpayne@knowledgeandsuccess.com*.

Top Personnel Firms

Thinking of outsourcing your employee search? Then you're going to want to engage a personnel firm. Here are some of the largest ones to choose from and the services they provide.

1. Adecco SA

The largest staffing firm in the world, not to mention the United States, employs 16,000 permanent colleagues and 450,000 temporary workers. Its 3,000 offices throughout fifty countries place temporary, full-time, clerical, industrial, and technical workers throughout its network of 500,000 clients.

www.adecco.com

2. ADP TotalSource

Formerly The Vincam Group, the professional employer organization (PEO) provides small and midsize businesses with staffing-related services. It establishes a co-employer relationship with clients by providing services in such areas as human resources, regulatory compliance and tax administration, employee benefits, payroll tax, and risk management.

www.adptotalsource.com

3. Allegis Group, Inc.

Allegis Group is one of the world's largest staffing and recruitment firms, with more than 300 offices in North America and Europe. Its operating companies include Aerotek (engineering, automotive, and scientific professionals for short- and long-term assignments), Mentor 4 (recruitment for accounting, human resources, and customer support positions), and TEKsystems (IT staffing and consulting).

www.allegisgroup.com

4. Bernard Haldane Associates

HaldaneOnline.com is specifically designed and directed toward the employer. With more than eighty locations internationally and more than 500 Haldane representatives serving clients worldwide.

www.haldaneonline.com/

5. Bob Allen Recruiting

Bob Allen Recruiting is an executive-recruiting firm specializing in the printing and packaging industry. They are a full-service recruitment and placement firm assisting companies fill openings in many production processes including web and sheet-fed offset, wide and narrow web Flexography, Rotogravure, digital and screen printing.

www.boballenrecruiting.com/

6. Caliper Human Strategies

Caliper has advised more than 25,000 companies—including FedEx, Avis, and some of the fastest-growing smaller firms—on employee selection, employee development, team building, and organizational development.

www.calipercorp.com

Source: The Vault (*www.thevault.com*)—The Internet's ultimate destination for insider company information, advice, and career management services. Contact them at 150 West 22nd St., New York, NY 10011.

Ways to Defend an Unemployment Claim

After you fire an employee, or someone quits working for you, one of the tasks that remains is dealing with the issue of unemployment benefits for that worker. If the benefit is warranted, then fine. But if a benefit is applied for, and if it's not deserving, you should fight it. Unemployment claims, whether fair or not, will raise your rates. So here's a few ways to defend yourself against a wrongful unemployment claim.

1. Just give the facts.

Typically, the report will ask how long the employee worked for you, what his or her earnings were, whether the worker quit voluntarily or was dismissed, and what the facts surrounding the termination were. Don't give just a one-word explanation—but don't write a whole novel either! A few sentences should do it.

2. Go to the hearing.

You should have a presence at any hearings, formal or informal, before the state unemployment insurance officials. This is the only effective way to present your side and to respond to any false or incomplete statements your ex-employee might make. The "burden of proof" is on the employer—that means it's up to you to prove your statements, by testifying or presenting documents. The supervisor who actually witnessed the misconduct or other action that led to the termination should be present to testify; in most cases, that means you. It's a good idea to have an attorney represent you at any hearing, especially the first time you are involved in an unemployment case. Attorney representation becomes a virtual necessity if you lose at the hearing level and decide to appeal to the court.

3. If you learn new facts, report them to the state.

If you later learn of facts that would disqualify the claimant for benefits (for example, he or she turned down a job offer, went on a long vacation without looking for work, or refused to take the old job back if you offered to rehire the worker), report these facts to the state unemployment agency.

4. If you lose, file an appeal.

If the employee is found eligible for benefits despite your objections, follow up with an appeal to the administrative agency and (if you lose again) to the courts, unless, of course, your lawyer tells you this would be fruitless in your particular case.

5. Don't let a possible claim stop you.

Even though a successful unemployment claim may raise your tax rates, don't let the fear of a rate increase keep you from firing an employee who is truly dragging your business down. One bad apple can destroy the morale of an entire office.

Source: ItsSimple.biz (*www.itssimple.biz*)—A very popular free Internet resource center that assists small business owners by providing valuable information, guidance, and business-development tools. ItsSimple.biz is a free Internet resource center to assist small business owners. Contact them at 316 California Ave., Suite 433, Reno, NV 89509; (775) 324-2900.

Steps to Take Before Firing Your Employee

One of the most difficult tasks you will face as a business owner will be firing employees. Employees who consistently break the rules, do not perform the functions of their job, or cause difficulties for your business can be a strain on the work environment, your cash flow, and even disrupt your business from thriving and performing as

expected. This list will give you steps and hints for terminating employees or associates.

1. Document, document, document

The first step is to make sure you have all the documentation you need. When you give verbal warnings, be sure to document them properly. Make a case for this specific situation by documenting everything you did before making the decision to release the employee. Document anything that shows that you tried to solve things to the better. Your business should have a well-documented procedure for what it expects from employees and anything that is considered grounds for immediate dismissal. Be sure to use these as guidelines and consult with a lawyer experienced in HR questions if necessary.

2. Have witnesses

Have a friend, family member, or business partner assist in any paperwork and any issues that arrive from the employee. Not only does this representative help with anything you might forget, they also serve as a witness if any lawsuit arises. This will be difficult for either one of you, but in the end it will be well worth the effort.

3. Just give the facts

Explain to the employee the performance you have expected, the steps you have taken to help them meet that performance, and that he or she has not met them. Do not say more than you have to; just state why the person is being dismissed and fill out any exit paperwork. If you are upset, cool down before talking. If you have to fire somebody over the phone because he or she is in a different location, advise the employee that you have somebody with you listening to the conversation. Make it very clear that you are in control and prepared.

4. Establish exit procedures

Make sure you back up any important files before firing the employee and take steps to lock the person out of any computer system. Change all passwords, but make sure the employee does not realize that before the actual moment of truth. Fire someone on a Monday and not on Friday. Employees fired on Fridays have the whole weekend to stew, while those fired on Mondays usually are more upbeat because they have the week ahead of them. Be sure to explain when the last paycheck is coming, when benefits terminate, and any information regarding extending health coverage or any other details (if this applies to your situation). Remember to keep the meeting short and to the point. Explain to the other team members that you fired the individual without going into too many details. They do not need to know all the details, but you need to make sure that they understand that this was not a personal dispute between you and the employee fired. You want employees to be honest when disagreeing on something and not scared to get fired. When a new potential employer calls you for a reference, remember to just state the title and dates of employment. Specify that you are not able to provide any further information. Advise your remaining employees that your business policies specify that all calls for references have to go through HR (you?) or you. Document again how the complete process of firing went, what the employee had to say, and what happened.

Source: SmallBusinessLand (*www.smallbusinessland.com*)—A site that offers free knowledge for the small business community in the form of tutorials and articles to help small businesses succeed.

Checklist for Terminating an Employee

As an employer, you must be aware of legal claims that can arise from involuntary terminations of employees. Because of this, use a checklist to make sure the termination is appropriate. Here is an eight-step checklist to follow.

1. Why do you want to terminate the employee?

Explore the reasoning behind terminating the employee. As an employer, you should be able to answer this question in one to two sentences.

2. What alternatives have been considered?

Consider alternatives and consider why these alternatives might have been rejected. An alternative could have been suspension from pay or a final written warning.

3. What documentation is needed?

You will need to consider what documents will support the termination, whether the documentation is adequate to support the termination, and what other documentation can be prepared before the termination.

4. What written policies apply?

Consider what written policies or agreements will apply to the termination, such as your drug or sick day policy.

5. What was the past practice when similar situations happened?

Consider what you did in the past that would apply to this situation. Then, think about how you handled those situations.

6. What is the employee's protected status?

Determine whether the employee is in a protective class or recently engaged in a protected activity. If they have, determine how you can show that your employee's protected status or activity is not the reason for the termination.

7. What procedures have been followed?

Determine what procedures have been followed, whether they have been fair, and what further procedures such as exit interviews, final paychecks, and insurance notices, will be followed after the termination.

8. Anticipate problems and prepare for them.

Think about problems, questions, claims that may arise from the employee termination and what you will do to fairly address these issues.

Source: Lawrence C. Winger, Esq. (*http://userpages.prexar.com/lcw/lcw/*)—Winger has more than twenty-four years of experience in the area of labor and employment law. He has handled labor and employment law litigation matters such as National Labor Relations Board (NLRB) unfair labor practice trials; union picketing injunction litigation; age, sex, and handicap discrimination trials; sexual harassment jury trials; litigated wage and hour cases; wrongful discharge jury trials; severance pay litigation; NLRB unit determination hearings; NLRB unit clarification hearings; noncompetition agreement litigation; unemployment compensation litigation; and arbitrations. He can be reached at 75 Pearl Street, Suite 217, Portland, ME 04101; (207) 780-9920; fax: (207) 780-9923; e-mail: *lcw@ime.net.*

Considerations for Conducting a Fair Termination Meeting

A successful termination meeting should always be thought out and planned carefully. If you find yourself faced with a termination meeting, here is a list of considerations to help you conduct it fairly.

1. Review the employee's history

Make sure you go over your employees file before the meeting. Review documents from prior disciplinary discussions.

2. Plan what to say

Think and plan what you are going to say ahead of time. Get another company employee to role-play with you. This will help you avoid saying something you might regret later. Keep everything in the role-play confidential.

3. Make superiors aware of the reasons for termination

If applicable, let your superiors know the reasons the employee is being terminated. Also tell them the termination date.

4. Be ready for questions the employee will ask

Be prepared for any questions that the employee may ask you.

5. Have a list of the assets from the company the employee owes

Create a checklist for any company assets or other property that the employee should return.

A list will help you remember during the termination meeting.

6. Prepare a written termination notice before the meeting

Prepare a written termination notice in advance. Include in the notice any required insurance or benefit notices.

7. Consult with your legal counsel if you have questions

If questions arise, remember that you can always contact your legal counsel. They will assist you with questions about the process or the circumstances that have resulted in the involuntary termination.

8. Make sure you have a witness to the meeting

If you can, have a witness at the meeting. Tell this person what his or her role is. Also brief the witness on how to respond to any comments that may come up.

9. Change passwords the employee may have

If necessary, change all security passwords and locks. Remember PCs or any other bank transfer PIN numbers the employee could still have.

Source: Small Business Administration (*www.sba.gov*).

Managing Your Employees

Ways to Avoid Burnout

You've probably heard a great deal about the rewards of running your own business. But you must also be aware of the trade-offs and sacrifices that come with being in charge. Over time, those long hours, missed weekends, and pressure-packed deadlines may take their toll on your physical and emotional health, affecting relations with your employees, family, and friends in the process. Fortunately, our business coach provides here a few great ways to keep business burnout at bay.

1. Identify the stressors

What aspects of running your business regularly cause discomfort or even anxiety? Perhaps you dread mundane tasks like bookkeeping and filing reports, or having to make sales calls. You may have customers who are difficult to work with, or do not pay invoices on time—and, because you are responsible for everything your business does, you may find yourself obsessing about things beyond your control.

2. Delegate

One cure for an overburdened mind is to shed some of your responsibilities. Members of your staff with specific skills or leadership potential may be good candidates to take on certain functions. If you're a solo entrepreneur, it may be time to hire your first employee or outsource your administrative work to a part-timer.

3. Schedule some "me" time and stick with it

You follow a regular maintenance schedule for your equipment, so why not treat yourself the same way? A monthly lunch get-together with colleagues and designated family nights are great ways to get your mind off business issues and reconnect with the people who matter most to you. Even a quick walk around the block will do wonders to refresh your mind and spirit.

4. Consult your doctor

Regular check-ups, eating right, and sensible exercise will not only preserve your good health, but also help you better manage the demands of daily life.

5. Take care of #1

If you're run down, you'll burn out faster. Make sure you get enough sleep, eat right, exercise, and de-stress on a regular basis.

6. Get back in touch with the things you value

Is your work fulfilling and meaningful for you? If not, check in with your values. What's missing? Where are you compromising? What needs to be eliminated? What are you merely tolerating? Re-assess and re-adjust your priorities as needed. If you work for yourself, you're in control. Make the choices you want to make by honoring what's important for you.

7. Think outside the box and challenge yourself consistently

If work has become a chore or you're in a rut, try spicing things up a bit! Find innovative ways to do mundane tasks, create new products or services to add to your offering, improve performance, or tweak what you do best and make it even better.

8. Establish realistic expectations for what you can and cannot accomplish

If you find that you're driving yourself or your employees too hard, it may be time to let go of unrealistic expectations and readjust. Shorten your to-do list, give yourself some slack when needed, and know when to let up on yourself and others.

9. Learn to communicate clearly

Resolve conflicts, don't run from them. Let people know what you expect from them, and ask them what they expect from you. Be clear and concise with what you say, and how you say it. Listen closely to the people around you, it will teach them to listen closely to you.

10. Manage your time

Poor time management is another thing we do that leads to burnout. Set regular business hours. Make appointments with yourself to get things done—and keep them! Being on time counts, show up promptly for appointments and expect others to do the same.

11. Stop blaming yourself or others

If you're playing the "woulda, coulda, shoulda" game, perhaps it's time to re-evaluate your attitude. Blaming yourself or others for things that have gone wrong doesn't help. What does? Learn from your experiences and make changes to ensure that you get the results you want the next time.

12. Value yourself by establishing boundaries and limits

Learn how to do it in a way that is clear and consistent. Don't give away too much of your time. Let people know your policies and procedures. Be up-front with what's acceptable and what's not. Learn how to say no.

13. Deal with your emotions

Keeping your feelings inside usually leads to trouble. If you are feeling any kind of negative emotion, don't deny it. Instead, learn how to acknowledge your feelings, be up-front with them, and deal with the underlying causes.

14. Don't feel embarrassed to ask for help

Everybody needs a little help once in a while. You can't do everything yourself. Don't be afraid to ask friends or associates for help, or hire a professional when needed.

Source: Executive business coach and consultant Susan Martin. To find out how you can make more money with less effort and stress; visit Susan at *www.business-sanity.com* and subscribe to Business Sanity Tips.

Items to Include in an Employee Manual

Do your employees understand what's expected of them in any given situation? More important, do you know what you expect of your employees in a given situation? Regardless of the size of your business, the Employee Policy Manual is an essential management tool that communicates your rules and expectations to employees. Although the contents of the Employee Policy Manual will differ from business to business, all should contain the following main sections.

1. Employee code

Outline the basic elements such as working hours, vacation time, salary and benefits, overtime, orientation procedures, and performance evaluations. Also, include coverage of customer handling and other issues that arise during the normal course of the workday. Include job descriptions in this section as well.

2. Employee misconduct

Include a description of how employee misconduct will be addressed, including issues such as tardiness, persistent lateness, or employee theft.

3. Sexual misconduct

Even small and start-up businesses are advised to include a policy item outlining behaviors that are not acceptable within the workplace. Primarily designed to protect women in the workplace, these policies also advance strong guidelines to mitigate the occurrence of sexual misconduct in the work environment.

4. Health and safety guidelines

When employees share in the responsibility for health and safety issues, the entire business benefits. Guidelines must comply with applicable local, provincial, and federal legislation.

5. Internet policy

Include mention of appropriate Internet and e-mail usage. Be sure to specify that employees may not use company e-mail or other Internet components to conduct illegal activities, or to access or distribute pornography or copyrighted materials, such as the popular MP3 music files. Should you ever find yourself in court defending your business because an employee has used your e-mail system to send threatening or harassing e-mails, an Internet policy will be to your benefit.

Source: June Campbell of Nightcats Multimedia Productions (www .nightcats.com) provides writing services to business and organizations, and provides content to print and electronic publications. Her Web site currently offers a number of free and low-cost resources for entrepreneurs and operators of small businesses. Contact her at 103-145 West Keith Road, North Vancouver, BC, Canada V7M1L3; (604) 980-3261; or e-mail: campbelj@nightcats.com.

Reasons to Have an Employee Manual

The president of a large company was quoted as saying, "We've done away with our personnel manual. It got us into more trouble than it was worth." While most Human Resource directors and corporate CEOs understand why policies, procedures, and forms are necessary to effectively operate any organization, there are a few who establish them because "that is the way it has always been done." At the same time, there are many attorneys who will tell you that policies and procedures only place the company in situations loaded with liabilities because no policy manual can be without implied contracts. There are no endeavors without risk, but in personnel management, risk must and can be diminished. Here are the major reasons for establishing policies and procedures.

1. Minimizes danger of a lawsuit

In the absence of policies, past and present activities become policy. Since many of these practices are or can be discriminatory (because of a lack of consistency), the company is in greater danger of lawsuits and claims with government agencies than if they had carefully spelled out the company's expectations of the employee.

2. Provides management with sufficient discretionary powers

The contractual nature of policy manuals can be lessened considerably by providing management with sufficient discretionary powers to act in a number of ways under similar circumstances.

3. Maintains management discretion while firmly communicating mutual expectations

There is as much danger in saying too much as too little. What a handbook should do is to provide the most positive way of maintaining management discretion while firmly communicating mutual expectations. Manuals that are more than fifty pages long are probably replete with implied contracts. Further, they call for more frequent updating than policies that have left sufficient discretionary powers to give leeway in various situations.

4. Articulates rights of the employer and the obligations of the employee

Many policies and forms can and should have attendant disclaimers that articulate the rights of the employer and the obligations of the employee.

5. Establishes benefits and disciplinary policies

The employee deserves to know what is expected and what he or she can expect in return. Since job satisfaction is based upon rewards and expectations, it only makes sense to establish "benefits" and disciplinary policies.

6. Establishes well-written policies

By establishing well-written policies, the company can expect that supervisors and managers will (if properly trained) take approximately the same course of action in similar circumstances. It is not the handbook that is usually at fault but rather the way policies are administered or not administered by management.

7. Reduction of liabilities through structure and direct communication of rights and obligations are still best disseminated through an employee handbook

Until the laws and labor codes in the United States catch up with the realities of the workplace, reduction of liabilities through structure and direct communications of rights and obligations are still best disseminated through a handbook.

Source: Why and When Are Employee Handbooks Necessary, by Ethan A. Winning (www.ewin.com)—A popular consultant on human resources–related issues, he has published numerous books and articles on human resources. His firm provides manuals, forms, and formats that help employers to minimize implied contract liabilities. He can be reached at ewinning@ewin.com.

Top Ways to Maximize Your Training Dollars

Training is a win-win situation. It builds the competencies that strengthen both individual and organizational performance. But training can be expensive. Here is a list of some proven ways to reap the benefits of training while keeping costs under control.

1. Assess both the organization and individuals to determine training needs

Companies that train for the sake of training often miss important areas that would make a difference on return on investment (ROI). By using assessment tools to target training needs, companies can make sure their training dollars are well spent.

2. Identify the top three areas of training needed within the organization

In some organizations the urgent need is to begin training with the sales organization. In others, the greatest need is to develop senior level managers. Begin where the greatest impact will be realized. This will boost the morale of the organization more quickly, thus creating an atmosphere that welcomes change.

3. Create training goals

The best training program, if it is not in keeping with your organizational goals, will yield little fruit. Prioritizing training goals, and then implementing them in their order of importance, will save training dollars

4. Use mentoring and coaching to reinforce training

Mentoring and coaching are powerful ways to raise the bar of excellence and create a culture conducive to individual and organizational learning and growth.

5. Use batch training whenever possible

Training several people at a time is a very efficient use of training dollars. The group approach also reinforces learning as participants interact with each other as well as the instructor.

6. Measure results from training

It's relatively easy to measure sales training results. It's also possible to create measurements to determine pre-learning and post-learning performance in other areas. One strategy is to set up parallel projects for people who have been through training and those who haven't—and then measure performance of the two groups.

7. Use blended learning to cut costs

Technology has changed the way we learn. By launching training in a classroom setting, and then continuing the process via e-learning, it is possible to save on travel expenses as well as the cost of live instruction at training centers.

8. Enhance employee retention

A Louis & Harris Poll says that among employees who say their company offers little to no training, 41 percent plan to leave within a year. This underscores a key point: turnover is much more expensive than training.

9. Use biblio-training to supplement training programs

Books by great authors, recommended as a supplement to training, are a cost-effective way to increase learning and awareness throughout the organization. Having a person within the organization review new and great classics, and then share that information with others, is an inexpensive way to encourage personal and professional growth through reading.

Source: Mike McGrail (*www.mcgrailgroup.com*)—Mike McGrail's corporate experience includes sales and marketing management roles at IBM, Exxon and M&M Mars before founding The McGrail Group in 1990. Today The McGrail Group offers consulting and training in leadership, sales, and personal productivity, as well as in other management areas, to create an ideal environment for personal and organizational growth. Contact him at The McGrail Group, Inc., 800-459-7191 or *mike@mcgrailgroup.com*.

The Benefits of Running a Virtual Company

As a small business owner, you may be thinking about starting, or converting to, a virtual company. A virtual company is a great way to reduce the costs and headaches involved in the traditional office environment. Here is a list of just some of the many benefits of running a virtual company:

1. Reduces costs and overhead

Traditional companies experience the costs of rent, office supplies, and real estate–based employees (i.e., receptionists), to name a few. A virtual company, on the other hand, experiences more limited expenses; in the case of service or professional service businesses, a virtual company can eliminate most real-estate expenses, which is one of the two biggest expenses your company can incur.

2. Attracts high-quality talent

A virtual company can be a tremendous recruiting tool. A high percentage of skilled people for various reasons prefer not to work in a traditional office setting. You will also find many men and women on the parent track. Many of these people prefer to work out of their home. It allows them the time to take care of their children.

3. Allows more flexibility with strategic decisions

Many strategic decisions in a traditional company are tied to real estate. It is hard to be flexible when strategic and personnel decisions are based on real-estate expenses. It is hard to expand and contract to meet the economic realities of today when you have to link every strategic decision to the cost of real estate.

4. Provides new growth opportunities

For example, in a traditional company, if you have a project that you need ten additional people for, you will have to expand your office space and therefore may choose not to take on the project. With a virtual company, you do not have to worry about leasing space and determine whether you can get rid of the space when the project is complete.

5. Makes better use of the advantage of technology

In the last two years, wireless technology has allowed all of us the ability to connect faster with each other than ever before on the Internet. A virtual company can take advantage of the wireless benefit. Meeting rooms for virtual companies can be T-Mobile hot spots in Starbucks. There is no need to look for conference space. A virtual company gives you flexible technology in a world that is rapidly becoming wireless.

6. Decreases the amount of interruptions

In a traditional office environment, it can be hard to get away from coworkers who want to come into your office to chat. They take valuable time away from your work and make you less efficient. In a virtual company, it is easier for you to concentrate without those interruptions.

7. Decreases the times of meetings

With a virtual company, there is less of a tendency for lengthy and unproductive meetings. In a traditional company, you must coordinate for everyone to meet and then fix the date and the time, and drag everyone into the conference room, which can waste valuable time. In a virtual company, meeting times are decreased, allowing your company to be more productive.

8. Decreases or eliminates commuter time

Working in a virtual environment can also save time and money on your daily commute. In large urban areas, this can amount to a saving of between ten and twenty hours per week.

9. Increases employee morale

The virtual company also offers the benefit of a better work environment for you and your employees. It allows employees to work in a more "trusting" environment where there is the benefit of knowing that your employer trusts you to manage your time in a cost-effective manner resulting in a win-win for everyone.

Source: Jay Jaffe, president and CEO of Jaffe Associates (*www .jaffeassociates.com*)—He is an award-winning consultant who advises top attorneys and other professionals worldwide about how to turn their business goals into business achievements. Jaffe Associates is a virtual consultancy with professionals throughout the world collaborating via e-mail, instant messaging, white boards, and Web conferencing. Small Business Computing magazine named Jaffe Associates one of the 100 most tech-savvy small businesses in America and selected Jaffe as one of only ten to profile, in a feature aptly titled, "Virtually Brilliant." He can be contacted at (970) 748-0003 or by e-mail at *jaffej@jaffeassociates.com*.

Typical Performance Appraisal Questions

Most managers dread employee performance reviews. It is hard to win—you can never say enough good things, and one word of criticism is generally the only thing the employee will remember. The only way this ever gets better is with a lot of practice and a pretty thick skin. Here are some typical performance appraisal questions that should help you and your employee benefit from the process.

1. Productivity

What could I do to make your work more productive?

2. Training

What equipment or training do you need to do your best work that you don't have?

3. Company changes

What could the company change (or add or delete) that would help you do your work better?

4. Underutilized skills and abilities

What skills and abilities do you have that you think are underutilized?

5. Their opinions

Are there any other comments or opinions you would like to express?

Source: Jan B. King (*www.janbking.com*)—Former president and CEO of Merritt Publishing, one of the fifty largest woman-owned and run businesses in Los Angeles. King is currently an author and leads a consulting practice primarily devoted to helping traditional publishers, writers, and educators with content development and curriculum design for print publications and innovative Web sites. In addition, she teaches small business management and writes and speaks extensively on employee-ownership and participative management. Contact her at 531 Main Street, PMB 1161, El Segundo, CA 90245-3036; (310) 990-8807; e-mail: *jan@janbking.com*.

Steps for Dealing with a Problem Employee

Despite all our best efforts at "managing," we have very little control over other people's actions, including the people who work with or for us. We can inspire, motivate, guide, or threaten them, but the choice to act in a certain way is up to the individual. Today's workplaces are complex environments; it is a rare occasion when all employees get on together and work enthusiastically and constructively to achieve the goals of the business. Problem behavior on the part of employees can erupt for a variety of reasons. Here are ten tips for dealing with it.

1. Recognize that problem behavior usually has a history

It usually develops over time and seldom from a single incident. As a manager, it is your responsibility to be alert to the early warning signs and deal with the underlying causes before the situation reaches a crisis.

2. Assess your responsibility

If the problem is in your team, then you are at least partly responsible for it. Perhaps you were blind to the signs the individual was undoubtedly leaving, or you chose to ignore them and hope they would go away. Perhaps you hadn't been managing that individual's performance on a regular basis and so missed an opportunity to discover the problem earlier. Whatever the reason, responsibility lies with you in some part. You would be surprised how frequently it is the manager who has created or at least contributed to problems of employee behavior. Having an abrasive style, being unwilling to listen, and being inattentive to the nuances of employee behavior are all factors that contribute to the manager's need to thoroughly examine what is going on.

3. Don't focus only on the overt behavior

When confronted by an angry or upset employee, it's easy to attack the person and target their behavior rather than examine the underlying factors. Often, this takes patience, careful probing, and a willingness to forgo judgment until you really understand the situation.

4. Be attentive to the "awkward silence" and to what is not said

When an employee is obviously reluctant to communicate, it's almost a sure sign that more lurks beneath the surface. Often, employees will hold back because they feel unsafe. They may test the waters by airing a less severe or kindred issue to see what kind of a response they get. To get the full story and encourage forthrightness, the manager has to read between the lines and offer the concern and support necessary to get the employee to open up.

5. Clarify before you confront

Chances are, when an issue first surfaces, you will be given only a fragmentary and partial picture of the problem. You may have to dig deep to reach important facts, and talk to others who may be involved. One safe assumption is that each person will tend to present the case from his or her viewpoint, which may or may not be the way it really is. Discretion and careful fact-finding are often required to get a true picture.

6. Be willing to explore the possibility that you have contributed to the problem

This isn't easy, even if you have reason to believe it's so, because you may not be fully aware of what you have done to fuel the fire. Three helpful questions to ask yourself: Is this problem unique, or does it have a familiar ring as having happened before? Are others in my organization exhibiting similar behaviors? Am I partially the cause of the behavior I am criticizing in others? Once you understand how you

have contributed, you can decide to take action to make sure it doesn't happen again.

7. Plan your strategy

Start by defining, for yourself, what changes you would like to see take place, and then, follow this sequence: Meet with the person and let him or her know that there is a problem. State the problem as you understand it and explain why it is important that it be resolved. Gain agreement that you've defined the problem correctly, and that the employee understands that it must be solved. Ask for solutions, using open-ended questions such as: "What are you willing to do to correct this problem?" In some cases, you may have to make it clear what you expect. Get a dedication that the employee will take the required actions. Set deadlines for finishing the actions. In the case of a repeated problem, you may want to advise the employee of the consequences of failing to take corrective action. Follow up on the deadlines you've set.

8. Treat the employee as an adult and expect adult behavior

To some extent, expectation defines the result. If you treat the employee as a naughty child, then you should expect a naughty child to respond. If you indicate—by your actions or by the content or tone of your voice—that you expect adult behavior, then that's what you're likely to get.

9. Treat interpersonal conflicts differently

If the problem behavior stems from a personality conflict between two employees, have each one answer these questions: How would you describe the other person? How does he or she make you feel? Why do you feel that the other person behaves the way he or she does? What might you be able to do to alleviate the situation? What would you like the other person to do in return?

10. Gain agreement on the steps to be taken and the results expected

A problem is not really "fixed" until it stays fixed. Everyone involved must agree that the steps taken (or proposed) will substantially alleviate the problem. This includes you as manager and the steps you personally will take to ensure you are not contributing to similar problem in the future. Finally, agree how you will both monitor the issue. What needs to take place for you both to be satisfied that the issue has been completely resolved. Write this down and use it as your measure of success.

Source: Megan Tough, director, Complete Potential (*www.com pletepotential.com*)—A leadership and business coaching company based in Sydney, Australia. Contact her at her Web site or by telephone: 0412 500 663; outside Australia: +61 412 500 663.

Most Common Federal Labor Laws You Should Know

As a business owner or manager, you may be unaware of the many labor laws out there. The following are a few of the most common federal labor laws you should know from the U.S. Department of Labor.

1. Fair Labor Standards Act

The Department of Labor enforces the Fair Labor Standards Act (FLSA), which sets basic minimum wage and overtime pay standards. These standards are enforced by the Department's Wage and Hour Division, a program of the Employment Standards Administration. Workers who are covered by the FLSA are entitled to a *minimum wage* of not less than $5.15 an hour. Overtime pay at a rate of not less than one and one-half times their regular rate of pay is required after forty hours of work in a workweek. Certain exemptions apply to specific types of businesses or specific types of work. The FLSA does not, however, require severance pay, sick leave, vacations, or holidays.

2. Davis-Bacon and Related Acts

The Davis-Bacon and Related Acts require payment of prevailing wage rates and fringe benefits on federally financed or assisted construction.

3. Service Contract Act

The Service Contract Act requires payment of prevailing wage rates and fringe benefits on contracts to provide services to the federal government.

4. Contract Work Hours and Safety Standards Act

The Contract Work Hours and Safety Standards Act sets overtime standards for most federal service contracts, federally funded construction contracts, and federal supply contracts over $100,000.

5. Walsh-Healey Public Contracts Act

The Walsh-Healey Public Contracts Act requires payment of minimum wage rates and overtime pay on federal contracts to manufacture or provide goods to the federal government.

6. Family and Medical Leave Act

The Family and Medical Leave Act (FMLA) provides for up to twelve weeks of unpaid leave for certain medical and family situations (e.g., adoption) for either the employee or a member of the covered and eligible employee's immediate family; however, in many instances paid leave may be substituted for unpaid FMLA leave.

7. Immigration and Nationality Act of 1990

The Immigration and Nationality Act of 1990 applies to employers seeking to hire nonimmigrant aliens as workers in specialty occupations under H-1B visas.

8. Employee Retirement Income Security Act

Most private-sector health plans are covered by the Employee Retirement Income Security Act (ERISA). Among other things, ERISA provides protections for participants and beneficiaries in employee benefit plans (*participant rights*), including providing access to plan information. Also, those individuals who manage plans (and other fiduciaries) must meet certain standards of conduct under the fiduciary responsibilities specified in the law.

Source: Department of Labor (*www.dol.gov*)—Frances Perkins Building, 200 Constitution Avenue, NW, Washington, DC 20210; (866) 4-USA-DOL; TTY: (877) 889-5627.

Top Things You Should Know about the Americans with Disabilities Act

The Americans with Disabilities Act (ADA) prohibits discrimination against people with disabilities in employment, transportation, public accommodation, communications, and governmental activities. The ADA also establishes requirements for telecommunications relay services. Here are some things you and your employees should know about this important piece of legislation as it could significantly impact your business.

1. Employee rights

Individuals with disabilities are protected from discrimination in employment primarily by the Americans with Disabilities Act (ADA) and the Rehabilitation Act. The Department of Labor's Office of Disability Employment Policy (ODEP) provides publications and other technical assistance on the requirements of these laws. However, ODEP does not enforce these laws.

2. Employers' responsibilities

Employers with fifteen or more employees are prohibited from discriminating against people with disabilities by Title I of the Americans with Disabilities Act (ADA). In general, the employment provisions of the ADA require equal opportunity in selecting, testing, and hiring qualified applicants with disabilities; job accommodation for applicants and workers with disabilities when such accommodations would not impose "undue hardship"; and equal opportunity in promotion and benefits.

3. Hiring people with disabilities

The ODEP provides the following programs to help employers find qualified applicants with disabilities: The Employer Assistance Referral Network is a free, nationwide service that connects employers with job placement professionals who can identify qualified candidates with disabilities for their job openings in the company's geographic area. The Workforce Recruitment Program for College Students with Disabilities is a free, nationwide database of prescreened, qualified postsecondary students and recent college graduates with disabilities who are available for permanent and temporary positions. The ODEP also offers fact sheets to educate employers about laws pertaining to the hiring of people with disabilities.

4. Job accommodations

A job accommodation is a reasonable adjustment to a job or work environment that makes it possible for an individual with a disability to perform job duties. Determining whether to provide accommodations involves considering the required job tasks, the functional limitations of the person doing the job, the level of hardship to the employer, and other issues. The Job Accommodation Network (JAN), a service of the ODEP, provides a free consulting service on workplace accommodations.

5. Job search

The ODEP provides resources to help people with disabilities find employment. Job Links provides a list of employers who are interested in recruiting and hiring qualified individuals with disabilities for open positions in their companies. The Directory of State Liaisons provides state contacts on disability issues in each state. The president's New Freedom Initiative Grants fund innovative programs and technical assistance that aim to improve employment outcomes for adults and youth with disabilities. The ODEP administers these grants. Job search assistance is also available through local one-stop career centers.

6. Laws and regulations

The ADA is the disability-related law that many Americans are most familiar with because it applies to a far broader range of persons, organizations, and businesses than any laws that preceded or followed it. Various titles of the ADA apply in different circumstances. Title I prohibits private-sector employers who employ fifteen or more individuals and employment agencies, labor organizations, and joint labor/management committees from discriminating against qualified individuals with disabilities in all aspects of employment.

7. Small business and self-employment

Entrepreneurship is an exciting opportunity for people with disabilities to realize their full potential while becoming financially self-supporting. Some of the benefits of self-employment or small business ownership include working at home, control of your work schedule, and the independence that comes from making your own decisions. The ODEP provides information, counseling, and referrals about self-employment and small business ownership opportunities for people with disabilities through its Small

Business and Self-Employment Service. The service provides information about developing a business concept, obtaining capital, creating a marketing plan, and other business issues.

8. Social security

The Department of Labor does not enforce any part of the social security program. For information on social security, visit the Social Security Administration's Web site. The Department of Labor does play a role in the implementation of the Ticket to Work and Work Incentives Improvement Act (TWWIIA). Under this law, recipients of Social Security Income (SSI) and Social Security Disability Insurance (SSDI) will have greater choice in getting the services and technology they need to obtain employment. The objective of the program is to work with businesses, state vocational rehabilitation agencies, and other traditional and nontraditional service providers to prepare individuals with disabilities for work and link them with employers who want to hire qualified employees.

9. Statistics

The ODEP provides limited data on employment of people with disabilities. Detailed employment statistics on the overall American workforce can be found at the Department of Labor's Bureau of Labor Statistics (BLS).

10. Workers' compensation

Individuals injured on the job while employed by private companies should contact their state workers' compensation board. The Department of Labor does not handle workers' compensation claims relating to private employers.

Source: Department of Labor (*www.dol.gov*)—Contact them at Frances Perkins Building, 200 Constitution Avenue, NW, Washington, DC 20210; (866) 4-USA-DOL; TTY: 1-(877)-889-5627.

The Most Important Discrimination Laws

Everyone agrees that workplace discrimination has no place in the modern business world. But not everyone understands the laws that protect employees against discrimination. In this case, what you don't know can hurt you—especially if an aggrieved employee files a discrimination claim against your company. When employers violate workplace discrimination laws—whether deliberately or by accident—they face stiff legal and financial penalties, along with bad publicity, low employee morale, and other consequences. Here are some of the most important discrimination laws to keep in mind.

1. Civil Rights Act of 1964

The Civil Rights Act of 1964 prohibits employment discrimination based on race, color, religion, sex, or national origin. The Civil Rights Act of 1991 made major changes in the federal laws against employment discrimination enforced by EEOC. The act authorizes compensatory and punitive damages in cases of intentional discrimination, and provides for obtaining attorneys' fees and the possibility of jury trials.

2. Equal Pay Act of 1963 (EPA)

The Equal Pay Act of 1963 protects men and women who perform substantially equal work in the same establishment from sex-based wage discrimination. Employers may not reduce wages of either sex to equalize pay between men and women. A violation of the EPA may occur where a different wage was/is paid to a person who worked in the same job before or after an employee of the opposite sex. A violation may also occur where a labor union causes the employer to violate the law.

3. Age Discrimination in Employment Act of 1967 (ADEA)

The Age Discrimination in Employment Act of 1967 protects individuals who are forty years of age or older. An age limit may only be specified in the rare circumstance where age has been proven to be a bona fide occupational qualification (BFOQ); discrimination on the basis of age by apprenticeship programs, including joint labor-management apprenticeship programs; and denial of benefits to older employees. An employer may reduce benefits based on age only if the cost of providing the reduced benefits to older workers is the same as the cost of providing benefits to younger workers.

4. Americans with Disabilities Act of 1990 (ADA)

The ADA prohibits job discrimination by employers, with fifteen or more employees, against qualified individuals with disabilities. The Equal Employment Opportunity Commission (EEOC) has primary authority for enforcing the ADA. Most government contractors are covered by both Section 503 and the ADA. Only qualified individuals with disabilities are protected by Section 503 and the ADA. The person must have the necessary education, skills, or other job-related requirements. The person also must be able to perform the essential functions of the job—the fundamental job duties of the position he or she holds or desires—with or without reasonable accommodation. Reasonable accommodation may include, but is not limited to, making existing facilities used by employees readily accessible to and usable by persons with disabilities; job restructuring; modification of work schedules; providing additional unpaid leave; reassignment to a vacant position; acquiring or modifying equipment or devices; adjusting or modifying examinations, training materials, or policies; and providing qualified readers or interpreters. Reasonable accommodation may be necessary to apply for a job, to perform job functions, or to enjoy the benefits and privileges of employment that are enjoyed by people without disabilities. An employer is not required to lower production standards to make an accommodation. An employer generally is not obligated to provide personal use items such as eyeglasses or hearing aids.

5. Rehabilitation Act of 1973

Section 504 of the Rehabilitation Act of 1973 is a national law that protects qualified individuals from discrimination based on their disability. The nondiscrimination requirements of the law apply to employers and organizations that receive financial assistance from any federal department or agency, including the U.S. Department of Health and Human Services (DHHS). These organizations and employers include many hospitals, nursing homes, mental health centers, and human service programs. Section 504 forbids organizations and employers from excluding or denying individuals with disabilities an equal opportunity to receive program benefits and services. It defines the rights of individuals with disabilities to participate in, and have access to, program benefits and services.

Sources: Equal Employment Opportunity Commission (*www.eeoc.gov*), Department of Labor. (*www.dol.gov/esa*), and Department of Health and Human Services (*www.hhs.gov*).

Best Ways to Protect Your Assets Against Employee Litigation

According to our expert, employment litigation, has tripled in the past decade and accounts for more than one-third of all lawsuits filed in the federal courts of the United States. Here are some of the practical things you can do to protect yourself from losing everything if you should lose a future lawsuit.

1. Make an appointment with a casualty insurance agent

Insurance is the first defense against losing your personal assets because of a lawsuit. However, various policies have substantial limitations and restrictions that need to be understood. The next step is to find other ways to protect your assets that can't be insured against employee litigation claims.

2. If you own a business that has employees, form an LLC

A limited liability company is the preferred form of asset protection by most lawyers, for the active owners of a business. Owner/managers are still likely to be sued individually, but the risk is reduced with an LLC, particularly for owners who are not directly involved in the alleged violation of the employee's rights.

3. Joint ownership may be hazardous to your wealth

Don't put assets in joint ownership (with a spouse, parent, or children) without having a good reason and without the advice of competent legal counsel. The general rule is to avoid joint ownership, because those assets are subjected to a double risk. The creditors of both owners can attach any jointly held assets.

4. Find out which assets are protected in your state

Each state protects certain assets from the claims of creditors. Some states protect the equity in a homestead, the cash value of an annuity or life insurance policy, the assets in a partnership or limited liability company, or the assets in an irrevocable trust (for the benefit of others). Assets in a retirement savings plan are generally protected from creditors.

5. You can't lose what you don't own

If you are married and if various investments or bank accounts are owned by your spouse, those assets may be protected from your creditors—subject to the fraudulent transfer laws. On the other hand, you should not do this if your marriage isn't highly stable.

6. Don't rely on a domestic, revocable living trust for lawsuit protection

It may help to avoid some state probate expenses, but it does not remove your assets from your personal creditors.

7. Consider using a limited partnership or limited liability company

Savings and investments that are not protected by other means can be better protected by transferring ownership of those assets to a family-owned limited partnership or limited liability company. This is not an inexpensive way to protect your assets and is not appropriate for those with less than $250,000 of assets.

8. Have a detailed review of the form of title to your assets

A common problem is to set up a limited partnership or irrevocable trust or corporation to protect some of your assets and to fail to change the title to your property.

9. Don't ignore legal protocols

Respect the separation of ownership when you create limited partnerships, corporations, irrevocable trusts, or charitable entities. These are all creatures of the law. If you ignore the legal protocols, the courts can ignore the existence of these entities.

10. If you wait until you are sued, it's too late

You can't buy fire insurance after your house is on fire, and you can't protect your assets from a litigant after a cause of action has occurred. Asset-protection arrangements must be made when there is no threat of a potential claim on the horizon.

Source: Offshore Press, Inc. (*www.offshorepress.com*) has published a newsletter on asset-protection strategies since 1992. The current newsletter is called the International Wealth Protection Monitor. The company provides an online library of information about asset protection from litigation for subscribers and a free Web book on asset protection, which is available at *www.offshore press.com/protection/*.

Privacy Laws That Can Affect Your Business

Employers want to be sure their employees are doing a good job, but employees don't want their every sneeze or trip to the water cooler logged. That's the essential conflict of workplace monitoring. Here are some critical privacy rules that you should know.

1. Employee surveillance

Employers should carefully research local employee privacy laws. While the Federal Electronic Communications Privacy Act provides some protection for workers, the types of monitoring that may be conducted vary widely from state to state. Check the law in your state before beginning telephone, camera, computer, or any other type of electronic monitoring.

2. Personal appearance

Employers are generally free to set reasonable guidelines concerning neatness, dress, appearance, and hygiene. However, such codes are always in danger of legal attack, usually on the grounds that they are discriminatory or violate a person's right to privacy. In some states, employers requiring uniforms may be required to supply or compensate employees for the uniform. Check the law in your state before setting guidelines.

3. Off-duty behavior

In most states, employers may discipline or terminate employees for off-duty behavior that might embarrass the company or disrupt its operations, although some methods of obtaining information about off-duty conduct may infringe on privacy rights. Some states, such as Michigan and Illinois, restrict employers from gathering information regarding an employee's off-duty behavior. Check the law in your state before taking any action against an employee.

4. Drug and alcohol testing

The Supreme Court has upheld an employer's right to test employees for drugs and alcohol. However, some state and local governments have passed laws prohibiting testing, and the subject is always bound to raise privacy law issues. Check on the laws in your state before planning a testing policy.

5. Lie detector tests

The federal Polygraph Protection Act protects most American workers from taking a lie detector test as a condition of employment or continued employment. In many states, however, the law does not apply to applicants with law enforcement agencies, persons in sensitive positions relating to national security, or applicants with drug manufacturers and distributors.

6. Psychological and personality tests

Federal law does not prohibit an employer from requiring an employee or prospective employee to take a psychological or personality test. However, check the law in your state before requiring any candidate or existing employee to take such a test.

7. Searches

Private employers may generally conduct on-premises searches of employer-owned vehicles, equipment, desks, lockers, briefcases, and other items. In most states, searches of an employee's personal items may be legal if the employee had a reasonable expectation of privacy. Public employees enjoy constitutional protections that guard against many kinds of searches.

Sources: Privacy Rights Clearinghouse (*www.privacyrights.org*)— Contact them at 5th Ave., Suite B, San Diego, CA 92103; voice: (619) 298-3396. Business.gov (*www.business.gov*)—The U.S. government's official hub for business, Business.gov is a collaborative effort managed by the Small Business Administration.

Most Common Employee Notices to Be Posted in Your Workplace

Some federal and state agencies require that you post certain posters in the workplace where workers can see them. Typically, such posters are designed to inform workers about safety procedures, wage and hour laws, and other statutes and regulations. Are you required to hang this information?

1. Fair Labor Standards Act (FLSA)

Every employer of employees subject to the Fair Labor Standards Act's minimum wage provisions must post, and keep posted, a notice explaining the act in a conspicuous place in all of their establishments so as to permit employees to readily read it. The content of the notice is prescribed by the Wage and Hour Division of the Department of Labor.

2. Job safety and health protection

All covered employers are required to display and keep displayed, a poster prepared by the Department of Labor informing employees of the protections of the Occupational Safety and Health Act, PL 91-596, December 29, 1970, and its amendments.

3. Family and Medical Leave Act

All covered employers are required to display and keep displayed a poster prepared by the Department of Labor summarizing the major provisions of the Family and Medical Leave Act (FMLA) and telling employees how to file a complaint. The poster must be displayed in a conspicuous place where employees and applicants for employment can see it. A poster must be displayed at all locations even if there are no eligible employees.

4. Equal Employment Opportunity Act

Every employer covered by the nondiscrimination and EEO laws is required to post on its premises the poster, "Equal Employment Opportunity Is the Law." The notice must be posted prominently, where it can be readily seen by employees and applicants for employment. The notice provides information concerning the laws and procedures for filing complaints of violations of the laws with the Office of Federal Contract Compliance Programs (OFCCP).

5. Migrant and Seasonal Agricultural Worker Protection Act (MSPA)

Each farm labor contractor, agricultural employer, and agricultural association that is subject to the MSPA and that employs any migrant or seasonal agricultural worker(s) shall post and keep posted in a conspicuous place at the place of employment a poster prepared by the Department

of Labor, which explains the rights and protections for workers required under the MSPA.

6. Notice to Workers with Disabilities

Each farm labor contractor, agricultural employer, and agricultural association that is subject to the MSPA and that employs any migrant or seasonal agricultural worker(s) shall post and keep posted in a conspicuous place at the place of employment a poster prepared by the Department of Labor, which explains the rights and protections for workers required under the MSPA.

7. Employee Polygraph Protection Act

Every employer subject to the Employee Polygraph Protection Act (EPPA) shall post and keep posted on its premises a notice explaining the act, as prescribed by the secretary of labor. Such notice must be posted in a prominent and conspicuous place in every establishment of the employer where it can readily be observed by employees and applicants for employment.

8. Uniformed Services Employment and Reemployment Rights Act

Employers are required to provide to persons entitled to the rights and benefits under the Uniformed Services Employment and Reemployment Rights Act (USERRA), a notice of the rights, benefits, and obligations of such persons and such employers under USERRA. Employers may provide the notice, "Your Rights under USERRA," by posting it where employee notices are customarily placed. However, employers are free to provide the notice to employees in other ways that will minimize costs while ensuring that the full text of the notice is provided (e.g., by handing or mailing out the notice, or distributing the notice via electronic mail).

9. Davis-Bacon Act

Every employer performing work covered by the labor standards of The Davis-Bacon and Related Acts shall post a notice (including any applicable wage determination) at the site of the work in a prominent and accessible place where it may be easily seen by employees.

10. The Beck Poster

Executive Order 13201 (EO 13201) requires government contracts and subcontracts to include an employee notice clause requiring nonexempt federal contractors and subcontractors to post notices informing their employees that they have certain rights related to union membership and use of union dues and fees under federal law.

11. Service Contract Act

Every employer performing work covered by the Walsh-Healey Public Contracts Act or the McNamara-O'Hara Service Contract Act (SCA) is required to post a notice of the compensation required (including, for service contracts, any applicable wage determination) in a prominent and accessible location at the worksite where it may be seen by all employees performing on the contract.

Sources: Business.gov (*www.business.gov*)—The U.S. government's official hub for business, Business.gov is a collaborative effort managed by the U.S. Small Business Administration. Partner executive departments include Department of Commerce (DOC), Department

of Labor, Office of Small Business Programs (*www.dol.gov/osbp/sbrefa/poster/main.htm*)—Department of Labor, Frances Perkins Building, 200 Constitution Avenue NW, Washington, DC 20210; (866) 4-USA-DOL.

Things To Consider Before Hiring An Immigration Consultant

The complexity and ever-changing rules associated with immigration law increase the likelihood of deception by dishonest immigration consultants seeking to take advantage of businesses who want to legalize the immigration status of their current or prospective employees. Businesses who use these services may lose thousands of dollars, become subject to deportation proceedings or even be accused of attempting to file false papers with immigration authorities. Here is a list of things you should keep in mind when hiring an immigration consultant.

1. Who is allowed to represent me on immigration matters?

Know who you are dealing with. Ask about credentials and experience. Ask to see the consultant's diploma or license and ask for client recommendations. Federal law allows an attorney licensed in any state to appear before the U.S. Citizenship & Immigration Services ("USCIS"). The U.S. Department of Justice Executive Office for Immigration Review accredits certain organizations and non-lawyers to represent individuals before USCIS and immigration tribunals (Immigration Courts and the Board of Immigration Appeals). Only attorneys admitted to practice law in federal court can represent someone in the federal courts.

2. What should trigger suspicions?

Be wary of individuals offering inside connections with immigration authorities, or who otherwise suggest that they are able to guarantee results. Beware of notario fraud. Notaries public may take advantage of the literal Spanish translation of their title, *notario publicio*, a title describing an attorney in many Latin American countries. By taking advantage of the confusion, immigration consultants fraudulently claim expertise or promise results that they simply cannot deliver. An unwillingness to put a representation agreement in writing and demanding that all fees be paid in cash in advance are signals of potential fraud.

3. What should I keep in mind once I have hired an attorney or a consultant?

Make sure you understand the terms of any retainer agreement before signing. It should include all fees, and the nature of any representation. Request copies of any retainer agreements and any papers filed on your behalf. Keep detailed records of all payments and obtain receipts. Do not agree to sign any papers containing any false statements.

Source: Office of New York State Attorney General Eliot Spitzer (*www.oag.state.ny.us*)

Ways to Avoid Immigration Problems

U.S. employers must be very careful when they hire immigrants to work in the United States. On one hand, substantial penalties can be imposed against both companies and individuals who hire people not authorized to work in

this country. On the other hand, it is illegal to discriminate against immigrants who are authorized to work. Thus, employing some foreigners would violate the law, while refusing to employ others would violate the law. Our expert, an immigration law specialist, offers these tips to avoid problems.

1. Complete an I-9 form

Follow strictly the I-9 form that must be completed for each new hire. That form lists the documents that will establish an individual's authorization to work in the United States.

2. Audit supervisors' behaviors

Audit supervisors' behaviors to ensure that they are not treating some ethnic groups differently than others.

3. Tolerate accents

Tolerate accents unless they interfere with job performance. Further, impose "English only" rules only when absolutely necessary to the job.

4. Know job requirements

Be sure height and weight requirements are necessary for the job, since foreigners may have difficulty meeting those requirements.

5. During the interview, ask if he/she is authorized to work in the United States

During job interviews, ask whether an individual is authorized to work in the United States, not whether he or she is a U.S. citizen.

6. Obtain a copy of INS regulations

Finally, the Immigration and Nationalization Service (INS), the agency responsible for enforcement of the IRCA, has issued an extensive set of regulations implementing the act. Employers should obtain a copy of the INS regulations because they are an excellent guideline for complying with the IRCA.

Source: Dr. Steven E. Abraham, professor, Department of Management and Marketing, State University of New York at Oswego (*www.oswego.edu/~abraham*)—He teaches employment law, labor law, legal and social environment of business, labor relations, and human resource management. His primary research interest is the interrelationship between law and employment, and he has investigated this relationship both empirically and conceptually. Contact him at the Department of Management, State University of New York at Oswego, 316 Rich Hall, Oswego 13126; (315) 312-3307; e-mail: *abraham@Oswego.edu*.

Tips for Managing Remote Employees

Most organizations see one of the biggest challenges they face when implementing a telework program as managing mobile or remote workers. The biggest difference is the shift in management style from "eyeball management" (assuming workers are being productive because you physically see them at their desks working) to managing by results. Our expert believes that there are four main keys to managing remote employees. This list will help you work more successfully with your mobile workers and virtual teams.

1. Managing by results, not activity

It is easy to confuse activity with accomplishments. A manager's job is to provide specific, measurable, and attainable goals for the teleworker to meet so that he or she knows what must be done and when. These can include reports completed, number of calls made, number of support issues resolved, or any other appropriate measure of job productivity. It is important that the employee and manager arrive at a shared definition of the deliverables and timetable together. It also ensures that the goals and expectations are realistic.

2. Improving communication (staying connected)

This is one area of remote work that technology helps make easier every day. A variety of tools are available to make it easier than ever to stay in touch and collaborate. The most obvious way to ensure proper communication with teleworkers is to have defined working hours. Another common area of miscommunication and concern that tends to cause problems when dealing with remote workers is the timeliness of communication. An easy, but often overlooked, solution to this problem is to create a set schedule for voice and e-mail checking and responding. There are also a variety of activities managers can institute to make sure that remote employees are "connected" and still feel like part of the gang at the office. This includes having regularly scheduled phone calls, making sure to include remote workers in impromptu lunches and other social events, and routing more informal information, memos, and FYI items to them.

3. Handling meetings and schedules

There are a variety of Web-based groupware/virtual office and dedicated software solutions available to help organizations manage group schedules and shared calendars. This allows both on-site and off-site employees to always have access to current schedules and up-to-date information on last-minute scheduling changes. If you use technology properly, remote workers can use a combination of teleconferencing, videoconferencing, groupware, and Web conferencing to participate in meetings and attend presentations in real time without having to travel and waste valuable time. This also allows you to include remote workers in important ad hoc meetings that might arise.

4. Feedback and support

Regular meetings should be scheduled between managers and telecommuters to assess needs, give feedback, and discuss problems. This is an excellent opportunity to discuss the initially agreed-on scope of work to be done, timelines, and deadlines. Another important way to improve the relationship with remote or mobile workers is to be sure to include them in feedback and praise. Telecommuters don't have as many opportunities to bump into the boss or a manager, so some extra effort is required to provide it. Even using simple, quick ways of letting people know how they are doing such as a brief voice or e-mail, a quick note jotted in the margin of a report or memo, or a short chat when they are in the office can help make sure your employees get this much-needed feedback.

Source: Phil Montero is the founder and CEO of Montero Consulting, a workplace consulting firm that offers workshops and training on managing mobile workers, remote collaboration, improving virtual teams, and setting up virtual offices. Visit their Web site, http://YouCanWorkFromAnywhere.com, for articles, tips, strategies, and resources on all facets of distributed work.

Paying Your Employees

Most Important Wage Laws

The creation of a new business brings many new responsibilities, including compliance with federal wage and hour laws. What are the most important wage-related laws that could affect your business? Here are the top ones from the Department of Labor. Make sure you know these laws well!

1. Fair Labor Standards Act (FLSA)

The FLSA requires that most employees in the United States be paid at least the minimum wage (currently $5.15 per hour) and time and one-half their regular rate for hours worked beyond forty in a workweek. Youth under twenty years of age may be paid not less than $4.25 an hour during the first ninety consecutive calendar days of employment with an employer. The FLSA also includes child labor and recordkeeping provisions. The FLSA covers all workers who are engaged in or producing goods for interstate commerce or are employed in certain enterprises.

2. Child labor

The FLSA sets fourteen years of age as the minimum age for employment and restricts hours of work and allowable occupations for fourteen- and fifteen-year-olds. It also bans employment in specified hazardous occupations for those under eighteen years of age. Special rules apply to minors employed in agriculture.

3. Consumer Credit Protection Act (CCPA)

The CCPA's wage-garnishment provisions limit the amount of an individual's disposable income

that may be legally garnished and prohibit an employer from firing an employee whose pay is garnished for payment of any single debt.

4. The Davis-Bacon and Related Acts (DBRA)

The DBRA requires payment of prevailing wages and fringe benefits to laborers and mechanics employed by contractors and subcontractors engaged in federally financed and assisted construction projects.

5. McNamara-O'Hara Service Contract Act (SCA)

The SCA requires payment of prevailing wages and fringe benefits to service employees of contractors and subcontractors furnishing services to agencies of the U.S. government.

Source: Department of Labor (*www.dol.gov*).

Typical Questions about the Fair Labor Standards Act

The Fair Labor Standards Act (FLSA) establishes minimum wage, overtime pay, recordkeeping, and child labor standards affecting full-time and part-time workers in the private sector and in federal, state, and local governments. What other things do you need to know about this very law? Here they are.

1. When are pay raises required?

Pay raises are generally a matter of agreement between an employer and an employee (or the employee's representative). Pay raises to amounts above the federal minimum wage are not required by the FLSA.

2. Is extra pay required for weekend or night work?

Extra pay for working weekends or nights is a matter of agreement between the employer and the employee (or the employee's representative). The FLSA does not require extra pay for weekend or night work. However, the FLSA does require that *covered, nonexempt* workers be paid not less than time and one-half the employee's regular rate for time worked over forty hours in a workweek.

3. How much do employers with "tipped employees" have to pay?

Tip credit: Employers of "tipped employees" must pay a cash wage of at least $2.13 per hour if they claim a tip credit against their minimum wage obligation. If an employee's tips combined with the employer's cash wage of at least $2.13 per hour do not equal the minimum hourly wage, the employer must make up the difference. Certain other conditions must also be met.

4. How are vacation pay, sick pay, and holiday pay computed, and when are they due?

The FLSA does not require payment for time not worked, such as vacations, sick leave, or holidays (federal or otherwise). These benefits are matters of agreement between an employer and an employee (or the employee's representative).

5. How is severance calculated, and when is it due?

The FLSA requires payment of at least the minimum wage for all hours worked in a workweek and time and one-half an employee's regular rate for time worked over forty hours in a workweek. There is no requirement in the FLSA for severance pay. Severance pay is a matter of agreement between an employer and an employee (or the employee's representative). The Pension and Welfare Benefits Administration (PWBA) may be able to assist an employee who did not receive the severance pay required in his or her employment contract.

6. When must breaks and meal periods be given?

The FLSA does not require breaks or meal periods be given to workers. Some *states* may have requirements for breaks or meal periods. If you work in a state that does not require breaks or meal periods, these benefits are a matter of agreement between the employer and the employee (or the employee's representative).

7. Are periodic performance evaluations required?

The FLSA does not require performance evaluations. Performance evaluations are generally a matter of agreement between an employer and an employee (or the employee's representative).

8. When is overtime due?

For covered, nonexempt employees, the FLSA requires overtime pay at a rate of not less than one and one-half times an employee's regular rate of pay after forty hours of work in a workweek. Some exceptions to this forty-hour standard apply under special circumstances to police officers and firefighters employed by public agencies and to employees of hospitals and nursing homes. Some *states* have also enacted overtime laws. Where an employee is subject to both the state and federal overtime laws, the employee is entitled to overtime according to the higher standard (i.e., the standard that will provide the higher rate of pay).

9. How many hours per day or per week can an employee work?

The FLSA does not limit the number of hours per day or per week that employees age sixteen years and older can be required to work.

10. What are the rules concerning child labor?

An employee must be at least sixteen years old to work in most non-farm jobs and at least eighteen to work in nonfarm jobs declared hazardous by the secretary of labor. Youths fourteen and fifteen years old may work outside school hours in various non-manufacturing, non-mining, non-hazardous jobs under the following conditions: no more than three hours on a school day or eighteen hours in a school week; eight hours on a nonschool day or forty hours in a nonschool week. Also, work may not begin before 7 A.M. or end after 7 P.M., except from June 1 through Labor Day, when evening hours are extended to 9 P.M. Different rules apply in agricultural employment.

11. What about in special situations?

Employees under twenty years of age may be paid $4.25 per hour during their first ninety consecutive calendar days of employment with an employer. Certain full-time students, student learners, apprentices, and workers with disabilities may be paid less than the minimum wage under special certificates issued by the Department of Labor.

12. How many hours is full-time employment? How many hours is part-time employment?

The FLSA does not define full-time employment or part-time employment. This is a matter generally to be determined by the employer. Whether an employee is considered full-time or part-time does not change the application of the FLSA.

13. When can an employee's scheduled hours of work be changed?

The FLSA has no provisions regarding the scheduling of employees, with the exception of certain child labor provisions. Therefore, an employer may change an employee's work hours without giving prior notice or obtaining the employee's consent (unless otherwise subject to a prior agreement between the employer and employee or the employee's representative).

14. When is double time due?

The FLSA has no requirement for double-time pay. This is a matter of agreement between an employer and employee (or the employee's representative).

15. Is extra pay required for weekend or night work?

Extra pay for working weekends or nights is a matter of agreement between the employer and the employee (or the employee's representative). The FLSA does not require extra pay for weekend or night work. However, the FLSA does require that covered, nonexempt workers be paid not less than time and one-half the employee's regular rate for time worked over forty hours in a workweek.

16. Are pay stubs required?

The FLSA does require that employers keep accurate records of hours worked and wages paid to employees. However, the FLSA does not require an employer to provide employees pay stubs.

17. What notices must be given before an employee is terminated or laid off?

The FLSA has no requirement for notice to an employee prior to termination or lay-off. In some situations, the WARN Act provides for notice to workers prior to lay-off. Some states may have requirements for employee notification prior to termination or lay-off.

18. What if I violate the law?

The Department of Labor may recover back wages, either administratively or through court action, for the employees who have been underpaid in violation of the law. Violations may result in civil or criminal action. Fines of up to $11,000 per violation may be assessed against employers who violate the child labor provisions of the law and up to $1,100 per violation against employers who willfully or repeatedly violate the minimum wage or overtime pay provisions. This law prohibits discriminating against or discharging workers who file a complaint or participate in any proceedings under the act.

Source: Department of Labor, Employee Standards Administration: Wage and Hour Division (www.dol.gov)—Contact them at Frances Perkins Building, 200 Constitution Avenue NW, Washington, DC 20210; (877) 889-5627 or (866) 4-USWage.

Creative Employee Benefits

The Institute of Labor Relations' Annual Survey of employees consistently shows that employees want appreciation for a job well done, flexibility in work schedules, and belonging to a team (before money). These creative employee benefits, gathered from several closely held companies, parallel that list.

1. Flexible work schedules

Employees want the ability to set their work hours. For example, they pick 8:15 A.M. to 4:45 P.M. with a half-hour lunch because it matches their day care's schedule.

2. In-office nanny for employees

Parents who take their children to work can easily check in with them, eat lunch together, and be available in an emergency.

3. Emergency time bank

One company set up an annual, twenty-four-hour emergency bank for employees who lose a family member, confront an illness, or encounter family emergencies.

4. Incentives for sales results

Examples include shopping sprees for winning a proposal, theater tickets, gift certificates for dinner at high-end restaurants.

5. First Friday afternoon off for meeting monthly goals

An international marketing company rewarded all staff for meeting its monthly sales goal by giving the first Friday afternoon off. Friday afternoons are typically slow and in advance, the company notified all staff.

6. Celebrate birthdays, company anniversaries

One small company provided a budget for each supervisor to take each employee out to lunch on his or her company anniversary and also provided cake for each person's birthday.

7. Paid time at local food bank in lieu of being sent home with no pay when there is no production work

A mailing house provided this incentive so that employees did not lose pay because work was slow.

8. Two hours per month paid time off for volunteer work

This benefit is especially appreciated by parents of school-age children.

9. Pets at work

Several companies find that pets in the office create a more friendly office atmosphere and with proper policies rarely interfere with work.

10. Memberships to big-box stores

If your company purchases a membership to a warehouse store for its own supplies, then for the minimal cost, upgrade it to provide a membership to each employee.

11. Membership to fitness facilities

Encourage good health by providing a corporate membership to fitness facilities.

12. In-office chair massages and wellness services

You could schedule a regular day for chair massages or use them as a reward. Also, consider providing other wellness services like education on nutrition, fitness, and aging.

13. On-site exercise room

Encourage employees to take a break at work and stay fit. Employees in the "sandwich generation," who are taking care of children and elderly parents, especially appreciate this benefit.

14. Entertainment tickets

Purchase memberships to sporting or fine-arts events and rotate use of the tickets "within the office."

15. For personal service providers, offer free services every month and/or discounts to employees

For example, a day spa provides a free service to each employee each month and gives a discount on all other services. This encourages the employees to recommend services at a higher rate because of actual experience.

16. Golf lessons

If your business includes playing golf with clients, employees will appreciate the opportunity to fine-tune their game.

17. Nap room

Believe it or not, a technology company provided a room with cots because it found its programmers "got on a creative roll" and did not want to go home before they finished a sequence of coding.

18. Game room

The same software company offered a game room with pool and foosball, which helped programmers break through creative blocks.

Source: Pam Watson Korbel, MBA, a business coach, trainer, speaker, and author specializing in entrepreneurial business growth. She is CEO and business synergist of SmartGrowth, Inc. (www.smartgrowth.com) and can be reached at (303) 790-9131 or pam@smartgrowth.com.

Employee Benefits That You Are Required to Offer

Small employers are not required to provide retirement plans, health plans (except in Hawaii), dental plans, vision plans, life insurance plans, paid vacations, paid holidays, and paid sick leave. But there are certain benefits than a company, regardless of size, must provide to their employees. These mandatory benefits are listed here.

1. Time off to vote

You probably want your employees to be active in the community, and part of that activism involves voting in local, state, and federal elections. While there are no federal laws that require you to give employees time off to vote, thirty-two jurisdictions have laws that require private employers to give employees time off to vote; in many of these states, the employee must be paid for this time. Always check to see the policies of your state.

2. Time to serve on a jury

Employers of all sizes have to provide employees with jury duty leave. Both federal and state laws apply in this area. Employees have the right to take leaves of absence to serve as jurors in federal courts, under the Jury Systems Improvement Act. Under this federal law, an employer can be sued for discharging or otherwise intimidating an employee because of that employee's jury service. This applies only to service as a juror in federal court; it does not apply to service as a juror in state or local court. As you might have guessed, the state laws are the ones that protect employees who serve on state and local juries. The laws are not all exactly alike. Most states prohibit an employer from discharging someone who takes leave to serve on a jury. Some prohibit other forms of reprisal or threats of reprisal. Some treat violations as misdemeanors or as contempt of court; others authorize the employee to bring a court action for reinstatement and damages. Some states specifically say that an employer does not have to pay for the lost time or that it may set off from wages any money received by the employee for juror service.

3. Perform military service

There may come a time when you are faced with an employee who may need leave time to serve in the military. All employers, regardless of size, must provide military leaves of absences to employees. The rules governing your employees' rights are set forth in both federal and state law. What about reservists? As a private (i.e., nongovernmental) employer, you do not have to pay reservists during the period they are on active duty. While some employers have a policy that pays reservists the difference between their regular salary and their military pay, you are under no obligation to do so. Also, reservists generally must give you advance notice prior to leaving for active duty, except if military necessity prevents them from doing so. You also may choose to have a policy that makes clear what employees need to do to request military leave.

4. Comply with all requirements of workers' compensation

Every state has enacted workers' compensation laws to protect employees against loss of income and for medical payments due to a work-related injury, accident, illness, or disease. In the vast majority of states, workers' compensation coverage is mandatory. Before you set up your workers' compensation program, however, you should discuss it with your attorney to make sure that you're complying with all of the applicable laws. Do the laws apply to you? In most states, all employers who have at least one employee are covered. While some states exempt very small employers, they don't all have the same definition of what constitutes a small employer. The most common exemption is for employers with fewer than three employees, but some provide the exemption to employers with fewer than four and others to

employers with fewer than five. Of course, even if you're exempt, you can generally choose to participate in the state program.

5. Withhold FICA

The Federal Insurance Contributions Act (FICA) requires you to withhold two separate taxes from the wages you pay your employees: a social security tax and a Medicare tax. This law also requires you to pay the employer's portion of these taxes. Unless you have employees who receive tips, the employer's portion will be the same as the amount that you're required to withhold from your employees' wages. Each of the FICA taxes is imposed at a single flat rate. Currently, the social security tax rate for employees is 6.2 percent, and the Medicare tax rate is 1.45 percent. The taxes are unaffected by the number of withholding exemptions an employee may have claimed for income tax withholding purposes. Simply multiply an employee's gross wage payment by the applicable tax rate to determine how much you must withhold and how much you must pay.

6. Withhold FUTA

The Federal Unemployment Tax Act (FUTA) imposes a payroll tax on employers, based on the wages they pay their employees. You don't withhold the FUTA tax from an employee's wages; the business itself must pay this tax. You must pay the FUTA tax if during the current or the preceding calendar year, you meet either of the following tests: you pay wages totaling at least $1,500 to your employees in any calendar quarter, or you have at least one employee on any given day in each of twenty different calendar weeks (the 20 weeks need not be consecutive, and the "one employee" need not be the same individual). For this purpose, a "calendar week" is a period of seven successive days beginning with Sunday and ending at the close of the following Saturday. However, short weeks at the beginning and end of a calendar year are counted as calendar weeks. Once you meet either of the tests, you become liable for the FUTA tax for the entire calendar year and for the next calendar year as well. For example, if you first met the one-in-twenty test in December 2004, you would have been responsible for the tax with respect to the wages you paid during the entire 2004 calendar year as opposed to just the wages you paid after you met the test. You would also continue to be liable for the FUTA tax during the 2005 calendar year, even if you fail to meet both the wages-paid test and the one-in-twenty test during that year.

7. Contribute to state disability programs

If you happen to run your business in one of the handful of states where state-mandated temporary disability insurance programs are operated for the benefit of workers in the state, you can probably add to your payroll tax obligations a duty to withhold and/or pay taxes that fund the state's program. The jurisdictions where you may have to collect or pay disability insurance taxes are California, Hawaii, New Jersey, New York, Puerto Rico, and Rhode Island. Click on one of these areas on the map at *www.itssimple.biz* for information about their disability insurance taxes. The information includes a short description of the employment level

required to subject you to the state's tax; the tax rate, if any, applied when employers are personally liable for paying the state tax; the rate at which the tax is withheld from employees' wages; the maximum wage amount to which the state's tax applies; and the address of the agency that administers the state's tax.

Source: ItsSimple.biz (*www.itssimple.biz*)—A very popular free Internet resource center that assists small business owners by providing valuable information, guidance, and business-development tools. ItsSimple.biz is a free Internet resource center to assist small business owners. Contact them at 316 California Ave., Suite 433, Reno, NV 89509; (775) 324-2900.

Top Issues when Considering an Employee Raise

When you begin the process of paying employees, your first concerns will probably be related to deciding how much employees get paid. These issues revolve around the principle that you want to pay your employees enough to keep the good ones, but at the same time you can't afford to pay so generously that your business's cash flow is jeopardized. Here are the issues you should consider when addressing the "how much" question.

1. Compare what others are paying

Getting salary data is the first step in determining what "competitive" pay is for the work you want done. Why should you pay attention to what others are doing? You want to offer a competitive wage to make sure you attract the best candidates and retain the best employees, but you'll want to do it without putting yourself in the poorhouse. The best way to find out what a competitive wage is in your area is to find out what others are paying for the same type of work. So where do you go for quick data? There are a number of sources: the classified ads, networking, and public information such as the Bureau of Labor Statistics.

2. Negotiating a new hire's salary

When you make a job offer to an applicant, mention the salary that comes with the job. You may have already discussed it in the interview. If you have, use the job offer to confirm what you have told the candidate. You should know from your informal survey of what other companies are paying the salary or wage you want to offer the person you're hiring. What happens if the candidate wants more money? How can you negotiate with the applicant to mutually agreeable terms? Steps to consider as you decide how to handle this situation are deciding whether the candidate is worth it and making a counteroffer.

3. Giving employee raises

Besides deciding how much to pay new hires, the other major concern of employers related to paying employees is how much of a raise to give an existing employee. There are as many ways of determining this information as there are people determining it. There are two basic approaches to giving raises: give everybody the same percentage or dollar amount raise; or give employees different raises based on the *equity between base wages* and *performance*, also known as a merit system.

4. Using base wages to give raises

Before you can determine what a fair raise is for a current employee, compare what others are paying for the same job by doing some research. This research shouldn't occur only when you bring in a new employee. You should look at market conditions for your employees at least every two years. To stay competitive as an employer and retain your best employees, you'll have to keep on top of pay issues to make sure what you're paying is in line with the market for your area, your industry, and your job. Once you're convinced that your employees' pay is about what it should be for their occupation, if you have more than one employee, examine the pay equity within your business.

5. Examine pay compression

Do you have people who just joined the company who are making the same amount as people who have been there for years, but because of inflation the longtime employees' salaries did not keep pace with starting salaries of today? If this is the case, your company may be suffering from a problem common in business today called pay compression.

6. Combating pay compression

If senior employees find out that newcomers make as much as they do, you'll have problems with morale. Clearly, the only way around this problem is to make sure that long-term employees are paid more than newly hired employees. If market conditions require that you give new employees more pay, you'll have to give older employees at least a little more as well. Some business owners have the philosophy that raises should be linked strictly to the performance of the employee and that employee's contribution to the success of the business. If that's how you feel, you probably will not put as much credence in the idea that employees with more time in the business should make more than newcomers. In that case, focus on linking pay with performance.

7. Linking pay with performance

As a part of the process of coaching and motivating employees, most employers take some time every six months or every year to sit down with employees and discuss their performance. This practice is known as performance appraisal. In addition to talking with the employees about how they have been doing in performing their jobs, you can also use the performance appraisal to set goals for the employees for the period until the next time you evaluate performance.

8. How to link pay and performance

If you do decide to pay for performance, the hard part is making the connection between how well someone has performed and how much of a raise you'll give to that employee. There are some basic steps to follow in making that link: Know what your salary budget will be as a percentage of your *total* budget, considering your sales forecast for the coming year. Decide what form the raises will take. If you use actual dollars, make sure that the person who performs the best gets the most money. The problem becomes figuring out how to divide the money among performance appraisals on all employees. Rank employees based on their performance and the

criteria that you set for them. Divide the money according to that ranking.

9. Review your compensation package

A common occurrence among busy small employers is to develop a compensation package and then, in effect, put it in the back of the closet and forget about it. To keep your compensation package competitive and up-to-date, you'll need to periodically review it.

10. Review at regular intervals

Review your package at regular intervals, perhaps every year. The review doesn't have to be elaborate—it can consist merely of having your lawyer review it for legal compliance or getting some salary data to find out what other business are paying. Review the benefits you're offering when benefit contracts come up for negotiation. When it's time to renew a benefit contract, check with other providers to see if they can quote you a better rate for the same coverage. See if the coverage you're offering is in line with what others offer. Too little coverage may mean you need to consider additional benefits; too much may mean that employees don't need all the coverage you're paying for. Review your package if you notice a pattern beginning to emerge in which employees are leaving for better pay elsewhere. A constant flow of employees out the door may indicate that you're underpaying your employees. Get salary data to confirm your suspicions.

Source: CCH Business Owner's Toolkit: (*www.toolkit.cch.com*)— They provide advice, guides, legal tools, business models, and other resources to small business owners.

Top Employee Compensation Considerations

Small businesses have to be creative with compensation since few of them can match the pay and benefits offered by larger companies. Top performers want more than basic salary, benefits, and vacation days. Flexibility and the opportunity to share in future growth are major attractions for employees of small businesses. Used effectively, benefits, incentives, and deferred compensation are powerful tools. Here are some practical tips on using compensation and benefits to motivate employees.

1. Find out how your company compares

To compare your compensation and benefits with those of other employers and industry standards in your area, you can obtain information from sources such as the chamber of commerce, recruiting firms, industry associations, and studies conducted by firms and government agencies. Online sources include *www.salaries.com* and *www.salaryticker.com*. With this information, you will have a baseline for evaluating your compensation plan.

2. Look at the overall employee picture

By pulling together an updated summary of employee compensation and benefits, you can get a clear picture of the current situation. Many business owners are surprised when they see the information in an integrated way. There may be legal liability exposure if "new hires" are being paid more than long-term highly skilled (and older) employees. Benefits are costly and need to be carefully reviewed on a regular basis to ensure that the coverage is appropriate and the price is competitive.

3. Use compensation strategically

Employees respond positively to incentives. Incentive compensation is additional money (above base compensation) for achieving specific pre-established objectives or milestones. In most businesses, paying salespeople a commission for sales is standard practice. Commissions are usually highly effective in motivating salespeople. One approach is to extend the sales commission model of rewarding specific accomplishments to other positions in your company. For example, employees might receive a commission or bonus for achieving specific milestones such as completing a project on a tight deadline or developing an innovative solution.

4. Be careful what you ask for

There is an old saying: "Be careful what you ask for—because you may get it." Employees respond to incentives, so it is important to align your incentives with the company goals. If the two do not match, you will not get the desired results. Poorly designed incentive compensation can backfire and be counterproductive. Rewarding excellent performance with well-designed incentive compensation can create a prosperous business environment.

5. Change is tricky

If you already have a plan in place, changing is tricky. You must carefully plan any changes and clearly communicate them to motivate employee performance and achieve business results. Changes are disruptive and raise concerns with employees. To ensure a positive outcome, think about compensation in a comprehensive manner. Do not just add a 401k plan without looking at the overall picture.

6. Don't get lost in the details

Evaluating the alternatives can be overwhelming for small business owners who focus primarily on running the business. Examining the options can be like getting lost in the "trees" (details and issues) and losing sight of the "forest" (the business goals). Large corporations hire compensation experts to perform analyses, design models, and create complex, multifaceted compensation programs. Most small business owners, however, have neither the time nor personnel for such elaborate processes and hence must take a practical approach.

7. Get a second opinion

With the increasing costs of benefits (especially health care), it's more important than ever to be clear about your goals for benefits and budget. When your plan is renewing, don't just renew automatically. It's a good business practice to get a second opinion. According to Matt Hollister, president of Business Benefits, located in Clinton, Massachusetts, and on the Internet at *www.b-benefits.com*, common mistakes for benefits include being overly generous (such as paying 100 percent of the medical and dental coverage); not keeping employee records up-to-date; not communicating clearly with employees about costs and the need for changes in plans; and not checking with employees about what they want and how satisfied they are with the company's plans.

Source: Jean D. Sifleet, Esq., CPA, business attorney and consultant, and author of *Beyond 401(k)s for Small Business Owners—A Practical Guide to Incentive, Deferred Compensation and Retirement Plans* (John Wiley & Sons, 2004). She is also the author of *Advantage IP—Profit from Your Great Ideas* (Infinity, 2005), and numerous books and business publications. Her Web site *www.smartfast.com* is a recognized resource for practical information on business issues. Jean can be contacted at 120 South Meadow Road, Clinton, MA 01510; (978) 368-6104; e-mail: *jean@smartfast.com*.

Questions to Ask Before You Purchase Disability Insurance

How long could you or your employees manage without an income if you were unable to work due to sickness or injury? If more than ninety days would be a problem, you have probably already considered purchasing disability insurance. It's a smart move. Statistics compiled indicate that at age thirty, five out of nine people will be disabled for more than ninety days. At age fifty, it's one out of three. When you're shopping for a good policy, take your time and read the fine print. There are a lot of differences between policies and some key issues you should know about before you sign on the dotted line. The following questions to ask are provided by a Licensed Disability Consultant, based in Canada.

1. What is the length of the term?

If you have a stroke, for example, are you covered for thirty-six months or until age sixty-five? For some conditions, thirty-six months won't be enough.

2. How is disability defined?

If you can't work at your stated occupation, are you considered disabled, or will you be expected to get a job serving hamburgers if you are capable?

3. Is there a partial disability option?

Diseases like multiple sclerosis or diabetes, for example, often make it possible for you to work sporadically or part time. You don't want to discover that you are disqualified if you are able to work sporadically.

4. Are the premiums guaranteed?

If you start smoking or become high risk for disability in some way, can your premiums be raised?

5. Is there a cost-of-living rider?

A monthly income that seems adequate today may be way too little twenty years from now.

6. If you miss a payment, how much time before your policy is canceled?

You don't want to discover that your policy is canceled because your check was tied up in the mail, and you are three days late with a payment. Cancellation after thirty days is reasonable.

7. Is your company the First Payer or is there an Integration clause?

That is, if you are unable to work but have some other income, will your insurance policy deduct your other income from the payments (Integration), or will they pay you the full amount (First Payer)? It will make a difference if you believe your disability insurance will augment some other type of income, then discover too late that this will not be how it works.

8. Is your policy portable?

If you relocate to another area or country, can your policy go with you?

9. Is there some way you can check to ensure that the company has been solvent for several years?

If you purchase insurance with an unstable company, you will lose your premiums and your coverage if they go broke.

10. Are there tax benefits?

Your insurance agent or your accountant should be able to provide this information.

Source: June Campbell of Nightcats Multimedia Productions (*www .nightcats.com*) provides writing services to business and organizations, and provides content to print and electronic publications. June's Web site currently offers a number of free and low-cost resources for entrepreneurs and operators of small businesses. Contact her at 103-145 West Keith Road, North Vancouver, BC, Canada V7M1L3; (604) 980-3261; e-mail: *campbelj@nightcats.com*.

Questions to Ask a Prospective Employee Benefits Firm

Navigating through the maze of corporate health care benefits can be mind-boggling. Without the help of a good employee benefits firm, you could be spinning around in circles for months. You'll need someone whom you can trust to design for you and your employees a plan that fits everyone's needs at an affordable cost. Our expert, a benefits consultant himself, offers us this list of questions to ask when interviewing a potential firm.

1. Does my business qualify for group coverage for my employees? What percentage participation in the programs must I have to offer the coverage?

Usually a group is defined as two or more full-time employees. It can even be a husband and wife. In most cases, the employer has to underwrite the majority of the premiums, and there may be a minimum participation level by employees to qualify as a group. The broker would know the underwriting requirements of each carrier. The carriers will ask for a confidential census asking for demographic data on your employee work force such as sex, age and job title, and dates of service. This helps the carrier's underwriter assess the risk on the case and the pricing.

2. What percentage of your compensation is based on new or renewal business?

You want to know how much attention you may receive in the future once the broker gets your business. Chances are you may be referred to a less knowledgeable service person after the initial sale if they earn more money from for new business, rather than retaining older accounts. Brokers who are compensated equally on new and renewal business usually provide you the attention you deserve.

3. Should I go with a large brokerage firm or a small one?

A small business should contract with a medium-size brokerage firm where you will be a "bigger fish in a smaller pond" rather than a "small fish in a large pond." Huge firms are not organized to give small businesses the attention they deserve. Going with the smaller brokerage firm may not give you the latest and greatest technological tools, however. Check out the large firm's capabilities and see if they outweigh the advantages of the more personal attention and service a smaller firm would afford your business. Many times, they do not. The latest technology is only good if your basic needs for excellent service are met.

4. Which benefit carriers have the majority of your business?

A broker who uses only one or two insurance carriers may not have your best interests in mind. No single carrier can meet every client's needs in terms of industry, benefits, features, and price. Once a broker has your business, ask for a complete list of all insurance carriers that provided a quote or declined to quote your business. Make sure you ask for a detailed analysis of the top three to four carriers, with a cost and plan feature comparison. To make sure your broker does not influence you with their personal bias, do some "due diligence" yourself. Check with some of their other clients about the carriers you are most interested in, asking the client contact person questions about ease of administration and employee complaints.

5. How much are the commissions on my account?

Brokers should be up-front about this as it does vary from broker to broker and can range from 2 to 6 percent of monthly premiums for any products you purchase for your employees, added to those same premiums. This is what you pay each month for your broker's value-added services and assistance. Standard commissions vary depending on the type of insurance product, insurance carrier, and size of the case. On larger cases, broker commission may be negotiated. If your employee base and your business are large enough, you can negotiate a direct commission or flat payment to the broker from your firm and ask the carriers price minus their standard commissions. This way the broker acts as your paid consultant and there are fewer chances of conflicts of interest on their part.

6. What services do you offer and what level of service commitment will I receive?

As part of the services offered, insist on annually receiving a Form 5500 Annual Return/Report for Employee Benefit Plan for every line of coverage you have prior to the deadlines for submission to the Department of Labor. This is a federal ERISA requirement, and you should not have to worry about it. A good broker will also coordinate the open enrollment process after the contracts are awarded to the carriers and be an extra resource to make sure it goes smoothly and on time and assist you with educating your employees on how to use their benefits. Ask for a dedicated contact for any service issues or questions. A quality broker will personally answer your questions and visit you regularly, at least once every quarter. Your broker should act as an ongoing consultant to assist you in strategic planning for up to one to five years.

7. Ask your broker how they keep "on top" of their field and what certifications they have?

The world of insurance and benefits is constantly changing. A broker who does the minimum to keep his or her license current will not service you as well as an active professional who participates in professional trade associations where they learn about the latest products and service techniques. Most brokers have professional certifications from various insurance trade institutes that can confirm their basic body of knowledge and expertise.

8. How do I keep the broker's attention on my business and reduce the chance of complacency?

Interview rival brokers periodically—say, every two years—to match what your broker does for you against their offerings. It is a way for you to stay on top of the market of services to businesses and gives you leverage to get more out of your current broker relationship. If you find a big disparity between the market and what you get, it may be time for a change. Certainly, however, if you are getting excellent and appropriate service, stay put. In any event, you can only win by "shaking the tree" occasionally and the status quo in your broker relationships. They should work as hard to keep your business as they did to get it.

Source: Dan Curtin, principal and owner of Curtin Associates (*www.hrsolutions-socal.com*)—An HRCI-certified, recognized consultant, he advises small and medium-size businesses, manufacturers, and nonprofits on the West Coast about how to better manage their employees and stay in compliance with state and federal labor laws. He can be contacted at (323) 937-02612 or by e-mail at consultant@socal.com.

Things You Must Know about COBRA

In 1986, Congress passed the Consolidated Omnibus Budget Reconciliation Act (COBRA) health benefit provision, which amended the Employee Retirement Income Security Service Act, the Internal Revenue Code, and the Public Health Service Act to provide continuation of group health coverage that would otherwise be terminated. This law may affect you, so here are some things you need to know.

1. COBRA generally covers group health plans maintained by employers with twenty or more employees.

COBRA generally covers group health plans maintained by employers with twenty or more employees during 50 percent of the working days in the previous calendar year.

2. COBRA generally defines a group health plan as a plan that provides medical benefits.

COBRA generally defines a group health plan as a plan that provides medical benefits, which may include inpatient and outpatient hospital care, physician care, surgery and other major medical benefits, prescription drugs, and any other medical benefits such as dental and vision care.

3. Under COBRA, employees are entitled to continuation of their health insurance coverage.

Under COBRA, eligible employees and their qualified dependents are entitled to continuation of their health insurance coverage for up to thirty-six months, depending on the qualifying event.

4. The employee or qualified beneficiary may be required to pay all of the premium for the contribution period.

Under the law, the employee or qualified beneficiary may be required to pay all of the premium for the contribution period, plus up to 2 percent for administrative costs.

5. COBRA is governed by the U.S. Department of Labor.

The Department of Labor is the governing agency for COBRA.

Source: Paychex Inc. (*www.paychex.com*)—A recognized leader in the payroll and human resource services industry and a top national provider of payroll, human resource, and benefits outsourcing solutions for businesses in the United States.

Important Things to Know about Health Savings Accounts

Health savings accounts (HSAs) were created by the Medicare bill signed by President Bush on December 8, 2003, and are designed to help individuals save for future qualified medical and retiree health expenses on a tax-free basis. The following is a list of some of the important things to know about an HSA. For more details, visit the Department of Treasury's Web site.

1. What is a health savings account?

An HSA is an alternative to traditional health insurance; it is a savings product that offers a different way for consumers to pay for their health care. HSAs enable you to pay for current health expenses and save for future qualified medical and retiree health expenses on a tax-free basis. You must be covered by a High Deductible Health Plan (HDHP) to be able to take advantage of HSAs. An HDHP generally costs less than what traditional health care coverage costs, so the money that you save on insurance can therefore be put into the HSA. You own and control the money in your HSA. Decisions on how to spend the money are made by you without relying on a third party or a health insurer. You will also decide what types of investments to make with the money in the account in order to make it grow.

2. As an employer, do I own my employees' HSAs? Can I control how they spend the money in them?

No, you do not own your employees' HSAs. The employee fully owns the contributions to the account as soon as they are deposited, just as with a personal checking or savings account to which you would deposit their compensation.

3. My employees want to contribute to their HSAs but want to make sure they get a tax benefit out of doing so. How does that work?

Employee contributions can be made to HSAs on either an after-tax or pre-tax basis. If made on an after-tax basis, they should be counted as an above-the-line deduction on their tax return, effectively making their contributions tax-free. If they want to make the contribution pre-tax, it can be done through a Section 125 (also called a "salary reduction" or "cafeteria plan").

4. How much do I have to contribute to my employees' HSA?

As much or as little as you want (while staying below the legal limit on the account of $2,600 or $5,150 for employees with family coverage).

5. Do HSA contributions have to be made in equal amounts each month?

No, you can contribute in a lump sum or in any amounts or frequency you wish. However, keep in mind that the funds belong to the employee after they are deposited.

6. As an employer, do I have to contribute the same amount to every employee's HSA?

Employer contributions must be "comparable"—that is, they must be in the same dollar amount or same percentage of the employee's deductible for all employees in the same "class." You can vary the level of contributions for full-time versus part-time employees, and employees with self-only coverage versus family coverage. You do not need to consider employees who do not have HDHP coverage as they are not eligible for HSA contributions.

7. Our company offers benefits through a Section 125 plan, do contributions have to be comparable under these plans as well?

Section 125 plans (also known as "salary reduction" or "cafeteria" plans) must meet a different set of rules. Under these plans, contributions (both from the employer and/or the employee) must meet "nondiscrimination" rules. These rules require the employer to ensure that contributions do not favor higher compensated employees.

8. Our company wants to offer "matching" contributions, can we do that?

Yes, but your company can only offer matching contributions through a Section 125 plan. Remember that the nondiscrimination rules still apply.

9. I don't offer health insurance, but some of my employees have opened HSAs and I'd like to help them out. What can I do?

Your company can make pre-tax contributions to your employees' HSAs as long as you do so for all eligible employees. However, the comparability rules apply. If you have a Section 125 plan, then the nondiscrimination rules apply.

10. How are contributions treated for owners and shareholders of S corporations?

Owners and officers with greater than 2 percent share of a Subchapter S corporation cannot make pre-tax contributions to their HSAs through the company by salary reduction. In addition, any contributions made to their HSAs by the corporation are taxable as income. However, they can make their own personal contributions to their HSAs and take the "above-the-line" deduction on their personal income taxes.

11. How are contributions treated for partners in a partnership or limited liability company (LLC)?

Partners in a partnership or LLC cannot make pre-tax contributions to their HSAs through the partnership by salary reduction. However, they can make their own personal contributions to their HSAs and take the "above-the-line" deduction on their personal income taxes.

12. May a self-employed person contribute to an HSA on a pre-tax basis?

No. Self-employed persons may not contribute to an HSA on a pre-tax basis and may not take the amount of their HSA contribution as a deduction for SECA purposes. However, they may contribute to an HSA with after-tax dollars and take the "above-the-line" deduction.

Source: Department of the Treasury (*www.treasury.gov*)

Ways to Keep Health Insurance Costs Down

Health insurance costs never seem to stop going up. This yearly expense is not only significant, but worrying because it's very difficult to keep it under control. We went to our expert, an insurance professional, and asked him to perform a very difficult task: tell us some ways to lower health insurance costs. He said "no problem" and provided us with this list.

1. Provide as much information as possible when seeking quotes

When you put your health insurance out to bid, arrange to provide as much medical information as necessary to get accurate quotes. Many companies unwittingly accept unrealistic quotes that are rated up when the insurance carriers collect medical underwriting data from employees. To compare truly competitive quotes, be as informative as possible before you get the quotes. "Book" quotes may look inexpensive, but few companies actually get policies at "book" rates.

2. Transfer some costs to employees

The days when companies paid all health expenses are behind us. Many employees are now expected to pay some of their health insurance premiums in addition to copays and deductibles. Be careful to consider the impact on your employees' standard of living when transferring costs to them. Robust benefits plans may still entice employees to look elsewhere for work.

3. Offer Section 125 or cafeteria plans

IRS Section 125 rules allow companies to take pretax deductions for some employee-funded benefits. If your firm pays FICA matching taxes, your company may benefit from employee deductions. With Section 125 plans, employees save at least 15 percent (in federal withholding) of their pretax dollars. If they pay FICA taxes, they save an additional

7.65 percent. Other savings may be incurred depending on plan and state.

4. Help your employees reduce their out-of-pocket expenses

Provide tax-deferred flexible spending accounts (with debit cards where available) to employees. An employee family that spends $1,000 per year on copays, deductibles, and over-the-counter medicines may save $150, $220, or more with a flexible spending account (depending on their contributions). First-year contributions may be lower until employees become comfortable with how the plan works.

5. Use indemnity plans to cover catastrophic expenses

Deductibles of $500 to $1,000 are common today, but for the average employee one trip to the hospital can be a shock. Look into hospital indemnity plans to help cover these up-front costs. For example, you can increase your health insurance deductible from $500 to $1,500 and provide indemnity insurance to cover all or part of the deductible.

6. Use supplemental insurance to cover unexpected expenses

Many low-cost accident plans optionally cover illness as well as accidents. When combined with major medical plans that provide only limited hospitalization, accident/illness supplemental insurance offers more complete protection at a lower overall cost.

7. Offer voluntary benefits

Many employees will buy additional insurance to meet special needs. Some supplemental plans offer wellness benefits that significantly reduce employee costs as well as help encourage annual tests and examinations. Many supplemental plans can be included in Section 125 plans, thus providing employers and employees additional savings options.

8. Reach out to employees with growing families

Companies with young work forces can offer short-term disability to help employees meet expenses for several weeks' maternity leave. There may be a ten- to twelve-month qualifying period before employees can claim maternity benefits, so be sure to understand the policies before employees need to use them. Disability insurance can be offered on a voluntary basis. Studies indicate that a weekly phone call to employees taking short-term disability decreases off-work time and increases rates of return.

9. Look into health savings accounts and health reimbursement accounts

High income employees appreciate the tax-deferred savings and investment options provided with health savings accounts. Alternatively, employers appreciate the ability to designate how funds are spent through health reimbursement accounts. Some IRS rules may make one account more favorable than the other for your firm.

10. Offer a benefits bank

Some companies allocate a fixed amount of money per employee to be used to pay for additional, optional benefits. For example, employees with families may use the allocated funds

to pay for additional major medical coverage or supplemental accident insurance.

11. Organize group benefit meetings

When enrolling employees into your health plans, hold group meetings where employees can ask questions of qualified insurance professionals. Companies that hold enrollment meetings usually see higher participation in medical plans, especially voluntary plans.

Source: Michael Martinez is a licensed life, accident, health, HMO, property, and casualty insurance agent in Texas with Brown & Brown of Texas, Inc., a subsidiary of Brown & Brown, Inc., one of the world's largest insurance brokers. A freelance writer and author, he has published articles and books covering subjects such as health insurance, the works of J. R. R. Tolkien, salsa dancing, Business Basic programming, and search engine optimization. Visit *www .michael-martinez.com* or *www.bbtexas.com* for more information.

Top Questions To Ask Your Health Insurance Provider

Making the wrong choice when choosing health insurance can not only cost you money but bring on unnecessary problems for your valuable employees. The next time your health insurance comes up for renewal, it's a good idea to consider this list of questions to ask your current (or prospective) health insurance provider.

1. What is the financial strength of the insurance carrier?

Usually inquire through AM Best as to their financial ratings. The AM Best system is a standard used throughout the insurance industry. A-rated or better companies are financially sound. F-rated companies have failed financially. If the carrier is not financially secure you want to be sure you'll get claims paid. Also check with Standard and Poor's for claim paying ability and timeliness.

2. Is the carrier licensed in all states?

If your company requires health coverage in a state where the proposed carrier is not licensed to operate, confirm whether coverage will be provided to your employees before accepting the plan.

3. What kind of rate guarantees do the carriers have and for what period of time?

Some insurance carriers provide no rate guarantee. Other carriers will provide at least 6 to 12 months for their rate guarantees. A guaranteed rate means your premiums will not be increased beyond the agreed plan (subject to underwriting guidelines).

4. How does the carrier require you to submit claim information?

Some carriers accept claim filings over the Internet. Some carriers require that you submit the claims. Some carriers allow your provider to handle the claims for you. Does your provider offer this type of service?

5. What kind of medical provider network does the carrier have, such as local only or nationwide?

Some carriers use their own networks of doctors and hospitals. Other carriers may subscribe to third-party network operators. Some carriers may offer a choice. You need to know if your carrier offers a nationwide provider network so that you and your employees can find

doctors, hospitals, and other facilities. If a participant in your plan requires medical attention outside your home state, will the service they receive be considered In-network or Out-of-network? Out-of-network services entail higher deductibles and co-insurance percentages.

6. Will the premiums be composite or individual age rated?

Age-rating means that older employees' health insurance will be more expensive than younger employees' insurance. Most employers want a composite rate for all employees rather than age-rated.

7. How are multi-state locations affected by deductibles and waiting periods?

If your company operates multiple locations across several states, the states may require different deductibles and waiting periods. Some states may even require that you offer both PPO and HMO plans for the employees to choose from instead of one plan for the entire group. There may also be state-mandated coverages that differ from those of the home state where your company's plan is issued.

8. Will the carrier have plans that meet the requirements for HRA and HSA plans?

Tax-deferred health accounts are becoming popular. Health Reimbursement Accounts (commonly referred to as HRAs) and Health Savings Plans (commonly referred to as HSAs) are governed by different sets of rules set forth by the Internal Revenue Service. HSAs, designed for higher income employees, require higher deductibles than many typical major medical plan designs call for. Company owners may not be eligible to use HRAs. Be sure your carrier offers sufficient coverages for all classes of employees with respect to these types of supplemental plans.

9. Will the carrier administer Section 125 Premium Only Plans free of charge?

Some carriers offer these services for a fee. Other carriers provide them free of charge. Be sure you know in advance whether you will be billed for administering your Section 125 Premium Only Plans (commonly referred to as POP plans).

10. A question for the agent would be: "Do you have E&O coverage?"

Agents do make mistakes and it can be costly if litigation arrives on the scene. Errors and Omissions coverage protects the agent's assets from litigation, but it also protects his clients from costly oversights.

Source: Floyd Box (*www.btbenefits.com*) is president and co-principal of BT Benefits Inc., located near Houston, TX. With over 40 years' experience in the insurance industry, Floyd began his career at Allstate Insurance Company. Floyd has worked with several major companies who marketed directly to the Property and Casualty agencies. They specialize in Group Life, Group Health, Group Disability and Voluntary products as well as Section 125, HRA and HSA administration. Contact him at Floyd Box, LUTCF, BT Benefits, Inc, 19627 Holzwarth Road, Suite 400, Spring, TX 77388, (281) 350-4000, e-mail: *market@btbenefits.com*.

Typical Health Insurance Plans

Twenty-five years ago, most people in the United States had indemnity insurance coverage. But today, more than half of all Americans who have health insurance are enrolled in some kind of managed care plan, an organized way of both providing services and paying for them. Different types of managed care plans work differently and include preferred provider organizations (PPOs), health maintenance organizations (HMOs), and point-of-service (POS) plans. You've probably heard these terms before. But what do they mean, and what are the differences between them? And what do these differences mean to you? Here's a list to help you answer these questions.

1. Indemnity plan

With an indemnity plan (sometimes called fee-for-service), you can use any medical provider (such as a doctor and hospital). You or they send the bill to the insurance company, which pays part of it. Usually, you have a deductible—such as $200—to pay each year before the insurer starts paying. Once you meet the deductible, most indemnity plans pay a percentage of what they consider the "Usual and Customary" charge for covered services. The insurer generally pays 80 percent of these costs and you pay the other 20 percent, which is known as coinsurance. If the provider charges more than the Usual and Customary rates, you will have to pay both the coinsurance and the difference. The plan will pay for charges for medical tests and prescriptions as well as from doctors and hospitals. It may not pay for some preventive care, like checkups.

2. Preferred provider organization (PPO)

A PPO is a form of managed care closest to an indemnity plan. A PPO has arrangements with doctors, hospitals, and other providers of care who have agreed to accept lower fees from the insurer for their services. As a result, your cost sharing should be lower than if you go outside the network. In addition to the PPO doctors making referrals, plan members can refer themselves to other doctors, including ones outside the plan. If you go to a doctor within the PPO network, you will pay a copayment (a set amount you pay for certain services—say $10 for a doctor or $5 for a prescription). Your coinsurance will be based on lower charges for PPO members. If you choose to go outside the network, you will have to meet the deductible and pay coinsurance based on higher charges. In addition, you may have to pay the difference between what the provider charges and what the plan will pay.

3. Health maintenance organization (HMO)

HMOs are the oldest form of managed care plan. HMOs offer members a range of health benefits, including preventive care, for a set monthly fee. There are many kinds of HMOs. If doctors are employees of the health plan and you visit them at central medical offices or clinics, it is a staff or group model HMO. Other HMOs contract with physician groups or individual doctors who have private offices. These are called individual practice associations (IPAs) or networks. HMOs will give you a list of doctors from which to choose a primary care doctor. This doctor coordinates your care, which means that generally you must contact him or her to be referred to a specialist. With some HMOs, you will pay nothing when you visit doctors. With

other HMOs, there may be a copayment, like $5 or $10, for various services. If you belong to an HMO, the plan only covers the cost of charges for doctors in that HMO. If you go outside the HMO, you will pay the bill. This is not the case with point-of-service plans.

4. Point-of-service (POS) plan

Many HMOs offer an indemnity-type option known as a POS plan. The primary-care doctors in a POS plan usually make referrals to other providers in the plan. But in a POS plan, members can refer themselves outside the plan and still get some coverage. If the doctor makes a referral out of the network, the plan pays all or most of the bill. If you refer yourself to a provider outside the network and the service is covered by the plan, you will have to pay coinsurance.

Source: Department of Health and Human Services (*www.ahrq.gov*).

Typical ERISA Requirements

ERISA sets uniform minimum standards to ensure that employee benefit plans are established and maintained in a fair and financially sound manner. In addition, employers have an obligation to provide promised benefits and satisfy ERISA's requirements for managing and administering private pension and welfare plans. The Department of Labor's Employee Benefits Security Administration (EBSA), together with the Internal Revenue Service, has the statutory and regulatory authority to ensure that workers receive the promised benefits. The department has principal jurisdiction over Title I of ERISA, which requires persons and entities that manage and control plan funds to comply with the following requirements.

1. Manage the plan exclusively.

Plan for the exclusive benefit of participants and beneficiaries.

2. Refrain from conflict-of-interest transactions.

Carry out their duties in a prudent manner and refrain from conflict-of-interest transactions expressly prohibited by law.

3. Comply with limitations on certain plans investments.

Comply with limitations on certain plans' investments in employer securities and properties.

4. Makes sure you fund the benefits.

Fund benefits in accordance with the law and plan rules.

5. Report and disclose information.

Report and disclose information on the operations and financial condition of plans to the government and participants.

6. Provide documents to assure compliance with law.

Provide documents required in the conduct of investigations to assure compliance with the law.

Source: Department of Labor, Employment Standards Administrations Wage and Hour Division (*www.dol.gov*). Frances Perkins

Building 200 Constitution Avenue, NW, Washington, DC 20210; (877) 889-5627 or (866) 4-USWage.

Popular Types of Retirement Plans

Ready to set up a retirement plan for your employees? The following are some of the most popular types of these plans. Which one is right for you?

1. 401k plan

This is the most popular of the defined contribution plans and is most commonly offered by larger employers. Employers often match employee contributions.

2. 403b tax-sheltered annuity plan

Think of this as a 401k plan for employees of school systems and certain nonprofit organizations. Investments are made in tax-sheltered annuities or mutual funds.

3. SIMPLE IRA

The Savings Incentive Match Plan for Employees of Small Employers is one of the newest types of employer-based retirement plans. There is also a 401k version.

4. Profit-sharing plan

The employer shares company profits with employees, usually based on the level of each employee's wages.

5. Employee stock ownership plan (ESOP)

Employee stock ownership plans are similar to profit-sharing plans, except that an ESOP must invest primarily in company stock. Under an ESOP, the employees share in the ownership of the company.

6. Simplified employee pension (SEP)

Simplified employee pension plans are used by both small employers and the self-employed.

Source: Certified Financial Planner Board of Standards, Inc. (*www.cfp.net*) is a professional regulatory organization based in the United States that fosters professional standards in personal financial planning so that the public has access to and benefits from competent and ethical financial planning. Learn more about CFP Board by contacting them at 1670 Broadway, Suite 600, Denver, CO 80202; (888) 237-6275.

Reasons to Have a Retirement Plan

A retirement plan has lots of benefits—for you, your business, and your employees. Retirement plans allow investing in the future now for financial security when you and your employees retire. As a bonus, you and your employees get significant tax advantages and other incentives. Even the IRS agrees that there are good reasons to have a good retirement plan. Here are a few.

1. Tax-deductible contributions

In terms of benefits for your business, employer contributions are tax deductible.

2. Tax-free assets

Another benefit for your business is that the assets in your retirement plan grow tax-free.

3. Compounding interest

The assets in your retirement plan will grow with compounding interest

4. Tax credits and incentives

Your business may receive tax credits and other incentives for starting a retirement plan.

5. Attract and retain better employees

Another benefit to having a retirement plan allows you to attract and retain better employees, and consequently reduce new employee training costs.

6. Benefits for your employees

Tax on employee contributions is deferred until distributed.

7. Investment gains are not taxed

Another benefit to your employees is that investment gains are not taxed until distributed.

8. Retirement assets

Another benefit for your employees is the retirement assets can be carried from one employer to another.

9. Contributions can be made easily

Employees can make contributions easily through payroll deductions

10. Savers credit

Employees have the benefit of savers credit.

11. Allows your employees options

Another benefit for an employee is that flexible plan options are available to them.

12. Gives your employees financial security

Your employees will be granted better financial security when they retire.

Source: Internal Revenue Service (*www.irs.gov*).

Index

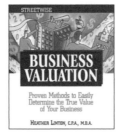

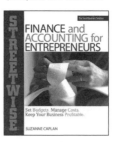
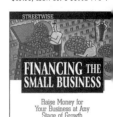

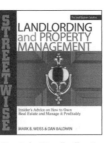
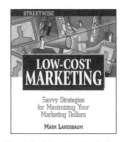

Streetwise® Managing a Nonprofit
John Riddle
$19.95; ISBN 10: 1-58062-698-X

Streetwise® Managing People
Bob Adams, et al.
$19.95; ISBN 10: 1-55850-726-4

Streetwise® Marketing Plan
Don Debelak
$19.95; ISBN 10: 1-58062-268-2

Streetwise® Maximize Web Site Traffic
Nobles and O'Neil
$19.95; ISBN 10: 1-58062-369-7

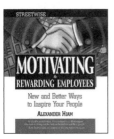

Streetwise® Motivating & Rewarding Employees
Alexander Hiam
$19.95; ISBN 10: 1-58062-130-9

Streetwise® Project Management
Michael Dobson
$19.95; ISBN 10: 1-58062-770-6

Streetwise® Restaurant Management
John James & Dan Baldwin
$19.95; ISBN 10: 1-58062-781-1

Streetwise® Sales Letters with CD
Reynard and Weiss
$29.95; ISBN 10: 1-58062-440-5

Streetwise® Selling on eBay®
Sonia Weiss
$19.95; ISBN 10: 1-59337-610-3

Streetwise® Small Business Book of Lists
Edited by Gene Marks
$19.95; ISBN 10: 1-59337-684-7

Streetwise® Small Business Start-Up
Bob Adams
$19.95; ISBN 10: 1-55850-581-4

Streetwise® Start Your Own Business Workbook
Gina Marie Mangiamele
$9.95; ISBN 10: 1-58062-506-1

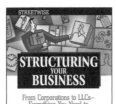

Streetwise® Structuring Your Business
Michele Cagan
$19.95; ISBN 10: 1-59337-177-2

Streetwise® Time Management
Marshall Cook
$19.95; ISBN 10: 1-58062-131-7